Academic Communities/ Disciplinary Conventions

Bonnie Beedles
Michael Petracca
University of California, Santa Barbara

Prentice
Hall

Prentice Hall, Upper Saddle River, New Jersey 07458

Library of Congress Cataloging-in-Publication Data

Beedles, Bonnie.
    Academic communities/disciplinary conventions / Bonnie Beedles, Michael Petracca.—
1st ed.
        p. cm.
    Includes bibliographical references and index.
    ISBN 0–13–040169–2
        1. College readers.   2. Interdisciplinary approach in eduction—Problems, exercises, etc.
    3. English language—Rhetoric—Problems, exercises, etc.   4. Academic writing—Problems,
    exercises, etc.   I. Petracca, Michael   II. Title.

PE1417 .B3945 2001
808'.0427—dc21

00–057103

Editor in chief: Leah Jewell
Acquisitions editor: Corey Good
Assistant editor: Vivian Garcia
Managing editor: Mary Rottino
Production liaison: Fran Russello
Editorial/production supervisor:
Bruce Hobart (Pine Tree Composition)
Prepress and manufacturing buyer:
Mary Ann Gloriande
Cover art director: Jayne Conte
Cover designer: Bruce Kenselaar
Marketing manager: Brandy Dawson

For Frances, who was behind me all along
and will be beside me from now on.
—BB

For my dear friends Violet Oaklander, Ph.D.,
and Peter Mortola, Ph.D.—and to LizaJane
Petracca and the memory of Minou
Petracca—all four of whom have made fre-
quent and creative use of the sand tray.
—MP

This book was set in 10/12 Times Roman by Pine Tree Composition, Inc.,
and was printed and bound by R.R. Donnelley & Sons Company.
The cover was printed by Phoenix Color Corp.

© 2001 by Prentice-Hall, Inc.
A Division of Pearson Education
Upper Saddle River, New Jersey 07458

Printed in the United States of America

10 9 8 7 6 5 4 3 2 1

ISBN 0-13-040169-2

Prentice-Hall International (UK) Limited, *London*
Prentice-Hall of Australia Pty. Limited, *Sydney*
Prentice-Hall Canada Inc., *Toronto*
Prentice-Hall Hispanoamericana, S.A., *Mexico*
Prentice-Hall of India Private Limited, *New Delhi*
Prentice-Hall of Japan, Inc., *Tokyo*
Pearson Education Asia Pte. Ltd., *Singapore*
Editora Prentice-Hall do Brasil, Ltda., *Rio de Janeiro*

CONTENTS

CHARLES HORTON COOLEY

> In our own life the intimacy of the neighborhood has been broken up by the
> growth of an intricate mesh of wider contacts which leaves us strangers to people
> who live in the same house.

ERVING GOFFMAN

> In everyday life, of course, there is a clear understanding that first impressions
> are important.

KENNETH GERGEN

> It is not simply the expansion of self through relationships that hounds one with
> the continued sense of "ought." There is also the seeping of self-doubt into every-
> day consciousness, a subtle feeling of inadequacy that smothers one's activities
> with an uneasy sense of impending emptiness.

Thelma and Louise *is seen, for example, to be either an imperfect satirical analogy of the woman's dilemma in contemporary America or an unrealistic female liberation fantasy that backhandedly supports reactionary violence.*

Rob Roy *and* Braveheart *reveal our culture's subconscious fear of the feminized man. The films portray gay men as destructive of manhood and virility and as a threat to the solidarity of the family.*

"Here I wish to challenge this myth. I want to argue that gay men and lesbians have not always existed. Instead, they are a product of history, and have come into existence in a specific historical era."

This episode crystallizes the irony that although American men tend to talk more than women in public situations, they often talk less at home. And this pattern is wreaking havoc with marriage.

Taking the similarities in the patterns of interruptions between adults and children and males and females to mean that females have an analogous status to children in certain conversational situations implies that the female has restricted rights to speak and may be ignored or interrupted at will.

sometimes trancelike fixity, thereby rendering ourselves captive audiences to mes-
sages that may be insidious in their rhetorical effect.

PREFACE

In everyday conversation, we call this text *AC/DC* rather than *Academic Communities/Disciplinary Conventions*. We like *AC/DC* because it's shorter and more sprightly, easy for students, professors, and ourselves to articulate out loud. We also like it because, as an acronym, *AC/DC* straddles the three major academic domains—the sciences, the social sciences, and the humanities—around which we've grouped the readings and writing assignments for this text. Within scientific fields such as physics and engineering, *AC/DC* refers to electrical current that either continually reverses direction, with the change in direction being expressed in hertz, or cycles per second (Alternating Current), or electrical current that flows in one direction (Direct Current). In the humanities, *AC/DC* is known to all popular music critics as a "heavy metal" band that was formed in 1974, produced sixteen albums, and influenced a number of other popular musical performers, such as Bonnie Raitt and the band Collective Soul. Finally, *AC/DC* is an old slang term that certain members of our culture use (sometimes in a derogatory fashion and sometimes not, depending on who is using it and how it is being used) to describe bisexuals: individuals who feel and/or who act out a sexual or romantic attraction directed toward members of more than one sex; of course, human sexuality and its conceptions by members of particular cultures fall within the purview of the social sciences.

We undertook to write this text because the University of California at Santa Barbara's Writing Program, where we teach, organizes its curriculum around a writing-in-the-disciplines approach: the fundamental notion that composition students benefit from writing in a variety of disciplinary contexts, so that skills learned in our courses will readily translate to the rest of their university education and beyond. Following this approach, one of our entry-level composition courses exposes students to readings from the sciences, social sciences, and humanities, giving them practice in writing within each of those disciplinary areas. In teaching this course, we found ourselves assembling photocopied readers based on certain broad themes—identity and consciousness, gender and sexuality, capital economies, and the environment—and this textbook evolved gradually from that ongoing course preparation process. We believe that by organizing the material in this way—that is, around broad content areas that are themselves actually an aggregation of many rich and lively subcategories—we enact the kind of interdisciplinary and intradisciplinary conversations that are at the heart of university research and writing.

We've taken great care in choosing topics and readings that will be interesting to students. Our experience with the growing readership of popular-culture-based texts, for example, confirms in our minds that students will be most engaged in the writing process when they're having fun with the material at hand. For that reason, *AC/DC* contains topics and readings that are both academically rigorous and accessible and engaging for students. Likewise, the sequence of activities we've built into each topical chapter's units—preparation for critical reading, textual examination, close reading questions, class discussion and freewriting prompts—is designed to maintain a high degree of student interest. Thus, while *AC/DC* involves students in serious academic approaches, it makes sure they find connections between the activities/materials and their own lives as bright twenty-somethings. Toward this end, while obviously paying homage to traditional disciplines such as psychology, sociology, literary studies, and biochemistry, we've also included relatively new and exciting fields such as evolutionary psychology, computer science, genetics, ethnic studies, lesbian and gay studies, and cultural studies.

Our students have responded very positively to the nascent, photocopied versions of this text, and we're confident that students will respond with even greater enthusiasm to *AC/DC*, with its more extensive list of readings, its further refinements of apparatus . . . and with its glossier pages and sturdier bindings!

We would like to thank the following reviewers: James Allen, College of DuPage; Todd Taylor, University of North Carolina; Tim Morris, University of Texas-Arlington; Sarah McLaughlin, Marie Cahil Devry Institute of Technology—Phoenix; Helen R. Andretta, York College—The City University of New York; Dr. Carol Kivo, Pepperdine University; Allene Cooper, Arizona State University; Margaret Colarelli, Northwood University; Joe Law, Wright State University; and Mary Ann Rudy, Chadron State College.

Bonnie Beedles
Michael Petracca

CHAPTER ONE

INTRODUCTION

SURGICAL SCRUBBING, BARBIE DOLLS, A GRECIAN URN, AND MUCH MORE: THE CHALLENGE OF UNIVERSITY WRITING

Students are often surprised when they enter college and encounter writing assignments that are much more difficult than those they received in high school. College freshmen report that the typical writing assignment in high school asked them to interpret *Romeo and Juliet* or to write a report on the life cycle of the flea. Many high school students learned the five-paragraph essay format, in which the introduction announces a thesis statement, three supporting points contained in three paragraphs expand on this thesis, and a conclusion restates the thesis, often in a somewhat repetitive manner. The five-paragraph essay was a valuable method for helping students learn to formulate thesis statements and to practice developing that thesis with examples and illustrations. However, now that you are at the university, your professors will ask you to take that process a step further—or, oftentimes, many steps further. In college, you will encounter a variety of writing forms and tasks in a variety of academic contexts. For example, you may be asked to write a microbiology lab exercise that investigates the effectiveness of surgical scrubbing on removing bacteria from the hands, an analysis of the persuasive techniques used in Barbie Doll advertisements for a mass communications course, an environmental impact study of the ecological impact of golf courses for an environmental studies class, a policy analysis for a political science course, as well as a literary interpretation of John Keats's "Ode on a Grecian Urn."

Although these assignments share certain qualities with the five-paragraph essay that you may have learned—namely, a clear focus or guiding thesis, concrete support, and logical development—they assume different forms and require attention to specialized purposes and audiences. You may find yourself surprised at both the variety of writing assignments that you'll encounter in college, as well as the frequency with which writing is assigned in courses that don't at first seem as though they would be writing-intensive. The truth is that writing is practiced extensively by scholars in all fields within the university (and, of course, by people outside the university as well).

By learning to communicate more effectively with words in a variety of academic situations, you will increase the probability of having your written work received enthusiastically by those who read it: a boon for professors and teaching assistants, who read hundreds of papers each year, and for yourself, since you will almost undoubtedly find your grade-point average moving in an upward direction. Our goal with this text is to introduce you to the major university disciplines, to provide you with examples of writing within these disciplines, and to give you practice in writing the kinds of documents that professors in these disciplines will require of you, so that when you move out into the greater academic community, you will feel prepared and confident to write whatever kinds of assignments you encounter, using language appropriate to the discourse communities in which they are situated.

ACADEMIC PROSE: SOME FORMAL CONSIDERATIONS

Before you examine the unique demands of writing for specific university disciplines, it is useful to examine the strategies that all writers use to develop arguments. The forms that these strategies assume are sometimes called *rhetorical modes,* because in different ways, they aim to persuade readers to accept a certain point or thesis. Rhetoric refers to the art of speaking and/or writing persuasively. It can be argued that all academic writing is persuasive: writers in the academy seek to convince their readers to accept that what they state is the "truth."

At the most basic level, writers may use autobiographical narrative to demonstrate personal engagement with a topic, to generate concrete examples, to explore personal opinions and feelings. An autobiographical narrative essay assignment might, for example, ask you to reflect on your experience with a particular concept, such as the "group solidarity" theory from sociology. Such an assignment seeks to increase your understanding of a theoretical concept by asking you to examine its implications in your own life. The majority of university-level writing, however, asks you to move beyond your own, personal perspective to examine the world at large.

When college-level writers begin to go outside themselves and engage more pointedly with the world of ideas, they use strategies such as *summary, description,* and *comparison/contrast* to develop their arguments. Summaries are compact presentations of material that appears elsewhere in more fully developed form. As such you might see the summary as a brief, neutral restatement of a source, such as an article or a portion of a book. Summary can be used to provide background information, to support subpoints in an essay, or to give readers a brief overview of material that is to follow, as in the case of a research article abstract.

A writing strategy that is ubiquitous in all forms of academic writing, description—as the name implies—means clear, detailed delineation of all the aspects of a subject under consideration. The "Methods" section of a science report, for example, must clearly describe the procedures undertaken in a particular experiment; the "Results" section of a psychological report must systematically describe the researchers' findings; an interpretive essay for an art history course must employ description to support the author's conclusions about a work of art; and a pop-culture analysis of graffiti art must first describe the artifacts in question, so that readers unfamiliar with the tagging of subway cars might understand the subject of the analysis.

The comparison/contrast essay is a form that you have probably used in limited ways and that writers of more sophisticated academic prose use frequently to point out similarities and differences between issues, ideas, points of view, practices, behaviors, traits, and qualities. An economics class might require you to compare and contrast the economic theories of Karl Marx and Adam Smith, pointing out areas of similarity and difference in their approaches to economic stratification. Through comparing the process of cell division in various organisms, scientists may uncover new general truths about cell biology. Since the very act of comparing related ideas, objects, events, or phenomena is a fundamental way of learning about these things, comparison is an integral part of all knowledge production in the academy.

All of these techniques—summary, description, comparison/contrast—are used in argumentative writing. At the heart of any consideration of argumentation are three components that form what many educators and theorists call the rhetorical triangle. In attempting to persuade a reader to adopt a particular point of view or thesis that you are developing in a given essay, you must keep in mind these three components. The first of these, *audience,* refers to the group of people to whom you are addressing a piece of writing. If you are writing to a group of tenured professors attending a biology conference, you will use language that is very different—more formal and, perhaps even to your point of view, stuffy—than if you are presenting a report on student activism to a meeting of your undergraduate student government. We adjust our rhetoric to the demands of different audiences all the time. For instance, if your best friend drops you off at a job interview, you will say something like "Seeya, bud," to your friend, and then switch to a more formal way of talking— "Very pleased to meet you, sir,"—as you encounter the new, more formal audience represented by a prospective employer. Indeed, sometimes people fail to land jobs when they don't adequately adjust their tone and word choice during a job interview. "Whassup, yo?" may work just fine with your friends, but Ms. Lewsite, the personnel officer at Global Tools, may not be down with your colloquial diction.

The second rhetorical consideration when writing persuasively has to do with your *purpose.* If you are writing an advertisement for the school newspaper, your purpose may be to convince people to come to the fund-raising movie screening that your sorority is presenting. Similarly, if you're writing a statistical analysis of worldwide population growth, your underlying purpose might be to convince readers that all nations need to adopt a zero-population-growth policy. On the other hand, your purpose in certain disciplinary settings might be to deliver information as objectively and with as little bias as possible.

Usually, however, even the most "objective" piece of academic writing has an underlying persuasive purpose. As a careful reader, it is important for you to begin to discern the rhetorical agendas underlying the texts that you read in this book and elsewhere. As a writer, you need to have at your disposal a range of techniques by which you can persuade audiences—either very subtly or more blatantly—to adopt the point of view or the thesis of the given piece you are writing. This consideration leads us to the third side of the rhetorical triangle, *argument,* which refers to the full palate of writerly tools—rhetorical modes, logical strategies, straightforward presentation of evidence—that writers use both to make valid points and sometimes even to mislead their readers . . . hopefully, more often the former.

One final form of writing that we will mention here is formal, academic research. Remember that report on the life cycle of the flea that you wrote for your junior high science class? You went to your school library's *World Book Encyclopedia,* copied several points that seemed relevant to the topic, wrote them down on a piece of lined notebook paper, and handed them in as "research." Whereas this method might have earned you an A in junior high school, university-level research writing requires a much more extensive, and even exhaustive, exploration of a variety of sources, from scholarly journals to books written on specific topics, to government publications, to World Wide Web sites and other electronic media. In addition to relying on these sophisticated secondary sources for your research, you will also be asked in certain courses to conduct your own primary research, and the data obtained through new methods of hands-on empirical observation will help to provide evidence in reports that you will then write. Therefore, in conjunction with learning new methods of conducting research, your job as a college-level research writer will require the more sophisticated skills of analysis and synthesis, that is, the ability to examine material methodically, to extract cogent points from it, to discern relationships between ideas, to present these ideas through quotation and paraphrase in your work, and to organize all the material into a logically sequenced essay form.

WRITING AS A PROCESS

Common to all these rhetorical modes—and to all genres or kinds of writing in the disciplines—is one central reality: you're going to have to write. Stated more positively, you're going to have the wonderful opportunity to analyze sources, to generate ideas, to put those ideas into a coherent assemblage of words (because doing that is what we readers have come to expect from texts), and to organize that material into a logically sequenced form, whether that form be a research essay, an environmental impact report, an explication/analysis of a poem, or a recommendation essay on global population growth. Although these tasks, when looked at in sum, may appear overwhelming, it often helps students to think of writing as a process and to separate that process into a series of discrete phases—broadly defined as prewriting, drafting, and revising—so that the entire enterprise becomes less scary and more easily accomplished.

Prewriting

Prewriting, the first phase of the writing process, was initially formulated by composition teachers who wanted to encourage fluency in their students by directing them to avoid the factors that often contribute to writer's block, brain cramp, and feelings of panic or aversion that people sometimes experience when faced with a writing task. In the prewriting phase, you don't have to concern yourself with correct grammar and spelling, coherent presentation of ideas, or logical sequence of supporting material. To the contrary, in this phase the only requirement is that you free up your creative/imaginative mind to generate ideas, connections between sources, genial turns of phrase: a wealth of written material you can use during the drafting phase, when you sit down to produce some actual college-level writing. Studies of the writing process of students and of professional writers alike have found that the more time writers spend prewriting, or "brainstorming" ideas, the less time they need to spend on the actual drafting of their essays, because they have generated more ideas. How many times have you sat down in front of the computer screen or a piece of blank paper with various ideas (or worse, no ideas!) in your head and tried to start right in on the introduction to an essay? Most of us find that endeavor particularly agonizing, and much of the agony can be obviated if time is spent on any method of prewriting ideas freely.

You may have heard of, or even practiced a number of prewriting strategies already. Certainly, at some point in your life, you have written a list, which is one of the most basic and commonly practiced forms of prewriting. With the *jot list,* for example, you simply jot down a series of ideas, phrases, unformed thoughts, or even pictures, one after the other. Having taken a few minutes to generate a rough list, you might then develop it into another prewriting form, the *outline:* a kind of shorthand, notational technique for setting ideas out in order. Keep in mind, however, that the outline is a fluid form that is not cast in concrete. It's more like Silly Putty, actually: as you think about your topic, you will undoubtedly twist, bend, break up, and rearrange the ordering of your ideas a number (often a large number) of times. The outline exists as a malleable frame, over which you will eventually build supporting paragraphs when you get to the drafting phase of the writing process.

Another prewriting activity—different from listing and outlining because it's less linear—is called *clustering,* a useful technique for finding associations between certain words and concepts that you may have generated in your preliminary list. In the process of clustering, you choose a word and write it down at the center of a piece of paper. Some teachers advise drawing a square or circle around that word, to separate it from all the other words you will write down subsequently. You then think of any word or phrase that relates to the word at the center of the page, and use lines to connect those phrases to the central word. For instance, in writing this section of *Academic Communities/Disciplinary Conventions,* we began by writing "PREWRITING" and then surrounded that word with key concepts— "makes writing task easier," "generate ideas," "before drafting," and so on—and tasks, such as "outline," "list," and "freewrite." Then we created another group of clusters, each around one of those new phrases, and we kept at this process until we had generated the nuclei for a series of supporting paragraphs, and gradually the material for this chapter took on the delightful and instructive form that you have before you right now.

In this text, we'll be concentrating on a version of the prewriting strategy called *freewriting.* Freewriting is a useful means of examining sources, noting sense impressions, and generating new ideas. A composition teacher named Peter Elbow developed this method, asserting that students could circumvent the nightmare of writer's block by writing anything that came into their minds, while at the same time recording external noises, scents, visual impressions, and physical sensations. The rationale underlying this technique is that the act of writing freely can release thoughts and ideas buried within our minds, which often censor free expression be-cause of feelings of fear, insecurity, or simple laziness. Thus, the single goal in freewriting is to keep writing, and to suspend other formal considerations, such as correct grammar, spelling, and so on. You just write and write for a certain period of time—say fifteen minutes. Occasionally you will find yourself at a loss for any-thing to say. In that case, just write, "I find myself at a loss for anything to say" or "This is an incredibly lame activity" or "I truly despise Beedles and Petracca and everything they stand for." Write that phrase over and over. We predict that you will soon become bored with the repeated wording and that your preconscious mind will start to provide some original notions and phrasings.

Freewriting can be either unfocused or focused. In the unfocused freewrite, you merely sit with a blank piece of paper or a new word processing file and let the words come, with no particular topic to explore. This technique can be useful when you face a writing task about which you feel you have no ideas, since often ideas lurk within us, buried beneath mundane concerns of insecurities. Unfocused freewriting is also valuable as a daily practice, to help dissociate you from the para-lyzing effects of self-criticism that too often accompany more structured forms of writing. For that reason, many composition instructors require that students keep daily journals of unfocused freewriting, and you may want to try doing this on your own as well. In *Academic Communities/Disciplinary Conventions,* the questions following every reading conclude with "Directed Freewrites," which are intended to help you generate ideas for essay assignments. Although not every "Directed Freewrite" in this text leads directly to every essay assignment to follow, the activ-ity of using freewriting to think through important issues will indirectly help you to write better essays about those issues. When you allow your subconscious mind free access to paper or a computer screen, it will reward you with startlingly original ideas and turns of phrase. Some of these you will end up using in your final drafts; others you will eventually discard as excessive, confusing, or inconsistent with the tone you're trying to establish in your essay or report.

Drafting

Here we'll consider the central concern for most students: turning prewritten material into a presentable piece of college-level prose. Now that you've done some freewriting, and perhaps listing and outlining as well, it's time to begin assembling that material in a more formal way. Since writing in the various university disciplines takes many forms, it's impossible to provide a single recipe that will enable you to construct any piece of writing that you may be assigned. To pick one small example: most writing teachers will tell you to avoid using passive verb constructions in your papers. Why use a stuffy-sounding construction such as "Many fabulous essays are written by university students," when you can eliminate the inactive "to be" verb construction ("essays are written") and can provide a more vigorously active subject simply by reversing the order of words: "University students write many fabulous essays"? This is excellent advice to students writing for the humanities and social sciences. However, you will discover that in some branches of the "hard" sciences, professors actually require that you use the passive voice for certain kinds of writing, such as lab reports, where the goal is to take the experimenter—the active subject—out of the equation as much as possible, for the sake of a rigorously objective tone.

The passive verb problem is a small example of the many ways in which writing conventions vary, depending on the rhetorical situation. Although we therefore cannot provide a template you can use to create all types of university-level writing, we can point out certain elements that most forms of college writing share. Foremost among these is the thesis: the main point of your piece of writing. It's safe to say that all forms of college writing will move toward developing a central assertion. In a humanities essay—say, for art history—a typical thesis might be that Andy Warhol's art incorporated the common and everyday in his works, and that one therefore cannot impose traditional criteria of art criticism on his work. A psychology report might have as its central assertion that, according to statistics generated through research, male and female substance abusers engage in family violence more frequently than do individuals who are not substance abusers. In the "hard" sciences, a chemistry report might have as its thesis that, after carrying out an assay of caffeine, theophylline, and xanthine by surface plasmon resonance sensors, it appears that selectivity of antipolymers is limited to their original print molecules and that they lack affinity for other drug molecules.

In each of these examples, the thesis is comprehensive but pointed: broad enough to embrace your paper's main supporting points, yet at the same time focused, so that you don't have to write a book-length manuscript to cover your topic adequately. Note also that each of the preceding theses embodies a forceful assertion: "one cannot impose traditional criteria of art criticism ..."; "substance abusers engage in family violence more frequently ..."; "selectivity of antipolymers is limited to. ..." Whenever the genre in which you are writing warrants it, you want your thesis statement to be a dynamic, vigorous assertion, instead of a question or a less-than-pointed summary of intention. As much as possible, avoid the ever-popular (and ever-boring), "In this art history paper, I am going to discuss the use of common and everyday images in Andy Warhol's art." Of course, you will find exceptions to this general principle, as in the case of certain scientific reports, which tend to sacrifice vigorous assertion for the sake of objective tone, but as a general goal, try to make your thesis statements as assertive as possible.

In most disciplinary writing—except for abstracts, one-paragraph summaries, and some science and social science reports—you will have an opening paragraph that presents your thesis, as well as some supporting paragraphs that develop it. As you begin to write your supporting paragraphs, it's important to keep your audience in mind (see the preceding discussion of rhetorical considerations). If you're not writing to a group of readers grounded in the discipline within which you are writing, then you will have to take special care to explain certain unfamiliar terms. In the previous chemistry example, if you were writing that antipolymer report for a group on non-chem majors, you would have to explain certain terms, such as theophylline, xanthine, plasmon resonance sensors, and antipolymers. On the other hand, were you writing this same report to your chemistry teaching assistant, then you'd be safe in assuming that these terms fall within the body of common knowledge that all chemists share, and you wouldn't have to explain them, although through your use of these terms, you will demonstrate that you understand their meaning.

Having settled on an audience, you next want to establish a tone. As mentioned before, certain types of writing, such as scientific reports, demand a relatively dry and detached tone, whereas other genres allow for more "creative" use of literary devices such as metaphors, sense imagery, humor, and narrative. Compare the following two supporting paragraphs, focusing specifically on tone:

> This particular bit of sandy coast is no Hades. Only an hour or so from Manhattan, the Jersey shore even seems like paradise to millions of people—the beach-blanket-and-sunscreen version of the great outdoors. But the way some critics see it, Sisyphus is here, in the form of a giant dredge more than half a mile out to sea. In an astounding feat of engineering, the dredge has vacuumed some 16,000 cubic yards of sand from the seafloor. And now it's pumping that sand through a 3,000-foot pipe to a spot on the beach not far from me. A great rushing slurry of water and sand is spewing out, part of three loads it will dump that day. (Luoma 50)

> The starling nest was found on 26 May at the edge of a field crop in a cultivated area containing some scattered trees. Grazing pastures and corn fields were located within 100 m of the nest area, and some

relictual patches of natural vegetation, including cardon and dagger cactus, mesquite, palo verde, Adam's tree, lomboy, and cholla bordered the area. The nest was in an old woodpecker hole in a 4.7 m cardon cactus. The nest cavity was 4.2 m above the ground, and the cavity entrance was oriented in a NNW direction. Two apparently healthy nestlings, almost fully feathered (ca 15 days old), were in the cavity. (Rodriguez-Estrella 533)

Both of these supporting paragraphs describe a natural setting from an environmentalist perspective. The first paragraph, typical of the kinds of creative nonfictional writing that one might do in many humanities-based disciplines or in more "popular" forms of writing such as journalism, uses literary devices such as mythical allusions ("Hades," "Sisyphus") and some vivid descriptions ("beach-blanket-and-sunscreen," "great rushing slurry," "spewing out") to create a sense of local color. Furthermore, the author does not distance himself at all from the subject. To the contrary, he uses the phrase "not far from me" to position himself squarely in the middle of the scene, thus placing the reader vicariously there as well. The author of the first paragraph fuses this relatively informal, lively tone with more objectively factual language ("16,000 cubic yards of sand," "3,000-foot pipe") to make his points about beach erosion.

By contrast, the authors of the second paragraph, which is lifted from a standard environmental impact report, create a more consistently distanced, scientific tone. The article presents much more factual data ("26 May," "within 100 m of the nest area," "NNW direction") than did the first paragraph, and there is a conspicuous absence of literary devices. Technical terms ("relictual patches," "nest cavity," "healthy nestlings") abound, and the authors do not refer to themselves in the first person. By choosing appropriate diction and stylistic features, the authors of both paragraphs have produced pieces of writing whose tone is completely appropriate to the genre for which they are writing.

Once you've decided on a tone for the body of your paper, you can begin to write the supporting paragraphs. In most types of academic writing, regardless of the discipline, a supporting paragraph will have a topic sentence that brings up a subpoint—perhaps one from your list or outline—and some elaboration on that point through the use of concrete evidence. The effective incorporation of evidence is the critical task in constructing your paper's supporting paragraphs. Your writing will convince readers to the degree that you make your arguments credible. It is concrete evidence that lends credibility to your arguments.

Evidence can be broken down into two broad categories, which are based on their source. *Primary evidence* consists of material derived firsthand, either by researchers in a particular field, or by yourself, through interviewing individuals, conducting your own empirical observations, distributing questionnaires and tabulating the results, or even by reading people's accounts of personal experiences on the World Wide Web. Researcher Jacques Barzun says that primary evidence is distinguished from secondary evidence "by the fact that the former gives the words of the witnesses or first recorders of an event—for example, the diaries of Count Ciano written under Mussolini's regime. The researcher, using a number of such primary sources, produces a secondary source."

Secondary evidence, then, consists mainly of secondary sources as defined by Barzun: articles written by scholars about original writings. You will find secondary evidence in academic journals, popular magazines, newspapers, textbooks, televised reports, and so on. While studying articles from these various media, it's important that you exercise your critical reading (or viewing and listening, in the case of television and radio) skills to maximum effect when evaluating the credibility of secondary evidence. Most secondary sources will include documentation (in the form of in-text citations or footnotes) or attribution (in the case of news reportage, whose validity depends on the accurate accounts of sources often gained firsthand), and it is important that you verify your secondary sources' validity whenever possible.

Should you find that two independent secondary sources agree, you can assume that the information is probably more credible than if you found only one secondary source making a particular truth claim. By contrast, if you find that two secondary sources present opposing views, it is crucial that you evaluate the credibility of each source and then decide which one you believe. Some criteria you can apply to secondary sources are the following:

- **Qualification:** What are the source's professional or personal credentials? Obviously, recognized experts in a given field carry more authority than do individuals who are relatively unknown.
- **Documentation:** Does the source provide accurate footnotes, citations, bibliography, and/or attribution?
- **Objectivity:** Does the source present material in a biased way, or is there a clear attempt to represent both sides of a given argument fairly? If the source is political, do you find evidence of an underlying ideological slant? If the source is commercial, do business-related considerations color the material?
- **Timeliness:** Is the source material current and up-to-date? Was a given article published fifty years ago, or last year? Generally, more recent articles reflect the current state of scholarship regarding a given topic and should therefore be favored.

Apply these criteria to all secondary sources, especially those derived from the internet: a truly democratic medium where anyone, from expert to crackpot extremist, has equal voice. In that way, you'll ensure that your evidence is of the highest quality, convincing to the most demanding of readers, such as your professors.

Quotations derived from secondary sources are perhaps the most common form of evidence used by academic writers to develop supporting paragraphs. A few simple rules apply to the incorporation of quotations within paragraphs. As much as possible, avoid beginning or ending a body paragraph with a quotation. Instead, first bring up an abstract concept in your own words; then use a "signal phrase," such as "according to Beedles" or "as Petracca says," that leads the reader into the quoted or paraphrased material, which you provide as evidence. Following the quote, insert another couple of sentences that keep the paragraph focused on your thesis, and make a transition into the next paragraph. Also, try not to make your quotations too long; use only quoted material that is necessary to support your abstract points. All of your secondary evidence should be footnoted or cited, using American Psychological Association or Modern Language Association guidelines, to dispel any suspicion of plagiarism. Finally, remember that you don't have to quote all secondary evidence directly. You can also paraphrase—that is, restate in your own words—certain passages, for the sake of stylistic variety. In fact, it's a good idea to have a fairly equal balance between quotations and paraphrases in your supporting paragraphs. Just make sure that you footnote or otherwise attribute your paraphrases, exactly as you would do with quotations.

Revising

You may, after having followed the preceding guidelines, have written such a perfect piece of prose that it needs no more work. Just turn it in to your teacher and wait for the paper to come back with a big red A on the title page. Too often, students take this approach to the writing process. Having finished the first draft, they feel it's good enough to turn in and therefore may neglect the very procedure that will ensure a good grade. That procedure is revision, which many writers believe to be the most important phase in the writing process. Successful writers celebrate the revision phase as a chance to refine their thesis, to reexamine stated opinions and claims, to reorder textual material to improve its logical flow, to insert new and improved phrasings, and to cut clunky or awkward passages.

The objective of the revision process is to end up with as flawless a final draft as possible, to give yourself a sense of satisfying closure—the heady satisfaction of a job well done—and to give your work the best chance of being embraced warmly by professors and teaching assistants. Many students find it useful to approach the revision with a concise list of guidelines, suggestions for approaching certain key points that are crucial to producing polished writing in the disciplines. Read over each of the following bulleted points, and make sure that your draft material conforms to the criteria outlined within each category.

- *Consistency* means a certain congruity of style that your written work will ideally maintain. You don't want to start out an essay or report in one tone—say, the relatively informal tone of the beach-based paragraph included earlier—and then veer into a much more formal tone, as illustrated by the second sample paragraph. During the consistency phase of the revision process, you will want to establish a voice appropriate to the genre in which you are writing and then to revise in order to maintain it.
- *Brevity* means resolutely cutting out the unnecessary words that infest even the best of first drafts like weevils in the oatmeal carton. Why say, "I invite you hereby to imbibe the very liquid caffeinated beverage contained in the container that you are presently holding within your fingers," when you can

say the same thing in fewer words, "Drink your coffee": a net savings of 87 percent? Check for wordiness, repetition, padding for the sake of additional paper length (professors always recognize this and hate it!). Revising for conciseness may require gouging out some of the wonderful phrases you generated in your freewriting, because they don't work in the context of the paper under consideration. It can be agonizing to eliminate the most exquisite sentence or the wittiest simile you ever wrote, but you sometimes have to do it. Save that brilliancy in a computer file, and use it later, in another paper.

- *Focus* and *coherence* mean making sure that your written work has a thesis— a main idea—and that your supporting paragraphs serve to develop that thesis. If you find yourself having strayed from the paper's thesis, either you will have to remove that digressive material, rewrite it, and reorder it to fit into the paper's developmental flow, or you will have to reconceive and rewrite your thesis. The writing process can be seen as cyclic: you come up with a thesis; you write about that thesis, thus leading you into new and unexpected intellectual territory; you revise your thesis on the basis of that new supporting material; you write some more supporting material, thereby causing you to revise your thesis further, and so on, until you have a thesis with which you are satisfied and supporting material that develops it coherently.

- *Correctness* refers to the proofreading process during which you read over your paper for stylistic issues and problems in spelling and grammar. Certain students—especially those who don't consider themselves as natural-born grammarians—may find the proofreading process scary. If you're one of those people, we suggest that you proof your papers by looking for one group of commonly made mistakes at a time. Start first with style, cutting out long, spaghetti-like strands of prepositional phrases, eliminating repetitive wordings. Avoid using passive verb constructions, unless you are writing in a discipline in which such syntax is the norm. Having proofread for stylistics, then check for grammar, spelling, and typos. If you're a computer user, you can inspect the latter two with the spell-checker that usually comes bundled with word processing softwave. There are many excellent writing reference guides on the market; these allow you easily to find information on punctuation, basic grammar, word choice, and documentation, and they usually cover "trouble areas" for writers whose native language is not English.

If you follow these straightforward guidelines, you will be better equipped to produce the kinds of writing assigned in all of your university classes. Although most of us are used to thinking of writing as a product—you manufacture a given piece of writing in order to show your professor that you understand the course material—it may be more useful for you to think of writing as a process, as outlined before: a thinking and inventing process in the prewriting phase; a process of communication in the drafting phase; and a process of clarification and refinement in the revision phase. Careful attention to all phases of this process will result in better writing "products."

THE ACADEMIC CONTEXT(S)

Imagine a student named Joe sitting in the lecture hall of his Sociology 1 class. One day the sociology professor announces the following essay assignment: "Analyze a social issue using either the functionalist or the social conflict paradigm."

At first Joe thinks this sounds doable—he's heard the word "analyze" before, and he even analyzed a poem once for his high school English class. However, on the night before the assignment's due date, Joe suddenly finds himself beset with a myriad of vexing questions. As he looks over news stories to analyze, he realizes that this kind of analysis might be different from the kind he used when he tried to make sense of that Nikki Giovanni poem in high school. And then there are the theoretical paradigms. How, exactly, is he supposed to use the functionalist paradigm? What is that paradigm, anyway? Joe has a vague idea that analysis means taking something apart and examining it in some way, but he's not sure what it means to analyze a social issue by using a particular theory. Joe begins to ask himself the question that students have asked themselves for centuries, since Socrates invented his method. "What does this crazy teacher want here, anyway?"

Although it's true that certain teachers do favor certain kinds of writing or emphasize certain thematic issues over others, the real questions Joe is asking himself at this point—although he may not know it yet—are, "What are the conventions for analytical writing in the discipline that calls itself sociology? How can I learn these conventions so that I can perform tasks such as the one my teacher just handed me?"

A somewhat cynical and easy answer to these questions would be, "Spend two years in sociology classes and it will eventually come to you," in the same way that, by living in France for two years, a reasonably intelligent American will eventually pick up some of the language. However, in a case like Joe's, when an assignment is due the next day, a background in writing in the disciplines can be extremely useful, if not downright lifesaving. Experts in the composition field have identified particular conventions in each of the disciplines that derive from each discipline's unique objects, methods, and linguistic conventions. In sociology, for example, theoretical perspectives such as functionalism and social conflict theory are used as tools for analyzing and thus for making sense of social phenomena; such knowledge would help Joe tackle the assignment successfully and without cancer-producing stress.

Universities have been set up not just to hand out diplomas to students who stick out their four or five years, but of more importance, to produce and disseminate knowledge. In order to accomplish this, universities have traditionally divided themselves into three major categories: the sciences, the social sciences, and the humanities. Broadly speaking, the sciences take the natural world as their object of study; thus, methods of empirical—that is, firsthand—investigation, observation, and experimentation form the foundation of all scientific inquiry. The "hard" sciences include disciplines such as physics, biology, zoology, chemistry, anatomy, and physiology, and for the purposes of this text, computer science.

The social sciences focus on the world of human action and interaction, and, like the sciences, the social sciences use methods of empirical observation and experimentation in order to understand the nature of human behavior. However, since many aspects of human activity are not open to investigation by the hard sciences, social scientists rely more on theorizing than on the "hard" empirical observations that are available to chemists and zoologists, for example. Social sciences include psychology, sociology, anthropology, communications, media study, economics, and political science.

The humanities concentrate on aesthetics and cultural production—that is, on artistic and creative human expression as well as on means of communicating, language being foremost among these. Humanities' methods rely more on interpretation than do the disciplines under the broad umbrellas of science and social science. However, it is important to keep in mind that all of these generalizations concerning method are just that—generalizations—and that a great deal of theorizing takes place in hard sciences such as physics (cosmology, for example), quite a bit of interpretation takes place in the social sciences, and so on.

Categories are useful for ordering ideas and objects, yet they are usually incapable of neatly containing everything we try to place within them. The categories used by universities to divide and define the parameters of human inquiry are not always as distinct as they might seem. All the disciplines are united in their efforts to discover what is true about the world in which we live, and although for the most part, each discipline looks at a particular aspect of this world, asking particular questions about it, there is sometimes overlap between the work of different fields. Scholars within one specialized area of inquiry often rely on discoveries made in other fields to augment their own work. Similarly, as we saw in our brief outline of the methods used in the disciplines, all disciplines rely on observation, and the experimental method is performed both in the sciences and in psychology, a social science.

Even though they look at different areas of life and ask very different kinds of questions about them, both scientists and social scientists employ some common strategies: they use quantitative observation methodologies, wherein they systematically observe particular phenomena; they posit hypotheses about the phenomena; they test their hypotheses through more observation; and they refine these hypotheses on the basis of their observations ultimately trying to arrive at the closest approximation to "truth" as possible. And even within the humanities, observation of objective cultural productions is necessary to the kinds of interrogations conducted within the humanistic disciplines.

Since all the disciplines rely on observation, practitioners within all the disciplines must confront the problems of objectivity and subjectivity. *Objectivity* refers to the ability to focus on a particular object under consideration, filtering out everything but that which is present and observable. This principle is the cornerstone of empirical methods in the sciences and thus is key in the social sciences as well. *Subjectivity* in this context refers to the subject who is conducting the observation, as separate from the object of study, and ultimately mediating the observation. All objectivity is hindered by subjectivity; the zoologist observing the mating behavior of the San Joaquin kit fox, the anthropologist cataloging the religious rituals of the Yanomamo Indians of Brazil, the drama critic watching the performance of Tennessee Williams's *Cat on a Hot Tin Roof,* all have to negotiate the interplay between the object under observation and their own ideas, expectations, beliefs, and biases. Scientists and social scientists especially try to maintain objectivity; they strive for it, but ultimately there is really no way to achieve total objectivity. Indeed, observing a phenomenon can alter that phenomenon, as, for instance, in the case of physicists attempting to define the properties of subatomic particles: the very act of observation alters the properties of the particles themselves.

Even if it were possible to observe some phenomena with total objectivity, human subjectivity inevitably intervenes when it becomes time to interpret the meaning of such phenomena. All disciplines engage in such interpretation, even though we tend to think that it is primarily humanities scholars whose job it is to infer meaning(s) in relatively ambiguous artifacts. All of the disciplines proceed by using the broadest common methodology; that is, all academicians use the skills of induction and deduction to arrive at meaning both generalized and specific. This process works in a kind of cyclical manner. Researchers look at events and objects in the external world and perceive certain similarities, patterns, and meanings. From that observation, these scholars will posit theories in order to make some general sense of what is being observed. They will then proceed to apply these theories to observable phenomena, and on the basis of such observation, will modify their theories—updating, clarifying them, bringing the body of shared knowledge in their discipline closer and closer to the "truth,"—at least as they see it. For instance, astronomers twenty years ago believed the universe to be static and unchanging, until they observed certain celestial bodies having a reddish tint. From this coloration—called a "red shift" in the parlance of astronomers—they deduced that some galaxies are in fact receding from us, and therefore they posited the notion of an expanding universe, which, in turn, caused them to infer a cause for this expansion, namely the "big bang" event that is now thought to be the point of origin of all existence as we know it.

Compounding the complexity of the subjectivity/objectivity issue is the fact that many scholars approach their objects of study from the perspective of theories to which they adhere. In the social sciences, for example, some psychologists interpret human behavior from a Freudian perspective—looking for the sexual drives underlying all human activities and artifacts—whereas Jungian theorists look for archetypal symbols such as the never-ending circle or the cross as they shed light on those human behaviors and artifacts. Likewise, theoretical perspectives for interpreting cultural artifacts abound in the humanities. The literary scholar writing from the perspective of the Marxist cultural critic will look at a given piece of writing, say a novel, for example, to identify the ways in which that novel reveals the economic stratification characteristic of Western capitalist culture. A Green theorist—as you will see later in this text—will look at a cereal box (no kidding!) to discover the ways in which people's attitudes toward the environment are shaped by what they read, see, and hear in the media. A feminist art historian might examine Botticelli's renderings of the female anatomy, comparing them with contemporary media representations of the "ideal" female body type, to show the evolution—

once again driven in no small part by the media—of our cultural notions of what is aesthetically beautiful and sexually appealing.

The Principle of Interdisciplinarity

Because the broad disciplinary categories of science, social science, and humanities share certain theories and practices in common, you will discover certain academic disciplines that do not fall readily into any single one of these umbrella categories. The discipline called history, for example, is considered by some to fall within the social sciences, because it concerns itself with human social behavior through time. But it also examines such behavior by analyzing cultural artifacts such as books, paintings, and fashion, and therefore in many ways resembles the activities of scholars in the humanities. Other academic disciplines such as religious studies, gender studies, and ethnic studies may be categorized either as social sciences or humanities, depending on the concerns and approaches of particular practitioners. For example, some religious studies scholars might approach a religious text such as the Dead Sea Scrolls as a kind of literary product and therefore be writing in the mode of humanities-based scholarship, whereas others might examine the cultural implications of those same texts, therefore more closely aligning themselves with the work of anthropologists who—as you now know—are social scientists.

Some disciplines represent a conflation of two fields that are ordinarily considered to be distinct and separate from one another. Evolutionary psychology is a recently emergent field that combines a social science emphasis on human social behavior with the natural sciences' evolutionary theory to posit new ways of understanding why we act in the strange and amazing ways that we can observe on the Jerry Springer show. Within certain disciplines, practitioners may also concentrate on areas traditionally considered to be outside the sphere of inquiry of that particular discipline. Within the humanities, for instance, philosophers of mathematics show how to derive the whole of arithmetic—often considered as the province of the sciences—in logical terms. Likewise, when they study the relation between human brain chemistry and behavior, some psychologists align themselves more with the natural sciences of biology and chemistry than with disciplines within the social sciences. In fact, the trend in psychology in recent years has been toward an emphasis on scientific methods and concerns, rather than on behaviorism; thus, drug therapy is now practiced as much as, if not more than, more traditional cognitive therapeutic approaches.

In part, such an emphasis is motivated by the incredible amounts of money available from drug companies for research and is due to the increased control of health maintenance organizations (HMOs) on the medical insurance industry. Drug therapies are a lot cheaper to administer than are the more time-consuming traditional "couch therapies" of traditional psychology; thus, the marketplace has partly influenced the "objective" pursuits of science. This example highlights an important element of the work of the disciplines. Although people often refer to university work as existing separate from the "real world," ensconced in the "ivory tower," the world intrudes in a number of ways into the supposedly rarefied world of universities.

Political movements, market forces, the directing of research funds by large corporations, the disbursement of scholarship monies and financial aid to some groups and not to others—these factors and others influence what gets studied in the halls of academia.

DISCIPLINARY CONVENTIONS

Even though there is much interdisciplinary overlap between the sciences, social sciences, and humanities, each of these fields of inquiry can be fruitfully considered as a different "discourse community," a group of people having common interests and shared ways of doing things, including ways of expressing their shared knowledge verbally—that is, with words on paper or on a computer screen. Remember Joe, our Sociology 1 student, who was struggling with the assignment that asked him to analyze a news event, using a sociological theory? Joe is systematically working through his general education requirements, and now we find him enrolled in a Music Appreciation class. An easy A, he thinks—that is, until the professor asks the class to write a music review of the city symphony's performance of J. S. Bach's Cantata No. 140.

Again, Joe is mystified, because he's not familiar with the conventions that are unique to the branch of the humanities known as musicology. Merely knowing that music is a discipline within the category of the humanities would help Joe discern the shape, voice, and the ways of presenting evidence and of interpreting the merits and meanings of a piece of artistic production that a music review requires. Furthermore, as it turns out, the music review is a very standard form that practitioners in that field use to share information and opinions about different musical products. The subgenre of the music review has a particular form with an agreed-on means of arranging ideas logically, a standard tone, and a common set of terms that everyone in the musicology field uses with the understanding that everyone else in the community knows what these terms mean.

It is these unique conventions of discourse communities that perplex students as they enter various disciplines for the first time. Not knowing the shared language (outsiders sometimes cynically call it jargon) and being unaware of the particular forms of sharing information verbally, students feel lost. Therefore, we would advise Joe not to drop out of college and join the army (which, he would sadly discover, has its own set of disciplinary conventions: "Drop down and give me 50, maggot!") but should instead familiarize himself with the conventions of the musicological review.

Some genres such as the music review are distinct and clearly defined, with somewhat rigid guidelines; others are more flexible. The science report, for example, follows a standard structure, one that reflects the scientific process itself. The science report starts with an abstract, that is, a summary of the entire report; follows with an introduction that reviews relevant studies and theories; and lays out the focus of the study being introduced, its research question(s), and hypotheses. The "Methods" section then describes the procedures used in the study, the "Results" section reports the findings, and the "Discussion" section interprets the meaning and significance of those findings. This format—sometimes with very slight variations—is what scientists expect to see when they look at research reports. Such standardization helps scientists conduct their work efficiently. Since science works by building on previous knowledge, scientists must be able to read a report and judge immediately whether the results are valid on the basis of the kinds of procedures used. They must be able to repeat accurately the procedures of studies to verify the results and ultimately arrive at relative "truths" based on the accumulation of shared knowledge.

There are a number of such standardized genres within other disciplines, such as the journal abstract, the legal brief, environmental impact reports, and position papers. In this textbook, we've taken a number of fascinating topics and provided a window into the ways that practitioners in different disciplines use a variety of perspectives and discipline-specific genres to approach issues within these topics. We have also included articles that have a "reader-friendly journalistic" tone as you might find in a "popular" magazine such as *Newsweek* or *Time,* along with more esoteric discipline-specific genres: the kinds of writing you will be likely to encounter when you move from the composition classroom and into the broader academy. In this way, *AC/DC* will introduce you to a wide variety of academic discourse communities, while making you increasingly sophisticated in reading and writing actual genre-specific prose.

In the third chapter of this book, for example, we have chosen the broad topic of "Gender and Sexuality" to frame a number of disciplinary points of view and modes of expression. In this chapter's communications unit, theoretical essays on differences in male and female communication styles appear alongside a report formatted in the experimental report style, wherein two researchers present their findings on power relations and their effects on male/female communication. Later, in the zoology unit of that chapter, two zoologists report their experimental findings on bird behavior, whereas two other pieces address animal behavior in a more journalistic fashion. Just as you will read examples of genre-specific writing in *Academic Communities/Disciplinary Conventions,* so too, you will be given assignments to produce your own essays that reflect the unique kinds of writing required in the various disciplines. Rather than extensively delineating all the rhetorical forms and disciplinary genres at the beginning of this text—an impossible and pointless task, without a disciplinary context in which to situate those forms—we will identify genres and rhetorical modes as they appear in the readings and writing assignments throughout *AC/DC.*

WRITING WITHIN THE DISCIPLINE OF COMPOSITION: A CASE STUDY

To give you a closer look at the kinds of work that scholars in the disciplines undertake, we are including an essay from our own field, that of composition and rhetoric. This sample "case study" essay will function in two ways: it will raise issues that are relevant to the work of this textbook: that is, it will to some extent introduce you to this textbook's guiding philosophies, and it will represent an example of a piece of writing performed in a specific discipline. Following the essay, we will "walk you through" the kinds of questions and prewriting tasks that you will find at the end of each reading in this textbook.

But first, here is a little background information, so as to acquaint you with the theoretical issues relevant to this essay from the discipline of composition studies. In the olden days (like fifteen years ago), writing instruction was typically viewed as the special province of English departments. English professors and graduate students in literary studies were the primary instructors of college composition, and writing assignments were given usually in relation to literature—perhaps a more sophisticated version of the writing you did for your high school English classes. Recently, however, composition theorists have been questioning this approach, since so much of the work of scholars in all fields involves writing, since the professional world requires a large amount of writing, and since these forms of writing are typically quite different from the kinds of personal and interpretive essays often assigned in composition courses with a literary emphasis. Thus, the movement known as writing across the curriculum evolved within the composition field.

The writing across the curriculum (WAC) movement attempted to broaden the focus of writing instruction beyond an English emphasis, to encompass the kinds of writing performed in all fields. Proponents of WAC believed that writing should be assigned and taught in all disciplines, because students would then have practice in a variety of written genres and because writing is believed to be an effective way of learning. In the simplest formulation, WAC asserts that through the process of writing about a subject area, students learn more about that subject. Many early WAC proponents envisioned the abolition of the college composition course (stop that cheering, dammit!), believing that as more professors within the disciplines required writing in their courses, the need for a separate college composition course would become obsolete.

Since those initial stages of WAC, another related movement has emerged within composition studies, which is called writing in the disciplines (WID). Proponents of WID support the WAC ideas about the importance of having students learn a variety of discipline-based discourses. However, the WID approach asserts that this kind of instruction can and should be conducted within composition courses. Some of the rationale for this approach is pragmatic: many professors in the disciplines have enough to do just teaching the content of their courses, and even when they require writing of their students, professors do not often have the time (or the interest) in teaching their students how to perform this writing. This was part of Joe's problem in our earlier examples, since in neither class was Joe given much guidance about how to write the assignments. Although these were fictional examples, this problem happens in the real world all the time, as you may be experiencing in some of your courses right now. For this reason, composition instructors with a WID orientation structure their courses around reading and writing from the different disciplines. Since you are reading this textbook, your instructor is aligning himself or herself with this philosophy.

Research in Writing
Across the Curriculum

BEGINNINGS

George A. McCulley

The following essay by George A. McCulley was written in the early days of WAC, when composition theorists were in the process of working out their pedagogical approaches. McCulley calls for research into the different kinds of writing performed in different disciplinary contexts. Since this article was written, researchers have filled in many of the gaps in our knowledge about these conventions, so that now composition instructors are generally well-equipped to teach the writing that is performed within the disciplines. As you read, pay attention to the intentional shifts in McCulley's writing style, and note the kinds of evidence he uses to make his points.

THREE SCENARIOS

Paritally hidden behind a stack of student papers that are waiting to be read, the phone rings. "Hi. This is Martie. I want to ask you a couple of questions. I assigned a term paper in my cellular biology course this quarter—no specific topic, just about something related to cellular biology. I tried peer critiques in the same course last year, but they didn't work out so well. Some students complained because they thought the students who critiqued their papers were dull—didn't know enough about the subject to offer helpful comments. I'd like to use peer critiques again, but I think I need some help. What do you think?" 1

"Well . . ." long pause. 2

Since Martie had attended one of our writing-across-the-curriculum workshops and had participated in peer critiques, she didn't want to know how peer critiques could be used; she *knew* the process. She knew what she expected in these papers, based on her experience and training in biology, but she wasn't quite sure how to articulate her expectations into specific 3 criteria that students could use to evaluate each other's papers during the critique sessions.

What criteria should be used to judge papers in Cellular Biology? What   4
do English teachers know about writing in biology? Do we know, for instance, if the rules of evidence are different in biology than in composition? In mathematics? In history? That is, in composition and literature we regularly accept (in fact, demand) authoritative opinion as sufficient evidence to support a point: "Which critics assert that Chaucer's *Troilus and Creseyde* had its roots in Boccaccio's *Decameron*?" But is authoritative opinion ever appropriate evidence in biology? If so, under what conditions? If not, what is appropriate evidence? Is writing in biology always grounded in the scientific method, from theory building to hypothesis testing? Or are there cases when the logic of narrative or some other type of reasoning is appropriate? If so, what are they? Do they also hold for physics? Elsewhere? All of these questions concerning writing in disciplines outside of English are important, yet remain largely unanswered.

*   *   *

Outside the third-story windows autumn sweeps through the campus,   5
day-glo red and gold. Inside the faculty lounge there is a din of lunch conversation:

"May I join you, George? I've been meaning to call you for a while."   6
"Sure! Sit down, Jon. What's up?"   7
"Well, as I'm sure you're aware, the College of Engineering has ap-   8
proved the development of 'writing-intensive' courses—you know, putting in as much writing as possible in some of our upper-division courses to improve content knowledge as well as writing ability. I think my 406 course would be a natural choice—course concepts highly interrelated, requiring the kind of synthesis that writing seems to develop so well. But I'm not quite sure how writing can be best integrated in the course."

Eagerly, "What's 406, Jon?"   9
"Microwave Devices."   10
"Oh . . ."   11
"Resonant cavities," "slow-wave structures," "two-cavity klystrons" and   12
much more make up the content of a "Microwave Devices" course in electrical engineering. Can writing effectively be used to teach at least part of this? If so, which part? How "rectangular, cylindrical, and re-entrant cavities" physically differ and how these differences "influence fields"? How "phase and group velocities" and "cutoff frequencies" are interrelated? How "slow-wave structures" get their name? Assuming that writing can help students learn about slow-wave structures and the rest, what types of writing assignments work best? Journal entries? Term papers? Essay examinations? Moreover, what works best within an hour-and-a-half, twice-weekly Microwave Devices course? Several short papers? One long paper?

Finally, even if answers to questions about effective writing assign-   13
ments, related to course content and physical constraints, are known, what
are the answers to these questions in other electrical engineering courses? In
mathematics courses? History courses? All courses across the curriculum?

*   *   *

The civil engineering professor steps in front of his Professional Prac-   14
tices class, cradling a small stack of one-page handouts in his left arm that
he begins to distribute as he tells the students:
"Today, we're going to work on developing a clear, technical style—   15
something that's very important in the career of a professional civil engineer.
We're going to use something called the 'Paramedic Technique' (Lanham,
1981), accurately named as I believe it helps breathe life back into moribund
writing."
After his discussion of the "Paramedic Technique," the students dive   16
in, reading something about the problems with the public address system
and the ceiling in the Michigan Tech ice arena:

> The Michigan Tech Ice Arena has a serious voice reproduc-
> tion problem during hockey games. In much of the seating
> area, the announcer is impossible to understand, due to the
> constant echo in near-capacity situations. Indirectly related
> is a ceiling paint problem—the paint is flaking off and land-
> ing on the ice, tripping up several hockey players. The sug-
> gestion to solve this problem and to also improve acoustical
> characteristics of the arena is to suspend a thin tarp of ma-
> terial just below the rafters. This material supposedly has
> some acoustical effectiveness. This suggestion must be an-
> alyzed for acoustical effectiveness, and possible alternative
> solutions must be explored. Changes in speaker tuning and
> positioning will also be considered.

The students begin by circling *is's, are's,* and every word resembling a   17
preposition. They ask "Who's kicking who" in each sentence, find it very
awkward to put "real" subjects and "active" verbs into some sentences, such
as "Changes in speaker tuning and positioning will also be considered," but
keep trying.
During the next class and throughout the rest of the quarter, the pro-   18
fessor encourages students to use the "Paramedic Technique" when editing
their writing. But he realizes that the students soon internalize the circling of
to be and prepositions—indeed, find these steps in the method tedious and
abandon them—so he deletes these steps in next quarter's course, only
mentioning the evils of *to be* verbs and prepositional strings in his opening
discussion of the technique. He wonders if he should go through the whole
process next term—or could he skip some of the prescribed steps?

These are real questions: Are there hallmarks of "good" writing that ⁣19 pervade most writing contexts, such as Lanham (1981), Williams (1981), Reddish (1983), and others suggest? Many authorities agree on the horrors of overly nominalized prose and convoluted syntax. But when does nominalization become extreme and syntax convoluted? Obviously the answer depends on the context. But what do we know of the rhetorical contexts in each discipline?

If there are truisms of good style that span most disciplines and con- ⁣20 texts, do the specific stylistic and editorial conventions change from discipline to discipline, from context to context? What do experienced readers in each discipline expect? In what situations? Fundamentally, what emphasis should be put on teaching specific stylistic and editorial conventions, particularly when many students will change careers several times during their lives? Odell, Goswami, and Quick (1983) believe that we should turn our attention from style and focus on invention, echoing the concern for process-oriented instruction that has permeated all levels of composition theory and practice in recent years. If Odell and his colleagues' reasoning is sound, and common sense suggests that it is, what invention strategies should be employed in each context? What are the questions about audience(s) and purpose(s) a civil engineer should answer before drafting an environmental impact statement? An accountant writing a letter to the file? And so forth . . .

Quite clearly, we don't yet know what the specific stylistic considera- ⁣21 tions across the curriculum are nor how important they may be. Nor do we know how invention can best be managed from biology to history, from philosophy to applied statistics.

WRITING TO COMMUNICATE

Kinneavy (1971) argues that we don't know much about the principles ⁣22 of logic, organization, and style in informative and exploratory discourses— the two primary aims of most lab reports in biology courses and many writing tasks in other disciplines. Other researchers who have carefully examined writing outside of the composition classroom echo Kinneavy's conclusions (e.g., see Odell and Goswami, 1982).

Writing texts in courses from law to engineering do exist. But most au- ⁣23 thorities, including some authors, admit that the general prescriptions for quality in too many texts are static, immune to the constantly changing contexts for writing, and largely ignorant of the specific logical, organizational, and stylistic requirements for separate writing tasks. Houp and Pearsall (1984), the authors of a widely used technical writing text, make this clear in their first chapter:

> Because the qualities of good reports vary from report to report, depending upon audience and objective, we cannot

offer . . . a list [the criteria for quality] that applies equally to all reports (pp. 8–9).

Of course, we can't determine the specific requisites of quality for every writing task. Nevertheless, if we are to make writing a viable concept in biology, physics, electrical engineering classes, and all across the curriculum, we must begin filling in the gaps in our knowledge of how writing is best used within the specific discourse aims across the curriculum. To do this, we must carefully investigate writing and the writing process in a myriad of contexts—that is, we must conduct research.

WRITING TO LEARN

Beyond the general speculations of Berthoff (1983), Britton (1970), Emig (1983), and Moffett (1981) and the seminal research of Applebee (1983), Britton, Burgess, Martin, McLeod, and Rosen (1975), we know little about the specifics of writing to learn. We don't know what content can be taught using writing, especially in the more scientific and technical areas. We also don't know if writing is a more effective means of teaching content than other more "traditional" methods. (Intuitively, most of us will agree that writing is not the most efficient pedagogical technique for teaching multiplication tables or other rote learning tasks.) Worse yet, we haven't done much to match types of writing (exposition, for instance) and their inherent logical and organizational structures with specific learning tasks. In general, Kinneavy (1971) suggests that if students are just acquainting themselves with the subject matter (such as "slow-wave structures" and "resonant cavities"), then the logic and organization of classification and narration would be most applicable, usually calling for an essay. But we aren't sure if this holds true for all new content in all areas. Following the same reasoning, it would appear that when students are asked to design, construct and test microwave devices, necessitating the use of "slow-wave structures" and "resonant cavities," then inductive and deductive logic and organization become necessary characteristics of reports and proposals. But again we aren't sure. Further, if students must understand the limitations of these concepts in the theory of microwave devices, where and why they don't work (applied research), or are asked to extend them, how they might be improved (basic research), then the logic and organization of evaluation and exploration (if any exists) become necessary and would require argumentative papers and theoretical treatises. We aren't certain, however.

Even if we did know what type of writing is best suited for what type of learning, we would still have to guess which physical constraints (class size, term length, credit hours) limit the usefulness of writing as a pedagogical technique. Since our hunches are often misleading, only research can answer our questions and guide us as to where (in electrical engineering and else-where) and how writing can be best used for teaching and learning.

RHETORICAL CONSIDERATIONS

In the last few years "packaged" editing schemes, like Lanham's 26 "Paramedic Technique" (1981), have exploded into the literature and texts on writing. Yet, just a decade before, some authorities, like Kinneavy (1971), were asking which stylistic and editorial conventions were appropriate to each discipline. Have we now discovered that there are no unique conven-tions, that they are the same everywhere?

Reddish (1983), writing about bureaucratic language, distinguishes 27 three styles of writing: simple ("Dick-and-Jane" style), complex (mature but graceful style), and "complexified" (a highly legalistic, convoluted style which largely ignores the rhetorical context within which the writing is placed). For Reddish and many others, then, "good" style largely depends on the rhetori-cal context—who is writing, for what purposes, and for whom. In this sense, good style is like good manners—what may be appropriate behavior at a white-tie dinner may not be necessary at McDonalds, although there are probably threads common to both situations. What we don't fully know is what readers need to make meaning out of written texts as the contexts for writing change and what, if any, are the universals of good style within all contexts.

This relativistic notion of good style is also much closer to the position 28 of others, like Odell and his colleagues (1983), who call for more specific knowledge about invention in varying contexts. If the elements of good style are dependent upon changing conditions, then logically the most effective invention strategies should also vary. Selzer's (1983) investigation of the composing processes of a practicing engineer, considered a successful writer, depicts that this engineer spends most of his composing time plan-ning. But is this engineer unique? Are the invention strategies he employs in planning common to other successful engineers? For most writing tasks? What about other professionals and nonprofessionals who must write to succeed on the job? And what is the interrelation between invention and style across disciplines, among writing tasks? Without at least partial an-swers to these questions, our efforts to foster and improve writing across the curriculum will be greatly handicapped.

WHY RESEARCH AND EVALUATION IN WRITING
ACROSS THE CURRICULUM PROGRAMS?

For Martie, the clear articulation of criteria for Cellular Biology papers 29 was essential to her efforts to instill writing in biology. For Jon, the knowl-edge of which type of writing could be best used to teach and extend which course concept made writing a fixture in his Microwave Devices course. For the civil engineering professor, the discovery of how style could be best taught in his Professional Practices course cemented his attention to style and opened his eyes to other rhetorical concerns in his civil engineering report writing courses.

Although these three scenarios, all brief and insular but typical, repre-   30 sent glances of the writing-across-the-curriculum program at Michigan Tech, they point out three strong reasons for conducting writing research across the curriculum:

1. to discover the uses and roles of writing to communicate across the curriculum;
2. to determine how writing can best be used to structure and improve learning across the curriculum;
3. to identify and develop the appropriate rhetorical concerns across the curriculum.

Individually, each of these three reasons represents strong motivation for conducting research in writing-across-the-curriculum programs, and together they comprise a compelling argument for making research central to such programs. But there are still other reasons.

Writing-across-the-curriculum programs require time and money. To   31 gain these resources, program developers need to demonstrate that their programs work and that classrooms are improving—the evaluation function of research. Evaluations, if properly designed, can tell us not only if our programs are working, but *why* they are working. Such evaluations add to program growth by providing diagnostic and prescriptive information as well as evaluative data; they do not just statistically assume that the program is as good as it is ever going to get. In evaluation jargon, these dynamic evaluations are known as formative evaluations; static assessments as summative evaluations. Obviously, if writing-across-the-curriculum programs are to succeed, satisfying the needs of administrators and/or funding agencies, and to improve, satisfying the need of students and teachers, our evaluations of them must be both formative and summative—that is, they must include research in its fullest sense.

With increasing frequency, faculty members outside of the English   32 area at our institution seek us out and ask questions like: "What do you think is the best way to incorporate writing into my CAD/CAM (computer-assisted design/computer-assisted manufacturing) course?" The gravity of such a question is hard to appreciate unless you have worked in an institution like Michigan Tech where engineering and the sciences are the popular concerns. All too often a well-intentioned faculty member, seated at a crowded luncheon table, prefaces a comment with: "You people in the humanities won't appreciate this, but . . ." Our best explanation of these surprising questions, which occur just about anywhere and anytime, even between periods at Tech hockey games, is that we are now seen as authorities in an area where a wide range of faculty have an interest. These "shared interests," more than anything else, have led to the collaborative research which has benefited us all, as Art Young accurately pointed out in the first chapter of this book.

Even at a technological university like Michigan Tech, the curriculum is extensive, from Outdoor Recreation Development in the School of Technology to Drill and Ceremonies in Army ROTC. Within this varied curriculum, the diversity of classrooms and instructors is large, and writing is beginning to pervade this spectrum of different courses and teachers. Students write "letters to the file" in their Accounting I and II courses, documenting their procedures. Students in an intermediate algebra course must summarize basic concepts in a journal. Students in many engineering courses write lab reports, field reports, proposals, feasibility studies and more, and it is the same in the life and physical sciences. Because we believe that writing should be at the center of the curriculum, we see the whole curriculum as a laboratory, full of opportunities. The questions within our own curriculum provide the motivation for research in writing across the curriculum.   ©

READING WITHIN THE DISCIPLINE OF COMPOSITION

In our introduction to the material you just read, we suggested that you pay attention to certain aspects of the text to follow. This is a device that we will employ at the beginning of each reading in this textbook, to focus your attention on certain points, techniques, logical strategies, or disciplinary features we believe a certain article or report models. With regard to the McCulley essay, we asked you to pay attention to the intentional shifts in his writing. One feature that you will notice from the very first sentence of this essay is that it begins with a relatively informal tone. Instead of having a complete first sentence, for instance, which would give the reader some sense of the essay's content, the author uses a sentence fragment, or heading, to introduce three seemingly unrelated stories. The two-word heading "Three Scenarios" leads us into a series of narratives, each alluding to concerns that people in different disciplines have about assigning writing in their classes.

The style that McCulley chooses to employ here looks like the kind that people in literary studies often hold as objects for analysis—namely, short stories—rather than the kind of expository prose one would expect to find in a research essay. We can deduce from this stylistic feature a number of points. George A. McCulley is a writing teacher who apparently identifies himself to some degree as a creative writer and has therefore issued himself license to take certain liberties with the traditional research essay format. McCulley's style also suggests a point about discipline-specific writing as well: creative license may be acceptable and even encouraged in some disciplines, such as the field of composition theory, but in other disciplines, you may be required to adhere more rigorously to more rigid rules and certain formats. Finally, the narrative style of this essay's opening provides us with anecdotal evidence for the thesis that McCulley develops in this essay, namely that successful implementation of WAC theories will require a certain amount of reeducation or rethinking for all instructors throughout the university community.

Besides asking you to look at the stylistic features of this essay, we also suggested in our introduction to the reading that you note the kinds of evidence McCulley relies on as he articulates his central points. He uses a combination of evidentiary forms; in addition to the brief narrative examples—themselves firsthand evidence of his thematic point—he also draws on previously published research, which he cites using the American Psychological Association–based parenthetical in-text citation format. The APA format is the standard citation method used by practitioners of the social sciences. Be aware, however, that APA is not the only citation format that researchers use. In most humanities-based disciplines, researchers use the Modern Language Association's (MLA) guidelines to parenthetical citation. In other fields, especially the hard sciences a more traditional citation format relying on footnotes and bibliography remains the preferred method for citing sources. In any case, although the disciplines employ these varying methods for citing secondary evidence, what they share is a reliance on the published work of others, both inside and outside their disciplinary spheres, to develop and lend credibility to their own arguments. By asking you to note McCulley's use of evidence, we were helping you to see some of the workings of composition studies as a discipline, as well as to direct your attention toward a model of presenting support that can help you in your own writing.

CRITICAL READING

Following each essay in this text, you will find a group of questions. These questions, which are labeled "Critical Reading," ask you to examine and often clarify key points within each reading. Critical reading, as we conceive of it here, is different from the activity you engage in when you read the latest *Thrasher* magazine or pick up a copy of *Cosmo*. Critical reading involves approaching a text from two levels simultaneously. On the literal level, you want to make sure you understand what all the words mean. What are the "tilted sedimentary strata" you encounter in a geology article? What are the "charmed quarks" you read about in a physics report? What is the "hegemony of oppressive cultural beliefs" that the cultural critic is noting? Understanding what authors are really saying means using dictionaries and other more discipline-specific resource materials to clarify any terms you find confusing or completely alien. This may seem to be obvious advice, but you'd be surprised at how many students will pass their eyes over a given page of text without stopping to clarify unknown terms. Avoiding such skimming can make the difference between complete bafflement, partial understanding, or full mastery over course materials.

Below the surface level of language, it is important that you begin not merely ingesting information passively but considering the implications and credibility of material as you read it. What are the underlying assumptions that a given author is making about a topic when writing about it? What theoretical biases might be coloring an author's interpretation of so-called objective data? What do these texts reveal about the cultural milieu in which they're created? What are the professional credentials of this author, anyway? These are all questions you should apply to every text you read, including those *Cosmo* and *Thrasher* articles, because to do less would be to allow yourself to become a mere passive recipient of predigested information, potentially subject to the manipulation of skilled rhetoricians. Our "Critical Reading" questions are designed to assist you in identifying words and phrases that might need further elucidation at the literal level, and to encourage you to question the assumptions, credentials, credibility, motives, and persuasive strategies used by the authors of the articles you read. Following the McCulley reading, we might ask the following Critical Reading question: How does McCulley end this chapter? What suggestions does he make to composition instructors in order to improve writing instruction across the university curriculum?

To answer this question, you would have to refer back to the end of the essay, where McCulley suggests that more empirical research be undertaken in order to discover "the uses and roles of writing to communicate across the curriculum"; to "determine how writing can best be used to structure and improve learning across the curriculum"; and to identify the unique forms and audiences of writing in particular disciplines. This question serves two purposes: it encourages you to focus on the thematic point the author is making about the need for increased research into writing across the curriculum; and it advocates the pursuit of firsthand, empirical research, the kind of activity in which social scientists routinely engage. This undertaking should, in turn, lead you to certain conclusions about composition theory as a discipline. Whereas, because of its close historical connection to the work done in English departments, most people might think of composition as a field in the humanities, it actually draws on the language conventions and research methods of both the humanities and the social sciences. In this case, McCulley is advocating that social-scientific methods of empirical observation be used to test and validate the theories of the field.

CLASS DISCUSSION

Following Critical Reading questions, you will find two suggestions for class discussion. For the McCulley essay, we might ask class members to reflect, as a group, on the kinds of writing assignments they have encountered thus far in their university careers. We might first ask you to discuss these assignments from the affective—that is, the emotional—level: how did you feel when your music professor asked you to write that review of Bach's Cantata and you had no idea what a musicological review was? After giving you an opportunity to vent your spleen about these sometimes confusing assignments, we might then ask you to discuss them on a more productively cognitive level: what kinds of writing activities have your humanities professors asked you to perform? Your social science professors and "hard" science professors? What elements did these assignments have in common? How did they differ? How do the features of these assignments relate to specific concerns of the discipline within which it is situated? The Class Discussion prompts are designed to engage the class in lively debate concerning the reading at hand, while at the same time planting seeds for future writing that you might undertake on a related topic.

DIRECTED FREEWRITES

The last feature you will find at the end of each reading in this book will be a brief and friendly freewriting suggestion based on the technique discussed earlier, in the writing process portion of this chapter. For the McCulley essay, we might ask you, as a freewriting assignment, to come up with a brief narrative scenario similar to the three ministories that McCulley provides at the beginning of his essay. These freewriting assignments are designed to help you engage with the topics being covered in the texts that you will be reading, and, once again, to help you generate ideas for the essay assignments that end each unit of this book.

CONCLUSION

So . . . now that you've seen an example of the kind of work we do in the field of composition, you have an increased degree of understanding, empathy—perhaps even pity—for us. But let us assure you: we like the work, and that's why we do it! We hope that as you move out into the broader academic community, you will feel similarly invigorated, inspired, and enthusiastic about some of the fields that you encounter, and that the reading and writing that you undertake while using *Academic Context/Disciplinary Conventions* will assist you in that process of self-discovery and increased knowledge.

CHAPTER TWO

IDENTITY
AND CONSCIOUSNESS

INTRODUCTION

In the introduction to his novel *Speaker for the Dead* award-winning science fiction writer Orson Scott Card tells the following anecdote:

> I remember well my summer as a performer at the Sundance Summer Theatre in Utah. I was a 19-year old trying to convince myself and others that I was a man, so with the other performers I became at least as profane—nay, foul-mouthed and filthy-minded—as the most immature of them. I worked hard to develop some fluidity and cleverness in my vulgarity, and won my share of laughs from the others. Yet during this whole time I lived with my parents, coming down the mountain at insane speeds late at night, only to end up in a home where certain words were simply never said. And I never said them. Not once did I slip and speak in front of my family the way I spoke constantly in front of the other performers at Sundance. This was not by an herculean effort, either. I didn't think about changing my behavior, it simply happened. When I was with my parents *I wasn't the same person.*
>
> I have seen this time and time again with my friends, with other family members. Our whole demeanor changes, our mannerisms, our figures of speech, when we move from one context to another. Listen to someone you know when they pick up the telephone. We have special voices for different people; our attitudes, our moods change depending on whom we are with. (xviii–xix)

Does this scenario sound familiar to you? Probably most of us have experienced the phenomenon Card describes here—being "different people" in different settings—which is one reason the topic of human identity and consciousness is so interesting and elusive. If we are so changeable in different contexts, what does this characteristic say about who we really are? Is there some core of "true self" underneath the various masks we put on for different people and different situations? It could be that these different "masks" are really not masks at all, as Card suggests; rather, they are different facets of our "true selves."

This perception leads logically to a myriad of fundamental questions concerning human individuality and awareness. What is a "true self"? Can we ever pin down a clear sense of our identities if they change so radically in different contexts, not to mention the fact that we change over time as we grow and, hopefully, mature? How do we become the unique individuals that we are? How much of a role does biology and "nature" play in this process, and how much is our identity a product of the cultures in which we live, or the "nurture" of our environments? Further, at the core of the self, what is the attribute we call consciousness? What processes are involved in thinking and awareness—both of the self and the world around us—and how does human consciousness differ from that of animals and the intelligent machines we are building in our own images? Does human consciousness transcend the physical body? Such questions about human identity and consciousness have fascinated scholars in the social sciences, hard sciences, and the humanities for centuries. Nearly every discipline within these categories has attempted to solve a different aspect of the puzzle that is humanity's essence.

Social scientists obviously have a major stake in studying the nature of human identity, since all the branches of the social sciences deal with human behavior and/or the underlying motives for behavior. Psychologists are the practitioners who primarily concern themselves with individual identity, although issues of individual identity invariably run into issues of group identity and influence. Sigmund Freud's work in human consciousness and identity formation influenced a very important field whose work continues to this day, now encompassing realms of neuro-chemistry and biology that Freud might never have imagined, except in his wildest cocaine-induced fantasies.

Psychologists routinely delve into different aspects of identity and consciousness, seeking to understand the unique functioning of human psychology. For example, psychological researcher David Feinstein has explored the ways that individuals use personal myths as organizing models that shape perception, understanding, and behavior. Such myths, primarily arising out of personal history and culture, are composed of postulates about oneself, one's world, and the relationship between the two. Individuals use these myths to "guide individual development, provide social direction, and address spiritual questions in a manner that is analogous to the way cultural myths carry out those functions for entire societies."

More hard science–oriented psychologists are discovering amazing things about brain chemistry and genetics that suggest that much of our human psychology is more biologically driven than behaviorists ever imagined. Still, the debates over the effects of nature versus nurture in forming individual psychology are far from resolved; most theorists at this point argue that a complex combination of biological and environmental factors make us into who we are. For example, observable changes in the brain chemistry of depressed patients receiving various combinations of therapies have led biopsychologists to theorize about the ways that factors in individual's early infant environment may actually alter the neural pathways in the brain, thus altering one's basic psychological makeup.

By contrast, sociologists investigate individual identity in relation to groups. Sociologists have contributed to our understanding of how our positions within certain identity categories—gender, race, ethnicity, nation, economic class, age, sexual orientation, for example—shape our individual identities. Frequently, "belonging" to a certain social group determines the advantages or disadvantages we may have, as we live in a society that, sociologists may argue, assigns differential power to individuals on the basis of group membership. Early social psychological work into the nature of in-groups and out-groups by the theorist Gordon Allport, for example, showed the importance of group memberships in influencing our behavior toward others who belong to groups outside our own. Further, his work helped to explain the ways in which prejudice—and its manifestations in discriminatory behavior—is largely based on our definitions of self in opposition to groups that fall outside our own.

The social science section in this chapter contains two units. Starting with the individual and his or her process of socialization and thus identity formation, we include a social psychology unit. This unit contains two "seminal" theories from social psychology that each, in slightly different ways, posit the individual as formed through social interactions. This unit concludes with a more recent essay in which a theorist explores the ways that consumerism and computer technology—something those earlier theorists of identity formation never dreamed of—is changing our notions of identity and its formation, expression, and evolution.

Many other disciplines within the social sciences concern themselves with questions of human identity and consciousness. Anthropologists, for example, have amassed a large body of information regarding the ways in which different cultures conceive of identity, the relations of the individual to the larger community, and the nature of human consciousness. Although the world's peoples are amazingly alike in many ways, the diversity in worldviews (and corresponding views of self) is, at the same time, startling.

Political science as a social science discipline has always concerned itself with issues of individual rights and responsibilities in relation to government and political order, and the history of Western beliefs about identity and individuality is intricately tied to the evolution of Western political and philosophical theory, from Descartes' "*cogito, ergo sum*" (I think, therefore I am) to Jean Jacques Rousseau's formulation of the social contract in which individuals implicitly agree to give up a certain amount of personal freedom in order to form societies in which their efforts at survival and prosperity are joined for the maximum benefit of all, to John Hobbes's view that our basic nature is to be brutish and nasty—thus societies work to civilize our beastly selves—to John Locke's more positive belief that human beings start out as a blank slate (*tabula rasa*) on which culture engraves certain ideals. All of these theories have had profound influence on the formation of Western political structures, which, in turn, profoundly influence the ways in which we conceive of our identities in our respective societies.

Clearly, religious studies as a discipline within the social sciences have a pointed interest in questions of human identity and consciousness, since all the world's religions have at their roots a basic concern with human subjectivity, agency, essence, and purpose. Religious studies investigate notions of human identity and consciousness from a number of angles, comparing the different religions' conceptions of human agency and positioning of the individual in the "large scheme of things." Religious conceptions of supreme being, the afterlife, beneficent cosmic forces, meditative practices and prayer, are all bound with notions of human consciousness as transcending earthly limitations of materiality and identity in differing ways. This chapter's religious studies unit focuses on a particular issue within the concern of this field, namely the effect of religion on one aspect of identity: morality. We present a thoughtful essay in which a writer argues that true Christian ideals are necessary both to individual human morality and thus to any kind of ethical political formations. The second piece in this unit presents an overview of various social science studies' findings that call into question the connection between religious affiliation and the ethical behavior of individuals.

At the heart of all scientific inquiry is the asking of questions about the ways in which the world—no, the universe—around us works. The distinction between science and other methods of knowledge acquisition, such as philosophy and religion, is grounded in the strategies and measures used to determine the underlying reasons—for example, "natural laws"—for the universe's complex workings. The basic strategies of science are observing and experimenting. Initial observations often generate research questions, which lead scientists to produce an interpretive account—scientists call it a hypothesis—intended to explain the event or object under observation. Scientists test their hypotheses either through more systematic observation or experimentation, or, as is most often the case, through combining both methods. In this way, scientists can move closer to the "truth" about the workings of the natural world, in all its myriad forms.

The first unit of this chapter's science section looks at one working of the natural world—that is, human consciousness—from the perspective of neuroscience: that branch of the hard sciences devoted to studying nerve cells and the way they work together to form the brain and nervous system. The central question of this unit is, Where does human thought and consciousness come from; is it simply a function of electrical and chemical processes at work within the brain, or are there more subtle and less easily observable phenomena at play? The unit presents researchers who answer this question from a variety of neuroscientific perspectives and who sometimes engage in heated debate in the process.

The chapter's science unit next examines human consciousness from the point of view of genetics: that branch of science devoted to studying inherited traits and their variation. Genetics occupies a pivotal location within the biological sciences, since it involves the observation of all living things and includes such subactivities as the analysis of DNA structures; the configurations of genes in various groups of organisms; inheritable diseases such as cancer; and possible genetic causes for conditions such as alcoholism. The central question on which this section of the chapter focuses is the timeless nature versus nurture debate: do people's individual characteristics—their "selves"—derive from purely genetic causes, do they come mainly from environmental causes such as family dynamics, or is personality the result of a complex interplay between these two forces? Researchers present cogent arguments for both sides of this debate, and we leave you to draw your own conclusions.

Finally, we explore consciousness from the point of view of computer science, the discipline that focuses on understanding and manipulating information through electronic means. A recently developed discipline, compared with that of genetics or neuroscience, computer science has evolved to include programming—that is, writing the actual code by which computers run—and studying the complex nature of information systems: theoretical substructures that are crucial to the formation and implementation of new computer-based applications. In this unit, several computer scientists discuss the theoretical implications of artificial intelligence, the simulation of human thought processes by computers. The central question in this section is, Will machines ever be able to learn—to gather information and the means of using that information—as human beings do? And if they do attain this ability, will they then have consciousness as we currently conceive of it?

Moving into the humanities unit, we continue our examination of artificial intelligence, in order to delineate concretely the distinction between hard sciences and the humanities. The readings in this unit focus on the same question with which the computer scientists grappled—namely, can machines think in the same way that humans do—but using a different methodology: whereas computer scientists consider practical applications of new technologies, philosophers engage in more abstract theorization about the moral, legal, religious, metaphysical, and artistic ideas that enable people to comprehend themselves and the world around them. The readings in this unit illustrate the ways in which philosophy—an ancient discipline that goes back literally thousands of years—considers contemporary issues such as machine-based thought.

In many ways, art runs parallel to philosophy, since the aesthetic productions of human beings throughout the ages have depicted and explored human selfhood. Art depicts life in all its manifold significations, often exploring the nature of human agency and of human striving. Thus, art critics and interpreters have extensively studied artistic expressions of issues related to identity and consciousness. Scholars of American literature, for example, have written widely on the ways that American literature has helped to construct definite notions of American identity as individualistic by frequently depicting nonconforming rebel figures. Literary characters such as Hawthorne's Hester Prynne, Melville's Captain Ahab, and Twain's Huck Finn are obvious examples of ways in which the American hero or antihero is figured as someone apart form the larger society, waging personal battles (which symbolize larger battles) against forces of conformity and constraint. Such a literary focus on lone individuals confronting obstacles to individuality out in the "wilderness" have become standard fare in American popular culture as well, from figures such as the mythic American cowboy of Western films (and Marlboro ads) to more recent versions of the action adventure hero in the Sylvester Stallone/Arnold Schwarzenegger mold. One of cultural studies' fundamental premises is that peoples' national—and thus, personal—identities are shaped by pervasive formulations such as these.

This chapter's humanities section contains an art section focusing on the work of one artist, the early-twentieth-century Mexican painter Frida Kahlo. The self-portrait is a form practiced by artists for hundreds of years, and Kahlo painted an extremely large number of self-portraits (55!) during her career. Artistic interpretations and critiques of the self-portrait in art provide an interesting way of exploring issues of self-creation and self-presentation, and Kahlo's work is especially useful in this regard, since she figured herself in very different ways throughout her body of self-portraits. We present several Kahlo self-portraits and follow these with a biographical essay and a scholarly discussion of the portrayal of self in her works. This focus on one particular artist will, we hope, lead you to explore the self in other artist's works, and will lead to further questions and possible answers regarding the nature of self and its constructions.

Before approaching the readings in this chapter, we'd like to invite you to think about this concept of identity on your own, and about what it means to have identity. Who are you, are there some core things about you that transcend all the different contexts in which you find yourself? How do you change in different situations? Also, think about how you got the way you are. What are the factors that have shaped your identity and sense of self? Do you think that this process is fairly complete? What factors do you envision that might affect your identity now and in the future? By considering the ways in which you conceive of the elusive concept known as "consciousness," you will come to a greater understanding of your own personal identity and through that process will arrive at a more comprehensive awareness of the kinds of questions that the scholars represented in this chapter confront in their work.

THINKING AND WRITING
IN THE SOCIAL SCIENCES

Unit 1:
Social Psychology—The Individual Self

PRIMARY GROUPS
Charles Horton Cooley

One of the most important thinkers in social psychology, Cooley posits that our identity develops through social interaction with "primary groups." According to Cooley, primary groups are the "spheres of intimate association and cooperation" that are "fundamental in forming the social nature and ideals of the individual." As you read, think about how different primary groups might exert different kinds of influences on a person's socialization processes.

Charles Horton Cooley (1864–1929) was born in Ann Arbor, Michigan. Cooley received a doctorate in sociology from the University of Michigan in 1894 where he taught as a professor for over thirty years. He wrote dozens of articles and published four books Human Nature and the Social Order, Social Organization, Social Process, *and* Life and the Student—*a book composed of extracts from a journal he kept throughout his life and from which this selection is taken. His early papers in social ecology and a few other contributions written in later years are available in a posthumous volume,* Sociological Theory and Social Research. *In addition to his publications, Cooley participated in the formation of the American Sociological Society in 1905 and became its president in 1918.*

By primary groups I mean those characterized by intimate face-to-face association and cooperation. They are primary in several senses, but chiefly in that they are fundamental in forming the social nature and ideals of the individual. The result of intimate association, psychologically, is a certain fusion of individualities in a common whole, so that one's very self, for many   1

---

purposes at least, is the common life and purpose of the group. Perhaps the simplest way of describing this wholeness is by saying that it is a "we"; it involves the sort of sympathy and mutual identification for which "we" is the natural expression. One lives in the feeling of the whole and finds the chief aims of his will in that feeling.

It is not to be supposed that the unity of the primary group is one of   2
mere harmony and love. It is always a differentiated and usually a competitive unity, admitting of self-assertion and various appropriative passions; but these passions are socialized by sympathy, and come, or tend to come, under the discipline of a common spirit. The individual will be ambitious, but the chief object of his ambition will be some desired place in the thought of the others, and he will feel allegiance to common standards of service and fair play. So the boy will dispute with his fellows a place on the team, but above such disputes will place the common glory of his class and school.

The most important spheres of this intimate association and coopera-   3
tion—though by no means the only ones—are the family, the play-group of children, and the neighborhood or community group of elders. These are practically universal, belonging to all times and all stages of development; and are accordingly a chief basis of what is universal in human nature and human ideals. The best comparative studies of the family, such as those of Westermarck or Howard, show it to us as not only a universal institution, but as more alike the world over than the exaggeration of exceptional customs by an earlier school had led us to suppose. Nor can anyone doubt the general prevalence of play-groups among children or of informal assemblies of various kinds among their elders. Such association is clearly the nursery of human nature in the world about us, and there is no apparent reason to suppose that the case has anywhere or at any time been essentially different.

As regards play, I might, were it not a matter of common observation,   4
multiply illustrations of the universality and spontaneity of the group discussion and cooperation to which it gives rise. The general fact is that children, especially boys after about their twelfth year, live in fellowships in which their sympathy, ambition, and honor are engaged even more often than they are in the family. Most of us can recall examples of the endurance by boys of injustice and even cruelty, rather than appeal from their fellows to parents or teachers—as, for instance, in the hazing so prevalent at schools, and so difficult, for this very reason, to suppress. And how elaborate the discussion, how cogent the public opinion, how hot the ambitions in these fellowships.

Nor is this facility of juvenile association, as is sometimes supposed, a   5
trait peculiar to English and American boys; since experience among our immigrant population seems to show that the offspring of the more restrictive civilizations of the continent of Europe form self-governing playgroups with almost equal readiness. Thus Miss Jane Addams, after pointing out that the "gang" is almost universal, speaks of the interminable discussion which every detail of the gang's activity receives, remarking that "in these social

folk-motes, so to speak, the young citizen learns to act upon his own determination."

Of the neighborhood group it may be said, in general, that from the 6
time men formed permanent settlements upon the land, down, at least, to
the rise of modern industrial cities, it has played a main part of the primary,
heart-to-heart life of the people. Among our Teutonic forefathers the village
community was apparently the chief sphere of sympathy and mutual aid for
the commons all through the "Dark" and Middle Ages, and for many purposes it remains so in rural districts at the present day. In some countries
we still find it with all its ancient vitality, notably in Russia, where the *mir,* or
self-governing village group, is the main theatre of life, along with the family,
for perhaps 50 million peasants.

In our own life the intimacy of the neighborhood has been broken up 7
by the growth of an intricate mesh of wider contacts which leaves us
strangers to people who live in the same house. And even in the country the
same principle is at work, though less obviously, diminishing our economic
and spiritual community with our neighbors. How far this change is a healthy
development, and how far a disease, is perhaps still uncertain.

Besides these almost universal kinds of primary association, there are 8
many others whose form depends upon the particular state of civilization;
the only essential thing, as I have said, being a certain intimacy and fusion
of personalities. In our own society, being little bound by place, people easily form clubs, fraternal societies and the like, based on congeniality, which
may give rise to real intimacy. Many such relations are formed at school and
college, and among men and women brought together in the first instance
by their occupations—as workmen in the same trade, or the like. Where
there is a little common interest and activity, kindness grows like weeds by
the roadside.

But the fact that the family and neighborhood groups are ascendant in 9
the open and plastic time of childhood makes them even now incomparably
more influential than all the rest.

Primary groups are primary in the sense that they give the individual 10
his earliest and completest experience of social unity, and also in the sense
that they do not change in the same degree as more elaborate relations, but
form a comparatively permanent source out of which the latter are ever
springing. Of course they are not independent of the larger society, but to
some extent reflect its spirit; as the German family and the German school
bear somewhat distinctly the print of German militarism. But this, after all, is
like the tide setting back into creeks, and does not commonly go very far.
Among the German, and still more among the Russian, peasantry are found
habits of free cooperation and discussion almost uninfluenced by the character of the state; and it is a familiar and well-supported view that the village
commune, self-governing as regards local affairs and habituated to discussion, is a very widespread institution in settled communities, and the

continuator of a similar autonomy previously existing in the clan. "It is man who makes monarchies and establishes republics, but the commune seems to come directly from the hand of God."

In our own cities the crowded tenements and the general economic 11 and social confusion have sorely wounded the family and the neighborhood, but it is remarkable, in view of these conditions, what vitality they show; and there is nothing upon which the conscience of the time is more determined than upon restoring them to health.

These groups, then, are springs of life, not only for the individual but 12 for social institutions. They are only in part moulded by special traditions, and, in larger degree, express a universal nature. The religion or government of other civilizations may seem alien to us, but the children or the family group wear the common life, and with them we can always make ourselves at home.

By human nature, I suppose, we may understand those sentiments 13 and impulses that are human in being superior to those of lower animals, and also in the sense that they belong to mankind at large, and not to any particular race or time. It means, particularly, sympathy and the innumerable sentiments into which sympathy enters, such as love, resentment, ambition, vanity, hero-worship, and the feeling of social right and wrong.

Human nature in this sense is justly regarded as a comparatively per- 14 manent element in society. Always and everywhere men seek honor and dread ridicule, defer to public opinion, cherish their goods and their children, and admire courage, generosity, and success. It is always safe to assume that people are and have been human. . . .

To return to primary groups: The view here maintained is that human 15 nature is not something existing separately in the individual, but a *group-nature or primary phase of society,* a relatively simple and general condition of the social mind. It is something more, on the one hand, than the mere instinct that is born in us—though that enters into it—and something else, on the other, than the more elaborate development of ideas and sentiments that makes up institutions. It is the nature which is developed and expressed in those simple, face-to-face groups that are somewhat alike in all societies' groups of the family, the playground, and the neighborhood. In the essential similarity of these is to be found the basis, in experience, for similar ideas and sentiments in the human mind. In these, everywhere, human nature comes into existence. Man does not have it at birth; he cannot acquire it except through fellowship, and it decays in isolation.

If this view does not recommend itself to common sense I do not know 16 that elaboration will be of much avail. It simply means the application at this point of the idea that society and individuals are inseparable phases of a common whole, so that wherever we find an individual fact we may look for a social fact to go with it. If there is a universal nature in persons there must be something universal in association to correspond to it.

What else can human nature be than a trait of primary group? Surely   17
not an attribute of the separate individual—supposing there were any such
thing—since its typical characteristics, such as affection, ambition, vanity,
and resentment, are inconceivable apart from society. If it belongs, then, to
man in association, what kind or degree of association is required to develop it? Evidently nothing elaborate, because elaborate phases of society
are transient and diverse, while human nature is comparatively stable and
universal. In short the family and neighborhood life is essential to its genesis
and nothing more is.

Here as everywhere in the study of society we must learn to see   18
mankind in psychical wholes, rather than in artificial separation. We must
see and feel the communal life of family and local groups as immediate
facts, not as combinations of something else. And perhaps we shall do this
best by recalling our own experience and extending it through sympathetic
observation. What, in our life, is the family and the fellowship; what do we
know of the we-feeling? Thought of this kind may help us to get a concrete
perception of that primary group-nature of which everything social is the outgrowth.   ©

CRITICAL READING

1. Sum up Cooley's theory in your own words.
2. How are Cooley's primary groups different from their implied opposite, secondary groups? Give some examples of secondary groups, and discuss the effects these might have on individuals' identities.
3. Cooley came up with his theories of socialization in the first decade of the twentieth century. In looking at today's world, do you think that there are factors in
   our current socialization that might modify or even invalidate Cooley's notion of
   primary groups?

CLASS DISCUSSION

1. As a class, discuss the last paragraph of Cooley's reading. What is he saying
   here? How might we answer the questions with which Cooley ends this paragraph?
2. Discuss how this very social definition of the individual conflicts with popular
   beliefs about individual autonomy, uniqueness, and identity.

DIRECTED FREEWRITE

Spend fifteen minutes writing about your own primary groups. What effect do you
think that they have had on who you are as a person?

THE PRESENTATION OF SELF

Erving Goffman

Goffman, a very influential thinker in sociology and social psychology, here discusses the ways in which we manage the presentation of our "selves" in face-to-face interactions with others. As you read, think about examples of the kinds of impression management that Goffman discusses. How do the impressions that we convey shape our perceptions of ourselves as well as the perceptions that others have of us?

Erving Goffman (1922–1988) was born in Manville, Alberta in Canada. He attended the University of Chicago where he received his Ph.D. in 1953. Goffman was a social scientist, professor, writer and ethnographer who was well known for his theories suggesting that routine social actions indicated that people naturally strove to formulate identities. Goffman held memberships in the American Academy of Arts and Sciences, the American Anthropological Association, and the American Sociological Association (President 1981–82). He taught at the University of California and the University of Pennsylvania and was the author of several texts including Forms of Talk *(1981 National Book Critics Circle Award nominee),* Gender Advertisements, Asylums: Essays on the Social Situation of Mental Patients and Other Inmates, *and* Presentation of Self in Everyday Life *from which this selection is taken. He was also a contributor to such periodicals as* Psychiatry *and the* American Journal of Sociology.

When an individual enters the presence of others, they commonly   1
seek to acquire information about him or to bring into play information about him already possessed. They will be interested in his general socioeconomic status, his conception of self, his attitude toward them, his competence, his trustworthiness, etc. Although some of this information seems to be sought almost as an end in itself, there are usually quite practical reasons for acquiring it. Information about the individual helps to define the situation, enabling others to know in advance what he will expect of them and what they may expect of him. Informed in these ways, the others will know how best to act in order to call forth a desired response from him.

For those present, many sources of information become accessible   2
and many carriers (or "sign-vehicles") become available for conveying this information. If unacquainted with the individual, observers can glean clues from his conduct and appearance which allow them to apply their previous

---

Source: From *The Presentation of Self in Everyday Life* by Erving Goffman. Copyright © 1959 by Erving Goffman. Used by permission of Doubleday, a division of Random House, Inc.

experience with individuals roughly similar to the one before them or, more important, to apply untested stereotypes to him. They can also assume from past experience that only individuals of a particular kind are likely to be found in a given social setting. They can rely on what the individual says about himself or on documentary evidence he provides as to who and what he is. If they know, or know of, the individual by virtue of experience prior to the interaction, they can rely on assumptions as to the persistence and generality of psychological traits as a means of predicting his present and future behavior.

However, during the period in which the individual is in the immediate presence of the others, few events may occur which directly provide the others with the conclusive information they will need if they are to direct wisely their own activity. Many crucial facts lie beyond the time and place of interaction or lie concealed within it. For example, the "true" or "real" attitudes, beliefs, and emotions of the individual can be ascertained only indirectly, through his avowals or through what appears to be involuntary expressive behavior. Similarly, if the individual offers the others a product or service, they will often find that during the interaction there will be no time and place immediately available for eating the pudding that the proof can be found in. They will be forced to accept some events as conventional or natural signs of something not directly available to the senses. In Ichheiser's terms, the individual will have to act so that he intentionally or unintentionally *expresses* himself, and the others will in turn have to be *impressed* in some way by him.   3

The expressiveness of the individual (and therefore his capacity to give impressions) appears to involve two radically different kinds of sign activity: the expression that he *gives,* and the expression that he *gives off.* The first involves verbal symbols or their substitutes which he uses admittedly and solely to convey the information that he and the others are known to attach to these symbols. This is communication in the traditional and narrow sense. The second involves a wide range of action that others can treat as symptomatic of the actor, the expectation being that the action was performed for reasons other than the information conveyed in this way. As we shall have to see, this distinction has an only initial validity. The individual does of course intentionally convey misinformation by means of both of these types of communication, the first involving deceit, the second feigning.   4

. . . Let us now turn from the others to the point of view of the individual who presents himself before them. He may wish them to think highly of him, or to think that he thinks highly of them, or to perceive how in fact he feels toward them, or to obtain no clear-cut impression; he may wish to ensure sufficient harmony so that the interaction can be sustained, or to defraud, get rid of, confuse, mislead, antagonize, or insult them. Regardless of the particular objective which the individual has in mind and of his motive for   5 having this objective, it will be in his interests to control the conduct of the others, especially their responsive treatment of him. This control is achieved largely by influencing the definition of the situation which the others come to formulate, and he can influence this definition by expressing himself in such a way as to give them the kind of impression that will lead them to act voluntarily in accordance with his own plan. Thus, when an individual appears in the presence of others, there will usually be some reason for him to mobilize his activity so that it will convey an impression to others which it is in his interests to convey. Since a girl's dormitory mates will glean evidence of her popularity from the calls she receives on the phone, we can suspect that some girls will arrange for calls to be made, and Willard Waller's finding can be anticipated:

> It has been reported by many observers that a girl who is called to the telephone in the dormitories will often allow herself to be called several times, in order to give all the other girls ample opportunity to hear her paged.

Of the two kinds of communication—expressions given and expressions given off—this report will be primarily concerned with the latter, with the more theatrical and contextual kind, the nonverbal, presumably unintentional kind, whether this communication be purposely engineered or not. As an example of what we must try to examine, I would like to cite at length a novelistic incident in which Preedy, a vacationing Englishman, makes his first appearance on the beach of his summer hotel in Spain: 6

> But in any case he took care to avoid catching anyone's eye. First of all, he had to make it clear to those potential companions of his holiday that they were of no concern to him whatsoever. He stared through them, round them, over them—eyes lost in space. The beach might have been empty. If by chance a ball was thrown his way, he looked surprised; then let a smile of amusement lighten his face (Kindly Preedy), looked round dazed to see that there *were* people on the beach, tossed it back with a smile to himself and not a smile *at* the people, and then resumed carelessly his nonchalant survey of space.
>
> But it was time to institute a little parade, the parade of the Ideal Preedy. By devious handlings he gave any who wanted to look a chance to see the title of his book—a Spanish translation of Homer, classic thus, but not daring, cosmopolitan too—and then gathered together his beach-wrap and bag into a neat sand-resistant pile (Methodical and Sensible Preedy), rose slowly to stretch at ease his

huge frame (Big-Cat Preedy), and tossed aside his sandals (Carefree Preedy, after all).

The marriage of Preedy and the sea! There were alternative rituals. The first involved the stroll that turns into a run and a dive straight into the water, thereafter smoothing into a strong splashless crawl towards the horizon. But of course not really to the horizon. Quite suddenly he would turn on to his back and thrash great white splashes with his legs, somehow thus showing that he could have swum further had he wanted to, and then would stand up a quarter out of water for all to see who it was.

The alternative course was simpler, it avoided the cold-water shock and it avoided the risk of appearing too high-spirited. The point was to appear to be so used to the sea, the Mediterranean, and this particular beach, that one might as well be in the sea as out of it. It involved a slow stroll down and into the edge of the water—not even noticing his toes were wet, land and water all the same to *him!*—with his eyes up at the sky gravely surveying portents, invisible to others, of the weather (Local Fisherman Preedy).

The novelist means us to see that Preedy is improperly concerned with the extensive impressions he feels his sheer bodily action is giving off to those around him. We can malign Preedy further by assuming that he has acted merely in order to give a particular impression, that this is a false impression, and that the others present receive either no impression at all, or, worse still, the impression that Preedy is affectedly trying to cause them to receive this particular impression. But the important point for us here is that the kind of impression Preedy thinks he is making is in fact the kind of impression that others correctly and incorrectly glean from someone in their midst. . . .   7

There is one aspect of the others' response that bears special comment here. Knowing that the individual is likely to present himself in a light that is favorable to him, the others may divide what they witness into two parts: a part that is relatively easy for the individual to manipulate at will, being chiefly his verbal assertions and a part in regard to which he seems to have little concern or control, being chiefly derived from the expressions he gives off. The others may then use what are considered to be the ungovernable aspects of his expressive behavior as a check upon the validity of what is conveyed by the governable aspects. In this a fundamental asymmetry is demonstrated in the communication process, the individual presumably being aware of only one stream of his communication, the witnesses of this stream and one other. For example, in Shetland Isle one crofter's wife, in   8 serving native dishes to a visitor from the mainland of Britain, would listen with a polite smile to his polite claims of liking what he was eating; at the same time she would take note of the rapidity with which the visitor lifted his fork or spoon to his mouth, the eagerness with which he passed food into his mouth, and the gusto expressed in chewing the food, using these signs as a check on the stated feelings of the eater. The same woman, in order to discover what one acquaintance (A) "actually" thought of another acquaintance (B), would wait until B was in the presence of A but engaged in conversation with still another person (C). She would then covertly examine the facial expressions of A as he regarded B in conversation with C. Not being in conversation with B, and not being directly observed by him, A would sometimes relax usual constraints and tactful deceptions, and freely express what he was "actually" feeling about B. This Shetlander, in short, would observe the unobserved observer.

Now given the fact that others are likely to check up on the more controllable aspects of behavior by means of the less controllable, one can expect that sometimes the individual will try to exploit this very possibility, guiding the impression he makes through behavior felt to be reliably informing. For example, in gaining admission to a tight social circle, the participant observer may not only wear an accepting look while listening to an informant, but may also be careful to wear the same look when observing the informant talking to others; observers of the observer will then not as easily discover where he actually stands. A specific illustration may be cited from Shetland Isle. When a neighbor dropped in to have a cup of tea, he would ordinarily wear at least a hint of an expectant warm smile as he passed through the door into the cottage. Since lack of physical obstructions outside the cottage and lack of light within it usually made it possible to observe the visitor unobserved as he approached the house, islanders sometimes took pleasure in watching the visitor drop whatever expression he was manifesting and replace it with a sociable one just before reaching the door. However, some visitors, in appreciating that this examination was occurring, would blindly adopt a social face a long distance from the house, thus ensuring the projection of a constant image. 9

This kind of control upon the part of the individual reinstates the symmetry of the communication process, and sets the stage for a kind of information game—a potentially infinite cycle of concealment, discovery, false revelation, and rediscovery. It should be added that since the others are likely to be relatively unsuspicious of the presumably unguided aspects of the individual's conduct, he can gain much by controlling it. The others of course may sense that the individual is manipulating the presumably spontaneous aspects of his behavior, and seek in this very act of manipulation some shading of conduct that the individual has not managed to control. This again provides a check upon the individual's behavior, this time his presumably uncalculated behavior, thus re-establishing the asymmetry of the 10 communication process. Here I would like only to add the suggestion that the arts of piercing an individual's effort at calculated unintentionality seem better developed than our capacity to manipulate our own behavior, so that regardless of how many steps have occurred in the information game, the witness is likely to have the advantage over the actor, and the initial asymmetry of the communication process is likely to be retained. . . .

In everyday life, of course, there is a clear understanding that first impressions are important. Thus, the work adjustment of those in service occupations will often hinge upon a capacity to seize and hold the initiative in the service relation, a capacity that will require subtle aggressiveness on the part of the server when he is of lower socioeconomic status than his client. W. F. Whyte suggests the waitress as an example: 11

> The first point that stands out is that the waitress who bears up under pressure does not simply respond to her customers. She acts with some skill to control their behavior. The first question to ask when we look at the customer relationship is, "Does the waitress get the jump on the customer, or does the customer get the jump on the waitress?" The skilled waitress realizes the crucial nature of this question . . .
>
> The skilled waitress tackles the customer with confidence and without hesitation. For example, she may find that a new customer has seated himself before she could clear off the dirty dishes and change the cloth. He is now leaning on the table studying the menu. She greets him, says, "May I change the cover, please?" and, without waiting for an answer, takes his menu away from him so that he moves back from the table, and she goes about her work. The relationship is handled politely but firmly, and there is never any question as to who is in charge.

When the interaction that is initiated by "first impressions" is itself merely the initial interaction in an extended series of interactions involving the same participants, we speak of "getting off on the right foot" and feel that it is crucial that we do so. Thus, one learns that some teachers take the following view: 12

> You can't ever let them get the upper hand on you or you're through. So I start out tough. The first day I get a new class in, I let them know who's boss. . . . You've got to start off tough, then you can ease up as you go along. If you start out easy-going, when you try to get tough, they'll just look at you and laugh.

. . . In stressing the fact that the initial definition of the situation projected 13
by an individual tends to provide a plan for the cooperative activity that follows—in stressing this action point of view—we must not overlook the crucial
fact that any projected definition of the situation also has a distinctive moral
character. It is this moral character of projections that will chiefly concern us in
this report. Society is organized on the principle that any individual who possesses certain social characteristics has a moral right to expect that others will
value and treat him in an appropriate way. Connected with this principle is a
second, namely that an individual who implicitly or explicitly signifies that he
has certain social characteristics ought in fact to be what he claims he is. In
consequence, when an individual projects a definition of the situation and
thereby makes an implicit or explicit claim to be a person of a particular kind,
he automatically exerts a moral demand upon the others, obliging them to
value and treat him in the manner that persons of his kind have a right to expect. He also implicitly foregoes all claims to be things he does not appear to
be and hence foregoes the treatment that would be appropriate for such individuals. The others find, then, that the individual has informed them as to what
is and as to what they *ought* to see as the "is."

One cannot judge the importance of definitional disruptions by the fre- 14
quency with which they occur, for apparently they would occur more frequently were not constant precautions taken. We find that preventive
practices are constantly employed to avoid these embarrassments and that
corrective practices are constantly employed to compensate for discrediting
occurrences that have not been successfully avoided. When the individual
employs these strategies and tactics to protect his own projections, we may
refer to them as "defensive practices"; when a participant employs them to
save the definition of the situation projected by another, we speak of "protective practices" or "tact." Together, defensive and protective practices
comprise the techniques employed to safeguard the impression fostered by
an individual during his presence before other. It should be added that while
we may be ready to see that no fostered impression would survive if defensive practices were not employed, we are less ready perhaps to see that
few impressions could survive if those who received the impression did not
exert tact in their reception of it.

In addition to the fact that precautions are taken to prevent disruption 15
of projected definitions, we may also note that an intense interest in these
disruptions comes to play a significant role in the social life of the group.
Practical jokes and social games are played in which embarrassments
which are to be taken unseriously are purposely engineered. Fantasies are
created in which devastating exposures occur. Anecdotes from the past—
real, embroidered, or fictitious—are told and retold, detailing disruptions
which occurred, almost occurred, or occurred and were admirably resolved.
There seems to be no grouping which does not have a ready supply of
these games, reveries, and cautionary tales, to be used as a source of

humor, a catharsis for anxieties, and a sanction for inducing individuals to be modest in their claims and reasonable in their projected expectations. The individual may tell himself through dreams of getting into impossible positions. Families tell of the time a guest got his dates mixed and arrived when neither the house nor anyone in it was ready for him. Journalists tell of times when an all-too-meaningful misprint occurred, and the paper's assumption of objectivity or decorum was humorously discredited. Public servants tell of times a client ridiculously misunderstood form instructions, giving answers which implied an unanticipated and bizarre definition of the situation. Seamen, whose home away from home is rigorously he-man, tell stories of coming back home and inadvertently asking mother to "pass the fucking butter." Diplomats tell of the time a near-sighted queen asked a republican ambassador about the health of his king.

To summarize, then, I assume that when an individual appears before others he will have many motives for trying to control the impression they receive of the situation. 16 ©

CRITICAL READING

1. What is the difference between expressions that one *gives* and the expressions that one *gives off*, in Goffman's theory? Provide examples of each kind of expression, and discuss why Goffman is most concerned with the expressions that people *give off*.
2. Goffman is the author of a "dramaturgical approach" to identity formation. How are his ideas here related to the concept of drama, or acting and staging?
3. How can we evaluate the validity of people's presentations of self? How can people manipulate such evaluations, and what purposes are served by this manipulation?

CLASS DISCUSSION

1. Discuss specific examples of expressions that people give off, and have members of the class act these out. Discuss the kinds of impressions conveyed by these expressions. Do certain situations seem to require more or less impression management? What are some of the strategies that people use in these situations to manage impressions?
2. How are the expressions that we give off related to our identities? Are we merely playing roles when we manage our expressions, or are these elements of our "true" selves? Is there any such thing as a "true" self? What would Goffman likely answer to this question?

DIRECTED FREEWRITE

Brainstorm about different kinds of situations in which people play particular roles in order to manage impressions. Describe several of these situations in detail, discussing the different actors' behaviors.

THE DISSOLUTION OF SELF

Kenneth Gergen

Gergen, in an essay written much more recently than the Cooley and the Goffman pieces, examines the ways in which concepts and experiences of the self have changed in the latter part of the twentieth century. As you read, notice to what extent you find yourself thinking of identity as a romanticist or as a modernist would think, according to Gergen. What does this tendency indicate about our postmodernism?

A graduate of Yale University (B.A.) and Duke (Ph.D.), Ken Gergen is currently a Professor of Psychology at Swarthmore College, Pennsylvania. He's written 12 books including Therapy as Social Construction, Realities and Relationships: Soundings in Social Construction, Toward Transformation in Social Knowledge, 2/e, *and the 1991 award-winning* The Saturated Self: Dilemmas of Identity in Contemporary Life *from which this selection is taken. Gergen has been awarded three Fulbright grants as well as a Guggenheim Fellowship, and the Alexander von Humbolt prize in the Humanities. Gergen has served as president of the Psychology & the Arts and Theoretical & Philosophical Psychology divisions of the American Psychological Association.*

. . . Cultural life in the twentieth century has been dominated by two 1 major vocabularies of the self. Largely from the nineteenth century, we have inherited a romanticist view of the self, one that attributes to each person characteristics of personal depth: passion, soul, creativity, and moral fiber. This vocabulary is essential to the formation of deeply committed relations, dedicated friendships, and life purposes. But since the rise of the *modernist* worldview beginning in the early twentieth century, the romantic vocabulary has been threatened. For modernists, the chief characteristics of the self reside not in the domain of depth, but rather in our ability to reason—in our beliefs, opinions, and conscious intentions. In the modernist idiom, normal persons are predictable, honest, and sincere. Modernists believe in educational systems, a stable family life, moral training, and rational choice of marriage partners.

Yet, as I shall argue, both the romantic and the modern beliefs about 2 the self are falling into disuse, and the social arrangements that they support are eroding. This is largely a result of the forces of social saturation.

Emerging technologies saturate us with the voices of humankind—both harmonious and alien. As we absorb their varied rhymes and reasons, they become part of us and we of them. Social saturation furnishes us with a multiplicity of incoherent and unrelated languages of the self. For everything we "know to be true" about ourselves, other voices within respond with doubt and even derision. This fragmentation of self-conceptions corresponds to a multiplicity of incoherent and disconnected relationships. These relationships pull us in myriad directions, inviting us to play such a variety of roles that the very concept of an "authentic self" with knowable characteristics recedes from view. The fully saturated self becomes no self at all. . . .

I . . . equate the saturating of self with the condition of *postmodernism.* 3
As we enter the postmodern era, all previous beliefs about the self are placed in jeopardy, and with them the patterns of action they sustain. Postmodernism does not bring with it a new vocabulary for understanding ourselves, new traits or characteristics to be discovered or explored. Its impact is more apocalyptic than that: the very concept of personal essences is thrown into doubt. Selves as possessors of real and identifiable characteristics—such as rationality, emotion, inspiration, and will—are dismantled. . . .

THE PROCESS OF SOCIAL SATURATION

A century ago, social relationships were largely confined to the dis- 4
tance of an easy walk. Most were conducted in person, within small communities: family, neighbors, townspeople. Yes, the horse and carriage made longer trips possible, but even a trip of thirty miles could take all day. The railroad could speed one away, but cost and availability limited such travel. If one moved from the community, relationships were likely to end. From birth to death, one could depend on relatively even-textured social surroundings. Words, faces, gestures, and possibilities were relatively consistent, coherent, and slow to change.

For much of the world's population, especially the industrialized West, 5
the small, face-to-face community is vanishing into the pages of history. We go to country inns for weekend outings, we decorate condominium interiors with clapboards and brass beds, and we dream of old age in a rural cottage. But as a result of the technological developments just described, contemporary life is a swirling sea of social relations. Words thunder in by radio, television, newspaper, mail, radio, telephone, fax, wire service, electronic mail, billboards, Federal Express, and more. Waves of new faces are everywhere—in town for a day, visiting for the weekend, at the Rotary lunch, at the church social—and incessantly and incandescently on television. Long weeks in a single community are unusual; a full day within a single neighborhood is becoming rare. We travel casually across town, into the countryside, to neighboring towns, cities, states; one might go thirty miles for coffee and conversation.

Through the technologies of the century, the number and variety of re-   6
lationships in which we are engaged, potential frequency of contact, expressed intensity of relationship, and endurance through time all are steadily
increasing. As this increase becomes extreme, we reach a state of social
saturation.

In the face-to-face community, the cast of others remained relatively   7
stable. There were changes by virtue of births and deaths, but moving from
one town—much less state or country—to another was difficult. The number
of relationships commonly maintained in today's world stands in stark contrast. Counting one's family, the morning television news, the car radio, colleagues on the train, and the local newspaper, the typical commuter may
confront as many different persons (in terms of views or images) in the first
two hours of a day as the community-based predecessor did in a month.
The morning calls in a business office may connect one to a dozen different
locales in a given city, often across the continent, and very possibly across
national boundaries. A single hour of prime-time melodrama immerses one
in the lives of a score of individuals. In an evening of television, hundreds of
engaging faces insinuate themselves into our lives. It is not only the immediate community that occupies our thoughts and feelings, but a constantly
changing cast of characters spread across the globe. . . .

POPULATING THE SELF

Consider the moments: 8

- Over lunch with friends, you discuss Northern Ireland. Although you
  have never spoken a word on the subject, you find yourself heatedly
  defending British policies.
- You work as an executive in the investments department of a bank. In
  the evenings, you smoke marijuana and listen to the Grateful Dead.
- You sit in a café and wonder what it would be like to have an intimate
  relationship with various strangers walking past.
- You are a lawyer in a prestigious midtown firm. On the weekends, you
  work on a novel about romance with a terrorist.
- You go to a Moroccan restaurant and afterward take in the latest show
  at a country-and-western bar.

In each case, individuals harbor a sense of coherent identity or self-   9
sameness, only to find themselves suddenly propelled by alternative impulses. They seem securely to be one sort of person, but yet another comes
bursting to the surface—in a suddenly voiced opinion, a fantasy, a turn of
interests, or a private activity. Such experiences with variation and self-
contradiction may be viewed as preliminary effects of social saturation. They
may signal a *populating of the self,* the acquisition of multiple and disparate

potentials for being. It is this process of self-population that begins to undermine the traditional commitments to both romanticist and modernist forms of
being. It is of pivotal importance in setting the stage for the postmodern turn.
Let us explore.

The technologies of social saturation expose us to an enormous range   10
of persons, new forms of relationship, unique circumstances and opportunities, and special intensities of feeling. One can scarcely remain unaffected
by such exposure. As child-development specialists now agree, the process
of socialization is lifelong. We continue to incorporate information from the
environment throughout our lives. When exposed to other persons, we
change in two major ways. We increase our capacities for *knowing that* and
for *knowing how.* In the first case, through exposure to others, we learn myriad details about their words, actions, dress, mannerisms, and so on. We ingest enormous amounts of information about patterns of interchange. Thus,
for example, from an hour on a city street, we are informed of the clothing
styles of blacks, whites, upper class, lower class, and more. We may learn
the ways of Japanese businessmen, bag ladies, Sikhs, Hare Krishnas, or
flute players from Chile. We see how relationships are carried out between
mothers and daughters, business executives, teenage friends, and construction workers. An hour in a business office may expose us to the political views of a Texas oilman, a Chicago lawyer, and a gay activist from San
Francisco. Radio commentators espouse views on boxing, pollution, and
child abuse; pop music may advocate machoism, racial bigotry, and suicide.
Paperback books cause hearts to race over the unjustly treated, those who
strive against impossible odds, those who are brave or brilliant. And this is
to say nothing of television input. Via television, myriad figures are allowed
into the home who would never otherwise trespass. Millions watch as talk-
show guests—murderers, rapists, women prisoners, child abusers, members of the KKK, mental patients, and others often discredited—attempt to
make their lives intelligible. There are few six year olds who cannot furnish
at least a rudimentary account of life in an African village, the concerns of divorcing parents, or drug-pushing in the ghetto. Hourly, our storehouse of social knowledge expands in range and sophistication.

This massive increase in knowledge of the social world lays the   11
ground work for a second kind of learning, a *knowing how.* We learn how to
place such knowledge into action, to shape it for social consumption, to act
so that social life can proceed effectively. And the possibilities for placing
this supply of information into effective action are constantly expanding. The
Japanese businessman glimpsed on the street today, and on the television
tomorrow, may well be confronted in one's office the following week. On
these occasions, the rudiments of appropriate behavior are already in place.
If a mate announces that he or she is thinking about divorce, the other's reaction is not likely to be dumb dismay. The drama has so often been played

out on television and movie screens that one is already prepared with multiple options. If one wins a wonderful prize, suffers a humiliating loss, faces temptation to cheat, or learns of a sudden death in the family, the reactions are hardly random. One more or less knows how it goes, is more or less ready for action. Having seen it all before, one approaches a state of ennui.

In an important sense, as social saturation proceeds we become pastiches, imitative assemblages of each other. In memory, we carry others' patterns of being with us. If the conditions are favorable, we can place these patterns into action. Each of us becomes the other, a representative, or a replacement. To put it more broadly, as the century has progressed, selves become increasingly populated with the character of others. . . .   12

MULTIPHRENIA

It is sunny Saturday morning, and he finishes breakfast in high spirits.   13
It is a rare day in which he is free to do as he pleases. With relish, he contemplates his options. The back door needs fixing, which calls for a trip to the hardware store. This would allow a much-needed haircut; and, while in town, he could get a birthday card for his brother, leave off his shoes for repair, and pick up shirts at the cleaners. But, he ponders, he really should get some exercise; is there time for jogging in the afternoon? That reminds him of a championship game he wanted to see at the same time. To be taken more seriously was his ex-wife's repeated request for a luncheon talk. And shouldn't he also settle his vacation plans before all the best locations are taken? Slowly, his optimism gives way to a sense of defeat. The free day has become a chaos of competing opportunities and necessities.

If such a scene is vaguely familiar, it attests only further to the pervasive effects of social saturation and the populating of the self. More important, one detects amid the hurly-burly of contemporary life a new constellation of feelings or sensibilities, a new pattern of self-consciousness. This syndrome may be termed *multiphrenia,* generally referring to the splitting of the individual into a multiplicity of self-investments. This condition is partly an outcome of self-population, but partly a result of the populated self's efforts to exploit the potentials of the technologies of relationship. In this sense, there is a cyclical spiraling toward a state of multiphrenia. As one's potentials are expanded by the technologies, so one increasingly employs the technologies of self-expressions; yet, as the technologies are further utilized, so do they add to the repertoire of potentials. It would be a mistake to view this multiphrenic condition as a form of illness, for it is often suffused with a sense of expansiveness and adventure. Someday, there may indeed be nothing to distinguish multiphrenia from simply "normal living."   14

However, before we pass into this oceanic state, let us pause to consider some prominent features of the condition. Three of these are especially noteworthy.   15

VERTIGO OF THE VALUED

With the technology of social saturation, two of the major factors tradi-   16
tionally impeding relationships—namely time and space—are both removed.
The past can be continuously renewed—via voice, video, and visits, for example—and distance poses no substantial barriers to ongoing interchange.
Yet this same freedom ironically leads to a form of enslavement. For each
person, passion, or potential incorporated into oneself exacts a penalty—a
penalty both of *being* and of *being with.* In the former case, as others are incorporated into the self, their tastes, goals, and values also insinuate themselves into one's being. Through continued interchange, one acquires, for
example, a yen for Thai cooking, the desire for retirement security, or an investment in wildlife preservation. Through others, one comes to value
whole-grain breads, novels from Chile, or community politics. Yet as Bud-
dhists have long been aware, to desire is simultaneously to become a slave
of the desirable. To "want" reduces one's choice to "want not." Thus, as others are incorporated into the self, and their desires become one's own, there
is an expansion of goals—of "musts," wants, and needs. Attention is neces-
sitated, effort is exerted, frustrations are encountered. Each new desire
places its demands and reduces one's liberties.

There is also the penalty of being with. As relationships develop, their   17
participants acquire local definitions—friend, lover, teacher, supporter, and
so on. To sustain the relationship requires an honoring of the definitions—
both of self and other. If two persons become close friends, for example,
each acquires certain rights, duties, and privileges. Most relationships of
any significance carry with them a range of obligations—for communication,
joint activities, preparing for the other's pleasure, rendering appropriate con-
gratulations, and so on. Thus, as relations accumulate and expand over
time, there is a steadily increasing range of phone calls to make and answer,
greeting cards to address, visits or activities to arrange, meals to prepare,
preparations to be made, clothes to buy, makeup to apply. . . . And with each
new opportunity—for skiing together in the Alps, touring Australia, camping in
the Adirondacks, or snorkling in the Bahamas—there are "opportunity costs."
One must unearth information, buy equipment, reserve hotels, arrange
travel, work long hours to clear one's desk, locate babysitters, dogsitters,
homesitters. . . . Liberation becomes a swirling vertigo of demands.

In the professional world, this expansion of "musts" is strikingly evident.   18
In the university of the 1950s, for example, one's departmental colleagues
were often vital to one's work. One could walk but a short distance for advice, information, support, and so on. Departments were often close-knit
and highly interdependent; travels to other departments or professional
meetings were notable events. Today, however, the energetic academic will
be linked by post, long-distance phone, fax, and electronic mail to likeminded scholars around the globe. The number of interactions possible in a

day is limited only by the constraints of time. The technologies have also stimulated the development of hundreds of new organizations, international conferences, and professional meetings. A colleague recently informed me that if funds were available, he could spend his entire sabbatical traveling from one professional gathering to another. A similar condition pervades the business world. One's scope of business opportunities is no longer so limited by geography; the technologies of the age enable projects to be pursued around the world. (Colgate Tartar Control toothpaste is now sold in over forty countries.) In effect, the potential for new connection and new opportunities is practically unlimited. Daily life has become a sea of drowning demands, and there is no shore in sight.

THE EXPANSION OF INADEQUACY

It is not simply the expansion of self through relationships that hounds one with the continued sense of "ought." There is also the seeping of self-doubt into everyday consciousness, a subtle feeling of inadequacy that smothers one's activities with an uneasy sense of impending emptiness. In important respects, this sense of inadequacy is a by-product of the populating of self and the presence of social ghosts. For as we incorporate others into ourselves, so does the range of proprieties expand—that is, the range of what we feel a "good," "proper," or "exemplary" person should be. Many of us carry with us the "ghost of a father," reminding us of the values of honesty and hard work, or a mother challenging us to be nurturing and understanding. We may also absorb from a friend the values of maintaining a healthy body, from a lover the goal of self-sacrifice, from a teacher the ideal of worldly knowledge, and so on. Normal development leaves most people with a rich sense of personal well-being by fulfilling these goals. 19

But now consider the effects of social saturation. The range of one's friends and associates expands exponentially; one's past life continues to be vivid; and the mass media expose one to an enormous array of new criteria for self-evaluation. A friend from California reminds one to relax and enjoy life; in Ohio, an associate is getting ahead by working eleven hours a day. A relative from Boston stresses the importance of cultural sophistication, while a Washington colleague belittles one's lack of political savvy. A relative's return from Paris reminds one to pay more attention to personal appearance, while a ruddy companion from Colorado suggests that one grows soft. 20

Meanwhile, newspapers, magazines, and television provide a barrage of new criteria of self-evaluation. Is one sufficiently adventurous, clean, well traveled, well read, low in cholesterol, slim, skilled in cooking, friendly, odor free, coiffed, frugal, burglar proof, family oriented? The list is unending. More than once, I have heard the lament of a subscriber to the Sunday *New York Times.* Each page of this weighty tome will be read by millions. Thus, each 21 page remaining undevoured by day's end will leave one precariously disadvantaged—a potential idiot in a thousand unpredictable circumstances.

Yet the threat of inadequacy is hardly limited to the immediate confrontation with mates and media. Because many of these criteria for self-evaluation are incorporated into the self—existing within the cadre of social ghosts—they are free to speak at any moment. The problem with values is that they are sufficient unto themselves. To value justice, for example, is to say nothing of the value of love; investing in duty will blind one to the value of spontaneity. No one value in itself recognizes the importance of any alternative value. And so it is with the chorus of social ghosts. Each voice of value stands to discredit all that does not meet its standard. All the voices at odds with one's current conduct thus stand as internal critics, scolding, ridiculing, and robbing action of its potential for fulfillment. One settles in front of the television for enjoyment, and the chorus begins: "twelve year old," "couch potato," "lazy," "irresponsible". . . . One sits down with a good book, and again: "sedentary," "antisocial," "inefficient," "fantasist". . . . Join friends for a game of tennis, and "skin cancer," "shirker of household duties," "underexercised," "overly competitive" come up. Work late and it is "workaholic," "heart attack–prone," "overly ambitious," "irresponsible family member." Each moment is enveloped in the guilt born of all that was possible but now foreclosed. 22

RATIONALITY IN RECESSION

A third dimension of multiphrenia is closely related to the others. The focus here is on the rationality of everyday decision-making instances in which one tries to be a "reasonable person." Why, one asks, is it important for one's children to attend college? The rational reply is that a college education increases one's job opportunities, earnings, and likely sense of personal fulfillment. Why should I stop smoking? one asks, and the answer is clear that smoking causes cancer, so to smoke is simply to invite a short life. Yet these "obvious" lines of reasoning are obvious only so long as one's identity remains fixed within a particular group. 23

The rationality of these replies depends altogether on the sharing of opinions—of each incorporating the views of others. To achieve identity in other cultural enclaves turns these "good reasons" into "rationalizations," "false consciousness," or "ignorance." Within some subcultures, a college education is a one-way ticket to bourgeois conventionality—a white-collar job, picket fence in the suburbs, and chronic boredom. For many, smoking is an integral part of a risky lifestyle; it furnishes a sense of intensity, offbeatness, rugged individualism. In the same way, saving money for old age is "sensible" in one family, and "oblivious to the erosions of inflation" in another. For most Westerners, marrying for love is the only reasonable (if not conceivable) thing to do. But many Japanese will point to statistics 24 demonstrating greater longevity and happiness in arranged marriages. Rationality is a vital by-product of social participation.

Yet as the range of our relationships is expanded, the validity of each   25
localized rationality is threatened. What is rational in one relationship is
questionable or absurd from the standpoint of another. The "obvious choice"
while talking with a colleague lapses into absurdity when speaking with a
spouse, and into irrelevance when an old friend calls that evening. Further,
because each relationship increases one's capacities for discernment, one
carries with oneself a multiplicity of competing expectations, values, and beliefs about "the obvious solution." Thus, if the options are carefully evaluated, every decision becomes a leap into gray vapors. Hamlet's bifurcated
decision becomes all too simple, for it is no longer being or non-being that is
in question, but to which of multifarious beings one can be committed.

CONCLUSION

So we find a profound sea change taking place in the character of so-   26
cial life during the twentieth century. Through an array of newly emerging
technologies, the world of relationships becomes increasingly saturated. We
engage in greater numbers of relationships, in a greater variety of forms,
and with greater intensities than ever before. With the multiplication of relationships also comes a transformation in the social capacities of the individual—both in knowing how and knowing that. The relatively coherent and
unified sense of self inherent in a traditional culture gives way to manifold
and competing potentials. A multiphrenic condition emerges in which one
swims in ever-shifting, concatenating, and contentious currents of being.
One bears the burden of an increasing array of oughts, of self-doubts and irrationalities. The possibility for committed romanticism or strong and single-minded modernism recedes, and the way is opened for the postmodern
being. . . .

As belief in essential selves erodes, awareness expands of the ways in   27
which personal identity can be created and recreated. . . . This consciousness
of construction does not strike as a thunderbolt; rather, it eats slowly and irregularly away at the edge of consciousness. And as it increasingly colors our understanding of self and relationships, the character of this consciousness
undergoes a qualitative change. . . . [P]ostmodern consciousness [brings] the
erasure of the category of self. No longer can one securely determine what it
is to be a specific kind of person . . . or even a person at all. As the category of
the individual person fades from view, consciousness of construction becomes focal. We realize increasingly that who and what we are is not so much
the result of our "person essence" (real feelings, deep beliefs, and the like),
but of how we are constructed in various social groups. . . . [T]he concept of
the individual self ceases to be intelligible. . . .   ©

CRITICAL READING

1. In your own words, define the key terms from Gergen's essay. These terms include social saturation, populating the self, and multiphrenia. After defining the terms, discuss how they relate to each other, and how they help to define the postmodern self.
2. Discuss how Gergen's ideas modify or nullify the perspectives of Cooley and Goffman.
3. Can you think of examples of your tastes, interests, and concerns being influenced by others in the ways that Gergen discusses in the first paragraph following the title "Vertigo of the Valued"? Describe these examples.

CLASS DISCUSSION

1. Explain and discuss Gergen's point that in contemporary life, "liberation becomes a swirling vertigo of demands." How do new technologies that Gergen doesn't mention play a role in this?
2. Test out Gergen's points that our identities are a "pastiche" or imitative assemblages of each other, so that we know how to act in certain situations because we've seen how others act on television and other media. Have members of the class list several kinds of situations that might be upsetting and then either discuss or act out the reactions that seem either appropriate or possible. Is there some consensus among students about the possible reactions? Where have students seen or heard of these reactions?

DIRECTED FREEWRITE

Freewrite about your own identity—what are its various aspects? Discuss things such as your values and beliefs; your behaviors (are these two always consistent, or do you ever behave in ways that violate the values you hold?); your likes and dislikes; your relationships with others and the roles you play in these; and your hobbies, tastes, and possessions, and what they mean to you. How are you different in different settings? How do you wish you were different? Why aren't you that way?

SOCIAL PSYCHOLOGY UNIT WRITING ASSIGNMENTS

1. An autobiographical narrative is one of the most basic rhetorical forms in that it focuses on one specific event or grouping of events from your life and it seeks to derive meaning from those events. This assignment modifies the autobiographical narrative slightly. This "analytical autobiography" assignment asks you to discuss the primary group or groups that have had the most significant effect on your sense of self and to explain precisely what kind of effect they have had. We're calling this an analytical autobiography because rather than just relating one incident in your personal history, we are asking you to relate a specific aspect of your history in relation to Cooley's theoretical concepts. Thus, this essay

should have a clear thesis statement that tells your reader exactly how the primary groups you are discussing have affected you.

Although focusing on ourselves and our experiences is useful for increasing our understanding of the concepts and of ourselves, social scientists focus more often on phenomena that can be observed more objectively. Thus, theories such as Cooley's or Goffman's might be used as lenses through which to view human interactions and behavior. The act of using theory to understand and make sense of phenomena is often called "analysis." Thus, another related assignment might be to apply Goffman's theory to a particular environment such as the classroom, a party, a family dinner, or a job interview. What are the typical ways that the various "actors" in these settings present themselves, and what are their reasons for doing so? For this kind of analysis, make sure to give your reader a clear sense of the overall point (thesis) you're making: what does Goffman's theory help you to understand about the particular set of actions you've observed?

2. Argument essays are one of the most common assignments given to undergraduate writers, in all kinds of different contexts within the university. Moreover, constructing effective arguments is an important part of getting things done in the world at large; political, social, and economic issues are debated and resolved on the basis of argument. Entire books can be and have been written on techniques of writing effective arguments; an entire discipline, classical rhetoric, is devoted to this undertaking.

Rather than explaining all the aspects of argument and rhetoric, we will limit our discussion of argument essays to a few key concerns. Arguments engage *issues*—problems, controversies, ideas—about which people disagree. In an argument essay, a writer then makes a *claim* about a particular, and a sufficiently narrow and focused, issue. That claim is the thesis. All claims should contain within them *reasons;* we take certain positions, or make certain claims because of facts *w, x, y,* and *z.* Of course, people make particular claims all the time that rest on nonfactual reasons and that rest on unsupported opinion, beliefs, preferences, and so forth, but the most effective and persuasive claims are supported by *evidence* and *logical reasoning.* Therefore, the fourth important element of an argument is evidence, and the fifth, logic. A writer makes claims for specific reasons, and those reasons are supported by evidence, which is interpreted, discussed, and structured logically. Two more concerns must be noted here. First, the writer of an effective argument must assess his or her *audience,* in order to make appropriate choices about the kinds of evidence to employ and about how to employ it. Clearly, addressing an audience that is already opposed to a particular claim requires different handling than for an undecided audience, or for an audience in agreement with the claim. Assessing one's audience leads to the second concern we must note: the necessity of addressing opposing arguments. In order to effectively argue a specific claim, the writer must be aware of the opposing arguments and must head these off at the pass, so to speak. Anticipating the objections that might be or have been raised against particular reasons for making a claim, or against specific evidence, helps to strengthen one's claim, if those objections are addressed—as shortsighted, incomplete, illogical, or inaccurate.

At this point, it's important to recognize that there are not only fact-based arguments, but also more subjective and opinion-based arguments. These different kinds of arguments are useful in different settings. In attempts to influence public policy, for instance, fact-based arguments are crucial, and one needs to rely on factual evidence, interpreted as objectively as possible, in order to persuade readers to accept particular political positions or policies. When it comes to theories and ideas, which are the focus of much work in academia, factual evidence is used as well, but arguments rely just as much logical reasoning. Another way to conceive of this process is to say that some arguments can be proved empirically, for example, the fact that these words are printed on a page, whereas some arguments lack complete empirical proof but instead can be supported through logical reasoning and sometimes ambiguous evidence. The assertions made by Cooley and Goffman in this unit about aspects of the socialization process are not unequivocally proved by the writers, but their theoretical arguments are nonetheless persuasive; we are meant to see that things could very likely happen in the ways these writers suggest, even if they and we can't know for sure that this is so. Similarly, when Gergen, at the end of his essay, states that "We realize increasingly that who and what we are is not so much the result of 'person essence' (real feelings, deep beliefs, and the like), but of how we are constructed in various social groups," he is not making a factual statement, but his argument has persuasive power as a very likely way of understanding identity today, when we look at the points he has raised in its support.

Therefore, this assignment asks you to write an argumentative essay in which you draw on your own experiences, observations, and reading, to question, confirm, or modify Gergen's points about postmodern identity. Responding to this idea will require you to look as objectively as possible at your own values, beliefs, preferences, behaviors, and to examine where they might have come from, and to look at your behavior in different social settings to see the differences or similarities between the person(s) you appear to be in these settings. Your essay, then, will make a claim about the relationship between your experiences and Gergen's point, and it will go on logically to discuss evidence from your own experiences and those you've learned about from observation and reading—citing concrete examples—in order to support your claim.

3. Each reading in this unit is a theoretical essay, putting forth each author's beliefs—based on previous theories, observations, and logic—about social-psychological processes. In this assignment, you are asked to play the role of a theorist, by articulating a theory of an individual's socialization process. Use ideas from Gergen's essay to modify a key element in either Cooley's or Goffman's theories, such as Cooley's notion of primary groups or Goffman's impression management. Write a short essay describing this new "hybrid" theoretical perspective.

Unit 2
Religious Studies—Religion and Moral Identity

RELIGION AND CRIME: DO THEY GO TOGETHER?

Lisa Conyers and Philip D. Harvey

Citing a number of social science studies that have examined the connections between religious beliefs and behavior, Conyers and Harvey attempt to debunk the notion that religious beliefs lead to ethical behavior. Their review of recent studies leads them to suggest the need for further insights into the ways that religion may impact altruism, group solidarity, and criminal acts. As you read, keep in mind this chapter's main topic of identity and consciousness. In your observations and experience, what kinds of effects on identity does religion seem to have? How might these observations be tested by social scientists?

Free Inquiry *is a journal published quarterly by the Council for Secular Humanism. It features both academic and popular writings dealing with secular humanism, atheism, church-state separation, and issues affecting the rights of religious minorities.*

Lisa Conyers is a writer and researcher based in Mount Vernon, Washington and Philip D. Harvey writes on a wide variety of public policy issues from Washington, D.C.

Charles W. Colson, the convicted Watergate felon, went on after prison to found a volunteer program for reforming prisoners. As part of that program, he advocated the broader use of religious values to help break "America's seemingly-indomitable cycle of crime." 1

In a talk before the National Press Club in Washington, D.C., Colson chided the media for giving "short shrift" to religious values, "including the acknowledgment of the relevance of morality in society." 2

Source: "Religion and Crime: Do they Go Together?" by Lisa Conyers & Philip D. Harvey in *Free Inquiry,* vol. 16, no. 3 (Summer 1996). Copyright © 1996 by Council for Democratic & Secular Humanism. Reprinted with permission from Free Inquiry Magazine.

But how relevant is religion to morality? Does religion make a person   3
more ethical? Can a strong dose of religion really reduce crime?

Surprisingly, recent research suggests that a religious person is more   4
likely to commit a crime than a non-religious person. One can even argue
that the more religious the society, the more likely it is to have high crime
rates.

What's more, studies indicate that a believer in a religion is less likely   5
to do a good deed than is a nonbeliever. Religion alone, many researchers
agree, does not determine personal moral behavior.

Renowned sociologist Alfie Kohn, author of *No Contest: The Case*   6
Against Competition and *You Know What They Say . . . The Truth About*
Popular Beliefs, has taken on the myths surrounding altruism and empathy
in his recent book, *The Brighter Side of Human Nature.* With this book he
continues his reasoned refutation of popular beliefs, proving that man is by
nature as likely to be altruistic as selfish, or gentle as opposed to aggressive. This book reviews the available research on the impact of religion on
behavior and brings us Kohn's conclusion that "religious faith appears to be
neither necessary for one to act pro-socially nor sufficient to ensure such
behavior."

Kohn adds there is "virtually no connection one way or the other" be-   7
tween religious belief or affiliation and pro-social social activities.

Among studies Kohn cites is one done on 700 city dwellers. It found   8
that religious people were no more likely to be sociable, helpful to neighbors, or eager to participate in neighborhood groups than non-religious
people.

In another study, researchers asked students about their religious affil-   9
iation and their willingness to cheat on a test. The majority of only one group
resisted cheating: atheists.

Kohn also describes an experiment in which researchers told students   10
that a person in another room had just fallen off a ladder. The finding: There
was no relationship between a student's belief in the Bible's accuracy and
his or her willingness to aid the ladder "victim."

Two thousand years of preachments about the Good Samaritan have   11
not changed an "obvious fact about altruism," explains Morton Hunt, another
avid researcher into human nature. People tend to practice altruism toward
those in their own group, Hunt says, but not those outside it, "for whom they
feel anything from indifference to hatred."

Hunt is the author of seventeen books in the behavioral and social sci-   12
ences, including the best-selling *The Universe Within* and *Profiles of Social*
Research: The Scientific Study of Human Interactions. He is a frequent
contributor to the *New York Times* magazine and is well known as a behavioral scientist. In his book Hunt cites extensive research done by Samuel
and Pearl Oliner on rescuers of Jews during World War II. Their analysis

shows that 90% of the rescuers had had religious upbringing, yet only 15% cited religion as the main reason for what they did. Further, there was no significant difference between the religiosity of rescuers and that of a control group.

In his book *The Compassionate Beast: What Science Is Discovering* 13 *About the Humane Side of Humankind,* Hunt writes: "It has not only been Goths, Huns and other barbarians who have relished slaughtering their enemies; civilized people, whose religions exalt altruism and the love of mankind, have done likewise."

Logician-philosopher Bertrand Russell went even further in Why I Am 14 Not a Christian:

> The more intense has been the religion of any period and the more profound has been the dogmatic belief, the greater has been the cruelty and the worse has been the state of affairs. . . .

You find as you look around the world that every single bit of progress 15 in humane feeling, every improvement in criminal law, every step towards the diminution of war, every step towards better treatment of the colored races, every moral progress that there has been in the world, has been consistently opposed by the organized churches of the world. [p. 20]

If religion does not deter war, can it at least deter crime? Is there any 16 evidence that Charles Colson's project to instill more religion in prisoners will cut the rate of violence? Not according to research by Lee Ellis of the University of North Dakota at Minot. Dr. Ellis has published widely in the social sciences on the topics of religiosity, criminal and violent behavior, rape and sexual behavior. He has devoted a lifetime to examining the relationship between religion and crime.

In comparing denominational religions, Ellis found Jews to be the least 17 criminal, by far, and Catholics the most. But a group showing a crime rate equal to or lower than that of Jews was one composed of people claiming no religious affiliation. Seeking further empirical confirmation, Ellis is conducting a study of 16,000 respondents to see if he can replicate those findings. Ellis is also conducting a comparison of crime rates with available information on religious affiliation by country, to see if he can further support his findings.

Sociologists William Sims Bainbridge and Rodney Stark of Towson 18 State University in Maryland differ with Ellis over the part religion plays in impeding crime. They argue that religion itself does not decide whether a person will commit a crime. What is crucial, they say, is whether the group or society to which that individual belongs is religious and enforces religious values. Any strong social group that molds behavior, even a high school sports team, can determine whether a person will behave morally.

Bainbridge and Stark support their views with analyses of large com-   19
puter databases. Their grist includes crime statistics from the Department of
Justice for every county in the country. It also contains data on religious
groups gathered by the Census Bureau and services for the study of religion.

In a brief demonstration of their database, Bainbridge showed a strong   20
correlation between areas of low church membership and larceny. He then
wiped out that correlation by introducing a second variable, transience. He
found that transience relates strongly, too, to many other crimes.

Bainbridge says: "Even if you do not consider yourself a religious per-   21
son, you are only a generation or two removed from a religious upbringing,
and you also live in a society in which the majority are religious, and religious values are ingrained in the laws and social rules of the society. Therefore, you are in fact influenced by religion and that religion instills values in
you. The United States is in fact a very religious country."

Evidence from other sources supports Bainbridge's last sentence. Sta-   22
tistics from *Where We Stand,* a book written by the World Rank Research
Team, suggests that 91% of the population in the United States believes in
God. That compares with 48% in the United Kingdom and 47% in Japan.

The percent of people who believe in their religious leaders is 43% in   23
the United States. It is only 6% in Japan and 3% in the United Kingdom and
Germany. The portion believing in hell is 76% in the United States. Compare that with 53% in Japan, 38% in Australia, 35% in the United Kingdom,
and 16% in Germany.

The Gallup Poll finds that 81% of people in the United States consider   24
themselves religious persons. That is two points lower than Italy, but well
ahead of Ireland, Spain, Great Britain, West Germany, Hungary, France,
and Scandinavia. Ireland far surpasses the United States in the number of
people who attend church at least weekly. Still, the United States leads
most other major countries by a wide margin.

Those figures, Ellis counters, simply prove the fallacy of Bainbridge's   25
argument. If America is very religious, and if religious communities thwart
crime, one would expect to find a very low crime rate in the United States.
The opposite is true; the United States is among the most criminal, violent
countries in the industrialized world.

Where We Stand cites these figures: The United States has 8.4 mur-   26
ders per 100,000 people. Rates in Germany, Australia, Portugal, France,
Denmark, and Canada range between 4.2 and 5.45. Rates in Greece, Austria, and the United Kingdom, Norway, Italy, Switzerland, Spain, and Belgium range between only 1.75 and 2.8.

The same report shows that the United States has 37.2 rapes per   27
10,000 people. The rate in Sweden is 15.7 and in Denmark, 11.23. Rates in
Ireland, Greece, Belgium, Austria, Spain, Luxembourg, Switzerland, France,

Finland, the United Kingdom, Norway, and Germany range between only 1.72 and 8.6.

The Untied States has 221 armed robberies per 100,000 people. 28 Spain tops that with 265. However, rates in Italy, Austria, the United Kingdom, Belgium, France, and Canada are much lower—between 50 and 94.

Such statistics, Ellis contends, shatter the main explanation Bainbridge 29 and Stark give for their contention that religion inhibits crimes. Ellis classifies their explanation as "group solidarity." It goes like this: those who participate in organized religion are members of a group that by definition does not condone crime. Therefore, they will be less likely to commit crimes.

Group solidarity is the most common explanation given by those who 30 view religion as a barrier to crime, Ellis discovered after analyzing more than fifty studies on the relationship between religion and criminality. He pinpointed three other explanations given by researchers.

One Ellis calls "coincidental." According to this theory, religious people 31 just happen to have social status or education levels that make them less likely to commit crimes. And non-religious people just happen to have other variables in their lives—such as drug use or frequent moves—that make them commit more crimes.

Ellis terms another theory "the Hell Fire explanation." It applies to 32 those religions that hold as a tenet an afterlife in which one pays for sins committed in life. Logically, this explanation goes, members of such churches would be less likely to commit crimes. Ellis notes, however, that counterbalancing such a threat is the fact that religions—such as Catholicism—that expound such theories also offer readily available absolution. That makes the real threat of hellfire remote.

Finally, Ellis identifies the "obedience-to-authority theory." This argues 33 simply that those who are members of organized religions exhibit strong willingness to submit to authority and are eager to do as told. Hence, they would be less likely to commit crimes that might anger the authority figure.

While dismissing each of those explanations as faulty, Ellis is embark- 34 ing on research into neurohormonal explanations of human behavior. He is trying to learn whether "arousal theory"—the theory that a person's need for arousal leads to certain behaviors—can explain crime.

Linking the theory to studies of religion and criminality, Ellis suggests 35 that those who can sit through church services have average levels of arousal. They do not need to engage in activities to get themselves aroused or excited. So, they may not commit as many crimes.

On the other hand, those who cannot sit still for church services may 36 have suboptimal arousal. They may need to engage in stimulating behavior, including crimes, to reach normal arousal levels. This research could support the view that it is not religion in itself that daunts crime. Rather, certain characteristics related to the activities surrounding religion happen to attract non-criminals. These activities include obedience and frequent attendance at church services.

The need for such research is becoming critical because the outcries 37 to fight crime become more strident every year.

The *Manchester Guardian* recently quoted the Archbishop of Canter- 38 bury, George Carey. He said that atheists cannot fully understand goodness and are less likely than believers to do good deeds without personal reward.

To cut crime and boost morality, clerics such as the Archbishop and 39 laypeople such as Colson are choosing what may be a perilously wrong weapon—religion. ©

CRITICAL READING

1. Discuss how group membership plays a role in altruistic behavior, according to work cited by Conyers and Harvey. Then discuss your own observations of and experiences with the effects of group membership on the treatment of others.
2. Explain the argument that religion alone does not decide whether a person will commit a crime. What other factors play a greater role, according to some researchers? Do some theorizing of your own—what factors besides religious affiliation can you think of that might influence criminal behavior? Are these factors perhaps strong enough to override an individual's religious beliefs?
3. Even if religion and lower crime rates are correlated, some researchers cited in this selection argue that reasons other than religious morality may explain the correlation. In your own words, sum up the arguments advanced by these researchers.

CLASS DISCUSSION

1. Conyers and Harvey point out that many people believe that religion positively influences morality. Discuss the logical basis for this view, or in other words, how might the argument for this positive influence work?
2. Why do social scientists study issues such as altruism, crime, and religion? Are there specific real-world applications for these kinds of studies and their findings? Discuss your answers, and then, as a class, theorize about other possible studies that could help shed light on the ways in which religion influences personal beliefs and behavior.

DIRECTED FREEWRITE

Freewrite for fifteen minutes about your own views and experiences with religion. To what extent has a religious upbringing influenced who you are? Or, if you weren't given a religious upbringing, do you think that absence has affected you, and if so, in what ways? In addition, explore your own sense of morality. Where did it come from? Does your behavior match your beliefs? You don't have to bare your soul here, but explore these issues within limits that are comfortable for you.

Can We Be Good Without God?

ON THE POLITICAL MEANING
OF CHRISTIANITY

Glenn Tinder

Tinder develops a complex argument regarding the relationship between true Christian beliefs and human morality, and ultimately he
links these to political ideology and practice, answering the question
raised in his title with a resounding "NO!" As you read, think about the
tone of this piece; does Tinder's tone shift around, or does it stay constant throughout? Where does he explicitly state his underlying assumptions, and how does laying his cards on the table in this way affect his
argument?

*Glenn E. Tinder received his B.A. from Pomona College, his M.A. from
Claremont Graduate School, and his Ph.D. from the University of California, Berkeley. He is currently a Professor Emeritus of Political Science at
the University of Massachusetts, Boston. His books include* The Political
Meaning of Christianity *and* Political Thinking.

We are so used to thinking of spirituality as withdrawal from the world   1
and human affairs that it is hard to think of it as political. Spirituality is personal and private, we assume, while politics is public. But such a dichotomy
drastically diminishes spirituality, construing it as a relationship to God without implications for one's relationship to the surrounding world. The God of
Christian faith (I shall focus on Christianity, although the God of the New
Testament is also the God of the Old Testament) created the world and is
deeply engaged in the affairs of the world. The notion that we can be related
to God and not to the world—that we can practice a spirituality that is not
political—is in conflict with the Christian understanding of God.

And if spirituality is properly political, the converse also is true, how-   2
ever distant it may be from prevailing assumptions: politics is properly spiritual. The spirituality of politics was affirmed by Plato at the very beginnings
of Western political philosophy and was a commonplace of medieval political thought. Only in modern times has it come to be taken for granted
that politics is entirely secular. The inevitable result is the demoralization of

Source: "Can We Be Good Without God?: On the Political Meaning of Christianity" by Glenn Tinder in *The Atlantic Monthly,* December 1989, pp. 69–88. Reprinted by permission of the author.

politics. Politics loses its moral structure and purpose, and turns into an affair of group interest and personal ambition. Government comes to the aid of only the well organized and influential, and it is limited only where it is checked by countervailing forces. Politics ceases to be understood as a pre-eminently human activity and is left to those who find it profitable, pleasurable, or in some other way useful to themselves. Political action thus comes to be carried out purely for the sake of power and privilege.

It will be my purpose in this essay to try to connect the severed realms of the spiritual and the political. In view of the fervent secularism of many Americans today, some will assume this to be the opening salvo of a fundamentalist attack on "pluralism." Ironically, as I will argue, many of the undoubted virtues of pluralism—respect for the individual and a belief in the essential equality of all human beings, to cite just two—have strong roots in the union of the spiritual and the political achieved in the vision of Christianity. The question that secularists have to answer is whether these values can survive without these particular roots. In short, can we be good without God? Can we affirm the dignity and equality of individual persons—values we ordinarily regard as secular—without giving them transcendental backing? Today these values are honored more in the breach than in the observance; Manhattan Island alone, with its extremes of sybaritic wealth on the one hand and Calcuttan poverty on the other, is testimony to how little equality really counts for in contemporary America. To renew these indispensable values, I shall argue, we must rediscover their primal spiritual grounds.

Many will disagree with my argument, and I cannot pretend there are no respectable reasons for doing so. Some may disagree, however, because of misunderstandings. A few words at the outset may help to prevent this. First, although I dwell on Christianity, I do not mean thus to slight Judaism or its contribution to Western values. It is arguable that every major value affirmed in Christianity originated with the ancient Hebrews. Jewish sensitivities on this matter are understandable. Christians sometimes speak as though unaware of the elemental facts that Jesus was a Jew, that he died before even the earliest parts of the New Testament were written, and that his scriptural matrix was not Paul's Letter to the Romans or the Gospel of John but the Old Testament. Christianity diverged from Judaism in answering one question: Who was Jesus? For Christians, he was the anticipated Messiah, whereas for traditional Jews (Paul and the first Christians were of course also Jews), he was not. This divergence has given Christianity its own distinctive character, even though it remains in a sense a Jewish faith.

The most adamant opposition to my argument is likely to come from protagonists of secular reason—a cause represented pre-eminently by the Enlightenment. Locke and Jefferson, it will be asserted, not Jesus and Paul, created our moral universe. Here I cannot be as disarming as I hope I was in the paragraph above, for underlying my argument is the conviction that Enlightenment rationalism is not nearly so constructive as is often supposed.

3

4

5

Granted, it has sometimes played a constructive role. It has translated certain Christian values into secular terms and, in an age becoming increasingly secular, has given them political force. It is doubtful, however, that it could have created those values or that it can provide them with adequate metaphysical foundations. Hence if Christianity declines and dies in coming decades, our moral universe and also the relatively humane political universe that it supports will be in peril. But I recognize that if secular rationalism is far more dependent on Christianity than its protagonists realize, the converse also is in some sense true. The Enlightenment carried into action political ideals that Christians, in contravention of their own basic faith, often shamefully neglected or denied. Further, when I acknowledged that there are respectable grounds for disagreeing with my argument, I had secular rationalism particularly in mind. The foundations of political decency are an issue I wish to raise, not settle.

CHRISTIAN LOVE

Love seems as distant as spirituality from politics, yet any discussion   6
of the political meaning of Christianity must begin by considering (or at least making assumptions about) love. Love is for Christians the highest standard of human relationships, and therefore governs those relationships that make up politics. Not that political relationships are expected to exhibit pure love. But their place in the whole structure of human relationships can be understood only by using the measure that love provides.

The Christian concept of love requires attention not only because it un-   7
derlies Christian political ideas but also because it is unique. Love as Christians understand it is distinctly different from what most people think of as love. In order to dramatize the Christian faith in an incarnate and crucified God, Paul spoke ironically of "the folly of what we preach," and it may be said that Christian love is as foolish as Christian faith. Marking its uniqueness, Christian love has a distinctive name, *agape,* which sets it apart from other kinds of love, such as *philia,* or friendship, and *eros,* or erotic passion.

When John wrote that "God so loved the world, that he gave his only   8
Son," he illuminated the sacrificial character of divine love. This is the mark of *agape.* It is entirely selfless. If one could love others without judging them, asking anything of them, or thinking of one's own needs, one would meet the Christian standard. Obviously, no one can. Many of us can meet the requirements of friendship or erotic love, but *agape* is beyond us all. It is not a love toward which we are naturally inclined or for which we have natural capacities. Yet it is not something exclusively divine, like omnipotence, which human beings would be presumptuous to emulate. In fact, it is demanded of us. *Agape* is the core of Christian morality. Moreover, we shall see, it is a source of political standards that are widely accepted and even widely, if imperfectly, realized.

The nature of *agape* stands out sharply against the background of or-   9
dinary social existence. The life of every society is a harsh process of mutual appraisal. People are ceaselessly judged and ranked, and they in turn
ceaselessly judge and rank others. This is partly a necessity of social and
political order; no groups whatever—clubs, corporations, universities, or nations—can survive without allocating responsibilities and powers with a degree of realism. It is partly also a struggle for self-esteem; we judge
ourselves for the most part as others judge us. Hence outer and inner pressures alike impel us to enter the struggle.

The process is harsh because all of us are vulnerable. All of us mani-   10
fest deficiencies of natural endowment—of intelligence, temperament, appearance, and so forth. And all personal lives reveal moral deficiencies as
well—blamable failures in the past, and vanity, greed, and other such qualities in the present. The process is harsh also because it is unjust. Not only
are those who are judged always imperfect and vulnerable, but the judges
are imperfect too. They are always fallible and often cruel. Thus few are
rated exactly, or even approximately, as they deserve.

There is no judgment so final nor rank so high that one can finally attain   11
security. Many are ranked high: they are regarded as able, or wise, or coura-
geous. But such appraisals are never unanimous or stable. A few reach sum-
mits of power and honor where it seems for a moment that their victory is
definitive. It transpires however, that they are more fully exposed to judgment
than anyone else, and often they have to endure torrents of derision.

Agape means refusing to take part in this process. It lifts the one who   12
is loved above the level of reality on which a human being can be equated
with a set of observable characteristics. The *agape* of God, according to
Christian faith, does this with redemptive power; God "crucifies" the observable, and always deficient, individual, and "raises up" that individual to new
life. The *agape* of human beings bestows new life in turn by accepting the
work of God.

The power of *agape* extends in two directions. Not only is the one who   13
is loved exalted but so is the one who loves. To lift someone else above the
process of mutual scrutiny is to stand above that process oneself. To act on
the faith that every human being is a beneficiary of the honor that only God
can bestow is to place oneself in a position to receive that honor. (That is
not the aim, of course; if it were, *agape* would be a way of serving oneself
and would thus be nullified.) *Agape* raises all those touched by it into the
community brought by Christ, the Kingdom of God. Everyone is glorified. No
one is judged and no one judges.

Here we come to the major premise (in the logic of faith, if not invari-   14
ably in the history of Western political philosophy) of all Christian social and
political thinking—the concept of the exalted individual. Arising from *agape,*
this concept more authoritatively than any other shapes not only Christian
perceptions of social reality but also Christian delineations of political goals.

THE EXALTED INDIVIDUAL

To grasp fully the idea of the exalted individual is not easy, but this is   15
not because it rests on a technical or complex theory. The difficulty of grasp-
ing the concept is due to its being beyond the whole realm of theory. It
refers to something intrinsically mysterious, a reality that one cannot see by
having someone else point to it or describe it. It is often spoken of, but the
words we use—"the dignity of the individual," "the infinite value of a human
being," and so forth—have become banal and no longer evoke the mystery
that called them forth. Hence we must try to understand what such phrases
mean. In what way, from a Christian standpoint, are individuals exalted? In
trying to answer this question, the concept of destiny may provide some
help.

In the act of creation God grants a human being glory, or participation   16
in the goodness of all that has been created. The glory of a human being,
however, is not like that of a star or a mountain. It is not objectively established but must be freely affirmed by the one to whom it belongs. In this
sense the glory of a human being is placed in the future. It is not a mere
possibility, however, nor does it seem quite sufficient to say that it is a moral
norm. It is a fundamental imperative, even though all of us, in our sinfulness,
to some degree refuse it. This fusion of human freedom and divine necessity may be summarily characterized by saying that the glory of an individual, rather than being immediately given, is destined.

Destiny is not the same as fate. The word refers not to anything terri-   17
ble or even to anything inevitable, in the usual sense of the word, but to the
temporal and free unfoldment of a person's essential being. A destiny is a
spiritual drama.

A destiny is never completely fulfilled in time, in the Christian vision,   18
but leads onto the plane of eternity. It must be worked out in time, however,
and everything that happens to a person in time enters into eternal selfhood
and is there given meaning and justification. My destiny is what has often
been referred to as my soul.

Realizing a destiny is not a matter of acquiescing in some form of re-   19
lentless causality. If it were, there would be no sin. A destiny can be failed or
refused. That is why it is not a fate. True, the very word "destiny" is indicative of necessity, but the necessity of a destiny is not like the necessity that
makes an object fall when it is dropped. Rather, it is the kind I recognize
when I face a duty I am tempted to evade and say to myself, "This I *must*
do." Yet my destiny has a weight unlike that of any particular duty, since it is
the life given to me by God. As is recognized in words like "salvation" and
"damnation," the call of destiny has a peculiar finality.

The *agape* of God consists in the bestowal of a destiny, and that of   20
human beings in its recognition through faith. Since a destiny is not a matter
of empirical observation, a person with a destiny is, so to speak, invisible,

But every person has a destiny. Hence the process of mutual scrutiny is in vain, and even the most objective judgments of other people are fundamentally false. *Agape* arises from a realization of this and is therefore expressed in a refusal to judge.

The Lord of all time and existence has taken a personal interest in every human being, an interest that is compassionate and unwearying. The Christian universe is peopled exclusively with royalty. What does this mean for society? 21

To speak cautiously, the concept of the exalted individual implies that governments—indeed, all persons who wield power—must treat individuals with care. This can mean various things—for example, that individuals are to be fed and sheltered when they are destitute, listened to when they speak, or merely left alone so long as they do not break the law and fairly tried if they do. But however variously care may be defined, it always means that human beings are not to be treated like the things we use and discard or just leave lying about. They deserve attention. This spare standard has of course been frequently and grossly violated by people who call themselves Christians. It has not been without force, however. Even in our own secularized times people who are useless or burdensome, hopelessly ill or guilty of terrible crimes, are sometimes treated with extraordinary consideration and patience. 22

The modest standard of care implies other, more demanding standards. Equality is one of these; *no one* is to be casually sacrificed. No natural, social, or even moral differences justify exceptions to this rule. Of course destinies make people not equal but, rather, incomparable; equality is a measurement and dignity is immeasurable. But according to Christian claims, every person has been immeasurably dignified. Faith discerns no grounds for making distinctions, and the distinctions made by custom and ambition are precarious before God. "Many that are first will be last, and the last first." Not only love but humility as well—the humility of not anticipating the judgments of God—impels us toward the standard of equality. 23

No one, then, belongs at the bottom, enslaved, irremediably poor, consigned to silence; this is equality. This points to another standard: that no one should be left outside, an alien and a barbarian. *Agape* implies universality. Greeks and Hebrews in ancient times were often candidly contemptuous of most of the human race. Even Jesus, although not contemptuous of Gentiles, conceived of his mission as primarily to Israel. However, Jesus no doubt saw the saving of Israel as the saving of all humankind, and his implicit universalism became explicit, and decisive for the history of the world, in the writings and missionary activity of Paul. Christian universalism (as well as Christian egalitarianism) was powerfully expressed by Paul when he wrote that "there is neither Jew nor Greek, there is neither slave nor free, there is neither male nor female; for you are all one in Christ Jesus." 24

Christian universalism was reinforced by the universalism of the later   25
Stoics, who created the ideal of an ell-embracing city of reason—*cosmopolis*. Medieval Christians couched their universalist outlook in Hellenic terms.
Thus two streams of thought, from Israel and Greece, flowed together. As a
result the world today, although divided among nations often ferociously
self-righteous and jealous, is haunted by the vision of a global community.
War and national rivalry seem unavoidable, but they burden the human conscience. Searing poverty prevails in much of the world, as it always has, but
no longer is it unthinkingly accepted in either the rich nations or the poor.
There is a shadowy but widespread awareness, which Christianity has had
much to do with creating, that one person cannot be indifferent to the destiny of another person anywhere on earth. It is hardly too much to say that
the idea of the exalted individual is the spiritual center of Western politics.
Although this idea is often forgotten and betrayed, were it erased from our
minds our politics would probably become altogether what it is at present
only in part—an affair of expediency and self-interest.

The exalted individual is not an exclusively Christian principle. There   26
are two ways in which, without making any religious assumptions, we may
sense the infinite worth of an individual. One way is love. Through personal
love, or through the sympathy by which personal love is extended (although
at the same time weakened), we sense the measureless worth of a few, and
are able to surmise that what we sense in a few may be present in all. In
short, to love some (it is as Dostoevsky suggested, humanly impossible to
love everyone) may give rise to the idea that all are worthy of love. Further,
the idea of the exalted individual may become a secular value through reason, as it did for the Stoics. Reason tells me that each person is one and not
more than one. Hence my claims upon others are rightfully matched by their
claims upon me. Simple fairness, which even a child can understand, is implicitly egalitarian and universal; and it is reasonable.

Can love and reason, though, undergird our politics if faith suffers a   27
further decline? That is doubtful. Love and reason are suggestive, but they
lack definite political implications. Greeks of the Periclean Age, living at the
summit of the most brilliant period of Western civilization, showed little consciousness of the notion that every individual bears an indefeasible and incomparable dignity. Today why should those who assume that God is dead
entertain such a notion? This question is particularly compelling in view of a
human characteristic very unlike exaltation.

THE FALLEN INDIVIDUAL

The fallen individual is not someone other than the exalted individual.   28
Every human being is fallen and exalted both. This paradox is familiar to all
informed Christians. Yet it is continually forgotten—partly perhaps, because
it so greatly complicates the task of dealing with evil in the world, and no
doubt partly because we hate to apply it to ourselves; although glad to recall

our exaltation, we are reluctant to remember our fallenness. It is vital to political understanding, however, to do both. If the concept of the exalted individual defines the highest value under God, the concept of the fallen individual defines the situation in which that value must be sought and defended.

The principle that a human being is sacred yet morally degraded is 29 hard for common sense to grasp. It is apparent to most of us that some people are morally degraded. It is ordinarily assumed, however, that other people are morally upright and that these alone possess dignity. From this point of view all is simple and logical. The human race is divided roughly between good people, who possess the infinite worth we attribute to individuals, and bad people, who do not. The basic problem of life is for the good people to gain supremacy over, and perhaps eradicate, the bad people. This view appears in varied forms: in Marxism, where the human race is divided between a world-redeeming class and a class that is exploitative and condemned; in some expressions of American nationalism, where the division—at least, until recently—has been between "the free world" and demonic communism; in Western films, where virtuous heroes kill bandits and lawless Indians.

This common model of life's meaning is drastically ir-religious, be- 30 cause it places reliance on good human beings and not on God. It has no room for the double insight that the evil are not beyond the reach of divine mercy nor the good beyond the need for it. It is thus antithetical to Christianity, which maintains that human beings are justified by God alone, and that all are sacred and none are good.

The proposition that none are good does not mean merely that none 31 are perfect. It means that all are persistently and deeply inclined toward evil. All are sinful. In a few sin is so effectively suppressed that it seems to have been destroyed. But this is owing to God's grace. Christian principles imply, not to human goodness, and those in whom it has happened testify emphatically that this is so. Saints claim little credit for themselves.

Nothing in Christian doctrine so offends people today as the stress on 32 sin. It is morbid and self-destructive, supposedly, to depreciate ourselves in this way. Yet the Christian view is not implausible. The twentieth century, not to speak of earlier ages (often assumed to be more barbaric), has displayed human evil in extravagant forms. Wars and massacres, systematic torture and internment in concentration camps, have become everyday occurrences in the decades since 1914. Even in the most civilized societies subtle forms of callousness and cruelty prevail through capitalist and bureaucratic institutions. Thus our own experience indicates that we should not casually dismiss the Christian concept of sin.

According to that concept, the inclination toward evil is primarily an in- 33 clination to exalt ourselves rather than allowing ourselves to be exalted by God. We exalt ourselves in a variety of ways: for example, by power, trying to control all the things and people around us; by greed, accumulating an inequitable portion of the material goods of the world; by self-righteousness, claiming to be wholly virtuous; and so forth. Self-exaltation is carried out sometimes by individuals, sometimes by groups. It is often referred to, in all of its various forms, as "pride."

The Christian concept of sin is not adequately described, however, 34 merely by saying that people frequently engage in evil actions. Our predisposition toward such actions is so powerful and so unyielding that it holds us captive. As Paul said, "I do not do what I want, but I do the very thing I hate." This does not imply, of course, that I am entirely depraved. If I disapprove of my evil acts, then I am partly good. However, if I persist in evil in the face of my own disapproval, then I am not only partly evil but also incapable of destroying the evil in my nature and enthroning the good. I am, that is to say, a prisoner of evil, even if I am not wholly evil. This imprisonment is sometimes called "original sin," and the phrase is useful, not because one must take the story of Adam's disobedience literally but because it points to the mysterious truth that our captivity by evil originates in a primal and iniquitous choice on the part of every person. I persistently fail to attain goodness because I have turned away from goodness and set my face toward evil.

The political value of the doctrine of original sin lies in its recognition 35 that our evil tendencies are not in the nature of a problem that we can rationally comprehend and deliberately solve. To say that the source of sin is sin is to say that sin is underivable and inexplicable. A sinful society is not like a malfunctioning machine, something to be checked and quickly repaired.

Sin is ironic. Its intention is self-exaltation, its result is self-debase- 36 ment. In trying to ascend, we fall. The reason for this is not hard to understand. We are exalted by God: in declaring our independence from God, we cast ourselves down. In other words, sin concerns not just our actions and our nature but also the setting of our lives. By sin we cast ourselves into a degraded sphere of existence, a sphere Christians often call "the world." Human beings belong to the world through sin. They look at one another as objects; they manipulate, mutilate, and kill one another. In diverse ways, some subtle and some shocking, some relatively innocuous and some devastating, they continually depersonalize themselves and others. They behave as inhabitants of the world they have sinfully formed rather than of the earth created by God. Original sin is the quiet determination, deep in everyone, to stay inside the world. Every sinful act is a violation of the personal being that continually, in freedom, vision, and love, threatens the world. The archetype of sin is the reduction of a person to the thing we call a corpse.

THE MAN-GOD VERSUS THE GOD-MAN

When the paradox of simultaneous exaltation and fallenness col- 37 lapses, it is replaced by either cynicism or (to use a term that is accurate but masks the destructive character of the attitude it refers to) idealism.

Cynicism measures the value of human beings by their manifest quali- 38
ties and thus esteems them very slightly. It concludes, in effect, that individuals are not exalted, because they are fallen. Idealism refuses this conclusion. It insists that the value of human beings, or of some of them, is very great. It is not so simplistic, however, as to deny the incongruity of their essential value and their manifest qualities. Rather, it asserts that this incongruity can be resolved by human beings on their own, perhaps through political revolution or psychotherapy. Human beings can exalt themselves.

We shall dwell in this discussion on idealism, partly because idealism 39
is much more tempting and therefore much more common than cynicism. Idealism is exhilarating, whereas cynicism, as anything more than a youthful experiment, is grim and discouraging. We shall dwell on idealism also because it is so much more dangerous than it looks. The dangers of cynicism are evident; that a general contempt for human beings is apt to be socially and politically destructive scarcely needs to be argued. But idealism looks benign. It is important to understand why its appearance is misleading.

Idealism in our time is commonly a form of collective pride. Human be- 40
ings exalt themselves by exalting a group. Each one of course exalts the singular and separate self in some manner. In most people, however, personal pride needs reinforcement through a common ideal or emotion, such as nationalism. Hence the rise of collective pride. To exalt ourselves, we exalt a nation, a class, or even the whole of humanity in some particular manifestation like science. Such pride is alluring. It assumes grandiose and enthralling proportions yet it seems selfless, because not one person alone but a class or nation or some other collectivity is exalted. It can be at once more extreme and less offensive than personal pride.

To represent the uncompromising and worldly character of modern 41
idealism we may appropriately use the image of the man-god. This image is a reversal of the Christian concept of the God-man, Christ. The order of the terms obviously is crucial. In the case of the God-man, it indicates the source of Christ's divinity as understood in Christian faith. God took the initiative. To reverse the order of the terms and affirm the man-god is to say that human beings become divine on their own initiative. Here pride reaches its most extreme development. The dignity bestowed on human beings by god, in Christian faith, is now claimed as a quality that human beings can acquire through their own self-creating acts.

In using the concept of the man-god, I do not mean to suggest that di- 42
vinity is explicitly attributed to certain human beings. Even propagandists, to say nothing of philosophers, are more subtle than that. What happens is simply that qualities traditionally attributed to God are shifted to a human group or type. The qualities thus assigned are various—perfect understanding, perhaps, or unfailing fairness. Illustrative are the views of three great intellectual figures, familiar to everyone, yet so diversely interpreted that the fundamental character of their thought—and their deep similarity—is sometimes forgotten.

Friedrich Nietzsche set forth the ideal of the man-god more literally   43
and dramatically than any other writer. Nietzsche's thinking was grounded in
a bitter repudiation of Christianity, and he devoted much of his life to scouring human consciousness in order to cleanse it of every Christian idea and
emotion. In this way his philosophy became a comprehensive critique of
Western civilization, as well as a foreshadowing of an alternative civilization.
It is, as practically everyone now recognizes, remarkable in its range, sub-
tlety, and complexity; Nietzsche is not easily classified or epitomized. It can
nevertheless be argued that the dramatic center of his lifework lay in the effort to overthrow the standard of Christian love and to wipe out the idea that
every human being deserves respect—leading Nietzsche to attack such
norms in the field of politics as equality and democracy. If Christian faith is
spurned, Nietzsche held, with the courage that was one of the sources of
his philosophical greatness, then Christian morality must also be spurned.
Agape has no rightful claim on our allegiance. And not only does *agape* lack
all moral authority but it has a destructive effect on society and culture. It inhibits the rise of superior human beings to the heights of glory, which, we realize at last, are not inhabited by God. By exalting the common person, who
is entirely lacking in visible distinction and glory, *agape* subverts the true
order of civilization. The divine quality that Nietzsche claimed for humanity
was power—the power not only of great political leaders like Julius Caesar
and Napoleon but also of philosophers, writers, and artists, who impose intricate and original forms of order on chaotic material. Such power, in the
nature of things, can belong only to a few. These few are human gods. Their
intrinsic splendor overcomes the absurdity that erupted with the death of the
Christian God, and justifies human existence.

Karl Marx is perhaps not only as well known among Christian intellec-   44
tuals as even the most celebrated theologians but also as influential. The familiar saying "We are all Marxists now" dramatizes the fact that Marx's
views on such matters as class and capitalism are part of the furniture of the
modern mind. Christian writers are not exceptions; spontaneously they think
in some measure in Marxist terms. A considerable number of them can
even be called Marxist Christians—an appellation fully justified in the case
of most liberation theologians. Marx has in that sense become a familiar
member of the Christian household. When he is thus domesticated, however, we tend to forget what he really thought. We may forget that he was as
apocalyptically secular and humanistic as Nietzsche, even though he dis-
dained the kind of elevated and poetic rhetoric that abounds in Nietzsche's
writings. He called for the entire transformation of human life by human beings, and this, in Marx's mind, included the transformation of nature. The universe was to become radically—in its roots, in its sources and standards—
human. True, like the Christians he scorned, and unlike Nietzsche, Marx was
egalitarian. The transformation of humanity and being was envisioned as the

work of multitudes, the proletariat, and not of exceptional individuals, and ahead lay justice and community rather than glorious solitude, as in Nietzsche. Nevertheless, Marx tacitly claimed for the proletariat qualities much like those attributed in the Old Testament to God—omniscience, righteousness, and historical sovereignty, all devoted to avenging past wrongs and transfiguring human existence.

Sigmund Freud, of course, avoided both the rhetoric of redemption and the thought; he regarded any great change in the character of human beings or the conditions of human life as unlikely, and by intention was a scientist, not a prophet or a revolutionary. He belongs among the heralds of the man-god, however, because of the conviction that underlay all his psychological investigations. Disorders of the soul, which for Christians derive in one way or another from sin, and hence in their ultimate origins are mysterious, Freud believed to be scientifically explicable. From this conviction it followed that the healing work Christians believe to be dependent on divine grace Freud could assign altogether to human therapy. The soul was thus severed from God (for Freud, a childish illusion) and placed in the province of human understanding and action. Not that psychoanalysis and Christianity are in all ways mutually exclusive; the many Christians who have learned from Freud testify to the contrary. But for Freud and his major followers, psychoanalysis is a comprehensive faith, not merely a set of useful hypotheses and techniques. As a faith, it attributes to humanity alone powers and responsibilities that Christians regard as divine. Human beings are exalted by virtue of purely human faculties. Freud's attitude of resignation was a matter mainly of temperament; his methods, theories, and basic assumptions have reinforced the efforts of human beings to seize the universal sovereignty that Christians assign exclusively to God.

Nietzsche, Marx, and Freud represent a movement by no means restricted to those who consciously follow any one of them or even to those familiar with their writings. Not only are we "all Marxists now"; it could be said with nearly equal justification that we are all Nietzscheans and Freudians. Most of have come to assume that we ourselves are the authors of human destiny. The term "man-god" may seem extreme, but I believe that our situation is extreme. Christianity poses sweeping alternatives—destiny and fate, redemption and eternal loss, the Kingdom of God and the void of Hell. From centuries of Christian culture and education we have come habitually to think of life as structured by such extremes. Hence Christian faith may fade, but we still want to live a destiny rather than a mere life, to transform the conditions of human existence and not merely to effect improvements, to establish a perfect community and not simply a better society. Losing faith in the God-man, we inevitably begin to dream of the man-god, even though we often think of the object of our new faith as something impersonal and innocuous, like science, thus concealing from ourselves the radical nature of our dreams.

45

46

POLITICAL IDOLATRY

The political repercussions are profound. Most important is that all log-   47
ical grounds for attributing an ultimate and immeasurable dignity to every
person, regardless of outward character, disappear. Some people may gain
dignity from their achievements in art, literature, or politics, but the notion
that all people without exception—the most base, the most destructive, the
most repellent—have equal claims on our respect becomes as absurd as
would be the claim that all automobiles or all horses are of equal excellence.
The standard of *agape* collapses. It becomes explicable only on Nietzsche's
terms: as a device by which the weak and failing exact from the strong and
distinguished a deference they do not deserve. Thus the spiritual center of
Western politics fades and vanishes. If the principle of personal dignity dis-
appears, the kind of political order we are used to—one structured by standards such as liberty for all human beings and equality under the law—
becomes indefensible.

Nietzsche's stature is owing to the courage and profundity that en-   48
abled him to make this all unmistakably clear. He delineated with overpowering eloquence the consequences of giving up Christianity, and every like
view of the universe and humanity. His approval of those consequences and
his hatred of Christianity give force to his argument. Many would like to think
that there are no consequences—that we can continue treasuring the life
and welfare, the civil rights and political authority, of every person without
believing in a God who renders such attitudes and conduct compelling. Nietzsche shows that we cannot. We cannot give up the Christian God—and the
transcendence given other names in other faiths—and go on as before. We
must give up Christian morality too. If the God-man is nothing more than an
illusion, the same thing is true of the idea that every individual possesses in-
calculable worth.

It is true, as we have seen, that love and reason provide intimations of   49
such worth—but intimations alone; they provide little basis for overruling the
conclusions of our senses. The denial of the God-man and of God's merciful
love of sinful humanity is a denial of destiny, and without destiny there is simply life. But life calls forth respect only in proportion to its intensity and quality.
Except in the case of infants and children, we ordinarily look on those lacking
in purposeful vitality with pity or disgust. Respect we spontaneously reserve
for the strong and creative. If it is life we prize, then institutions that protect and
care for people whose lives are faltering are worse than senseless. It is hard
to think of anyone else, with the single exception of Dostoevsky, who has understood all of this as profoundly as did Nietzsche.

Marx certainly did not. His mind was on matters of a different kind,   50
matters less philosophical. The result was an illogical humanitarianism.
Marx was incensed by the squalor in which the common people of his time
were forced to live and by the harsh conditions and endless hours of their

work. Marx sympathized deeply with the downtrodden and disinherited. But this expressed his personal qualities, not his philosophy or faith. His philosophy was a materialism that can be interpreted in differing ways but that implied, at the very least, that reality was not created by and is not governed by God, his faith was in science and human will. He provided no philosophical or religious grounds whatever for the idea that every person must be treated with care. In spite of Marx's humanitarianism, therefore, there is a link between Marxist thought and the despotic regimes that have ruled in his name. It is perfectly true, as his defenders aver, that Marx adhered to political principles quite unlike those manifest in the purges and prison camps of the Soviet Union. That such practices should claim the authority of his name is thus outrageous in a sense. Nonetheless, the connection between Marx himself and modern Marxist despots is not entirely accidental. They share the principle that a single individual does not necessarily matter.

If the denial of the God-man has destructive logical implications, it also 51 has dangerous emotional consequences. Dostoevsky wrote that a person "cannot live without worshipping something." Anyone who denies God must worship an idol—which is not necessarily a wooden or metal figure. In our time we have seen ideologies, groups, and leaders receive divine honors. People proud of their critical and discerning spirit have rejected Christ and bowed down before Hitler, Stalin, Mao, or some other secular savior.

When disrespect for individuals is combined with political idolatry, the 52 results can be atrocious. Both the logical and the emotional foundations of political decency are destroyed. Equality becomes nonsensical and breaks down under attack from one or another human god. Consider Lenin: as a Marxist, and like Marx an exponent of equality, under the pressures of revolution he denied equality in principle—except as an ultimate goal—and so systematically nullified it in practice as to become the founder of modern totalitarianism. When equality falls, universality is likely also to fall. Nationalism or some other form of collective pride becomes virulent, and war unrestrained. Liberty, too, is likely to vanish; it becomes a heavy personal and social burden when no God justifies and sanctifies the individual in spite of all personal deficiencies and failures.

The idealism of the man-god does not, of course, bring as an immedi- 53 ate and obvious consequence a collapse into unrestrained nihilism. We all know many people who do not believe in God and yet are decent and admirable. Western societies, as highly secularized as they are, retain many humane features. Not even tacitly has our sole governing maxim become the one Dostoevsky thought was bound to follow the denial of the God-man: "Everything is permitted."

This may be, however, because customs and habits formed during 54 Christian ages keep people from professing and acting on such a maxim even though it would be logical for them to do so. If that is the case, our position is precarious, for good customs and habits need spiritual grounds, and if those are lacking, they will gradually, or perhaps suddenly in some crisis, crumble.

To what extent are we now living on moral savings accumulated over 55 many centuries but no longer being replenished? To what extent are those savings already severely depleted? Again and again we are told by advertisers, counselors, and other purveyors of popular wisdom that we have a right to buy the things we want and to live as we please. We should be prudent and farsighted, perhaps (although even those modest virtues are not greatly emphasized), but we are subject ultimately to no standard but self-interest. If nihilism is most obvious in the lives of wanton destroyers like Hitler, it is nevertheless present also in the lives of people who live purely as pleasure and convenience dictate.

And aside from intentions, there is a question concerning conse- 56 quences. Even idealists whose good intentions for the human race are pure and strong are still vulnerable to fate because of the pride that causes them to act ambitiously and recklessly in history. Initiating chains of unforeseen and destructive consequences, they are often overwhelmed by results drastically at variance with their humane intentions. Modern revolutionaries have willed liberty and equality for everyone, not the terror and despotism they have actually created. Social reformers in the United States were never aiming at the great federal bureaucracy or at the pervasive dedication to entertainment and pleasure that characterizes the welfare state they brought into existence. There must always be a gap between intentions and results, but for those who forget that they are finite and morally flawed the gap may become a chasm. Not only Christians but almost everyone today feels the fear that we live under the sway of forces that we have set in motion—perhaps in the very process of industrialization, perhaps only at certain stages of that process, as in the creation of nuclear power—and that threaten our lives and are beyond our control.

There is much room for argument about these matters. But there is no 57 greater error in the modern mind than the assumption that the God-man can be repudiated with impunity. The man-god may take his place and become the author of deeds wholly unintended and the victim of terrors starkly in contrast with the benign intentions lying at their source. The irony of sin is in this way reproduced in the irony of idealism: exalting human beings in their supposed virtues and powers, idealism undermines them. Exciting fervent expectations, it leads toward despair.

IDEOLOGY AND AMBIGUITY

Practically everyone today agrees that "being good," in a political 58 sense, depends on recognizing the measureless worth of the human being. When this recognition is translated into ideological terms, such as liberalism and conservatism, however, agreement vanishes. The main moral assumption underlying the discussion above becomes controversial. Nevertheless, we have to ask what the ideological implications of Christianity are, for this is simply to inquire about the practical meaning of the ideas that we have been discussing and thus to carry the argument to its logical conclusion.

In asking about ideology, however, we immediately encounter some- 59 thing that seemingly undermines any ideological commitment. This is an implicit political ambiguity. This ambiguity is deeply rooted in Christian principles, and must at the outset be taken into account.

In the Christian view, while every individual is exalted, society is not. 60 On the contrary, every society is placed in question, for a society is a mere worldly order and a mere human creation and can never do justice to the glory of the human beings within it. The exaltation of the individual reveals the baseness of society. It follows that our political obligations are indeterminate and equivocal. If we recognize what God has done—so Christian principles imply—we shall be limitlessly respectful of human beings but wary of society. Yet human beings live in society, and we meet them there or not at all. Hence we cannot stand wholly apart from society without failing in our responsibilities to the human beings whom God has exalted. So far as we are responsive to God, we must live within human kingdoms as creatures destined to be fellow citizens in God's Kingdom. This obligation gives rise to a political stance that is ambiguous and, in a world of devastatingly unambiguous ideologies, unique: humane and engaged, but also hesitant and critical.

Christianity implies skepticism concerning political ideals and plans. 61 For Christianity to be wedded indissolubly to any of them (as it often has been, "Christian socialism" and Christian celebrations of "the spirit of democratic capitalism" being examples) is idolatrous and thus subversive of Christian faith.

Trying to take into account both the profound evil in human nature and 62 the immense hope in the human situation, as Christians must, leads inevitably to what reformers and radicals—particularly those of the Third World, surrounded as they are by impoverished multitudes—are apt to regard as fatal equivocations. It leads, as I have already indicated, to a critical spirit and to qualified commitments. It would be easy to charge that such a posture reflects the self-interest and complacency of those who do not suffer from the injustice characterizing existing structures. Equivocation, it may be said, is one of the luxuries of bourgeois life in the industrial world.

Still, a Christian in the United States, without being particularly discern- 63 ing or morally sensitive, can see at least two things not so clearly visible to Third World Christian writers, particularly those liberation theologians who long for immediate social transformation. One of these is the universal disaster of revolution. There is perhaps not a single example in our time of a determined effort to produce swift and sweeping change which has not ended in tyranny; such efforts have often also ended in abominations, such as those witnessed in recent times in Cambodia, incalculably worse than those perpetrated by the old social order.

The second thing a Christian in a prosperous industrial nation can see 64 is visible because it is near at hand: that life can be culturally vulgar, morally degraded, and spiritually vacuous even under conditions of substantial justice. Not that justice has been fully achieved in the United States. But it has been approximated closely enough for us to begin to gauge its significance. We can begin to see that justice does not necessarily mean an entirely good society. The great masses of people in the United States enjoy historically unprecedented prosperity, in stark contrast with conditions in the Third World. Accompanying his prosperity, however, are signs—too numerous and flagrant to need mentioning—of moral cynicism, spiritual frivolity, and despair. If revolutions make plain the power of sin—its ability to captivate idealistic reformers—mass society displays the ingenuity of sin. Human beings in their passion for justice have not devised institutions that they cannot in their pride and selfishness outwit.

It may seem that the ideological meaning of Christianity is becoming 65 clear: Christianity is solidly, if covertly, on the side of the status quo. It is conservative. There are good reasons for arguing, however, that Christianity cannot logically be conservative but is rather—in its own distinctive fashion—radical.

A HESITANT RADICALISM

The Christian record in the annals of reform, it must be granted, is not 66 impressive. Christians have accepted, and sometimes actively supported, slavery, poverty, and almost every other common social evil. They have often condemned such evils in principle but failed to oppose them in practice. Faith does not necessarily conquer selfishness and is particularly unlikely to do so when connected with an established religion and thus with privileged groups. That Christianity has in various times and places, and in various ways, been an established religion is perhaps the major reason why it has been implicated in injustices such as slavery, serfdom, and the oppressive wage labor of early capitalism.

Nevertheless, Christianity in essence is not conservative. The notion 67 that it is (the historical record aside) probably stems mainly from the fact that Christians share with conservatives a consciousness of the fallibility of human beings. The two camps occupy common anthropological ground. But the consciousness of human fallibility is far keener among Christians than among conservatives, for Christians are skeptical of human arrangements that typically command deep respect in conservatives. Thus, Christians cannot logically assume that the antiquity of institutions provides any assurance of their justice or efficacy. They realize, if they consult Christian principles, that long-standing customs and traditions embody not only the wisdom of generations but also the wickedness—in particular, the determination of dominant groups to preserve their powers and privileges.

Christians are also mistrustful of aristocracies and elites. Conserva- 68 tives typically commend the rule of long-ascendant minorities, those certified by the established order as wise and noble. But Paul, addressing early Christians in Corinth, noted that "not many of you were wise according to worldly standards, not many were powerful, not many were of noble birth." New Testament passages indicate that Christ had a special concern for the despised and disinherited, the ignorant and unsophisticated. "God chose what is foolish in the world to shame the wise." The attitude expressed in such a passage is remote from the typical conservative reverence for minorities of inherited rank and traditional learning.

Conservatives (like non-Christian radicals) commonly assume that sin 69 can be circumvented by human skill. In the conservative view, allowing only those institutional changes that are gradual and protracted, and according authority to traditional elites, will accomplish this. For Christians, sin is circumvented only by grace. It is certainly not circumvented by society, the form that sinful men and women give to the fallen world.

In America conservatives believe that sin is effectively redirected to the 70 common good through the market. The alchemy of capitalist competition transmutes sin into virtue. But it is difficult to see how any Christian who fully grasps Christian principles can be an unqualified supporter of capitalism. Insofar as the market governs social relations, people are forced into acquisitive rivalry; to count in any way on a gift of "daily bread" rather than on money in the bank would be the mark of a fool. Acquisitive success is candidly equated with virtue and personal worth naively measured in material terms. Charity is often bestowed on the needy, but it is a matter of personal generosity, not of justice or community; and it is unsanctioned in capitalist theory. No principles could be more thoroughly anticommunal than those of capitalism. Indeed, capitalism is probably more anticommunal in theory than in practice for human beings cannot be as consistently selfish and calculating as capitalist doctrine calls on them to be. Capitalism has one bond with Christianity—the premise that human beings are ordinarily selfish. A system that enables an industrial society to achieve a degree of order and efficiency without depending on either human goodness or governmental coercion cannot be entirely despised. Nevertheless, even if capitalism worked as well as its supporters claim, it would by Christian standards fail morally and spiritually.

But if Christians are more pessimistic about human beings and about 71 social devices like the market than are conservatives, how can they act on the side of serious social change? How can they do anything but cling to all institutions, however unjust, that counteract the chaotic potentialities of human beings and achieve some sort of order? There are three answers to these questions.

First of all, Christian ideas place one in a radical—that is, critical and ad-   72
verse—relationship to established institutions. The Kingdom of God is a judgment on existing society, and a symbol of its impermanence. Jesus was
crucified because his presence and preaching were profoundly unsettling to
reigning religious and political groups. Jesus did not seek the violent overthrow
of these groups, but neither did he show much concern for their stability.

Further, these attitudes have to be acted on. This is a matter of spiri-   73
tual integrity. To anticipate the coming of the Kingdom of God is merely sentimental, a private frivolity, unless one tries to reshape society according to
the form of the imminent community, a form defined by equality and universality and requiring particular attention to the disinherited and oppressed.

Finally, however, to take it for granted that all attempted reforms will   74
fail would be as presumptuous as to assume that they will succeed. It is not
only sinful human beings who are at work in history, Christians believe, but
God as well. *Agape* is not merely a standard of personal conduct, powerless
over events. In exalting individuals, it discloses the inner meaning of history.
To practice love is to be allied with the deepest currents of life. From a
Christian standpoint, a frightened refusal of all social change would be
highly inappropriate.

Clearly the immediate political aims of Christians are not necessarily   75
different from those of secular radicals and reformers. Their underlying attitudes are different, however. The Christian sense of the depth and stub-
bornness of evil in human beings, along with the faith that the universe
under the impetus of grace is moving toward radical re-creation, gives a distinctive cast to the Christian conception of political action and social
progress.

Secular conceptions of reform are apt to be characterized by optimistic   76
oversimplifications and distortions. American reformers, for example, typically assume that human beings are both reasonable and just and that
beneficent social change is therefore easy. The main thing necessary, after
identifying a problem, is to devise and propagate a rational solution.
Poverty, crime, class conflict, war, and all other great social evils can gradually but surely be eliminated. Good will and intelligence, well organized and
fully informed (through the studies of social scientists), will suffice. Such illusions stem from a dilemma noted above. It is difficult for secular reformers
to reconcile their sense of the dignity of individuals with a recognition of the
selfishness and perversity of individuals. They are thus led persistently to
exaggerate human goodness. Trying to match their view of human nature
with their belief in human dignity, they fail to see how human beings actually
behave or to understand the difficulties and complexities of reform.

Tocqueville suggested approvingly that Christianity tends to make a   77
people "circumspect and undecided," with "its impulses . . . checked and its
works unfinished." This expresses well the spirit of reform inherent in Christian faith. Christianity is radical, but it is also hesitant. This is partly, of

course, because Christianity restrains our self-assurance. Efforts at social transformation must always encounter unforeseen complexities, difficulties, limits, and tragedies. Caution is in order. But Christian hesitancy has deeper grounds than prudence and more compelling motives than wariness of practical blunders. Hesitation expresses a consciousness of the mystery of being and the dignity of every person. It provides a moment for consulting destiny. Recent decades have seen heroic political commitments in behalf of social reform, but hesitation has been evident mainly in the service of self-interest. Christian faith, however, suggests that hesitation should have a part in our most conscientious deeds. It is a formality that is fitting when we cross the frontier between meditation and action. And like all significant formalities, it is a mark of respect—for God and for the creatures with whom we share the earth.

Some will dislike the implication that "being good" consists in being radical; others will think it strange to link radicalism with hesitation or religious faith. I suggest, however, that the main task facing political goodness in our time is that of maintaining responsible hope. Responsible hope is hesitant because it is cognizant of the discouraging actualities of collective life; it is radical because it measures those actualities against the highest standards of imagination and faith. Whether so paradoxical a stance can be sustained without transcendental connections—without God—is doubtful. [78]

We live in a disheartening century—"the worst so far," as someone has said. There have never before been wars so destructive as the series of conflicts that erupted in 1914; never have tyrannies been so frenzied and all-consuming as those established by Nazism and communism. All great political causes have failed. Socialism has eventuated in the rule either of privileged ideological bureaucrats or of comfortable, listless masses; liberal reform in America has at least for a time passed away, leaving stubborn injustices and widespread cynicism; conservatism has come to stand for an illogical combination of market economics an truculent nationalism. Most of the human race lives in crushing poverty, and the privileged minority in societies where industrial abundance undergirds a preoccupation with material comfort and an atmosphere of spiritual inanity. [79]

It is not just that hope itself is difficult to maintain in our situation. One is forced, so to speak, to hope alone. After all that has happened, in what party or cause or movement can one find a hope that can be unreservedly shared? Inherent in the disheartenment of our century is the impossibility of believing any longer in political commitment. And to draw back from commitment is to face political solitude. The individual must find a way of standing for authentic values with little or no human support. A radicalism that is hesitant must also be solitary. [80]

If the great causes and movements all have failed, and unqualified political commitments have become impossible, why not, as Paul asked, eat [81] and drink, since tomorrow we die? This is a question that secular reason should take far more seriously than it ever has.

It is a question to which all of us need an answer. The need is partly 82 political. There can be no decent polities unless many people can resist the historical discouragement so natural in our times. The consumer society and fascism exemplify the possible outcome when nations are populated predominantly by people incapable of the hesitation in which reality needs to be faced or the hope in which it must be judged and reshaped.

The need is also personal. In its depths the life of an individual is his- 83 torical and political because it is one with the lives of all human beings. To despair of history is to despair of one's own humanity. Today we are strongly tempted to split the individual and history, the personal and the political. When this occurs, personal being is truncated and impoverished. People in earlier times of bewilderment and disillusionment, such as the era of the downfall of the ancient city-state system, were similarly tempted, and a standard of life first clearly enunciated by Epicurus in the aftermath of the Macedonian conquest of the city-states is still, in the twentieth century, attractive. Epicurus called for withdrawal from public life and political activity; he argued that everything essential to one's humanity, such as friendship, can be found in the private sphere. Personal life thus is salvaged from the raging torrent of history. But it is also mutilated, for it is severed from the human situation in its global scope and its political contours.

The absorption of Americans in the pleasures of buying and consum- 84 ing, of mass entertainment and sports, suggests an Epicurean response to our historical trials. The dangers—erosion of the grounds of political health and impairment of personal being—are evident.

Being good politically means not only valuing the things that are truly 85 valuable but also having the strength to defend those things when they are everywhere being attacked and abandoned. Such strength is exemplified by Dietrich Bonhoeffer, the great German pastor and theologian, who uncompromisingly opposed the Nazi regime from the beginning, even to the extent of returning to Germany from a guaranteed haven in America to join the anti-Hitler resistance. Arrested by the Gestapo, he was killed at the end of the war. One of Bonhoeffer's prayers, composed in prison, was, "Give me the hope that will deliver me from fear and faintheartedness." Much that I have tried to say in the preceding pages might be summarized simply in this question: If we turn away from transcendence, from God, what will deliver us from a politically fatal fear and faintheartedness? ©

CRITICAL READING

1. Explain the concept of *agape*. Then go on to explore whether it's possible to reconcile the notion that *agape* is impossible for human beings to practice, and yet, according to Christian morality, the practice of *agape* is essential for human morality.

2. Explain why the Christian concept of the exalted individual is crucial to Western political life, according to Tinder.
3. In writing, work out what Tinder means when he writes on page 79 that we are all Marxists, Nietzcheans, and Freudians. Then look around in current popular culture, and discuss examples of cultural productions that seem to promote or illustrate the belief that we are the authors of our own destiny.

CLASS DISCUSSION

1. Discuss the tone used by Tinder in this piece. In what ways does he adopt a formal, didactic tone? And where do you see his using a more conversational tone? What purpose does this dual voice serve for advancing his argument?
2. Explore the ways in which this essay fits within the topic of "Identity and Consciousness." Tinder approaches these issues philosophically. What are some other ways that religious studies scholars might approach these related issues of religion, ethics, identity, and consciousness?
3. If students have read the Conyers and Harvey piece, discuss how Tinder might account for the lack of correlation between religion and morality found by the studies that Conyers and Harvey cite.

DIRECTED FREEWRITE

Explore some of the issues Tinder raises, particularly about morality and Christian ideals. Can moral behavior be justified on any other than religious grounds? And what about religions other than Christianity? Then go on to explore what a true Christian individual would be like. Do you know any people who could qualify for this?

RELIGIOUS STUDIES UNIT WRITING ASSIGNMENTS

1. The significant experiences in your life—the joys, disappointments, initiations, humiliations, narrow escapes, and religious climaxes that are a part of your unique history—helped form the person you are now. This piece of writing, a true autobiographical narrative, should focus on an incident in which you grappled with a moral dilemma, in relation to your religious and/or family upbringing. The first stage in this process involves a bit of prewriting in whatever form is comfortable for you. Think back through your life, and then write about any special incidents that fit the moral/religious question just stated. Don't necessarily filter out those incidents that seem tangentially related to the topic; sometimes seemingly unimportant events can turn out to be the most special and illuminating. Also, unless you want to write a ten-page paper, keep your listed or clustered incidents brief—a few hours or at most a single day. The story can be either uplifting or tragic, but it should tell the reader something about you. That "something" will be your thesis.
2. Write an argument essay in which you support a position (or claim) about the relationship between morality and religious identity. Focus on a relationship that is in some way connected to one or both of the readings in this unit. You might, for

example, argue for or against one of Tinder's assertions. Use findings from studies cited in the Conyers and Harvey piece to help support your position. Although your own personal opinions might help to inspire your argument, for this assignment, make sure that you don't take a position that can be supported only through personal opinion. Instead, rely on empirical evidence. Refer to Writing Assignments 2 in Unit 1 of this chapter for more discussion of argument.

The most important consideration in a piece of college-level argumentative writing is that it persuade your reader that the claim your paper advances is valid. A successful argumentative essay wins readers over to your viewpoint. Therefore, at the beginning of this essay assignment, it's a good idea for you to consider the members of your audience, so that you can avoid the pitfall of "antirhetoric": that is, using arguments that might alienate or offend them. Initially you want to grab your readers' attention, toward which end you might use a brief story, quotation, bit of humor, or controversial statement. Next, you will need to articulate your claim or position in a focused, assertive thesis statement, which will assist you in concentrating on your central point, as you write the first draft of your argumentative piece. On what reasons does your claim rest? Decide which reasons you will focus on, and go on to explain and support them by using sound evidence and logic. Include both primary and secondary evidence, in the form of statistics, quotations from readings, and firsthand interviews, along with your own opinions and responsible (that is, credible and grounded in fact) appeals to your readers' emotions. Finally, you will want to restate your most persuasive points, so that your readers will end up changing—or at least, questioning—their ways of thinking and may even adopt a certain course of action that your thesis suggests.

3. This assignment falls into the category of an article critique, a genre of writing that one might be asked to do as an undergraduate in a social science or a science course. The skills involved here are useful in a number of ways; critiquing the research of others is essential to study in any discipline. Moreover, such critique involves the kinds of critical thinking that is essential in all facets of life. Writing up the results of one's critique is a useful enterprise as well; as you can see in the Conyers and Harvey piece and as you'll find if you peruse almost any academic journal, writers in academia frequently write reviews of others' work. Additionally, when reporting the findings of one's own studies, reviewing and critiquing other related studies is a necessary part of the research process and of the experimental report format in which that research is documented. Thus, in this assignment, we ask you to find an experimental report of a study conducted to explore the relationship between religious affiliation and moral or altruistic behavior. (A note about the experimental report format: this format originated in the sciences, where the chief method of collecting primary data is experimentation. Although some social scientists do conduct experiments, the vast majority of social science research comes from observation of preexisting phenomena, rather than from experiments that are set up to create some condition. Such observations are more generally referred to as "studies," not "experiments." So, even though the genre

used to report both experiments and studies is usually referred to as an experimental report, it need not only describe experiments.)

The experimental report format is fairly standard, consisting of different sections, the abstract, introduction (sometimes called a literature review), methods, results, and, lastly, a discussion or a conclusion section. The abstract is usually placed apart from the essay text, after the essay title, and it is often further set apart from the text of the report through the use of italics and/or font that is smaller than the rest of the report. Abstracts sum up the major elements of the entire report, from the research question, the methods of study used to try to answer it, the overall results of the study, and the conclusion or interpretation that the researcher(s) arrived at on the basis of these results.

After the abstract, the text of the report starts with an introduction, which usually has no heading to indicate that's what it is, but all experienced readers of these reports know what to expect at the beginning of an experimental report. These introductions are more straightforward than the introductions you may be accustomed to reading or writing in argumentative essays. The experimental report's introduction typically describes the overall topic under which the report's research question falls. The introduction states the researcher's question or set of questions, and notes the hypotheses held by the researcher—the answer or results expected from the question(s). Such hypotheses are usually justified by reference to the findings and/or the theories of other researchers. Introductions also usually review other work that is relevant to the study reported (hence, the alternate title of "literature review"), showing the connections between those works and the current study, and critiquing the other work if necessary.

A description of the current study's methods of inquiry comprises the next section of the report, and this section usually is headed by the word "Methods." This description is a crucial part of the report, as it allows other researchers and scholars to evaluate the validity of the author(s)' findings on the basis of the ways in which the study was carried out. Next, the report contains a "Results" section, where the findings are reported in objective terms—"just the facts, ma'am." This section will typically contain charts, tables or graphs, reporting statistical findings in visual terms, while also reporting them, and perhaps summing them up within the text of the section. In the next section, usually called "Discussion" but sometimes "Conclusions," or sometimes even united with the results section and headed "Results and Discussion," the researchers interpret the meaning of those objective findings just reported. Such meaning is usually arrived at through the application of particular theoretical perspectives. For example, a sociologist might find that members of a particular group that is not accorded much respect in American society, for example, welfare recipients, are reluctant to identify themselves as such when they interact with others. The researcher might then explain this phenomenon by using Erving Goffman's theory of "stigma," which argues that negative stigmas attached to certain groups or individuals on the basis of societal norms, will help to dictate how members of those groups feel about their identity within the group.

Now that we have described the basic features of the experimental report, take a look at some examples of this genre of writing that are included in this textbook. You can find one written by Candace West and Don Zimmerman, researchers in communications, in the social science section in Chapter 3. Also in that chapter, the science section contains a zoologists' report entitled "Sex Roles, Parental Experience and Reproductive Success of Eastern Kingbirds, *Tyrannus tyrannus*." Notice that although the terms used for headings will sometimes change, for example, West and Zimmerman refer to their "Results" section as "Findings," the order in which information is presented in nearly always standardized.

Now that you know what kind of article to look for in this assignment, you may choose to locate one of the studies cited by Conyers and Harvey or to find one of your own. You should choose your article with care, since many of these kinds of reports employ sophisticated language and statistical methods, so that some studies will thus be easier for you to understand than others. Given your level of knowledge at this point, our article critique assignment is more narrow than these critiques can be. First, we will outline the typical elements of an article critique, then we'll describe the more focused version that we are assigning here.

Typically, an article critique contains the following sections: Thesis, Methods, Evidence, Contribution to the Literature, and Recommendation. The author's task is to evaluate these elements and thus ultimately to convey the overall usefulness of the report.

Our scaled-down version of this critique will ask you to eliminate the evaluation of the report's methods, since you may not be equipped at this point in your studies to judge the adequacy of social science methodologies and the way that they are employed. Additionally, your section on the report's contribution to the literature will not address the usual issues that article critiques encompass in this section. Instead of relating the report to a wide range of current work on the topic, we will ask you to relate the report only to any of the relevant work cited in the Conyers and Harvey piece in this unit. Thus your article critique should do the following: (a) Your thesis section should identify the report's thesis. Sometimes such a thesis will not be stated in a sentence or two, but rather will be more complex and/or will be spread throughout a section of the report. The thesis in these reports consists of a summation of the researcher(s)' findings, often coupled with a statement regarding the importance or the usefulness of those findings. We leave it to you to determine where such points will usually appear. (b) Include a methods section, but rather than evaluating the methods, simply sum up what methods of study the author or authors used. (c) Your next section should sum up the evidence that the report contains in support of its thesis. Discuss what kind of evidence it is, and use your common sense to evaluate briefly how credible that evidence appears to be. (d) As we already stated, in the section on the report's contribution to the literature, discuss how this report's findings relate to any of the related work discussed by Conyers and Harvey. (e) In the last section on recommendations, state your overall evaluation of this article. Discuss such considerations as what the benefit of this work is and who that benefit would serve. This section is where the thesis to your critique will be located, so you must clearly state your evaluation here.

THINKING AND WRITING IN THE SCIENCES

Unit 1:

Neuroscience—Identity: A Function of the Brain, or Something More?

THE GREAT UNKNOWN

Robert M. Hazen

In this article, the author discusses a Massachusetts Institute of Technology's *Technology Review* reader survey that was conducted to probe the relative importance of certain key scientific questions. The survey found that readers—themselves scientists—most often asked questions concerning the mind, brain, and the nature of consciousness. As you read, pay attention to the distinctions that scientists draw between what is scientific and what falls outside the scope of science: what kinds of issues can scientists claim as their own, and what issues do they consider nonscientific. What criteria make some issues truly "scientific"?

Robert M. Hazen received his Ph.D. from Harvard in 1975. He is currently a research scientist at the Geophysical Laboratory at the Carnegie Institution of Washington, D.C., and is the Clarence Robinson professor of earth science at George Mason University. His primary research interest involves understanding relations between crystal structure and physical properties, in particular for high-pressure phases. He recently published a new book, Why Aren't Black Holes Black? The Unanswered Questions at the Frontiers of Science.

In July, we asked readers to pick the most compelling questions facing science today. . . . *Technology Review* readers posed more than 100 different questions, but almost a third of all respondents—by far the largest group—placed questions about the mind, the brain, and the nature of consciousness near the top of their lists. Among the varied questions related to this topic were: How does the mind work? What are emotions? What is

1

Source: From "The Great Unknown" (Most Asked Questions in Science)" by Robert M. Hazen in *Technology Review,* vol. 100, no. 8. (November/December 1997). Copyright © 1997 by Massachusetts Institute of Technology Alumni Association. Reprinted by permission of Copyright Clearance Center on behalf of MIT Alumni Assn.

love? Can we build a conscious machine? What is the origin of creativity? What do dreams mean? Why do we respond to music?

These questions contrast with our more narrowly focused question: "What are the physical origins of memory?" which one reader described as "almost laughably simple" in comparison with the attempt to understand consciousness. Many of science's deepest thinkers, including Nobel Prize winners Francis Crick and Gerald Edelman, and mathematician Roger Penrose, would agree with *Technology Review* readers that the latter "What is consciousness?" is the most fundamental unanswered question concerning the brain. Crick, who defines consciousness as "attention and short-term memory," has called for an intensified research effort in his book *The Astonishing Hypothesis.* 2

But the distinction between questions about memory and those about consciousness raise a key point about the nature of science. For a question to be scientific, it must be answerable through a reproducible process of observation, experiment, and theory. Is the study of consciousness, as opposed to the physical brain, scientific? Many researchers, including Stanford computer scientist Terry Winograd and the late physicist Richard Feynman, are not persuaded that it's possible to find a concrete physiological definition of consciousness, much less an unambiguous experimental protocol for its study, any time soon. They contend that since a clear research strategy is lacking, consciousness must for the time being lie outside the domain of science. 3

Indeed, most unanswered questions about human thought seem to fall somewhere in the nebulous realm between philosophy and science. What is an idea? What is an emotion? What does it mean to be curious or to know something? It's hard to see how these abstract questions can be reduced in any neat way to a collective property of brain tissues, nor is it obvious how to make the giant leap from the concept of thought to a reproducible experiment in the lab. 4

The problem of consciousness has been pondered by myriad scientists and philosophers, from avowed reductionists who expect that thought and emotion can be explained by neurons alone to skeptics who deny any hope of physical understanding. University of California philosopher David Chalmers adopts a useful intermediate view by dividing the question "What is consciousness?" into what he calls the "easy problem" and the "hard problem." 5

The easy problem focuses on mechanics of consciousness: How can humans isolate external stimuli and react to them? How does the brain process information to control behavior? How can we articulate information about our internal state? Neurobiologists have long tackled aspects of these questions, which are amenable to systematic study in much the same way that researchers probe the physical mechanisms of memory. Perhaps, with many decades of intense research, such questions can be answered. 6

The hard problem, on the other hand, relates to the intangible connections between the physical brain and self-awareness, emotion, perception, and 7 reasoning. How can music evoke a sense of longing, or a poem deep sadness? How does reading a book stimulate curiosity or frustration? What are the physical structures and processes that produce love, fear, melancholy, or greed?

Some researchers believe that, in due time, an understanding of consciousness will follow naturally from research on the physical brain. Others argue for a radically new perspective. Chalmers, for example, makes the startling proposition that consciousness must be accepted as a characteristic of the universe completely distinct from previously recognized physical attributes, such as matter, energy, forces, and motions. Perhaps, he says, consciousness is an (as yet unrecognized) intrinsic property of information. 8

What is consciousness? For the time being, scholars cannot even agree on what exactly the question means, much less imagine the form an answer might take. For as far into the future as anyone cares to foresee, this greatest mystery of the human mind may remain. 9

Memories are different; they are more tangible and tightly defined. At one level, memories are a kind of information that can be stored, recalled, altered, or deleted—all familiar tasks in the computer age. It's conceivable that each memory is stored in the brain as a molecule or set of molecules that carries a message. Alternatively, memories might be hard-wired into networks of brain cells, or maybe they consist of electrical potentials that pervade the whole brain. Whatever the nature of memories, we can hold out the hope that answers will yield to clever and persistent study. 10

There's another reason why the quest to understand memory holds a central position in the study of the human brain. Awareness, perception, and thinking depend on receiving information through our senses and analyzing that information in the context of learned patterns of experience—patterns recorded as memories. We cannot be self-aware without a remembered context of existence and personal history. Understanding the physical basis of memories, therefore, is an essential step to knowing what it is to be human—to be conscious of memories. © 11

CRITICAL READING

1. Explain the statement, "For a question to be scientific, it must be answerable through a reproducible process of observation, experiment, and theory." How is such a position key to all scientific endeavor?
2. What is a reductionist, as described in the fifth paragraph of this article? What is a skeptic, as that term pertains to this debate about human consciousness?
3. Explain the universal consciousness theory as proposed by Chalmers in the eighth paragraph. What does Chalmers mean when he says that "consciousness is an (as yet unrecognized) intrinsic property of information"?
4. How is memory different from thought, according to this article? Explain the statement, "We cannot be self-aware without a remembered context of existence and personal history."

CLASS DISCUSSION

1. From your own experience in the "hard" sciences, cite examples of other, non-mind-related, scientific questions that you have encountered and perhaps investigated. How did "observation, experiment, and theory" factor into the pursuit of these scientific questions?
2. In your opinion, is the study of consciousness scientific? Explain what aspects of such study might be considered scientific and what aspects might be considered outside the scope of science, and why. Then discuss how such beliefs place you in the reductionist or the skeptic camp, somewhere in between, or in some entirely different theoretical camp.

DIRECTED FREEWRITE

In your humble opinion, what is an idea? What is a thought? Where do these things come from, and why? Run with these elusive concepts, and see where the writing takes you.

THE PUZZLE OF CONSCIOUS EXPERIENCE

David J. Chalmers

In this article, philosopher of consciousness David Chalmers discusses one of the most profound mysteries of human existence: namely, consciousness. He believes that science alone cannot explain the mystery behind conscious experience. Rather, he suggests that a more comprehensive theory is necessary to explain the nature of consciousness. As you read, look for the ways in which Chalmers develops his new theory: how does he incorporate physical systems and psychophysical laws into his comprehensive approach to this issue?

David J. Chalmers studied mathematics at Adelaide University and as a Rhodes Scholar at the University of Oxford. He has a Ph.D. in philosophy and cognitive science from Indiana University and is currently a professor of philosophy at the University of Arizona. Chalmers' primary areas of interest are in consciousness, artificial intelligence, computation, and in related areas of cognitive science and metaphysics. Among his many activities, Chalmers is on the board of directors of the Association for the Scientific Study of Consciousness, an associate editor of Psyche *(an interdisciplinary e-journal on consciousness), philosophy of mind editor for the Stanford Encyclopedia of Philosophy, and is on the executive committee of the Society for Philosophy and Psychology. In 1996, he published his first book,* The Conscious Mind.

Source: "The Puzzle of Consciousness" by David J. Chalmers in *Scientific American*, December 1995. Reprinted by permission of the author.

Conscious experience is at once the most familiar thing in the world 1
and the most mysterious. There is nothing we know about more directly
than consciousness, but it is extraordinarily hard to reconcile it with everything else we know. Why does it exist? What does it do? How could it possibly arise from neural processes in the brain? These questions are among
the most intriguing in all of science.

From an objective viewpoint, the brain is relatively comprehensible. 2
When you look at this page, there is a whir of processing: photons strike
your retina, electrical signals are passed up your optic nerve and between
different areas of your brain, and eventually you might respond with a smile,
a perplexed frown or a remark. But there is also a subjective aspect. When
you look at the page, you are conscious of it, directly experiencing the images and words as part of your private, mental life. You have vivid impressions of colored flowers and vibrant sky. At the same time, you may be
feeling some emotions and forming some thoughts. Together such experiences make up consciousness: the subjective, inner life of the mind.

For many years, consciousness was shunned by researchers studying 3
the brain and the mind. The prevailing view was that science, which depends on objectivity, could not accommodate something as subjective as
consciousness. The behaviorist movement in psychology, dominant earlier
in this century, concentrated on external behavior and disallowed any talk of
internal mental processes. Later, the rise of cognitive science focused attention on processes inside the head. Still, consciousness remained off-limits,
fit only for late-night discussion over drinks.

Over the past several years, however, an increasing number of neuro- 4
scientists, psychologists and philosophers have been rejecting the idea that
consciousness cannot be studied and are attempting to delve into its secrets. As might be expected of a field so new, there is a tangle of diverse
and conflicting theories, often using basic concepts in incompatible ways.
To help unsnarl the tangle, philosophical reasoning is vital.

The myriad views within the field range from reductionist theories, ac- 5
cording to which consciousness can be explained by the standard methods
of neuroscience and psychology, to the position of the so-called mysterians,
who say we will never understand consciousness at all. I believe that on
close analysis both of these views can be seen to be mistaken and that the
truth lies somewhere in the middle.

Against reductionism I will argue that the tools of neuroscience cannot 6
provide a full account of conscious experience, although they have much to
offer. Against mysterianism I will hold that consciousness might be explained by a new kind of theory. The full details of such a theory are still out
of reach, but careful reasoning and some educated inferences can reveal
something of its general nature. For example, it will probably involve new
fundamental laws, and the concept of information may play a central role.
These faint glimmerings suggest that a theory of consciousness may have
startling consequences for our view of the universe and of ourselves.

THE HARD PROBLEM

Researchers use the word "consciousness" in many different ways. To 7
clarify the issues, we first have to separate the problems that are often clustered together under the name. For this purpose, I find it useful to distinguish between the "easy problems" and the "hard problem" of
consciousness. The easy problems are by no means trivial—they are actually as challenging as most in psychology and biology—but it is with the
hard problem that the central mystery lies.

The easy problems of consciousness include the following: How can a 8
human subject discriminate sensory stimuli and react to them appropriately?
How does the brain integrate information from many different sources and
use this information to control behavior? How is it that subjects can verbal-
ize their internal states? Although all these questions are associated with
consciousness, they all concern the objective mechanisms of the cognitive
system. Consequently, we have every reason to expect that continued work
in cognitive psychology and neuroscience will answer them.

The hard problem, in contrast, is the question of how physical 9
processes in the brain give rise to subjective experience. This puzzle involves the inner aspect of thought and perception: the way things feel for
the subject. When we see, for example, we experience visual sensations,
such as that of vivid blue. Or think of the ineffable sound of a distant oboe,
the agony of an intense pain, the sparkle of happiness or the meditative
quality of a moment lost in thought. All are part of what I am calling
consciousness. It is these phenomena that pose the real mystery of
the mind.

To illustrate the distinction, consider a thought experiment devised by 10
the Australian philosopher Frank Jackson. Suppose that Mary, a neuroscientist in the 23rd century, is the world's leading expert on the brain
processes responsible for color vision. But Mary has lived her whole life in a
black-and-white room and has never seen any other colors. She knows
everything there is to know about physical processes in the brain—its biology, structure and function. This understanding enables her to grasp everything there is to know about the easy problems: how the brain discriminates
stimuli, integrates information and produces verbal reports. From her knowledge of color vision, she knows the way color names correspond with wave-
lengths on the light spectrum. But there is still something crucial about color
vision that Mary does not know: what it is like to experience a color such as
red. It follows that there are facts about conscious experience that cannot
be deduced from physical facts about the functioning of the brain.

Indeed, nobody knows why these physical processes are accompa- 11
nied by conscious experience at all. Why is it that when our brains process
light of a certain wavelength, we have an experience of deep purple? Why
do we have any experience at all? Could not an unconscious automaton

have performed the same tasks just as well? These are questions that we would like a theory of consciousness to answer.

I am not denying that consciousness arises from the brain. We know,   12
for example, that the subjective experience of vision is closely linked to processes in the visual cortex. It is the link itself that perplexes, however. Remarkably, subjective experience seems to emerge from a physical process. But we have no idea how or why this is.

IS NEUROSCIENCE ENOUGH?

Given the flurry of recent work on consciousness in neuroscience and   13
psychology, one might think this mystery is starting to be cleared up. On closer examination, however, it turns out that almost all the current work addresses only the easy problems of consciousness. The confidence of the reductionist view comes from the progress on the easy problems, but none of this makes any difference where the hard problem is concerned.

Consider the hypothesis put forward by neurobiologists Francis Crick   14
of the Salk Institute for Biological Studies in San Diego and Christof Koch of the California Institute of Technology. They suggest that consciousness may arise from certain oscillations in the cerebral cortex, which become synchronized as neurons fire 40 times per second. Crick and Koch believe the phenomenon might explain how different attributes of a single perceived object (its color and shape, for example), which are processed in different parts of the brain, are merged into a coherent whole. In this theory, two pieces of information become bound together precisely when they are represented by synchronized neural firings.

The hypothesis could conceivably elucidate one of the easy problems   15
about how information is integrated in the brain. But why should synchronized oscillations give rise to a visual experience, no matter how much integration is taking place? This question involves the hard problem, about which the theory has nothing to offer. Indeed, Crick and Koch are agnostic about whether the hard problem can be solved by science at all.

The same kind of critique could be applied to almost all the recent   16
work on consciousness. In his 1991 book *Consciousness Explained,* philosopher Daniel C. Dennett laid out a sophisticated theory of how numerous independent processes in the brain combine to produce a coherent response to a perceived event. The theory might do much to explain how we produce verbal reports on our internal states, but it tells us very little about why there should be a subjective experience behind these reports. Like other reductionist theories, Dennett's is a theory of the easy problems.

The critical common trait among these easy problems is that they all   17
concern how a cognitive or behavioral function is performed. All are ultimately questions about how the brain carries out some task—how it discriminates stimuli, integrates information, produces reports and so on. Once

neurobiology specifies appropriate neural mechanisms, showing how the functions are performed, the easy problems are solved.

The hard problem of consciousness, in contrast, goes beyond problems about how functions are performed. Even if every behavioral and cognitive function related to consciousness were explained, there would still remain a further mystery: Why is the performance of these functions accompanied by conscious experience? It is this additional conundrum that makes the hard problem hard. 18

THE EXPLANATORY GAP

Some have suggested that to solve the hard problem, we need to bring in new tools of physical explanation: nonlinear dynamics, say, or new discoveries in neuroscience, or quantum mechanics. But these ideas suffer from exactly the same difficulty. Consider a proposal from Stuart R. Hameroff of the University of Arizona and Roger Penrose of the University of Oxford. They hold that consciousness arises from quantum-physical processes taking place in microtubules, which are protein structures inside neurons. It is possible (if not likely) that such a hypothesis will lead to an explanation of how the brain makes decisions or even how it proves mathematical theorems, as Hameroff and Penrose suggest. But even if it does, the theory is silent about how these processes might give rise to conscious experience. Indeed, the same problem arises with any theory of consciousness based only on physical processing. 19

The trouble is that physical theories are best suited to explaining why systems have a certain physical structure and how they perform various functions. Most problems in science have this form; to explain life, for example, we need to describe how a physical system can reproduce, adapt and metabolize. But consciousness is a different sort of problem entirely, as it goes beyond the explanation of structure and function. 20

Of course, neuroscience is not irrelevant to the study of consciousness. For one, it may be able to reveal the nature of the neural correlate of consciousness—the brain processes most directly associated with conscious experience. It may even give a detailed correspondence between specific processes in the brain and related components of experience. But until we know why these processes give rise to conscious experience at all, we will not have crossed what philosopher Joseph Levine has called the explanatory gap between physical processes and consciousness. Making that leap will demand a new kind of theory. 21

A TRUE THEORY OF EVERYTHING

In searching for an alternative, a key observation is that not all entities in science are explained in terms of more basic entities. In physics, for example, space-time, mass and charge (among other things) are regarded as 22 fundamental features of the world, as they are not reducible to anything simpler. Despite this irreducibility, detailed and useful theories relate these entities to one another in terms of fundamental laws. Together these features and laws explain a great variety of complex and subtle phenomena.

It is widely believed that physics provides a complete catalogue of the 23 universe's fundamental features and laws. As physicist Steven Weinberg puts it in his 1992 book *Dreams of a Final Theory,* the goal of physics is a "theory of everything" from which all there is to know about the universe can be derived. But Weinberg concedes that there is a problem with consciousness. Despite the power of physical theory, the existence of consciousness does not seem to be derivable from physical laws. He defends physics by arguing that it might eventually explain what he calls the objective correlates of consciousness (that is, the neural correlates), but of course to do this is not to explain consciousness itself. If the existence of consciousness cannot be derived from physical laws, a theory of physics is not a true theory of everything. So a final theory must contain an additional fundamental component.

Toward this end, I propose that conscious experience be considered a 24 fundamental feature, irreducible to anything more basic. The idea may seem strange at first, but consistency seems to demand it. In the 19th century it turned out that electromagnetic phenomena could not be explained in terms of previously known principles. As a consequence, scientists introduced electromagnetic charge as a new fundamental entity and studied the associated fundamental laws. Similar reasoning should apply to consciousness. If existing fundamental theories cannot encompass it, then something new is required.

Where there is a fundamental property, there are fundamental laws. In 25 this case, the laws must relate experience to elements of physical theory. These laws will almost certainly not interfere with those of the physical world; it seems that the latter form a closed system in their own right. Rather the laws will serve as a bridge, specifying how experience depends on underlying physical processes. It is this bridge that will cross the explanatory gap.

Thus, a complete theory will have two components: physical laws, 26 telling us about the behavior of physical systems from the infinitesimal to the cosmological, and what we might call psychophysical laws, telling us how some of those systems are associated with conscious experience. These two components will constitute a true theory of everything.

SEARCHING FOR A THEORY

Supposing for the moment that they exist, how might we uncover such 27 psychophysical laws? The greatest hindrance in this pursuit will be a lack of data. As I have described it, consciousness is subjective, so there is no direct way to monitor it in others. But this difficulty is an obstacle, not a dead end. For a start, each one of us has access to our own experiences, a rich trove that can be used to formulate theories. We can also plausibly rely on indirect information such as subjects' descriptions of their experiences. Philosophical arguments and thought experiments also have a role to play. Such methods have limitations, but they give us more than enough to get started.

These theories will not be conclusively testable, so they will inevitably   28
be more speculative than those of more conventional scientific disciplines. Nevertheless, there is no reason they should not be strongly constrained to account accurately for our own first-person experiences, as well as the evidence from subjects' reports. If we find a theory that fits the data better than any other theory of equal simplicity, we will have good reason to accept it. Right now we do not have even a single theory that fits the data, so worries about testability are premature.

We might start by looking for high-level bridging laws, connecting   29
physical processes to experience at an everyday level. The basic contour of such a law might be gleaned from the observation that when we are conscious of something, we are generally able to act on it and speak about it— which are objective, physical functions. Conversely, when some information is directly available for action and speech, it is generally conscious. Thus, consciousness correlates well with what we might call "awareness": the process by which information in the brain is made globally available to motor processes such as speech and bodily action.

The notion may seem trivial. But as defined here, awareness is objec-   30
tive and physical, whereas consciousness is not. Some refinements to the definition of awareness are needed, in order to extend the concept to animals and infants, which cannot speak. But at least in familiar cases, it is possible to see the rough outlines of a psychophysical law: where there is awareness, there is consciousness, and vice versa.

To take this line of reasoning a step further, consider the structure   31
present in the conscious experience. The experience of a field of vision, for example, is a constantly changing mosaic of colors, shapes and patterns and as such has a detailed geometric structure. The fact that we can describe this structure, reach out in the direction of many of its components and perform other actions that depend on it suggests that the structure corresponds directly to that of the information made available in the brain through the neural processes of awareness.

Similarly, our experiences of color have an intrinsic three-dimensional   32
structure that is mirrored in the structure of information processes in the brain's visual cortex. This structure is illustrated in the color wheels and charts used by artists. Colors are arranged in a systematic pattern—red to green on one axis, blue to yellow on another, and black to white on a third. Colors that are close to one another on a color wheel are experienced as similar. It is extremely likely that they also correspond to similar

perceptual representations in the brain, as part of a system of complex three-dimensional coding among neurons that is not yet fully understood. We can recast the underlying concept as a principle of structural coherence: the structure of conscious experience is mirrored by the structure of information in awareness, and vice versa.

Another candidate for a psychophysical law is a principle of organizational invariance. It holds that physical systems with the same abstract organization will give rise to the same kind of conscious experience, no matter what they are made of. For example, if the precise interactions between our neurons could be duplicated with silicon chips, the same conscious experience would arise. The idea is somewhat controversial, but I believe it is strongly supported by thought experiments describing the gradual replacement of neurons by silicon chips. The remarkable implication is that consciousness might someday be achieved in machines. 33

INFORMATION: PHYSICAL AND EXPERIENTIAL

The ultimate goal of a theory of consciousness is a simple and elegant set of fundamental laws, analogous to the fundamental laws of physics. The principles described above are unlikely to be fundamental, however. Rather they seem to be high-level psychophysical laws, analogous to macroscopic principles in physics such as those of thermodynamics or kinematics. What might the underlying fundamental laws be? No one knows, but I don't mind speculating. 34

I suggest that the primary psychophysical laws may centrally involve the concept of information. The abstract notion of information, as put forward in the 1940s by Claude E. Shannon of the Massachusetts Institute of Technology, is that of a set of separate states with a basic structure of similarities and differences between them. We can think of a 10-bit binary code as an information state, for example. Such information states can be embodied in the physical world. This happens whenever they correspond to physical states (voltages, say); the differences between them can be transmitted along some pathway, such as a telephone line. 35

We can also find information embodied in conscious experience. The pattern of color patches in a visual field, for example, can be seen as analogous to that of the pixels covering a display screen. Intriguingly, it turns out that we find the same information states embedded in conscious experience and in underlying physical processes in the brain. The three-dimensional encoding of color spaces, for example, suggests that the information state in a color experience corresponds directly to an information state in the brain. We might even regard the two states as distinct aspects of a single information state, which is simultaneously embodied in both physical processing and conscious experience. 36

A natural hypothesis ensues. Perhaps information, or at least some in- 37
formation, has two basic aspects: a physical one and an experiential one.
This hypothesis has the status of a fundamental principle that might underlie
the relation between physical processes and experience. Wherever we find
conscious experience, it exists as one aspect of an information state, the
other aspect of which is embedded in a physical process in the brain. This
proposal needs to be fleshed out to make a satisfying theory. But it fits
nicely with the principles mentioned earlier—systems with the same organization will embody the same information, for example—and it could explain
numerous features of our conscious experience.

The idea is at least compatible with several others, such as physicist 38
John A. Wheeler's suggestion that information is fundamental to the physics
of the universe. The laws of physics might ultimately be cast in informational
terms, in which case we would have a satisfying congruence between the
constructs in both physical and psychophysical laws. It may even be that a
theory of physics and a theory of consciousness could eventually be consol-
idated into a single grander theory of information.

A potential problem is posed by the ubiquity of information. Even a 39
thermostat embodies some information, for example, but is it conscious?
There are at least two possible responses. First, we could constrain the fundamental laws so that only some information has an experiential aspect,
perhaps depending on how it is physically processed. Second, we might bite
the bullet and allow that all information has an experiential aspect—where
there is complex information processing, there is complex experience, and
where there is simple information processing, there is simple experience. If
this is so, then even a thermostat might have experiences, although they
would be much simpler than even a basic color experience, and there would
certainly be no accompanying emotions or thoughts. This seems odd at first,
but if experience is truly fundamental, we might expect it to be widespread.
In any case, the choice between these alternatives should depend on which
can be integrated into the most powerful theory.

Of course, such ideas may be all wrong. On the other hand, they might 40
evolve into a more powerful proposal that predicts the precise structure of
our conscious experience from physical processes in our brains. If this project succeeds, we will have good reason to accept the theory. If it fails, other
avenues will be pursued, and alternative fundamental theories may be developed. In this way, we may one day resolve the greatest mystery of the
mind.   ©

CRITICAL READING

1. How does the author define consciousness early in this article? What are the traditional scientific views of and approaches to consciousness, according to
   Chalmers?

2. How have "an increasing number of neuroscientists, psychologists and philosophers" been overturning the traditional scientific view of consciousness? How does the author respond to the specific claims of neuroscience and "mysterianism"?

3. What is the "hard problem" of consciousness, in the view of this author? How does the example of Mary, the fictional twenty-third-century neuroscientist, illustrate the hard problem?

4. What specific solutions does Chalmers propose to answer the hard problem of consciousness? How does he differentiate between "physical laws" and "psychophysical laws?" How do these two groups of laws work together to explain consciousness?

5. What does Chalmers mean by "the concept of information"? How does this concept help address the hard problem of consciousness, in the author's view?

CLASS DISCUSSION

1. Consider your position relative to the author's statement, "I will argue that the tools of neuroscience cannot provide a full account of conscious experience, although they have much to offer." In what ways can consciousness be explained by medical/scientific study of the brain as an organ of the body, and in what ways is such study too limited and limiting?

2. Discuss the concept of information, as Chalmers describes it here. What previous experience with the concept of information do you bring to this discussion? In your opinion, is this concept useful in addressing the hard problem of human consciousness?

DIRECTED FREEWRITE

Explore Chalmers's discussions of physical and psychophysical laws. As you write, mull over the merits and deficiencies of these approaches to consciousness, and see whether you can come up with some new laws of your own (one point of extra credit for every new law you devise in the next fifteen minutes!).

WHY NEUROSCIENCE MAY BE ABLE TO EXPLAIN CONSCIOUSNESS

Francis Crick and Christof Koch

In this piece, biologist Francis Crick and professor of computation and neural systems Christof Koch take issue with some of the arguments expressed by Chalmers in the previous article. Here, the authors insist that scientifically understanding the brain itself will answer the "big questions" about human consciousness. As you read, notice the ways in which colleagues in a given discipline—or, in this case, individuals who come from different disciplines but focus on a common topic—engage in a sometimes heated debate, oftentimes expressing differences of opinion without "pulling punches." Pay special attention to the ways in which the authors acknowledge respect for the contrasting opinions of others, while asserting the validity of their own arguments.

Francis Harry Compton Crick was born on June 8th, 1916, in Northampton, England. He earned a B.Sc. in physics from University College in 1937, and his Ph.D. from Caius College in 1954. With J. D. Watson and M.H.F. Wilkins he was presented with a Lasker Foundation Award in 1960. Crick was awarded the Prix Charles Leopold Meyer of the French Academy of Sciences in 1961. In 1962 he won the Award of Merit of the Gairdner Foundation and was elected as a Foreign Honorary Member of the American Academy of Arts and Sciences. Together with J. D. Watson he was a Warren Triennial Prize Lecturer in 1959 and received a Research Corporation Award in 1962. In 1964, he and J. D. Watson won the Nobel Prize in Medicine for their discoveries concerning the molecular structure of nuclear acids. Francis Crick is currently a Kieckhefer Distinguished Research Professor at the Salk Institute for Biological Studies in San Diego.

Christof Koch was born on November 13, 1956 in Kansas City, Missouri and proceeded to grow up all over the world—including Rabat/Morocco and Bonn/Germany. He graduated from the Lycée Descartes in 1974 with a French Baccalauréat. By 1982, Koch had earned an M.A. and Ph.D. in Physics and Philosophy from the Max-Planck-Institute for Biological Cybernetics in Tübingen, Germany. After 4 years as a post-doctoral fellow at the Artificial Intelligence Laboratory at the Department of Psychology at MIT, he joined the California Institute of Technology's newly started Computation and Neural Systems operation, where he is now an Executive Officer and Professor of Computation and Neural Systems responsible for running the K-Lab.

We believe that at the moment the best approach to the problem of explaining consciousness is to concentrate on finding what is known as the 1 neural correlates of consciousness—the processes in the brain that are most directly responsible for consciousness. By locating the neurons in the cerebral cortex that correlate best with consciousness, and figuring out how they link to neurons elsewhere in the brain, we may come across key insights into what David J. Chalmers calls the hard problem: a full accounting of the manner in which subjective experience arises from these cerebral processes.

We commend Chalmers for boldly recognizing and focusing on the   2
hard problem at this early stage, although we are not as enthusiastic about some of his thought experiments. As we see it, the hard problem can be broken down into several questions: Why do we experience anything at all? What leads to a particular conscious experience (such as the blueness of blue)? Why are some aspects of subjective experience impossible to convey to other people (in other words, why are they private)? We believe we have an answer to the last problem and a suggestion about the first two, revolving around a phenomenon known as explicit neuronal representation.

What does "explicit" mean in this context? Perhaps the best way to define it is with an example. In response to the image of a face, say, ganglion   3
cells fire all over the retina, much like the pixels on a television screen, to generate an implicit representation of the face. At the same time, they can also respond to a great many other features in the image, such as shadows, lines, uneven lighting and so on. In contrast, some neurons high in the hierarchy of the visual cortex respond mainly to the face or even to the face viewed at a particular angle. Such neurons help the brain represent the face in an explicit manner. Their loss, resulting from a stroke or some other brain injury, leads to prosopagnosia, an individual's inability to recognize familiar faces consciously—even his or her own, although the person can still identify a face as a face. Similarly, damage to other parts of the visual cortex can cause someone to lose the ability to experience color, while still seeing in shades of black and white, even though there is no defect in the color receptors in the eye.

At each stage, visual information is reencoded, typically in a semihierarchical manner. Retinal ganglion cells respond to a spot of light. Neurons in   4
the primary visual cortex are most adept at responding to lines or edges; neurons higher up might prefer a moving contour. Still higher are those that respond to faces and other familiar objects. On top are those that project to pre-motor and motor structures in the brain, where they fire the neurons that initiate such actions as speaking or avoiding an oncoming automobile.

Chalmers believes, as we do, that the subjective aspects of an experience must relate closely to the firing of the neurons corresponding to those   5
aspects (the neural correlates). He describes a well-known thought experiment, constructed around a hypothetical neuroscientist, Mary, who specializes in color perception but has never seen a color. We believe the reason Mary does not know what it is like to see a color, however, is that she has never had an explicit neural representation of a color in her brain, only of the words and ideas associated with colors.

In order to describe a subjective visual experience, the information has   6
to be transmitted to the motor output stage of the brain, where it becomes
available for verbalization or other actions. This transmission always involves reencoding the information, so that the explicit information expressed
by the motor neurons is related, but not identical, to the explicit information
expressed by the firing of the neurons associated with color experience, at
some level in the visual hierarchy.

It is not possible, then, to convey with words and ideas the exact na-   7
ture of a subjective experience. It is possible, however, to convey a difference between subjective experiences—to distinguish between red and
orange, for example. This is possible because a difference in a high-level visual cortical area will still be associated with a difference in the motor
stages. The implication is that we can never explain to other people the nature of any conscious experience, only its relation to other ones.

The other two questions, concerning why we have conscious experi-   8
ences and what leads to specific ones, appear more difficult. Chalmers proposes that they require the introduction of "experience" as a fundamental
new feature of the world, relating to the ability of an organism to process information. But which types of neuronal information produce consciousness?
And what makes a certain type of information correspond to the blueness of
blue, rather than the greenness of green? Such problems seem as difficult
as any in the study of consciousness.

We prefer an alternative approach, involving the concept of "meaning."   9
In what sense can neurons that explicitly code for a face be said to convey
the meaning of a face to the rest of the brain? Such a property must relate
to the cell's projective field—its pattern of synaptic connections to neurons
that code explicitly for related concepts. Ultimately, these connections extend to the motor output. For example, neurons responding to a certain face
might be connected to ones expressing the name of the person whose face
it is and to others for her voice, memories involving her and so on. Such associations among neurons must be behaviorally useful—in other words,
consistent with feedback from the body and the external world.

Meaning derives from the linkages among these representations with   10
others spread throughout the cortical system in a vast associational network, similar to a dictionary or a relational database. The more diverse
these connections, the richer the meaning. If, as in our previous example of
prosopagnosia, the synaptic output of such face neurons were blocked, the
cells would still respond to the person's face, but there would be no associated meaning and, therefore, much less experience. A face would be seen
but not recognized as such.

Of course, groups of neurons can take on new functions, allowing   11
brains to learn new categories (including faces) and associate new categories with existing ones. Certain primitive associations, such as pain, are to
some extent inborn but subsequently refined in life.

Information may indeed be the key concept, as Chalmers suspects.   12
Greater certainty will require consideration of highly parallel streams of information, linked—as are neurons—in complex networks. It would be useful to
try to determine what features a neural network (or some other such computational embodiment) must have to generate meaning. It is possible that
such exercises will suggest the neural basis of meaning. The hard problem
of consciousness may then appear in an entirely new light. It might even
disappear.   ©

CRITICAL READING

1. Why do the authors feel that "locating the neurons in the cerebral cortex that correlate best with consciousness" will yield "a full accounting of the manner in
   which subjective experience arises from these cerebral processes"?
2. Explain the term "explicit neuronal representation," as discussed by the authors
   of this article. How does this concept help develop the authors' thesis that studying brain function will shed light on the issue of human consciousness?
3. What is the concept of "meaning," according to the authors? How does this "alternative approach" facilitate our understanding of consciousness? Explain the
   difficult phrase, "its pattern of synaptic connections to neurons that code explicitly for related concepts," in the context of the authors' discussion of meaning.

CLASS DISCUSSION

1. Discuss the pros and cons of the authors' assertion that a study of brain mechanisms—neurons, synapses, and so on—will yield a comprehensive understanding of human consciousness. What specific evidence do they bring to bear on
   this argument? Cite personal experience that either supports or calls into question the authors' thesis here.

DIRECTED FREEWRITE

Read over this brief essay, and write down the main points in the essay, but in a
more conversational and less academic tone. Use everyday words to explain some
of the "fifty-cent words" here, and express the points in this article in a way that
your fifteen-year-old sibling (or cousin) could understand.

NEUROSCIENCE UNIT WRITING ASSIGNMENTS

1. The act of summarizing—describing the key points of something in a condensed
   form, is a very important and versatile skill. You already know how to summarize, of course; we do it all the time on an informal basis. For example, in describing an incident to a friend, either verbally or in a letter or an e-mail
   message, we usually condense the story down to its key points, rather than relating every single detail (or perhaps you've listened in agony as someone told
   a story that wasn't condensed into summary form, and therefore you can

understand the importance of summarizing). In the academic setting, summary appears in all kinds of forms. Writers summarize another scholar's theories or ideas, in order to use, modify, or dispute them. A student studying for an exam needs to be able to summarize a large body of information, at least mentally, in order to complete the exam. Research papers rely on good summary skills, and the kind of close and careful reading that summary requires is a skill that is crucial to all academic—as well as most professional—activities.

This assignment, therefore, asks you to write a three-page summary of Chalmers's essay. Start your summary with a short, objective introduction to the topic engaged by Chalmers, and state the author's main point, or his thesis, in your introduction. In the summary that follows, recount what you take to be the key points of Chalmers's essay, rephrasing them in your own words, and clearly indicating how these key points relate to Chalmers's thesis. Imagine that your reader is a peer, is not a science major, and has not read this essay; thus, all the reader will ever know about these ideas will come from you, and you may need to simplify and provide explanations for some of Chalmers's more difficult concepts and terminology. When the reader has finished reading your summary, he or she should have a thorough understanding of Chalmers's ideas.

One of the challenges of writing good summaries is the ability to rephrase others' ideas into one's own words. It is important that in your summary, you rely on this rephrasing, called paraphrasing, rather than quoting. Your summary might contain one or two quotations, but overall, your summary should be written by you, not Chalmers. Appropriate paraphrasing requires that you change the words as well as the sentence structures of the author's original work. The best way to arrive at clear paraphrasing is to read and reread the original work thoroughly, and then to put the work away as you attempt to restate the author's ideas. Then go back to the text, and check your work for accuracy. If you try to rephrase Chalmers's words with the essay right in front of you, you will be too focused on his exact words to easily come up with your own. In a summary, you may organize the original author's points into an order that makes sense to you, or you may stay with the organization of the original work.

2. An important kind of writing in the sciences is sometimes called, by writing teachers anyway, process analysis. In process analysis, one describes a particular process in step-by-step detail. Description, of any kind, is key in science; as we noted in Chapter 1, establishing the validity of data requires the scientists who generated the data to describe very clearly what process—of experimentation or observation—he or she used to arrive at the data. There are two kinds of process descriptions; one, like the description of how an experiment was conducted, is called an "informational" process, which describes a process that has already been completed. The second kind, called a "directional" process, describes how to do something, as in giving directions for loading software on a computer, or for baking a cake. As you may have learned, when instructions for completing a process are provided, clarity and precision are very important. These qualities are important when describing the completion of different processes as well.

Write an essay in which you describe the writing process that you followed in writing a specific paper for a specific class, from beginning to end. This could be an assignment for another class you are currently taking or could be one that you completed in this class. Your description should be as detailed as possible, using specific examples from your experience and proceeding in an orderly, step-by-step fashion.

The structure of process essays is dictated by the structure of the step-by-step procedure being described. Still, you need to think about the overall unity and coherence of your essay, and a good way to ensure unity is by starting your essay with an introduction that contains a thesis statement giving an overview, or overall characterization of the process that you followed and that you will go on to elaborate on in the remainder of the essay. Don't write a statement that says, "In this essay I will describe the process I followed in writing such and such a paper"; rather, sum up an overall characterization of your particular process. Doing this means that your thesis (and even your entire introductory paragraph) should probably be written last—after you have delineated the process and can then step back and find a succinct way to characterize it in the introduction. Throughout your essay, be sure to use clear transitional words and phrases that indicate the movement to each step of the process.

This assignment not only is intended as an exercise in writing clear descriptive prose but also is meant to focus you on your own writing process itself, helping you to look at all of its constituent elements, and perhaps to see where you could spend more time and energy. After you have completed a rough draft of this essay, you might want to take a look at the discussion of one model writing process in Chapter 1 and to think about how your own process differs from, improves on, or pales in comparison with that particular process.

3. Write an essay in which you argue in favor of a particular approach (or set of approaches) to the study of consciousness. You might organize this essay by first summarizing each of the various approaches to consciousness, as suggested by the three readings in this section, and then going on to provide reasons—in the form of evidence from the text, from your personal experience and from your freewriting—for favoring one approach over another. Refer to the discussion of argument essays in the Social Psychology unit of this chapter for more on writing effective arguments.

Unit 2
Computer Science— Can Computers Think?

IN THE MACHINE: ARTIFICIAL CONSCIOUSNESS
The Economist

This piece of journalism from the broad field of economics discusses the recently published writings of physicist Rodney Cotterill, who theorizes about what constitutes consciousness. His views on the role that physical movement plays on awareness and on the ability to have ideas are discussed, along with possible applications for artificial consciousness. As you read, notice the way the author of this article "hooks" the reader's attention with a provocative question: one of many opening techniques—along with quotations, brief stories, statistics, and controversial statements—that you can use to open your own essays. Notice also the ways in which three disciplines—economics, physics, and computer science—converge and overlap as the subject of human consciousness is explored by the writer of this article and its subject, Dr. Cotterill.

Founded in 1843, The Economist *is a weekly magazine of international news and business that reports and analyzes several topics including world affairs, politics and government, business and finance, economics, science and technology, and the arts and multimedia. It is one of the leading sources of business information and opinion on international business and politics.*

Why can you not tickle yourself? And what does that have to do with 1 artificial consciousness? Quite a lot, according to Rodney Cotterill, a physicist at the Danish Technical University in Lyngby. After years of pondering the workings of the brain, Dr. Cotterill believes he has found the quintessence of consciousness. For good measure, he has also applied for a

---

patent covering a circuit design for conscious computers, and is discussing possible applications with several companies.

The nature of consciousness is shrouded in controversy. Theologians, 2 philosophers, biologists and computer scientists all have their pet theories. So, to understand how Dr. Cotterill's computers might work, it is necessary to understand his views of consciousness.

His is a classical outlook that can be traced to the philosophers and 3 scientists of the first half of this century, who saw muscular movement as the key to understanding consciousness. They believed that a person's main source of information about the world comes through movement. Even vision depends on the tiny scanning movements the eye makes to keep the photosensitive cells of the retina refreshed with new information. So, the theory goes, consciousness must be intimately related to muscles.

This view is no longer fashionable, thanks to the obsession during the 4 past few decades with unmuscular electronic computers as potential agents of artificial intelligence. But being old-fashioned does not necessarily mean being wrong.

Like many of his fellow physicists, Dr. Cotterill is intrigued by how artifi- 5 cial neural networks—vast arrays of interconnected electronic processors— might mimic the real networks of nerve cells in the brain. But whereas many neural-network enthusiasts hope that consciousness will emerge automatically if their machines become sufficiently complex, Dr. Cotterill thinks that something fundamental is still missing in such machines. That something is linked to the particular way in which brains communicate with muscles.

Consider what happens when you reach for a glass. Signals to the 6 brain from the eyes and fingers (called afference in the biological jargon) keep it informed about how the task is progressing. Signals from the brain to the fingers and eyes (called efference) make the necessary adjustments to avoid an accident. But at the same time another type of signal, called an efference copy, is sent out to other parts of the brain. In simple terms, the efference copy warns the brain's sensory-receptor areas about what the muscles are about to do. Hence, since it is anticipated, self-tickling is not very stimulating.

Certain nerve cells in the brain are activated only if they receive effer- 7 ence copy and related afference within about two-tenths of a second of each other. This seems to be a way of discriminating between events that the brain has caused in the environment and those over which it has no control, and thus distinguishing self and non-self, a central aspect of consciousness.

It is the efference copy that Dr. Cotterill believes is the crucial ingredi- 8 ent of consciousness. Without it, all there is is a computer-controlled robot. With it, the computer-robot becomes aware that it is in control of itself.

Efference copy can be produced by a brain even when no muscles   9
move. According to Dr. Cotterill, thought itself may be efference copy looping round and round in a way that allows a brain to simulate vision, speech
and other faculties without actually moving a muscle. Such simulations can
lead to new associations of muscular movements—associations which are
more commonly known as ideas.

Dr. Cotterill's arguments, which have just been published in the *Jour-*   10
nal of Consciousness Studies, are unlikely to be endorsed universally. But
having identified a loop in the brain which he thinks others have overlooked,
he is already toying with a host of possible applications of computers containing an artificial version of it. Video games and stockmarket analysis are
two areas where he sees a big potential.

The key to such applications will be for the computer to probe its envi-   11
ronment in an electronic analogy of motion and, at the same time, warn itself of what it is doing by sending itself artificial efference copy—thus
keeping constant track of the relationship between its own actions and the
reactions of the environment. Dr. Cotterill does not expect the first computers of this sort to soliloquise spontaneously. But they should show rudimentary signs of consciousness, such as hesitancy and the ability to change
their "minds." Such traits are absent from most forms of artificial intelligence.
Their presence, hopes Dr. Cotterill, will make computer games more fun,
and financial forecasting more lucrative.   ©

CRITICAL READING

1. According to Cotterill, what are people's main sources of information about the
   world? How does Cotterill move from this theory to more specific notions about
   artificial intelligence?
2. What do the words "afference" and "efference" mean, "in biological jargon," according to this article? What is "efference copy," and how does this latter term
   relate to Cotterill's theories concerning human consciousness and artificial intelligence?
3. Why does the author several times bring up tickling in this article? What does
   the phenomenon of tickling tell us about people's awareness of themselves and
   of the world around them?

CLASS DISCUSSION

1. According to the author of this article, "Doctor Cotterill's arguments, which
   have just been published in the *Journal of Consciousness Studies,* are unlikely to
   be endorsed universally." On the basis of your reading thus far in this chapter,
   discuss some theorists who might take exception to Cotterill's theories of consciousness.
2. At the end of this article, the author says, "Dr. Cotterill does not expect the first
   computers of this sort to soliloquise [to reveal its thoughts when alone or

unaware of the presence of others, as a character in a Shakespeare play might do] spontaneously. But they should show rudimentary signs of consciousness, such as hesitancy and the ability to change their 'minds.'" Using this chapter's readings and your own experience as evidence, generate a list of other "signs" of consciousness, and explain why each of these signs should be considered as an indicator of conscious activity taking place.

DIRECTED FREEWRITE

Imagine a conversation between Dr. Cotterill and any one or more of the other theorists of consciousness presented in this chapter. Write a scene of dialogue, in which these theorists argue—either logically, or emotionally, or both—the merits of their own particular approaches to human consciousness. Feel free to let your dialogue resolve to a conclusion that mirrors your own views on the subject of consciousness, or to let the argument become increasingly personal and even violent, if that's the direction in which your creative imagination leads you.

I PROCESS THEREFORE I AM

Clive Davidson

In this *Science* magazine article, the author discusses artificial intelligence researchers Igor Aleksander and Marvin Minsky, who believe in the possibility of creating more "conscious" machine intelligence. Both researchers are developing sophisticated neural networks and computer programs, which they believe will mimic—and perhaps eventually even surpass—human consciousness. As you read, note the ways in which academicians within relatively insular discourse communities engage in friendly and constructive dialogue with each other: a dialectical process of difference and resolution that leads to progress in both theoretical constructions and practical applications within scholarly fields.

> *Clive Davidson has written on science and technology for a wide range of United Kingdom, United States, and European publications, including* New Scientist, The Guardian, *and* Wired. *He has written extensively on new technologies for the financial press, both in the United Kingdom and the United States. He is a contributing editor to the investment banking magazine* Risk.

Source: "I Process, Therefore I Am" by Clive Davidson in *New Scientist,* March 27, 1993, vol. 137, no. 1866. Reprinted by permission of New Scientist.

Computers can perform a broad range of tasks that involve reasoning, learning, planning and other functions usually associated with human intelligence. Does that make these machines intelligent? Some scientists and philosophers argue that mechanical intelligence is not the same as mind: computers can never be conscious of their thoughts and actions and so lack an essential part of human intelligence. Not everyone agrees: the assertion that machines could be conscious unites two leading researchers who have otherwise disagreed on the best way to push forward the frontiers of machine intelligence.

Opinion has long been divided as to how best to achieve machine intelligence. Igor Aleksander, professor of neural systems engineering at Imperial College, London, belongs to the school which wants to develop intelligent machines by mimicking the way the human brain is built. He believes that a number of attributes of consciousness can now be "captured" in neural networks—computer systems which mimic the workings of the brain. Marvin Minsky, director of the Artificial Intelligence Laboratory of the Massachusetts Institute of Technology in the US is identified with an opposing school, which favours creating complex computer software that mimics the characteristics of human intelligence. Like Aleksander, Minsky believes that machines could be conscious—possibly even more conscious than humans.

THINKING ABOUT THINKING

Minsky is one of the founding fathers of artificial intelligence. He began his career in 1951 shortly after the first electronic computers appeared. At the time, the British mathematician and computer pioneer Alan Turing was publicly speculating that, by the turn of the century, it would be generally accepted that, machines could think. Minsky says he had been "thinking about thinking" since high school. He started investigating models of networks made up of simple processing units modelled on brain nerve cells, or neurons, but gradually became disillusioned with their potential.

In 1969, Minsky and a colleague at MIT, Seymour Papert, published a book, called *Perceptron,* pointing out the limitations of the main neural network model of the time, the "perceptron." In their view, intelligence could never emerge from such models of the human brain—what they called the "bottom-up" approach. Instead, they argued for a "top-down" approach to artificial intelligence—imitating human intelligence by programming computers to process information by manipulating symbols that represented knowledge and rules. The book put a brake on research on neural networks for more than a decade, and Minsky's top-down approach became synonymous with the term artificial intelligence, or AI.

The paths of Aleksander and Minsky crossed briefly in the late 1960s, when Aleksander worked at Minsky's AI laboratory at MIT. Here Aleksander studied the role of feedback in complex systems, a concept which was later to become central to the learning process in neural networks. But while Minsky's views caused the tide of research in the 1970s to flow strongly towards symbolic processing, Aleksander was one of the few researchers who held firm to the belief that neural models offered the best approach to computation and artificial intelligence. He moved to Brunel University, London, where in 1981 with colleagues Bruce Wilkie and John Stonham he built Wisard, the first large-scale neural network for commercial use.

In the brain, neurons are connected in complex networks where input   6
from, say, the nerve cells of the eye, generates patterns of activity in particular centers of the brain, such as the primary visual cortex. Wisard had a quarter of a million artificial neurons—simple processing elements based on memory chips—linked by adjustable connections. It demonstrated that neural networks could be trained relatively quickly to perform certain tasks that had proved difficult or impossible for symbolic processing systems—in particular the tasks of recognising shapes and patterns.

Giving machines vision is a task AI researchers seriously underesti-   7
mated. Minsky, for instance, is reported to have given the problem of machine vision to a student at MIT in the 1960s to solve as a summer project. Writing programs to analyze images captured with cameras, however, has proved enormously difficult.

Neural networks are not programmed. Instead they "learn" to solve   8
problems from examples. For instance, if a network is to recognise faces, it is first presented with a number of examples of faces. Images of the faces are captured by a camera, converted to digital data and presented individually to the network as input. The input will trigger patterns of activity, or "states," in the network, which will result in an output. The connections between the artificial neurons are adjusted by the learning program so that a particular input—an individual's face—always results in the same pattern of activity and gives the same output.

Wisard caused excitement because, against expectations, it was able   9
to recognise individual human faces after only 20 seconds' training. Since then, Wisard has been put to work in factories, picking out defective components on production lines, and in banks, where it identifies bank notes at high speed.

Aleksander is now working with Stonham, Thomas Clarke and Man-   10
issa Wilson at Imperial College and Brunel University on a neural net system called Magnus that could be used to control a mobile robot. Magnus differs from Wisard in that it simulates the neurons and their interconnections in software on an ordinary workstation computer rather than being constructed from thousands of chips linked together. Aleksander claims that when Magnus is completed it will demonstrate characteristics, such as learning, language and knowledge representation, which are normally associated with consciousness.

Magnus operates using what Aleksander calls "iconic representations."   11
These are patterns of activity in the network which represent objects in the
real world. The iconic representations are the equivalent of mental images,
and will be used to translate instructions given in everyday language into actions by the robot. Aleksander says that in the first experiments, Magnus is
operating in a restricted world with objects such as a pyramid, sphere and
cube, which it views via a camera. The researchers have already trained the
system to link iconic representations to the patterns of activity, or states, associated with camera images of the real world objects and their language
symbols. They have also trained it to associate a term such as "left" with the
camera view moving to the left and to create iconic representations for relationships such as "on top of" or "to the right of."

MENTAL IMAGES FOR ROBOTS

The aim of the experiments is to show how a robot driven by a neural   12
network could operate by associating language, images and actions. For example, the sentence "Pick up the pyramid and put it on the cube" will be represented by a sequence of iconic patterns of activity in the network, and the
robot's actions could be associated with these. Conversely, when the robot
views a scene, the objects in view and their relationships would trigger
iconic representations which could be used to "output" language that describes the scene. Iconic representations are a machine equivalent of mental images, and therefore a step towards machine consciousness, says
Aleksander.

He says it will avoid the problems that the symbolic school of AI, pro-   13
moted by Minsky, have run into when interpreting instructions for robots to
manipulate objects. The archetype of such systems is SHRDLU (a non-
sense word made by the order of keys on a linotype machine, like QWERTY
on a typewriter), a computer program developed in 1968 by Terry Winograd,
another student of Minsky's. With SHRDLU, the operator could communicate with the computer about a simple world comprising a box, a number of
blocks and a robot arm. But before answering questions or performing actions in the blocks world, SHRDLU had to analyse the typed-in instructions.
And interpreting everyday language requires a knowledge of semantics, a
large number of rules of syntax and a large body of general knowledge. For
example, SHRDLU could not interpret the question "How many blocks go on
top of one another to make a steeple?," which requires an understanding
that the phrase "go on top of one another" must not be taken literally.

According to Aleksander, Magnus will avoid these problems by dealing   14
with language in a way more akin to humans—associating words and
phrases with mental imagery. "Language is a representation of the real
world. It squeezes the real world into the things you can say and eventually
write," he says. "AI people have taken these linguistic strings and tried to

present them in a computer in an unambiguous way, and have run into trouble. Very small changes in a sentence represent things that are completely different in the real world. They are unable to deal with this."

What Aleksander has done is different. He is not trying to represent 15 the linguistic strings but to represent the effects in the real world that gave rise to those linguistic strings. "That makes language understanding easier as you only need to ensure that the linguistic strings trigger the right representations," he says.

"Consciousness is very heavily dependent on having a learning sys- 16 tem that can represent the world more or less as it is. AI has always tried to do the representation at the symbolic level—so it has lost mental imagery which seems to me to be the crux of consciousness."

The Magnus project is ambitious. Aleksander has a reputation as a sci- 17 entific showman, and is confident his approach will pay off. In discussing consciousness, Aleksander refers to the definition in *Chambers 20th Century English Dictionary:* "The waking state of the mind; the knowledge the mind has of anything." The "waking state of the mind" is a synthesis of many things, says Aleksander and he postulates a number of attributes—learning, language, planning, attention and inner perception—that are prerequisite for the existence of consciousness. It is now possible, he claims, to demonstrate that a general neural system can possess each of these five attributes.

His first attribute, learning, is fundamental to neural networks. Instead 18 of being programmed like conventional computers, neural networks learn from examples. The language and planning attributes derive from the ability of a neural network to create internal states—that is, particular patterns of activity—in response to sequences of perceptual input and to generate appropriate actions based on these states. The creation of internal states in response to perceptual input is the equivalent of language, suggests Aleksander. Planning requires the internal state to be split, with part representing the target state, while the other part learns a sequence of states that leads to the target state.

Attention, says Aleksander, is the "ability to select perceptual input" or 19 to focus on aspects of the inner state. For example, a human might think of a cat and then focus on its ears, tail, fur and so on. A neural network will respond, or "attend" to new input, but if the input is static or a number of inputs are present, some form of stimulus is required to keep it attentive. This can be achieved by applying a "burst of noise"—a sudden, arbitrary but temporary change to the network's variables. The "burst of noise" stimulus is so important for attention in neural networks that Aleksander thinks it would be worth looking for the mechanism in biological systems.

Inner perception Aleksander describes as "a sensed inner state." In a 20 neural network the "inner state" is the state, or pattern of activity learnt, in response to an input from the outside world. These patterns of activity can be stored in a computer memory and retrieved when required.

Aleksander acknowledges that his set of attributes is minimal. But 21
were an organism to possess all the properties they imply, he says, "the organism would be ready for exposure to critics who have to define what else
it should have in order for them to believe that consciousness had actually
been isolated."

Inner perception is the point where the views of Aleksander and Min- 22
sky begin to overlap. For Minsky, memory of inner states is the key attribute
of consciousness. "When somebody says they are conscious, what they are
saying is 'I remember a little bit about the state of my mind a few moments
ago'," says Minsky. Most of the things that are attributed to consciousness
are to do with this short-term memory, he says. "If you can't think about or
reason about what your mind was doing a minute ago then you say 'That
was unconscious.'"

Minsky's definition of consciousness is typically simple and clear: 23
"Consciousness is being aware of what is happening in the world and in
one's mind." Short-term memory is easy to achieve in a conventional serial
computer, says Minsky. For example, the symbol-manipulating language
LISP, the most popular AI programming language in the US, has a "trace"
function. A computer can be programmed to keep a record of all its internal
states and then to trace back through these. For a human to do the same
would require the ability to go back through brain states to find the point
where there was a particular response to certain stimuli.

"The human brain has only very limited records of what it has been 24
doing recently. A machine could be vastly more conscious than a person
because we didn't evolve for that," says Minsky. "Now some people will
jump up and be angry and say you mean machines are smarter. No, I'm
saying it would be easy to be extremely conscious—but that doesn't mean
you would know what to do with it."

Minsky admits to "mocking consciousness," but this is because he ab- 25
hors the mystification that surrounds many of the terms in the AI debate.
Consciousness is "one of those words we have for things we don't understand," he says. Because we do not understand these things they are often
confused with vital forces, he says. To use words like "consciousness,"
"mind" and "intelligence" in an ill-defined way can be a strategy for avoiding
thinking about difficult phenomena. "Consciousness is something we [hu-
mans] only use a little bit. We don't have much of it and we boast about it
too much."

MISCHIEVOUS HUMOUR

Behind the provocation there is a wisp of mischievous humour and an 26
attempt to force people to think about difficult subjects. Minsky sees himself
as something of a Socrates, challenging received ideas, vague terminology
and "bad thinking."

There is little doubt that the views of Aleksander and Minsky on con- 27
sciousness will stir controversy. Consciousness is currently the focus of
considerable philosophical and scientific discussion. Two of the fiercest critics of AI, philosopher John Searle and mathematician and physicist Roger
Penrose, have drawn a firm line between machines and consciousness.

According to Searle, mental phenomena are caused by neurophysio- 28
logical processes in the brain. The brain is not a digital computer but a "specific biological organ." Consciousness, he argues, "is a natural biological
phenomenon." For Penrose, consciousness "is such an important phenomenon that I simply cannot believe that it is something just 'accidentally' con-
jured up by complicated computation."

Aleksander will no doubt be challenged that the Magnus project does not 29
substantiate his claims regarding machines and consciousness. He will, for instance, have to demonstrate that the project meets "the law of requisite variety."
This was devised in the 1960s by W. Ross Ashby, a researcher in cybernetics,
a precursor to AI. To paraphrase, the law says that an AI system must contain
variety of information equivalent to the variety of information in the problem to
which it is applied. If it does not it cannot provide a solution. As language interpretation is key to Aleksander's views on consciousness and machines, the language element of the project must demonstrate requisite variety. This would
have to include the ability to apply common-sense understanding—for example,
interpreting how many objects "go on top of one another" in a nonliteral way.

Common sense is a challenge for Minksy, too. A machine could have 30
a high level of consciousness but not use it in any meaningful way, he says.
Consciousness is not the issue in the quest for intelligent machines: the
need is to endow them with common sense. Even the most sophisticated of
present-day robots cannot perform a mundane task like cleaning a house.
To do so a robot would require a vast amount of everyday knowledge ranging from the force of gravity to the brittleness of glass—so that it would know
that a glass that is dropped will break.

AI systems are currently restricted by the lack of this kind of general 31
knowledge, and Minsky believes that "every country should have a pro-
gramme to make a common-sense computer." As a model he cites the Cyc
project initiated in the mid-1980s by Douglas Lenat at the Microelectronics
and Computer Technology Corporation in Austin, Texas. Cyc will be a mammoth accumulation of common-sense knowledge that an intelligent machine
might require to perform everyday tasks and interpret everyday situations.
Lenat aims to have 10 million interconnected facts keyed into the computer
database by 1995. Cyc will one day be able to offer its knowledge to other
specialised computer programs, Lenat believes.

Minsky has also modified his views on neural networks since his dev- 32
astating critique in 1969. More sophisticated neural network architectures
than the perceptron model plus more advanced software methods have
overcome the limitations that he and Papert outlined. Also neurological

research has greatly increased our knowledge about the brain. The discovery of many different specialised centres in the brain led Minsky to formulate a theory that the mind is a "society" of interlinked and cooperating parts, a theory he explores in his recent novel, *The Turing Option* (Viking), written with Harry Harrison. He speculates that a thinking machine of the future "might look like the brain with hundreds of neural nets."

Aleksander and Minsky are no strangers to controversy. Their views   33
are often provocative and Minsky at least has a reputation for thought-provoking speculation while leaving others to work out the details. But both men are continuing to push the frontiers of artificial intelligence, and they have made it clear that this frontier now extends to consciousness. The debate and the research have a long way to go.   ©

CRITICAL READING

1. According to this article, Aleksander is attempting to simulate the way that the human brain is built, while Minsky is using complex computer programs to replicate the characteristics of human intelligence. Describe briefly the methods that each computer scientist is using to accomplish his respective task.
2. Explain the term "neural network," as it relates to the subject of artificial intelligence. What was the "perceptron"? How did this device anticipate the research that's being done in the field of AI today?
3. How does a computer-based neural network learn and adapt, according to this article? By what means can a neural network use disparate examples to solve complex problems?
4. What is Magnus, and what are its possible future applications? What are the "iconic representations" by which Magnus operates? What is the system known as SHRDLU, and how does it help computer operators to "communicate" with neural networks?

CLASS DISCUSSION

1. Explain how the technology developed by Aleksander could associate "language, images, and actions" to drive a fully functioning robot. How will this robot's behavior be similar to human thought and action, in your view, and in what ways will it be fundamentally different?
2. Aleksander says, "Consciousness is very heavily dependent on having a learning system that can represent the world more or less as it is. AI has always tried to do the representation at the symbolic level—so it has lost mental imagery which seems to me to be the crux of consciousness." Discuss what the computer scientist means by this assertion, in light of this article's discussion of artificial intelligence. How do Aleksander's "linguistic strings" replicate the "lost mental imagery" that is the foundation of consciousness, in the view of the scientist?
3. In what ways will machines surpass the human brain, in the view of Minsky? In his view, do these areas of superiority make advanced computers "smarter" than

human beings? Discuss your own reasons for agreeing or disagreeing with Minsky's position on this point.

DIRECTED FREEWRITE

Summarize the controversy between AI pioneers, such as Aleksander and Minsky, and detractors, such as Penrose and Searle, who, according to this article, "have drawn a firm line between machines and consciousness." What qualities of human consciousness cannot be replicated by computers, according to the detractors? How might Aleksander and Minsky respond to these skeptical arguments concerning the ability of AI to replicate human consciousness?

TERMINATORS: THE ROBOTS THAT RODNEY BROOKS AND HANS MORAVEC IMAGINE WILL SUCCEED HUMANS, NOT SERVE THEM

Mark Dery

Author Dery presents two major approaches to the study of artificial intelligence, the "bottom-up" approach and the "top-down" approach. The author compares the theories and applications of two AI pioneers, Rodney Brooks and Hans Moravec. Brooks, a proponent of the bottom-up approach, has developed an insect-sized robot that has been programmed to behave in the same manner as a cockroach; this sort of robotic device, he speculates, many dominate the "post-biological" world. Moravec, on the other hand, believes that the progress of artificial intelligence lies in the ability of the robot to recognize pieced-together models of the world; these allow the robot to "think" its way through a path of obstacles. As you read, consider your own views regarding the underlying premise of both of these researchers: that robots will become commonplace and even be able to think and respond in the way their human creators do. In your view, can human consciousness ever be replicated—or even surpassed—by an artificially intelligent machine?

Mark Dery is a cultural critic. He is an occasional writer for The New York Times Magazine, Rolling Stone, The Village Voice Literary Supplement, Suck, *and* Feed, *and a frequent lecturer in the United States and Europe on new media, fringe thought, and unpopular culture. Dery has published some works including* Escape Velocity: Cyberculture at the End of the Century *and a collection of essays entitled* The Pyrotechnic Insanitarium: American Culture on the Brink. *He also edited* Flame Wars: The Discourse of Cyberculture.

Data, the chalk white android with the positronic brain, was pondering   1
the meaning of life.

In a recent episode of *Star Trek: The Next Generation,* Data enlisted   2
the aid of the *Enterprise*'s Dr. Crusher in his struggle to crack the toughest
nut of all. "I am curious as to what transpired between the moment when I
was nothing more than an assemblage of parts," Data said, puzzled, "and
the next moment, when I became alive. What is it that endowed me with
life?" To which the doctor replied, "Scientists and philosophers have been
grappling with that question for centuries without coming to any conclusion."

A neat dodge and a forgivable one. Even in *The Next Generation's*   3
twenty-fourth century, apparently, the life-giving spark that transforms a
bucket of bolts into a sentient being remains a mystery. One thing seems
certain, however: When we build a machine so intelligent that it seems alive,
we will fashion it in our own likeness, à la Dr. Frankenstein—"a man of science who sought to create a man after his own image," to quote the 1931
classic film.

Data, a cross between the Tin Woodman and the "soft" man vilified by   4
Robert Bly, is only the latest in a long line of humanoid robots. His family
tree includes Robby the Robot, the talkative boiler in *Forbidden Planet* who
could brew bourbon and speak 187 languages; R2D2 and C-3PO, the inter-
galactic Laurel and Hardy in *Star Wars;* Rachael, the sexy "replicant" who
beds the hard-boiled protagonist in *Blade Runner;* and Ash and Bishop, the
corporate droids in the *Alien* trilogy. All resemble humans in appearance or
behavior; even the manhunting Terminator, a steely skeleton beneath its
synthetic skin, looks and acts like Stanley Kowalski on steroids.

But Data and his mythic forebears live in a future that may never be.   5
Increasingly, artificial-intelligence researchers are moving away from the
human paradigm in their quest to create silicon consciousness from "an assemblage of parts." Intelligent machines will look less like Data and more
like the microscopic mites that already share our apartments, subsisting on
dust motes and traces of food. Stranger still, such robots won't display the
egghead propensities of Data and his chess-playing, cocktail-mixing kin;
they'll behave more like nest-building termites or swarms of bees.

In their embrace of creepy-crawly alternatives to the anthropomorphic   6
model familiar from science fiction, visionary roboticists are following a path
that could lead to a future of unutterable strangeness. The more radical
among them suggest that present attempts to build battery-powered household helpers may ultimately yield robots that will struggle toward evolution's

putative peak—human intelligence—and surpass it. If two of the field's visionary roboticists, Rodney Brooks and Hans Moravec, have their way, the human gene code may one day find itself out of a job, outperformed by artificial creatures that Brooks surmises "may be alien enough that we won't be able to appreciate them or they us."

Though they once shared an office at Stanford University's Artificial Intelligence Laboratory, Brooks and Moravec are now poles apart in theoretical terms. Brooks, an associate professor in the Department of Electrical Engineering and Computer Science at MIT, is without doubt the most vocal proponent of what is known as the bottom-up approach to artificial intelligence. He believes that sensorimotor skills, not higher-level thought processes, are the foundation on which intelligence is built. In other words, robots are going to have to learn to crawl before they learn to think. Brooks argues that intelligent inorganic life will evolve, like organic life before it, from simpler organisms. He dismisses as hopelessly misguided the top-down school of thought, which holds that artificial intelligence must set its sights on the supposed zenith of human intellectual achievement, pure reasoning. 7

Brooks's many-legged robots are inspired not by articulate, tool-using hominids that walk upright but by things that creep—ants, termites and the like. Brooks has drawn on studies by researchers who poke electrodes into the neural pathways of insects trudging on treadmills in an attempt to correlate the creatures' neural activity with their motor functions. "They come up with a set of condition-action rules that the insect seems to be following," says Brooks. "They validate them through computer simulations, and then we take those sets of rules and implement them on the robots." What crawl off the workbench are astonishingly lifelike robots that not only resemble bugs but behave like them, too. 8

Brooks is building a world that is not so much inhuman as "posthuman," to borrow a phrase from Bruce Sterling's cyberpunk novel *Schismatrix*. He imagines a future in which the membrane between animate and inanimate is highly permeable, a Disney cartoon come to life where even chairs and tables sense and react. "Everything around us will be roboticized," says Brooks. "Normally passive elements will be active; 'smartness' will be oozing everywhere. We'll be surrounded by intelligent objects in the same way that we're surrounded by plastics now. You'll go into a department store and buy this element and install it in your house; then, when you get three or four of them installed, they'll start communicating with each other, coupling and cooperating, and you'll end up with a smart house." 9

While Brooks contemplates ways to get small, Hans Moravec spends his days at a place that has staked its claim on the opposite end of the scale. Carnegie Mellon's Field Robotics Center, of which Moravec's Mobile Robot Laboratory is a part, is driven, according to Moravec, by director 10

William Whittaker's passion for "big things—big mountains, big robots and big projects." Although Moravec has all but abandoned hands-on robotics for more theoretical pursuits, his contributions to the study of mobile systems, manipulators, computer vision and programming have proven invaluable to those at work FRC robots.

The center's big machines are housed in two barn-size buildings nestled in a hollow on the university campus. The Tessellator, a rectangular vehicle with one long arm and omnidirectional wheels that allow it to float sideways with eerie grace, is under construction in the hangarlike building called the highbay; if approved by NASA, it will rewaterproof the underside of the space shuttle with toxic chemicals, a hazardous, laborious task for human workers. 11

Parked close by are the Navlabs (Navigation Laboratories), scary vehicles that use electric steering, computer-controlled hydraulic drives and a small fortune in technology—video cameras, laser range finders, sonar and supercomputers—to drive themselves. Funded by ARPA, the Department of Defense's Advanced Research Projects Agency, the Navlabs may one day end up transporting materiel in war zones or functioning as platforms for weapons systems. "As researchers, we're more interested in robotic delivery vehicles and smart highways, where cars drive themselves," says former Navlabs project manager Kevin Dowling, who takes pains to point out that Carnegie Mellon is not involved in classified military projects. 12

Even so, Navlab 2, whose chassis is based on a humvee that did a tour of duty in the gulf war, looks battlefield mean. A brutish, I-brake-for-nothing mountain of metal, it formerly sported a sign reading NOBODY ON BOARD. 13

Awesome as the Navlabs are, they're fossils to Moravec. He maintains that lumbering monsters intended for hazardous military or industrial applications, as well as mindlessly repetitive assembly-line robots, are single-celled organisms on the evolutionary time line of artificial intelligence. In Moravec's view, tomorrow belongs to the mass-produced, general-purpose robot for the home that he believes will be a reality by 1998, ready to weed the lawn, whip up a gourmet meal, give the car a tuneup and vacuum. (The Jetsons' vacuuming robot springs, apparently, from a deep-rooted desire; Brooks claims that marketing surveys have determined that what the American consumer wants out of a domestic robot, more than anything else, is a clean carpet.) 14

Moravec envisages a stainless-steel servant with five wheeled legs, two arms ending in humanoid hands, sonar sensors and a pair of color-TV cameras for eyes. The robot's ability to "maintain representations, at varying levels of abstraction and precision, of the world around it" is all-important, Moravec asserts in his 1988 book *Mind Children: The Future of Robot and Human Intelligence.* He writes, "In these internal models of the world I see the beginnings of awareness in the minds of our machines—an awareness I believe will evolve into consciousness comparable with that of humans." 15

Moravec, needless to say, spends much of his mental life in the distant   16
future. He takes up where Brooks leaves off, theorizing a "post-biological"
future in which Homo sapiens has been rendered irrelevant by its highly
evolved artificial offspring—superintelligent mechanisms that almost certainly will not inhabit humanoid bodies and may not resemble anything we
have ever seen.

In *Mind Children,* Moravec conjures trillion-limbed machine flora—robot   17
bushes whose stems branch into ever more delicate, ever more numerous
twigs, culminating, finally, in a dizzying array of microscopic cilia. "Such machines could carry on our cultural evolution, including their own construction
and increasingly rapid self-improvement, without us, and without the genes
that built us," Moravec writes. "When that happens, our DNA will find itself out
of a job, having lost the evolutionary race to a new kind of competition."

A marathon runner whose wardrobe leans toward Reeboks and leather   18
jackets, Brooks exudes a jittery, adolescent energy. Over sushi he answers
questions while rolling—and rerolling and re-rerolling—his paper napkin into a
pencil-thin tube. His unruly chestnut curls and bright, intense eyes make him
look younger than his thirty-eight years. His accent, flat and twangy with the
strains of Adelaide, Australia, where Brooks grew up, turns even the most innocent remark into a wisecrack.

"I'm much shorter term than Hans," says Brooks around a bite of sushi.   19
"I only think a couple hundred years ahead." Brooks wants to see his ideas
soldered together into something he can touch. "I don't want to think about
things I'm not going to get a chance to build," he says.

In pursuit of attainable goals, Brooks has focused for the most part on   20
near-term, low-cost projects. Working small is one way of keeping budgets
manageable, and the mechanical creatures turned out by the Mobile Robot
Project under Brooks's guidance have set new standards for miniaturization.
Squirt, a wheeled, cubic-inch-size mite built in 1988 to prove just how small
a robot could be, thinks it's a cockroach. The microbot cowers under furniture or in dark corners, listening for loud sounds; when the noises have
faded, Squirt creeps warily from its hiding place in search of new cover,
near the noises' point of origin.

Research scientist Anita Flynn, who collaborated with Brooks on   21
Squirt, believes that electronic cockroaches are an intermediate stage in the
evolution of gnat robots—millimeter-size robots etched on computer chips.
She dreams of a computer chip that can "get up and walk." In a world measured in microns, computing power comes cheap; through very large-scale
integration, the processing power of a computer can be scrunched onto an
integrated circuit chip. Propulsion is another matter: The bulk of Squirt's
mass is taken up by motors and batteries. But if a robot's hardware could be
squeezed down to the size of its computer-chip brains, armies of invisible
minions would be at our beck and call.

As part of her Ph.D. thesis, Flynn is investigating micromotors—micro- 22
scopic motors chiseled out of silicon and set spinning when electricity is
zapped through a ring of piezoelectric crystals. Miniature—though far from
microscopic—piezoelectric motors are already used in some autofocus
cameras. Moreover, researchers at Cornell University and UC Berkeley are
experimenting with structures carved in layers on silicon chips; a chemical
bath eats away the scaffolding, and the structure unfolds and locks in place,
like a self-erecting tent. "It's not a robot yet," says Brooks, "but the individual
elements have been demonstrated."

Brooks, together with Flynn and then-graduate student Lee Tavrow, 23
applied for a patent for the "3-D fabrication of a gnat robot." In a 1989 essay
titled "Twilight Zones and Cornerstones: A Gnat Robot Double Feature," the
trio declared: "We want to build gnat-sized robots, a millimeter or so in diam-
eter. They will be cheap, disposable, totally self-contained autonomous
agents able to do useful things. . . . Gnat robots are going to change the
world."

But not tomorrow. For now, speck-size robots whose computers, mo- 24
tors, sensors and limbs can fit on a silicon chip are a distant mirage—not
that that stops Brooks and his colleagues from thinking up jobs for gnat robots. In "Twilight Zones," the authors sketch scenarios involving medical
gnat robots that unclog arteries, mend severed neurons or crawl across
eyeballs to perform retinal surgery. Mass-produced using techniques already employed to fabricate computer chips, gnat robots would be sufficiently cheap for consumers to assign millions of them, all working in
concert, to a single task, no matter how mundane. Imagine two-tone gnat
robots that cling, like infinitesimal flecks of paint, to the exterior of your
house and, when you're tired of the color, "repaint" it simply by rolling over;
gardening gnat robots that clamber up grass blades and nibble your lawn
short; coiffure gnat robots that roost on your scalp, rearranging your hair
and holding it in place.

Brooks's interest in robots that can dance on the head of a pin is 25
rooted in his realization that in the natural world, small size and smaller
brainpower aren't necessarily barriers to evolutionary success. "I spent
many hours with Hans Moravec at Stanford in the Seventies, when he was
working on his Ph.D. thesis, a robot called the Cart," Brooks recalls. The
Cart was the first vision-equipped robot to venture into the crowded, confusing world beyond the static, neatly geometric laboratory environment. Re-
motely controlled by computer, it scanned its surroundings with a TV
camera, locating objects and planning its route. After ten or fifteen minutes'
worth of rumination, it would lurch forward a yard, stop and take stock of its
place in the world. "Using one of the biggest computers around at the time, it
took five hours to reach its destination," says Brooks. "It didn't seem too impressive, compared to an insect flying around."

How, wondered Brooks, could a more or less brainless creature ac- 26
complish in seconds what robots linked to supercomputers puzzled over for
hours? Certainly, the conundrum had little to do with computer technology,
whose giddy speedup had seen ENIAC—a room-size vacuum-tube-
powered monster that in 1946 was the first programmable electronic computer—shrink to a transistorized machine in the Fifties, a boxful of integrated
circuits in the Sixties and a chip-driven PC in the Seventies. Perhaps the
flaw lay in the premises on which the study of artificial intelligence was
based, assumptions cemented in place at the legendary Dartmouth conference in 1956.

For two months, mathematician John McCarthy, computer scientist 27
Marvin Minsky and other brash young minds grappled with the question
posed by Alan Turing, one of the founding fathers of computer science:
Can machines think? Out of this watershed colloquium came the classical
top-down postulate that any thinking machine must emulate the problem-
solving ability associated with rational thought. For a machine to be truly
intelligent, adherents argue, it must possess the symbol-manipulating, rule-
implementing proficiency that characterizes human reasoning.

Robotics, presumably, was mere brawn; teaching a machine to walk 28
should be child's play after untangling the Gordian knot of human thought.
An intelligent robot would construct a mental map of its environment, plot a
course from point A to point B and, after much deliberation, take one small
step for tin man. Unfortunately, while computers soon learned to play chess,
solve calculus problems and prove geometric theorems, their motor skills
were put to shame by toddlers.

In his book in progress, *The Age of Mind,* Moravec recalls experiments 29
in the late Sixties and early Seventies by McCarthy's research group at
Stanford and Minsky's at MIT: "[They] connected television cameras and
robot arms to their computers so 'thinking' programs could begin to collect
information directly from the real world. The early results were like a cold
shower. While the pure reasoning programs did their jobs about as well and
fast as college freshmen, the best robot control programs . . . took hours to
find and pick up a few blocks on a table top, and often failed completely,
performing much worse than a six-month-old child."

Decades later, computers play chess on a grandmaster level but no 30
robot yet exists that can locate and manipulate actual chess pieces with the
unthinking ease that comes naturally to human infants. Moravec, Brooks
and many other artificial-intelligence theorists now believe that sensory perception and motor control, not rational thought, are what the human brain
does best. None of us uses trigonometry to calculate the trajectory of his
hand before lifting cup to lip; evolution has consigned such functions to the
lowest levels of unconscious data processing. By comparison, as Moravec
notes in *The Age of Mind,* rational thought of the sort used in playing chess
is a relatively recent arrival, "perhaps less than 100,000 years old."

Why not do away with the symbol-juggling, cognitive brain altogether, 31
Brooks speculated, and route sensor data directly to motor responses? Of
course, the resultant robot would be more insectoid than humanoid—an affront to those who contend that humankind is the crown of creation—but
beetles and their brethren have proven surprisingly durable in the Darwinian
road test.

Brooks threw down the gauntlet at "Pixels to Predicates," a 1983 semi- 32
nar. "I gave a talk," he says, "and I drew this diagram—this was my divine inspiration, the basis for everything I've done since—in which I had the world out
here, feeding into perception, and then I had another box over here called action, and both boxes overlapped completely. Up here, I had an observer, observing the interaction of perception and action; cognition is in the mind of the
observer, not in the system itself. What I'm saying is that there is no box inside
me that does the cognition; an observer may impute such a box—'Ah, he's
doing that because he's decided that'—and if you ask me, I'll give you an explanation, but it's just this thin layer of consciousness trying to make up a story
about what happens down below. In fact, cognition is nowhere."

An assistant professor at Stanford at the time of the fateful lecture, 33
Brooks left shortly thereafter to take up residence at MIT, where he, Anita
Flynn and a graduate student named Jonathan Connell set to work on a
robot that embodied his theories. The fruit of their labors, in 1986, was a
squat, wheeled contraption named Allen, who resembled a trash-compacted
R2D2, his electronic innards exposed for all to see.

Allen's software was based on Brooks's concept of stimulus-response 34
behavior, refined into a scheme dubbed "subsumption architecture." Subsumption architecture consists of a stack of behavior modules—low-level,
real-time behaviors ("avoid obstacle") on the bottom; higher-level, goal-
oriented directives ("explore") at the top—that permit a robot to generate complex behaviors from simple responses. Allen, for example, had three layers of
control: The first required that the robot avoid both static and dynamic obstacles; the second motivated it to wander about randomly (all the while avoiding
obstacles); and the third suppressed the desire to meander aimlessly and directed it to move toward distant points located by its sonar range sensors.

Behavior, rather than being controlled by a centralized brain, emerges 35
from a series of parallel activities, one behavior subsuming the others as circumstances require. The elaborate planning and mapping that forces conventional laboratory robots to rely on the processing power of off-board
computers, thus slowing them to a crawl, is jettisoned. In fact, the computer
to which Allen was yoked soon proved unnecessary: Brooks's approach,
being simpler, required far less number crunching.

More recent generations of robots have earned Brooks's group its un- 36
official tag (the Insect Lab) and motto (Fast, Cheap and Out of Control).
Genghis, the first of the lab's legged progeny, was the brain-child of Colin
Angle, a gifted undergraduate who had come to MIT to "major in whatever

lets me build the coolest stuff." And Genghis, so named, says Angle, because it "stomps over things" like the Mongolian conqueror, is nothing if not cool. Bequeathed twelve layers of behavior, the foot-long robot scrambles over mountains made of textbooks and plods inexorably on, pursuing human prey with the aid of a cluster of sensors that gives its "head" a distinctly buggy appearance.

Attila, Genghis's direct descendant, calls to mind a four-pound taran- 37
tula in a suit of armor. Rigged with ten microprocessors, twenty-three motors and 150 sensors, the high-tech arachnid can hoist itself onto ten-inch-high ledges and scrabble up near-vertical inclines. When powered up, Attila wriggles its legs in a manner disconcertingly reminiscent of a dying insect. In actuality, the robot's flailings are a means of gathering information about its environment. Within minutes, the six legs have "learned" how to coordinate themselves, and Attila is on the prowl—in search, no doubt, of a Lilliputian Tokyo to terrorize.

Emergent behavior like Attila's, the result of independent limbs following 38
simple rules, manifests itself as emergent social behavior, or "swarm intelligence," when groups of behavior-based robots interact, their decentralized activities working toward a common goal. Think of bees: Their almost robotic activity—governed, again, by simple rules—produces wonderfully complex hives. Drawing on studies conducted by ethologists analyzing ant colonies as self-organizing systems, Brooks and his associates are attempting to program twenty identical robots to behave like social insects, collaborating on collective tasks. Small, boxy things that scoot along on wheels, the better to seize objects in their pincerlike grippers, they resemble heavily armored toasters. Brooks hopes they'll act like bees.

At IS Robotics, Brooks's start-up in Cambridge, Massachusetts, MIT 39
graduate turned company president Colin Angle and a small staff are pursuing the roboticist's dream of "a robot invasion of the solar system"—"nerd herds" of galactic explorers. Like the late science-fiction writer Isaac Asimov (who coined the word *robotics*), Brooks dreams of off-world colonies. But he hopes to realize his visions of extraterrestrial settlements in a manner unlike anything imagined by Asimov. Classic Asimov titles like *I, Robot* are populated by chrome-skinned robots with photoelectric eyes and positronic brains (that's where Data got his); Brooks's far less anthropocentric future would find human explorers sharing new worlds with artificial intelligences possessed of nonhuman psychologies and nonhuman bodies.

"Let's grab a salad," says Brooks, "and I'll tell you a story about ter- 40
mites." He moves purposefully toward the salad bar, lacquered bowl in hand. "There's a particular termite that builds large structures by following some very simple rules," he begins, piling unfamiliar, seaweedy greens in his bowl. "These termites pick up wood chips, chewing them in their mandibles and then randomly spitting them out, imprinted with a pheromone that dies away over time. Now, the only additional rule is that if a termite

detects that pheromone, the probability of it disgorging a spitball goes up, so that as you increase the density of termites in an area, the chance of them coming across spitballs which still have pheromones that haven't yet dissipated goes up.

"You start to see little accumulations of two, three, four spitballs," Brooks continues, "and as you increase the density even more, you get a perfect hexagonal pattern of spitballs, because if you go through the differential equations, that's the maximum density of these piles you can get. The termites are not measuring this hexagonal pattern; it all comes from this statistical picking up and dropping, with this high probability. So you can actually get complex structures produced by individuals following very simple rules; you don't have to have a global plan in the minds of robots in order to get these structures." 41

Bowl mounded high, Brooks leads the way back to the table, where he sets to work on his salad. "The challenge," he says, "is to find similar sorts of rules if you want, say, hordes of robots to produce nice troughs for lunar dwellings. NASA would have to bury the habitation modules for a lunar base below the surface to avoid the radiation. My idea is to send a horde of these social robots five years ahead of time. You don't control them from Earth; they just dig these long trenches that are programmed into their nature. If one robot breaks down, another one pushes it aside—just like ants building an anthill, carrying off the dead ants to get them out of the way." 42

Brooks's reflex-driven, or "behavior-based," approach to AI is not without its critics. Marvin Minsky, the field's patron saint, once twitted him by saying, "Hey, maybe we should all just devote ourselves to replicating insect intelligence." 43

Moravec, who enjoys an affable sparring relationship with Brooks, offers a more charitable critique of his colleague. Ensconced in his office in the Mobile Robot Lab, Moravec leans back in his chair pensively; a finger smooths an eyebrow obsessively, as if to iron out the wrinkles in his thoughts. 44

Permanently shadowed eyes—Moravec keeps hacker's hours, working late into the night—dominate a pale, round face. It is a face one sees frequently in paintings by Austrian artists, a fact that falls into place when Moravec remarks that although his family moved to Canada when he was four, he was born in Kautzen, a small town in northern Austria. Where Brooks is animated, contentious, Moravec is measured, reflective. But his composed demeanor conceals a restless, insatiably curious mind that never winds down; asked a question, he invariably responds with a chapter. 45

"Rod's approach is the first approach," Moravec says. "It's not a dead end, since any robot will want reflexes; your ancestors were once worms and worked entirely by reflex, and now those same reflexes are what makes your hand withdraw, *fast,* if you put it on a hot plate. Robots that model their worlds and reason about them will still have reflexes, so Rod's approach will 46 be a small part of these future robots. But I don't think you can build a robot that's going to run a company based on insect reflexes."

Moravec's strategy bears a closer resemblance to traditional AI than to   47
Brooks's bottom-up approach. Moravec believes that "evidence grids"—internal models of the world, collaged from sensor data, that will enable robots to navigate their surroundings—are an essential step toward the creation of mobile machines with human intelligence. In 1988, he test drove his theory with Uranus, a squat, wheeled robot whose distinguishing feature is a pair of TV-camera eyes attached to a mast jutting from its topside. Using stereo vision and sonar, Uranus was able to paint a remarkably accurate picture of the world, permitting the robot to thread its way through cluttered obstacle courses at the eye-blurring speed of about three quarters of a mile per hour.

Recently, Moravec stumbled on a shortcut to the perfection of his evi-   48
dence grids and hence, he believes, to artificial intelligence itself. The roboticist spent his 1992 sabbatical at Cambridge's Thinking Machines Corporation, home to W. Daniel Hillis's massively parallel computer, the Connection Machine—an inscrutable black monolith studded with winking red lights that looks like Darth Vader's refrigerator. When Moravec arrived, eager to begin work on a 3-D version of the grid, the latest generation of Hillis's machine was not quite ready. "I decided to develop my program on a regular workstation with an eye to transferring it later," says Moravec. "As it turns out, I wrote the best program I've ever written in my life; it's so awesomely fast that I never had to transfer it. This is the program that's going to control the robots that dust and vacuum your house *this decade.*"

Such cymbal-crash pronouncements are typical of Moravec, who shares   49
Brooks's love of the grand gesture. His evolution from practical roboticist to cloud-dwelling theorist nearly complete, he spares no hyperbole in his descriptions of the coming post-biological age. *Mind Children,* for example, opens with a statement calculated to cause apoplectic seizures in humanist quarters: "I believe that robots with human intelligence will be common within fifty years."

Human culture, according to Moravec, represents the first nongenetic   50
instance of data transferal from one generation to another; animals rely on their gene codes to pass useful behavior on to their descendants, but humans store accumulated knowledge in books, still and moving images and, increasingly, electronic media. We have already outpaced biological evolution, he asserts, and will beget our mind children—robots possessed of human-level intelligence—as soon as the processing power required for humanlike computers becomes available.

Moravec, an unreconstructed mechanist, believes that the mind is sim-   51
ply a soft machine; equivalence, therefore, is merely a matter of computing speed. Ten tera-ops should do the trick, by Moravec's reckoning. That's 10 trillion operations per second, light-years beyond a state-of-the-art PC chip like Intel's recently debuted Pentium, capable of 112 million instructions per second. Based on his calculation that there has been a *trillionfold* increase

in the amount of computation a dollar will buy since the invention of the punch-card tabulator shortly before the turn of the century, Moravec projects the arrival of a ten-tera-ops machine by 2010.

At which point buckle your seat belt, because evolution's warp drive is going to engage. Astronomically intelligent robots, "looking quite unlike the machines we know," writes Moravec, "will explode into the universe, leaving us behind in a cloud of dust." Robots capable of enginering their own evolution will quickly surpass human equivalence, he theorizes, leapfrogging up the scale of intelligence to a level that defies human comprehension. Downloading human consciousness into computers is one of Moravec's strategies for keeping pace with his superevolved creations. With dubious relish, he describes a robot surgeon removing the crown of a person's skull and using high-resolution magnetic-resonance measurements to create a computer simulacrum of the subject's neural architecture. Layer by layer, the brain is scanned, simulated and surgically removed. In time, the brainpan is empty; the robot disconnects all life-support systems, and the body goes into convulsions and expires. The subject's consciousness, meanwhile, is curiously unconcerned, wandering wraithlike through cyberspace. Eternity is his or hers to spend, pinwheeling past constellations of data or downloaded into an android whose servomechanical muscles never tire, whose memory banks are never short-circuited by age.

The Age of Mind—described by the author as "a more coherent sequel" to *Mind Children*—is subtitled *Transcending the Human Condition Through Robots.* Assuming a priori the revolution in machine intelligence foretold in his earlier book, Moravec time warps his reader to a universe watched over by godlike machines who may choose, for old times' sake, to digitize the human race and preserve it in a computer-generated world—the virtual equivalent of the Kryptonian city in a bottle in Superman's Fortress of Solitude.

"I go past human equivalents into whole robot ecologies, from micro-bots to enormous machines," says Moravec. He hypothesizes the emergence of robot companies that churn out all manner of necessities and luxuries, creating a utopia in which the workweek dwindles to nothing and every human need is attended to. But conspicuous consumption proves no match for robotic efficiency, and as ever smaller amounts of their energies are spent on their Terran creators, the machines turn their attention heavenward. Boldly they go, turning whole planets into the raw material for their automated manufacturing processes. It is a sci-fi take on laissez-faire capitalism that would gladden the heart of William F. Buckley, Jr.

"All of this will happen in the context of our current social structures," says Moravec. "I think it's a very natural way for it to happen. The robots' behavior is shaped entirely by the requirements of competition, except that the mechanisms that further this are ultra-intelligence, exotic physics, incredible technology." Moravec has a discomfiting habit of shifting into the present tense when discussing such matters, as if their inevitability were a given. "After a while," he continues, "they've expanded to cover all available space, and activity takes place

52

53

54

55

at sub-sub-subatomic levels, but because matter is used so efficiently, the world inside the computer simulation, or cyberspace, is much bigger than the physical world ever was. At which point the robots become obsolete, and we enter the age of mind, where there's no more overt physical activity at all; everything is happening at such a subtle level that it's essentially computation."

Moravec's universe-size computer simulation is inhabited by down-   56
loaded human minds and "unhuman disembodied superminds, engaged in affairs . . . that are to human concerns as ours are to bacteria." Humanity, in such a cosmos, will be a passing thought in the mind of a cybergod. "Human beings will be the smallest of the small in this universe, although occasionally some supermind will re-create them just by thinking about them," says Moravec matter-of-factly. "To the supermind, it will be just a stray thought, of course, but to the human beings it will be a whole universe."

In the present, however, machine intelligence is typified by Polly, a   57
stumpy, barrel-shaped robot cobbled together by Ian Horswill, a graduate student in Brooks's Mobile Robot Project. Polly, whose name indicates the parrotlike nature of its linguistic abilities, displays its visual acuity by giving tours of the AI lab in a fuzzy, metallic voice Horswill describes as "Stephen Hawking on Thorazine."

Polly is easily confused. During a demonstration, the robot took wrong   58
turns and incorrectly identified various areas, requiring frequent assistance from its chagrined creator. "Some of the hardware's acting up," Horswill said. "Polly is hallucinating random objects." Polly, however, remained sanguine. "Follow-me," it chirred. "I-can-avoid-obstacles-follow-corridors-recognize-places-and-navigate-from-point-to-point.   By-the-way-I-don't-understand-anything-I'm-saying."

Silicon godhood, for Polly at least, seems far away indeed. Nonethe-   59
less, unrepentant anthropocentrists shouldn't feel too reassured. In the field of artificial intelligence, the technical and the philosophical intertwine; Brooks's bug-bots and Moravec's post-biological flights of fancy have done much to dislodge the age-old notion that humanity has been given dominion over all things, for all time.

Christopher Evans, writing in 1979, on the eve of the PC revolution, fore-   60
saw the psychological consequences of Brooks's and Moravec's work carried to its ultimate conclusion. "How will we feel at the realization that the gap between ourselves and the Ultra-Intelligent Machines is unbridgeable," he wrote in *The Micro Millennium*, "and that any advances we make will be easily outdistanced by their superlative endeavors?" Not that the view of ourselves propounded by Brooks and Moravec isn't unsettling enough as it is. If, as Brooks suggests, "cognition is nowhere," what, then, is human consciousness?

The skin crinkles impishly at the corners of Brooks's eyes. "Conscious-   61
ness," he says, "is this high-level interface that God put in there so he could check out thoughts quickly; he didn't want to have to mess with the details one by one. This way, he can find the good and bad thoughts easily."   ©

CRITICAL READING

1. What is the author's point in discussing in the first portion of this essay the various pop-cultural representations (such as Data from *Star Trek: The Next Generation*) of robots and androids? What does he mean when he says, "Data and his forebears live in a future that may never be"?
2. What does Dery mean by "the bottom-up approach to artificial intelligence," as propounded by Brooks? What is the "top-down school," and why does Brooks criticize that approach to constructing intelligent robotic systems?
3. Explain the "divine inspiration" that Brooks presented in his 1983 seminar. What was his central thesis regarding human consciousness and its relation to robotic systems?
4. What is "swarm intelligence" as it relates to insects? How does this concept carry over into the realm of artificial intelligence?

CLASS DISCUSSION

1. What is Moravec's view of the future, as regards the interrelationship between human beings and machines? Discuss worldviews that coincide with and/or differ from Moravec's. How does your worldview coincide with Moravec's, and in what ways does it differ?
2. What are the advantages of small size, in the view of Brooks? Generate a list of real-world examples that support Brooks's belief that small size can be a definite advantage for certain life-forms, both organic and artificial.
3. What is Minsky suggesting when he criticizes Brooks's approach to artificial intelligence, joking, "Hey, maybe we should just devote ourselves to replicating insect intelligence." Divide the class into supporters and critics of Brooks's "behavior-based" approach, and engage in a debate concerning its pros and cons in theory and practice.

DIRECTED FREEWRITE

1. Following up on the author's fanciful discussion of possible future incarnations of robots—"intelligent machines will look . . . more like the microscopic mites that already share our apartments"—let your imagination range over possible future applications of robotic technology, as suggested both by this article and by other pieces of writing in this unit.
2. Alternatively, write for seventeen minutes on these questions: Is it ethically appropriate to create creatures that might eventually replace us on this planet? Is our development of robots a phenomenon that could be considered akin to evolution in the same sense that we evolved from and have replaced earlier forms of life?

COMPUTER SCIENCE UNIT WRITING ASSIGNMENTS

1. The memo is a very common genre of writing used by scientists and engineers. Memos are written usually to make a request, an announcement, or to report something. The latter type of memo is generally longer—two pages or more—

than the request or announcement memos; may include appendix items or illustrations; and may be broken into sections. In this assignment, we are using the shorter announcement type of memo. Imagine that you are a scientist working on one of the AI projects described in Dery's article. Bearing in mind the projects that Dery describes, be creative and imagine a discovery that would significantly advance the work of either Brooks or Moravec. Then write a memo announcing that discovery and indicating when and where you will give a presentation of your discovery to the rest of the laboratory's scientists. Adhere to the conventions for the memo that we will outline here for you.

Since announcement or request memos are usually read quickly, the writer needs to get to the point quickly, even in the first sentence, and usually needs to conclude in less than a page. Keep sentences clear, short, and to the point. Assume that your discovery is important, that you are excited about it, and that you want as many other scientists to attend your presentation as possible. Decide how much you need to include in this particular announcement—while it should be concise, it should also clearly convey the importance of your work. Therefore, consider questions such as these: Should you briefly describe the discovery? Should you state the importance of your discovery to the work of the lab as a whole? The information you include should be carefully grouped into several short paragraphs, and these paragraphs should be presented in "block" form, with two spaces between them rather than indentations indicating the paragraph breaks. Single-space the lines within your paragraphs. Your last paragraph should announce the time, place, and date of your presentation; obviously, this assignment asks you to invent these kinds of details. At the top left corner of the memo, type "To:" followed by the name of the recipient(s) of the memo; double-spaced below that, type "From:" followed by your name; double-spaced below that, type "Subject:" and include a brief summation of your subject.

2. Write an essay exploring the specific ways that "intelligent machines" might change our lives. You might choose to focus on the application of machines or robotics to everyday life and task performance, or you might choose to consider broader issues, such as the entire composition of human society, our relationships to work, our relationships to each other and/or to the machines in our midst—any of the changes that you can foresee as possibilities, given the kind of research described in this unit. Use one or all of the essays in the unit to support the logic of your ideas.

Alternatively, you could write an essay exploring the assertion in Mark Dery's article that in the future, intelligent machines will be so alien "that we won't be able to appreciate them and they us." Write about the possible future implications of such human/robot "alienation." How might our lives be affected by this kind of relationship?

Essays that explore a complex topic usually arrive at a conclusion or a point, on the basis of such exploration; arrive at a question or set of questions; or review the different conclusions and questions that others have come up with in relation to the topic. One can often find this kind of essay in newspapers and magazines, where an author provides the reader with an overview of current thought or work on a topic, and raises salient issues, questions, and implications inherent in that work. Hopefully, our description is sounding familiar here, as you just read two essays that exemplify this kind of writing; Clive Davidson and Mark Dery both explore scientific work on artificial intelligence in their essays, ultimately raising more questions than they answer. Thus your essay for this assignment should be driven by the questions that these issues raise about our lives, our social organizations and institutions and the way that machines of the future might impact these. Rather than synthesizing the work of others, as Davidson and Dery do, you will be generating your own questions, derived from the essays of this unit, and you will thoughtfully discuss these questions in your essay.

One challenge in this assignment is your essay organization. Rather than writing an essay that simply presents a string or a list of different questions and their discussion, you will need to think carefully about how your questions relate to each other, and take care to sequence them so that each question leads logically to the next, presenting a logical progression of related ideas and issues, explored in relation to a common focus on the issues at stake here.

3. In Jack Copeland's *Artificial Intelligence: A Philosophical Introduction,* AI researcher Herbert Simon says, "It is not my aim to surprise or shock you—but the simplest way I can summarize is to say that there are now in the world machines that can think, that can learn and that can create. Moreover, their ability to do these things is going to increase rapidly until—in a visible future—the range of problems they can handle will be coextensive with the range to which the human mind has been applied." Write a relatively formal academic research essay of eight to ten pages, in which you summarize the basic philosophical and/or practical approaches that have been posited with regard to "intelligent" computers, and from that research develop a thesis which reflects your own feelings and thoughts about this topic. Although you will be incorporating secondary evidence in your paper (see Chapter 1 for an explanation of the different kinds of evidence), the paper that results from your research must be original; that is, it must contain insights and information that are new to you. For the purposes of this essay, you may assume that the other members of your class—and not scientists at a professional conference—are the audience. Write a paper that is appropriate and comprehensible for this audience, and that they will find interesting and informative as well. Use a documentation style—either MLA or APA in-text (numbers in parentheses within the body of the paper) or footnotes—that reflect the rhetorical conventions and styles of the academic discipline in which your topic area is situated. Your essay should be based on a variety of sources, including books, periodicals, professional journals, newspapers, and computer-based media such as the World Wide Web, accessible through web browsers such as Netscape. If possible, it should also include firsthand findings from interviews, questionnaires, or experiments.

THINKING AND WRITING IN THE HUMANITIES

Unit 1
Philosophy—Thinking Machines, Take Two

CAN MACHINES THINK? MAYBE SO, AS DEEP BLUE'S CHESS PROWESS SUGGESTS

Robert Wright

This article, written for a popular magazine rather than a scholarly journal, discusses the philosophical debate regarding man-made, sentient intelligence, focusing specifically on the social-theological implications of chess champion Gary Kasparov's difficulty in beating the latest IBM computer chess program. The essay further discusses artificial intelligence theories of philosopher David Chalmers, as embodied in his new book, *The Unconscious Mind*. As you read, note the lack of objectivity that the author displays in this piece, as in the phrases "most of us are so abject that not even Kasparov can save us" and "Some laypeople (like me, for example)." How does this tone differ from that of academics writing for science-based disciplines within the academy?

Robert Wright is a senior editor at The New Republic, *a contributor to* Time *(from which this piece is taken), and a contributor to* Slate *online magazine, where his column "The Earthling" appears monthly. He has also written for* The Atlantic Monthly *and* The New Yorker. *He previously worked at* The Sciences *magazine, where his writings on science, technology, and philosophy won the National Magazine Award for Essay and Criticism. Wright has also written several books including* Three Scientists and Their Gods: Looking for Meaning in an Age of Information, *which was nominated for a National Book Critics Circle Award, and* The Moral Animal, *which was named by* The New York Times Book Review *as one of the eleven best books of 1994.*

When Garry Kasparov faced off against an IBM computer in last   1
month's celebrated chess match, he wasn't just after more fame and
money. By his own account, the world chess champion was playing for you,
me, the whole human species. He was trying, as he put it shortly before the
match, to "help defend our dignity."

Nice of him to offer. But if human dignity has much to do with chess   2
mastery, then most of us are so abject that not even Kasparov can save us.
If we must vest the honor of our species in some quintessentially human
feat and then defy a machine to perform it, shouldn't it be something the average human can do? Play a mediocre game of Trivial Pursuit, say? (Or
lose to Kasparov in chess?)

Apparently not. As Kasparov suspected, his duel with Deep Blue in-   3
deed became an icon in musings on the meaning and dignity of human life.
While the world monitored his narrow escape from a historic defeat—and at
the same time marked the 50th birthday of the first real computer, ENIAC—
he seemed to personify some kind of identity crisis that computers have induced in our species.

Maybe such a crisis is in order. It isn't just that as these machines get   4
more powerful they do more jobs once done only by people, from financial
analysis to secretarial work to world-class chess playing. It's that, in the
process, they seem to underscore the generally dispiriting drift of scientific
inquiry. First Copernicus said we're not the center of the universe. Then
Darwin said we're just protozoans with a long list of add-ons—mere "survival machines," as modern Darwinians put it. And machines don't have
souls, right? Certainly Deep Blue hasn't mentioned having one. The better
these seemingly soulless machines get at doing things people do, the more
plausible it seems that we could be soulless machines too.

But however logical this downbeat argument may sound, it doesn't ap-   5
pear to be prevailing among scholars who ponder such issues for a living. That
isn't to say philosophers are suddenly resurrecting the idea of a distinct, immaterial soul that governs the body for a lifetime and then drifts off to its
reward. They're philosophers, not theologians. When talking about some conceivably nonphysical property of human beings, they talk not about "souls" but
about "consciousness" and "mind." The point is simply that as the information
age advances and computers get brainier, philosophers are taking the ethereal existence of mind, of consciousness, more seriously, not less. And one
result is to leave the theologically inclined more room for spiritual speculation.

"The mystery grows more acute," says philosopher David Chalmers,   6
whose book *The Conscious Mind* will be published next month by Oxford
University Press. "The more we think about computers, the more we realize
how strange consciousness is."

Though chess has lately been the best-publicized measure of a ma-   7
chine's humanity, it is not the standard gauge. That was invented by the
great British computer scientist Alan Turing in a 1950 essay in the journal

Mind. Turing set out to address the question "Can machines think?" and proposed what is now called the Turing test. Suppose an interrogator is communicating by keyboard with a series of entities that are concealed from view. Some entities are people, some are computers, and the interrogator has to guess which is which. To the extent that a computer fools interrogators, it can be said to think.

At least that's the way the meaning of the Turing test is usually put. In truth, midway through his famous essay, Turing wrote, "The original question, 'Can machines think?,' I believe to be too meaningless to deserve discussion." His test wasn't supposed to answer this murky question but to replace it. Still, he did add, "I believe that at the end of the century the use of words and general educated opinion will have altered so much that one will be able to speak of machines thinking without expecting to be contradicted." 8

Guess again. With the century's end in sight, no machine has consistently passed the Turing test. And on those few occasions when interrogators have been fooled by computers, the transcripts reveal a less-than-penetrating interrogation. (Hence one problem with the Turing test: Is it measuring the thinking power of the machines or of the humans?) 9

The lesson here—now dogma among researchers in artificial intelligence, or AI—is that the hardest thing for computers is the "simple" stuff. Sure they can play great chess, a game of mechanical rules and finite options. But making small talk—or, indeed, playing Trivial Pursuit—is another matter. So too with recognizing a face or recognizing a joke. As Marvin Minsky of the Massachusetts Institute of Technology likes to say, the biggest challenge is giving machines common sense. To pass the Turing test, you need some of that. 10

Besides, judging by the hubbub over the Kasparov match, even if computers could pass the test, debate would still rage over whether they think. No one doubted Deep Blue's chess skills, but many doubted whether it is a thinking machine. It uses "brute force"—zillions of trivial calculations, rather than a few strokes of strategic Big Think. ("You don't invite forklifts to weightlifting competitions," an organizer of exclusively human chess tournaments said about the idea of man-vs.-machine matches.) On the other hand, there are chess programs that work somewhat like humans. They size up the state of play and reason strategically from there. And though they aren't good enough to beat Kasparov, they're good enough to leave the average Homo sapiens writhing in humiliation. 11

Further, much of the progress made lately on the difficult "simple" problems—like recognizing faces—has come via parallel computers, which mirror the diffuse data-processing architecture of the brain. Though progress in AI hasn't matched the high hopes of its founders, the field is making computers more like us, not just in what they do but in how they do it—more like us on the inside. 12

So machines can think? Not so fast. Many people would still say no. When they talk about what's inside a human being, they mean way inside— 13 not just the neuronal data flow corresponding to our thoughts and feelings but the thoughts and feelings themselves. You know: the exhilaration of insight or the dull anxiety of doubt. When Kasparov lost Game 1, he was gloomy. Could Deep Blue ever feel deeply blue? Does a face-recognition program have the experience of recognizing a face? Can computers—even computers whose data flow precisely mimics human data flow—actually have subjective experience? This is the question of consciousness or mind. The lights are on, but is anyone home?

For years AI researchers have tossed around the question of whether   14
computers might be sentient. But since they often did so in casual late-night conversations, and sometimes in an altered state of consciousness, their speculations weren't hailed as major contributions to Western thought. However, as computers keep evolving, more philosophers are taking the issue of computer consciousness seriously. And some of them—such as Chalmers, a professor of philosophy at the University of California at Santa Cruz—are using it to argue that consciousness is a deeper puzzle than many philosophers have realized.

Chalmers' forthcoming book is already making a stir. His argument has   15
been labeled "a major misdirector of attention, an illusion generator," by the well-known philosopher Daniel Dennett of Tufts University. Dennett believes consciousness is no longer a mystery. Sure there are details to work out, but the puzzle has been reduced to "a set of manageable problems."

The roots of the debate between Chalmers and Dennett—the debate   16
over how mysterious mind is or isn't—lie in the work of Dennett's mentor at Oxford University, Gilbert Ryle. In 1949 Ryle published a landmark book called *The Concept of Mind.* It resoundingly dismissed the idea of a human soul—a "ghost in the machine," as Ryle derisively put it—as a hangover from prescientific thought. Ryle's juiciest target was the sort of soul imagined back in the 17th century by René Descartes: an immaterial, somewhat autonomous soul that steers the body through life. But the book subdued enthusiasm for even less supernatural versions of a soul: mind, consciousness, subjective experience.

Some adherents of the "materialist" line that Ryle helped spread in-   17
sisted that these things don't even exist. Others said they exist but consist simply of the brain. And by this they didn't just mean that consciousness is produced by the brain the way steam is produced by a steam engine. They meant that the mind is the brain—the machine itself, period.

Some laypeople (like me, for example) have trouble seeing the differ-   18
ence between these two views—between saying consciousness doesn't exist and saying it is nothing more than the brain. In any event, both versions of strict materialism put a damper on cosmic speculation. As strict materialism became more mainstream, many philosophers talked as if the mind-body problem was no great problem. Consciousness became almost passé.

Ryle's book was published three years after ENIAC's birth, and at first 19
glance his ideas would seem to draw strength from the computer age. That, at
any rate, is the line Dennett takes in defending his teacher's school of thought.
Dennett notes that AI is progressing, creating smart machines that process
data somewhat the way human beings do. As this trend continues, he believes, it will become clearer that we're all machines, that Ryle's strict materialism was basically on target, that the mind-body problem is in principle
solved. The title of Dennett's 1991 book says it all: *Consciousness Explained.*

Dennett's book got rave reviews and has sold well, 100,000 copies to 20
date. But among philosophers the reaction was mixed. The can-do attitude that
was common in the decades after Ryle wrote—the belief that consciousness is
readily "explained"—has waned. "Most people in the field now take the problem
far more seriously," says Rutgers University philosopher Colin McGinn, author
of *The Problem of Consciousness.* By acting as if consciousness is no great
mystery, says McGinn, "Dennett's fighting a rearguard action."

McGinn and Chalmers are among the philosophers who have been 21
called the New Mysterians because they think consciousness is, well, mysterious. McGinn goes so far as to say it will always remain so. For human
beings to try to grasp how subjective experience arises from matter, he
says, "is like slugs trying to do Freudian psychoanalysis. They just don't
have the conceptual equipment."

Actually there have long been a few mysterians insisting that the glory 22
of human experience defies scientific dissection. But the current debate is
different. The New Mysterians are fundamentally scientific in outlook. They
don't begin by doubting the audacious premises of AI. O.K., they say,
maybe it is possible—in principle, at least—to build an electronic machine
that can do everything a human brain can do. They just think people like
Dennett misunderstand the import of such a prospect: rather than bury old
puzzles about consciousness, it resurrects them in clearer form than ever.

Consider, says Chalmers, the robot named Cog, being developed at 23
M.I.T.'s artificial-intelligence lab with input from Dennett . . . Cog will someday have "skin"—a synthetic membrane sensitive to contact. Upon touching
an object, the skin will send a data packet to the "brain." The brain may then
instruct the robot to recoil from the object, depending on whether the object
could damage the robot. When human beings recoil from things, they too
are under the influence of data packets. If you touch something that's dangerously hot, the appropriate electrical impulses go from hand to brain,
which then sends impulses instructing the hand to recoil. In that sense, Cog
is a good model of human data processing, just the kind of machine that
Dennett believes helps "explain" consciousness.

But wait a second. Human beings have, in addition to the physical data 24
flow representing the heat, one other thing: a feeling of heat and pain, subjective experience, consciousness. Why do they? According to Chalmers,
studying Cog doesn't answer that question but deepens it. For the moral of

Cog's story seems to be that you don't, in principle, need pain to function like a human being. After all, the reflexive withdrawal of Cog's hand is entirely explicable in terms of physical data flow, electrons coercing Cog into recoiling. There's no apparent role for subjective experience. So why do human beings have it?

Of course, it's always possible that Cog does have a kind of consciousness—a consideration that neither Dennett nor Chalmers rules out. But even then the mystery would persist, for you could still account for all the behavior by talking about physical processes, without ever mentioning feelings. And so too with humans. This, says Chalmers, is the mystery of the "extraness" of consciousness. And it is crystallized, not resolved, by advances in artificial intelligence. Because however human machines become—however deftly they someday pass the Turing test, however precisely their data flow mirrors the brain's data flow—everything they do will be explicable in strictly physical terms. And that will suggest with ever greater force that human consciousness is itself somehow "extra."

Chalmers remarks, "It seems God could have created the world physically exactly like this one, atom for atom, but with no consciousness at all. And it would have worked just as well. But our universe isn't like that. Our universe has consciousness." For some reason, God chose "to do more work" in order "to put consciousness in."

When Chalmers says "God," he doesn't mean—you know—God. He's speaking as a philosopher, using the term as a proxy for whoever, whatever (if anyone, anything) is responsible for the nature of the universe. Still, though he isn't personally inclined to religious speculation, he can see how people who grasp the extraness of consciousness might carry it in that direction.

After all, consciousness—the existence of pleasure and pain, love and grief—is a fairly central source of life's meaning. For it to have been thrown into the fabric of the universe as a freebie would suggest to some people that the thrower wanted to impart significance.

It's always possible that consciousness isn't extra, that it actually does something in the physical world, like influence behavior. Indeed, as a common-sense intuition, this strikes many people as obvious. But as a philosophical doctrine it is radical, for it would seem to carry us back toward Descartes, toward the idea that "soul stuff" helps govern the physical world. And within both philosophy and science, Descartes is dead or, at best, on life support. And the New Mysterians, a pretty hard-nosed group, have no interest in reviving him.

The extraness problem is what Chalmers calls one of the "hard" questions of consciousness. What Dennett does, Chalmers says, is skip the "hard" questions and focus on the "easy" questions—and then title his book *Consciousness Explained*. There is one other "hard" question that Chalmers emphasizes. It—and Dennett's alleged tendency to avoid such questions—

is illustrated by something called pandemonium, an AI model that Dennett favors.

According to the model, our brain subconsciously generates competing theories about the world, and only the "winning" theory becomes part of consciousness. Is that a nearby fly or a distant airplane on the edge of your vision? Is that a baby crying or a cat meowing? By the time we become aware of such images and sounds, these debates have usually been resolved via a winner-take-all struggle. The winning theory—the one that best matches the data—has wrested control of our neurons and thus of our perceptual field.

As a scientific model, pandemonium has virtues. First, it works; you can run the model successfully on a computer. Second, it works best on massively parallel computers, whose structure resembles the brain's structure. So it's a plausible theory of data flow in the human brain, and of the criteria by which the brain admits some data, but not other data, to consciousness.

Still, says Chalmers, once we know which kinds of data become part of consciousness, and how they earned that privilege, the question remains, "How do data become part of consciousness?" Suppose that the physical information representing the "baby crying" hypothesis has carried the day and vanquished the information representing the rival "cat meowing" hypothesis. How exactly—by what physical or metaphysical alchemy—is the physical information transformed into the subjective experience of hearing a baby cry? As McGinn puts the question, "How does the brain 'turn the water into wine'?"

McGinn doesn't mean that subjective experience is literally a miracle. He considers himself a materialist, if in a "thin" sense. He presumes there is some physical explanation for subjective experience, even though he doubts that the human brain—or mind, or whatever—can ever grasp it. Nevertheless, McGinn doesn't laugh at people who take the water-into-wine metaphor more literally. "I think in a way it's legitimate to take the mystery of consciousness and convert it into a theological system. I don't do that myself, but I think in a sense it's more rational than strict materialism, because it respects the data." That is, it respects the lack of data, the yawning and perhaps eternal gap in scientific understanding.

These two "hard" questions about consciousness—the extraness question and the water-into-wine question—don't depend on artificial intelligence. They could occur (and have occurred) to people who simply take the mind-as-machine idea seriously and ponder its implications. But the actual construction of a robot like Cog, or of a pandemonium machine, makes the hard questions more vivid. Materialist dismissals of the mind-body problem may seem forceful on paper, but, says McGinn, "you start to see the limits of a concept once it gets realized." With AI, the tenets of strict materialism are being realized—and found, by some at least, incapable of explaining certain parts of human experience. Namely, the experience part.

Dennett has answers to these critiques. As for the extraness problem,   36
the question of what function consciousness serves: if you're a strict materialist and believe "the mind is the brain," then consciousness must have a
function. After all, the brain has a function, and consciousness is the brain.
Similarly, turning the water into wine seems a less acute problem if the wine
is water.

To people who don't share Dennett's philosophical intuitions, these ar-   37
guments may seem unintelligible. (It's one thing to say feelings are generated by the brain, which Chalmers and McGinn believe, but what does it
even mean to say feelings are the brain?) Still, that doesn't mean Dennett is
wrong. Some people share his intuitions and find the thinking of his critics
opaque. Consciousness is one of those questions so deep that frequently
people with different views don't just fail to convince one another, they fail
even to communicate. The unintelligibility is often mutual.

Chalmers isn't a hard-core mysterian like McGinn. He thinks a solution   38
to the consciousness puzzle is possible. But he thinks it will require recognizing that consciousness is something "over and above the physical" and
then building a theory some might call metaphysical. This word has long
been out of vogue in philosophy, and even Chalmers uses it only under
duress, since it makes people think of crystals and Shirley MacLaine. He
prefers "psychophysical."

In *The Conscious Mind,* Chalmers speculatively sets out a psy-   39
chophysical theory. Maybe, he says, consciousness is a "nonphysical" property of the universe vaguely comparable to physical properties like mass or
space or time. And maybe, by some law of the universe, consciousness accompanies certain configurations of information, such as brains. Maybe information, though composed of ordinary matter, is a special incarnation of
matter and has two sides—the physical and the experiential. (Insert *Twilight
Zone* music here.)

In this view, Cog may indeed have consciousness. So might a pande-   40
monium machine. So might a thermostat. Chalmers thinks it quite possible
that AI research may someday generate—may now be generating—new
spheres of consciousness unsensed by the rest of us. Strange as it may
seem, the prospect that we are creating a new species of sentient life is now
being taken seriously in philosophy.

Though Turing generally shied away from such metaphysical ques-   41
tions, his 1950 paper did touch briefly on this issue. Some people, he noted,
might complain that to create true thinking machines would be to create
souls, and thus exercise powers reserved for God. Turing disagreed. "In attempting to construct such machines we should not be irreverently usurping
his power of creating souls, any more than we are in the procreation of children," Turing wrote. "Rather we are, in either case, instruments of his will
providing mansions for the souls that he creates."   ©

CRITICAL READING

1. Why, according to this article, was the world so interested in the chess match between Kasparov and Deep Blue, that the contest "became an icon in musings on the meaning and dignity of human life"?
2. Explain what is meant by "the Turing test." How does it work, and what is it designed to prove? What, according to this test, is the deciding factor in whether a machine can "think"?
3. What message is implied in the statement, "You don't invite forklifts to weight-lifting competitions"? How does this message factor into the debate about whether or not machines can truly think?
4. How does Chalmers's theory differ from that of Dennett? What is meant by the term "New Mysterians" as it applies to Chalmers and other philosophers who share his views?

CLASS DISCUSSION

1. Explain the implied meaning in Wright's statement, "The better these seemingly soulless machines get at doing things people do, the more plausible it seems that we could be soulless machines too." Argue for or against the philosophical position underlying this assertion by Wright.
2. Who or what is Cog? How does his/its development reflect arguments currently raging over the nature of human and artificial intelligence? Discuss whether you believe Cog "does have a kind of consciousness."

DIRECTED FREEWRITE

Situate yourself somewhere within the debate between Dennett and Chalmers regarding artificial intelligence. Briefly summarize each philosopher's theoretical position, and then state your own preference: to which of these positions do you most closely adhere, and why?

DANIEL C. DENNETT, MATERIALIST PHILOSOPHER

Robert Killheffer

In this article from *Omni* magazine, the author interviews philosopher Dennett, who, as we have seen from previous articles, believes that the mind arises completely from the physical activity of the brain and dismisses the existence of the soul or spirit. In this interview, Dennett discusses the theories contained in his book *Consciousness Explained*, present research into artificial intelligence and possible future applications for AI, evolutionary theory, and a number of other far-flung topics. As you read, pay attention to the interview format here. While you will rarely write a paper that consists mainly of interview material as this article does, you will sometimes want to incorporate interviews as primary evidence, especially in reports and essays for social science courses, such as psychology and sociology.

Robert Killheffer attended Yale, where he minored in computer science and majored in medieval history. Killheffer served as Executive Producer of Omni's *live Web shows and events and was on the charter staff of* TV Guide Online *as the science fiction producer. Later, he joined Simon & Schuster's online division, where he developed Web sites and interactive CD-ROMs for their Star Trek books. He has since directed development of Web sites at several other publishing houses. Additionally, he has written on computers, computer culture, brain science, archaeology, and other related topics for various publications including* Omni, The Washington Post, Newsweek, Penthouse, *and* Publishers Weekly. *An expert in science fiction film and literature, he has also contributed a column to* The Magazine of Fantasy and Science Fiction *and was a staff member and managing editor of* The New York Review of Science Fiction.

It's hard to reconcile what I know of Daniel Dennett—unflinching   1
philosopher of mind, tenacious and learned reasoner, challenger of our comfortable illusions—with the man in knee-length shorts greeting me from the front step of his nineteenth-century farmhouse. A man who keeps two pigs, bottles homemade apple cider, and looks forward to raking up a good crop of blueberries later in the season. Before we start discussing the origins of life and the nature of consciousness, we fire up his old International Harvester tractor for a tour of the acreage. We talk about his distant relatives—the first exit on I-95 as you cross the Maine border is Dennett Road—

---

and he teaches me a thing or two about farming that he's picked up over the 24 summers that he has spent here.

In fact it's no paradox. His very earthiness is a main reason Dennett 2 has been able to reach so far beyond the tight circles of philosophical academia with books such as *Consciousness Explained,* and recently, *Darwin's Dangerous Idea.* The term "philosophy" might conjure images of impenetrable prose and irrelevant arguments, but Dennett's work avoids the dreary formal logic and technical jargon clogging other philosophical texts. He makes his abstract points about the nature of mind and processes of evolution vivid and accessible with real-life anecdotes and easy-to-try thought experiments. One need hardly hold a Ph.D. to appreciate his ideas. Although he's most concerned with his books' reception among colleagues, he has relished responses from high-school students, dentists, and used-car salesmen. An artist in Germany used one suggested experiment from *Consciousness Explained* to create a recent work. (The two may co-author a paper detailing the results for a psychological journal.)

Educated at Harvard and Oxford, Dennett, 53, heads the Center for Cog- 3 nitive Studies at Tufts University, where he's taught since 1971. Over the years he has become perhaps the most uncompromising and outspoken proponent of a materialist philosophy of mind. According to Dennett and other materialists, the mind—everything that makes up you, your thoughts, feelings, dreams, desires—arises entirely from the brain's physical activity. There are no ethereal spirits or immortal soul, just the wet matter between our ears.

In explaining how selves need no souls, Dennett borrows the concept of 4 memes from the British zoologist Richard Dawkins. Simply put, memes can be any sort of cultural unit, ideas transmittable from person to person—the idea of the wheel, wearing clothes, chess, basketball, catchy songs or jingles: Greensleeves is a meme. Comparable to genes in that they reproduce and mutate over time, memes make the elements of culture into an evolutionary system like biology. Those memes in our brains (you could say those memes "infecting" us), give us the makings of a self. The 'I' is a cultural artifact, the product of the acquisition of memes. The very idea of self could well be considered a meme.

If that sounds rather hard-nosed and, well, materialist, it's no surprise. 5 Calm, self-assured, and affable, Dennett nevertheless makes no bones about his convictions. In *Darwin's Dangerous Idea,* he declares unequivocally that evolution "is as secure an example of a scientific fact as the roundness of the earth." He has no patience with adherents of what he calls a "mind-first" cosmology—where the material world arises out of "consciousness," ours, God's, or someone's, rather than the other way around—nor does he tolerate the illogical contortions underlying creationist beliefs. Paraphrasing Aristotle, he says, "If you can find someone who denies the law of noncontradiction, it's like talking to a cabbage."

In *Darwin's Dangerous Idea,* he takes to task evolutionist Stephen Jay 6 Gould, mathematical physicist Roger Penrose, and linquist Noam Chomsky, as well as fellow philosophers. In some cases it's just polite professional disagreement, but in others there's a distinctly personal note to the criticism. "I have been harsh on a variety of people," Dennett admits, "but I think without exception the people I've gone after I might classify as bullies. If there's one thing I really don't like it's when a very influential, charismatic, and brilliant person engages in willful caricature of the opposition. When I see that I see red."

Not surprisingly, he's got enemies in the neurosciences, linguistics, biology, and elsewhere, as well as philosophy. Some of Dennett's critics consider his eclecticism an excuse to dismiss his arguments, claiming only a specialist could evaluate the research in any area well enough to comment on it. But to Dennett and others in his camp, the synthetic approach offers the only hope of addressing the big questions of the origins of life and consciousness. "You're going to have to be bold," he says. If any one word could sum up the man who would title his book *Consciousness Explained,* that's certainly it. —Robert K. J. Killheffer   7

Omni: How did your colleagues react to *Consciousness Explained?*   8

Dennett: In general I've been delighted, because certainly it's been   9
taken very seriously—everybody seems to have to deal with it one way or another. At one extreme are people who, to my surprise and dismay, have been unable to take seriously the book's radical challenge. They think, Well, that just can't be. [Philosopher] Ned Block seems to be one of those who still hasn't come to grips with the real possibility I'm right. And lots of others just found the message too radical for them. One neat thing was that people in the neurosciences responded by saying, Well, I thought I was a good materialist until you showed me just how counterintuitive materialism really is. Now that I see what I have to jettison from my traditional worldview to be a good materialist, maybe dualism looks a bit better.

This pleases me because I wanted to show that materialism isn't this   10
simple, intuitive, "the mind is the brain" concept. They're facing the problems in some regard more forthrightly than materialists still trying to cling to what I call a Cartesian materialism. They threw away the interactionism [mindbody dualism!] but kept the place where it all comes together, the Cartesian theater [control center in the brain!]. My goodness, people have defended that view vigorously. That's been perhaps the most interesting aspect of the response. And some scientists have shown me that their own work could be reinterpreted to support and extend my views. Rod Brooks of MIT said, "We think you're right about consciousness and would like to try to model some of them in this robot." I thought, great! That's like being handed Aladdin's lamp!

Omni: What should be the relationship between philosophy and neuro-   11
science?

Dennett: Most of what's done by philosophers of mind is really not of   12
much help to cognitive and neuroscientists. It's infighting that has to go on

but other disciplines can avert their eyes. It doesn't matter to them yet. But if you view philosophy of mind as a branch of philosophy of science, whose point is to clarify and alleviate conceptual problems arising in science, then the work is important to neuroscientists who now can see that arguments and analyses I give help them avoid going down mistaken avenues. Of course there's still a fairly overwhelming legacy of antitheoretical bias in the neurosciences. Even today neuroscientists who don't keep their fingers wet are in jeopardy of not being taken seriously.

Omni: Are Roger Penrose's objections to AI based on a similar bias? 13

Dennett: In his case it's a very specific mislocation of the issue. He 14 gets it in his head that what a mathematician means by an algorithm is the same as what AI people have meant by algorithms, and that's really not true. Thinking the way mathematicians think, an algorithm is a terminating Turing machine that probably does a certain thing—[a series of instructions that] computes a specific function. Thinking that way, then AI has almost never been concerned with algorithms. [AI researchers take "algorithm" to mean a set of instructions that can be followed by rote, but need not have any goal, specific purpose, or end! So the whole point of *The Emperor's New Mind* is sort of misbegotten. It's really a sort of stunning error on Penrose's part, because he quite innocently went ahead treating algorithms the wrong way. It's time for Emily Litella to come out and say, Nevermind!

We had a debate at Dartmouth last spring where he presented chap- 15 ters of his new book, *Shadows of the Mind,* and I presented portions of my Penrose chapter form *Darwin's Dangerous Idea.* Although Penrose has now recognized that this is not a small loophole but a major gap in his argument, I don't think he's really confronted it properly. He still fails to make his case, but at least sees this is a bigger problem than he'd realized.

Omni: What about Penrose's notion that microtubules in neurons—so 16 small that the behavior of single electrons can have a strong effect—are a likely brain site for significant quantum mechanical effects? And that these quantum effects, such as the simultaneous existence of several probability states for a single particle, somehow give rise to consciousness?

Dennett: The microtubules—Stuart Hameroff's ideas. I got a good in- 17 troduction to that from Stuart and Roger at a workshop two years ago in Lapland, up with the reindeer and midnight sun. On the one hand, Penrose was right to recognize that the neuroscience in *The Emperor's New Mind* was woefully inadequate and sketchy and he had to find some base of operations if he was going to continue that argument. I think Hameroff's ideas are dubious at best, and this is not a good wagon for Penrose to hitch on to. But there it is; he's become enthusiastic about it. If you're looking to find magnification of quantum effects in the nervous system, microtubules are as good a place as any to start. But Hameroff's claims strike me as confused.

Omni: You mean the inhibition of quantum effects in microtubules is 18 what produces unconsciousness in anesthesia?

Dennett: I challenged Hameroff if as an anesthesiologist he'd ever as-   19
sisted in an operation to reattach a severed limb. He said no. And I said, "If I
understand you right, according to your theory of consciousness, you really
ought to anesthetize the severed limb before it's reattached. Because after
all, it's got a full dose of microtubles in it, and if consciousness depends on
the operation of microtubules, then that arm is feeling pain before it's reattached." My impression then was that it had never occurred to him—he
didn't have a good answer for it.

Omni: More basically, is some sort of magnification of quantum effects   20
really vital to any scientific explanation of consciousness?

Dennett: In 1984 in *Elbow Room,* I discussed the question of whether   21
quantum randomness is necessary to get free will. It's easy enough theoretically to install it, but, I argued, nobody had ever shown it was necessary.
You could get pseudorandomness, as it were, much cheaper at a macroscopic level by just adding a sort of number generator providing you with a
coin-flip, whenever you need one. Pseudorandomness apparently gives you
all the power you'd ever get from quantum randomness. You want randomness, you can install it in the nervous system. What good does it do you?

It's conceivable that computation at the molecular level matters, but   22
nobody has given a good reason to think it does. Penrose imagines he has
because he thinks he's shown that human mathematicians can do something no Turing machine can do, and that to him presents something of a
dilemma to the materialist: Either we have to be frank dualists, or we'll have
a revolution in physics. His argument is just broken-backed, so he hasn't
found a reason for going quantum.

Omni: Penrose really can't swallow straight, unmitigated materialism?   23

Dennett: Penrose wants a skyhook, a deus ex machina, an exemption   24
from mechanism, from algorithmic mindless processes. Darwin suggests all
design in natures can be explained in terms of mechanisms—what I call
"cranes"—of one Darwinian algorithmic process piled on top of another. To
me this is the best, most beautiful idea I've ever encountered.

Omni: By cranes you mean more complex intermediary mechanisms—   25
perfectly consistent with Darwinian process—that help promote evolutionary
change?

Dennett: Right. But others find it oppressive, and for them the search   26
has always been to find some gap that could not be leapt by cranes, mere
mechanism, where you must have a skyhook to help you up to the next
level. Noam Chomsky, when he resists evolutionary accounts of the creation of the language organ, would probably like it to be a skyhook, a sort
of gift from God that sets us apart from the rest of mechanical creation and
is inexplicable in terms of brute mechanism. Penrose is forthright in saying
he finds the idea of AI offensive and wants to show artificial intelligence
can't be right. At first, I blush to say, I didn't connect this desire to his
openly expressed doubt about standard Darwinian theory of natural selec-

tion. Then I realized he's almost obliged to be a skeptic about evolution, because AI and evolution are just the same story on a different time scale. Natural selection says we're the descendants of robots, little tiny macromolecular robots, and we're composed of robots. And that's what AI says. To be a skeptic about strong AI and not be a skeptic about evolution, you'd have to maintain that, although we descend from a long line of robots, at some point shazam!—something marvelous happens so we cease to be just a collection of robots.

Omni: You take on another popular scientist, Stephen Jay Gould, in 27 your new book. What's your objection to his views?

Dennett: Steve has been out to attack a notion of a global progress 28 and goal-directedness in evolution. But that is not the view of evolutionists; it's a lay view of evolution, and a silly one. So if that's Gould's target, what's he going on about? Nobody in the field accepts that view.

Omni: So your argument is with Gould's rhetoric, when he makes it 29 seem his view marks a revolution in science?

Dennett: He certainly presented *Wonderful Life* as a view supposed to 30 upset the evolutionary establishment. If what he's saying is that many people outside biology continue to think because we're one of the end-products to date of evolution, this is a process destined and supposed to produce us—that's wrong. He's right; that's wrong. But gosh, I can't think of anybody in the sciences who's asserted that view since Darwin!

Omni: So a goal-directed view of evolution is incorrect? 31

Dennett: On a global scale, it's always a mistake to think about 32 progress—after all, we may blow ourselves up next week, and then it won't have looked like progress, will it? But on shorter time scales, there is progress. Of course there's progress in evolution. There's hill-climbing going on on many scales in many dimensions all the time. And three is in culture, too. Some people have a hard time believing I'm not after Steve Gould the man. I'm really after an unfortunately effective myth he's put out there that I think has to be revised. I've tried to leave Steve as much room as possible to say, "Oh, thanks, Dan, I hadn't realized the rhetoric had some of these untoward effects." But that's not what he's said so far. A few years ago, my literary agent, John Brockman, arranged for us to have lunch with him and Danny Hills from Thinking Machines. It was terribly tense.

My effort there was to give Steve the skyhook/crane distinction, and de- 33 fine the difference between good reductionism and greedy reductionism. Good reductionists think it can all be done without skyhooks; greedy reductionists think it can all be done without even cranes. Then I proposed we were all in agreement about one thing, weren't we? We were all at least good reductionists. Danny said, "Yeah, sure." When I turned to Steve, he wouldn't agree. It [no skyhooks] was a mechanistic reductionism he really didn't like.

Omni: Why do scientists like Gould and Penrose find the Darwinian 34 model so oppressive?

Dennett: One reason is built right into the scientific enterprise. When   35
scientists experiment, they presuppose they are independent, outside of the
phenomenon being studied. As Freeman Dyson points out in *Disturbing the
Universe,* the scientist is disturbing the universe to see what happens. To do
that you have to think of yourself as outside it. If the experimenter is part of
the fabric of the universe, maybe it's an illusion that you can "objectively"
disturb the universe—it's just one part of the universe disturbing another.

I don't see this as a formal contradiction. If so, science would fall apart.   36
It's an approximation, idealization, but one built into the heart of the scientific method. The desire for that idealization to be the literal truth may be
what fuels our unwillingness to be considered a mechanism. Many people
are quite willing to play a geographical game. They've given up their toes,
legs, immune system, metabolism, and retreated back into the brain—the
only place that really matters. The rest can all be mechanism, but please let
consciousness be exempt from that.

Omni: Why is Darwin's idea dangerous? For whom?   37

Dennett: It's dangerous to those who have staked everything on a   38
mind-first vision of how the universe works. It's threatening to them because
it's science—the very same science that builds the bridges they drive over
and makes possible the television they watch. That very same science, just
as objective and reliable, is showing all these processes they thought had to
have divine explanation ultimately don't.

People who've mistakenly thought ethics and morality depend on this   39
mind-first version will find the whole foundation of their sense of what life is
about overturned. That's dangerous, because it's upsetting. There's a real
conflict between that worldview and the Darwinian one. All I can say is most
of what people hold dear in the traditional worldview—and, I'd argue, everything that really matters to that worldview—is preserved in the Darwinian
view in adjusted form. There's plenty of meaning, morality, love, and hate—
everything great and important to us has a version that survives healthier
than ever.

Omni: What would be different about morality in Darwin's version?   40

Dennett: Let's take abortion. Everybody agrees you have to draw a   41
line somewhere. It's not an ideological but a practical question. The tradi-
tionalist thinks or hopes there will be a joint at which nature is carved that
will settle this issue, an essential divide. Darwin shows nature doesn't have
that kind of joint. Whatever decision we make will be to some degree arbitrary. That doesn't mean we can't have reasons for it. It's like the law that
says you can't get a driver's license till you're 16 or 18. Everybody knows it's
arbitrary, but people don't lie awake at night worrying about the injustice of
it, because they realize it's an arbitrary point. Good moral reasons exist for a
dividing line and nobody should suppose some imaginably discoverable set
of facts would do better. We'll have to do that with abortion and moral issues

such as the medical definition of death. Darwinism shows that hope for a more principled dividing line on these issues is forlorn.

Omni: Is some resistance a kind of laziness, a not wanting to do the work of deciding for ourselves? 42

Dennett: I wouldn't label it laziness so much as a distaste for what seems an unprincipled decision. They don't want to give up a view that would rule from on high. The Ten Commandments, law of Islam, Talmud, or whatever, lay it on the line. People don't relish casting adrift from those traditional anchors. Real points of confrontation are often, and maybe in most regards for good reason, glossed over. People don't want to start fights. There's been a tendency to be too tolerant of woollyheaded compatibilist thinking about evolution. It's not such a hard pill to swallow, some say. Well, it is a hard pill to swallow, but swallow it. 43

Omni: Some would see your position as atheistic. Do you describe yourself as such? 44

Dennett: I'm actually closer to a pantheist. At the end of *Darwin's Dangerous Idea* I say, look, the world itself, this unique, marvelous, fantastic thing sort of created itself ex nihilo, and that's what's sacred, right there. It isn't the atheism of "nothing's sacred"; it isn't nihilism, but by any other lights it's atheism. 45

Omni: What about some less admirable purposes to which people have put Darwin's ideas over the years—racial divisions, fascism? 46

Dennett: Social Darwinism, eugenics, Nazism . . . No question. Darwinism has inspired some pernicious, even obscene social movements and political doctrines. Then so has Platonism and Einsteinian relativity theory, though perhaps not as badly. Darwin's idea is so seductive. It's very easy to get a cheap version of it and then run off half-cocked, thinking you've got the blessings of science for one dismal misconstrued idea or another. I'm embarrassed to say I've fallen for some bad arguments, then woken up saying, My gosh, how could I have fallen for that? It's tricky stuff. These ideas seem tailor-made for enthusiasm of both the good and bad sort. People get a little Darwin under their belt, and they're off and running. 47

Omni: How can we avoid such pitfalls? 48

Dennet: First, we have to think about what matters and why. Few would agree with B. F. Skinner that the survival of culture in its present form is the end-all and be-all. Most of us would think we shouldn't even try to identify the summum bonum for all people and time. We should ask: What seems to matter the most and to go on mattering the most to most of us for as far as we can foresee? If it turns out that half a million years from now our descendants don't give a hoot for liberty, art, or love . . . well, it's good we didn't make horrendous sacrifices now that they might have liberty, art, and freedom then. It'd be hubris to suppose what matters most to us now is always going to matter most to everybody and should matter most forever. 49

Omni: Darwinian ideas don't specify values, then. It's what you do with   50
them?

Dennett: Sure, and that's a message I'm sure Gould and I agree on.   51
That's what made social Darwinism so pernicious, and what makes pop sociobiology so bad. It makes the elementary mistake of supposing that an implied value of the process that got us here is to be extrapolated into the
future.

Omni: Can Darwinian theory be useful to people in the humanities?   52

Dennett: Yes, my own semicasual survey of thinking among critics is   53
that they've all seen the wisdom of abandoning a pure Cartesian mind-first
author-first view. What's the death of the author—deconstruction—all
about? That's bread and butter to these people. They've all seen what to
flee. But my gosh, they've been all over the map about where to go from
there, so we've had a lot of dreary exaggeration of different sorts of post-
modernist, relativist baloney.

There was a time when my hunch that the truth about DNA was going   54
to turn out to be much more "deconstructionist" than its turned out to be.
Many biologists thought so too, that context must rule expression of DNA,
so there'd be very little interspecies translation possibility. Each species
would have its own DNA ideo ect its own textual tradition. But it doesn't turn
out that way. When you lift glow-in-the-dark genes from fireflies and put 'em
in plants they glow in the dark. That's an absolutely antideconstructionist
fact. It's like taking a sentence out of the Gilgamesh and putting it into a
Saul Bellow novel and it means the same thing there!

What we're learning about DNA is that although in principle there's this   55
complete contextuality, and the reader makes all the difference, in practice,
it doesn't make all the difference. There's a tremendous amount of constraint, like the cryptographer's constraint. Cryptographers have always
known that if you can find any sizable chunk of cipher text, any decoding at
all, you've found the decoding. That principle is being shown to apply in at-
tenuated form to DNA, so we find that things like the genes for "eyeness" in
Drosophila are recognizably the same as a gene in mice for their eyes. In literature we'll realize "in principle" any text can be read as any other: *Moby
Dick* is a tract on petunias—sure. Try it. It doesn't work.

Omni: Some people will complain you're forcing this Darwinian idea on   56
them, that they like their traditional worldview better.

Dennett: I'm not making up these facts or discovering them. I'm doing   57
what I can to show what the implications are and aren't. These cats are already out of the bag. It's just a question of not confusing them with other
cats people think may be out of that bag. If, when I initially thought about it,
the balance would have come out negatively, I wouldn't have written the
book. I'd have thought, this is mischief, doing damage; it's intellectual van-
dalism. On the contrary, the vision of things we hold dear is more elegant,
more real, has more detail. It's more awe-inspiring than the vision it replaces.

So people are trading up to a more adult and wonderful idea. But a lot of people don't want to be adults. Some regret the passage of childhood, and in many regards so do I. It'd be wonderful to be able to experience the world through five-year-old eyes. But people grow up, and the human race is growing up. And it's time to be grownups.   ©

CRITICAL READING

1. What are "memes," as described by British zoologist Richard Dawkins? How does this term relate to Dennett's opinions about self and soul?
2. Explain the term "quantum randomness." How does it differ from "pseudorandomness," and how do both these terms relate to theories concerning the human nervous system, in the view of Dennett?
3. What is the "goal-directed view of evolution" as explained here? Why, in Dennett's mind, is it wrong to discuss evolution as "progress"?

CLASS DISCUSSION

1. In this article, the author/interviewer situates himself clearly outside the discourse community of philosophers, with phrases like "The term 'philosophy' might conjure images of impenetrable prose and irrelevant arguments" and "Dennett's work avoids the dreary formal logic and technical jargon clogging other philosophical texts." Why does the author adopt this tone when discussing philosophy as it is currently practiced at the academy? On the basis of your experience with philosophy, discuss whether you agree or disagree with Killheffer's assessment of that particular academic discipline.
2. Dennett says, "If there's one thing I really don't like it's when a very influential, charismatic, and brilliant person engages in willful caricature of the opposition. When I see that I see red." How does this statement by Dennett characterize the theoretical debates that sometimes take place within academic discourse communities? What would be the alternative to the kinds of intellectual "mud-slinging" Dennett alludes to here?
3. Why do some people find Darwin's ideas "dangerous," in Dennett's opinion? Discuss your own feelings about Darwinian theory: what parts of it, if any, ring true for you, and what parts of it challenge your own views of the world as you conceive of it?

DIRECTED FREEWRITE

Dennett makes the assertion, "Natural selection says we're the descendants of robots, little tiny macromolecular robots, and we're composed of robots." Spend some time explaining what this statement means in light of what you know about Darwinian theory, and then let yourself explore in writing the possible implications of this notion for human life and consciousness as we know it.

COG AS A THOUGHT EXPERIMENT

Daniel C. Dennett

The two previous articles in this unit discussed the artificial intelligence philosophies and inventions of Daniel Dennett, head of the Center for Cognitive Studies at Tufts University. The first article in this unit was written in a journalistic style, and the second took the form of an introduction and interview. Here we have an article written not about Dennett, but by the philosopher himself. In the introduction to *Academic Contexts,* we promised that we'd provide not only popular readings about topics in the disciplines but also pieces not by journalists but by actual practitioners writing within their fields, primarily to other academics. You will probably find Dennett's article somewhat difficult, because it uses terms and methodologies with which you are unfamiliar, unless you're a philosophy major with a specialization in artificial intelligence. As you read, therefore, don't fret if you are unable to grasp every methodological nuance of Dennett's piece. Rather, read this article as you would read a historical novel set in Shakespeare's time: Although you might not understand every word and although you might not recognize every cultural artifact mentioned, the overall context of the piece will suggest meaning, and—in the case of Dennett's article—you will find yourself enriched for having plunged into a fascinating, if somewhat alien, intellectual milieu.

Daniel C. Dennett was born in Boston in 1942. He received his B.A. in philosophy from Harvard in 1963 and a Ph.D. in philosophy from Oxford in 1965. He's written several books including Content and Consciousness, Brainstorms, Elbow Room, The Intentional Stance, Consciousness Explained, Darwin's Dangerous Idea, Kinds of Minds, *and* Brainchildren: A Collection of Essays 1984–1996. *He is also the author of over a hundred scholarly articles on various aspects on the mind, published in journals ranging from* Artificial Intelligence *and* Behavioral and Brain Sciences *to* Poetics Today *and the* Journal of Aesthetics and Art Criticism. *He has received two Guggenheim Fellowships and a Fulbright Fellowship. Dennett was elected to the American Academy of Arts and Sciences in 1987. He was the Co-founder (in 1985) and Co-director of the Curricular Software Studio at Tufts, and has helped to design museum exhibits on computers for the Smithsonian Institution, the Museum of Science in Boston, and the Computer Museum in Boston. He is currently a Distinguished Arts and Sciences Professor of Philosophy, and Director of the Center for Cognitive Studies at Tufts University.*

In her presentation at the Monte Verità workshop, Maja Mataric   1
showed us a videotape of her robots cruising together through the lab, and

Source: "Cog as a Thought Experiment" by Daniel C. Dennett from *Robotics and Autonomous Systems,* vol. 20, June 1997. Reprinted with permission from Elsevier Science.

remarked, aptly: "They're flocking, but that's not what they think they're doing." This is a vivid instance of a phenomenon that lies at the heart of all the research I learned about at Monte Verità: the execution of surprisingly successful "cognitive" behaviors by systems that did not explicitly represent, *and did not need to explicitly represent,* what they were doing. How "high" in the intuitive scale of cognitive sophistication can such unwitting prowess reach? All the way, apparently, since I want to echo Maja's observation with one of my own: "These roboticists are doing philosophy, but that's not what they think they're doing." It is possible, then, even to do philosophy—that most intellectual of activities—without realizing that that is what you are doing. It is even possible to do it well, for this is a good, new way of addressing antique philosophical puzzles.

Then why on earth do I point this out? Why do I want to make these   2
thinkers self-conscious about their activities? Won't they thereby run the usual risks of self-consciousness: a sudden deterioration in performance, diminished spontaneity, awkward re-working of already graceful competences? Yes, I might unleash monsters: roboticists who fancy themselves philosophers—an ugly prospect! But an underappreciated fact—underappreciated by this "intelligence without representation" gang—is that *sometimes* the deliberate and accurate representation, and even rerepresentation, of one's activities does yield huge increments in competence, in comprehension. I think the gains are worth the risks, but then I would; I'm a philosopher. In what follows, I will address those who engage in this research directly, rather than speaking about their work in the third person, since what I am offering is not just disinterested commentary, but advice—take it or leave it.

Why do I say you're doing philosophy? Because both your topics and   3
your methods are those of philosophy—except where they are improvements thereon. Topics first. You are asking *very* abstract, general questions about the conditions under which perception, action, intelligence, and yes, even consciousness, can emerge in the world. This is a point that is often noted in passing by people in AI or ALife: by looking at deliberately simplified and artificial cases, you get to explore the fundamental requirements, the minimal conditions under which various necessary components of cognition can be obtained.

As for methods, you share with philosophy and traditional AI a funda-   4
mental reliance on thought experiments. In fact, one might say that the whole field consists of nothing but thought experiments. Not "regular" experiments? What about all the data-gathering on your robots' behaviors? Do mere thought experiments ever yield graphs? The key difference is that when the data don't come out the way you expected, you get to tinker with the robots, tuning them into conformity with the point you were setting out to demonstrate. The improvement over traditional, philosophical methods is that your thought experiments are prosthetically controlled and enhanced by the requirement that you actually make your models and demonstrate their

competences. In philosophers' thought experiments, the sun always shines, the batteries never go dead, and the actors and props always do exactly what the philosophers' theories expect them to do. There are no surprises for the creators of the thought experiments, only for their audience or targets. As Ronald de Sousa has memorably said, much of philosophy is "intellectual tennis without a net." Your thought experiments have nets, but they are of variable height. "Proof of concept" is usually all you strive for, though sometimes that's all you get even though you are striving for more.

Don't change! I think that the tactic of varying the degree of difficulty, 5 the degree of ambitiousness, of your demonstrations until you can find a feat that you can get to work is a perfectly acceptable practice. It is not "unprincipled"; it is shrewd, resourceful, opportunistic in a good sense. But outsiders often have difficulty seeing this. Workers in more traditional fields are dubious of demos that seem to help themselves at every turning to whatever simplifications are imposed on the demonstrator by the hard realities of practice. But how else are we going to find paths through this foggy world of cognition? The abstemious routes (one neuron at a time, or one rat at a time, or one day of field observations at a time, or . . .) are myopic, slow-motion trudges that are manifestly in need of some guidance and inspiration from high-flying scouts who are willing to live dangerously. At the same time, the advice I give to my philosopher colleagues and students is that they ought to consider flying at a somewhat lower altitude, taking on some of the problems of implementation, some of the real-world difficulties that you address. Their speculations are too easy, too unconstrained, too abstract to be trustworthy. The way to find the right level is to do some floating and see what works.

Traditional philosophical methodology does offer one practice that is 6 not very apparent in your work, and might be, on occasion, a major corrective to your ways of thinking: historical scholarship. In the "hard" sciences, cumulative progress more or less obviates the need for contemporary students to have a detailed knowledge of the history of their field. There are historians of mathematics, physics, or chemistry who will dispute this vigorously, but they have a hard sell. Does today's biochemist really need to retrace the stumbling steps of the alchemists of yore, or re-create the long and arduous path of specific arguments that unified organic and inorganic chemistry? Aside from the sheer drama of it, does today's gene sequencer need to have an accurate knowledge of just how Crick and Watson reasoned their way beyond the confusions of their day about the chemistry of the vehicles of heredity? But in philosophy, to move to the other extreme, the only discernible dimension of progress is the replacement of one set of mistakes by another: thanks to our appreciation of the works of Plato, Aristotle. Descartes, Kant, etc., we don't make *their* mistakes any more—or at least not all of them. But since those philosophers were not dummies, their mistakes were not obvious, and are typically still enticing to the uninitiated, because they concern questions that are still non-routine, still unclear. These perennially tempting bad ideas are, you might say, slop basins of attraction that continue to exert their pull. The only way to protect yourself from these tempting errors is to study them in situ. Or get a good philosopher to explain them to you, in terms you can appreciate. You might like to supplement your current methods, then, with a little traditional philosophical investigation—reading a few books and articles, for instance—but not all that many.

One contribution of philosophy to an enterprise like this is simply to put   7
your questions in the larger context of human curiosity, both lay and professional. For instance, in his 1995 course notes, Rolf Pfeifer announces: "Our main goal is to relate behavior to internal mechanisms," which is fine, of course, but many bystanders are going to say, "Behavior is all very well, but what about consciousness? Where does that come in?" It is worth remembering that to the average layperson, "conscious robot" is an oxymoron, a contradiction in terms. They are supremely confident that no mere "automaton" will ever be conscious. Meanwhile, our professional colleagues in cognitive science want to see more cognitive behaviors than mere phototaxis and herding, as Phil Husbands said in his presentation. They recognize that one must start with something simple, but they are skeptical that "more of the same" will ever add up to the sorts of cognitive competences they study from a more top-down perspective. Putting these two sorts of curiosity together, we can join our bystanders in wondering if there is a distinction between mere "sentience" on the one hand and fancier cognition (and human-style consciousness) on the other, and we may also want to address and question of whether even simple sentience is beyond our current models.

Fig. 1 shows a putative table of increasing sophistication, with natural   8
entities lined up opposite their artificial counterparts, starting with parts-of-agents (transducers, pseudo- or micro-agents) and arriving via paths of increasing complexity and sophistication of both living and non-living agents at the (current) summit: Cog on the left and conscious human beings on the right. If we grant that all these entities, on both the artificial and natural side of the ledger, are equipped with varying degrees of *sensitivity,* we may ask whether some distinct phenomenon, *sentience,* makes its appearance somewhere on this trajectory, and if so, at what level of sophistication? Concentrate first on the right hand, natural side: Surely a cone cell in the retina is not sentient all by itself, whatever sentience is, nor is the vestibular ocular reflex machinery or the immune system or the temperature-maintenance system. And moving to whole agents, are jellyfish sentient, or are they merely sensitive and adaptive? And plants? Perhaps most people would reserve sentience for animals somewhere higher up the complexity ladder (fish yes, insects maybe—that sort of thing). If naive intuition puts the emergence of sentience fairly high up on this scale, it is no wonder that few if any observers are comfortable with the claim that any existing robots on the left

From "mere sensitivity" to consciousness?	
artificial	*natural*
transducers	
bimetallic spring	rhodopsin molecule
photocell	cone cell
pseudo- (or micro-) agents	
thermostat	temperature maint. syst.
camera	VOR, vergence control, etc.
agents	
"robocteria"	bacteria, spermatazoa, . . .
"animats"	amoebas, jellyfish, . . .
. . . ?	plants?
. . . ?	fish, reptiles, . . .
. . . ?	birds, mammals, . . .
Cog	people

Fig. 1.

exhibit sentience (let alone consciousness), since for all their cleverness, they are surely at or below the level of unicellular organisms in their sophistication. We should not be bound by naive intuition, however, or feel particularly obligated to answer the questions posed on its behalf. We do well to recognize, nevertheless, that this is the mindset of the onlookers, and if we are misunderstood in our pronouncements, it may well be because we haven't taken that mindset into account.

What is sentience? In my new book, *Kinds of Minds,* 1996, I argue that   9
the widely shared idea that *there is* a basic, animal sort of consciousness ("sentience") which some animals have and plants lack is an illusion, but it is undeniable that naive intuition suggests that sentience is something more than sensitivity, that

$$\text{sentience} = \text{sensitivity} + X.$$

And what is *X?* Are we leaving something out on the left-hand side? Rod Brooks spoke, amusingly, of "the Juice." We might well suspect, with Brooks, that we haven't got the Juice *yet,* but I gather we would also all declare that as far as we can see, we don't need any radically new breakthroughs (quantum gravity, psi-forces, morphic resonances, *élan vital,* ectoplasm) to add the Juice, or *X,* at some later stage. How will we ever test our common conviction? We shouldn't be impatient for a "scientific proof," but if we want some sanity checks along the way. Cog is a project that ought to provide insights, if not an outright answer, by attempting to model at the highest level (on the pretheoretical, intuitive scale of Fig. 1).

We want the behaviors (internal and external) exhibited by Cog to par-   10
allel those of a human infant, and eventually of course, an adult. We want

first proto-language and later language to crown our efforts; we want Cog to manifest curiosity, insight, fear, hope, pleasure, comprehension, friendship, . . . the works. Also we want to do this by building Cog out of "more of the same," proceeding just as evolution has proceeded, piling complexity on complexity. Cog must be always a going bodily concern, in which the particularly human competences—and tell-tale pathologies—can *emerge* from the interaction of all this new growth. We would love to see Cog exhibit paranoia or left neglect or obsessive-compulsive disorder as a result of a naturally arising imbalance or breakdown. Other pathological symptom clusters would not be welcome: for instance, coma, or autism.

Autism is a particularly automaton-like condition, as the term suggests, 11 so providing Cog with the wherewithal to avoid autism, to establish and maintain normal contact with human beings, is an important priority. How should we do it? By installing what Alan Leslie has called a TOMM or Theory of Mind Mechanism? This can be understood in a strong or a vacuous sense. In the vacuous sense, the TOMM is simply whatever features of Cog's brain prevent Cog from being autistic; in the strong sense, it suggests a Fodorian "module," a GOFAI organ equipped with axioms of belief and desire expressed with the use of multi-place predicates, a theorem-prover, and capable of deriving predictions along these lines:

Bel_{ego} {the candy is in the box}
Bel_{ego} {Bel_x [the candy is in the jar]}
Bel_{ego} {Des_x [that x obtain the candy]}

ergo:

Bel_{ego} {x *will look in the jar*}

Adding a GOFAI "module" of this sort at Cog's "summit" to handle what George Bush might call the vision thing is literally the last thing the Cog team would do. The GOFAI methodology, and GOFAI structures, are just too brittle, too unbiological. They are wrong as process models even if they are sometimes valuable ways of characterizing the competence (under idealized conditions). If we want to build a TOMM in the evolutionary, behavior-based spirit shared by the Monte Verità participants, how might we proceed? A few steps can be seen. Consider Elaine Morgan's comment:

> The heart-stopping thing about the new-born is that, from
> minute one, there is somebody there. Anyone who bends
> over the cot and gazes at it is being gazed back at.

As an observation about how we human observers instinctively react 12 to eye contact, this is right on target, but it thereby shows that we can be easily misled. Cog's video camera eyes, unseeing as they still are, will saccade to focus on a newly arrived person who enters the room, and then track that person as he or she moves. Being tracked in this way is an oddly unsettling experience even for those in the know. Also staring into Cog's eyes while Cog stares mindlessly back can be quite "heart-stopping" to the uninitiated. Not surprisingly, this natural—indeed involuntary—tendency to draw the conclusion that "there is somebody there" has, in the natural world, a powerful element of truth. A built-in capacity for good gaze monitoring is a natural enabler of (not quite a logical prerequisite for) *unthinking* second-order intentionality, of the sort exhibited by piping plovers when they lead the predator away from the vulnerable nest by feigning injury. Gaze monitoring is also a natural enabler of *shared attention,* which in turn plays a crucial role, as Baron-Cohen shows, in developing language and other interpersonal skills. (I have begun collecting observations on eye contact from primatologists and ethologists. They note a striking difference between, for instance, the great apes and all other primates. To what extent does this explain only our *intuitive sense of greater kinship*—that "there is somebody there" inside the chimpanzee-suit—and to what extent does it mark a theoretically important difference? If and when Cog's eye-contact and gaze-monitoring skills are put to work in creating higher levels of shared understanding between Cog and its human companions we will surely get a better grip on this question.

I have argued that linguistic skills, especially their proto-versions in   13
such phenomena as infant babbling and semi-understood self-commentary (self-admonition, self-description) probably play a crucial role in permitting the infant brain to develop skill at "labeling" and then "manipulating" some of its own internal representations, representations that had heretofore been "embedded" in the sorts of computational architectures that are fine for insects and simple animals (and human infants), but not for mature human cognition. Alan Turing, as so often before, points to one of the keys to progress: "If the untrained infant's mind is to become an intelligent one, it must acquire both discipline and initiative." The initiative must be an outgrowth of Cog's innate curiosity (or what I call epistemic hunger, which is trivially present in transducers, but must be an active feature of larger sub-systems), while the discipline Turing speaks of comes, I suspect, as a byproduct of the talents for speaking and listening, to oneself and others. That is a contentious claim much in need of further defense and investigation.   ©

CRITICAL READING

1. Dennett says that roboticists' "topics and methods" are "those of philosophy." Explain what he means by the topics and methods of philosophy, and the ways that roboticists' ideas and practices resemble those of philosophers.
2. Explain the meanings suggested by the figure labeled "From 'mere sensitivity' to consciousness?" What does ending the figure's title with a question mark tell

you about the nature of Dennett's research—and about much of the research being undertaken in this field?

3. Even if you aren't a math major, you can probably explain the meaning of the equation "sentience = sensitivity + X." What is the quality to which Dennett humorously refers as "the Juice"?

CLASS DISCUSSION

1. How would you characterize the tone of Dennett's article? Who comprise his audience? If you find that Dennett deviates from standard academic writing practices in certain ways, what reasons might he have for doing this?

2. How do robotic experiments represent an "improvement over traditional, philosophic methods," in the view of Dennett? Do you think he is being completely serious when he makes such a claim? Why, or why not?

DIRECTED FREEWRITE

1. Write for a while on the following questions: How are roboticists "doing philosophy," even though they don't know that they're doing philosophy, in the view of Dennett? What does it mean to "do philosophy" in the field of artificial intelligence, as you have read in this unit?

2. Imagine you're Cog, the fruit of many artificial intelligence researchers' extensive theorizing and mechanical tinkering. What do you think about yourself and your "life," if anything? What do you want to do with your "life"? What do you want to say to Dennett and his colleagues? As much as possible, let your writing reflect the ways in which Cog might actually "think."

PHILOSOPHY UNIT WRITING ASSIGNMENTS

1. Write a summary of Wright's essay. Start your summary with a short, objective introduction to the topic engaged by Wright, and state the author's main point, or his thesis, in your introduction. In the summary that follows, recount what you take to be the key points of Wright's essay, rephrasing them in your own words and clearly indicating how these key points relate to Wright's thesis. Imagine that your reader is a peer, is not a philosophy major, and has not read Wright's essay; thus, since all that the reader will ever know about these ideas will come from you, you may need to simplify and provide explanations for some of the more difficult concepts and terminology that Wright discusses. When the reader has finished reading your summary, he or she should have a thorough understanding of the ideas Wright deals with.

For a more detailed discussion of summary, see item 1 of the Writing Assignments at the end of the Neuroscience unit of this chapter.

2. The activity of synthesizing different points of view is central to a number of different kinds of academic writing. For example, comparison/contrast essays embody the most basic form of synthesis: you are putting together two different

points of view or sets of information, usually in order to arrive at a conclusion—perhaps about which point of view is most credible, or how the two points of view could be combined, or what kinds of solutions to problems are suggested by one or both points of view. The important point here is that regardless of the conclusion reached, compare and contrast is usually done for some purpose, even if you have written compare and contrast essays in English classes that seemed to serve no other purpose than performing an academic exercise. The exercise alone is worthwhile, since most academic research relying on secondary sources involves synthesizing many more than two viewpoints; therefore, this is a skill that once mastered (or at least practiced extensively) will translate to any number of research-based assignments you will encounter as you move into more advanced courses.

This particular synthesis activity asks you to explore the relationship between two views of conciousness—one contained in a science fiction movie and the other being a philosophical position. Watch the science fiction movie *Dark City,* which is available on video. As you watch, take notes about what the movie has to say about human souls/consciousness and about what our "humanness" is composed of. Then write an essay in which you compare and contrast the movie's take on the issue to either the materialist or the mysterian views of consciousness, as these are described in the readings of this unit.

The kinds of prewriting techniques we outlined in the introduction to *Academic Contexts* provided groundwork for synthesizing related materials. Clustering, listing, and outlining are efficient and painless tools that can help you discover the relationships between certain authors' ideas, opinions, presented data, and your own reaction to these things as you view and/or read them. Reread the essays in this unit, and sketch out the characteristics of each school of thought—materialist and mysterian. Then compare these positions with what you noted about the movie and its vision of consciousness, deciding which viewpoint from the readings provides the most interesting comparisons and contrasts. Use this process then to devise a rough working thesis, perhaps one that notes the central points of comparison and contrast, and what these then lead you to conclude about theories of consciousness.

3. Dialogue has a venerable history in the field of philosophy, dating back at least as far as the ancient Greek philosophers Socrates and Plato. For example, Plato's *Republic,* wherein he lays out criteria for what he views as an ideal society, is written as a discussion between Socrates and others. While Socrates expounds on certain characteristics of the imagined society, his listeners question him and thus prod his further elucidation of ideas. Discussion or dialogue (dialogue usually means that two people are engaged in communication; discussion would include more than two) are useful ways of both working out complex ideas, as well as representing them. Although the dialogue is not a common mode of writing, and you may never be asked to write such a thing, the skills involved in constructing your dialogue in this assignment are useful for all other types of writing. You will draw on your critical reading and summarizing skills first in

understanding, and then in representing, sometimes complex points from the readings; you will be performing the strategy of comparison and contrast; and you will be practicing skills of argumentation, and in the oral context wherein the art of persuasion (classical rhetoric) first developed.

Write an imagined dialogue between two individuals who are exploring questions of human consciousness. While we would like you to position each individual in your dialogue as adhering to a particular and opposed theoretical camp, imagine that your discussants are not trained philosophers but instead are educated individuals who have no particular expertise in these matters but who nonetheless have ideas about these issues. Imagine that one of the discussants leans toward believing in the materialist view of mind and consciousness—the viewpoint of Daniel Dennett—and the other aligns herself with the "new mysterian" camp, as represented by David Chalmers's ideas in Wright's article. Imagine each individual as attempting to explain his or her own perspective as well as critiquing the other's viewpoint. You can decide how firmly you wish your characters to hold their beliefs; the opposition between these individuals could remain intact throughout the discussion, or one or both of the individuals could end up questioning and/or even rejecting the original position held. Use information from any or all of the readings in this unit to help flesh out each position, remembering to represent some of the points in terms that are simpler than those used in the articles, especially in the Kilheffer and Dennett pieces. This assignment, as alluded to before, will utilize your skills of summary and of comparison and contrast (a form of synthesis). Your prewriting should involve summarizing—and simplifying—the features of the different positions, and then comparing and contrasting them. The points of agreement and disagreement between the two perspectives will help you proceed to a first draft of your discussion; isolate the key points on which you will focus, and use these to form the basis of your essay.

Alternatively, you could formulate your own position on consciousness, such as one that includes the theological concept of spirit, and write a discussion between a person taking that position, and either a materialist or a new mysterian.

Unit 2

Art History—Frida Kahlo and Artistic Identity

Frida Kahlo Self-Portraits

MY NURSE AND I, **1937**
THE TWO FRIDAS, **1939**
HENRY FORD HOSPITAL, **1932**

My Nurse and I, 1937.
Oil on sheet metal, 12 × 13⅝ in. Collection, Fundacion Dolores Olmedo, Mexico

The Two Fridas, 1939
Oil on canvas, $68\frac{1}{8} \times 68\frac{1}{8}$ in. Collection, Instittuto Nacional de Bellas Artes, Museo de Arte Moderno, Mexico

Henry Ford Hospital, 1932
Oil on sheet metal, 12 × 15 in. Collection, Fundacion Dolores Olmedo, Mexico

DIRECTED FREEWRITE

Before tackling the readings on Frida Kahlo's work, freewrite your own response to these paintings. First, discuss what you like and/or don't like about them. What overall meanings seem to be conveyed in each individual painting? Do you notice any recurring images or themes in these paintings? If so, discuss how images are used in each painting. How different are the paintings from one another? Do you get an overall impression of Frida Kahlo's sense of her identity? If so, try to describe what she might be saying about herself.

EXCERPTS FROM *FRIDA KAHLO: THE BRUSH OF ANGUISH*

Martha Zamora

In this biographical piece, Zamora outlines the major events in Kahlo's life, a life that is marked by physical illness and a sense of loneliness interrupted at times by passionate—and often painful—relationships with others. As you read, think about the ways in which the events recorded by Zamora seem present in the paintings with which we opened this unit.

Martha Zamora is currently a resident of Palo Alto but she has also lived for many years in Mexico, South America, and Europe. She has written and spoken extensively on Kahlo's life and work. Zamora is an authority on the San Francisco murals of Diego Rivera and is currently writing a guidebook about them. She has written and edited several books on Frida Kahlo including The Letters of Frida Kahlo: Cartas Apasionadas, Frida Kahlo: 'I Painted My Own Reality' *and* Frida Kahlo: The Brush of Anguish *from which this passage is taken.*

THE BEGINNING

Rain in the morning in Coyoacán, for her birth as well as her death. 1 Magdalena Carmen Frida Kahlo Calderón came into the world on the sixth of July, 1907, maybe in the family home, the Casa Azul, as she always claimed, maybe down the street at her grandmother's house, as shown in the official registry of her birth.

An hour by streetcar from Mexico City, Coyoacán was surrounded by flat, 2 open land, cornfields, and ranches. Frida absorbed the history and habits of every corner of the village; she explored its river, markets, churches, and plazas. She knew when the street markets and neighborhood fairs would be held, which street vendors sold the best quesadillas, and where to buy the most amusing toys. She spent hours strolling the streets with her friends, talking to merchants and shoeshine boys, and roaming the verdant parks and gardens.

The Casa Azul, a rambling, blue structure in colonial style, was built by 3 Guillermo Kahlo a few years before Frida's birth. Tall, shuttered windows opened to the street, and within, a series of interconnected rooms surrounded a large inner patio. Frida's part-Indian mother, Matilde Calderón, a rigidly conventional woman, was a meticulous housekeeper and a devout Catholic. She frequently took communion, went to confession, and said the rosary in the late afternoon with relatives and friends. She chose not to raise

Source: Excerpted from *Frida Kahlo: The Brush of Anguish* by Martha Zamora. Reprinted by permission of Chronicle Books.

her husband's two daughters by a previous marriage, sending them off to live in a convent orphanage. Her relationship with her own four daughters was strained as well; the oldest two married and left home at very young ages. By the time Frida was in her teens, her mother was in poor health and struggling with the family's finances. Although Matilde Calderón's letters prove otherwise, Frida once said with irony that her mother couldn't read or write, but she certainly could count money. [. . .]

At about this time Frida announced to friends, "You don't know what I would give to have a child by Diego Rivera." Her fellow students were stupefied, for despite their admiration for his talent as a painter, they saw him as a fat, untidy, bulging-eyed married man. Rivera was then working on his frescoes at the school, and Frida subjected him to her tricks. Once she soaped the school steps, hoping to make him slip and fall; other times she teased his wife, Lupe Marín, about other women in Diego's life. 4

Frida fell in love, however, with the charismatic leader of the Cachuchas, Alejandro Gómez Arias, an intelligent, attractive, well-mannered young man of a good family. "We were very good friends all our lives; we were more than sweethearts but never had wedding plans or anything like that, because we were still very young," Gómez Arias has said. Frida's ardent correspondence with Alejandro reveals her maturation from a young girl into a woman. Years later she said, "For me, Alex ignited love, the ambition to know, to know it all." 5

Frida's precocious behavior worried her parents. Societal restraints on women were severe, and even the concept of coeducation was upsetting to the families of proper young ladies. But Frida enjoyed flouting the rules, whether by a small transgression like wearing bobby socks, prohibited by the school dress code, or by a deviation as extreme as a sexual adventure with an older woman. This affair and other relationships not only scandalized her family but caused Frida to be ostracized by many of her schoolmates. Her passionate temperament had little respect for limitations, and Frida was not ashamed of her blossoming sexuality. She wrote to Gómez Arias: "I don't care. I like myself the way I am." 6

Guillermo Kahlo's business began to flounder while Frida was attending the Prepa, and as his financial situation worsened, he was forced to mortgage the Casa Azul. In order to help out, Frida enrolled in a business school in 1925 and learned to type. Her first jobs in a pharmacy and lumber yard office were unsuccessful, but eventually she was employed as an apprentice in an engraving studio. 7

That same year, on September 17, Frida and Alejandro spent the afternoon wandering among the colorful street stalls set up for Mexican National Day celebrations. On boarding a train to return to Coyocán, Frida discovered that she had lost a little toy parasol Alejandro had just bought for her. They retraced their steps, and when it couldn't be found, they bought a *balero,* a cup-and-ball. 8

A bus happened by, a brightly painted new one with two long benches   9
along the sides. Frida and Alejandro felt lucky to catch it. The driver, rushing
to cross the busy city on the way out of town, boldly tried to pass in front of a
turning streetcar. He didn't succeed: the heavy streetcar moved forward and
collided with the bus, pushing relentlessly into its side and pressing against
the benches where the passengers sat.

Gómez Arias still marvels at the elasticity of the vehicle, remembering   10
that he felt his knees pressing against those of the person sitting across
from him, just before the bus shattered to pieces. He regained consciousness underneath the streetcar, with the darkness of the metal chassis above
him and a terrible fear that it would continue moving and mangle him. When
he was able to sit up, he noticed that the front of his coat had somehow disappeared. He set out to find Frida.

At the moment of the accident, Frida was more concerned about the   11
loss of her new toy, which had flown out of her hand, then she was with the
seriousness of the collision. Alejandro found her bathed in blood, without
her clothes, virtually impaled on the rod of a metal handrail. A bag carried by
a passenger had spilled gold powder all over, and Frida's bloodied body
was sprinkled with it. Curious onlookers cried, "Help for the little ballerina!"

An overall-clad worker, whom Alejandro thought he recognized as an   12
employee of the Prepa, looked at Frida and said, "That has to be taken out
of her." With no more ado he pulled the metal rod out of Frida's body to the
terrible sound of breaking bones. Alejandro, horrified, carried her to a pool
hall across the street, put her on a table, and covered her with the shreds of
his ruined coat. They waited for an ambulance as Frida screamed in pain.

The wounded victims were taken to a nearby Red Cross hospital and   13
divided into two groups: those who would receive immediate medical attention and those who, because of their grave condition, were considered beyond help. Frida was placed in the second group, and only after the shaken
Alejandro pleaded with doctors, begging them to help, did they attend her.

A description of the wounds Frida suffered in the accident was com-   14
piled by her doctor in a clinical history years later: "Fracture of the third and
fourth lumbar vertebrae; pelvic fractures; fracture of the right foot; dislocation of the left elbow; deep abdominal wound produced by a metal rod entering through the left hip and exiting through the genitals. Acute peritonitis;
cystitis with drainage for several days." In other versions Frida added in-
juries, such as fractures of a cervical vertebra and two ribs, eleven fractures
in the right leg, and dislocation of the left shoulder.

Frida always maintained that the metal rod pierced her uterus and   15
emerged through her vagina. "[That's when] I lost my virginity," she said.
Gómez Arias says that "the wound was much higher up and hit the pelvic
bone; the invention of the point of exit was to hide other things." She would
also identify the accident as the cause of her inability to bear children, but it
was only one of her many explanations for that condition.

Frida told Alejandro, "In this hospital, death dances around my bed at night." But Frida's youth and characteristic vitality pulled her through. She was able to return home after a month, although she was almost completely immobilized by splints protecting her various fractures. Friends from school visited her frequently at first, but the long distance to her home in Coyocán eventually discouraged regular visits; she began to feel out of touch. Although her health might have allowed it, Frida never resumed her studies. 16

In June 1927 she wrote, "Monday, they're going to change my cast for the third time, this time to keep me immobilized without being able to walk for two or three months, until my spine knits together perfectly, and I don't know if afterwards they'll have to operate on me. . . . Every day I'm skinnier, and when you come back, you're really going to be in for a shock when you see how horrible I am with this dreadful apparatus. Afterward, I'm going to be a thousand times worse, so you can just imagine: after having been lying down for a month (the way you left me) and another month with two different devices, and now another two months flat on my back put in a coating of plaster, then six months again with the lighter apparatus so I can walk. . . . Is that enough to drive a person crazy, or not?" 17

On September 9, 1927, she noted, "On the seventeenth it will be two years since our tragedy. For sure I certainly will remember it terribly well, although it's stupid, isn't it? I haven't painted anything new (and won't), until you come back. . . . I've suffered terribly, and I'm almost neurotic, and I've let myself become such an ignoramus, I'm totally demoralized." And eight days later: "I'm still very sick and almost without any hope. As always, nobody believes it. Today is the seventeenth of September, the worst day of all because I'm alone." 18

Among the vague diagnoses and suggested treatments mentioned in Frida's letters were thermocauterization, an operation to graft a piece of bone from her leg, the discovery of a lesion on her sciatic nerve, and constant changes of immobilizing corsets in different materials. Undoubtedly her recovery and moods were affected by the household gloom dictated by her parents' poor health and the family's precarious economic situation. The Casa Azul was still mortgaged, and at one point all the fine furnishings had to be auctioned off. Her mother's daily bad humor coupled with her father's misanthropic behavior caused her to describe her home as "one of the saddest I have ever seen." 19

A Prepa friend who remained close to Frida during her recuperation was Germán de Campo. A man of ardent political convictions, he was a major influence on the ideologically leftist road she took then and maintained all her life. De Campo introduced Frida to the weekly salons of painters, writers, photographers, and intellectuals held by Tina Modotti, the strikingly beautiful Italian who had come to Mexico from the United States with photographer Edward Weston. Modotti, an outstanding photographer herself and Weston's protégé, worked for the muralists and was not only a 20 model for Diego Rivera but probably the reason he separated at that time from his wife, Lupe Marín.

Frida admired Modotti above all for her political militancy and the prac- 21
tical way she applied the strength of her convictions to her daily actions. Modotti apparently sponsored Frida's entry into the Communist party. Her hair now cut very short and styled close to her head, Frida no longer wore the white blouse of her student days, but was more apt to be seen in the distinctive red shirt of the party. (A Rivera mural, *Distributing Arms,* in Mexico City's Ministry of Public Education, portrays both Modotti and a red-shirt-clad Frida.)

One account suggests that Frida renewed her acquaintance with 22
Diego Rivera at a Modotti soiree where he impressed her with a show of flamboyant behavior, using a pistol to shoot a phonograph. Frida told another story in an interview with the Mexican journalist Bambi:

"I took four little pictures to Diego who was painting up on the scaffolds 23
at the Ministry of Public Education. Without hesitating a moment I said to him, 'Diego, come down,' and so, since he is so humble, so agreeable, he came down. 'Look, I didn't come to flirt with you or anything, even though you are a womanizer, I came to show you my painting. If it interests you, tell me so, if it doesn't interest you, tell me that too, so I can get to work on something else to help out my parents.' He told me, 'Look, I'm very much interested in your painting, especially this self-portrait which is the most original. The other three seem to me to be influenced by what you've seen. Go on home, paint a picture, and next Sunday, I'll come to see it and tell you.' So I did, and he said, 'You have talent.'"

Diego told biographer Gladys March a similar story, adding that when 24
he learned that the young woman who had sought his opinion of her paintings was Frida Kahlo, he immediately remembered the little girl who long ago had taunted his wife Lupe Marín in the halls of the Prepa and had been such a troublesome youngster to the school authorities.

True to his word, Rivera came to call on that Sunday, and many oth- 25
ers. Frida became "the most important thing in my life," he said, and on August 21, 1929, they were married in the historic town hall of Coyocán.

THE OTHER ACCIDENT

"When I was seventeen, Diego began to fall in love with me," Frida 26
once explained to a journalist (subtracting three years from her age). "My father didn't like him because he was a Communist and because they said he looked like a fat, fat, fat Breughel. They said it was like an elephant marrying a dove. Nevertheless, I arranged everything in the Coyocán town hall for us to be married on the twenty-first of August, 1929." To a friend, Frida said, "I have suffered two serious accidents in my life, one in which a street car ran over me. . . . The other accident is Diego."

It was Diego Rivera's first legal marriage, although there had been 27
many women in his life and two other long-term relationships. The Russian
artist Angelina Beloff lived with him as his common-law wife for ten years in
Paris during the 1910s; she bore him a son, who died at an early age. Another lover, Marievna Vorobiev-Stebelska, also had a child by him, a daughter, whom he did not acknowledge as his own for many years. In 1922 in a
church ceremony, Diego married the beautiful Mexican Lupe Marín, with
whom he had two daughters. According to Mexican law, which required a
civil ceremony, this union was not legal, but it was considered a serious
commitment by the couple. However, a divorce was not necessary when
Diego decided to marry Frida.

"I borrowed petticoats, a blouse, and a rebozo from the maid, fixed the 28
special apparatus on my foot so it wouldn't be noticeable, and we were married. Nobody went to the wedding, only my father, who said to Diego, 'Now,
look, my daughter is a sick person and all her life she's going to be sick.
She's intelligent but not pretty. Think it over awhile if you like, and if you still
wish to marry her, marry her, I give you my permission.'" According to
Diego, Frida's father added he rightfully had to warn him that she was *un
demonio,* a devil.

"Then they gave us a big party in Roberto Montenegro's house. Diego 29
got horrendously drunk on tequila, waved his pistol about, broke some
man's little finger, and destroyed some other things. Afterward, we got mad
at each other; I left crying and went home. A few days went by and Diego
came to get me and took me to his house at 104 Reforma."

Tina Modotti wrote to Edward Weston in September 1929: "Had I not 30
told you Diego had gotten married? I intended to. A lovely nineteen-year-old
girl, of German father and Mexican mother; a painter herself." Modotti added
in Spanish, "A ver que sale!" (Let's see how it works out!)

Many others were struck by the incongruity of the petite, young Frida 31
marrying the overweight, middle-aged artist. When her school friends heard
about her marriage, they were shocked and surprised, considering it *una
cosa monstruosa,* a hideous thing. But Frida was the last unmarried daughter of ill parents in sad financial straits. Her decision had pragmatic as well
as romantic repercussions; in fact, Diego paid off the mortgage on her parents' home.

Certainly the striking pair's marriage, reported widely in the interna- 32
tional press, offered Frida an opportunity to move not only in Mexican but
leading European and American artistic and intellectual circles; she relished
the contacts she made and the attention she received as the wife of a famous artist. But perhaps ultimately she was attracted by an attribute described by each of Diego's previous companions, his dynamism, by which
he vitalized everything and everyone who came near him. He was possessed of a great and genuine warmth along with a capacity for charmingly
tender gestures.

Frida began her married life in Diego's house in the first block of Mex-   33
ico City's Avenida Reforma. In an interview she said, "For furniture we had a
narrow bed, a dining set that Frances Toor (editor of *Mexican Folkways*)
gave us with a long black table, and a little yellow kitchen table that my
mother gave us. We arranged it out of the way in one corner for the collection of archaeological pieces. We couldn't have a child, and I cried incon-
solably, but I distracted myself fixing meals, cleaning house, painting at
times, and going along with Diego each day to the scaffolds. He really liked
me to come along bringing his lunch in a basket covered with flowers."

Hospitably, if unpredictably, Diego's ex-wife Lupe Marín took the   34
young newlywed under her wing, going with her to buy pots and pans and
kitchen things, then teaching her to prepare Diego's favorite dishes. Frida
painted Lupe's portrait as a gift in thanks for the cooking lessons.

Shortly after their marriage, the couple moved to Cuernavaca, where   35
Diego had been commissioned by U.S. Ambassador Dwight W. Morrow to
paint a mural in the historic colonial palace of Hernan Cortés. While Diego
tackled long work days, Frida passed the time visiting neighboring villages
with a friend, Luis Cardoza y Aragón, who was living with them. He remem-
bers with affection, "Frida was what she always was, a marvelous woman.
There was a spark in her that was growing and beginning to light up her
canvases, to light up her life and, in turn, the lives of others."

In the fall of 1930, Frida for the first time traveled out of Mexico. She   36
and Diego went to San Francisco, where he had commissions to paint two
murals. While he worked on the scaffolds at the Pacific Stock Exchange
Luncheon Club and the California School of Fine Arts (now the San Francisco Art Institute), she explored the streets of Chinatown and the North
Beach area near their studio living quarters. She visited with the wives of his
assistants and other artists they knew. Together they often played "Exquisite Cadavers," drawing by turns on a piece of paper folded in equal sections,
each player inventing a part of the human body without knowing what had
been drawn by the preceding person. When the paper was unfolded, the hi-
larious result was revealed, to which Frida always added the most erotic
and audacious details.

In San Francisco Frida and Diego attracted the attention not only of   37
artist friends but of wealthy art patrons and prominent business figures, beginning the torrent of adulation, praise, and later, controversy that would accompany Diego throughout his U.S. visit. They made a dramatic couple: the
dark and slender beauty in long Mexican dress with her elaborate jewelry,
the genial, towering fat man in rumpled suit and broad-brimmed hat. The
press loved them, and newspaper coverage was extensive wherever they
went.

Meanwhile, Frida was sketching and making pictures of herself and of   38
friends. She painted a double portrait of herself and Diego for Albert Bender,
an influential businessman and philanthropist who had intervened with the

State Department to get Diego an entry visa in spite of his Communist ties; he also helped them financially by purchasing Diego's work and by encouraging friends to do so. In one corner of the double portrait, using a motif from Mexican folk art, Frida painted on a ribbon held in the beak of a dove, "Here you see us, I, Frida Kahlo, with my adored husband. I painted these portraits in the beautiful city of San Francisco, California, for our friend, Mr. Albert Bender, and it was in the month of April in the year 1931."

During the six months they spent in San Francisco, Frida was briefly 39 hospitalized for a problem with her foot. Her physician, Dr. Leo Eloesser, became a lifelong friend and adviser. She painted *Portrait of Dr. Leo Eloesser* for him in thanks and perhaps as compensation.

After a short trip to Mexico in the summer of 1931, the Riveras re- 40 turned to the United States, this time to New York for a major exhibition of Diego's work at the Museum of Modern Art, only the second one-person show held there. Once again the center of attention, Diego and Frida were feted by New York's business and art elite, including John D. and Abby Rockefeller, who became patrons. Frida at first took a dislike to the crowded city, and Diego had little time for her as he prepared for the exhibition's opening. But as the months went by, Frida began to meet and enjoy new friends with whom she could explore Manhattan.

Diego's career next took them, in the spring of 1932, to Michigan 41 where the Detroit Arts Commission had invited him to create an extensive series of murals at the Detroit Institute of Arts. Diego again immersed himself in his work, putting in long, arduous days with his assistants. It was a lonely time for Frida. Her stay in Detroit was also marked by a serious medical problem. On the fourth of July, in the midst of severe hemorrhaging, she was rushed to Henry Ford Hospital.

In the retelling, and in a painting, Frida claimed to have lost a baby. 42 Her extreme isolation in a strange land, coupled with her apparently conflicted emotions about having a child, is movingly recalled in *Henry Ford Hospital* (1932). She expressed the dramatic event in this small painting with strongly contrasted colors in a simple but effective style that disregards scale or proportion.

Later that year Frida made a brief trip back to Mexico on another sad 43 occasion, the death of her mother, after which she painted *My Birth* (1932). She was creating many works now, experimenting with techniques, painting on tin, making lithographs, even trying her hand at fresco. More noteworthy was a change in content: her work was beginning to emphasize terror, suffering, wounds, and pain.

Homesick for her family and friends, Frida yearned to return perma- 44 nently to Mexico. But when Diego completed the Detroit murals, they moved back to New York where he was installing a large mural at Rockefeller Center. When work was nearing completion, Diego was discharged from the project because he refused Nelson Rockefeller's request that he remove a portrait of Lenin from the composition. The clash generated world-wide publicity, to Diego's great pleasure, but the mural was eventually destroyed.

Diego and Frida stayed in New York a few months longer, during which   45
time he did a number of other murals. Frida painted the ironic *My Dress Hangs There (New York)* (1933), in which a Tehuantepec costume hangs on a clothesline strung between two classic columns. They support American icons, a white enamel toilet and a gilt athletic trophy. No life force vitalizes the intensely colored canvas: Frida herself is no longer in New York.

Diego finally and reluctantly agreed to return to Mexico in late 1933. In   46
a few months they were settled in San Angel in the novel twin houses designed for them by their artist friend Juan O'Gorman. Built in a functional style, the larger building was Diego's studio; the smaller one, living space and Frida's studio. One house was blue, the other bright pink, with a light blue stairway and wrought ironwork painted red. A bridge at the level of the rooftop terrace connected the two structures, and encircling both houses like a fence, a line of gray-green cactus contrasted beautifully with the brilliant colors of the painted buildings.

Diego told journalists that the houses had been designed to "guaran-   47
tee domestic tranquillity," but the couple found little peace. Diego's displeasure at being forced to return to Mexico was visible and audible for a long time. Something worse marred the domestic scene, an event that perhaps caused Frida the greatest agony of her life. During 1934 Diego began a love affair with her younger sister, Cristina.

Frida was aware that Diego spread his affections around, and she ex-   48
cused him, saying, "How would I be able to love someone who wasn't attractive to other women?" She developed a defense: at the first pang of jealousy or sense of abandonment, she would pretend to others that she and Diego had an ideal union of unbroken devotion, despite his numerous casual and short-lived adventures with the admiring women who flocked around him. But the affair with Cristina, Frida's dearest family member and confidante, was too much. Frida took an apartment in Mexico City for a time, trying in vain to find an independent life.

But for all the strength of her personality, Frida felt insecure without   49
Diego to praise her talents, cleverness, and beauty. When he withdrew from her, feelings of abandonment overwhelmed her. In July 1935, she fled to New York. There she resolved to accept her husband's wayward behavior; as she wrote Diego, she "loved him more than her own skin." According to her husband, she returned to him in Mexico "with slightly diminished pride, but not with diminished love." They established a pact that allowed frequent escapades for both, but with the mutual understanding that the affairs were something apart from their own special and intimate relationship . . .

After her husband's involvement with her sister, Frida herself engaged   50
in a number of love affairs of varying duration and intensity. Some friends believed these dalliances were merely in retaliation for Diego's transgres-

sions; others felt they were expressions of her own sexual amorality. Whichever they were, she plunged into each liaison with a headlong passion, which typically extinguished itself rapidly. These fiery, fleeting relationships included the American sculptor Isamu Noguchi, who came to Mexico to do a mural; at least two Spanish refugees whom the Riveras helped during their first years of exile in Mexico; Heinz Berggruen, whom she met in San Francisco; and the painter Ignacio Aguirre. There were also a number of trysts with women . . .

Even though Frida's liaisons allowed her to reaffirm her power of attraction and to counteract the pain of her husband's escapades, her primary and exclusive love for Diego never abated. Once the flood of romantic passion had ebbed, she wanted to return to the firm ground of her true love, to Diego.   51

Perhaps Frida's most fascinating and unlikely affair was with Leon   52
Trotsky. The Russian leader had been exiled from the Soviet Union by Joseph Stalin in 1929, and after a few years in Turkey, France, and Norway, he found himself with an expired Turkish passport, no government wanting to admit him, and in urgent need of political asylum. Friends asked Rivera to intervene with the Mexican government. Diego was not only successful in convincing President Lázaro Cárdenas to grant asylum, but he offered Frida's Casa Azul as a permanent residence for the Trotskys.

In January 1937 Trotsky and his wife, Natalia Sedova, arrived by   53
steamship at the Mexican port of Tampico. The couple settled in at the house in Coyoacán, which had been modified for their safety into a virtual fortress with organized shifts of guards, barricades, covered windows, and alarm systems.

Trotsky was a vigorous man, fifty-seven years old, tall, dashing, and   54
full of energy. According to Jean van Heijenoort, Trotsky's secretary, Frida and Trotsky's interest in one another was soon apparent to many. Frida behaved coquettishly, frequently using the word "love" when speaking to him. She communicated easily with him in English, which had the advantage of excluding his wife, who didn't understand the language. Trotsky slipped letters into books he loaned to Frida, and they held clandestine meetings in Cristina Kahlo's nearby house . . .

These years, in which Frida met a stimulating parade of international   55
personalities and withstood the emotional somersaults of her sexual relationships, were among the most productive of her artistic career. Besides the self-portrait she dedicated to Trotsky, she painted *The Deceased Dimas* (1937), *My Nurse and I* (1937) (one of Frida's favorites), *What the Water Gave Me* (1938), *Self-Portrait (Fulang Chang and I)* (1937), and other works. She exhibited *My Grandparents, My Parents, and I (Family Tree)* (1936) in a group show at the National Autonomous University of Mexico's Department of Social Action. She was busy preparing for her first solo exhibition, to be held in November 1938 at the Julian Levy Gallery in New York, where she traveled toward the end of the year. Shortly before, she had been

thrilled by the first sale of her pictures to the actor and collector Edward G. Robinson, who was visiting Mexico. Until then she had been content to give away her paintings, but now an American connoisseur had paid for her work. Frida arrived in New York in a confident mood. Her exhibition was well received by public and critics, and she sold a fair number of pictures . . .

Frida arrived home [after a trip to Paris] in April 1939, feeling more   56
sure of herself as an artist than ever before. Her pictures were selling and had merited praise from the most severe critics; she was not the least bit disturbed by critical comments from those horrified by her sanguinary and shocking themes. Frida looked forward to being truly independent and supporting herself by painting. She was feeling equally secure about her attractiveness as a mature woman, one who captivated prominent industrialists and distinguished political figures as well as famous artists and writers.

But Frida's new-found security collapsed soon after her return, when   57
she was confronted with Diego's request for a divorce. Manuel González Ramírez, one of Frida's Cachucha friends from the Prepa, acted as her lawyer in preparing the papers. "I arranged the dissolution of the bonds, and I knew very well how sad she felt about the separation," he declared. "She was lost in a limbo bordering on despair."

A single reason for the divorce is hard to find. Perhaps Diego found   58
out about her affair with Trotsky. Perhaps Frida expressed displeasure at Diego's dalliance with American film star Paulette Goddard, who was staying at the San Angel Inn right across from their house. In a letter to a friend, Frida blamed Diego's ex-wife, Lupe Marín, for causing the divorce. Rivera's statement to journalists explained it as "purely a matter of legal convenience in the style of modern times. We did it for the purpose of bettering Frida's legal position. There are no sentimental, artistic, or economic reasons."

Frida was devastated, and she became deeply depressed. Suddenly   59
living alone, she was compelled to produce enough work to support herself. Paradoxically, the mental anguish and turmoil of her personal predicament resulted in some of her finest painting. The only large-scale canvases she ever made were done at this time: *The Two Fridas* (1939), a double self-portrait painted a few months after her separation and in the worst moments of her emotional crisis, and *The Wounded Table* (1940), a self-portrait in which Frida is embraced by a bizarre, oversized Judas figure, while a macabre skeleton twirls a lock of her hair.

Both paintings were exhibited in January 1940 in Mexico City at the   60
important *International Surrealism Exhibition* in Inés Amor's Gallery of Mexican Art. *The Two Fridas* was next exhibited in New York in the Museum of Modern Art's exhibition *Twenty Centuries of Mexican Art*. Not until seven years later was *The Two Fridas* sold, to the Institute of Fine Arts in Mexico. *The Wounded Table,* last exhibited in Warsaw in 1955, reportedly was sent to the Soviet Union as a gift from the Mexican Communist party; its whereabouts are now unknown.

Another fine self-portrait is *Self-Portrait with Cropped Hair* (1940). It 61 was inspired by Frida's defiant act of cutting her long hair, which Diego adored. The lyrics and notes of a popular song are displayed across the top: "Look, if I used to love you, it was because of your hair, now that you're *pelona,* I don't love you anymore." *Pelona,* a slang word of the sort Frida liked to use, means bald or shorn.

Frida's generally poor physical condition was exacerbated by ex- 62 tremely heavy drinking, and after the divorce her health deteriorated rapidly. She continued to suffer from the circulatory problems that had plagued her since 1934, when five joints on the toes of her right foot had been removed. General fatigue and back pain were always with her.

In May 1940, a pro-Stalinist group involving the artist Siqueiros made 63 an unsuccessful attack on Trotsky's life. A second attempt, on August 20, succeeded. Trotsky was fatally hit on the head with a climbing ax by a So- viet agent, Ramón Mercader. Since Frida had known Mercader in Paris as well as Mexico, she was among the many suspected accomplices. She and her sister Cristina were questioned for hours by the police.

The stress of the police interrogation only intensified the gravity of 64 Frida's already weakened physical condition. Diego was in San Francisco, painting a mural. When he heard how ill Frida was, he suggested that she consult with Dr. Eloesser, who had followed her medical history for the last decade. In September Frida flew to San Francisco. Eloesser prescribed ab- solute rest, a special nutritious diet, electro and calcium therapies, and ab- stinence from alcohol. This treatment, combined with Diego's tender sympathy, improved her health tremendously.

Eloesser was instrumental in more than the momentary improvement 65 of Frida's physical well-being. He urged the couple to reconcile, and on Diego's fifty-fourth birthday, December 8, 1940, they were married again. Frida went home to Mexico two weeks later, followed in a few months by Diego. They were ready to renew their life as partners.

But it was not the same Frida going back into the marriage. Despite 66 her continued enjoyment of public attention, she was no longer an impul- sive, flirtatious, and charming adolescent. The reality of her thirty-three years must have confronted her. Frida rejoined Diego with her eyes open, accepting the complexities of her own personality as well as his. She began to craft her own ambiance, a personal world apart from the one she shared with her husband.

Frida was so completely convinced of the necessity for this change 67 that shortly after her return from San Francisco she moved back to Coyoacán to the Casa Azul, determined to build an independent life for her- self. There she created the rest of her pictorial autobiography, never going back to stay in the studio next door to her husband's. Diego could live with her or not, sleep in Coyoacán or at his studio in San Angel. Frida would not move out of her refuge again.   ©

CRITICAL READING

1. Now that you've read about the circumstances that inspired Kahlo's painting *Henry Ford Hospital*, how is the meaning changed or clarified for you? What kinds of significance do the images take on?
2. Discuss the other two paintings in this unit in light of the biographical details with which you now are familiar. What images do you see that aren't easily reduced to a biographical interpretation?
3. Zamora asserts that throughout her life, Kahlo had a habit of exaggerating or stretching the truth about herself; Zamora calls this a "calculated fabrication for dramatic effect." Discuss the ways in which Zamora's biography focuses on specific events that help to achieve a similar kind of effect. How do Kahlo's self-portraits achieve their dramatic effect?

CLASS DISCUSSION

1. A prominent theme running through Zamora's biography of Kahlo is the artist's struggles for independence and autonomy, most obviously in her relationship with Diego Rivera. Discuss whether you can identify aspects of this theme in the three self-portraits that began this unit.
2. Discuss how the circumstances under which Kahlo first began painting self-portraits might influence one's reaction to them. Many art critics have cautioned that, even though Kahlo's work is intensely autobiographical, one cannot assume there are simple and direct relationships between her work and her biography. Discuss how you think this point applies in Kahlo's case.

DIRECTED FREEWRITE

Explore the ways in which your initial reactions to Kahlo's self-portraits have been changed or complicated (or not) after reading about the artist's life.

THE SELF-PORTRAITS
Sarah M. Lowe

In this chapter from her monograph on Frida Kahlo's life and work, Lowe focuses on Kahlo's self-portraits, discussing them in relation to Kahlo's life and beliefs, as well as to larger movements in art. In the introduction to her book, Lowe writes that "Kahlo's paintings, especially her self-portraits, created a rupture in the history of art by overturning expectations of the image of woman in art. Kahlo's radical structuring of her self, her actual self-construction, marks a resistance to objectification rarely seen in art. She is, ironically, both the subject and the object of her own gaze." Keep these ideas in mind as you read Lowe's analysis of Kahlo's self-portraits.

Sarah M. Lowe is an art historian and curator who is currently working on her Ph.D. in art history at the City University of New York. She's worked on several art texts including Frida Kahlo, Tina Modotti Photographs, and The Diary of Frida Kahlo: An Intimate Self-Portrait from which this essay is taken. She has also curated an exhibition of Modotti's work for the Philadelphia Museum of Art, a show now traveling around the country that is believed to be the first comprehensive gathering of Modotti's photographs.

I write because one day when
   I was an adolescent,
I looked in the mirror and no one
   was there.
Can you believe it? Complete
   nothingness.
And then, beside me "others"
   assumed great importance.
      —Rosario Castellanos

Substitute the word "paint" for "write" and Castellanos's stanza recapitulates the most striking quality of Frida Kahlo's work: she created images in which she could be sure she existed. Indeed, the fundamental theme in Kahlo's work was herself, and it can be no coincidence that her first oil painting was a self-portrait, a bold, unabashed image in which she evokes Italian Renaissance portraiture. Kahlo represented her face in over fifty-five other works (nearly one third of her oeuvre). Her earliest style, modeled on a European tradition, was modified after a few years, and Kahlo invented her own strategies by which she made visible the invisible, made real the imagined. 1

In her self-portraiture, Kahlo continually undertakes to situate herself   2
at the intersection of various levels of being. In the broadest sense, Kahlo
explores her condition as Mexican, as woman, and as disabled in relation to
each other: these lives, these selves, compensate for each other, act as
foils for one another, offer refuge. Each of Kahlo's portraits maps her tenuous hold on her self, allowing her to negotiate a way to exist, a way to position herself in the world.

At a more complex level, Kahlo's self-portraits are remarkable in that   3
they gave visibility to events and emotions that had rarely, if ever, been represented in, much less acknowledged, as legitimate subjects for art. Her
self-portraits fuse a public self with an inner, psychic self in a manner that
declares the traditional mind/body separation as simply an inadequate, perhaps irrelevant, concept. If the model of Descartes' assertion *cogito, ergo
sum* is understood to have influenced a modern notion of self, Kahlo's self-
portraits tell us that for her, to have a body, even to have pain, is to exist.

Kahlo's extraordinary production holds a unique position in the history   4
of self-portraiture, an art-historical genre whose own history provides a
background against which to measure the meaning and relevance of
Kahlo's work. Artists have rendered themselves with pigment and in stone
since as early as the Old Kingdom of ancient Egypt. The Western tradition
continued through the Romans who were renown for their objective, unide-
alized portraiture, especially during the Hellenistic period. In the Middle
Ages, self-portraits were generally used by artists to indicate authorship, as
a signature on their work, while portraiture customarily signified the sitter's
status or function, what one did in social, religious or political life. Personality only became a subject in portraiture with the dawning of the Renaissance. The credo of the period, "Man [sic] is the measure of all things,"
engendered the notion of individuality and personal temperament. Thus, as
the ascendance of man made itself felt on the cultural fabric of the Renaissance, so the portrait became a vehicle for affirming the singularity of one's
own personality. Moreover, the careful attention paid to the face, a mirror to
the mind, revealed the psychological dimensions of the sitter. Indeed, with
the perfection of the glass mirror—a fourteenth-century Venetian invention—Renaissance artists began to portray their own faces, and a new understanding of artistic personality as depicted in self-portraiture emerged.

Modeling her *Self-Portrait Wearing a Velvet Dress* after Bronzino's   5
1540 Mannerist portrait *Eleanor of Toledo,* Kahlo not only announces her
aspirations to create "high art," she also reminds us of Alberti's speculation
that Narcissus, who saw his reflection in the water, was the real inventor of
painting. So, too, self-portraiture was the origin of Kahlo's art. Apparent in
even this first painting as Kahlo's unrelenting gaze, which she casts in a mirror, at herself, in order to render herself in paint. The intensity of her glance
creates the illusion of disclosure, when, in fact, from here on, Kahlo perfects
a style that allows her to hide her emotional life behind a masklike face.

There is an ambiguity in this first painting. Against the background of   6
dark blue stylized waves and a mysterious mountain, Kahlo paints herself
as regal and distanced, regarding the viewer with disdain. Or does she? On
second glance Kahlo appears unsure, timid, and even vulnerable. By elon-
gating her torso and neck, and clothing herself in a deep burgundy robe she
renders herself aristocratic and aloof, but at the same time, the open velvet
gown and pale skin against the red and black brocade leaves her looking
hesitant and defenseless.

Kahlo's gaze rivets our attention. These conflicting interpretations of   7
the image result from her impassive face; the masklike quality of her expression heightens the sense both of Kahlo's aloofness and of her vulnerability.
In short, she expresses the polarities of her personality in this remarkable
first self-portrait . . .

Women artists who paint self-portraits have had to overcome an   8
already-given meaning—the equation of female self-reflection with "Vani-
tas." They have also had to reinvent images of the self that are, nevertheless, inscribed within a patriarchal order, one which defines women first in
sexual terms. Women are traditionally denied access to venues for presenting their own sense of self, and in light of these proscriptions, Kahlo's production is especially remarkable. Her construction of self is at once complex
and astonishingly straightforward: without a hint of self-pity or sentimentality, Kahlo depicts her dreams, fears, passions, and pain with a forthrightness that defies social and artistic restrictions . . .

Kahlo's, small, almost miniature painting, *Self-Portrait on the Border*   9
Between Mexico and the United States, painted during her visit to Detroit in
1932, is a strong example of her political acumen and insight. Kahlo's per-
spicacious allegory of the political arrangements between these two countries places at its center a full-length self-portrait, indicating Kahlo's sense of
a personal position in a larger political arena, or if you will, an early twentieth-
century avowal of the politics of the personal. Kahlo's figure stands at the divide of two landscapes, the past on the left and the present on the right. On
the Mexican land a pyramid in ruins stands in an arid landscape, while on
the right, undifferentiated American skyscrapers become the modern equivalent of this ancient temple. Where the cosmic forces of the sun and moon
clash to create Mexican culture on the left, the Ford factory, whose smokestacks bellow exhaust, gives forth the American flag, a cynical implication
that Ford not only makes cars but also creates national identity, literally out
of thin air. In the Mexican foreground, desert flora thrive and their roots (one
of Kahlo's favored themes, which indicates life), extend deep into the earth.
The only thing that flourishes in the sea of concrete on the right are sinister
self-replicating machines that evoke Marcel Duchamp's *Passage from the
Virgin to the Bride* (1912), and a trio of modern electrical appliances: a loud-
speaker, a searchlight and a generator that is plugged into the pedestal
upon which Kahlo places herself.

This image concretizes Kahlo's feelings of apprehension toward Amer- 10
ican imperialist policies, opinions already formulated shortly after her return
to Mexico from San Francisco and expressed in a letter to a friend:

> Mexico is as always, disorganized and gone to the devil, the
> only thing that it retains is the immense beauty of the land
> and of the Indians. Each day the United States' ugliness
> steals away a piece of it, it is a sad thing but people must eat
> and it can't be helped that the big fish eats the little one.

The profound contrast between Mexican values and those Kahlo encountered
in the United States (also addressed in *My Dress Hangs There,* done within a
year of her Detroit self-portrait) served to crystalize her political attitudes.

Self-Portrait on the Border Between Mexico and the United States also 11
reveals much about Kahlo's perceptions of her relationship with her husband,
especially when read in contrast to Rivera's epic *Portrait of Detroit,* which he
painted in the courtyard of the Detroit Institute of Arts, a project funded by
Henry Ford. While in Detroit, Kahlo and Rivera toured the Ford Motor Company's River Rouge complex in nearby Dearborn, and other factories in the
vicinity. Rivera was dazzled by Detroit, which represented to him the center of
American industry and the American worker. He aspired, he said, to place "the
collective hero, man-and-machine, higher than the old traditional heroes of art
and legend." Kahlo's opinion of Detroit was both more restrained and more
critical, and in a somewhat mocking tone, she writes to a friend:

> Diego is working very happily here . . . He is enchanted with
> the factories, the machines, etc., like a child with a new toy.
> The industrial part of Detroit is really most interesting, the
> rest is, as in all of the United States, ugly and stupid.

Not only with words but also in her painting, Kahlo seems to be poking fun 12
at Rivera's grandiose stance. In their art Kahlo and Rivera proceed with diamet-
rically opposed models. He advances a grand symbolism, a macrocosm, that
takes as its starting point an anonymous worker and ultimately creates an idealized vision removed from the reality of concrete experience. Kahlo, on the other
hand, paints in microcosm, with herself and her personal experience standing in
the field of cosmic phenomenon. In order to ground her image in the personal,
Kahlo invokes a formal model drawn from popular art: a young girl's confirmation picture. Although she cloaks herself in distinctly Mexican dress and appears
to be standing demurely on a pedestal, Kahlo mocks her submission by choosing to hold a cigarette in place of a fan, the required accoutrement of a lady.
Thus, in a parody of the confirmation picture wherein girls offered their devotion
to Christ, Kahlo seems to offer herself as a Mexican version of the New Woman.

The nearly miniature size of Kahlo's work, its private symbolic realm, in 13
such marked contrast to Rivera's monumental, public fresco, might mitigate

against comparing the two. But this is precisely where Kahlo's motive lies: she reinvents history painting as she parodies Rivera's mural. She reduces Rivera's grand symbolism into distilled opposites, thus intensifying the message.

Several months before Kahlo painted her Detroit self-portrait, she pro- 14 duced a double portrait of herself and Rivera in commemoration of their wedding, *Frida Kahlo and Diego Rivera* an in doing so constructed an image of their marriage that she simultaneously desired and resisted. On the one hand, she explicitly depicts herself playing the role of muse/wife to the genius/husband: she tilts her head hesitatingly, while Rivera holds the tools of their trade. On the other hand, Kahlo's love for Rivera in no way diminished her capacity for recognizing the limitations of this role. Kahlo counters her diffidence within the image with a stylistic paradigm that signals her move into the arena from which she establishes her stance of defiance.

In *Frida Kahlo and Diego Rivera,* Rivera looks like a large boy: Kahlo 15 takes years off his face, shortens his pants slightly, and paints him with a sheepish look on his face. The formality of the composition allows Kahlo to distance herself from Rivera, not only by contrasting his enormous bulk to her petite presence, but also by painting in a "primitivizing" way. Here, and in other work, Kahlo uses structures of popular imagery, specifically, the space typical of the unschooled ex-voto painters. Part of the appeal of these images was their immediacy and graphic legibility. Kahlo adapted their small size to her intensely personal images and even painted on tin, as was the practice of most of these untrained artists. The field she and Rivera occupy is rudimentarily painted with little detail and only summarily suggested. To strengthen the allusion to nonmodern art (in contrast to her self-conscious "modern" style of her Adelita paintings), Kahlo includes a pink bird bearing a message, a device used by colonial portrait painters to convey essential information about the sitters. Thus Kahlo effectively separates herself from Rivera, mapping out her own artistic terrain.

Kahlo takes a step beyond self-definition, to self-creation in a strange, 16 even fantastic image, *My Birth,* painted in 1932. Kahlo does not simply depict her artistic genesis but reinvents the unknowable moment of her actual birth. It is a disturbing image on many levels: the austere setting, the utter isolation of the draped birthing woman depicted without a head, and the unusual viewpoint that results in a contorted and misshapen figure. This monstrous figure is reminiscent of the bizarre beings who populate the morality paintings of Hieronymus Bosch, as well as of marginalia in Gothic manuscripts, which also appear to have moralizing overtones, both of which appealed to Kahlo. In purely iconographic terms, however, *My Birth* is a radical adaptation of the established depiction of the goddess Tlazolteotl, who is traditionally shown in the act of childbirth. Kahlo proposes this Aztec convention (known to her through figures collected by Rivera) as a model for her imaginary image of her recent past, creating an updated, graphically present image of this Precolumbian patroness of childbirth. Years later when Rivera used the image of Tlazolteotl in his mural *History of Medicine in Mexico* in the Hospital de la Raza, he lifts an image directly from a sixteenth-century codex because his interest was with archaeological exactitude. His allusion is pat and stylized. In contrast, Kahlo transformed the appropriate Meso-American goddess, depicting herself born in the image of her Mexican past.

Kahlo set *My Birth* within the ex-voto format, an especially appropriate   17
choice since the ex-voto customarily represents a supernatural event, which this surely is. The ex-voto mixes fact and fantasy, depicting an image of divine intervention to commemorate the miraculous recovery from a sickness or an accident. It pictures two registers of reality: the earthly—an incident recorded with journalistic verity—and the divine—in the form of a patron saint shown floating above the victim. Rivera commented astutely on the artist's conception of the ex-voto:

> . . . believing only in miracles and the reality of beings and
> things, he paints both of these in the retablo [ex-voto] . . .
> he makes miraculous events ordinary and turns everyday
> things into miracles.

This fusion of the real and the imaginary was enormously appealing to Kahlo, and it was this aspect of the ex-voto that she appropriated for her work.

Yet while using the form of the ex-voto, Kahlo forgoes any specific   18
Catholic sense, and, in lieu of a mystical guardian, she places on the wall in this sparse room a retablo of the Mater Dolorosa (Mother of Sorrows), another popular idiom for the expression of piety. Kahlo said that the Madonna was included not for religious reasons, but as a "memory image," because a similar retablo was present when she was born. The Virgin is depicted not with her usual crown of thorns, but pierced with daggers, a peculiarly Mexican artistic innovation, presiding over the bloody birth of full-grown Frida. Significantly though, this is the most important among traditional depictions of the Virgin without Christ and was invoked by believers to guard against sorrow or pain, or at the hour of death, which presents a paradox in this case.

It is likely that Kahlo identified with the Mater Dolorosa, who is often   19
depicted shedding tears of sorrow for her lost Son. In at least eight formal self-portraits—and in several letters where she drew caricatures of herself—Kahlo painted symbolic tears on her face. She even modified Imogen Cunningham's portrait of her by drawing tears right on the photograph. Perhaps biography may be used to corroborate the suggested affinity, for in Kahlo's mind, the three miscarriages/abortions she endured were literally lost children. A figure from popular legend, La Llorona, the Weeping Woman, further establishes the association of tears and loss of a child, for like the

Mother of Sorrows, La Llorona mourns her dead child. Thus, the tears on Kahlo's self-portraits recall her loss—she displaces her own mourning onto the Virgin. Other instances of Kahlo's conscious and unconscious use of Catholic imagery has been insightfully discussed from a psychoanalytic perspective, especially the relation of her use of heart imagery with the mystic visions of St. Teresa of Avila.

The bottom of *My Birth* is blank, in the place of the inscription that all 20
ex-votos bear and that usually served to concretize the event, recording the precise time, date, and players. Kahlo favored the ex-voto format throughout her career, though her secularized images never invoked a beneficent god.

A work conceptually related to *My Birth* is *My Nurse and I,* painted in 21
1937. In both images, Kahlo is reinventing a formative event in her life, giving a context to her current self-knowledge. Just as she had once pictured herself as heir to the *soldadera* and thus the descendant of the first modern woman of Mexico, so in *My Nurse and I* Kahlo charts her ancestral heritage back to precolonial Mexico, depicting herself nourished by a Precolumbian wet nurse. Kahlo's strategy for establishing her heritage is similar to Michelangelo's self-mythologizing—he relates to Vasari the story of being nursed by a stonecutter's wife in the Arezzo countryside, from whom he had "sucked in the hammer and chisels I use for my statues." Both artists were indeed suckled by wet nurses, and both merge this primal experience with their artistic origins and their cultural inheritance.

In *My Nurse and I* Kahlo's full-grown head appears in jarring dispropor- 22
tion to the circumstances (as it does in *My Birth*), signaling her centrality to the image, indeed marking her as creator of the image. The face of the nurse is painted as a stone mask from the Teotihuacán culture, while the figure was inspired by a Jalisco funerary figure of a nursing mother in Kahlo's collection. Of course, neither painting is intended as a literal representation of an event, but rather as a projection into the past that enables Kahlo to formulate a self in the present. Indeed, at one level, *My Birth* functions as a double self-portrait: Kahlo identifies with both figures and so manages to give birth to herself, in the image and by creating it.

Both *My Nurse and I* and *My Birth* create a visual testimony to a cul- 23
tural, even historical memory that Kahlo claims for herself. It is likely that Kahlo conceived them as part of a series she planned of important moments in her life, an agenda that bears a remarkable similarity to the pictorial codices that describe Aztec customs and beliefs. Following the Spanish invasion of Mexico in the early sixteenth century, the Aztec tradition of manuscript painting was co-opted by the viceregal government and was used by secular and ecclesiastical authorities alike to improve their knowledge of, and thus strengthen their control over, the native population. The codices that survive are cultural encyclopedias or dictionaries with pictographic information, ranging from topographic data, to historical accounts of migrations, to particulars about the Aztec calendar and its feasts. The effectiveness of

the codices demanded visual legibility and detailed enumerations, usually in both Nahuatl, the Aztec language, and in Spanish. Kahlo mapped her life cycle from birth (*My Birth*) through infancy (*My Nurse and I*), in childhood (*My Grandparents, My Parents and I*) and adolescence (*Self-Portrait, 1926*), to marriage (*Frida Kahlo and Diego Rivera*). In effect, her project is analogous to the codices: charting vital information, conveying her own history, recording her experiences.

Kahlo's self-representation as Mexican implies a multileveled association: for understanding oneself as Mexican is to be inscribed in overlapping cultures. The experience of colonization, the struggle for independence, and the articulation of an artistic identity free from cultural imperialism was always at the center of Kahlo's art. Her unwillingness to be labeled forced her to confront and reclaim her heritage, to search for political, cultural, and personal identity that is the core of her life and art, as it is for many artists and writers of Latin America. It is remarkable that Kahlo, as a woman artist, marshaled the spiritual will and physical wherewithal to realize that knowing oneself was not enough: she had to reinvent herself to become herself. [24]

An even more explicit example of Kahlo's affirmation of her Aztec descent is evident when, in the late 1930s, she adopted the Nahuatl name Xochítl, which she used as her signature on several self-portraits. Her choice is laden with connotations: *xochítl* means "flower" in Nahuatl, and thus she invokes Xochiquetzal (literally "Precious Flower"), the Aztec goddess of flowers and grain and patroness of weavers, embroiderers, and significantly, of painters. She is also the patroness of harlots, and thus ironically, the goddess of love. Xochítl is also a day sign in the Aztec month, and those born under its sign were destined to be painters or workers in all crafts that imitate nature. Like her artist friends Geraldo Murillo, who called himself Dr. Atl after the Aztec day sign for water, and Carmen Mondragón, who changed her name to Nahui Olín, the Aztec sun god, Kahlo's choice reflects her self-invention as an artist and her identification with her Indian past. [25]

The specific flower with which Kahlo identifies—what she calls "the flower of life"—is the blood-red blossom of the nopal cactus. For Kahlo its visual similarity to female sexual parts is its appeal. For example, in *My Grandparents, My Parents and I,* Kahlo paints it as a kind of displaced uterus, the site of her conception, which occurs in the foreground of the painting. The sexual content of *Fruit of the Earth* from 1938 depends upon the ripe, red fruit of the cactus flower. However, by signing her letters to her lover Nickolas Muray, "Xochítl," and from her painting *Xochítl, Flower of Life* done in 1938, it is apparent that she also has the flower's resemblance to a love act in mind. [26]

It was Kahlo's custom, as friends and the press habitually noted, to dress in indigenous Mexican clothes. She favored the long dresses from the Tehuantepec region, embellishing herself with Pre-columbian earrings, [27] necklaces, and bracelets. In part, Kahlo was motivated by a conscious dis-regard of appropriate bourgeois behavior, but it was equally a stance of soli-darity with those classes and races that wore and produced these beautiful objects. Accordingly, in many self-portraits Kahlo wears native blouses and skirts, with special care paid to her hair, which was often rolled with brightly colored wool cords or fabrics into a headdress known as *tlacoyal.* So careful was Kahlo's attention to detail, that the origin of each outfit can be deter-mined, thus tangibly communicating important information about her culture, as well as herself as a Mexican woman. It should be noted that Kahlo's Mexican dress, and her use of Mexican sources was not simply a matter of conforming with the current impulse of Mexicanidad and the indigenist movement; Kahlo embraced her Mexican heritage because it gave her strength. She drew upon a multiplicity of sources, constructing a polyse-mous self, one grounded in a native, but also female, existence . . .

28   The complex, idiosyncratic imagery of Kahlo's paintings are thus not easily read nor always logically intelligible, and in the case of *Self-Portrait with Thorn Necklace and Hummingbird* painted in 1940, the many layers of association create an intricate series of meanings. Native symbols and im-ported Catholic symbols converge in this painting, and they interact to cre-ate a truly syncretic image. On the most obvious level, the necklace of thorns alludes to Christ's passion, symbolism Kahlo has drawn from her Catholic upbringing. As a portrait, it also evokes the miracle of St. Veronica, who, after wiping the Savior's brow, found His image with the crown of thorns mysteriously transferred onto her veil. Moreover, Veronica (from "vera icon") herself is associated with the surcease from flowing blood. In addition to Christian allusions, Kahlo draws from her Mexican heritage, making reference to Aztec tradition of divinatory rituals entailing self-mortification with maguey thorns. The dead hummingbird around her neck and the butterflies in her hair are Aztec symbols that signify the souls of dead warriors.

29   The absolute frontality of this pose, unusual for Kahlo, and the utter lack of depth transform the image into a secular icon. The monkey, an om-nipresent pet, which makes its appearance in eight self-portraits, functions like a religious attribute and further underscores the iconic quality of the image. Kahlo may also be referring to the Aztec conception of a *nahual,* or animal alter ego. The ancient Mexicans believed their gods had the capacity to transform themselves into animals at will. Kahlo often depicts herself with her pets, including dogs and parrots, an allusion to this belief. The cat, on the other hand, seems to be a more generalized symbol of death, imparting an ominous sense of doom.

30   Iconographic analysis of Kahlo's paintings cannot "explain" their mean-ing. But sorting out the various connotations indicates the level of Kahlo's sophisticated and discriminate choices and suggests how her self-portraits are significant at many levels of meaning. Kahlo never represented a single

self but always a multicultural one. By mingling symbols from a diverse body of beliefs, she manages to reveal relations between things known and unknown.

On this occasion Kahlo brought together diverse cultural references in 31 a self-portrait; at other times she was unable to achieve this fusion. The other-worldly quality of Kahlo's 1939 image, *The Two Fridas* can be understood as pictorial manifestations of contradictory self-images. The two Fridas cannot logically (either physically or emotionally) share the same space. Kahlo establishes two images of herself, divided and yet allied, contrasting but nevertheless corresponding to the same body. Virtually all Kahlo's self-portraits navigate her ego among political, social, and emotional structures: she conceives of herself as Mexican, female, and physically damaged. Her portraits are plastic evidence of her will to contextualize herself—they are testimony to her search for existential meaning in a world of doubt. For Kahlo, neither ego nor personality define her: it is the indisputable existence of her body, transmitted from mirror to canvas, that brings her closest to being.

Against a cloudy sky painted in a manner reminiscent of her treatment 32 of the *pedregal,* Kahlo seats the two Fridas on a rustic, caned bench in a nondescript space. Rivera referred to this style as "occult materialism," and the fact that the two Fridas also share a circulatory system may account for his assessment. The mystical association is further implied since the Frida on the right holds a small emblem of Rivera, like the emblems associated with the *monjas coronadas.* Kahlo depicts the two Fridas separated by a generation, differentiated by their clothing: on the left she is dressed in traditional Victorian dress, and on the right she wears a Tehuana skirt and blouse. In an interview at the time the image was finished, Kahlo is said to have remarked on the identities of the two Fridas: one was the self that Rivera once loved and the other, the one he no longer loved. This cryptic, and ultimately unsatisfactory explanation, one that, indeed, transcends a biographical reading alluding to her divorce, indicates Kahlo's unfailing acknowledgment of the mutability of social meanings. For what the two Fridas share, significantly, is a symbiotic physiological existence—their bodies remain immutable and constant, while their costumes shift their meanings in the cultural realm of signification. Kahlo is not merely expressing aspects of her personality but constructing alternative selves, creating her own personae. This image is not a self-analysis but a self-invention. While acknowledging that she is subject to prescriptive patriarchal power structures beyond her control, Kahlo works from her own self-knowledge to create other possibilities for her selves.

Kahlo also explores the social construct of "woman" in *Self-Portrait* 33 *with Cropped Hair* from 1940. She puts forth not an analysis of her own identity, but an exegesis of the cultural definition of femininity. For what Kahlo eliminates from her self-image are the social trappings of womanhood: long hair, dresses, and even modest posture. In light of the proscription against cross-dressing that dates at least to biblical scripture [Deuteronomy 22:5], and in light of the claim of social-anthropologists that clothing not only grants, but produces social meaning, this image of transgression is astoundingly daring. Wearing an oversized man's suit, holding a pair of scissors where a "lady" would hold a fan, looking directly at the viewer, Kahlo challenges the viewer to see her as a woman. Ever conscious of the meaning of costume, Kahlo's deliberate refusal to acquiesce to conventional modes of dress signals her declaration of independence. By adapting the trappings of authority, she readily acknowledges the power such a masquerade confers. Kahlo's images invert traditional expectations and thus question the viability of constructing a female self using male-created forms of expression. The lines from a popular song painted above the figure of Kahlo point out how women's status relies upon elements of social signification (clothing, conduct, physical beauty), and how resistance to prescribed modes of behavior is rewarded with, in this case, emotional disenfranchisement.

> Look, if I loved you, it was for
>   your hair,
> Now that you're bald, I no longer
>   love you.

The animation of Kahlo's sheared tresses, as they twist and slither around her, as if energized by their new-found freedom, inevitably recall the roots and veins that appear with regularity in Kahlo's work. She often painted tendrils, roots, nerves, vines, imagery derived, in part, from her physiological knowledge: veins carry blood, and roots bring nourishment just as nerves transmit pain. Where in other cases, for example *Self-Portrait on the Border Between Mexico and the United States, The Dream, Self-Portrait as a Tehuana, Two Nudes in the Jungle,* and *Roots,* roots signify a groundedness, an interconnection with all life, here, severed from their origin, the tendrils of hair are rendered incapable of providing stability or nurture. Nothing grounds the figure except Kahlo's unyielding gaze with which she engages the viewer.

The immobile face characteristic of *Self-Portrait with Cropped Hair,* 34 and almost every self-portrait, reads as a mask, an interpretation Kahlo not only acknowledged but courted. Her calculated effort to disguise her emotions and hide her feelings while she relentlessly depicts her life on canvas produces an ever-present tension in her images. On the one hand, Kahlo delivers astonishingly personal portraits while, on the other, she intentionally withholds vital information. Her omission is self-conscious and internalized: indeed, she refers to herself as "la gran ocultadora," a not-easily translatable phrase, since, like Kahlo's aesthetic, it is synthetic. Perhaps "the great unrevealed one" gets at the sense of her deliberately-sought ambiguity.

Kahlo's *The Mask,* painted in 1945, addresses forthrightly the issues   35
around identity and exposure and is a particularly arresting image for a
painter who focused so intensely on her own face. At first glance, Kahlo
seems to be seeking respite from her own intense gaze, from introspection,
and from self-construction by taking on another's view. Yet Kahlo was remarkably able to deny herself as art object. Nowhere does she present her
body according to the traditional notions of the female body in art. She is,
both to herself and to her viewer, the object of the gaze. Kahlo manages to
participate in and then protest against the social construction of herself as
woman. It is the mask that allows her to call attention to this construction, as
it allows her an "other" personality.

In contrast to the many images of Kahlo that obscure her personality,   36
Self-Portrait with Loose Hair from 1947 is one of her most disarmingly can-
did images. Kahlo forgoes all accessories, omitting her pets and elaborate
headdresses, and includes only a modest succulent growing from the rocky
pedregal of the background. *Self-Portrait with Loose Hair* is reminiscent of
her first self-portrait: they share understatement and constraint less evident
in most of the others. Both act as a kind of reckoning, the earlier coming to
terms with her new life, the later coming to terms with who she is at age
forty, in an arrestingly direct way . . .

The pain and suffering so conspicuous in Kahlo's later work lead some   37
to interpret her paintings as unmediated illustrations of biographic events.
Her paintings that are admittedly grounded in actual incidents are diminished
without the broader significance that a careful visual interpretation can provide. *Henry Ford Hospital,* depicting her anguished, indeed, life-threatening
miscarriage in 1932, is an image that marks the beginning of the style and
content Kahlo would develop over the next twenty years. It brings together
formal constructions based on Mexican traditions, as well as what can be
called a Modernist vision of the body in the brave new world.

Much has been made of Kahlo's longing for a child: her prophetic ado-   38
lescent declaration that she would have Diego Rivera's child is invariably
cited as the beginning of this subject. Her bloody images of her many ill-
advised pregnancies and subsequent agonizing miscarriages or therapeutic
abortions work in concert with other images—of germination, of birth, of nurturing, and even of Rivera cradled in her arms—to convey a lifelong despair
at barrenness. But in the context of Mexican social codes, where having a
child, indeed, where motherhood itself, not only was an indispensible aspect
of femininity but virtually defined womanhood, Kahlo's desperation is readily
understandable. Without suffrage, women in Mexico had no officially sanctioned political life and were thus confined to a domestic role. The public
and private dichotomy maintained a strict separation between the genders,
and yet Kahlo's imagery manages to shatter the laws of patriarchy. Her
painting moves into an alternative space, not simply critical of the status quo
but maneuvering itself beyond it, charting other avenues of possibilities.

The image that most vividly marks the beginning of Kahlo's journey 39
into alternative visions is *Henry Ford Hospital,* painted at the time Rivera
was working on his murals for the Detroit Institute of Arts. It is a stunning
work, not only for its entirely original imagery, but for the way Kahlo assem-
bles objects that for her symbolize the bewildering emotions and sensations
of her month-long ordeal of miscarriage. Six objects circle Kahlo, each tied
to her with a red veinlike ribbon. In the center is the fetus she lost, an excru-
ciatingly accurate portrait of her miscarried child. To his left, Kahlo paints a
medical model, science's idea of what is inside a woman, an image of what
she lacks. Diagonally across, on the lower right-hand side, is a rendering of
her own pelvis, the guilty party: her broken bones, a result of her accident,
which prevent her from carrying her baby to term and are damaged further
by sexual intercourse.

These objects pose little confusion in this context and seem logical in- 40
clusions. However, the other three items are mystifying, and without Kahlo's
own words, they would be difficult to interpret. The snail, at first a seemingly
whimsical choice, in fact embodies for Kahlo the *experience* of an abortion,
which was slow, and in her words, "soft, covered and at the same time,
open." This extraordinary transformation of a horrifying experience into a
tangible and, significantly, animal form is paradigmatic of the nature of
Kahlo's symbolism. Feelings, sensations are converted into concrete objects, which stand in for deeply felt interior processes. The bruise-colored
orchid at the bottom center of the painting, a flower given her by Diego, was
included, according to Kahlo, to mix a sexual metaphor with the sentimental.
The last object is a machine whose function is unknown. Kahlo had an understandable aversion to machines: it was, after all, a machine that caused
her injury in 1925. Her abhorrence is made utterly clear in her *Self-Portrait
on the Border Between Mexico and the United States* where she contrasts
the diverse fruit of Mexico's earth and history with the mechanical reproduction of homogeneous automatons and proliferation of monolithic, uniform
skyscrapers. She said that she invented the image of the machine in *Henry
Ford Hospital* "to explain the mechanical part of the whole business"—presumably, the operation and the hospital, and even Gringolandia. Kahlo was
surely aware of the irony that, while she lay in a hospital bed at the mercy of
the tools of modern medical science, Rivera was busy painting a homage to
the age of the machine.

In this image, as in others, Kahlo presents herself in an entirely un- 41
charted space, both literally and figuratively. The bird's-eye view of Kahlo
naked in a hospital bed, which floats in an unarticulated space in front of the
Detroit skyline, underscores the no-man's-land in which she finds herself.
The painting is original in conception and in construction, for Kahlo has radically reformulated the space of the ex-voto. The miraculous scene of the ex-
voto, which traditionally takes place in a nonspecific indoor space, is here
modernized, as is the miracle to which the votive painting refers. Kahlo pays

a tribute, however ambivalent, to the miracle of modern medicine. She paints herself literally as the object of the gaze, but not simply a male gaze, but specifically a medical gaze, eyed and controlled by science. Like her predecessors Modersohn-Becker and Valadon when Kahlo paints herself without clothing, she eschews the traditional role of object of desire.   ◎

CRITICAL READING

1. Discuss how Kahlo's self-portraits are "significant at many levels of meaning" by referring to different points raised in Lowe's discussion.
2. Respond to Lowe's assertion that Kahlo's "construction of self is at once complex and astonishingly straightforward: without a hint of self-pity or sentimentality, Kahlo depicts her dreams, fears, passions, and pain with a forthrightness that defies social and artistic restrictions" (page 187). What evidence do you see in Kahlo's paintings that supports and/or refutes any aspect(s) of this statement?
3. Discuss the ways in which Kahlo's self-portraits seem to deliver "On the one hand, . . . astonishingly personal portraits while, on the other, she intentionally withholds vital information" (page 195). Does this statement contradict Lowe's earlier point about the straightforwardness of Kahlo's construction of self? Why, or why not?

CLASS DISCUSSION

1. Discuss recurring images in Kahlo's paintings, perhaps listing them on the board. Lowe offers various interpretations of these images, for example, on page 187, she states that roots in Kahlo's paintings indicate life, then later, on page 195, she adds that roots "signify a groundedness, an interconnection with all life . . ." As a class, make a list of interpretations, both from Lowe's essay and from the students' own ideas. Discuss how these interpretations relate to the different levels of meaning in Kahlo's works.
2. Discuss why, given her position as a woman in Mexico in the 1930s, the image of giving "birth to herself" (page 191) and participating in and then protesting "against the social construction of herself as a woman" (page 194) would be so important in Kahlo's work.

DIRECTED FREEWRITE

For at least fifteen minutes, write continuously about issues of identity and art. What are some other examples of visual artists' works that depict the self? What kinds of meanings about the nature of identity itself get articulated in art? What kinds of visual art do you like, and why? What kinds of images depicted in art—self-portraits, landscapes, still lifes, abstract designs, and the like—appeal to you, and why? What do your tastes in art say about you as a person, if anything?

ART HISTORY UNIT WRITING ASSIGNMENTS

1. Descriptive writing is used in a number of different contexts and can be approached in a number of ways, depending on that context. The writing of interpretive essays in the humanities involves the writer in description; one must clearly describe the elements of a painting, a poem, or a play that one is interpreting. Thus, description usually appears as an element within larger pieces of writing, as in the interpretive essay, or as in other kinds of writing, such as the experimental report in science or social science, or as an element of an argument essay when detailed description of a problem or a particular social context is needed to help situate an argument. In order to practice this kind of writing, this assignment asks you to write two short, purely descriptive essays on one of Frida Kahlo's paintings that is not included in this unit.

 Descriptive writing can be characterized as either objective, impressionistic, or subjective. Pure objectivity in description is challenging for human beings, since we view all things through subjective eyes; however, in the context of science and social science, academic writers typically strive to be as objective as possible in their descriptive writing—although these fields are much more self-conscious about the impossibility of true objectivity than ever before. The humanities allow for more subjectivity, to a point; writers in the arts have to be able objectively to view artifacts in order then to arrive at reasonable interpretations of their meaning; but in writing, objective views of art objects tend to be combined with the writer's more subjective interpretations. In this assignment, we'd like you to try your hand at objective description of the Kahlo painting you have chosen, wherein you restrict yourself to describing only what you see, without either interpreting its meaning or characterizing its effect. Then follow this with a short, impressionistic description, where you allow your own feelings and responses to the piece to inform the description of what you see. In impressionistic description, you do not necessarily have to cover every single detail in the painting; in fact, that could lead to a very tedious piece of writing. Instead, you should carefully select the elements on which you will focus and should describe your impressions of these. The elements you describe ought to relate to each other in some way, and they might all culminate in an overall impression, or several major impressions.

 Descriptive writing requires the writer to make some careful choices about organization. Where should your description begin? If you jump around in a disorderly fashion, describing this element over here, and then another one over there, your description won't clearly convey the relationships between the elements in the painting. In visual description, orderliness can be achieved by describing the object as the eye would encounter it; thus, you might decide to start from the most dominant image in the painting, its focal point. Or you might decide that it makes sense to move from left to right in the painting, or from right to left, or top to bottom, and so on. Another approach, especially relevant in impressionistic description, is to describe the overall view of the painting, then to move in and describe the various elements that make up this overview. These are just some approaches—you can come up with your own, referring to the work you have chosen, but just make sure that you do make a careful decision about how to order your points.

2. Art historians and art critics rely on the historical context in which an artist lived and worked to help elucidate the concerns and the meanings of particular art works. The simplest way of representing history is in a chronological narrative, which is essentially an objective account of the significant events of a particular historical period or of the elements of a particular historical event. Of course, deciding which details are important, and which are not, is not an objective endeavor, and such choices will be relevant in the following assignment.

Do some research on the historical period in which Frida Kahlo lived and worked. Look at Mexican history of the period, as well as American and world history. Then it is up to you, given what you know now about Kahlo's work and her biography, to decide what aspects of that history might be relevant to an understanding of Kahlo's work. Select either a set of important events or one particular significant event, and then tell its story in chronological order and great detail.

3. The essay by Lowe is an example of the kind of interpretive writing that scholars in the humanities routinely produce. Critical interpretation of this kind involves describing the artifacts from a relatively objective point of view: what are the specific qualities exhibited by the artifact? In the case of paintings, these would be vibrancy of color, use of negative space, degree to which the images are "photographically" representative, use of symbols and archetypal imagery, historical context, and so on. After describing the artifact, the critic has to step back from objective observation and ask questions about how the elements within the work may relate to each other. Questions such as these help the critic to interpret the underlying "meaning" of the piece; what messages are implied in the artifact, such as Picasso's *Guernica,* which intentionally illustrates the horrors of war, or what meanings—perhaps not consciously intentional by the artist—can be derived from the work in question?

The process is not quite this simple, of course. Critics typically bring to bear a number of tools to aid in and influence their interpretation. These tools include such things as prior knowledge of the artist's biography and the artist's other work, knowledge of the historical context in which the work was created, and specific theoretical alignments that influence the critic's interpretation. The interpretive piece by Lowe is an example of an art critic's interpreting artifacts through the lens of a loose theoretical alignment with feminist theory; thus Lowe focuses on Kahlo's depictions of gender identity, and argues specific interpretations that are colored by this perspective. Interpretive essays—whether theoretically informed or not—have as their thesis the critic's particular "take" on what the artwork (or, in Lowe's case, a group of works) is saying and on how it is saying this.

For this assignment, we ask you to engage in critical interpretation—a process that in your case will not involve the application of a particular theory to your interpretation unless you already identify yourself with a certain theoretical perspective, such as Freudian psychology, feminism, or environmentalism. Pick the self-portraits of another twentieth-century artist, such as Francis Bacon, David Hockney, or the photographer Cindy Sherman, and write a critical interpretation of what the artworks might be suggesting about the artist's identity or about the nature of identity in general.

Write one version of this paper based solely on your own interpretation of the images in the artist's work, and then write a second version incorporating the critical interpretations of at least two other art critics. The argument about the self-portraits' meanings should then be revised in relation to the critics' views. Follow this second essay with a one-page discussion of the ways in which your analysis of the art changed, or not, and why.

A second alternative for this assignment is to stay focused on the work of Frida Kahlo, and write an essay addressing the following issues (or others of your own or your instructor's choice). Diego Rivera once said that Kahlo was "an artist who tore open her chest and heart to reveal the biological truth of her feelings." Clearly, when viewing her self-portraits, elements of Kahlo's feelings and life experiences are represented. Such representation can sometimes make an artist's work seem too personal, so that viewers are not able to connect with the paintings through any kind of identification with Kahlo's feelings. Check out a book of Kahlo's self-portraits from the library, then write an essay in which you use points from Zamora's biographical piece and from the self-portraits themselves to explore this issue of personal versus more universal or general expression of feelings. What elements of Kahlo's self-portraits seem relevant to the "human experience" in general or to a specific group's identity and experience such as Mexicans or women or Mexican women? What elements (if any) seem purely personal? Your essay should be focused around a central argument (your thesis statement) about Kahlo's work and its relation to aspects of human experience.

CHAPTER THREE

GENDER
AND SEXUALITY

INTRODUCTION

One half of the world cannot understand the pleasures of the other.
—Jane Austen (1775–1817)

According to sociologists, when people encounter strangers, the first thing they notice is the stranger's gender.[1] The perception of another person's femaleness or maleness is typically automatic, instantaneous, and unconscious. Clearly, for a number of reasons, gender is one of the most important aspects of who we are and of how we relate to others. Similarly, sexuality plays a huge role in the lives of human beings, both as individuals and as a species.

Although closely linked, gender and sexuality are actually not the same thing. Some key terms for our discussion, and for this unit as a whole, are *sex, gender,* and *sexuality.* Sex, on the context of human identity, is a biological classification determined by reproductive organs, genetic makeup, and hormones; gender, by contrast, refers to the cultural definitions applied to a person's sex. In our contemporary culture, we refer to those individuals with ovaries, vaginas, two X chromosomes, and so forth, as women; accompanying this sexual identity, there are a number of gender-specific qualities we associate with those who occupy it, such as the propensity to be nurturing.

Biological functions of men and women have been the source of many behavioral characteristics that we ascribe to the genders. Obviously, women carry and give birth to children, and this distinction relates to the designation of nurturing.

---

[1]The second thing, by the way, is usually race.

However, we know that men are also fully capable of nurturing children, and there isn't a purely biological reason for women to do the bulk of the child rearing. Cultures play a huge role in how the activities and characteristics ascribed to men and women are defined, deployed, and valued, and these definitions are subject to change. For example, many of the gender roles traditionally applied to women in the United States—such as the quaint and antiquated notion that women are generally passive and dependent—have been challenged by women (and some men) in the past thirty years or so.

Sexuality, as a term in this discussion, refers to a person's orientation toward a specific gender (or genders) as objects of sexual desire. Because the dominant form of sexuality in most societies is heterosexuality, people often conflate gender and sexuality, as in the assumption that members of the masculine gender "naturally" desire members of the feminine gender and that masculine and feminine therefore equate with heterosexuality. Lovemaking itself has thus become normalized as an act of intercourse between two partners of the opposite sex, and this circumstance is part of the reason that homosexual men and women have often been stereotyped as having feminine or masculine traits and behaviors, respectively. The reality of the situation, of course, is more complex: one's sex does not necessarily predict one's gender identity, and one's gender identity does not necessarily predict one's sexual orientation. And sexuality is not so neatly characterized as either heterosexual or homosexual—plenty of people desire intimacy with both men and women, or they change their objects of desire at various times in their lives. This multiplicity of possibilities has been characterized by Sigmund Freud, the "father of psychology," as *polymorphous perversity,* and Freud thought that this was a stage that individuals had to move through in order to arrive at a more "healthy" sexual self. Today, with our increased questioning of such binaristic categories, these issues are much more complicated, and yet we are much more free to examine them.

Gender and sexuality are important topics in all disciplines of the university, studied from a multiplicity of perspectives. In the humanities, literary scholars look at the gender and sexual relations between men and women in works of literature. The literary critic Leslie Fiedler, for example, argued several decades ago that in the canon of American fiction, depictions of heterosexual marriages are noticeably rare. Instead, we have numerous great books about solitary men who go out on some kind of quest, sometimes with a male sidekick, such as Huckleberry Finn and his friend Jim. Paintings, similarly, are interesting artifacts to examine in terms of gender and sexuality; viewing paintings from various periods can indicate what that culture's period's standards of beauty and sensuality were, and it's frequently astonishing to see how much those standards have changed. Likewise, a survey of popular music from the twentieth century shows that love—and often, the pain associated with it—inspires more songs than any other aspect of human life.

Social scientists have always been preoccupied with this important area of life. Freud's work in psychology wasn't the first to delve into these matters, but certainly his sometimes controversial and oft-disputed theories of gender identity formation and sexuality have been the most enduring. Theorizing that the sex instinct is one of the most powerful in the human being and that the functioning of civilized societies relied on the effective suppression and control of these instincts, Freud developed a very detailed and complex model of how he believed the process of socialization occurred in children and of what could go wrong in this process. Later psychologists have studied the issues in other ways, developing theories that add to Freud's or developing entirely different notions of gender socialization and sexual function/dysfunction.

One of the problems subsequent social scientists have pointed out about Freud's work, for example, is that Freud was not attuned to the specificities of the particular cultural/historical context in which he observed human behavior. Thus he believed that his theories provided universal paradigms for explaining human development. The anthropologist Margaret Mead, among many subsequent others, helped to overturn such ideas. When she studied cultures outside the Western cultural context, Mead found a great deal of variation in gender roles and sexual behavior, adding evidence to the "nurture" side of the debate about whether "nature or nurture"—biological characteristics or culturally created ones—creates human behavior. In so doing, Mead helped to modify theories of universalists such as Freud.

Sociologists, since they are concerned with group interaction, have added much to our knowledge of gender and sex. For example, studies have shown that parents treat their children—from the very beginning of their lives—differently, depending on their sex, socializing boys to be more aggressive and sports-oriented than girls, for example. Although boys and girls, and women and men, are different, they are in theory treated equally under the law. So another interesting discipline in the social sciences, political science, is concerned with laws and policies addressing gender equality (among other things, of course).

Gender and sexuality are approached differently by scientists, who are more concerned with the biological aspects of these matters. Whereas social scientists have traditionally focused on the "nurture" side of the nature/nurture question, scientists are concerned with the role that nature plays in creating who we are and how we function; and the evidence they present indicates that biology plays a large role in who we are as sexual individuals and as gendered social creatures. For example, recent scientific work in genetics has led a number of social scientists to reevaluate certain theories about gender socialization. Most current findings confirm what would seem to be commonsense wisdom: that nature and nurture work *together,* through a wide range of subtle and complex dynamics, to produce gendered individuals.

This chapter explores these dynamics from our interdisciplinary perspective, beginning with the humanities, whose first unit centers on the contemporary practice of film interpretation. Movies are inescapable aspects of American popular culture; even if one doesn't attend movies, it would be nearly impossible to avoid the advertising, the videos, the critical reviews, and the merchandising that generally surround movies today. In the academic discipline known as film studies, scholars have traditionally focused their attention on such American "classic" films as Orson Welles's *Citizen Kane,* as well as works by foreign directors such as Federico

Fellini, Ingmar Bergman, and Akira Kurosawa. In more recent years, however, film scholars—like their counterparts in literary studies—have turned their attention to more popular genres, examining horror flicks, romantic comedies, musicals, and even pornographic movies. Many scholars of popular culture argue that products of mass culture deserve academic scrutiny, since they reflect a particular culture's values, practices, and beliefs; and thus they tell us much about ourselves, while at the same time, they exert a strong influence on what we believe and how we behave. Thus, our film studies unit, rather than offering readings that employ the technical vocabulary of film analysis, presents two interpretive essays dealing with three popular films, examining the ways they reflect and reinforce certain beliefs about acceptable gender roles.

This chapter's second humanities unit, centering on lesbian and gay studies, includes two readings that address gay and lesbian history in the United States. It should be noted that lesbian and gay studies as a field is considered interdisciplinary: scholars in this area come from literary studies, sociology, psychology, genetics, history, and so forth. The historical readings in this unit look at early-twentieth-century gay identity and gay life, examining ways in which capitalism helped create the conditions in which a gay identity could emerge.

In the social science section of this chapter, the first unit comes from the discipline of communications. As in many social sciences, communications is a field that is approached in ways that are "applied," as well as ways that are "theoretical." Theoretical study of communication issues is ultimately applied to various sites in which communication takes place. The readings in this unit deal with interpersonal communication styles of men and women, presenting some theoretical work on male/female communication styles, a study of gendered power differences and conversation patterns.

Our second social science unit represents some readings from a relatively new and controversial field of inquiry, sometimes called evolutionary psychology and sometimes sociobiology. Evolutionary psychology applies the chief paradigm of the biological sciences, evolutionary theory, to explain the social behavior of human beings. First articulated by Edwin O. Wilson, this interdisciplinary field, linking psychology, sociology, and biology, holds that each of us is programmed by biology to pass along our genes and that most of our behavior is motivated by this instinctual desire. In this light, nature is seen as favoring certain psychological traits that enhance the probability that an individual will pass along his or her genetic code. Some evolutionary psychologists focus chiefly on human genes as their unit of study, others focus on hormones—those produced prior to birth, or after the onset of puberty—to explain behavior, especially gender and sexual behavior, whereas other researchers focus primarily on the human brain itself. Readings in this unit provide some specific insights into evolutionary psychology and its application to human sexual behavior.

Biochemistry is the discipline we take up in the first unit of this chapter's science section. As the name indicates, biochemistry deals with the chemistry of living matter. This unit explores biochemists' work in identifying brain chemicals and neurological pathways that control the complex human experience of love. This unit confronts a provocative question: if we are encoded by genetics and prodded by chemicals to "fall in love," then what are we to make of that all-important feeling, and how do we value it? The two readings presented in this unit are popular accounts that synthesize recent findings about the biomechanics involved in producing loving feelings. They demonstrate how scientists use evolutionary theory to interpret the results of experiments on brain chemistry and functioning, and they provide additional evidence for the biological determination of people's sociosexual behavior.

Broadly defined as the branch of biology dealing with animals, zoology—the focus of this chapter's second science unit—is a discipline under which a wide variety of specialties—for example, ornithology (the study of birds), herpetology (the study of reptiles), entomology (the study of insects), and arachnology (the study of spiders)—are grouped. Zoology encompasses studies of such things as the physiology of the cardiovascular, respiratory, and autonomic nervous systems of vertebrates, marine ecology or biology, marsupial reproduction and development, the structure and function of single cells, and evolutionary biology. Furthermore, zoologists engage in taxonomy, the science of describing, identifying, naming, and classifying organisms. Although zoologists study animal behavior on its own terms—without resorting to simplistic comparisons with human behavior—nonetheless, comparisons of human and animal behavior are useful for some fields such as evolutionary psychology. Readings in this unit therefore cite studies of animal behavior to help support claims about human sexual behavior and its evolutionary purposes. In this way, studies of animal biology and behavior further our knowledge of the world around us and indirectly help us to understand ourselves better.

Before beginning this chapter, you might make a list of stereotypes concerning masculinity and femininity: ones that you've observed in other people, or even in yourself. Notice the complementary nature of these stereotypes, the ways that these are structured as binarisms, just as man/woman is. For example, we traditionally have believed that femininity involves passivity and dependence, whereas masculinity is active and independent. After making this list, think about the extent to which these stereotypes are currently supported or challenged by those around you. For instance, you might realize that certain gender-related attitudes are being reinforced by some peers and certain radio-talk-show hosts, whereas other stereotypes are being challenged by social critics whom you encounter in your university career, by scientists and scholars. Having initially examined these preconceptions will open you to the ideas and opinions expressed in the following textual pieces.

THINKING AND WRITING IN THE HUMANITIES

Unit 1

Film Studies—Real Wild Women/ Wild Real Men

Before reading each (or either) of these essays, rent the videos for the films, and watch them. Then write your own interpretation of what you think that these films have to say, or have to show, about gender roles, and about heterosexual relationships and/or homosexual relationships, or about nonsexual friendships.

SEDUCTION AND BETRAYAL IN THE HEARTLAND: *THELMA AND LOUISE*

Jack Boozer

While noting the multiple interpretations and mixed reviews generated in response to the 1991 Ridley Scott action-drama movie *Thelma and Louise,* Jack Boozer of Georgia State University advances his own argument about what the movie has to say about feminine gender roles, and about Hollywood movie genres. Asserting that the film is a reinvention of the "road rebel" movie tradition, Boozer believes that *Thelma and Louise* invites a consideration of that tradition from a feminine perspective. At times difficult, this essay's prose may present some problems for readers inexperienced with the terms that today's humanities scholars use to interpret cultural artifacts; keep a good dictionary handy, and refer to it as you read, and stick with the essay. As you read, notice Boozer's lengthy sentence structures and the way that complicated ideas are conveyed within these sentences. How might using shorter, simpler sentences change the tone of this piece?

Jack Boozer received his Ph.D. from Emory University. He was a postdoctoral Visiting Scholar in Graduate Cinema Studies at New York University, and in film and literature at the University of Massachusetts (Amherst), at the University of California, Berkeley, and at the City College

Source: "Seduction and Betrayal in the Heartland: *Thelma & Louise*" by Jack Boozer in *Literature Film Quarterly,* vol. 23, no. 3, July 1995. Copyright © 1995 by Salisbury State University. Reprinted with permission of *Literature Film Quarterly.*

of New York Graduate Center. He has written several articles on film including "Bending Phallic Patriarchy in The Crying Game*" and "Wall Street:* The Commodification of Perception.*" He has also published chapters in the following books:* The Films of Oliver Stone, Authority and Transgression in Literature and Film, Cultural Power, Cultural Literacy, *and* Retrofitting Blade Runner. *His most recent article is "The Lethal Femme Fatale in the Noir Tradition." He is currently an associate professor in film in the department of communication at Georgia State University and is completing a book on business and career films.*

Thelma and Louise is a popular commercial film that has stirred extensive critical discussion of the woman's place in Hollywood action drama. With its self-conscious gender switch on road film outlaws, it has provoked a fresh consideration of sexual stereotyping in film genre and in cultural ideology generally. But writer Callie Khouri and producer-director Ridley Scott's film is more than a satire on patriarchal presumption. As I hope to demonstrate, *Thelma and Louise* not only invites consideration of Hollywood's road rebel history from a feminine perspective, but relates it to a deeper problem of subjectivity in contemporary . . . culture.   1

The media response to this film was immediate and provocational. After placing *Thelma and Louise* with other 1991 productions that concern women's revenge such as *Mortal Thoughts, V.I. Warshawski,* and *Sleeping With the Enemy, Time* magazine's June 24 cover story, "Gender Bender," goes on to assert that "A white-hot debate rages over whether *Thelma and Louise* celebrates liberated females, male bashers—or outlaws." Richard Schickel's byline is accompanied by one from Margaret Carlson, who denies the film's claim to a feminist sensibility altogether because of its reliance on a male action mode. Either way, the confrontational gender stance identified in and extrapolated from the film by *Time's* writers and editors exemplifies the news media's tendency to over-simplify and exploit topical social conflicts represented in cultural narratives. This reductionist approach to a complex film typifies the effects of commercial pressures in mass market journalism and hardly moves beyond the kind of solicitous oppositionalism that characterizes American sociopolitical debate. Schickel's symptomatic reading of *Thelma and Louise* may be correct when he asserts that it "is satirically aware of the violent and depersonalizing traditions of our visual popular culture." But exactly how this film links its particular images of "violent and depersonalizing . . . popular culture" (which sounds like an entity one could blame) into specific chains of meaning remains to be interpreted.   2

Some of these linkages have been addressed in recent symposia on this film carried in *Cineaste* and *Film Quarterly*. The authors in both publications tend to mistrust this popular movie's rather comfortable inclinations toward violent Hollywood spectacle. *Thelma and Louise* is seen, for example, to be either an imperfect satirical analogy of the woman's dilemma in con-   3

temporary America, or an unrealistic female liberation fantasy that backhandedly supports reactionary violence. To what extent the film's violent fantasy
seduction is modified by a self-consciousness of generic and mythic traditions is generally recognized by Leo Braudy, who writes in *Film Quarterly:*

> Many of the more ridiculous attacks against the film took its
> assertions as somehow realistic arguments about women,
> men, guns, and violence. But however real *Thelma and
> Louise* may be, it's not realistic. Its violence erupts within a
> hard-edged satire of wannabe heroism . . . and it builds to
> its conclusion through a series of scenes that emphasize
> the way in which Scott and Callie Khouri's main characters
> move out of this heightened satiric reality into myth.

While I agree with the broad outline of Braudy's assessment, exactly   4
how this text conflates its characters' "consumer identity" with genre and
gender concerns requires elaboration.

GENRE AND GENDER

Associations with the promise of the West and the problems of west-   5
ern migration have been fundamental to the history of road outlaw films as
they are to most Westerns. Both genres look to a mythical natural world,
which still exists in the studio era Western but can only be fruitlessly sought
in the road outlaw film. While ruggedly individualistic classical Western heroes frequently appear out of a vaguely defined state of nature only to return
to it after resolving society's problems, classical outlaws of the road film
begin as members of society who seek escape from or revolt against it.
Their reactive travel odyssey is an effort to overcome their disenfranchised
status within the community, and to locate a better alternative outside of it.
But the Hollywood road outlaw film, born during the Depression years, is already associated nostalgically with a closed frontier. This closure alters frontier notions of self-law and limitless migration and suggests instead an irony
that is indigenous to this subgenre: The protagonist is increasingly entrapped (and usually martyred) the more desperately he/she seeks emanci-
pation. Because this film form implies modernity's confrontation with the
frontier's disappearance, it can also heighten the audience's awareness of
fundamental contradictions in American ideology, where the celebration of
individual freedom and enterprise has simultaneously permitted a history
of colonialistic exploitation.

In the classical road film, mainstream social attitudes and authority   6
usually appear at best injudicious, although the male protagonist's method
of confrontation and escape also seems doomed, as does the enrollment of
a woman as fellow fugitive, who might point to an alternative family/commu-
nity base in the future. Female road outlaws have usually been represented
either as innocent girlfriends and wives, who stand beside their man and

suggest the hope of peaceful family alternatives, or as *femmes fatales,* who betray the male protagonist and the family ideal out of greed. In *You Only Live Once* (1937), Sylvia Sidney plays the faithful wife who tries to escape to Canada with her fugitive husband and their new baby. Their effort to sustain their family is opposed in the film to a highly politicized and vindictive social authority that finally guns them down. Postwar road films such as *White Heat* and *Gun Crazy* of 1949, on the other hand, are more likely to indict principal female characters whether they are mothers, girlfriends, or wives, and to make them significant scapegoats for failed mainstream conventions and values. The character played by Peggy Cummings in *Gun Crazy,* for example, is even more aggressive and ruthless with a gun than is her spouse, which is atypical of the outlaw couple narrative. But she is finally killed by her husband in crime, becoming the extreme that proves the rule. Presumably, nothing is more threatening to patriarchal conventions than a woman who resorts to the tools of aggressive defiance.

Countercultural, antiheroic rebels of the road (who also share historical   7 ties to the tragic heroes of American urban gangsterdom) begin to appear in the late sixties, although the woman figure continues mainly to perform a supporting role to the male protagonist. *Bonnie and Clyde* (1967) features the economically embittered Clyde, who initiates the ingenue Bonnie into bank thefts as a social act. And in *Thieves Like Us* (a 1974 remake of the postwar *They Live By Night*), the woman's odyssey continues to be defined as a romantic choice first and a political choice only secondarily. Unlike the title characters of history and legend in *Bonnie and Clyde* or in *Butch Cassidy and the Sundance Kid* (1969), however, Thelma and Louise are disinclined to rob banks or trains as a calculated lifestyle. They are neither accomplices to nor promoters of male violence, much less neo *femmes noir* who seek financial advantage from it. Although *Thelma and Louise* shares some of the tragi-comic tone of those films, it is twice removed from their nostalgic/revisionary play on Western historicism.

Hints of a significant gender shift in the dominant road protagonist is   8 first notable in Goldie Hawn's role in *Sugarland Express* (1974), where she plays a mother who is determined at all costs to recover her child from a foster home. But as Marsha Kinder points out in her discussion of that character, the "nature of her strength is ambiguous," particularly since she gets her husband killed in the process of getting her baby back. The mother is represented as an "irresponsible child" as much as she is one who "bravely succeeds in fighting the system." Furthermore, because her provocation is presented in purely maternal terms (as it was, incidently, in the factual basis for this story), it remains bound to mainstream traditions.

Thelma and Louise has more important associations with *Easy Rider*   9 (1969) and the way that film indicts a stringent social conformity, rather than institutional enforcement, as its central concern. It is true that the romantic counterculturalism represented in *Easy Rider* hardly begins to problematize a sexism that is directly challenged in the contemporary text. But both films highlight the larger social forces that drive their heroes to desperate acts and futile escape efforts. The laid-back motorcyclists in *Easy Rider,* suddenly wealthy from an illegal drug sale, attempt to travel peacefully across the continent looking for escape and legitimacy, only to run headlong into a violent prejudice that belies America's belief in individual opportunity. "They're gonna talk to you and talk to you and talk to you about individual freedom," the Jack Nicholson character warns his new sidekicks before he is killed, "But they see a free individual, it's gonna scare 'em. . . . It makes 'em dangerous." This theme is expanded in the popular lyrical music of exuberance and then broken dreams that follows the open air flight of Wyatt (Captain America) and Billy, just as it later does *Thelma and Louise.* But the earlier, low-budget film lacks the audiovisual density that is such a significant backdrop in Ridley Scott's work, where the musical score contributes to an often ironic and self-reflexive commentary.

Easy Rider glorifies the wide open spaces of the Southwest that can   10
support an alternative family farm or a struggling communal experiment, but nature in *Thelma and Louise* is at best a last vestige of mother earth under stress, capable only of a metaphorical promise of reintegration. Late in the film, a few nostalgic cowboys on horseback and their longhorn steer momentarily block the women's escape route. But this pastoral setting is soon juxtaposed with a police helicopter that swoops from every angle in pursuit. Scott's cinematic portraits of the highway that stretches through Monument Valley to the desert's horizon is already representative of a Western genre artifact, which can only trap this contemporary female duo in the illusion of flight. Their physical isolation within the big frame is related to their inability to escape their social experience, which has further distanced them from anything transformational in nature. In the film's opening section, their nearest association with the natural is fishing gear they don't know how to use, and a hand gun initially intended to scare away marauding bears.

Unlike the bad culture/good nature antinomy still being tested in *Easy*   11
Rider, Thelma and Louise face the uninviting options of poor jobs and marriages, the meat market hustle of pleasure dens like the Silver Bullet, or its horrific parking lot from which flight seems impossible. Where woman has at best represented a nurturing escape from socioeconomic realities for the male hero in patriarchal narratives, there is no analogous alternative haven for woman through man, whose largely objective psychosocial roles have been directly aligned with the cultural dominant. Hence, the confrontation with patriarchal authority by Thelma and Louise in their flight toward a no longer viable frontier takes the specific form of a rejection of oppressive masculine protectionism.

In more recent road outlaw films such as *Something Wild* (1986), *Wild*   12
at Heart (1990), and *True Romance* (1991), the fugitives' motivations are more psychologically idiosyncratic than in *Thelma and Louise.* The hetero-

sexual couples in these three films tend to commit crimes out of spontaneous convenience and role-playing. They are more enthralled with fulfilling
the images of cultural models such as Louise Brooks, Elvis Presley, or
James Dean than with struggling for social justice. Moreover, they are pursued by mafia types (prompted by a psychopathic mother in *Wild at Heart*)
even more extreme than the institutional authorities, which has the effect of
further complicating heretofore more simplistic, populist ideological polarities. These young couples may challenge social convention or even crime,
and may succeed in expanding the limits of social accommodation, but their
pop culture image-consciousness encloses them within artifice. They long
mainly for a nostalgic, traditional gender and family organization, and thus
remain within an endless circulation of cultural quotations characteristic of
postmodern hegemony.

Thelma and Louise also avoids the trap of superficial gender-war   13
movies, typified by female-abuse-and-knee-jerk-revenge plots. In *Lipstick*
(1976), for example, the woman victim of rape pursues and ultimately de-
stroys her original attacker, much as the abused woman in *Sleeping With
the Enemy* finally kills her assailant. In different interviews, Ridley Scott
has insisted that *Thelma and Louise* is "not about rape. It's about choices
and freedom" or "about looking at someone's history." And his film's emphasis does shift in the second half from the protagonists' forced response
to abusive males and legalities to their shared determination to regain
control of their private destinies. Louise is no more against Thelma's
sexual awakening with the hitchhiker than Thelma is against Louise making her own decision about commitment to Jimmy. Nor do they reject the
possibility of positive heterosexual relationships in the utopian future of
Mexico.

As a gender transformation of the American road genre, *Thelma and*   14
Louise refuses to take itself too seriously. The text finally inscribes the
comedic disorientation of most of its characters into a larger context of
meaning, where neither gender is well served by the current state of heterosexual dynamics. The frustration both women experience with their male
counterparts is reflected back on their men's failures to maintain what they
assume to be the proper masculine image. The lone Jamaican bicyclist
notwithstanding, the inability of any of these characters to fulfill either their
own or their mate's expectations underlines the contemporary strains on the
heterosexual unit as a viable social or romantic haven.

Margaret Carlson's concern that Thelma and Louise fail to show the in-   15
timacy characteristic of female friends may have some justification. But that
they "become like any other shoot-first-and-talk-later action heroes," whose
violent skills are central to their identity, is contrary to the narrative intent
that affords them a charmed escape. After the Harlan Puckett episode, the
women are not forced into shootouts so common to couple and buddy initiation films. Louise is shocked when Thelma pulls a gun on a suddenly

terrified macho state trooper. And their target practice destruction of a phal-lic silver tanker truck comes only after a hearing in which the half-wit driver is given an opportunity to apologize for his sexist insults. When Thelma dons the trucker's filthy cap emblazoned with an American flag, her retalia-tion against working class misogyny begins to include his chauvinistic brand of patriotism.

Thelma and Louise are hardly gritty idealists or vigilantes in revolt 16 against corrupt bureaucracy or men generally. Nor is their inadvertent use of weapons a "Fembo" gender variation on fascistic militancy that would pay homage to it. They do follow generic convention in their ability to shoot straight and temporarily to foil the police, yet they are not working them-selves up toward an apocalyptic proving ground of blazing weapons. They constantly articulate and interrogate their impulses, repeatedly checking by phone to clarify their status. Louise explains in her last call to the police: "Got some kind of snowball effect going here. . . . Would you believe me if I told you this whole thing was an accident?" Louise's assumption of a te-dious, difficult, and unsympathetic legal process prompts her to explain to Thelma that even if they were eventually to go free from prison for their crimes, it would be at the price of "ruining their lives." To which Thelma replies, "Gee, the law is some tricky shit ain't it?" reducing the arcana of pa-triarchal legal procedures to an offhand joke.

The experience of Louise and Thelma is offered as a self-consciously 17 *hypothetical* possibility of feminine response to male aggression. The violent signifiers of the women's handguns finally go unused against the rifles held by the lawmen. Their choice in the end to grasp hands and kiss, to drive over the cliff rather than to face the further violation of bullets or prison, is hardly a proud warrior code of death by arms (as in *Butch Cassidy and the Sundance Kid*). Their suicide conclusively negates the self-righteous glory of violent confrontation; it points instead to a subjective, sisterly bond dedi-cated to mythic if not immediately realizable alternatives. This inclination is made implicitly by the film's framing apparatus. The opening credits are placed over a night-into-day shot of a dirt road winding toward a mountain range, and the film ends with a shot of the women's suspended leap of faith out over a reversed mountain range (the Grand Canyon), which is faded up to white. This closing still frame of the happy tandem driving into air is asso-ciated with the Polaroid two-shot briefly frozen on the screen just before their initial departure from home, and seen again (blowing off the back seat) at the film's conclusion. Such an aesthetically controlled encapsulation of their experience moves away from the spectacle of polarizing action drama and supports instead a more existential reading of their reach for liberation. Whether the mythopoeic tendency of this closing image compromises the film's satiric bite remains open to question.

What Thelma learns from the hard-traveled Louise is not simply to be 18 wary of phallocentric control. She also learns to embrace movement and action and choice as viable alternatives to her initial masochistic passivity. As Louise is prone to say, "You get what you settle for." In other words, *Thelma and Louise* turns the trajectory of its road film duo not so much into a male bashing spectacle as into a metaphor of the longing for a more active and assertive feminine principal of subjectivity.   ©

CRITICAL READING

1. Feminism can be defined simply as a political and theoretical movement concerned with establishing legal, economic, and social equality between men and women. Discuss the points in Boozer's essay that support an argument that *Thelma and Louise* is a feminist film.

2. In the second paragraph of his essay, Boozer notes his qualified agreement with *Time* magazine writer Richard Schickel's assertion that *Thelma and Louise* is "satirically aware of the violent and depersonalizing traditions of our popular culture." First, think about examples of "violent and depersonalizing traditions of our popular culture," and then write about the ways in which *Thelma and Louise* satirically portrays this tradition rather than simply adding another unself-conscious portrayal to this kind of film portrayal. What characters, events, and attitudes in the film seem satirical? Further, what is being satirized here? Draw on points in Boozer's essay for your answer.

3. In your own words, rephrase Boozer's statement on page 213 that Thelma and Louise's "inadvertent use of weapons" is not a "'Fembo' gender variation on fascistic militancy that would pay homage to it."

CLASS DISCUSSION

1. As a class, come up with a general list of American culture's traditional stereotypes of femininity and masculinity. Then discuss examples of how *Thelma and Louise* enacts and questions these stereotypes.

2. Discuss other action-drama films depicting two male buddies out on the road, committing or combating crime. How are men and women typically portrayed in these movies? Are Thelma and Louise heroines? Why, or why not? Discuss the film's ending, and what students make of it. What might the ending say about women's roles in current American culture? Does the ending signify anything hopeful, or is it portraying a negative view of women's current status?

DIRECTED FREEWRITE

Now that you've read a critical interpretation of *Thelma and Louise,* go back to the original interpretation you made before completing the reading (see headnote). Write about any ways that your own points have been altered, reinforced, or unchanged by any of Boozer's points, and then discuss the reasons, based on logic and evidence, for the current state of your views on this movie's meanings.

MASCULINITY AND MARGINALITY
IN *ROB ROY* AND *BRAVEHEART*

James R. Keller

Keller focuses on one particular aspect of the films *Rob Roy* and *Braveheart* in this essay, arguing about the ways that gay male stereotypes and characters in these films serve to define the masculinity of the heroes in specific ways. In arguing his reading of the film, Keller makes a broader argument about the relationship between stereotypes of gay men and cultural norms of masculinity and heterosexuality in American culture. As you read, note where you find Keller's points persuasive and where not, and think about ways he uses evidence from the films to support his points.

James R. Keller is a Full Professor of English and Director of the Honors College at Mississippi University for Women. He received a Ph.D. from the University of South Florida in 1991. Keller has written two books: Princes, Soldiers, and Rogues: The Politic Malcontent of Renaissance Drama *and* Anne Rice and Sexual Politics: The Early Novels. *He has written articles in a number of areas including Renaissance literature, cultural studies, gay and lesbian studies, drama, and film. He is currently at work on his third book, tentatively titled* Queer Friendly Film and TV.

The release and success of films such as *The Crying Game* (1992), *Philadelphia* (1994), *To Wong Fu, Thanks for Everything, Julie Newmar* (1995), and *The Birdcage* (1996) would seem to suggest that the mainstream movie industry has softened its anti-homosexual bias so well documented in Vito Russo's book *The Celluloid Closet.* However, Hollywood's portrayals of gay men as villains and buffoons are seldom far beneath the surface of even the most positive gay characterizations. Consider, for instance, that all four of the above-mentioned films include characters who are antagonistic toward the gay characters, thus reinforcing the cultural presumption that homophobia is instinctual: In *The Crying Game* the central character, played by Stephen Rea, actually vomits when he realizes that he has made love to a transsexual. In *Philadelphia* Denzel Washington, who plays a legal advocate, must struggle to overcome his own revulsion toward the dying, gay protagonist (Tom Hanks). The drag queens in both *To Wong Fu* and *The Birdcage* are forced to run or hide from police officers and politicians, respectively, whenever they leave the narrow confines of the big-city bar circuit.

Source: "Masculinity and Marginality in 'Rob Roy' and 'Braveheart'" by James R. Keller in *Journal of Popular Film and Television,* vol. 24, no. 4, Winter 1997. Copyright © 1997 by Heldref Publications. Reprinted with the permission of the Helen Dwight Reid Educational Foundation. Published by Heldref Publications, 1319 Eighteenth St., NW, Washington, DC 20036-1802.

Most public discussions of homosexuality are accompanied by alterna-   2
tive and often openly antagonistic perspectives. The American public has
been conditioned to conceptualize the gay lifestyle as the inferior half of sociosexual binarism—heterosexual/homosexual. This polarity, in the public
consciousness, duplicates and encompasses still more basic binary and hierarchical assumptions shared by much of our culture: natural/unnatural,
normal/abnormal, health/sickness, and masculine/feminine. However, it is
the last of these polarities that appears to be the current preoccupation
within recent debates over the "place" of gays in U.S. society. In the popular
mind, gay men and lesbians breach the neatly defined and strictly policed
gender divisions within our culture. Recent scholars within the field of men's
studies have defined gay men as the "symbolic repository of all that is excluded from hegemonic masculinity." The opposition between gay male and
straight male has been used within the conceptual framework of numerous
writers and filmmakers. Films such as *Rob Roy* and *Braveheart* are structured on a dichotomy that codes homosexuality as the negation of traditional
masculinity.

Michael Caton-Jones's *Rob Roy* (MGM, 1995) is one of two recent   3
films that depict the struggle of the Scottish for self-determination. However,
the film's narrative is less about early-eighteenth-century Scotland than
about American family values and traditional masculinity. Robert Roy Mac-
Gregor (Liam Neeson), his wife Mary (Jessica Lange), and their two children
are an anachronism, an American, bourgeois family living in the preindustrial Scottish Highlands. Their peace is disturbed by an effeminate British
fop and swordsman Archibald Cunningham (Tim Roth), who is in the employ
of the Marquis of Montrose (John Hurt). Cunningham hounds Rob Roy virtually to death, and his removal becomes vital to the maintenance of the family and the MacGregor clan. The film juxtaposes two separate masculinities:
that of the Scottish highlander and that of the British fop.

Archibald Cunningham's behavior sets him up as the antithesis of the   4
MacGregor clan and its values of honor, fidelity, and fraternity; but mostly
Cunningham is contrasted with the brutish masculinity of Rob. The effeminacy of the eighteenth-century fop was notorious, and Tim Roth's "Archie" is
no exception: he bows, smirks, lisps, and poses. Although Archie is heterosexual in his choice of sexual partners, his appearance and behavior are
negative stereotypes of the twentieth-century gay man. In the eighteenth
century, the fop was commonly associated with same-sex eroticism involving adolescent boys despite his reputation as a womanizer. In *Rob Roy,* a
substantial part of the dialogue and imagery is committed to maintaining the
association between Archie and same-sex practices. When Archie first
meets the Duke of Argyll, the duke playfully inquires whether he is a "bug-
gerer of boys," to which Cunningham responds, "In my own defense, I
thought him a girl at the moment of entry." The duke quips, reinforcing
Archie's sexual ambiguity, "Archie could not tell ass from quim."

Archie's mannerisms do not at all correspond with the gender codes of   5
twentieth-century America. Even when he defeats the duke's champion in a
sword fight, he does so with dainty swordsmanship. Indeed, the contrast between the Scotsman Gutherie's broadsword and Archie's rapier forms a
symbolic contrast between the film's competing masculinities. Gutherie
wields his broadsword with powerful and awkward strokes while Archie
sweeps his lighter sword nimbly and artfully. The "gentler party is the surest
winner," to the watching characters' surprise.

The audience's anxiety over Archie's sexuality is permitted to linger   6
through one intervening scene in which Rob and his wife make love. The
couple's sexual dalliance, coded as legitimate because they are married, is
immediately followed by the sexual transgression of Archie, who deflowers
the serving maid Betty. Later, when Archie is awakened by Montrose's
agent Killern, he perpetuates the homoerotic imagery associated with him:
"Do you think I want to wake up and see some bloody Scotsman staring
down at me?" Later when Betty asks to become his permanent partner,
Archie responds:

> You think me a gentleman because I have linen and can
> manage a lisp. I am but a bastard abroad, seeking my for-
> tune and the favors of great men, as big a whore as my
> mother ever was.

He abandons Betty when she becomes pregnant, telling her to "root it out."
He explains that "love is but a dung heap" and he "but a cock that crawls
upon it to crow."

Archie's sexual marauding extends beyond the seduction and discard-   7
ing of serving maids. When he is commissioned by Montrose to hunt down
the insolent and rebellious Rob Roy, Archie uses the Scotsman's wife in the
execution of his designs. He rapes Mary and burns their house, hoping that
the crimes will inspire Rob to seek revenge. However, Mary recognizes
Archie's intentions and refuses to tell her husband of the incident. Eve
Kosofsky Sedgewick's theory of homosocial bonding, in which the aggression and desire between men is mediated through a female, helps to define
the nature of Archie Cunningham's destructive gesture. Archie rapes Rob's
wife to guarantee that the two men have a private encounter of their own—
that they have the opportunity to work out their aggressions on each other.
In the brief exchange between Mary and Archie after the rape, he uses
sword/phallus imagery to describe the score that must be settled between
the two men. He describes Rob:

> Such a man will need to see blood on his blade before
> honor is satisfied. Tell him Archie Cunningham is at his ser-
> vice.

"Blood on his blade" may be an image of phallic penetration—for the ho-mosocial bonding has a homoerotic subtext. However, when Rob learns of the rape of Mary, he is already Archie's prisoner. In a verbal exchange be-tween the two men, Rob calls the Englishman a "violator of women": Archie responds, "I had hoped you'd have come to me much sooner on that score." To enrage Rob, Archie describes the rape in a parody of "kiss-and-tell" male bonding: "Your wife was far sweeter forced than many are willing . . . not all of her objected."

In contrast to Archie Cunningham, Rob Roy is constructed as the quin-   8
tessential family man, who looks after not only his wife and children but also his clan. Archie's villainy is punctuated by Rob's fatherly advice to his two sons, "never mistreat a woman or malign a man." Of course, those pieces of wisdom, intended to help Rob's boys become men, are the antitheses of the crimes committed by Montrose and Archie. The former desires to enlist Rob's assistance in maligning the Duke of Argyll, and Archie's abuses of women are already documented. The communal values of the clan are also distinguished from the solitude and murderous selfishness of Archie. While the MacGregor clan celebrates the thousand-pound loan intended to propel them into the cattle-marketing business, Archie pursues Allen McDonald (Eric Stoltz) through the forest to rob and murder him. Moreover, Archie's refusal to take responsibility for the child he fathered is opposed to Rob's embracing of the child of rape. Whereas the fop encourages the abortion of his own child, Rob raises a bastard as legitimate.

Rob's position as the symbolic repudiation of subversive desire is rein-   9
forced by dialogue. As Rob prepares to abandon his family in anticipation of the arrival of Montrose's troops, Mary asks him if he will seek comfort from a sheep while hiding from the English. Rob retorts that he will pick one that "does not bleat so bitterly." Absent is the suggestion that he would seek the company of his clansmen, an idea unthinkable for a family man such as Rob. The couple would never joke about Rob having sex with a man. The negation of any homoeroticism associated with Rob is continued when Archie Cunningham arrives at the household and demands the "outlaw Mac-Gregor." Mary defends her husband's masculinity: "If you think he'd be lying in his bed waiting for you, you're more a fool than you look." Her statement can be seen as a negation of the idea that, symbolically, Archie could be Rob's bed partner and that Rob would allow himself to be the subject of Archie's violation.

Rob's honor is set against the deceit of the Englishmen, particularly   10
Archie. He offers his word as collateral for the thousand-pound loan: the Englishman requires Rob's family land. The naive honesty of the Scotsman is intended to be a refreshing break from the corruption and cynicism of the courtly world. When brought before Montrose to answer for his insolence, Rob reveals the plot against him perpetrated by Archie and Killern. Mon-trose asks for evidence, and Rob gives only his word. The suspicious

marquis responds, "It will take more than that." Rob then offers Archie's "nature" as evidence against him: the sexual renegade is also the social outlaw. The refusal of the marquis to recognize the Scotsman's veracity is offered as a sign of the former's corruption. Archie is indeed deceitful and unprincipled, but Rob mistakes the extent to which Montrose and Archie are in league to take his land.

There are stronger visual images that reinforce the opposition between the two masculinities. Rob is a kilt-wearing Scotsman who is often dirty. (He is, however, domesticated, taking a bath in the loch before entering his wife's bed.) He is the ideal of athletic masculinity—large and powerful, capable of enduring much pain. Archie, as stated before, is by twentieth-century standards effeminate: he wears powdered wigs, makeup, and fancy clothes. His movements are slow, affected, and dainty, and he holds his hands erect but limp-wristed. When the men finally settle their score at the end of the film, masculine brawn prevails over gentility. Although Archie is clearly the better swordsman, bringing Rob to his knees, the latter has greater endurance. As Archie waits to strike the mortal blow, Rob grasps the blade of the Englishman's sword, and with his free arm, virtually chops Archie in half with a single stroke—one we are led to believe Archie could never muster. 11

The contest between brawn and effeminacy is settled in favor of brawn, but what does this mean in terms of gender politics? The prioritizing of Rob's lifestyle within the film is not deconstructed. Indeed, it is reconstructed. Whereas much of Archie's actions and successes seem to suggest that effeminacy and deceit can win out over honesty and sheer strength, the conclusion restores the traditional hierarchical opposition between the competing values, raising the communal over the individual, honor over deceit, monogamy over promiscuity, brawn over gentility and art, the provincial over the urban, the plebeian over the aristocratic, and the Scottish over the English. The technique employed in the vilification of the Englishmen includes feminizing them. One might argue that such behavior was commonplace among heterosexual men in the eighteenth century, so such a portrayal is not ultimately homophobic, but the eighteenth-century audience is not watching the film; a late-twentieth-century American audience is, an audience that recognizes the stereotypes of the gay male. Despite the images of Archie Cunningham sexually exploiting women, his language, his mannerisms, and his behavior identify him as homosexual and, in the context of the film, as the antithesis of masculinity, honor, family, and integrity. He is successful in winning out over more masculine males through cunning, but eventually sheer strength and endurance prevail. Archie is constructed as a violent threat to the social peace, quick to anger and quick to kill. 12

Mel Gibson's *Braveheart* (Paramount, 1995) deals with some similar themes, particularly the juxtaposition of competing masculinities. I do not claim to be the first to recognize the potential homophobia of this film. In nine separate cities, the Gay and Lesbian Alliance against Defamation 13

(GLAAD) led protests against the film, protests prompted by the film's controversial portrayal of the English Prince Edward. Although the prince seems to have a minor role within the film, he is symbolically central, acting as a contrast to the portrait of William Wallace (Mel Gibson), the Scottish rebel.

Seldom in recent films has there been a more stereotypical and nega- 14 tive portrayal of a gay man than that offered in *Braveheart.* Edward (Peter Hanly) is a throwback to the characters of earlier decades. He is constructed as vain, frivolous, and effeminate. While his father wages war and handles the serious business of the state, Edward frolics and poses with his courtly friends, ignoring his wife and infuriating his father. The king, Edward Longshanks (Patrick MacGoohan), must slap his son to make him respectful of authority and sensible long enough to address the Scottish rebellion seriously. In another scene, while his father and William Wallace are busy attending to the affairs of war, the prince is shown vainly posing and modeling his new clothes in front of a mirror, surrounded by an entourage of courtly butterflies, who all, shortly thereafter, swish down the hallway and out of sight. In the most damaging scene of the film, Edward's lover attempts to discuss the appropriate military strategy to put down rebellion and is tossed out of a window by the king to the laughter and occasional applause of the movie-going audience. The implicit message here is that gays have no place in the serious affairs of men. Edward's lover is killed because he presumed to knowledge about war, because he presumed to participate in the decision-making process of the state. The most persistent criticism of Prince Edward is related to his marriage. He refuses to embrace and comfort his wife, and it is here that the link between the prince and William Wallace is made.

Gibson's William Wallace, like Rob Roy, is represented as the ideal of 15 raw manhood. At the beginning of the film, what appears to be a brawl between Wallace and another arrogant young Scotsman is in actuality a meeting of old friends, Wallace playfully punches his buddy in the face to greet him after a long absence, a behavior that constitutes the antithesis of Edward's amorous preoccupation with his friends. Moreover, the image of Edward preening himself before a mirror is contrasted to the image of Wallace, covered in the blood of battle, shouting "Freedom!" As in *Rob Roy,* the Scotsman is shown to have more integrity than the usurping, effeminate Englishman. Whereas Wallace struggles for freedom, the English struggle to maintain domination and tyranny. Wallace's homosocial commitment to his men is set against Edward's seeming indifference when his lover is killed by the king, thus invoking the heterosexist presumption that no real affection could exist between gay men. Wallace is subject to constant betrayal, while the two Edwards deceitfully exploit his betrayers. Wallace's single shortcoming is his trust of other men, a flaw that Edward Longshanks manipulates to his advantage by enlisting the loyalties of Robert the Bruce with a promise of a Scottish throne. It is through treachery and subversion that Wallace is given up to his enemies and executed.

Wallace's marriage is an important point of divergence between the two representations of masculinity. Wallace secretly woos his wife (Catherine McCormack) in a romantic fashion. And contrary to Edward's matrimonial indifference, Wallace vows to make war on the English when they kill his wife. Contrary to Edward's vain preoccupations, Wallace almost single-handedly wipes out an entire regiment, driving the English from the province. The traditional man could never patiently brook his wife's violation, because the crime is as much against his honor as against her body. It is the structural device of the two wives in the film (Wallace's and Edward's) that produces some of the most important issues in the film. William Wallace is "evened" with them, "wife for wife." However, he does not kill the English princess (Sophie Marceau), since such an action would undermine his own masculine honor and remove his motivation for righteous indignation. He falls in love with her, meets her in secret, as he did his wife, with the implication that the English cannot satisfy their women—a compromising of their masculinity. It is here that the link between Edward's and Wallace's manhood becomes most plain. What entitles a man to be a leader of men is his willingness and capacity to satisfy a woman. Prince Edward is symbolically excluded from this realm: Wallace's triumph is his emasculation of the English monarchy. 16

What then are the politics of *Braveheart's* homophobic portrayal of Prince Edward? The director constructs Edward as the symbolic antithesis of manhood, incapable and unworthy of a place within the affairs of war and government. By defining Wallace's manhood in contrast to Edward's, Gibson invites a comparison of their politics. If Wallace fights for honor, justice, trust, integrity, and freedom, then the future Edward II must signify the negation of all these concepts. The effect of this portrayal is to construct the male homosexual as a representation of all that is repugnant. 17

I contend that the values embraced by William Wallace and Rob MacGregor are clearly intended to refer to contemporary American politics; thus the implicit message of the films reinforces the conservative agendas of the past decade and perpetuates the current trend to scapegoat homosexuals. In Archibald Cunningham and Prince Edward we see the revival of the homosexual villains and buffoons that Vito Russo described in his book. The sexual marauding of Archie Cunningham reveals the potential for violence and social chaos inherent in those unwilling to conform to American sexual norms. The depiction of Edward suggests that gay men are too frivolous, ineffectual, and vain to be trusted with the serious affairs of heterosexual men. *Rob Roy* and *Braveheart* reveal our culture's subconscious fear of the feminized man. The films portray gay men as destructive of manhood and virility and as a threat to the solidarity of the family. © 18

CRITICAL READING

1. Sum up Keller's argument in your own words, and then discuss whether you find the argument, or any parts of it, persuasive or not. Which points are more persuasive than others, and why?
2. Discuss Keller's statement in the second paragraph that "In the popular mind, gay men and lesbians breach the neatly defined and strictly policed gender divisions within our culture." How are gender divisions in American culture defined? In what ways and for whom are gender divisions strictly policed? Discuss stereotypes of gays and lesbians that illustrate Keller's point about "breaching" the gender divisions.
3. Keller argues that while the character Archibald Cunningham in *Rob Roy* is ostensibly heterosexual, the film nonetheless uses his character to illustrate a number of negative homosexual stereotypes. How does the film portray such sexual ambiguity, and why, according to Keller, does it attempt this portrayal?

CLASS DISCUSSION

1. What implicit messages about gay men are portrayed by these films, according to Keller? How do these messages fit (or not) with cultural stereotypes of gays? Do we as a culture seem to fear the "feminized man," as Keller asserts? What evidence from the culture at large might one draw on to support this assertion?
2. Regardless of what one thinks of Keller's interpretation, it is self-evident that stereotypes of gay men do cast them as effeminate, so Keller's points about these movies seem to fit into larger cultural beliefs. Then, at the end of Keller's essay, he broadens his point in the last paragraph when he argues that gays are portrayed in society at large as "a threat to the solidarity of the family." Discuss how this supposed threat gets played out in our cultural discourse about homosexuality.

DIRECTED FREEWRITE

Read the following assertions, and then write continuously for twenty minutes in agreement with either of them: (1) These are just movies, so there's no need to spend time analyzing them. (2) Movies have an impact on us, so it's important to look at the messages they convey.

FILM STUDIES UNIT WRITING ASSIGNMENTS

1. An influential literary scholar named Stanley Fish has written in his book *Is There a Text in This Class?* of the ways that interpretations of particular texts—poems, novels, films, paintings, songs, and so forth—are influenced as much by our membership in an "interpretive community" as by the details of the text itself. We all belong to communities that share an understanding of meaning. As members of the American community, most of us would look at a picture of Uncle Sam pointing his "I Want You" finger and would know that this image means service to one's country, patriotism, and loyalty. And further, veterans of

a war might interpret this image differently than would antiwar protesters. Someone living during World War II, will view the image differently than would someone born in the 1970s. These memberships in different communities shape our perceptions of things. Write an essay in which you critically examine your own interpretation(s) of one of the three films featured in this unit, according to your identities, beliefs, and experiences, and what communities you belong to. You can choose to focus either on your reaction to interpretations offered by Boozer or Keller, or on your own independent interpretation. What aspects of your own identity and experience might play a role in forming your views of the film? How might these aspects of who you are shape how you view the movie and its meanings?

2. As Jack Boozer notes in his essay on *Thelma and Louise,* critics have viewed the film in a number of different ways. The chief issue of the "debate" over the film concerns whether the film celebrates "liberated females, male bashers—or outlaws" (Boozer, second paragraph). In "The Many Faces of 'Thelma and Louise,'" in a Winter 1991 edition of *Film Quarterly,* Harvey A. Greenberg sums up the debate:

> The film has been variously interpreted as feminist manifesto (the heroines are ordinary women, driven to extraordinary ends by male oppression) and as profoundly antifeminist (the heroines are dangerous phallic caricatures of the very macho violence they're supposedly protesting). Some critics have discerned a lesbian subtext (that final soul kiss at the abyss); others interpret this reading as a demeaning negation of feminine friendship that flies in the face of patriarchal authority. (20)

> New York *Daily News* columnist Richard Johnson argues that the film "justifies armed robbery, manslaughter, and chronic drunken driving as exercises in consciousness raising," and further claims it is "degrading to men, with pathetic stereotypes of testosterone-crazed behavior."

> Take up one of these positions, and write an essay arguing either for or against the interpretation, using specific details from the movie and from Boozer's essay, if applicable, to support your interpretation. Read the discussion of critical interpretation essays in the next assignment.

3. Find a film that portrays the kind of quintessential traditional masculinity as discussed by Keller, and analyze the ways this film puts forth its definitions of manliness. Westerns, action-adventure films, and suspense thrillers are good movies in which to find these kinds of portrayals. In your interpretive essay, focus on how the film sets up oppositions to the masculine ideal in other characters such as women, effeminate men, children, and so on. Make an argument about how these oppositions and other elements in the movie help to present a specific version of masculinity, in the way that Keller does.

> The essays by Boozer and Keller represent examples of the kinds of interpretive writing that scholars in the humanities routinely produce. Critical interpretation of this kind involves describing the artifacts from a relatively objective point

of view: what are the specific qualities exhibited by the artifact? In the case of films, these qualities would be characterization, camera angles, dialogue, and scenery. After describing the artifact, the critic has to step back from objective observation and ask questions about how the elements within the work may relate to each other. Questions such as these help the critic to interpret the underlying meaning of the film; what messages are implied in the artifact, or, what meanings—perhaps not consciously intentional by the film's director—can be derived from the work in question?

The process is not quite this simple, of course. Critics typically bring to bear a number of tools to aid in and influence their interpretation. These tools include such things as the filmmaker's other work, knowledge of the historical context in which the work was created, and specific theoretical alignments that influence the critic's interpretation. The writers of both interpretive pieces in this unit are influenced by feminist, gender, and gay and lesbian theory, and these alignments lead the critics to focus on depictions of gender and sexuality. Interpretive essays—whether theoretically informed or not—have as their thesis the critic's particular "take" on what the art is saying and on how it is saying this. This assignment is asking you to employ Keller's perspective as the theoretical lens through which you view and interpret a film.

4. Both of the essays in this unit concern themselves with gender crossings and with traditional gender roles and their violations. Write an essay comparing and contrasting the portrayals of traditional or nontraditional gender roles in a recent film with those depictions in either *Thelma and Louise, Rob Roy,* and/or *Braveheart.* Make sure your essay makes a specific point about the relationship between the gender roles depicted in the two films with which you are dealing, drawing on points from Boozer's or Keller's essays where applicable. For a more detailed discussion of comparison and contrast (which is a kind of synthesis writing), see assignment 2 on page 165 in the Philosophy unit of Chapter 2.

Unit 2
Lesbian and Gay Studies— Hidden Histories

CAPITALISM AND GAY IDENTITY
John D'Emilio

In this provocative essay, John D'Emilio argues that the rise of capitalism in the nineteenth century caused some fundamental changes in society (and particularly in the family)—changes that helped lead to the creation of a gay and lesbian identity. A crucial distinction underlying D'Emilio's argument is that of gay activities as distinct from gay identity; although gay activity seems to have always been around, D'Emilio advances the position that gayness as an identity came into being only in the late nineteenth and early twentieth centuries. Such an assertion places D'Emilio in the "social constructionist" camp, that is, in opposition to "essentialist," who argue that homosexual identity is something inherent in the nature of certain individuals and that lesbians and gay men have always been around. D'Emilio argues that certain conditions of society "construct" the gay/lesbian identity. Think about the implications of such an argument, which suggests the possibility of further change—in sexual identities, in the structure of the family, of gender roles, perhaps. As you read, keep in mind this possibility for change, perhaps envisioning future changes that could occur in these (or other) areas of human life.

John D'Emilio is a Professor of Gender & Women Studies, and History, at the University of Illinois at Chicago. He is the author or editor of several books, including: Sexual Politics, Sexual Communities: The Making of a Homosexual Minority in the United States, 1940–1970; Intimate Matters: A History of Sexuality in America; Making Trouble: Essays on Gay History, Politics, and the University; *and* Creating Change: Sexuality, Public Policy, and Civil Rights. *He was the founding director of the Policy Institute of the National Gay and Lesbian Task Force, which conducts research and does strategic planning on gay, lesbian, bisexual, and transgender issues. The recipient of fellowships from the National Endowment for the Humanities and the Guggenheim Foundation, he is currently writing a biography of Bayard Rustin, an American pacifist and civil rights leader.*

For gay men and lesbians, the 1970s were years of significant 1
achievement. Gay liberation and women's liberation changed the sexual
landscape of the nation. Hundreds of thousands of gay women and men
came out and openly affirmed same-sex eroticism. We won repeal of
sodomy laws in half the states, a partial lifting of the exclusion of lesbians
and gay men from federal employment, civil rights protection in a few dozen
cities, the inclusion of gay rights in the platform of the Democratic Party, and
the elimination of homosexuality from the psychiatric profession's list of
mental illnesses. The gay male subculture expanded and became increasingly visible in large cities, and lesbian feminists pioneered in building alternative institutions and an alternative culture that attempted to embody a
liberatory vision of the future.

In the 1980s, however, with the resurgence of an active right wing, gay 2
men and lesbians face the future warily. Our victories appear tenuous and
fragile; the relative freedom of the past few years seems too recent to be
permanent. In some parts of the lesbian and gay male community, a feeling
of doom is growing: analogies with McCarthy's America, when "sexual perverts" were a special target of the Right, and with Nazi Germany, where
gays were shipped to concentration camps, surface with increasing frequency. Everywhere there is the sense that new strategies are in order if we
want to preserve our gains and move ahead.

I believe that a new, more accurate theory of gay history must be part 3
of this political enterprise. When the gay liberation movement began at the
end of the 1960s, gay men and lesbians had no history that we could use to
fashion our goals and strategy. In the ensuing years, in building a movement without a knowledge of our history, we instead invented a mythology.
This mythical history drew on personal experience, which we read backward
in time. For instance, most lesbians and gay men in the 1960s first discovered their homosexual desires in isolation, unaware of others, and without
resources for naming and understanding what they felt. From this experience, we constructed a myth of silence, invisibility, and isolation as the essential characteristics of gay life in the past as well as the present.
Moreover, because we faced so many oppressive laws, public policies, and
cultural beliefs, we projected this into an image of the abysmal past: until
gay liberation, lesbians and gay men were always the victims of systematic,
undifferentiated, terrible oppression.

These myths have limited our political perspective. They have con- 4
tributed, for instance, to an overreliance on a strategy of coming out—if
every gay man and lesbian in America came out, gay oppression would
end—and have allowed us to ignore the institutionalized ways in which homophobia and heterosexism are reproduced. They have encouraged, at
times, an incapacitating despair, especially at moments like the present:
How can we unravel a gay oppression so pervasive and unchanging?

There is another historical myth that enjoys nearly universal accep- 5
tance in the gay movement, the myth of the "eternal homosexual." The argument runs something like this: gay men and lesbians always were and
always will be. We are everywhere; not just now, but throughout history, in
all societies and all periods. This myth served a positive political function in
the first years of gay liberation. In the early 1970s, when we battled an ideology that either denied our existence or defined us as psychopathic individuals or freaks of nature, it was empowering to assert that "we are
everywhere." But in recent years it has confined us as surely as the most
homophobic medical theories, and locked our movement in place.

Here I wish to challenge this myth. I want to argue that gay men and 6
lesbians have *not* always existed. Instead, they are a product of history, and
have come into existence in a specific historical era. Their emergence is associated with the relations of capitalism; it has been the historical development of capitalism—more specifically, its free labor system—that has
allowed large numbers of men and women in the late twentieth century to
call themselves gay, to see themselves as part of a community of similar
men and women, and to organize politically on the basis of that identity. Finally, I want to suggest some political lessons we can draw from this view of
history.

What, then, are the relationships between the free labor system of 7
capitalism and homosexuality? First, let me review some features of capitalism. Under capitalism, workers are "free" laborers in two ways. We have the
freedom to look for a job. We own our ability to work and have the freedom
to sell our labor power for wages to anyone willing to buy it. We are also
freed from the ownership of anything except our labor power. Most of us do
not own the land or the tools that produce what we need, but rather have to
work for a living in order to survive. So, if we are free to sell our labor power
in the positive sense, we are also freed, in the negative sense, from any
other alternative. This dialectic—the constant interplay between exploitation
and some measure of autonomy—informs all of the history of those who
have lived under capitalism.

As capital—money used to make more money—expands, so does this 8
system of free labor. Capital expands in several ways. Usually it expands in
the same place, transforming small firms into larger ones, but it also expands by taking over new areas of production: the weaving of cloth, for instance, or the baking of bread. Finally, capital expands geographically. In
the United States, capitalism initially took root in the Northeast, at a time
when slavery was the dominant system in the South and when noncapitalist
Native American societies occupied the western half of the continent. During
the nineteenth century, capital spread from the Atlantic to the Pacific, and in
the twentieth, U.S. capital has penetrated almost every part of the world.

The expansion of capital and the spread of wage labor have effected a   9
profound transformation in the structure and functions of the nuclear family,
the ideology of family life, and the meaning of heterosexual relations. It is
these changes in the family that are most directly linked to the appearance
of a collective gay life.

The white colonists in seventeenth-century New England established   10
villages structured around a household economy, composed of family units
that were basically self-sufficient, independent, and patriarchal. Men,
women, and children farmed land owned by the male head of household. Although there was a division of labor between men and women, the family
was truly an interdependent unit of production: the survival of each member
depended on the cooperation of all. The home was a workplace where
women processed raw farm products into food for daily consumption, where
they made clothing, soap, and candles, and where husbands, wives, and
children worked together to produce the goods they consumed.

By the nineteenth century, this system of household production was in   11
decline. In the Northeast, as merchant capitalists invested the money accumulated through trade in the production of goods, wage labor became more
common. Men and women were drawn out of the largely self-sufficient
household economy of the colonial era into a capitalist system of free labor.
For women in the nineteenth century, working for wages rarely lasted beyond marriage; for men, it became a permanent condition.

The family was thus no longer an independent unit of production. But   12
although no longer independent, the family was still interdependent. Because capitalism had not expanded very far, because it had not yet taken
over—or socialized—the production of consumer goods, women still performed necessary productive labor in the home. Many families no longer
produced grain, but wives still baked into bread the flour they bought with
their husbands' wages; or, when they purchased yarn or cloth, they still
made clothing for their families. By the mid-1800s, capitalism had destroyed
the economic self-sufficiency of many families, but not the mutual dependence of the members.

This transition away from the household family-based economy to a   13
fully developed capitalist free labor economy occurred very slowly, over almost two centuries. As late as 1920, 50 percent of the U.S. population lived
in communities of fewer than 2,500 people. The vast majority of blacks in
the early twentieth century lived outside the free labor economy, in a system
of sharecropping and tenancy that rested on the family. Not only did independent farming as a way of life still exist for millions of Americans, but even
in towns and small cities women continued to grow and process food, make
clothing, and engage in other kinds of domestic production.

But for those people who felt the brunt of these changes, the family   14
took on new significance as an affective unit, an institution that produced not
goods but emotional satisfaction and happiness. By the 1920s among the

white middle class, the ideology surrounding the family described it as the means through which men and women formed satisfying, mutually enhancing relationships and created an environment that nurtured children. The family became the setting for a "personal life," sharply distinguished and disconnected from the public world of work and production.

The meaning of heterosexual relations also changed. In colonial New England, the birthrate averaged over seven children per woman of childbearing age. Men and women needed the labor of children. Producing offspring was as necessary for survival as producing grain. Sex was harnessed to procreation. The Puritans did not celebrate *hetero*sexuality but rather marriage; they condemned *all* sexual expression outside the marriage bond and did not differentiate sharply between sodomy and heterosexual fornication. 15

By the 1970s, however, the birthrate had dropped to under two. With the exception of the post–World War II baby boom, the decline has been continuous for two centuries, paralleling the spread of capitalist relations of production. It occurred even when access to contraceptive devices and abortion was systematically curtailed. The decline has included every segment of the population—urban and rural families, blacks and whites, ethnics and WASPs, the middle class and the working class. 16

As wage labor spread and production became socialized, then, it became possible to release sexuality from the "imperative" to procreate. Ideologically, heterosexual expression came to be a means of establishing intimacy, promoting happiness, and experiencing pleasure. In divesting the household of its economic independence and fostering the separation of sexuality from procreation, capitalism has created conditions that allow some men and women to organize a personal life around their erotic/emotional attraction to their own sex. It has made possible the formation of urban communities of lesbians and gay men and, more recently, of a politics based on a sexual identity. 17

Evidence from colonial New England court records and church sermons indicates that male and female homosexual behavior existed in the seventeenth century. Homosexual *behavior,* however, is different from homosexual *identity.* There was, quite simply, no "social space" in the colonial system of production that allowed men and women to be gay. Survival was structured around participation in a nuclear family. There were certain homosexual acts—sodomy among men, "lewdness" among women—in which individuals engaged, but family was so pervasive that colonial society lacked even the category of homosexual or lesbian to describe a person. It is quite possible that some men and women experienced a stronger attraction to their own sex than to the opposite sex—in fact, some colonial court cases refer to men who persisted in their "unnatural" attractions—but one could not fashion out of that preference a way of life. Colonial Massachusetts even had laws prohibiting unmarried adults from living outside family units. 18

By the second half of the nineteenth century, this situation was notice- 19
ably changing as the capitalist system of free labor took hold. Only when *individuals* began to make their living through wage labor, instead of as parts
of an interdependent family unit, was it possible for homosexual desire to
coalesce into a personal identity—an identity based on the ability to remain
outside the heterosexual family and to construct a personal life based on attraction to one's own sex. By the end of the century, a class of men and
women existed who recognized their erotic interest in their own sex, saw it
as a trait that set them apart from the majority, and sought others like themselves. These early gay lives came from a wide social spectrum: civil servants and business executives, department store clerks and college
professors, factory operatives, ministers, lawyers, cooks, domestics,
hoboes, and the idle rich: men and women, black and white, immigrant and
native born.

In this period, gay men and lesbians began to invent ways of meeting 20
each other and sustaining a group life. Already, in the early twentieth century, large cities contained male homosexual bars. Gay men staked out
cruising areas, such as Riverside Drive in New York City and Lafayette Park
in Washington. In St. Louis and the nation's capital, annual drag balls
brought together large numbers of black gay men. Public bathhouses and
YMCAs became gathering spots for male homosexuals. Lesbians formed
literary societies and private social clubs. Some working-class women
"passed" as men to obtain better paying jobs and lived with other women—
lesbian couples who appeared to the world as husband and wife. Among
the faculties of women's colleges, in the settlement houses, and in the professional associations and clubs that women formed one could find lifelong
intimate relationships supported by a web of lesbian friends. By the 1920s
and 1930s, large cities such as New York and Chicago contained lesbian
bars. These patterns of living could evolve because capitalism allowed individuals to survive beyond the confines of the family.

Simultaneously, ideological definitions of homosexual behavior 21
changed. Doctors developed theories about homosexuality, describing it as
a condition, something that was inherent in a person, a part of his or her
"nature." These theories did not represent scientific breakthroughs, elucida-
tions of previously undiscovered areas of knowledge; rather, they were an
ideological response to a new way of organizing one's personal life. The
popularization of the medical model, in turn, affected the consciousness of
the women and men who experienced homosexual desire, so that they
came to define themselves through their erotic life.

These new forms of gay identity and patterns of group life also re- 22
flected the differentiation of people according to gender, race, and class that
is so pervasive in capitalist societies. Among whites, for instance, gay men
have traditionally been more visible than lesbians. This partly stems from
the division between the public male sphere and the private female sphere.

Streets, parks, and bars, especially at night, were "male space." Yet the greater visibility of white gay men also reflected their larger numbers. The Kinsey studies of the 1940s and 1950s found significantly more men than women with predominantly homosexual histories, a situation caused, I would argue, by the fact that capitalism had drawn far more men than women into the labor force, and at higher wages. Men could more easily construct a personal life independent of attachments to the opposite sex, whereas women were more likely to remain economically dependent on men. Kinsey also found a strong positive correlation between years of schooling and lesbian activity. College-educated white women, far more able than their working-class sisters to support themselves, could survive more easily without intimate relationships with men.

Among working-class immigrants in the early twentieth century, closely 23
knit kin networks and an ethic of family solidarity placed constraints on individual autonomy that made gayness a difficult option to pursue. In contrast,
for reasons not altogether clear, urban black communities appeared relatively tolerant of homosexuality. The popularity in the 1920s and 1930s of
songs with lesbian and gay male themes—"B.D. Woman," "Prove It on Me,"
"Sissy Man," "Fairey Blues"—suggests an openness about homosexual expression at odds with the mores of whites. Among men in the rural West in
the 1940s, Kinsey found extensive incidence of homosexual behavior, but,
in contrast with the men in large cities, little consciousness of gay identity.
Thus even as capitalism exerted a homogenizing influence by gradually
transforming more individuals into wage laborers and separating them from
traditional communities, different groups of people were also affected in different ways.

The decisions of particular men and women to act on their erotic/emo- 24
tional preference for the same sex, along with the new consciousness that
this preference made them different, led to the formation of an urban subculture of gay men and lesbians. Yet at least through the 1930s this subculture
remained rudimentary, unstable, and difficult to find. How, then, did the
complex, well-developed gay community emerge that existed by the time
the gay liberation movement exploded? The answer is to be found during
World War II, a time when the cumulative changes of several decades coa-
lesced into a qualitatively new shape.

The war severely disrupted traditional patterns of gender relations and 25
sexuality, and temporarily created a new erotic situation conducive to homosexual expression. It plucked millions of young men and women, whose sexual identities were just forming, out of their homes, out of towns and small
cities, out of the heterosexual environment of the family, and dropped them
into sex-segregated situations—as GIs, as WACs and WAVEs, in same-sex
rooming houses for women workers who relocated to seek employment. The
war freed millions of men and women from the settings where heterosexuality was normally imposed. For men and women already gay, it provided an

opportunity to meet people like themselves. Others could become gay because of the temporary freedom to explore sexuality that the war provided.

Lisa Ben, for instance, came out during the war. She left the small California town where she was raised, came to Los Angeles to find work, and lived in a women's boarding house. There she met for the first time lesbians who took her to gay bars and introduced her to other gay women. Donald Vining was a young man with lots of homosexual desire and few gay experiences. He moved to New York City during the war and worked at a large YMCA. His diary reveals numerous erotic adventures with soldiers, sailors, marines, and civilians at the Y where he worked, as well as at the men's residence club where he lived, and in parks, bars, and movie theaters. Many GIs stayed in port cities like New York, at YMCAs like the one where Vining worked. In his oral histories of gay men in San Francisco, focusing on the 1940s, Allan Bérubé has found that the war years were critical in the formation of a gay male *community* in the city. Places as different as San Jose, Denver, and Kansas City had their first gay bars in the 1940s. Even severe repression could have positive side effects. Pat Bond, a lesbian from Davenport, Iowa, joined the WACs during the 1940s. Caught in a purge of hundreds of lesbians from the WACs in the Pacific, she did not return to Iowa. She stayed in San Francisco and became part of a community of lesbians. How many other women and men had comparable experiences? How many other cities saw a rapid growth of lesbian and gay male communities?

The gay men and women of the 1940s were pioneers. Their decisions to act on their desires formed the underpinnings of an urban subculture of gay men and lesbians. Throughout the 1950s and 1960s, the gay subculture grew and stabilized so that people coming out then could more easily find other gay women and men than in the past. Newspapers and magazines published articles describing gay male life. Literally hundreds of novels with lesbian themes were published. Psychoanalysts complained about the new ease with which their gay male patients found sexual partners. And the gay subculture was not just to be found in the largest cities. Lesbian and gay male bars existed in places like Worcester, Massachusetts, and Buffalo, New York; in Columbia, South Carolina, and Des Moines, Iowa. Gay life in the 1950s and 1960s became a nationwide phenomenon. By the time of the Stonewall Riots in New York City in 1969—the event that ignited the gay liberation movement—our situation was hardly one of silence, invisibility, and isolation. A massive, grass-roots liberation movement could form almost overnight precisely because communities of lesbians and gay men existed.

Although gay community was a precondition for a mass movement, the oppression of lesbians and gay men was the force that propelled the movement into existence. As the subculture expanded and grew more visible in the post–World War II era, oppression by the state intensified, becoming more systematic and inclusive. The Right scapegoated "sexual perverts" during the McCarthy era. Eisenhower imposed a total ban on the employment of gay women and men by the federal government and government contractors. Purges of lesbians and homosexuals from the military rose sharply. The FBI instituted widespread surveillance of gay meeting places and of lesbian and gay organizations, such as the Daughters of Bilitis and the Mattachine Society. The Post Office placed tracers on the correspondence of gay men and passed evidence of homosexual activity on to employers. Urban vice squads invaded private homes, made sweeps of lesbian and gay male bars, entrapped gay men in public places, and fomented local witch hunts. The danger involved in being gay rose even as the possibilities of being gay were enhanced. Gay liberation was a response to this contradiction.

Although lesbians and gay men won significant victories in the 1970s 29
and opened up some safe social space in which to exist, we can hardly claim to have dealt a fatal blow to heterosexism and homophobia. One could even argue that the enforcement of gay oppression has merely changed locales, shifting somewhat from the state to the arena of extralegal violence in the form of increasingly open physical attacks on lesbians and gay men. And, as our movements have grown, they have generated a backlash that threatens to wipe out our gains. Significantly, this New Right opposition has taken shape as a "pro-family" movement. How is it that capitalism, whose structure made possible the emergence of a gay identity and the creation of urban gay communities, appears unable to accept gay men and lesbians in its midst? Why do heterosexism and homophobia appear so resistant to assault?

The answers, I think, can be found in the contradictory relationship of 30
capitalism to the family. On the one hand, as I argued earlier, capitalism has gradually undermined the material basis of the nuclear family by taking away the economic functions that cemented the ties between family members. As more adults have been drawn into the free labor system, and as capital has expanded its sphere until it produces as commodities most goods and services we need for our survival, the forces that propelled men and women into families and kept them there have weakened. On the other hand, the ideology of capitalist society has enshrined the family as the source of love, affection, and emotional security, the place where our need for stable, intimate human relationships is satisfied.

This elevation of the nuclear family to preeminence in the sphere of 31
personal life is not accidental. Every society needs structures for reproduction and childbearing, but the possibilities are not limited to the nuclear family. Yet the privatized family fits well with capitalist relations of production. Capitalism has socialized production while maintaining that the products of socialized labor belong to the owners of private property. In many ways, childrearing has also been progressively socialized over the last two centuries, with schools, the media, peer groups, and employers taking over functions that once belonged to parents. Nevertheless, capitalist society

maintains that reproduction and childrearing are private tasks, that children "belong" to parents, who exercise the rights of ownership. Ideologically, capitalism drives people into heterosexual families: each generation comes of age having internalized a heterosexist model of intimacy and personal relationships. Materially, capitalism weakens the bonds that once kept families together so that their members experience a growing instability in the place they have come to expect happiness and emotional security. Thus, while capitalism has knocked the material foundation away from family life, lesbians, gay men, and heterosexual feminists have become the scapegoats for the social instability of the system.

This analysis, if persuasive, has implications for us today. It can affect 32 our perception of our identity, our formulation of political goals, and our decisions about strategy.

I have argued that lesbian and gay identity and communities are his- 33 torically created, the result of a process of capitalist development that has spanned many generations. A corollary of this argument is that we are *not* a fixed social minority composed for all time of a certain percentage of the population. *There are more of us* than one hundred years ago, more of us than forty years ago. And there may very well be more gay men and lesbians in the future. Claims made by gays and nongays that sexual orientation is fixed at an early age, that large numbers of visible gay men and lesbians in society, the media, and the schools will have no influence on the sexual identities of the young, are wrong. Capitalism has created the material conditions for homosexual desire to express itself as a central component of some individuals' lives; now, our political movements are changing consciousness, creating the ideological conditions that make it easier for people to make that choice.

To be sure, this argument confirms the worst fears and most rabid 34 rhetoric of our political opponents. But our response must be to challenge the underlying belief that homosexual relations are bad, a poor second choice. We must not slip into the opportunistic defense that society need not worry about tolerating us, since only homosexuals become homosexuals. At best, a minority group analysis and a civil rights strategy pertain to those of us who already are gay. It leaves today's youth—tomorrow's lesbians and gay men—to internalize heterosexist models that it can take a lifetime to expunge.

I have also argued that capitalism has led to the separation of sexual- 35 ity from procreation. Human sexual desire need no longer be harnessed to reproductive imperatives, to procreation; its expression has increasingly entered the realm of choice. Lesbians and homosexuals most clearly embody the potential of this split, since our gay relationships stand entirely outside a procreative framework. The acceptance of our erotic choices ultimately depends on the degree to which society is willing to affirm sexual expression as a form of play, positive and life-enhancing. Our movement may have begun as the struggle of a "minority," but what we should now be trying to "liberate" is an aspect of the personal lives of all people—sexual expression.

Finally, I have suggested that the relationship between capitalism and 36 the family is fundamentally contradictory. On the one hand, capitalism continually weakens the material foundation of family life, making it possible for individuals to live outside the family, and for a lesbian and gay male identity to develop. On the other, it needs to push men and women into families, at least long enough to reproduce the next generation of workers. The elevation of the family to ideological preeminence guarantees that capitalist society will reproduce not just children, but heterosexism and homophobia. In the most profound sense, capitalism is the problem.

How do we avoid remaining the scapegoats, the political victims of the 37 social instability that capitalism generates? How can we take this contradictory relationship and use it to move toward liberation?

Gay men and lesbians exist on social terrain beyond the boundaries of 38 the heterosexual nuclear family. Our communities have formed in that social space. Our survival and liberation depend on our ability to defend and expand that terrain, not just for ourselves but for everyone. That means, in part, support for issues that broaden the opportunities for living outside traditional heterosexual family units: issues like the availability of abortion and the ratification of the Equal Rights Amendment, affirmative action for people of color and for women, publicly funded daycare and other essential social services, decent welfare payments, full employment, the rights of young people—in other words, programs and issues that provide a material basis for personal autonomy.

The rights of young people are especially critical. The acceptance of 39 children as dependents, as belonging to parents, is so deeply ingrained that we can scarcely imagine what it would mean to treat them as autonomous human beings, particularly in the realm of sexual expression and choice. Yet until that happens, gay liberation will remain out of our reach.

But personal autonomy is only half the story. The instability of families 40 and the sense of impermanence and insecurity that people are now experiencing in their personal relationships are real social problems that need to be addressed. We need political solutions for these difficulties of personal life. These solutions should not come in the form of a radical version of the pro-family position, of some left-wing proposals to strengthen the family. Socialists do not generally respond to the exploitation and economic inequality of industrial capitalism by calling for a return to the family farm and handicraft production. We recognize that the vastly increased productivity that capitalism has made possible by socializing production is one of its progressive features. Similarly, we should not be trying to turn back the clock to some mythic age of the happy family.

We do need, however, structures and programs that will help to dis- 41 solve the boundaries that isolate the family, particularly those that privatize childrearing. We need community- or worker-controlled daycare, housing where privacy and community coexist, neighborhood institutions—from medical clinics to performance centers—that enlarge the social unit where each of us has a secure place. As we create structures beyond the nuclear family that provide a sense of belonging, the family will wane in significance. Less and less will it seem to make or break our emotional security.

In this respect gay men and lesbians are well situated to play a special 42 role. Already excluded from families as most of us are, we have had to create, for our survival, networks of support that do not depend on the bonds of blood or the license of the state, but that are freely chosen and nurtured. The building of an "affectional community" must be as much a part of our political movement as are campaigns for civil rights. In this way we may prefigure the shape of personal relationships in a society grounded in equality and justice rather than exploitation and oppression, a society where autonomy and security do not preclude each other but coexist.   ©

CRITICAL READING

1. D'Emilio notes on page 230 that "Among whites, gay men have traditionally been more visible than lesbians." Describe how he accounts for this discrepancy. Can you think of other reasons why this discrepancy has existed?
2. D'Emilio focuses on the contradictions inherent in capitalism's relation to the nuclear family unit. Explain his argument about this situation.
3. Discuss what D'Emilio regards as the necessary elements leading to the gay-rights movement of the 1970s.

CLASS DISCUSSION

1. Discuss the movement from economically interdependent family units to the modern family constructed around emotional interdependence. How does this shift affect views toward heterosexual marriage and about the role of sex in people's lives, according to D'Emilio?
2. As a class, explore the role of our consumer capitalist economy in shaping areas of our lives other than the family and the aspects of sexual identity that D'Emilio discusses. In other words, explore the ways in which one might logically extend D'Emilio's analysis to examine the broader influence of our economic system on our lives in general. Also discuss the relationship between the ideals inherent in capitalism and the ideals of our governmental system, representative democracy.

DIRECTED FREEWRITE

We are currently experiencing a revolutionary shift in our economic and social life due to changes enabled by computer technology, and many argue that this shift is just as monumental as the change to a capitalist economy, as discussed by D'Emilio. Think about the current state of the American family, and explore the ways in which any changes from the ideal articulated in D'Emilio's essay might be related to our changing economic structures.

LESBIAN AND GAY STUDIES UNIT WRITING ASSIGNMENTS

1. Write an essay exploring how our current period of rapid economic change that has been brought on by technology and its attendant result, globalization, might affect the composition of the family and our views regarding sexuality. D'Emilio makes a case for the changes brought on by an earlier economic shift; we are now in a period in which another huge shift is occurring, and one can argue that it's already affecting the family structure. Thus, we have politicians and commentators calling for a return to "traditional family values." But in a totally changed economic and social landscape, such traditional values and family structures may not apply, just as the economically organized colonial family didn't fit into the industrialized, capitalistic society created in the nineteenth century.

2. Historians rely on primary documents when trying to reconstruct historical periods, and sometimes a dearth of documents makes such reconstruction difficult or even impossible. Further, sometimes documents alone do not show the whole picture; for example, in trying to document events occurring in a colonized society, the written record might have been produced by the ruling colonizers, whereas the perspectives of the people who are colonized might not appear in written form. Other kinds of primary information can thus fill in gaps left by written documents. The eye-witness testimony of people, collected through written transcription of their remembrances, is called oral history.

   Many people are used to thinking of history as the recounting of lives of "great" men—and perhaps women—great wars, cataclysmic events, and so on, whereas accounts of the everyday lives of average people living in particular settings yield important—and often fascinating—information about particular time periods and cultures.

   The gathering and the reporting of oral histories can be accomplished in a number of ways. In this assignment, we ask you to interview someone you know who has lived during a time period, or lived in a place, that you have not experienced, or someone who has experienced life during an interesting time period or participated in a particular historical event. Or, in keeping with this unit's focus, you may choose to interview someone whose race, gender, sexual orientation, or economic class somehow helped to shape that person's experiences of otherwise "ordinary" events. For example, a woman who obtained a degree in the mostly male field of engineering would be a good candidate, as would a Latino member of an all-white fraternity or company.

   You will then have to shape selected parts of your interview findings into an essay. Doing this will require you to narrow your focus to one important event described by your interviewee or to one related set of experiences; thus, your essay will have some thematic unity. Start the essay with an introduction; in your words, give your reader some background information, such as the general outlines of the interviewee's life and/or the historical context within which this oral history fits. Then report the material you obtained in your interview, choosing the most important words from the interviewee and substituting paraphrasing when he or she goes into detail that you deem unnecessary, or when she or he makes a long-winded transition from one point to the next. A logical way to structure this material would be first to report the experiences that led up to the main event or experience, next to describe the main event itself, and then to discuss the either aftereffects of the event or the person's thoughts or feelings about it. Then provide your own conclusion, perhaps briefly summarizing the experiences covered and reflecting on their larger significance or relation to traditional historical accounts.

Interviewing itself requires some planning, and here are some brief suggestions. Set an undisturbed time slot in which to meet with your subject. Although you want to have enough time to cover important issues, you will also need to limit your time so that you don't end up with an overwhelming amount of material. Bring a tape recorder and a pad of paper to the interview, and tape-record the whole thing. In addition, take notes on the progression of the subject's story so that you'll have an easier time locating certain points or details when you go to review your material. Make sure you come to the interview prepared, having done some reading on the time period in which this person lived, and with some questions already formulated. Limit your questions to the particular area you are most interested in, but also be open to new ideas that might arise in your interviewee's story. Be analytical: You should not only ask questions that address what happened but also should ask your interviewee how he or she felt about what happened, or what his or her opinion was about the events. Lastly, be courteous and patient; make sure to express your gratitude to your subject for talking with you.

3. Write a short essay analyzing several items that you own, just as a historian in the future might write. Imagine that you are a historian who is trying to understand the features of, say, college student life in the late twentieth century. Pick several key items of yours that you think relate to this topic, and discuss the conclusions and interpretations about the features of college life in this particular era that could be drawn from these items. As much as possible, try to step out of your own understanding of these items, and view them as a stranger might—a stranger who probably has a very different view of college students and college life than you do.

4. Book reviews are an arena in which scholars in a particular discipline engage in dialogue with each other: the academic book reviewer communicates to other academics who want to know the value of a book, and also communicates to or with the author of the book under review. Book reviews are written in all disciplines, and although some disciplines' reviews have specific characteristics, the description we provide here generally applies to all the disciplines' book reviews. The primary objective of all book reviews, however, is to convey to readers whether a book is worth their effort to read and/or buy. Book reviews generally address three areas: (1) Book reviews *describe* the book under review, meaning that you'll supply some summary of the book's main points and describe its general scope, overall organization, and theoretical approach. (2) Book reports *explain* what the author of the book is attempting to accomplish with this

book and how the book fits in with existing scholarship. (3) Book reviews *evalu- ate* the extent to which a book has accomplished what its author intended it to do; here the writer typically makes a recommendation about the book's value.

Most academic journals contain book reviews, so in preparing for this as- signment, you should go and read some samples of book reviews in history jour- nals. Notice how the authors of these address the three areas that we laid out before, and notice that they don't always describe, explain, and evaluate a book in that order.

Choose a book that relates broadly to the historical issues raised in this unit; for example, you might choose a book on the experiences of a marginalized group other than lesbians and gays, during a particular period, or you may choose something addressing more recent—or more ancient—gay and lesbian history. Another topic might be another aspect of city life in the early twentieth century or during the nineteenth century.

In any case, choose a book written within the last five to ten years, and be sure to read it carefully. You will also need to skim some of the other material written on this subject so that you have a sense of how your chosen book relates to similar work in history. Take extensive notes as you read, keeping in mind the three areas your review must cover.

THINKING AND WRITING
IN THE SOCIAL SCIENCES

Unit 1
Communications—He Said/She Said

SEX, LIES, AND CONVERSATION
Deborah Tannen

Deborah Tannen, a linguistics professor at Georgetown University, has studied and written widely about communication styles of men and women, and the ways in which these differing styles can lead to misunderstanding. This adaptation of a newspaper article explores these issues, pointing out a number of ways that miscommunication plays out and arguing that because men and women are socialized so differently, we ought to view communication between them as a kind of cross-cultural communication. As you read, think about the role that interpretation plays in all communication and the way that different interpretations lead to miscommunication. Think about your own experiences in conversation with men or women, and then decide whether Tannen's assertions apply to your experiences.

> *Deborah Tannen is best known as the author of* You Just Don't Understand: Women and Men in Conversation; Talking from 9 to 5: Women and Men in the Workplace; Language, Sex, and Power; *and* The Argument Culture, *which received the Common Ground Book Award. Deborah Tannen is a frequent guest on television and radio news and information shows. Dr. Tannen has appeared on several major television and radio shows including* The NewsHour with Jim Lehrer, 20/20, 48 Hours, CBS News, ABC World News Tonight, Oprah, Good Morning America, CNN, Larry King, Hardball, *and* NPR. *She has been featured in and written for most major newspapers and magazines including* The New York Times, Newsweek, Time, USA Today, People, The Washington Post, *and* The Harvard Business Review. *Deborah Tannen is a member of the linguistics department faculty at Georgetown University, where she is one of only four individuals who holds the distinguished rank of University Professor. She has published sixteen books and over 85 articles and is the recipient of four honorary doctorates.*

I was addressing a small gathering in a suburban Virginia living   1
room—a women's group that had invited men to join them. Throughout the
evening, one man had been particularly talkative, frequently offering ideas
and anecdotes, while his wife sat silently beside him on the couch. Toward
the end of the evening, I commented that women frequently complain that
their husbands don't talk to them. This man quickly concurred. He gestured
toward his wife and said, "She's the talker in our family." The room burst into
laughter; the man looked puzzled and hurt. "It's true," he explained. "When I
come home from work I have nothing to say. If she didn't keep the conversation going, we'd spend the whole evening in silence."

This episode crystallizes the irony that although American men tend to   2
talk more than women in public situations, they often talk less at home. And
this pattern is wreaking havoc with marriage.

The pattern was observed by political scientist Andrew Hacker in the   3
late '70s. Sociologist Catherine Kohler Riessman reports in her new book
Divorce Talk that most of the women she interviewed—but only a few of the
men—gave lack of communication as the reason for their divorces. Given
the current divorce rate of nearly 50 percent, that amounts to millions of
cases in the United States every year—a virtual epidemic of failed conversation.

In my own research, complaints from women about their husbands   4
most often focused not on tangible inequities such as having given up the
chance for a career to accompany a husband to his, or doing far more than
their share of daily life—support work like cleaning, cooking, social arrangements and errands. Instead, they focused on communication: "He doesn't
listen to me," "He doesn't talk to me." I found, as Hacker observed years before, that most wives want their husbands to be, first and foremost, conversational partners, but few husbands share this expectation of their wives.

In short, the image that best represents the current crisis is the stereo-   5
typical cartoon scene of a man sitting at the breakfast table with a newspaper held up in front of his face while a woman glares at the back of it,
wanting to talk.

LINGUISTIC BATTLE OF THE SEXES

How can women and men have such different impressions of commu-   6
nication in marriage? Why the widespread imbalance in their interests and
expectations?

In the April issue of *American Psychologist,* Stanford University's   7
Eleanor Macoby reports the results of her own and others' research showing their children's development is most influenced by the social structure of
peer interactions. Boys and girls tend to play with children of their own gender, and their sex-separate groups have different organizational structures
and interactive norms.

I believe these systematic differences in childhood socialization make   8
talk between women and men like cross-cultural communication, heir to all
the attraction and pitfalls of that enticing but difficult enterprise. My research
on men's and women's conversations uncovered patterns similar to those
described for children's groups.

For women, as for girls, intimacy is the fabric of relationships, and talk   9
is the thread from which it is woven. Little girls create and maintain friendships by exchanging secrets; similarly, women regard conversation as the
cornerstone of friendship. So a woman expects her husband to be a new
and improved version of a best friend. What is important is not the individual
subjects that are discussed but the sense of closeness, of a life shared, that
emerges when people tell their thoughts, feelings, and impressions.

Bonds between boys can be as intense as girls', but they are based   10
less on talking, more on doing things together. Since they don't assume talk
is the cement that binds a relationship, men don't know what kind of talk
women want, and they don't miss it when it isn't there.

Boys' groups are larger, more inclusive, and more hierarchical, so   11
boys must struggle to avoid the subordinate position in the group. This may
play a role in women's complaints that men don't listen to them. Some men
really don't like to listen, because being the listener makes them feel one-
down, like a child listening to adults or an employee to a boss.

But often when women tell men, "You aren't listening," and the men   12
protest, "I am," the men are right. The impression of not listening results
from misalignments in the mechanics of conversation. The misalignment begins as soon as a man and a woman take physical positions. This became
clear when I studied videotapes made by psychologist Bruce Dorval of children and adults talking to their same-sex best friends. I found that at every
age, the girls and women faced each other directly, their eyes anchored on
each other's faces. At every age, the boys and men sat at angles to each
other and looked elsewhere in the room, periodically glancing at each other.
They were obviously attuned to each other, often mirroring each other's
movements. But the tendency of men to face away can give women the impression they aren't listening even when they are. A young woman in college was frustrated: Whenever she told her boyfriend she wanted to talk to
him, he would lie down on the floor, close his eyes, and put his arm over his
face. This signaled to her "He's taking a nap." But he insisted he was listening extra-hard. Normally, he looks around the room, so he is easily distracted. Lying down and covering his eyes helped him concentrate on what
she was saying.

Analogous to the physical alignment that women and men take in con-   13
versation is their topical alignment. The girls in my study tended to talk at
length about one topic, but the boys tended to jump from topic to topic. The
second-grade girls exchanged stories about people they knew. The second-
grade boys teased, told jokes, noticed things in the room and talked about

finding games to play. The sixth-grade girls talked about problems with a mutual friend. The sixth-grade boys talked about 55 different topics, none of which extended over more than a few turns.

LISTENING TO BODY LANGUAGE

Switching topics is another habit that gives women the impression men aren't listening, especially if they switch to a topic about themselves. But the evidence of the 10th-grade boys in my study indicates otherwise. The 10th-grade boys sprawled across their chairs with bodies parallel and eyes straight ahead, rarely looking at each other. They looked as if they were riding in a car, staring out the windshield. But they were talking about their feelings. One boy was upset because a girl had told him he had a drinking problem, and the other was feeling alienated from all his friends. 14

Now, then a girl told a friend about a problem, the friend responded by asking probing questions and expressing agreement and understanding. But the boys dismissed each other's problems. Todd assured Richard that his drinking was "no big problem" because "sometimes you're funny when you're off your butt." And when Todd said he felt left out, Richard responded, "Why should you? You know more people than me." 15

Women perceive such responses as belittling and unsupportive. But the boys seemed satisfied with them. Whereas women reassure each other by implying, "You shouldn't feel bad because I've had similar experiences," men do so by implying. "You shouldn't feel bad because your problems aren't so bad." 16

There are even simpler reasons for women's impression that men don't listen. Linguist Lynette Hirschman found that women make more listener-noise, such as "mhm," "uhuh," and "yeah," to show "I'm with you." Men, she found, more often give silent attention. Women who expect a stream of listener-noise interpret silent attention as no attention at all. 17

Women's conversational habits are as frustrating to men as men's are to women. Men who expect silent attention interpret a stream of listener-noise as overreaction or impatience. Also, when women talk to each other in a close, comfortable setting, they often overlap, finish each other's sentences and anticipate what the other is about to say. This practice, which I call "participatory listenership," is often perceived by men as interruption, intrusion and lack of attention. 18

A parallel difference caused a man to complain about his wife, "She just wants to talk about her own point of view. If I show her another view, she gets mad at me." When most women talk to each other, they assume a conversationalist's job is to express agreement and support. But many men see their conversational duty as pointing out the other side of an argument. This is heard as disloyalty by women, and refusal to offer the requisite support. It is not that women don't want to see other points of view, but that 19 they prefer them phrased as suggestions and inquiries rather than as direct challenges.

In his book *Fighting for Life,* Walter Ong points out that men use "ago-   20
nistic" or warlike, oppositional formats to do almost anything; thus discussion becomes debate, and conversation a competitive sport. In contrast, women see conversation as a ritual means of establishing rapport. If Jane tells a problem and June says she has a similar one, they walk away feeling closer to each other. But this attempt at establishing rapport can backfire when used with men. Men take too literally women's ritual "troubles talk," just as women mistake men's ritual challenges for real attack.

THE SOUNDS OF SILENCE

These differences begin to clarify why women and men have such dif-   21
ferent expectations about communication in marriage. For women, talk creates intimacy. Marriage is an orgy of closeness: you can tell your feelings and thoughts, and still be loved. Their greatest fear is being pushed away. But men live in a hierarchical world, where talk maintains independence and status. They are on guard to protect themselves from being put down and pushed around.

This explains the paradox of the talkative man who said of his silent   22
wife, "She's the talker." In the public setting of a guest lecture, he felt challenged to show his intelligence and display his understanding of the lecture. But at home, where he has nothing to prove and no one to defend against, he is free to remain silent. For his wife, being home means she is free from the worry that something she says might offend someone, or spark disagreement, or appear to be showing off; at home she is free to talk.

The communication problems that endanger marriage can't be fixed by   23
mechanical engineering. They require a new conceptual framework about the role of talk in human relationships. Many of the psychological explanations that have become second nature may not be helpful, because they tend to blame either women (for not being assertive enough) or men (for not being in touch with their feelings). A sociolinguistic approach by which male-female conversation is seen as cross-cultural communication allows us to understand the problem and forge solutions without blaming either party.

Once the problem is understood, improvement comes naturally, as it   24
did to the young women and her boyfriend who seemed to go to sleep when she wanted to talk. Previously, she had accused him of not listening, and he had refused to change his behavior, since that would be admitting fault. But then she learned about and explained to him the differences in women's and men's habitual ways of aligning themselves in conversation. The next time she told him she wanted to talk, he began, as usual, by lying down and covering his eyes. When the familiar negative reaction bubbled up, she reassured herself that he really was listening. But then he sat up and looked at

her. Thrilled, she asked why. He said, "You like me to look at you when we talk, so I'll try to do it." Once he saw their differences as cross-cultural rather than right and wrong, he independently altered his behavior.

Women who feel abandoned and deprived when their husband won't   25 listen to or report daily news may be happy to discover their husbands trying to adapt once they understand the place of small talk in women's relationships. But if their husbands don't adapt, the women may still be comforted that for men, this is not a failure of intimacy. Accepting the difference, the wives may look to their friends or family for that kind of talk. And husbands who can't provide it shouldn't feel their wives have made unreasonable demands. Some couples will still decide to divorce, but at least their decisions will be based on realistic expectations.

In these times of resurgent ethnic conflicts, the world desperately   26 needs cross-cultural understanding. Like charity, successful cross-cultural communication should begin at home.   ©

CRITICAL READING

1. Discuss what Tannen means when she says that talk between women and men is "like cross-cultural communication, heir to all the attraction and pitfalls of that enticing but difficult enterprise"? Explain what Tannen suggests causes this "cultural" difference. Ultimately, what does Tannen believe are the benefits of viewing communication in this way, as opposed to traditional psychological explanations for male/female communication differences?
2. Describe the ways in which body language plays a role in miscommunications between men and women. Why do you think boys/men and girls/women assume such different body positions in conversation?
3. What do you think of the assertion Tannen cites by Walter Ong, that "men use 'agonistic' or warlike, oppositional formats to do almost anything; thus discussion becomes debate, and conversation a competitive sport"? Describe some examples (either real or invented) that might illustrate this argument, and some that exemplify an opposing viewpoint as well.

CLASS DISCUSSION

1. Tannen begins her essay by describing an encounter with a married couple at a women's group. Discuss how this encounter and how this couple's different views of their communication exemplify a number of the concepts that Tannen deals with in her essay.
2. As a class, discuss Tannen's points in the seventh through the eleventh paragraphs about the "systematic differences in childhood socialization" that help lead to differences in male and female communication styles. Compare this assertion to classmates' childhood experiences, and discuss how these experiences relate to male and female communication styles.

DIRECTED FREEWRITE

Describe a conflict you have experienced in trying to discuss something with a member of the opposite sex (or invent a conflict). Then discuss how your application of some of Tannen's ideas might have helped to resolve, or at least explain, the conflict.

WOMEN'S PLACE IN EVERYDAY TALK: REFLECTIONS ON PARENT-CHILD INTERACTION

Candace West and Don H. Zimmerman

This study by West and Zimmerman is graying at the temples, having been reported in 1975, yet we include it here as a good example of two things. First, it demonstrates work in the field of communications into gendered conversational patterns, work that, while directed at an academic audience, is fairly comprehensible to readers outside the field of communication scholarship; and second, since the study builds on previous work that West and Zimmerman conducted, it is a good example of the ways in which knowledge in disciplines is constructed in tiny increments of increased knowledge. Although parts of this study may prove a bit difficult for undergraduate readers, stick with it so that you can get a picture of how some research in communications is conducted. And even though the methods of the research and some of the theoretical language may be challenging, focus as you read on the underlying concepts employed here and the conclusions that the authors generate.

Don H. Zimmerman received his Ph.D. from the University of California, Los Angeles. He is a professor of sociology at the University of California, Santa Barbara. His most recent publications include "The Interactional Organization of Calls for Emergency Assistance," "Identity, Context and Interaction" and "Observations on the Display and Management of Emotion in Naturally Occurring Activities: The Case of 'Hysteria' in Calls to 9-1-1" (with Jack Whalen). His current research interests include the interactional organization of talk in institutional settings and peer interaction among very young children.

Candace West received her B.A., M.A., and Ph.D. in sociology from the University of California, Santa Barbara. She is currently a sociology professor at the University of California, Santa Cruz. Her research interests include language and social interaction; sociology of gender; conversation analysis and microanalysis and medicine. West has published several articles in a range of journals including Discourse and Society, Social Science and Medicine, *and* Social Problems *from which this selection is taken. Additionally, her articles have been featured in various texts including* Common Bonds, Different Voices: Race, Class and Gender *and* The Psychology of Gender.

In this paper, we compare the results of our previous study of interruptions in same-sex and cross-sex conversations (Zimmerman and West, 1975) with similar data from parent-child verbal interaction and find that there are striking similarities between the pattern of interruptions in male-female interchanges and those observed in the adult-child transactions. We use the occasion of this comparison to consider several possible interactional consequences of interruption in conversation, particularly as these consequences relate to the issue of dominance in face-to-face interaction. 1

INTRODUCTION

It is sometimes said that children should be seen and not heard and that they should speak only when spoken to. To be sure, situations abound in which children are seen and most definitely heard without prior invitation to talk from adults. Nevertheless, these maxims do tell us that children have restricted rights to speak resulting in special problems in gaining adults' attention and engaging them in conversation. For example, Sacks (1966) has observed that children frequently use the form "D'ya know what?" when initiating talk with an adult. The answer to this particular question is ordinarily another question of the form "What?" and the adult so responding finds that he/she has given the child opportunity to begin an utterance to which a listener attends—at least for the moment. 2

Fishman (1975) observed that in fifty-two hours of tape-recorded conversation collected from three couples the women employed the "D'ya know what?" opening twice as frequently as men. Overall, the women asked almost three times as many questions as the men. The implication is, of course, that the greater reliance on such question forms by women stems from *their* limited rights as co-conversationalists with men. 3

The difficulties children encounter in verbal interaction with adults follow perhaps from their presumed lack of social competence. A child is a social actor whose opinion may not be taken seriously and whose verbal and non-verbal behavior is subject to open scrutiny, blunt correction, and inattention. It is thus potentially illuminating when parallels between the interaction of adults and children and men and women are observed. 4

Goffman (1974), characterizes the relation of middle-class parents to their children in face-to-face situations as one of benign control. The child is granted various privileges and the license to be a child, i.e., merely to play at or practice coping with the manifold demands of the social occasion. 5

Goffman (1976:72–73) notes that "there is an obvious price that the child must pay for being saved from seriousness," a price that includes suffering parents' intervention in his/her activities, being discussed in the presence of others as if absent, and having his/her "time and territory . . . seen as expendable" due to the higher priority assigned to adult needs. This sort of relation in face-to-face interaction can characterize other encounters between subordinate and superordinate parties:

> It turns out . . . that in our society whenever a male has dealings with a female or a subordinate male (especially a younger one), some mitigation of potential distance and hostility is quite likely to be induced by application of the parent-child complex. Which implies that, ritually speaking, females are equivalent to subordinate males and both are equivalent to children (Goffman, 1976:73).

Perhaps this ritual equivalence of women and children includes as a common condition the risk that their turns at talk will be subject to interruption and hence control by a superordinate.

In this paper, we compare the results of our previous study of interruptions in same-sex and cross-sex conversations (Zimmerman and West, 1975) with similar data from parent-child verbal interaction and find striking similarities between the pattern of interruptions in male-female interchanges and those observed in the adult-child transactions. We use the occasion of this comparison to consider the function of interruptions in verbal exchanges, particularly in conversations between parties of unequal status. Since interruptions are a type of transition between speakers, our point of departure in this as well as the previous paper is the model of turn-taking in conversation advanced by Harvey Sacks, Emanuel Schegloff and Gail Jefferson (1974) which provides a systematic approach to speaker alternation in naturally occurring conversation. 6

THE TURN-TAKING MODEL

Sacks, *et al.* (1974) suggest that speech exchange systems in general are arranged to ensure that (1) one party speaks at a time and (2) speaker change recurs. These features organize casual conversation, formal debate, and high ceremony. Conversation is distinguished from debate and ceremony by variable distribution of turns, turn length, and turn content. 7

A turn consists of not merely the temporal duration of an utterance but of the right and obligation to speak allocated to a particular speaker. Turns are constructed out of what Sacks *et al.* (1974) call "unit-types" which can consist of words, phrases, clauses, or sentences. Unit-types are projective, that is they provide sufficient information prior to their completion to allow the hearer to anticipate an upcoming transition place. 8

Sacks *et al.* (1974) represent the mechanism for speaker transition as an 9
ordered set of rules speakers use to achieve a normatively constrained order
of conversational interaction. For each possible transition place, these rules
provide, in order of priority: that (1) current speaker may select the next
speaker, e.g., by using a term of address, and if not choosing to do so, that (2)
a next speaker may self-select, and if not, that (3) the current speaker may
continue. The exercise of any of these three options recycles the rule-set to
the first option. The operation of the rule-set accounts for a number of regularly
occurring features of observed conversations—including the alternation of
speakers in a variable order with brief (if any) gaps or overlaps between turns,
as well as variable length of turns. That is, the model provides for the systematic initiation, continuation and alternation of turns in everyday conversation.
Our concern here is with the phenomenon of simultaneous speech, i.e., the
occurrence and distribution of overlap among categories of speakers.

Elsewhere (Zimmerman and West, 1975:114) we have defined overlap 10
as a brief stretch of simultaneous speech initiated by a "next" speaker just
before the current speaker arrives at a possible transition place, often in a
situation where the current speaker has elongated the final syllable of
his/her utterance (Cf. Sacks, *et al.* 1974:706–708; Jefferson and Schegloff,
1975:3):

(T14:213–214)   B2: Um so where's your shoror-sorORity
                     house. Is it on campus or off: :?
                 B1:   [No] it's
                     off=all thuh sororities and fraternities
                     are off campus.

The significance of overlap occurring in such an environment follows from
the fact that speakers apparently "target" the starting of their stream of
speech just at completion by the current speaker (Jefferson and Schegloff,
1975). When successfully managed, the next-speaker "latches" his/her utterance to the utterance of the preceding speaker as in the following:

(Jefferson and Schegloff, 1975:3)
            Earl: How's everything *look*.=
            Bud: =Oh looks pretty *goo*:d,

Jefferson and Schegloff (1975:3) also observe that the addition of tag-ques-
tions or conjunctions to a possibly complete utterance furnishes another
locus for overlap:

(Sacks, *et al.,* 1974:703, n. 12)
            Bert: Uh *you* been down here before ⌈havenche⌉
            Fred: ⌊Yeh.   ⌋

(T14:59–60)   B1: I don't like it at all ⌈but- ⌉
              B2:   ⌊You d⌋ on't

An interruption, in contrast, involves a "deeper" intrusion into the inter-   11
nal structure of the speaker's utterance, i.e., prior to a possible transition place:

(T1:114–115)   A1: It really sur ⌈prised me becuz-⌉
                A2:   ⌊It's jus' so smo :g⌋ gy . . .

Thus, what we call "overlaps" (Sacks, *et al.* use the term to refer to all   12
instances of simultaneous speech) are events occurring in the immediate
vicinity of a possible transition place and can be seen as generated by the
ordinary workings of the turn-taking system (cf. Sacks, *et al.,* 1974:
706–708). Interruptions, however, do not appear to have a systemic basis in
the turn-taking model as such, i.e., they are not products of the turn-
constructional and turn-allocation procedures that make up the model.
Moreover, there is nothing in the model to suggest that patterned asymmetries should occur between particular categories of speakers. Quite to the
contrary, the model is posited to hold for all speakers and all conversations
(cf. Sacks, *et al.,* 1974:700) and represents a mechanism for the systematic
allocation of turns across two or more speakers while minimizing gap and
overlap.

Viewed strictly in terms of the turn-taking model, then, the deep incur-   13
sion into the turn-space of a current speaker constitutes a violation of turn-
taking rules. Interruptions accomplish a number of communicative acts,
among them the exhibition of dominance and exercise of control in face-to-
face interaction.

FINDINGS

Our preliminary findings (Zimmerman and West, 1975), suggested   14
marked asymmetries in overlaps, interruptions, and silences between same-
sex and cross-sex conversational pairs. These interactional episodes were
(like the parent-child segments introduced below) selected from longer
stretches of talk by excerpting all topically coherent segments exhibiting (a)
two or more noticeable silences between speaker turns or (b) two or more
instances of simultaneous speech, without regard for who overlapped
whom. That is, they were selected precisely because of the presence of
gaps and overlaps. Three fourths of the exchanges between eleven adult
male-female, ten adult male-male, and ten adult female-female parties were
recorded in coffee shops, drug stores, and other public places in a university
community; the remainder in private dwellings (cf. Zimmerman and West,
1975:111–112).

The same-sex transcripts displayed silences in nearly equal distribu-   15
tions between partners. And while overlaps occurred with greater frequency
than interruptions, both were distributed symmetrically between male-male
and female-female speakers. In all, there were seven interruptions in the

same-sex conversations coming from three transcripts: in two of these there were three interruptions, and in one of them, a single interruption. These were divided as equally as possible between the two parties in each conversation: 2 vs. 1, 2 vs. 1, and 1 vs. 0. By comparison, cross-sex conversations displayed gross asymmetries. Interruptions were far more likely to occur than overlaps, and both types of simultaneity were much more frequently initiated by males than females. For example, forty-six out of forty-eight, or 96%, of the interruptions were by males to females. Females, on the other hand, showed a greater tendency toward silence, particularly subsequent to interruption by males. These patterned asymmetries—most striking in the case of interruption—led us to conclude tentatively that these females' rights to complete a turn were apparently abridged by males with impunity, i.e., without complaint from females.

Recall Goffman's (1976:73) observation that children—in interaction with adults—are accorded treatment characteristically extended to "non-persons," i.e., their status as coparticipants in conversation is contingent on adult forebearance, and their "time and territory may be seen as expendable." If we regard conversational turn-space as the "time and territory" of a speaker, then the tendency of males to interrupt females implies that women's turn at talk is—at least some of the time—expendable and that women can be treated conversationally as "non-persons." With these considerations in mind, we present our parent-child transcripts. [16]

Five interactions between parents and children were recorded in a physician's office, either in the open waiting room, or in the examination room before the doctor-patient interaction began. Each author inspected the transcripts of these exchanges to locate instances of simultaneous speech. In the five parent-child exchanges, we found seventeen instances of simultaneity, of which fourteen were interruptions. Of the fourteen, twelve or 86%, were by the adult. The remaining two interruptions were by the same child to an adult (trying to get her attention). [17]

Hence the striking asymmetry between males and females in the initiation of interruptions is reproduced in the transcripts of parent-child conversation. However, in contrast to the broader range of situations where the adult conversations were recorded, the parent-child segments are two party conversations drawn from a single setting. But one might argue that interactions between children and their parents in other, more relaxed situations might have a markedly different character. The pertinent point, in any event, is whether or not interruptions occur *when* the issue of who is to control the interaction is salient. Hence, the conversational exchanges recorded in the physician's office, while insufficient in themselves to establish the point, do suggest that interruptions are employed by the dominant party, the adult, to effect control in the exchange. Let us consider some of the ways interruptions may function to achieve control and to display dominance in both parent-child and male-female conversations. [18]

DISCUSSION

Taking the similarities in the patterns of interruptions between adults   19
and children and males and females to mean that females have an analogous status to children in certain conversational situations implies that the
female has restricted rights to speak and may be ignored or interrupted at
will. However, we suggest that the exercise of power by the male (or, for
that matter, the parent) is systematic rather than capricious, and is thus subject to constraint. That is, wholesale trampling of speaker rights, even in the
case of children, is not culturally approved, and those speakers who indiscriminately interrupt or otherwise misuse their conversational partner are
subject to characterization as rude, domineering, or authoritarian. We believe interruptions are a tool used to fashion socially appropriate interactional *displays* which both exhibit and accomplish proper relationships
between parties to the interaction.

Parent-Child Interaction

A common-sense observation about physicians' offices is: many (if not   20
most) young children are apprehensive about what will happen to them
there. Moreover, parents are likely to feel some anxiety about the behavior
of their children in that setting: control over the child is necessary to insure
cooperation in the medical examination, to suppress protest or other expressions of reluctance to participate, and to prevent uninvited handling of
equipment in the examining room (cf. Goffman, 1976). We can thus expect
interactions of the following sort:

    Child: But I don't wanna shot! ((sobs)) you said (x)
              said you said ⌈I   ⌉
    Parent: ⌊Look⌋ just be quiet and take that
              sock off or you'll get *more* than just a shot!

Or:

    Child: If I got one wi⌈th a   ⌉
    Parent: ⌊Leave⌋ that alone Kurt
    (1.8)
    Child: Huh?
    Parent: Don't touch that roller

The rule-set described earlier is a system of rules governing the con-   21
struction of speaker turns and the transitions between them. Observance of
these rules results in the distribution of opportunities to speak among participants and hence, the allocation of a segment of time to the speaker. The
time slot under control of a speaker is potentially (a) a time when the
speaker may engage in activities other than speaking, e.g. handling some
object, and (b) a time when the speaker's utterance itself may unfold as a
definite *action,* e.g. as a complaint or insult. The turn-taking system assigns

the current turn-holder the right to that interval, to reach at least a first possible transition place (Sacks, *et al.,* 1974:706) and the listenership of those present and party to the talk ratifies that right. Given that many utterances project not only their ending but their sense as well (cf. Jefferson, 1973:54–60), to listen (or to be witness to some unfolding behavior), is an *act* in its own right according at least provisional approval or acquiescence to the action heard (or witnessed), and acknowledging the right of the speaker to be speaking. What is said and *listened to* combine to permit inferences about the character and relationship of the speaker and hearer.

Thus, in the case of the parent-child interactions discussed above, 22 adult forebearance of the child's protest or failure promptly to disrobe could be seen as tolerance of—if not acquiescence to—the child's "unruly" behavior. If the child is simultaneously engaged in taking a turn at talk *and* some problematic non-verbal behavior, or if *what* the child is using the turn to do (e.g., to protest) is problematic, then the parent's presumed obligation to correct or control the child's behavior may take precedence over the child's already uncertain right to complete a turn. Moreover, the parent's intrusion into the child's turn *exhibits* the adult's control over the situation and the child, displaying it to the parent, the child, and to any others witnessing the interaction. The parent's failure to act in problematic situations also shows a lack of control or the child's dominance. Insofar as the parent-child relationship is *essentially* asymmetrical by our cultural standards, those occurrences warranting adult intervention may warrant interruption of the child's turn at talk as well.

Woman's Place

The similarity between parent-child and male-female conversational 23 patterns in our data has been noted. The suggested parallel is clear: men interrupt women in situations where women's verbal or non-verbal behavior is somehow problematic, as in the following:

Female: Both really (#) it just strikes me as too
1984ish y'know to sow your seed or whatever
(#) an' then have it develop miles away not
caring i⌈f   ⌉
Male: ⌊Now:⌋ : it may be something uh quite
different (#) you can't make judgments like
that without all the facts being at your
disposal

Or:

Female: I guess I'll do a paper on the economy business
he laid out last week if ⌈I can   ⌉
Male: ⌊You're⌋ kidding!
That'd be a *terrible* topic.

And:

    Female: So uh you really can't bitch when you've got
           all those on the same day (4.2) but I uh *asked*
           my physics professor if I couldn't chan⌈ge that⌉
    Male: ⌊Don't ⌋ touch that
    (1.2)
    Female: What?
    (#)
    Male: I've got everything jus' how I want it in that
           notebook (#) you'll screw it up leafin' *through*
           it like that.

Our reflections here touch on three matters. First, we take the view 24
that the use of interruptions by males is a *display* of dominance or control to
the female (and to any witnesses), just as the parent's interruption communicates an aspect of parental control to the child and to others present. Second, the use of interruptions is *in fact* a control device since the incursion
(particularly if repeated) disorganizes the local construction of a topic, as in
the following:

    Female: How's your paper coming?=
    Male: Alright I guess (#) I haven't done much in
           the past two weeks
    (1.8)
    Female: Yeah::: know how that⌈can⌉
    Male: ⌊Hey⌋ ya' got an extra cigarette?
    (#)
    Female: Oh uh sure ((hands him the pack))
           like *my*⌈pa ⌉
    Male: ⌊How⌋ 'bout a match?
    (1.2)
    Female: Ere ya go uh like *my*⌈pa   ⌉
    Male: ⌊Thanks⌋
    (1.8)
    Female: Sure (#) I was gonna tell you⌈my⌉
    Male: ⌊Hey⌋ I'd really like
           ta' talk but I gotta run (#) see ya
    (3.2)
    Female: Yeah

Third, and perhaps most important, the occurrence of asymmetrical interruption signals the presence of issues pertinent to the activation of dominating
behavior by the male. That is, just as the physician's examining room is a
setting likely to engender adult concerns for control of the child (and hence,
interruption of the child's utterance, among other things) so too may various

occasions, *and the talk within them* trigger male displays of dominance and female displays of submission. Thus, the presence of male-initiated simultaneity—particularly interruptions—provides a clue where to search in interactional materials to find the particulars accounting for the occurrence of situationally induced attempts at dominance, in part through the suspension or violation of the rule set. Those "situational inducements", viewed from within the matrix of our present culture, constitute the warrant for interruption of the female by the male.

CONCLUDING REMARKS

These are preliminary findings, based on suggestive but far from definitive results. We report them here to show their potential significance for the study of gender behavior. The notion that language and speech communicate the cultural significance of gender is reflected by the growing literature in this area (cf. Key, 1975; Lakoff, 1975; and Thome and Henley, 1975). Earlier research has utilized verbal interaction as an index of power in familial interaction (Farina and Holzberg, 1968; Hadley and Jacob, 1973; and Mishler and Waxler, 1968). 25

However, the use of features of conversational interaction as measures of power, dominance and the like has produced inconclusive—and sometimes contradictory—findings (cf. Shaw and Sadler, 1969) in the absence of an explicit model of conversational interaction *per se.* The work of Sacks, Schegloff, and Jefferson (1974) provides a theoretical basis for analyzing the very organization of such social interaction. We have tried to sketch the outlines of an approach to the study of male-female interaction utilizing this model. 26

APPENDIX

Our transcript techniques and symbols are based on those devised by Gail Jefferson in the course of research undertaken with Harvey Sacks. Techniques are revised, symbols added or dropped as they seem useful to the work. There is no guarantee that the symbols or transcripts alone would permit the doing of any unspecified research tasks; they are properly used as an adjunct to the tape recorded materials. 27

Transcribing Convention

(x) I've (x) I've met him once	Parentheses encasing an "x" indicate a hitch or stutter on the part of the speaker.
[ ] J: Well really ⌈I⌉ K: ⌊I⌋don't	Brackets around portions of utterances indicate that the portions bracketed overlap one another. Portions to the left and right of these denote those portions of utterances in the clear.

I know, but-	A hyphen at the end of a word indicates that the utterance is cut short at that point.
::: Well::: now	Colons indicate that the immediately prior syllable is prolonged.
= A: "Swat I said= B: = But you didn't	An equal sign is used to indicate that no time elapses between the objects "Latched" by the marks. Often used in transcribing it can also mean that a next speaker starts at precisely the end of a current speaker's utterance.
_____	Underscoring is utilized to represent heavier emphasis (in speaker's pitch) on words so marked.
?, !, ,, . Are you sure?	Punctuation marks are used for intonation, not grammar.
((softly)) Ha ((chuckles))	Double parentheses enclose "descriptions," not transcribed utterances.
(#) But (#) you said	Score sign indicates a pause of one second or less that wasn't possible to discriminate precisely.
(1.2)	Numbers encased in parentheses indicate the seconds and tenths of seconds ensuing between speaker's turns. They may also be used to indicate the duration of pauses internal to a speaker's turn.
(T15:50–60)	Designations appearing to the left of transcribed examples in parentheses refer to the transcript in which the example may be located, where (a) a citation indicates that it is borrowed from published material, and (b) a code indicates that it comes from other sources.
	Transcripts with no designation in the left margin are drawn from the corpus analyzed in Zimmerman and West (1975). ◎

CRITICAL READING

1. What is the point of comparing findings on male-female conversation patterns with those between children and adults? What assumptions underlie this comparison?
2. West and Zimmerman found that in conversations between men and women, the men interrupted the females fairly frequently, and the females remained silent at these points—seeming to allow such interruptions. Why do you think that the women did this? Do you think that such conversational patterns are common between men and women today? Have things changed much in twenty-five years?
3. What role does listening play in West and Zimmerman's conceptualization of conversation?

CLASS DISCUSSION

1. As a class, examine some of the writing in this report. Note places in the report in which the ideas are clearly communicated and places in which they are not. For example, look at the first paragraph of the Discussion section, and discuss its features—are aspects of the paragraph confusing because of lack of knowledge of the readers, in the way that the sentences are ordered, or the use or lack of transitions? Similarly, look at any confusing sentences, and work out their meaning. Discuss other ways of structuring the sentences if the class finds that it is indeed their structure, rather than their content, that is confusing (see, for example, the fifth sentence in the second paragraph of the Parent-Child Interaction Section).

2. What may be achieved, according to West and Zimmerman, by interruptions in parent-child and male-female conversation? What evidence do they give to support this notion?

DIRECTED FREEWRITE

Write a dialogue between a man and a woman that enacts the patterns that West and Zimmerman found. Incorporate elements of their study's findings by considering these questions: Who interrupts whom, and when does interruption seem to occur most? What function(s) is/are served by interruption? How does the interrupted party in the conversation respond? Then write another male-female dialogue that you view as egalitarian, one that doesn't contain the patterns discussed by West and Zimmerman.

COMMUNICATIONS UNIT WRITING ASSIGNMENTS

1. Write a process essay in which you describe, in step-by-step detail, how one might apply Tannen's ideas (and, perhaps, some of your own that relate to Tannen's points) to resolve a specific communication conflict between a woman and a man.

    The purpose of process analysis, as a mode of writing, is either to describe how something is/was done—we can term this kind of process analysis as "informational"—or, in the case of "directional" process essays, to tell a reader how to do something. The directional process analysis is most familiar to us as instructions for assembling something or as recipes for cooking food. In the case of this paper, since you are being asked to describe how something should be done and are giving instructions, your essay is directional.

    When describing a process, it is logical to proceed from the beginning to the completion of something. In this case, because you are describing the entire process of resolving a conflict, you should be as detailed as possible, so that a reader could easily carry out your instructions.

    Typically, the structure of process essays is dictated by the structure of the step-by-step procedure being described. Still, you need to think about the overall unity and coherence of your essay, and a good way to ensure unity is by starting your essay with an introduction that contains a thesis statement giving an overview, or overall characterization of the process you will be describing, and even further, perhaps by explaining its purpose.

2. In its broadest sense, to analyze something means carefully and critically to examine it, often looking at the individual parts that make up the whole thing, whatever that thing may be. A more specific kind of analysis is practiced by academics all the time, and many of the readings in this textbook apply this kind of analysis. Here we refer to analysis as the application of particular theoretical perspectives to specific phenomena, in an effort to understand the meaning or significance of those phenomena. For example, in West and Zimmerman's study of verbal interactions, the writers state early on that they will use Sacks, Schegloff, and Jefferson's model of turn-taking in conversation, and the use of this model, or theory, or paradigm provides a useful way for West and Zimmerman to understand the phenomena under study, and in turn helps them to arrive at their own (preliminary) theories of verbal interaction. As they note at the end of their piece, "The work of Sacks, Schegloff, and Jefferson (1974) provides a theoretical basis for analyzing the very organization . . . social interaction. We have tried to sketch the outlines of an approach to the study of male-female interaction utilizing this model."

Other examples of this kind of theoretical analysis are found elsewhere in this textbook when, for example, art critics and film critics apply principles of feminist theory to specific art works and films, thus arriving at particular kinds of interpretations of those works (see the Art History unit in Chapter 2 and the Film Studies unit in this chapter). Unlike West and Zimmerman, when the writers in these humanities disciplines conduct their critical interpretations, they don't explicitly identify the theoretical perspectives they are employing; experienced readers in these disciplines learn the features of particular theoretical camps and recognize their implicit use. Similarly, your professors in various college courses may not tell you their theoretical alignments, but these typically shape the professors' approaches to the subject matter of the courses you take. One more example of an implicitly theoretical approach is evident in John D'Emilio's essay on capitalism and gay identity in the Lesbian and Gay Studies unit of this chapter. D'Emilio's analysis of historical forces and their effects on family structure and identity arises out of Marxist theory; typically referred to as "materialist," Marxist theory stresses the importance of economic systems and forces in shaping social phenomena—a position that seems like good common sense to us today but that was a novel perspective in Marx's time.

In your experiences with college writing, you will have ample opportunities to practice the kind of analysis we are discussing, and you will do so in a number of different kinds of essays, or genres of writing. For this assignment, we ask you to write an analytical essay in which you apply Deborah Tannen's viewpoints to West and Zimmerman's findings on verbal interaction, or apply Tannen's perspective to Mills's ideas about non-verbal language cues. If we apply Tannen's ideas to these phenomena, what do we see? What does this theoretical approach allow us to conclude about the phenomena under analysis? The answer to questions like these ends up constituting the thesis statement of your essay; thus, you will have to do a lot of prewriting in which you explore the relations between Tannen's ideas and the phenomena you've chosen to analyze, and out of this exploration, begin to construct a thesis that sums up that relation, or what that relation reveals.

3. Since West and Zimmerman's study is twenty-five years old and since they note that their findings were preliminary, do some library research to locate several more recent studies into male-female conversation patterns. Then, write a synthesis essay in which you update West and Zimmerman's most basic suggestions regarding interruptions, expressions of power, dominance and control in male-female dialogue, and/or female submissive behavior. Update the findings either by adding further insight gained in subsequent research or by discussing contradictory findings.

You may have already encountered synthesis, in the form of a comparison and contrast assignment on page 165. That assignment noted that comparison and contrast is the synthesis of two things. Synthesis more broadly applies to the uniting of any number of sources or things; thus, research papers are a kind of synthesis essay. You could, then, think of this assignment as a miniresearch paper, and as such, it must do certain things.

Synthesis essays and research papers can be categorized as primarily argumentative or explanatory—just as the purpose of nearly all academic writing is to inform or to persuade, or some combination of both. Whereas an argument synthesis seeks to advance a somewhat controversial or disputed position by combining a number of sources on an issue, an explanatory synthesis seeks to explain the various sides to an issue or elements of a topic. This assignment, then asks for explanatory synthesis, as you describe for your reader how current studies relate to the older West and Zimmerman work.

As the word "synthesis" implies, you won't be simply describing the studies and findings that you discover, however. You will need to make a point—your own point, distilled from the readings—about what the current research has concluded about issues of male-female verbal communication, and you must relate that point to West and Zimmerman's ideas. It's a good idea to start at a broad level, as male-female verbal communication indicates, and then as you review various readings, start to focus on a more specific aspect of this topic that relates to the West and Zimmerman piece.

The process of prewriting for this essay will require you to spend time carefully reading and rereading the studies you find and to take notes listing the connections between the readings, searching for ways to narrow your focus, and thus to pull the points from the readings together around that focus. After you note connections between the readings, you can start to formulate a preliminary thesis statement that sums up the overall relationship and focus in the readings on which your essay will focus. Go back and forth between rereading the essays, adding to your notes and refining your thesis.

Then, when you begin to think about the structure of your essay and are ready to start drafting, you ought to plan to organize your essay around the points that you are dealing with and explaining, rather than around the different studies or readings you are using as sources. Remember the word "synthesis," and all that it implies: a synthesis is a true blending of things, and if your essay simply describes each study or reading, your essay will seem disjointed rather than pulled together and unified.

Unit 2
Evolutionary Psychology—
Love, Homo Sapiens Style

CHAPTER 1 FROM
THE EVOLUTION OF DESIRE:
STRATEGIES OF HUMAN MATING
David Buss

In this opening chapter of his book on evolutionary psychology's theories about human sexual behavior, Buss defines crucial elements of Darwin's theory of evolution and focuses on how they relate to human mating practices. Thus, this reading serves as an excellent introduction to the ways in which evolutionary psychologists employ Darwin's ideas and to the kinds of explanations for human sexual behavior that such applications lead to. As you read, pay attention to the ways that Buss both explains and supports the points he makes here.

David Buss received his undergraduate degree in psychology from the University of Texas and his Ph.D. from the University of California, Berkeley. He is currently at the University of Texas at Austin where he is a professor of psychology who teaches courses in human mating and evolutionary psychology. Buss is also an internationally known expert in the areas of sex, emotions, and human mating. He has won the APA Distinguished Scientific Award for Early Career Contribution to Psychology and the G. Stanley Hall Award. Additionally, he serves on the Board of Directors for the International Society for the Study of the Individual Differences, on the Executive Council of the Human Behavior and Evolution Society, and as Director of the International Consortium of Social and Personality Psychologists. Buss is the author of various articles and texts including Sex, Power, Conflict; The Dangerous Passion: Why Jealousy Is as Necessary as Love and Sex; *and* The Evolution of Desire: Strategies of Human Mating *from which this article is taken.*

Human mating behavior delights and amuses us and galvanizes our   1
gossip, but it is also deeply disturbing. Few domains of human activity generate as much discussion, as many laws, or such elaborate rituals in all cultures. Yet the elements of human mating seem to defy understanding.
Women and men sometimes find themselves choosing mates who abuse
them psychologically and physically. Efforts to attract mates often backfire.
Conflicts erupt within couples, producing downward spirals of blame and despair. Despite their best intentions and vows of lifelong love, half of all married couples end up divorcing.

Pain, betrayal, and loss contrast sharply with the usual romantic no-   2
tions of love. We grow up believing in true love, in finding our "one and
only." We assume that once we do, we will marry in bliss and live happily
ever after. But reality rarely coincides with our beliefs. Even a cursory look
at the divorce rate, the 30 to 50 percent incidence of extramarital affairs,
and the jealous rages that rack so many relationships shatters these illusions.

Discord and dissolution in mating relationships are typically seen as   3
signs of failure. They are regarded as distortions or perversions of the natural state of married life. They are thought to signal personal inadequacy,
immaturity, neurosis, failure of will, or simply poor judgment in the choice of
a mate. This view is radically wrong. Conflict in mating is the norm and not
the exception. It ranges from a man's anger at a woman who declines his
advances to a wife's frustration with a husband who fails to help in the
home. Such a pervasive pattern defies easy explanation. Something
deeper, more telling about human nature is involved—something we do not
fully understand.

The problem is complicated by the centrality of love in human life.   4
Feelings of love mesmerize us when we experience them and occupy our
fantasies when we do not. The anguish of love dominates poetry, music, literature, soap operas, and romance novels more than perhaps any other
theme. Contrary to common belief, love is not a recent invention of the
Western leisure classes. People in all cultures experience love and have
coined specific words for it. Its pervasiveness convinces us that love, with its
key components of commitment, tenderness, and passion, is an inevitable
part of the human experience, within the grasp of everyone.

Our failure to understand the real and paradoxical nature of human   5
mating is costly, both scientifically and socially. Scientifically, the dearth of
knowledge leaves unanswered some of life's most puzzling questions, such
as why people sacrifice years of their lives to the quest for love and the
struggle for relationship. Socially, our ignorance leaves us frustrated and
helpless when we are bruised by mating behavior gone awry in the workplace, on the dating scene, and in our home.

We need to reconcile the profound love that humans seek with the   6
conflict that permeates our most cherished relationships. We need to square

our dreams with reality. To understand these baffling contradictions, we must gaze back into our evolutionary past—a past that has grooved and scored our minds as much as our bodies, our strategies for mating as much as our strategies for survival.

EVOLUTIONARY ROOTS

More than a century ago, Charles Darwin offered a revolutionary explanation for the mysteries of mating. He had become intrigued by the puzzling way that animals had developed characteristics that would appear to hinder their survival. The elaborate plumage, large antlers, and other conspicuous features displayed by many species seemed costly in the currency of survival. He wondered how the brilliant plumage of peacocks could evolve, and become more common, when it poses such an obvious threat to survival, acting as an open lure to predators. Darwin's answer was that the peacock's displays evolved because they led to an individual's reproductive success, providing an advantage in the competition for a desirable mate and continuing that peacock's genetic line. The evolution of characteristics because of their reproductive benefits, rather than survival benefits, is known as sexual selection.   7

Sexual selection, according to Darwin, takes two forms. In one form, members of the same sex compete with each other, and the outcome of their contest gives the winner greater sexual access to members of the opposite sex. Two stags locking horns in combat is the prototypical image of this intrasexual competition. The characteristics that lead to success in contests of this kind, such as greater strength, intelligence, or attractiveness to allies, evolve because the victors are able to mate more often and hence pass on more genes. In the other type of sexual selection, members of one sex choose a mate based on their preferences for particular qualities in that mate. These characteristics evolve in the other sex because animals possessing them are chosen more often as mates, and their genes thrive. Animals lacking the desired characteristics are excluded from mating, and their genes perish. Since peahens prefer peacocks with plumage that flashes and glitters, dull-feathered males get left in the evolutionary dust. Peacocks today possess brilliant plumage because over evolutionary history peahens have preferred to mate with dazzling and colorful males.   8

Darwin's theory of sexual selection begins to explain mating behavior by identifying two key processes by which evolutionary change can occur: preferences for a mate and competition for a mate. But the theory was vigorously resisted by male scientists for over a century, in part because the active choosing of mates seemed to grant too much power to females, who were thought to remain passive in the mating process. The theory of sexual selection was also resisted by mainstream social scientists because its portrayal of human nature seemed to depend on instinctive behavior, and thus   9 to minimize the uniqueness and flexibility of humans. Culture and consciousness were presumed to free us from evolutionary forces. The breakthrough in applying sexual selection to humans came in the late 1970s and 1980s, in the form of theoretical advances initiated by my colleagues and me in the fields of psychology and anthropology. We tried to identify underlying psychological mechanisms that were the products of evolution—mechanisms that help to explain both the extraordinary flexibility of human behavior and the active mating strategies pursued by women and men. This new discipline is called evolutionary psychology.

When I began work in the field, however, little was known about actual   10
human mating behavior. There was a frustrating lack of scientific evidence on mating in the broad array of human populations, and practically no documented support for grand evolutionary theorizing. No one knew whether some mating desires are universal, whether certain sex differences are characteristic of all people in all cultures, or whether culture exerts a powerful enough influence to override the evolved preferences that might exist. So I departed from the traditional path of mainstream psychology to explore which characteristics of human mating behavior would follow from evolutionary principles. In the beginning, I simply wanted to verify a few of the most obvious evolutionary predictions about sex differences in mating preferences; for example, whether men desire youth and physical attractiveness in a mate and whether women desire status and economic security. Toward that end, I interviewed and administered questionnaires to 186 married adults and 100 unmarried college students within the United States.

The next step was to verify whether the psychological phenomena un-   11
covered by this study were characteristic of our species. If mating desires and other features of human psychology are products of our evolutionary history, they should be found universally, not just in the United States. So I initiated an international study to explore how mates are selected in other cultures, starting with a few European countries, including Germany and the Netherlands. I soon realized, however, that since European cultures share many features, they do not provide the most rigorous test for the principles of evolutionary psychology. Over a period of five years, I expanded the study to include fifty collaborators from thirty-seven cultures located on six continents and five islands, from Australia to Zambia. Local residents administered the questionnaire about mating desires in their native language. We sampled large cities, such as Rio de Janeiro and São Paulo in Brazil, Shanghai in China, Bangalore and Ahmadabad in India, Jerusalem and Tel Aviv in Israel, and Tehran in Iran. We also sampled rural peoples, including Indians in the state of Gujarat and Zulus in South Africa. We covered the well educated and the poorly educated. We included respondents of every age from fourteen through seventy, as well as places in the entire range of political systems from capitalist to communist and socialist. All major racial

groups, religious groups, and ethnic groups were represented. In all, we surveyed 10,047 persons worldwide.

This study, the largest ever undertaken on human mating desires, was   12
merely the beginning. The findings had implications that reached into every sphere of human mating life, from dating to marriage, extramarital affairs, and divorce. They were also relevant to major social issues of the day, such as sexual harassment, domestic abuse, pornography, and patriarchy. To explore as many mating domains as possible, I launched over fifty new studies, involving thousands of individuals. Included in these studies were men and women searching for a mate in singles bars and on college campuses, dating couples at various stages of commitment, newlywed couples in the first five years of marriage, and couples who ended up divorced.

The findings from all of these studies caused controversy and confu-   13
sion among my colleagues, because in many respects they contradicted conventional thinking. They forced a radical shift from the standard view of men's and women's sexual psychology. One of my aims . . . is to formulate from these diverse findings a unified theory of human mating, based not on romantic notions or outdated scientific theories but on current scientific evidence. Much of what I discovered about human mating is not nice. In the ruthless pursuit of sexual goals, for example, men and women derogate their rivals, deceive members of the opposite sex, and even subvert their own mates. These discoveries are disturbing to me; I would prefer that the competitive, conflictual, and manipulative aspects of human mating did not exist. But a scientist cannot wish away unpleasant findings. Ultimately, the disturbing side of human mating must be confronted if its harsh consequences are ever to be ameliorated.

SEXUAL STRATEGIES

Strategies are methods for accomplishing goals, the means for solving   14
problems. It may seem odd to view human mating, romance, sex, and love as inherently strategic. But we never choose mates at random. We do not attract mates indiscriminately. We do not derogate our competitors out of boredom. Our mating is strategic, and our strategies are designed to solve particular problems for successful mating. Understanding how people solve those problems requires an analysis of sexual strategies. Strategies are essential for survival on the mating battlefield.

Adaptations are evolved solutions to the problems posed by survival   15
and reproduction. Over millions of years of evolution, natural selection has produced in us hunger mechanisms to solve the problem of providing nutrients to the organism; taste buds that are sensitive to fat and sugar to solve the problem of what to put into our mouths (nuts and berries, but not dirt or gravel); sweat glands and shivering mechanisms to solve the problems of

extreme hot and cold; emotions such as fear and rage that motivate flight and fight to combat predators or aggressive competitors; and a complex immune system to combat diseases and parasites. These adaptations are human solutions to the problems of existence posed by the hostile forces of nature—they are our survival strategies. Those who failed to develop appropriate characteristics failed to survive.

Correspondingly, sexual strategies are adaptive solutions to mating   16
problems. Those in our evolutionary past who failed to mate successfully failed to become our ancestors. All of us descend from a long and unbroken line of ancestors who competed successfully for desirable mates, attracted mates who were reproductively valuable, retained mates long enough to reproduce, fended off interested rivals, and solved the problems that could have impeded reproductive success. We carry in us the sexual legacy of those success stories.

Each sexual strategy is tailored to a specific adaptive problem, such as   17
identifying a desirable mate or besting competitors in attracting a mate. Underlying each sexual strategy are psychological mechanisms, such as preferences for a particular mate, feelings of love, desire for sex, or jealousy. Each psychological mechanism is sensitive to information or cues from the external world, such as physical features, signs of sexual interest, or hints of potential infidelity. Our psychological mechanisms are also sensitive to information about ourselves, such as our ability to attract a mate who has a certain degree of desirability. The goal of this book is to peel back the layers of adaptive problems that men and women have faced in the course of mating and uncover the complex sexual strategies they have evolved for solving them.

Although the term *sexual strategies* is a useful metaphor for thinking   18
about solutions to mating problems, it is misleading in the sense of connoting conscious intent. Sexual strategies do not require conscious planning or awareness. Our sweat glands are "strategies" for accomplishing the goal of thermal regulation, but they require neither conscious planning nor awareness of the goal. Indeed, just as a piano player's sudden awareness of her hands may impede performance, most human sexual strategies are best carried out without the awareness of the actor.

SELECTING A MATE

Nowhere do people have an equal desire for all members of the oppo-   19
site sex. Everywhere some potential mates are preferred, others shunned. Our sexual desires have come into being in the same way as have other kinds of desires. Consider the survival problem of what food to eat. Humans are faced with a bewildering array of potential objects to ingest—berries, fruit, nuts, meat, dirt, gravel, poisonous plants, twigs, and feces. If we had no taste preferences and ingested objects from our environment at random,

some people, by chance alone, would consume ripe fruit, fresh nuts, and other objects that provide caloric and nutritive sustenance. Others, also by chance alone, would eat rancid meat, rotten fruit, and toxins. Earlier humans who preferred nutritious objects survived.

Our actual food preferences bear out this evolutionary process. We [20] show great fondness for substances rich in fat, sugar, protein, and salt and an aversion to substances that are bitter, sour, and toxic. These food preferences solve a basic problem of survival. We carry them with us today precisely because they solved critical adaptive problems for our ancestors.

Our desires in a mate serve analogous adaptive purposes, but their [21] functions do not center simply on survival. Imagine living as our ancestors did long ago—struggling to keep warm by the fire; hunting meat for our kin; gathering nuts, berries, and herbs; and avoiding dangerous animals and hostile humans. If we were to select a mate who failed to deliver the resources promised, who had affairs, who was lazy, who lacked hunting skills, or who heaped physical abuse on us, our survival would be tenuous, our reproduction at risk. In contrast, a mate who provided abundant resources, who protected us and our children, and who devoted time, energy, and effort to our family would be a great asset. As a result of the powerful survival and reproductive advantages that were reaped by those of our ancestors who chose a mate wisely, clear desires in a mate evolved. As descendants of those people, we carry their desires with us today.

Many other species have evolved mate preferences. The African vil- [22] lage weaverbird provides a vivid illustration. When the male weaverbird spots a female in the vicinity, he displays his recently built nest by suspending himself upside down from the bottom and vigorously flapping his wings. If the male passes this test, the female approaches the nest, enters it, and examines the nest materials, poking and pulling them for as long as ten minutes. As she makes her inspection, the male sings to her from nearby. At any point in this sequence she may decide that the nest does not meet her standards and depart to inspect another male's nest. A male whose nest is rejected by several females will often break it down and start over. By exerting a preference for males who can build a superior nest, the female weaverbird solves the problems of protecting and provisioning her future chicks. Her preferences have evolved because they bestowed a reproductive advantage over other weaverbirds who had no preferences and who mated with any males who happened along.

Women, like weaverbirds, prefer men with desirable "nests." Consider [23] one of the problems that women in evolutionary history had to face: selecting a man who would be willing to commit to a long-term relationship. A woman in our evolutionary past who chose to mate with a man who was flighty, impulsive, philandering, or unable to sustain relationships found herself raising her children alone, without benefit of the resources, aid, and protection that another man might have offered. A woman who preferred to mate with a reliable man who was willing to commit to her was more likely to have children who survived and thrived. Over thousands of generations, a preference for men who showed signs of being willing and able to commit to them evolved in women, just as preferences for mates with adequate nests evolved in weaverbirds. This preference solved key reproductive problems, just as food preferences solved key survival problems.

People do not always desire the commitment required of long-term 24 mating. Men and women sometimes deliberately seek a short-term fling, a temporary liaison, or a brief affair. And when they do, their preferences shift, sometimes dramatically. One of the crucial decisions for humans in selecting a mate is whether they are seeking a short-term mate or a long-term partner. The sexual strategies pursued hinge on this decision. This book documents the universal preferences that men and women display for particular characteristics in a mate, reveals the evolutionary logic behind the different desires of each sex, and explores the changes that occur when people shift their goal from casual sex to a committed relationship.

ATTRACTING A MATE

People who possess desirable characteristics are in great demand. 25 Appreciating their traits is not enough for successful mating, just as spying a ripe berry bush down a steep ravine is not enough for successful eating. The next step in mating is to compete successfully for a desirable mate.

Among the elephant seals on the coast of California, males during the 26 mating season use their sharp tusks to best rival males in head-to-head combat. Often their contests and bellowing continue day and night. The losers lie scarred and injured on the beach, exhausted victims of this brutal competition. But the winner's job is not yet over. He must roam the perimeter of his harem, which contains a dozen or more females. This dominant male must hold his place in life's reproductive cycle by herding stray females back into the harem and repelling other males who attempt to sneak copulations.

Over many generations, male elephant seals who are stronger, larger, 27 and more cunning have succeeded in getting a mate. The larger, more aggressive males control the sexual access to females and so pass on to their sons the genes conferring these qualities. Indeed, males now weigh roughly 4,000 pounds, or four times the weight of females, who appear to human observers to risk getting crushed during copulation.

Female elephant seals prefer to mate with the victors and thus pass on 28 the genes conferring this preference to their daughters. But by choosing the larger, stronger winners, they also determine the genes for size and fighting abilities that will live on in their sons. The smaller, weaker, and more timid males fail to mate entirely. They become evolutionary dead ends. Because only 5 percent of the males monopolize 85 percent of the females, selection pressures remain intense even today.

Male elephant seals must fight not just to best other males but also to   29
be chosen by females. A female emits loud bellowing sounds when a
smaller male tries to mate with her. The alerted dominant male comes
bounding toward them, rears his head in threat, and exposes a massive
chest. This gesture is usually enough to send the smaller male scurrying for
cover. Female preferences are one key to establishing competition among
the males. If females did not mind mating with smaller, weaker males, then
they would not alert the dominant male, and there would be less intense selection pressure for size and strength. Female preferences, in short, determine many of the ground rules of the male contests.

People are not like elephant seals in most of these mating behaviors.   30
For example, whereas only 5 percent of the male elephant seals do 85 percent of the mating, more than 90 percent of men are able at some point in
their lives to find a mate. Male elephant seals strive to monopolize harems
of females, and the winners remain victorious for only a season or two,
whereas many humans form enduring unions that last for years and
decades. But men and male elephant seals share a key characteristic: both
must compete to attract females. Males who fail to attract females risk being
shut out of mating.

Throughout the animal world, males typically compete more fiercely   31
than females for mates, and in many species males are certainly more ostentatious and strident in their competition. But competition among females is
also intense in many species. Among patas monkeys and gelada baboons,
females harass copulating pairs in order to interfere with the mating success
of rival females. Among wild rhesus monkeys, females use aggression to interrupt sexual contact between other females and males, occasionally winning the male consort for herself. And among savanna baboons, female
competition over mates serves not merely to secure sexual access but also
to develop long-term social relationships that provide physical protection.

Competition among women, though typically less florid and violent   32
than competition among men, pervades human mating systems. The writer
H. L. Mencken noted: "When women kiss, it always reminds one of prize
fighters shaking hands." This book shows how members of each sex compete with each other for access to members of the opposite sex. The tactics
they use to compete are often dictated by the preferences of the opposite
sex. Those who do not have what the other sex wants risk remaining on the
sidelines in the dance of mating.

KEEPING A MATE

Keeping a mate is another important adaptive problem; mates may   33
continue to be desirable to rivals, who may poach, thereby undoing all the
effort devoted to attracting, courting, and committing to the mate. Furthermore, one mate may defect because of the failure of the other to fulfill his or

her needs and wants or upon the arrival of someone fresher, more compelling, or more beautiful. Mates, once gained, must be retained.

Consider the *Plecia nearctica,* an insect known as the lovebug. Male 34 lovebugs swarm during the early morning and hover a foot or two off the ground, waiting for the chance to mate with a female. Female lovebugs do not swarm or hover. Instead, they emerge in the morning from the vegetation and enter the swarm of males. Sometimes a female is captured by a male before she can take flight. Males often wrestle with other males, and as many as ten males may cluster around a single female.

The successful male departs from the swarm with his mate, and the 35 couple glides to the ground to copulate. Perhaps because other males continue to attempt to mate with her, the male retains his copulatory embrace for as long as three full days—hence the nickname "lovebug." The prolonged copulation itself functions as a way of guarding the mate. By remaining attached to the female until she is ready to deposit her eggs, the male lovebug prevents other males from fertilizing her eggs. In reproductive currency, his ability to compete with other males and attract a female would be for naught if he failed to solve the problem of retaining his mate.

Different species solve this problem by different means. Humans do 36 not engage in continuous copulatory embraces for days, but the problem of holding on to a mate is confronted by everyone who seeks a long-term relationship. In our evolutionary past, men who were indifferent to the sexual infidelities of their mates risked compromising their paternity. They risked investing time, energy, and effort in children who were not their own. Ancestral women, in contrast, did not risk the loss of parenthood if their mates had affairs, because maternity has always been 100 percent certain. But a woman with a philandering husband risked losing his resources, his commitment, and his investment in her children. One psychological strategy that evolved to combat infidelity was jealousy. Ancestral people who became enraged at signs of their mate's potential defection and who acted to prevent it had a selective advantage over those who were not jealous. People who failed to prevent infidelity in a mate had less reproductive success.

The emotion of jealousy motivates various kinds of action in overt re- 37 sponses to a threat to the relationship. Sexual jealousy, for example, may produce either of two radically different actions, vigilance or violence. In one case, a jealous man might follow his wife when she goes out, call her unexpectedly to see whether she is where she said she would be, keep an eye on her at a party, or read her mail. These actions represent vigilance. In the other case, a man might threaten a rival whom he spotted with his wife, beat the rival with his fists, get his friends to beat up the rival, or throw a brick through the rival's window. These actions represent violence. Both courses of action, vigilance and violence, are different manifestations of the same psychological strategy of jealousy. They represent alternative ways of solving the problem of the defection of a mate.

Jealousy is not a rigid, invariant instinct that drives robotlike, mechani- 38
cal action. It is highly sensitive to context and environment. Many other behavioral options are available to serve the strategy of jealousy, giving
humans a flexibility in tailoring their responses to the subtle nuances of a situation. . . .

REPLACING A MATE

Not all mates can be retained, nor should they be. Sometimes there 39
are compelling reasons to get rid of a mate, such as when a mate stops providing support, withdraws sex, or starts inflicting physical abuse. Those who
remain with a mate through economic hardship, sexual infidelity, and cruelty
may win our admiration for their loyalty. But staying with a bad mate does
not help a person successfully pass on genes. We are the descendants of
those who knew when to cut their losses.

Getting rid of a mate has precedent in the animal world. Ring doves, 40
for example, are generally monogamous from one breeding season to the
next, but they break up under certain circumstances. The doves experience
a divorce rate of about 25 percent every season; the major reason for
breaking their bond is infertility. When a ring dove fails to produce chicks
with one partner during a breeding season, he or she leaves the mate and
searches for another. Losing an infertile mate serves the goal of reproduction for ring doves better than remaining in a barren union.

Just as we have evolved sexual strategies to select, attract, and keep 41
a good mate, we have also evolved strategies for jettisoning a bad mate. Divorce is a human universal that occurs in all known cultures. Our separation
strategies involve a variety of psychological mechanisms. We have ways to
assess whether the costs inflicted by a mate outweigh the benefits provided.
We scrutinize other potential partners and evaluate whether they might offer
more than our current mate. We gauge the likelihood of successfully attracting other desirable partners. We calculate the potential damage that might
be caused to ourselves, our children, and our kin by the dissolution of the
relationship. And we combine all this information into a decision to stay or
leave.

Once a mate decides to leave, another set of psychological strategies 42
is activated. Because such decisions have complex consequences for two
sets of extended kin who often have keen interests in the union, breaking up
is neither simple nor effortless. These complex social relationships must be
negotiated, the breakup justified. The range of tactical options within the
human repertoire is enormous, from simply packing one's bags and walking
away to provoking a rift by revealing an infidelity.

Breaking up is a solution to the problem of a bad mate, but it opens up 43
the new problem of replacing that mate. Like most mammals, humans typically do not mate with a single person for an entire lifetime. Humans often

reenter the mating market and repeat the cycle of selection, attraction, and retention. But starting over after a breakup poses its own unique set of problems. People reenter the mating market at a different age and with different assets and liabilities. Increased resources and status may help one to attract a mate who was previously out of range. Alternatively, older age and children from a previous mateship may detract from one's ability to attract a new mate.

Men and women undergo predictably different changes as they divorce and reenter the mating market. If there are children, the woman often takes primary responsibility for child rearing. Because children from previous unions are usually seen as costs rather than benefits when it comes to mating, a woman's ability to attract a desirable mate often suffers relative to a man's. Consequently, fewer divorced women than men remarry, and this difference between the sexes gets larger with increasing age. . . . 44

CONFLICT BETWEEN THE SEXES

The sexual strategies that members of one sex pursue to select, attract, keep, or replace a mate often have the unfortunate consequence of creating a conflict with members of the other sex. Among the scorpionfly, a female refuses to copulate with a courting male unless he brings her a substantial nuptial gift, which is typically a dead insect to be consumed. While the female eats the nuptial gift, the male copulates with her. During copulation, the male maintains a loose grasp on the nuptial gift, as if to prevent the female from absconding with it before copulation is complete. It takes the male twenty minutes of continuous copulation to deposit all his sperm into the female. Male scorpionflies have evolved the ability to select a nuptial gift that takes the female approximately twenty minutes to consume. If the gift is smaller and is consumed before copulation is completed, the female casts off the male before he has deposited all his sperm. If the gift is larger and takes the female more than twenty minutes to consume, the male completes copulation, and the two then fight over the leftovers. Conflict between male and female scorpionflies thus occurs over whether he gets to complete copulation when the gift is too small and over who gets to use the residual food resources when the gift is larger than needed. 45

Men and women also clash over resources and sexual access. In the evolutionary psychology of human mating, the sexual strategy adopted by one sex can trip up and conflict with the strategy adopted by the other sex in a phenomenon called strategic interference. Consider the differences in men's and women's proclivities to seek brief or lasting sexual relations. Men and women typically differ in how long and how well they need to know someone before they consent to sexual intercourse. Although there are many exceptions and individual differences, men generally have lower thresholds for seeking sex. For example, men often express the desire and 46 willingness to have sex with an attractive stranger, whereas women almost invariably refuse anonymous encounters and prefer some degree of commitment.

There is a fundamental conflict between these different sexual strate- 47
gies: men cannot fulfill their short-term wishes without simultaneously interfering with women's long-term goals. An insistence on immediate sex interferes with the requirement for a prolonged courtship. The interference is reciprocal, since prolonged courting also obstructs the goal of ready sex. Whenever the strategy adopted by one sex interferes with the strategy adopted by the other sex, conflict ensues.

Conflicts do not end with the wedding vows. Married women complain 48
that their husbands are condescending, emotionally constricted, and unreliable. Married men complain that their wives are moody, overly dependent, and sexually withholding. Both sexes complain about infidelities, ranging from mild flirtations to serious affairs. All of these conflicts become understandable in the context of our evolved mating strategies.

Although conflict between the sexes is pervasive, it is not inevitable. 49
There are conditions that minimize conflict and produce harmony between the sexes. Knowledge of our evolved sexual strategies gives us tremendous power to better our own lives by choosing actions and contexts that activate some strategies and deactivate others. Indeed, understanding sexual strategies, including the cues that trigger them, is one step toward the reduction of conflict between men and women.

CULTURE AND CONTEXT

Although ancestral selection pressures are responsible for creating the 50
mating strategies we use today, our current conditions differ from the historical conditions under which those strategies evolved. Ancestral people got their vegetables from gathering and their meat from hunting, whereas modern people get their food from supermarkets and restaurants. Similarly, modern urban people today deploy their mating strategies in singles bars, at parties, through computer networks, and by means of dating services rather than on the savanna, in protected caves, or around primitive campfires. Whereas modern conditions of mating differ from ancestral conditions, the same sexual strategies operate with unbridled force. Our evolved psychology of mating remains. It is the only mating psychology we have; it just gets played out in a modern environment.

To illustrate, look at the foods consumed in massive quantities at fast 51
food chains. We have not evolved any genes for McDonald's, but the foods we eat there reveal the ancestral strategies for survival we carry with us today. We consume in vast quantities fat, sugar, protein, and salt in the form of burgers, shakes, french fries, and pizzas. Fast food chains are popular precisely because they serve these elements in concentrated quantities.

They reveal the food preferences that evolved in a past environment of scarcity. Today, however, we overconsume these elements because of their evolutionarily unprecedented abundance, and the old survival strategies now hurt our health. We are stuck with the taste preferences that evolved under different conditions, because evolution works on a time scale too slow to keep up with the radical changes of the past several hundred years. Although we cannot go back in time and observe directly what those ancestral conditions were, our current taste preferences, like our fear of snakes and our fondness for children, provide a window for viewing what those conditions must have been. We carry with us equipment that was designed for an ancient world.

Our evolved mating strategies, just like our survival strategies, may be currently maladaptive in the currencies of survival and reproduction. The advent of AIDS, for example, renders casual sex far more dangerous to survival than it ever was under ancestral conditions. Only by understanding our evolved sexual strategies, where they came from and what conditions they were designed to deal with, can we hope to change our current course. 52

One impressive advantage humans have over many other species is that our repertoire of mating strategies is large and highly sensitive to context. Consider the problem of being in an unhappy marriage and contemplating a decision to get divorced. This decision will depend upon many complex factors, such as the amount of conflict within the marriage, whether one's mate is philandering, the pressure applied by relatives on both sides of the family, the presence of children, the ages and needs of the children, and the prospects for attracting another mate. Humans have evolved psychological mechanisms that consider and weight the costs and benefits of these crucial features of context. 53

Not only individual but also cultural circumstances vary in ways that are critical for evoking particular sexual strategies from the entire human repertoire. Some cultures have mating systems that are polygynous, allowing men to take multiple wives. Other cultures are polyandrous, allowing women to take multiple husbands. Still others are monogamous, restricting both sexes to one marriage partner at a time. And others are promiscuous, with a high rate of mate switching. Our evolved strategies of mating are highly sensitive to these legal and cultural patterns. In polygynous mating systems, for example, parents place tremendous pressure on their sons to compete for women in an apparent attempt to avoid the mateless state that plagues some men when others monopolize multiple women. In monogamous mating cultures, in contrast, parents put less pressure on their sons' strivings. 54

Another important contextual factor is the ratio of the sexes, or the number of available men relative to available women. When there is a surplus of women, such as among the Ache Indians of Paraguay, men become more reluctant to commit to one woman, preferring instead to pursue many casual relationships. When there is a surplus of men, such as in contempo- 55 rary cities of China and among the Hiwi tribe of Venezuela, monogamous marriage is the rule and divorce rates plummet. As men's sexual strategies shift, so must women's, and vice versa. The two sets coexist in a complex reciprocal relation, based in part on the sex ratio.

From one perspective, context is everything. Contexts that recurred over evolutionary time created the strategies we carry with us now. Current contexts and cultural conditions determine which strategies get activated and which lie dormant. To understand human sexual strategies, this book identifies the recurrent selection pressures or adaptive problems of the past, the psychological mechanisms or strategic solutions they created, and the current contexts that activate some solutions rather than others. 56

BARRIERS TO UNDERSTANDING HUMAN SEXUALITY

Evolutionary theory has appalled and upset people since Darwin first proposed it in 1859 to explain the creation and organization of life. Lady Ashley, his contemporary, remarked upon hearing about his theory of our descent from nonhuman primates: "Let's hope that it's not true; and if it is true, let's hope that it does not become widely known." Strenuous resistance continues to this day. These barriers to understanding must be removed if we are to gain real insight into our sexuality. 57

One barrier is perceptual. Our cognitive and perceptual mechanisms have been designed by natural selection to perceive and think about events that occur in a relatively limited time-span—over seconds, minutes, hours, days, sometimes months, and occasionally years. Ancestral humans spent most of their time solving immediate problems, such as finding food, maintaining a shelter, keeping warm, selecting and competing for partners, protecting children, forming alliances, striving for status, and defending against marauders, so there was pressure to think in the short term. Evolution, in contrast, occurs gradually over thousands of generations in tiny increments that we cannot observe directly. To understand events that occur on time scales this large requires a leap of the imagination, much like the cognitive feats of physicists who theorize about black holes and eleven-dimensional universes they cannot see. 58

Another barrier to understanding the evolutionary psychology of human mating is ideological. From Spencer's theory of social Darwinism onward, biological theories have sometimes been used for political ends—to justify oppression, to argue for racial or sexual superiority. The history of misusing biological explanations of human behavior, however, does not justify jettisoning the most powerful theory of organic life we have. To understand human mating requires that we face our evolutionary heritage boldly and understand ourselves as products of that heritage. 59

Another basis of resistance to evolutionary psychology is the naturalistic fallacy, which maintains that whatever exists should exist. The naturalis- 60 tic fallacy confuses a scientific description of human behavior with a moral prescription for that behavior. In nature, however, there are diseases, plagues, parasites, infant mortality, and a host of other natural events which we try to eliminate or reduce. The fact that they do exist in nature does not imply that they should exist.

Similarly, male sexual jealousy, which evolved as a psychological 61 strategy to protect men's certainty of their paternity, is known to cause damage to women worldwide in the form of wife battering and homicide. As a society we may eventually develop methods for reducing male sexual jealousy and its dangerous manifestations. Because there is an evolutionary origin for male sexual jealousy does not mean that we must condone or perpetuate it. Judgments of what should exist rest with people's value systems, not with science or with what currently exists.

The naturalistic fallacy has its reverse, the antinaturalistic fallacy. 62 Some people have exalted visions of what it means to be human. According to one of these views, "natural" humans are at one with nature, peacefully coexisting with plants, animals, and each other. War, aggression, and competition are seen as corruptions of this essentially peaceful human nature by current conditions, such as patriarchy or capitalism. Despite the evidence, people cling to these illusions. When the anthropologist Napoleon Chagnon documented that 25 percent of all Yanomamö Indian men die violent deaths at the hands of other Yanomamö men, his work was bitterly denounced by those who had presumed the group to live in harmony. The antinaturalistic fallacy occurs when we see ourselves through the lens of utopian visions of what we want people to be.

Opposition also arises to the presumed implications of evolutionary 63 psychology for change. If a mating strategy is rooted in evolutionary biology, it is thought to be immutable, intractable, and unchangeable; we are therefore doomed to follow the dictates of our biological mandate, like blind, unthinking robots. This belief mistakenly divides human behavior into two separate categories, one biologically determined and the other environmentally determined. In fact, human action is inexorably a product of both. Every strand of DNA unfolds within a particular environmental and cultural context. Within each person's life, social and physical environments provide input to the evolved psychological mechanisms, and every behavior is without exception a joint product of those mechanisms and their environmental influences. Evolutionary psychology represents a true interactionist view, which identifies the historical, developmental, cultural, and situational features that formed human psychology and guide that psychology today.

All behavior patterns can in principle be altered by environmental inter- 64 vention. The fact that currently we can alter some patterns and not others is a problem only of knowledge and technology. Advances in knowledge bring about new possibilities for change, if change is desired. Humans are extraordinarily sensitive to changes in their environment, because natural selection did not create in humans invariant instincts that manifest themselves in behavior regardless of context. Identifying the roots of mating behavior in evolutionary biology does not doom us to an unalterable fate.

Another form of resistance to evolutionary psychology comes from the 65 feminist movement. Many feminists worry that evolutionary explanations imply an inequality between the sexes, support restrictions on the roles that men and women can adopt, encourage stereotypes about the sexes, perpetuate the exclusion of women from power and resources, and foster pessimism about the possibilities for changing the status quo. For these reasons, feminists sometimes reject evolutionary accounts.

Yet evolutionary psychology does not carry these feared implications 66 for human mating. In evolutionary terms, men and women are identical in many or most domains, differing only in the limited areas in which they have faced recurrently different adaptive problems over human evolutionary history. For example, they diverge primarily in their preference for a particular sexual strategy, not in their innate ability to exercise the full range of human sexual strategies.

Evolutionary psychology strives to illuminate men's and women's 67 evolved mating behavior, not to prescribe what the sexes could be or should be. Nor does it offer prescriptions for appropriate sex roles. It has no political agenda. Indeed, if I have any political stance on issues related to the theory, it is the hope for equality among all persons regardless of sex, regardless of race, and regardless of preferred sexual strategy; a tolerance for the diversity of human sexual behavior; and a belief that evolutionary theory should not be erroneously interpreted as implying genetic or biological determinism or impermeability to environmental influences.

A final source of resistance to evolutionary psychology comes from the 68 idealistic views of romance, sexual harmony, and lifelong love to which we all cling. I cleave tightly to these views myself, believing that love has a central place in human sexual psychology. Mating relationships provide some of life's deepest satisfactions, and without them life would seem empty. After all, some people do manage to live happily ever after. But we have ignored the truth about human mating for too long. Conflict, competition, and manipulation also pervade human mating, and we must lift our collective heads from the sand to see them if we are to understand life's most engrossing relationships.   ©

CRITICAL READING

1. Explain why Buss uses the word "strategies" to characterize human sexual behavior. How are these strategies different from the kinds of strategies we usually deal with, such as strategies for accomplishing a project or strategies developed by generals in a war? What are these strategies ultimately meant to accomplish?

2. Point out some of the ways in which Buss's tone, word choice, and style make clear the theoretical nature of evolutionary psychology and some of the ways that his descriptions sound as if he is describing fact. Is this treatment likely to confuse a reader, or not?
3. Describe the different kinds of evidence that Buss uses to support his points and thus advance his argument.

CLASS DISCUSSION

1. While Buss is careful to point out that evolutionary psychology's insights do not doom human beings to certain "natural" behaviors, discuss how the theory's premises about human behavior could be used to justify certain kinds of behavior, and discuss what the costs or benefits of this justification might be for human societies.
2. As a class, explore the different barriers to understanding the evolutionary psychology of human mating, as discussed by Buss. Also, look at the reason Buss gives for scientists' century-long resistance to Darwin's theory of sexual selection, as outlined in the third paragraph in the "Evolutionary Roots" section and discuss the ways in which beliefs and attitudes serve to obscure the "objective" goals of science.

DIRECTED FREEWRITE

Consider the "nature versus nurture" debate, and evolutionary psychology's contribution to it. Brainstorm some human behaviors that, from a commonsense standpoint, appear to be related more to biology/genetics and those that seem more environmental or learned. Then examine the ways that you think biology and the environment might work together to produce certain qualities in us.

OUR CHEATING HEARTS

Robert Wright

In this piece written for a mass audience, Robert Wright describes evolutionary psychology and its theories about the evolutionary purpose of human male and female sexual behavior—most notably, infidelity in relationships. Men and women have different reproductive functions, and evolutionary psychologists such as Wright believe that these different functions underlie some of the different ways that men and women commit infidelity when involved in ostensibly monogamous relationships. Such issues raise interesting moral questions, as Wright notes near the end of his essay. As you read, notice the language Wright uses: where does he clearly indicate the theoretical nature of evolutionary psychology's insights, and where does his language imply that these insights are factual and proven?

Robert Wright is a senior editor at The New Republic, *and a contributor to* Slate *online magazine and* Time *from which this article is taken. Wright has also written for* The Atlantic Monthly, The New Yorker, *and* The Sciences *magazine where his articles on science and technology won the National Magazine Award for Essay and Criticism. In addition to his journalistic writings, Wright has also written several books including* The Moral Animal: Evolutionary Psychology and Everyday Life; Nonzero: The Logic of Human Destiny, *and* Three Scientists and Their Gods: Looking for Meaning in an Age of Information, *which was nominated for a National Book Critics Circle Award.*

The language of zoology used to be so reassuring. Human beings were called a "pair-bonding" species. Lasting monogamy, it seemed, was natural for us, just as it was for geese, swans and the other winged creatures that have filled our lexicon with such labels as "lovebirds" and "lovey-dovey." Family values, some experts said, were in our genes. In the 1967 best seller *The Naked Ape,* zoologist Desmond Morris wrote with comforting authority that the evolutionary purpose of human sexuality is "to strengthen the pair-bond and maintain the family unit." 1

This picture has lately acquired some blemishes. To begin with, birds are no longer such uplifting role models. Using DNA fingerprinting, ornithologists can now check to see if a mother bird's mate really is the father of her offspring. It turns out that some female chickadees (as in "my little chickadee") indulge in extramarital trysts with males that outrank their mates in the social hierarchy. For female barn swallows, it's a male with a long tail that makes extracurriculars irresistible. The innocent-looking indigo bunting has a cuckoldry rate of 40%. And so on. The idea that most bird species are truly monogamous has gone from conventional wisdom to punctured myth in a few short years. As a result, the fidelity of other pair-bonding species has fallen under suspicion. 2

Which brings us to the other problem with the idea that humans are by nature enduringly monogamous: humans. Of course, you don't need a Ph.D. to see that till-death-do-we-part fidelity doesn't come as naturally to people as, say, eating. But an emerging field known as evolutionary psychology can now put a finer point on the matter. By studying how the process of natural selection shaped the mind, evolutionary psychologists are painting a new portrait of human nature, with fresh detail about the feelings and thoughts that draw us into marriage—or push us out. 3

The good news is that human beings are designed to fall in love. The   4
bad news is that they aren't designed to stay there. According to evolutionary psychology, it is "natural" for both men and women—at some times,
under some circumstances—to commit adultery or to sour on a mate, to
suddenly find a spouse unattractive, irritating, wholly unreasonable. (It may
even be natural to *become* irritating and wholly unreasonable, and thus hasten the departure of a mate you've soured on.) It is similarly natural to find
some attractive colleague superior on all counts to the sorry wreck of a
spouse you're saddled with. When we see a couple celebrate a golden anniversary, one apt reaction is the famous remark about a dog walking on
two legs: the point is not that the feat was done well but that it was done at
all.

All of this may sound like cause for grim resignation to the further de-   5
cline of the American family. But what's "natural" isn't necessarily unchangeable. Evolutionary psychology, unlike past gene-centered views of human
nature, illuminates the tremendous flexibility of the human mind and the
powerful role of environment in shaping behavior. In particular, evolutionary
psychology shows how inhospitable the current social environment is to
monogamy. And while the science offers no easy cures, it does suggest avenues for change.

The premise of evolutionary psychology is simple. The human mind,   6
like any other organ, was designed for the purpose of transmitting genes to
the next generation; the feelings and thoughts it creates are best understood in these terms. Thus the feeling of hunger, no less than the stomach,
is here because it helped keep our ancestors alive long enough to reproduce and rear their young. Feelings of lust, no less than the sex organs, are
here because they aided reproduction directly. Any ancestors who lacked
stomachs or hunger or sex organs or lust—well, they wouldn't have become
ancestors, would they? Their traits would have been discarded by natural
selection.

This logic goes beyond such obviously Darwinian feelings as hunger   7
and lust. According to evolutionary psychologists, our everyday, ever shifting attitudes toward a mate or prospective mate—trust, suspicion, rhapsody,
revulsion, warmth, iciness—are the handiwork of natural selection that remain with us today because in the past they led to behaviors that helped
spread genes.

How can evolutionary psychologists be so sure? In part, their faith   8
rests on the whole data base of evolutionary biology. In all sorts of species,
and in organs ranging from brains to bladders, nature's attention to the sub-
tlest aspects of genetic transmission is evident. Consider the crafting of primate testicles—specifically, their custom tailoring to the monogamy, or lack
thereof, of females. If you take a series of male apes and weigh their testicles (not recommended, actually), you will find a pattern. Chimpanzees and
other species with high "relative testes weight" (testes weight in comparison

to body weight) feature quite promiscuous females. Species with low relative testes weight are either fairly monogamous (gibbons, for example) or systematically polygynous (gorillas), with one male monopolizing a harem of females. The explanation is simple. When females breed with many males, male genes can profit by producing lots of semen for their own transportation. Which male succeeds in getting his genes into a given egg may be a question of sheer volume, as competing hordes of sperm do battle.

THE TROUBLE WITH WOMEN

Patterns like these, in addition to showcasing nature's ingenuity, allow   9
a kind of detective work. If testicles evolved to match female behavior, then they are clues to the natural behavior of females. Via men's testicles, we can peer through the mists of prehistory and see how women behaved in the social environment of our evolution, free from the influence of modern culture; we can glimpse part of a pristine female mind.

The relative testes weight of humans falls between that of the chim-   10
panzee and the gorilla. This suggests that women, while not nearly so wild as chimpanzee females (who can be veritable sex machines), are by nature somewhat adventurous. If they were not, why would natural selection divert precious resources to the construction and maintenance of weighty testicles?

There is finer evidence, as well, of natural female infidelity. You might   11
think that the number of sperm cells in a husband's ejaculate would depend only on how long it has been since he last had sex. Wrong. What matters more, according to a recent study, is how long his mate has been out of sight. A man who hasn't had sex for, say, a week will have a higher sperm count if his wife was away on a business trip than if she's been home with the flu. In short, what really counts is whether the woman has had the opportunity to stray. The more chances she has had to collect sperm from other males, the more profusely her mate sends in his own troops. Again: that natural selection designed such an elaborate weapon is evidence of something for the weapon to combat—female faithlessness.

So here is problem No. 1 with the pair-bond thesis: women are not by   12
nature paragons of fidelity. Wanderlust is an innate part of their minds, ready to surface under propitious circumstances. Here's problem No. 2: if you think women are bad, you should see men.

THE TROUBLE WITH MEN

With men too, clues from physiology help uncover the mind. Consider   13
"sexual dimorphism"—the difference between average male and female body size. Extreme sexual dimorphism is typical of a polygynous species, in which one male may impregnate several females, leaving other males without offspring. Since the winning males usually secure their trophies by

fighting or intimidating other males, the genes of brawny, aggressive males get passed on while the genes of less formidable males are deposited in the dustbin of history. Thus male gorillas, who get a whole haremful of mates if they win lots of fights and no mates if they win none, are twice as big as females. With humans, males are about 15% bigger—sufficient to suggest that male departures from monogamy, like female departures, are not just a recent cultural invention.

Anthropology offers further evidence. Nearly 1,000 of the 1,154 past or present human societies ever studied—and these include most of the world's "hunter-gatherer" societies—have permitted a man to have more than one wife. These are the closest things we have to living examples of the "ancestral environment"—the social context of human evolution, the setting for which the mind was designed. The presumption is that people reared in such societies—the !Kung San of southern Africa, the Ache of Paraguay, the 19th century Eskimo—behave fairly "naturally." More so, at least, than people reared amid influences that weren't part of the ancestral environment: TVs, cars, jail time for bigamy. 14

There are vanishingly few anthropological examples of systematic female polygamy, or polyandry—women monopolizing sexual access to more than one man at once. So, while both sexes are prone under the right circumstances to infidelity, men seem much more deeply inclined to actually acquire a second or third mate—to keep a harem. 15

They are also more inclined toward the casual fling. Men are less finicky about sex partners. Prostitution—sex with someone you don't know and don't care to know—is a service sought overwhelmingly by males the world round. And almost all pornography that relies sheerly on visual stimulation—images of anonymous people, spiritless flesh—is consumed by males. 16

Many studies confirm the more discriminating nature of women. One evolutionary psychologist surveyed men and women about the minimal level of intelligence they would accept in a person they were "dating." The average response for both male and female: average intelligence. And how smart would the potential date have to be before they would consent to sex? Said the women: Oh, in that case, markedly above average. Said the men: Oh, in that case, markedly below average. 17

There is no dispute among evolutionary psychologists over the basic source of this male open-mindedness. A woman, regardless of how many sex partners she has, can generally have only one offspring a year. For a man, each new mate offers a real chance for pumping genes into the future. According to the *Guinness Book of Records,* the most prolific human parent in world history was Moulay ("The Bloodthirsty") Ismail, the last Sharifian Emperor of Morocco, who died in 1727. He fathered more than 1,000 children. 18

This logic behind undiscerning male lust seems obvious now, but it wasn't always. Darwin had noted that in species after species the female is 19 "less eager than the male," but he never figured out why. Only in the late 1960s and early 1970s did biologists George Williams and Robert Trivers attribute the raging libido of males to their nearly infinite potential rate of reproduction.

WHY DO WOMEN CHEAT?

Even then the female capacity for promiscuity remained puzzling. For women, more sex doesn't mean more offspring. Shouldn't they focus on quality rather than quantity—look for a robust, clever mate whose genes may bode well for the offspring's robustness and cleverness? There's ample evidence that women are drawn to such traits, but in our species genes are not all a male has to offer. Unlike our nearest ape relatives, we are a species of "high male-parental investment." In every known hunter-gatherer culture, marriage is the norm—not necessarily monogamous marriage, and not always lasting marriage, but marriage of some sort; and via this institution, fathers help provide for their children. [20]

In our species, then, a female's genetic legacy is best amplified by a mate with two things: good genes and much to invest. But what if she can't find one man who has both? One solution would be to trick a devoted, generous and perhaps wealthy but not especially brawny or brainy mate into raising the offspring of another male. The woman need not be aware of this strategy, but at some level, conscious or unconscious, deft timing is in order. One study found that women who cheat on mates tend to do so around ovulation, when they are most likely to get pregnant. [21]

For that matter, cheating during the infertile part of the monthly cycle might have its own logic, as a way (unconsciously) to turn the paramour into a dupe; the woman extracts goods or services from him in exchange for his fruitless conquest. Of course the flowers he buys may not help her genes, but in the ancestral environment, less frivolous gifts—notably food—would have. Nisa, a woman in a !Kung San hunter-gatherer village, told an anthropologist that "when you have lovers, one brings you something and another brings you something else. One comes at night with meat, another with money, another with beads. Your husband also does things and gives them to you." [22]

Multiple lovers have other uses too. The anthropologist Sarah Blaffer Hrdy has theorized that women copulate with more than one man to leave several men under the impression that they might be the father of particular offspring. Then, presumably, they will treat the offspring kindly. Her theory was inspired by langur monkeys. Male langurs sometimes kill infants sired by others as a kind of sexual icebreaker, a prelude to pairing up with the (former) mother. What better way to return her to ovulation—by putting an emphatic end to her breast-feeding—and to focus her energies on the offspring to come? [23]

Anyone tempted to launch into a sweeping indictment of langur moral- 24
ity should first note that infanticide on grounds of infidelity has been acceptable in a number of human societies. Among the Yanomamö of South
America and the Tikopia of the Solomon Islands, men have been known to
demand, upon marrying women with a past, that their babies be killed. And
Ache men sometimes collectively decide to kill a newly fatherless child. For
a woman in the ancestral environment, then, the benefits of multiple sex
partners could have ranged from their sparing her child's life to their defending or otherwise investing in her youngster.

Again, this logic does not depend on a conscious understanding of it. 25
Male langurs presumably do not grasp the concept of paternity. Still, genes
that make males sensitive to cues that certain infants may or may not carry
their genes have survived. A gene that says, "Be nice to children if you've
had lots of sex with their mothers," will prosper over the long haul.

THE INVENTION AND CORRUPTION OF LOVE

Genes don't talk, of course. They affect behavior by creating feelings 26
and thoughts—by building and maintaining the brain. Whenever evolutionary psychologists talk about some evolved behavioral tendency—a polyga-
mous or monogamous bent, say, or male parental investment—they are
also talking about an underlying mental infrastructure.

The advent of male parental investment, for example, required the in- 27
vention of a compelling emotion: paternal love. At some point in our past,
genes that inclined a man to love his offspring began to flourish at the expense of genes that promoted remoteness. The reason, presumably, is that
changes in circumstance—an upsurge in predators, say—made it more
likely that the offspring of undevoted, unprotective fathers would perish.

Crossing this threshold meant love not only for the child; the first step 28
toward becoming devoted parents consists of the man and woman developing a mutual attraction. The genetic payoff of having two parents committed
to a child's welfare seems to be the central reason men and women can fall
into swoons over one another.

Until recently, this claim was heresy. "Romantic love" was thought to 29
be the unnatural invention of Western vulture. The Mangaians of Polynesia,
for instance, were said to be "puzzled" by references to marital affection. But
lately anthropologists have taken a second look at purportedly loveless cultures, including the Mangaians, and have discovered what nonanthropolo-
gists already knew: love between man and woman is a human universal.

In this sense the pair-bonding label is apt. Still, that term—and for that 30
matter the term love—conveys a sense of permanence and symmetry that
is wildly misleading. Evolution not only invented romantic love but from the
beginning also corrupted it. The corruption lies in conflicts of interest inherent in male parental investment. It is the goal of maximizing male invest-

ment, remember, that sometimes leads a woman to infidelity. Yet it is the preciousness of this investment that makes her infidelity lethal to her mate's interests. Not long for this world are the genes of a man who showers time and energy on children who are not his.

Meanwhile, male parental investment also makes the man's naturally 31 polygynous bent inimical to his wife's reproductive interests. His quest for a new wife could lead him to withdraw, or at least dilute, investment in his first wife's children. This reallocation of resources may on balance help his genes but certainly not hers.

The living legacy of these long-running genetic conflicts is human jeal- 32 ousy—or, rather, human jealousies. In theory, there should be two kinds of jealousy—one male and one female. A man's jealousy should focus on sexual infidelity, since cuckoldry is the greatest genetic threat he faces. A woman, though she'll hardly applaud a partner's strictly sexual infidelity (it does consume time and divert some resources),should be more concerned with emotional infidelity—the sort of magnetic commitment to another woman that could lead to a much larger shift in resources.

David Buss, an evolutionary psychologist at the University of Michigan, 33 has confirmed this prediction vividly. He placed electrodes on men and women and had them envision their mates doing various disturbing things. When men imagined sexual infidelity, their heart rates took leaps of a magnitude typically induced by three cups of coffee. They sweated. Their brows wrinkled. When they imagined a budding emotional attachment, they calmed down, though not quite to their normal level. For women, things were reversed: envisioning emotional infidelity—redirected love, not supplementary sex—brought the deeper distress.

That jealousy is so finely tuned to these forms of treachery is yet more 34 evidence that they have a long evolutionary history. Still, the modern environment has carried them to new heights, making marriage dicier than ever. Men and women have always, in a sense, been designed to make each other miserable, but these days they are especially good at it.

MODERN OBSTACLES TO MONOGAMY

To begin with, infidelity is easier in an anonymous city than in a small 35 hunter-gatherer village. Whereas paternity studies show that 2% of the children in a !Kung San village result from cuckoldry, the rate runs higher than 20% in some modern neighborhoods.

Contraceptive technology may also complicate marriage. During 36 human evolution, there were no condoms or birth-control pills. If an adult couple slept together for a year or two and produced no baby, the chances were good that one of them was not fertile. No way of telling which one, but from their genes' point of view, there was little to lose and much to gain by ending the partnership and finding a new mate. Perhaps, some have speculated, natural selection favored genes inclining men and women to sour on a mate after long periods of sex without issue. And it is true that barren marriages are especially likely to break up.

Another possible challenge to monogamy in the modern world lies in   37 movies, billboards and magazines. There was no photography in the long-ago world that shaped the human male mind. So at some deep level, that mind may respond to glossy images of pinups and fashion models as if they were viable mates—alluring alternatives to dull, monogamous devotion. Evolutionary psychologist Douglas Kenrick has suggested as much. According to his research, men who are shown pictures of *Playboy* models later describe themselves as less in love with their wives than do men shown other images. (Women shown pictures from *Playgirl* felt no such attitude adjustment toward spouses.)

Perhaps the largest modern obstacle to lasting monogamy is eco-   38 nomic inequality. To see why, it helps to grasp a subtle point made by Donald Symons, author of the 1979 classic *The Evolution of Human Sexuality*. Though men who leave their wives may be driven by "natural" impulses, that does not mean men have a natural impulse designed expressly to make them leave their wives. After all, in the ancestral environment, gaining a second wife didn't mean leaving the first. So why leave her? Why not stay near existing offspring and keep giving some support? Symons believes men are designed less for opportune desertion than for opportune polygyny. It's just that when polygyny is illegal, a polygynous impulse will find other outlets, such as divorce.

If Symons is right, the question of what makes a man feel the restless-   39 ness that leads to divorce can be rephrased: What circumstances, in the ancestral environment, would have permitted the acquisition of a second wife? Answer: possessing markedly more resources, power or social status than the average Joe.

Even in some "egalitarian" hunter-gatherer societies, men with slightly   40 more status or power than average are slightly more likely to have multiple wives. In less egalitarian preindustrial societies, the anthropologist Laura Betzig has shown, the pattern is dramatic. In Incan society, the four political offices from petty chief to chief were allotted ceilings of seven, eight, 15 and 30 women. Polygyny reaches its zenith under the most despotic regimes. Among the Zulu, where coughing or sneezing at the king's dinner table was punishable by death, his highness might monopolize more than 100 women.

To an evolutionary psychologist, such numbers are just extreme ex-   41 amples of a simple fact: the ultimate purpose of the wealth and power that men seek so ardently is genetic proliferation. It is only natural that the exquisitely flexible human mind should be designed to capitalize on this power once it is obtained.

Thus it is natural that a rising corporate star, upon getting a big promo-   42 tion, should feel a strong attraction to women other than his wife. Testosterone—which expands a male's sexual appetite—has been shown to rise in nonhuman primates following social triumphs, and there are hints that it does so in human males too. Certainly the world is full of triumphant men— Johnny Carson, Donald Trump—who trade in aging wives for younger, more fertile models. (The multi-wived J. Paul Getty said, "A lasting relationship with a woman is only possible if you are a business failure.")

A man's exalted social status can give his offspring a leg up in life, so   43
it's natural that women should lust after the high-status men who lust after them. Among the Ache, the best hunters also have more extramarital affairs and more illegitimate children than lesser hunters. In modern societies, contraception keeps much of this sex appeal from translating into offspring. But last year a study by Canadian anthropologist Daniel Pérusse found that single men of high socioeconomic status have sex with more partners than lower-status men.

One might think that the appeal of rich or powerful men is losing its   44
strength. After all, as more women enter the work force, they can better afford to premise their marital decisions on something other than a man's income. But we're dealing here with deep romantic attractions, not just conscious calculation, and these feelings were forged in a different environment. Evolutionary psychologists have shown that the tendency of women to place greater emphasis than men on a mate's financial prospects remains strong regardless of the income or expected income of the women in question.

The upshot of all this is that economic inequality is monogamy's worst   45
enemy. Affluent men are inclined to leave their aging wives, and young women—including some wives of less affluent men—are inclined to offer themselves as replacements.

Objections to this sort of analysis are predictable: "But people leave   46
marriages for emotional reasons. They don't add up their offspring and pull out their calculators." True. But emotions are just evolution's executioners. Beneath the thoughts and feelings and temperamental differences marriage counselors spend their time sensitively assessing are the stratagems of the genes—cold, hard equations composed of simple variables: social status, age of spouse, number of children, their ages, outside romantic opportunities and so on. Is the wife really duller and more nagging than she was 20 years ago? Maybe, but maybe the husband's tolerance for nagging has dropped now that she is 45 and has no reproductive future. And the promotion he just got, which has already drawn some admiring glances from a young woman at work, has not helped.

Similarly, we might ask the young, childless wife who finds her hus-   47
band intolerably insensitive why the insensitivity wasn't so oppressive a year ago, before he lost his job and she met the kindly, affluent bachelor who seems to be flirting with her. Of course, maybe her husband's abuses are quite real, in which case they signal his disaffection and perhaps his

impending departure—and merit just the sort of pre-emptive strike the wife is now mustering.

THE FALLOUT FROM MONOGAMY'S DEMISE

Not only does male social inequality favor divorce. Divorce can also re- 48
inforce male social inequality; it is a tool of class exploitation. Consider Johnny Carson. Like many wealthy, high-status males, he spent his career dominating the reproductive years of a series of women. Somewhere out there is a man who wanted a family and a pretty wife and, if it hadn't been for Johnny Carson, would have married one of these women. And if this man has managed to find another woman, she was similarly snatched from the clutches of some other man. And so on—a domino effect: a scarcity of fertile females trickles down the social scale.

As theoretical as this sounds, it cannot help happening. There are only 49
about 25 years of fertility per woman. When some men dominate more than 25 years' worth, some man somewhere must do with less. And when, in addition to all the serial husbands, you count the men who live with a woman for five years before deciding not to marry her, and then do it again (perhaps finally at 35 marrying a 28-year-old), the net effect is not trivial. As some Darwinians have put it, serial monogamy is tantamount to polygyny. Like polygyny, it lets powerful men grab extra sexual resources (a.k.a. women), leaving less fortunate men without mates—or at least without mates young enough to bear children. Thus rampant divorce not only ends the marriages of some men but also prevents the marriage of others. In 1960, when the divorce rate was around 25%, the portion of the never married population age 40 or older was about the same for men and women. By 1990, with the divorce rate running at 50%, the portion for men was larger by 20% than for women.

Viewing serial monogamy as polygyny by another name throws a kink 50
into the family-values debate. So far, conservatives have got the most political mileage out of decrying divorce. Yet lifelong monogamy—one woman per man for rich and poor alike—would seem to be a natural rallying cry for liberals.

One other kind of fallout from serial monogamy comes plainly into focus 51
through the lens of evolutionary psychology: the toll taken on children. Martin Daly and Margo Wilson of McMaster University in Ontario, two of the field's seminal thinkers, have written that one of the "most obvious" Darwinian predictions is that stepparents will "tend to care less profoundly for children than natural parents." After all, parental investment is a precious resource. So natural selection should "favor those parental psyches that do not squander it on nonrelatives"—who after all do not carry the parent's genes.

Indeed, in combing through 1976 crime data, Daly and Wilson found 52
that an American child living with one or more substitute parents was about

100 times as likely to be fatally abused as a child living with biological parents. In a Canadian city in the 1980s, a child age two or younger was 70 times as likely to be killed by a parent if living with a stepparent and a natural parent than if living with two natural parents.

Of course, murdered children are a tiny fraction of all children living 53 with stepparents; divorce and remarriage hardly amount to a child's death warrant. But consider the more common problem of nonfatal abuse. Children under 10 were, depending on their age and the study in question, three to 40 times as likely to suffer parental abuse if living with a stepparent and a biological parent instead of two biological parents.

There are ways to fool Mother Nature, to induce parents to love chil- 54 dren who are not theirs. (Hence cuckoldry.) After all, people cannot telepathically sense that a child is carrying their genes. Instead they rely on cues that in the ancestral environment would have signaled as much. If a woman feeds and cuddles an infant day after day, she may grow to love the child, and so may the woman's mate. This sort of bonding is what makes adopted children lovable (and is one reason relationships between stepparent and child are often harmonious). But the older a child is when first seen, the less profound the attachment will probably be. Most children who acquire stepfathers are past infancy.

Polygynous cultures, such as the 19th century Mormons, are routinely 55 dismissed as cruelly sexist. But they do have at least one virtue: they do not submit children to the indifference or hostility of a surrogate father. What we have now—serial monogamy, quasi-polygyny—is in this sense worse than true polygyny. It massively wastes the most precious evolutionary resource: love.

IS THERE HOPE?

Given the toll of divorce—on children, on low-income men, and for that 56 matter on mothers and fathers—it would be nice to come up with a magic monogamy-restoration plan. Alas, the importance of this task seems rivaled only by its difficulty. Lifelong monogamous devotion just isn't natural, and the modern environment makes it harder than ever. What to do?

As Laura Betzig has noted, some income redistribution might help. One 57 standard conservative argument against antipoverty policies is their cost: taxes burden the affluent and thus, by lowering work incentive, reduce economic output. But if one goal of the policy is to bolster monogamy, then making the affluent less so would help. Monogamy is threatened not just by poverty in an absolute sense but also by the relative wealth of the rich. This is what lures a young woman to a wealthy married or formerly married man. It is also what makes the man who attracts her feel too good for just one wife.

As for the economic consequences, the costs of soaking the rich might 58 well be outweighed by the benefits, financial and otherwise, or more stable marriages, fewer divorces, fewer abused children and less loneliness and depression.

There are other levers for bolstering monogamy, such as divorce law. 59
In the short run, divorce brings the average man a marked rise in standard of living, while his wife, along with her children, suffers the opposite. Maybe we should not lock people into unhappy marriages with financial disincentives to divorce, but surely we should not reward men for leaving their wives either.

A MORAL ANIMAL

The problem of divorce is by no means one of public policy alone. 60
Progress will also depend on people using the explosive insight of evolutionary psychology in a morally responsible way. Ideally this insight would lead people to subject their own feelings to more acute scrutiny. Maybe for starters, men and women will realize that their constantly fluctuating perceptions of a mate are essentially illusions, created for the (rather absurd, really) purpose of genetic proliferation, and that these illusions can do harm. Thus men might beware the restlessness designed by natural selection to encourage polygyny. Now that it brings divorce, it can inflict great emotional and even physical damage on their children.

And men and women alike might bear in mind that impulses of wan- 61
derlust, or marital discontent, are not always a sign that you married the "wrong person." They may just signify that you are a member of our species who married another member of our species. Nor, as evolutionary psychiatrist Randolph L. Nesse has noted, should we believe such impulses are a sign of psychopathology. Rather, he writes, they are "expected impulses that must, for the most part, be inhibited for the sake of marriage."

The danger is that people will take the opposite tack: react to the new 62
knowledge by surrendering to "natural" impulses, as if what's "in our genes" were beyond reach of self-control. They may even conveniently assume that what is "natural" is good.

This notion was common earlier in this century. Natural selection was 63
thought of almost as a benign deity, constantly "improving" our species for the greater good. But evolutionary psychology rests on a quite different world view: recognition that natural selection does not work toward overall social welfare, that much of human nature boils down to ruthless genetic self-interest, that people are naturally oblivious to their ruthlessness.

George Williams, whose 1966 book *Adaptation and Natural Selection* 64
helped dispel the once popular idea that evolution often works for "the good of the group," has even taken to calling natural selection "evil" and "the enemy." The moral life, in his view, consists largely of battling human nature.

Darwin himself believed the human species to be a moral one—in fact, 65
the only moral animal species. "A moral being is one who is capable of

comparing his past and future actions or motives, and of approving or disapproving of them," he wrote.

    In this sense, yes, we are moral. We have at least the technical capacity 66 to lead an examined life: self-awareness, memory, foresight and judgment. Still, chronically subjecting ourselves to moral scrutiny and adjusting our behavior accordingly is hardly a reflex. We are potentially moral animals—which is more than any other animal can say—but we are not naturally moral animals. The first step to being moral is to realize how thoroughly we aren't. ©

CRITICAL READING

1. What reasoning and evidence does Wright use to support his point that evolutionary psychology's theories won't necessarily add to the "decline of the American family"? (See the fifth paragraph.)
2. Describe the different kinds of behavior that we might consider antisocial, or in some cases, criminal, that evolutionary psychology seems to explain, such as the high rate of child abuse in families with stepparents.
3. In your own words, summarize the argument that economic inequality poses a threat to monogamy within a society.

CLASS DISCUSSION

1. Discuss the possible social purposes of ideas and institutions that contradict the insights of evolutionary psychology. For instance, Wright asserts that from an evolutionary standpoint, lust is critical to human reproduction, yet according to many systems of morality and religious thought, lust is considered wrong or sinful. What social purpose is served by such condemnation? Consider other beliefs and social practices that Wright calls into question from an evolutionary standpoint, such as the belief that women are far less inclined to sexual infidelity than are men, or the adherence to the institution of monogamous "til-death-do-us-part" marriage.
2. The media have been reporting the theoretical premises of evolutionary psychology as regards human sexuality for a while now. It seems to be an idea that fascinates the media and, one assumes, its consumers. As a class, consider the reasons why a genetic explanation for male and female behavior in sex and relationships might be so fascinating to us today.

DIRECTED FREEWRITE

Referring to the issues of moral choice and human nature raised at the end of Wright's essay, discuss the possible effects on society if mass numbers of people chose to react to evolutionary psychology's insights by "surrendering to 'natural' impulses, as if what's 'in our genes' were beyond reach of self-control" (the fifth paragraph from the end). Be imaginative: feel free to imagine possible positive as well as negative effects.

EVOLUTIONARY PSYCHOLOGY UNIT WRITING ASSIGNMENTS

1. Write an essay analyzing specific "mating" patterns you've observed either in yourself or in someone whom you know well and can interview extensively, and relate these to the theoretical perspectives of evolutionary psychology. How can you see your behaviors fitting into some of the patterns that Buss discusses? For a detailed discussion of analysis, see assignment 2 on page 268 of this chapter's Communications unit.

2. On the basis of evolutionary psychology's insights into human sexual behavior, write an essay arguing that heterosexual, monogamous marriage ought to be either preserved or abolished, drawing on points in Wright's essay, as well as on your own opinions and ideas, if relevant. If you argue for the abolition of marriage as we now know it, propose something else in its place, something that more closely fits our supposed "natural" inclinations. Consider such issues as social order and organization, propagation of the species (as well as overpopulation!), and gender roles. For a discussion of argument, see assignment 2 on page 60 in the Social Psychology unit of Chapter 2.

3. The term "research design" is used to refer to the procedures that one plans to use in conducting a study. The research design can be thought of as the "methods" section of a scientific report; however, whereas "methods" sections describe a study that has been conducted, the research design describes a study that will be conducted. A social scientist preparing to conduct a study might write an informal research design in order to help conceptualize the elements of the study's method; a research design might be included in a grant proposal or a prospectus, in which a researcher is requesting funds or permission to conduct research and therefore need to lay out clearly the study's procedures for the readers of the proposal.

   Imagine that you are a graduate student in sociology, psychology, or communications, and that you are interested in the theories of evolutionary psychology. You are planning to conduct an empirical study in order to test out some claims of evolutionary psychologists, such as that of the study Wright mentions that found men and women possess different kinds of jealousy (the last three paragraphs). Imagine a way to study this issue empirically—that is, firsthand, before the "Modern Obstacles to Monogamy" section gathering your own data, rather than relying on secondary sources from the studies of others—but don't simply replicate any of the studies described by Wright. Be creative. Imagine that your research design will eventually be revised and will fit into a grant proposal from the Unlimited Funds for Social Science Research Foundation, and that you are expecting to receive a hefty grant, so that your study can be elaborate and expensive.

   Your research design will thus provide a detailed description of your study's proposed procedures. These procedures can be broken down into the following issues: the method of study you will use (we'll say more about this later) and the sample you will study—how many people will you study, what kinds of people will make up your sample? Do you need a random sampling of people, or are you interested in a specific population? How will you select your participants? You will need to describe the location in which your study will be conducted and how long you expect it to take. In addition to covering these procedural matters, your research design ought to begin with an introduction that describes what exactly you will be trying to find out with this study; in other words, what is your research question? If you like, you may also state a hypothesis in your introduction; hypotheses are essentially your informed estimate of what your study will show.

Since this is a student exercise and since you are most likely not graduate students in the social sciences, your description of the study methodology doesn't have to be as detailed and precise as the studies cited by Wright. The assignment just asks you to use common sense and to decide what kind of study methodology will best give you the kind of information you want. Methodology refers to the accepted methods that social scientists use when conducting empirical research. Distributing self-administered surveys (the participants fill out the surveys themselves) to gather information about some aspect of life is a common methodology; interviewing is a more in-depth kind of survey method; experimentation, wherein aspects of life are studied in a controlled, artificially created environment, is a methodology that is mostly used in psychology. A number of different kinds of observation methods are useful as well; for example, overt participant observation means that the researcher participates with those he or she is studying and that those being studied know they're being studied; covert participant observation means that the subjects under study do not know they're being scrutinized. In nonparticipant observation, the researcher stands outside what he or she is observing, such as public behavior, and records observations. These are some common social science methods, and there are others we don't need to get into here. This sketch of methods is enough to help you decide what method to imagine for your study, and you can use your imagination as well as your common sense to design the details of how you will employ your method of choice.

THINKING AND WRITING
IN THE SCIENCES

Unit 1:
Biochemistry—What's Chemistry Got to Do With It?

CAN'T DO WITHOUT LOVE: WHAT SCIENCE SAYS ABOUT THOSE TENDER FEELINGS

Shannon Brownlee

This article originally appeared in the popular news magazine *U.S. News and World Report;* thus, it is an example of the ways in which scientific research is reported in the popular media. Sometimes when journalists report about scientists' work, their language and tone tend to make the findings of these scientists more definitive and conclusive than they really are. Newspaper articles, for example, often bear titles such as "Aspirin Found to Prevent Heart Attacks." And when a reader scrutinizes the evidence for such a claim, she or he finds that the finding reported in the headline is based on one study conducted on a relatively small sample of participants and that the scientists who conducted the study do not go as far as to claim that they've proven that aspirin prevents heart disease but do claim that their finding suggests this might be the case and so merits further study. This is how knowledge in science is constructed: in tiny increments, evidence piled on evidence before anything is "proven." As you read Brownlee's article, notice where she makes the scientific findings about love sound conclusive, and where she uses language that qualifies certain findings.

Shannon Brownlee, was born and raised in Honolulu. She attended the University of California, Santa Cruz as a biology major and studied dolphin acoustics while earning her M.A. Brownlee later moved to New York where she wrote for Discover *magazine and* Sports Illustrated. *She is now a science writer with* U.S. News & World Report *where she has been for the past twelve years. As for her chosen area of interest, Brownlee states, "Sports teams and politicians win or lose year in, year out, but scientists are continually offering something new about the world and about human beings."*

Love has toppled kings, inspired poets, sparked wars, soothed beasts, and changed the course of history. It is credited for life's greatest joys, blamed for the most crushing sorrows. And of course, it "makes the world go round." 1

All of which is no surprise to biologists. They know that love is central to human existence. We are not just programmed for reproduction: The capacity for loving emotions is also written into our biochemistry, essential if children are to grow and to thrive. And love's absence can be devastating: The loss of a spouse often hastens death in older people. 2

Now researchers are beginning to sort out how body and mind work together to produce the wild, tender, ineffable feelings we call love. They have found, for example, that oxytocin, a chemical that fosters the bond between mothers and children, probably helps fuel romantic love as well. Brain chemicals that blunt pain and induce feelings of euphoria may also make people feel good in the company of lovers. And certain other mammals share many of the same neural and chemical pathways involved in human love—though no one knows if they feel a similar swooning intensity of emotion. 3

Far from reducing love's thrill to dry facts, biologists' efforts underscore the emotion's importance. "We evolved as social organisms," says University of Maryland zoologist Sue Carter. "The study of love tells us that we have a biology that allows us to be good to each other." 4

MOTHER, MOTHER

Love began with motherhood. For mammalian young to survive, mothers must invest considerable time and energy in them. Of course, the varying growth rates of mammalian species require some mothers to invest more time and energy than others. An elephant seal suckles her pup for only a few weeks before abandoning it; other species, including elephants, some primates, and especially people, lavish attention on their young for years. 5

With the help of oxytocin, doting mothers are able to cater to their offspring's every whim and whimper. When females of most mammalian species give birth, their bodies are flooded with oxytocin, known since 1906 as a hormone that stimulates uterine contractions and allows the breasts to "let down" milk. But oxytocin also acts as a neurotransmitter, or chemical messenger, that can guide behavior. Without it, a ewe cannot recognize her own lamb. A virgin female rat given a shot of oxytocin will nuzzle another female's pups, crouching over them protectively as if they were her own. 6

Oxytocin has even more dramatic effects on human mothers, inducing a tender openness that fosters maternal devotion. As a mother breastfeeds, oxytocin levels rise in her blood. She also scores higher on psychological measures of "social desirability," the urge to please others, according 7 to Kerstin Uvnas-Moberg of Sweden's Karolinska Institute. Mothers with higher levels of oxytocin are more sensitive to other people's feelings and better at reading nonverbal cues than those with lower levels. This makes sense, says Uvnas-Moberg, because oxytocin is thought to bind to centers in the brain involved with emotion. In her most recent experiments, the scientist has found that oxytocin acts as a natural tranquilizer, lowering a new mother's blood pressure, blunting her sensitivity to pain and stress, and perhaps helping her view her child more as a bundle of joy than as a burden.

Studies of a small rodent known as the prairie vole, a cuddly ball of fur   8 whose mating bond of lifelong monogamy would put most human couples to shame, indicate oxytocin may also play a role in the heady feelings associated with romance. "You just can't imagine how much time these animals spend together. Prairie voles always want to be with somebody," says Carter. The voles' undying devotion is the work not only of oxytocin but also of a related hormone, vasopressin. When single male and female prairie voles meet, they commence a two-day-long bout of sex that releases oxytocin in the female's brain, bonding her to the male. Deprived of the chemical, she finds him no more appealing than any other vole. Given an injection of oxytocin, she will prefer the vole she's with, whether or not they have consummated their relationship. Vasopressin inspires similar ardor in the male, who prefers his mate's company above all others, guarding his family against intruders with a jealous husband's zeal.

Like some human playboys, male prairie voles seem to get a kick out   9 of courtship mixed with danger. Carter and colleague Courtney DeVries made young unmated voles swim for three minutes before allowing them to meet a prospective mate. The exercise elevated the animals' stress hormones, which are also heightened by fear. But while females scurried off after the swim without bonding to the males as they normally would male voles bonded faster than ever.

LURE OF THE FORBIDDEN

Human beings—unlike rodents—are not entirely slaves to their hor-   10 mones. But the behavior of voles may hold clues to why men and women sometimes hold divergent views of sex and romance. While many women prefer candlelight and sweet talk, men are more apt to welcome a roll in the hay anytime, anywhere. For some men (and some women), sex is especially enticing when forbidden. Carter and DeVries suspect stress hormones can interfere with oxytocin's action in the brain, keeping a female vole from bonding, and perhaps preventing most women from finding danger sexually exciting. Vasopressin, in contrast, appears to work better in the presence of certain stress hormones, possibly making danger an aphrodisiac for many males.

Love's other messengers in the brain are the endorphins, or brain opi-   11 ates—the body's own version of drugs such as heroin and morphine. High levels of brain opiates kill pain and induce a state of happy relaxation. Low levers are associated with unpleasant feelings. Researchers believe the power of endorphins to affect mood may play a crucial role in bonding.

Compelling evidence for this notion comes from recent studies of female talapoin monkeys, animals that form what in humans would be termed friendships. While male talapoins are bellicose and standoffish, female talapoin friends spend as much as a third of their day grooming each other and twining their long tails together. Barry Keverne, a primatologist at Cambridge University in England, has found that when talapoin friends who have been separated are reunited, they commence grooming enthusiastically—and their endorphins skyrocket to double the usual level. Separated monkeys given a low dose of morphine, however, show little interest in grooming upon reunion: Since their opiate levels are already high, they don't need each other to feel good again. "It's not surprising that the same opioid system that evolved to modulate physical pain also can soothe the pain of social isolation," says Jaak Panksepp of Ohio's Bowling Green State University.   12

Indeed, research on opiates suggests the flip side of love is not hate, but grief. "Biochemically, loss of love, or grief, is the inverse of love," says Keverne. Nobody has yet proved that people get an endorphin kick out of love or friendship. But the human brain shares so much of its emotional chemistry with close evolutionary relatives, it's not unlikely that human lovers and friends enjoy a soothing surge of endorphins, when they meet—and miss that feeling when separated.   13

Passionate or platonic, love affects the whole body, setting the heart pounding, making the stomach do flip-flops, and of course, lighting the loins on fire. These visceral sensations are the work of the vagus nerve, which traces a meandering path through the body, coordinating the activities of internal organs, says the University of Maryland's Stephen Porges. The vagus ferries signals between our innards and our brains, conveying information upward about our internal state and sending orders down from the brain to the heart, the stomach, the lungs, and the sex organs.   14

Without the vagus, says Porges, love would be impossible. One part of the nerve is evolutionarily ancient, controlling primitive functions such as sex, hunger, and fear. This "old" vagus responds to oxytocin and serves as the pathway between sexual organs and the brain for feelings of both arousal and satiation after sex. But Porges argues that in mammals, newer branches of the vagus also connect emotional brain centers with the heart, the face, and the vocal equipment, helping to coordinate feelings with facial and verbal expression. The "new" vagus also helps slow the heart and keep the body calm enough for the brain to pay attention to emotional signals from other people. Without this, says Porges, "we can't modulate our interiors enough to express or read emotions."   15

In other words, the poets and bards were right about one thing: The heart speaks the language of love. As English poet W. H. Auden wrote,   16

Where love is strengthened, hope restored, / In hearts by chemical accord.
It may not literally skip a beat at the sight of one's desire or break with sorrow, but the heart's rhythms are exquisitely tuned to love.   ©

CRITICAL READING

1. After reading Brownlee's article and noting the presence or absence of qualify-
   ing language when reporting the scientific findings, what overall impression
   about the validity and conclusiveness of the findings are you as the reader left
   with? How do you think that this overall impression is conveyed?
2. Explain the roles played in love by the male hormone vasopressin, stress hormones, and endorphins, as described by Brownlee.
3. Discuss the way that the vagus nerve operates in relation to feelings of love.
   How does it seem to work differently for passionate versus platonic love?

CLASS DISCUSSION

1. Discuss whether you think that scientific findings establishing a biochemical
   component to love will diminish the "magical" feelings we attribute to love. Will
   love be in any way diminished if its function for humans as well as it causes are
   fully elucidated by scientists?
2. Look at the first sentence of Brownlee's fourth paragraph, and discuss your reactions to that statement.
3. What role does the heart seem to play in feelings of love, and do the heart's
   workings correspond with our popular conceptions of the heart's relation to
   love?
4. If you have read the Evolutionary Psychology unit, discuss how the findings reported here about brain chemistry and hormones relate to the evolutionary psychologists' theories of male and female sexual behaviors and attitudes.

DIRECTED FREEWRITE

Write a brief love story about two people meeting and falling in love, and use the
terms and concepts from Brownlee's article to describe and explain what happens
between the lovers.

AFTER ALL, MAYBE IT'S . . . BIOLOGY

Helen E. Fisher

Fisher's article is another example of a journalistic account of scientific findings; this article originally appeared in *Psychology Today,* which usually contains articles about psychologists' and scientists' findings but which is written for an audience that isn't necessarily familiar with psychological and scientific jargon. As you read this article, which looks at courtship and relationship behaviors from a biological perspective, pay attention to the types of evidence that Fisher uses to support various points, and notice which pieces of evidence seem to have more validity than others.

Helen E. Fisher is a Research Professor and member of the Center for Human Evolutionary Studies in the Department of Anthropology at Rutgers University. From 1984 to 1994 she was Research Associate in the Department of Anthropology at The American Museum of Natural History. She received her Ph.D. in Physical Anthropology at the University of Colorado. Her books include The First Sex: The Natural Talents of Women and How They are Changing the World; Anatomy of Love: The Natural History of Monogamy, Adultery and Divorce; *and* The Sex Contract: The Evolution of Human Behavior. *Her publications also include articles featured in a range of publications including* The Journal of NIH Research, The American Journal of Physical Anthropology, The New York Times Book Review, Psychology Today, *and* Natural History. *Since 1983, Dr. Fisher has served as an anthropological commentator and consultant for businesses and the media. Her contracts include those with NBC's Today Show, WNET TV (New York), The BBC, The Canadian Broadcasting Corporation, The Reader's Digest and Time-Life books. For her work in communicating anthropology to the lay public, Fisher received the American Anthropological Association's "Distinguished Service Award" in 1985.*

In an apocryphal story, a colleague once turned to the great British geneticist J. B. S. Haldane, and said, "Tell me, Mr. Haldane, knowing what you do about nature, what can you tell me about God?" Haldane replied, "He has an inordinate fondness for beetles." Indeed, the world contains over 300,000 species of beetles. I would add that "God" loves the human mating game, for no other aspect of our behavior is so complex, so subtle, or so pervasive. And although these sexual strategies differ from one individual to the next, the essential choreography of human courtship, love, and marriage has myriad designs that seem etched into the human psyche, the product of time, selection, and evolution. They begin the moment men and women get within courting range—with the way we flirt. 1

In describing these strategies, I make no effort to be "politically cor-   2
rect." Nature designed men and women to work together. But I cannot pretend that they are alike. They are not. And I have given evolutionary and
biological explanations for their differences where I find them appropriate.

FLIRTING

Women from places as different as the jungles of Amazonia, the sa-   3
lons of Paris, and the highlands of New Guinea apparently flirt with the
same sequence of expressions.

First the woman smiles at her admirer and lifts her eyebrows in a swift,   4
jerky motion as she opens her eyes wide to gaze at him. Then she drops
her eyelids, tilts her head down and to the side, and looks away. Frequently
she also covers her face with her hands, giggling nervously as she retreats
behind her palms. This sequential flirting gesture is so distinctive that [Ger-
man ethologist Irenaus] Eibl-Eibesfeldt is convinced it is innate, a human female courtship ploy that evolved eons ago to signal sexual interest.

Men also employ courting tactics similar to those seen in other   5
species. Have you ever walked into the boss's office and seen him leaning
back in his chair, hands clasped behind his head, elbows high, and chest
thrush out? Perhaps he has come from behind his desk, walked up to you,
smiled, arched his back, and thrust his upper body in your direction? If so,
watch out. He may be subconsciously announcing his dominance over you.
If you are a woman, he may be courting you instead.

The "chest thrust" is part of a basic postural message used across the   6
animal kingdom—"standing tall." Dominant creatures puff up. Codfish bulge
their heads and thrust our their pelvic fins. Snakes, frogs, and toads inflate
their bodies. Antelope and chameleons turn broadside to emphasize their
bulk. Mule deer look askance to show their antlers. Cats bristle. Pigeons
swell. Lobsters raise themselves onto the tips of their walking legs and extend their open claws. Gorillas pound their chests. Men just thrust out their
chests.

"COPULATORY" GAZE

The gaze is probably the most striking human courting ploy. Eye lan-   7
guage. In Western cultures, where eye contact between the sexes is permitted, men and women often stare intently at potential mates for about two to
three seconds during which their pupils may dilate—a sign of extreme interest. Then a starer drops his or her eyelids and looks away.

No wonder the custom of the veil has been adopted in so many cul-   8
tures. Eye contact seems to have an immediate effect. The gaze triggers a
primitive part of the human brain, calling forth one of two basic emotions—
approach or retreat. You cannot ignore the eyes of another fixed on you;
you must respond. You may smile and start conversation. You may look

away and edge toward the door. But first you will probably tug at an earlobe, adjust your sweater, yawn, fidget with your eyeglasses, or perform some other meaningless movement—a "displacement gesture"—to alleviate anxiety while you make up your mind how to acknowledge this invitation, whether to flee the premises of stay and play the courting game.

BABOON LOVE

Baboons gaze at each other during courtship too. These animals may have branched off of our human evolutionary tree more than 19 million years ago, yet this similarity in wooing persists. As anthropologist Barbara Smuts has said of a budding baboon courtship on the Eburru cliffs of Kenya, "It looked like watching two novices in a singles bar." 9

The affair began one evening when a female baboon, Thalia, turned and caught a young male, Alex staring at her. They were about 15 feet apart. He glanced away immediately. So she stared at him—until he turned to look at her. Then she intently fiddled with her toes. On it went. Each time she stared at him, he looked away; each time he stared at her, she groomed her feet. Finally Alex caught Thalia gazing at him—the "return gaze." 10

Immediately he flattened his ears against his head, narrowed his eyelids, and began to smack his lips, the height of friendliness in baboon society. Thalia froze. Then, for a long moment, she looked him in the eye. Only after this extended eye contact had occurred did Alex approach her, at which point Thalia began to groom him—the beginning of a friendship and sexual liaison that was still going strong six years later, when Smuts returned to Kenya to study baboon friendships. 11

AT THE BAR

Could these courting cues be part of a larger human mating dance? 12

According to David Givens, an anthropologist, and Timothy Perper, a biologist, who spent several hundred hours in American cocktail lounges watching men and women pick up each other, American singles-bar courtship has several stages, each with distinctive escalation points. I shall divide them into five. The first is the "attention getting" phase. Young men and women do this somewhat differently. As soon as they enter the bar, both males and females typically establish a territory—a seat, a place to lean, a position near the jukebox or dance floor. Once settled, they begin to attract attention to themselves. 13

Tactics vary. Men tend to pitch and roll their shoulders, stretch, exaggerate their body movements. Instead of using the wrist to stir a drink, men often employ the entire arm, as if stirring mud. The normally smooth motion necessary to light a cigarette becomes a whole-body gesture, ending with an elaborate shaking from the elbow to extinguish the match. 14

Then there is the swagger with which young men often move to and   15
fro. Male baboons on the grasslands of East Africa also swagger when they
foresee a potential sexual encounter. A male gorilla walks back and forth
stiffly as he watches a female out of the corner of his eye. The parading gait
is known to primatologists as bird-dogging. Males of many species also
preen. Human males pat their hair, adjust their clothes, tug their chins, or
perform other self-clasping or grooming movements that diffuse nervous energy and keep the body moving.

Young women begin the attention-getting phase with many of the   16
same maneuvers that men use—smiling, gazing, shifting, swaying, preening, stretching, moving in their territory to draw attention to themselves.
Often they incorporate a battery of feminine moves as well. They twist their
curls, tilt their heads, look up coyly, giggle, raise their brows, flick their
tongues, lick their upper lips, blush, and hide their faces in order to signal, "I
am here."

Some women also have a characteristic walk when courting; they arch   17
their backs, thrust out their bosoms, sway their hips, and strut. No wonder
many women wear high-heeled shoes. This bizarre Western custom, invented by Catherine de Medici in the 1500s, unnaturally arches the back,
tilts the buttocks, and thrusts the chest out into a female come-hither pose.
The clomping noise of their spiky heels helps draws attention too.

KEEPING TIME

Body synchrony is the final and most intriguing component of the   18
pickup. As potential lovers become comfortable, they pivot or swivel until
their shoulders become aligned, their bodies face-to-face. This rotation toward each other may start before they begin to talk or hours into conversation, but after a while the man and woman begin to move in tandem. Only
briefly at first. When he crosses his legs, she crosses hers; as he leans left,
she leans left; when he smoothes his hair, she smoothes hers. They move
in perfect rhythm as they gaze deeply into each other's eyes.

Called interactional synchrony, this human mirroring begins in in-   19
fancy. By the second day of life, a newborn has begun to synchronize its
body movements with the rhythmic patterns of the human voice. And it is
now well established that people in many other cultures get into rhythm
when they feel comfortable together. Our need to keep each other's time
reflects a rhythmic mimicry common to many animals. Chimps sometimes
sway from side to side as they stare into one another's eyes just prior to
copulation. Cats circle. Red deer prance. Howler monkeys court with rhythmic tongue movements. Stickleback fish do a zigzag jig. From bears to beetles, courting couples perform rhythmic rituals to express their amorous
intentions.

WOOING MESSAGES

Human courtship has other similarities to courtship in "lower" animals. 20 Normally people woo each other slowly. Caution during courtship is also characteristic of spiders. The male wolf spider, for example, must enter the long, darker entrance of a female's compound in order to court and copulate. This he does slowly. If he is overeager, she devours him.

Men and women who are too aggressive at the beginning of the court- 21 ing process also suffer unpleasant consequences. If you come too close, touch too soon, or talk too much, you will probably be repelled. Like wooing among wolf spiders, baboons, and other creatures, the human pickup runs on message. At every juncture in the ritual each partner must respond correctly, otherwise the courtship fails.

THE DINNER DATE

Probbly no ritual is more common to Western would-be lovers than the 22 "dinner date." If the man is courting, he pays—and a woman instinctively knows her partner is wooing her. In fact, there is no more widespread courtship ploy than offering food in hopes of gaining sexual favors. Around the world men give women presents prior to lovemaking. A fish, a piece of meat, sweets, and beer are among the delicacies men have invented as offerings.

This ploy is not exclusive to men. Black-tipped hang flies often catch 23 aphids, daddy longlegs, or houseflies on the forest floor. When a male has felled a particularly juicy prey, he exudes secretions from an abdominal scent gland that catch the breeze, announcing a successful hunting expedition. Often a passing female hang fly stops to enjoy the meal—but not without copulating while she eats.

"Courtship feeding," as this custom is called, probably predates the di- 24 nosaurs, because it has an important reproductive function. By providing food to females, males show their abilities as hunters, providers, worthy procreative partners.

ODOR LURES

Every person smells slightly different; we all have a personal "odor 25 print" as distinctive as our voice, our hands, our intellect. As newborn infants we can recognize our mother by her smell. Both men and women have "apocrine" glands in their armpits, around their nipples, and in the groin that become active at puberty. These scent boxes differ from "eccrine" glands, which cover much of the body and produce an odorless liquid, because their exudate, in combination with bacteria on the skin, produce the acrid, gamy smell of perspiration.

Today in parts of Greece and the Balkans, some men carry their hand- 26
kerchiefs in their armpits during festivals and offer these odoriferous tokens
to the women they invite to dance: they swear by the results.

But could a man's smell actually *trigger* infatuation in a woman? This 27
possible link between male essence and female reproductive health may
provide a clue to attraction. Women perceive odors better than men do.
They are a hundred times more sensitive to Exaltolide, a compound much
like men's sexual musk; they can smell a mild sweat from about three feet
away; and at midcycle, during ovulation, women can smell men's musk
even more strongly. Perhaps ovulating women become more susceptible to
infatuation when they can smell male essence and are unconsciously drawn
toward it to maintain menstrual cycling.

A woman's or a man's smell can release a host of memories too. So 28
the right human smell at the right moment could touch off vivid pleasant
memories and possibly ignite that first, stunning moment of romantic adoration.

But Americans, the Japanese, and many other people find odors offen- 29
sives; for most of them the smell of perspiration is more likely to repel than to
attract. Some scientists think the Japanese are unduly disturbed by body
odors because of their long tradition of arranged marriages: men and women
were forced into close contact with partners they found unappealing. Why
Americans are phobic about natural body smells, I do not know. Perhaps our
advertisers have swayed us in order to sell their deodorizing products.

LOVE MAPS

A more important mechanism by which human beings become capti- 30
vated by "him" or "her" may be what sexologist John Money calls your love
map. Long before you fixate on Ray as opposed to Bill, Sue instead of Ceci-
ley, you have developed a mental map, a template replete with brain circuitry that determines what arouses you sexually, what drives you to fall in
love with one person rather than another.

These love maps vary from one individual to the next. Some people 31
get turned on by a business suit or a doctor's uniform, by big breasts, small
feet, or a vivacious laugh. But averageness still wins. In a recent study, psychologists selected 32 faces of American Caucasian women and, using
computers, averaged all of their features. Then they showed these images
to college peers. Of 94 photographs of real female faces, only four were
rated more appealing than these fabrications.

As you would guess, the world does not share the sexual ideals of 32
Caucasian students from Wyoming. Despite wildly dissimilar standards of
beauty and sex appeal, however, there are a few widely shared opinions
about what incites romantic passion. Men and women around the world are

attracted to those with good complexions. Everywhere people are drawn to partners whom they regard as clean. And men in most places generally prefer plump, wide-hipped women to slim ones. Looks count.

So does money. From rural Zulus to urban Brazilians, men are at- 33 tracted to young, good-looking, spunky women, while women are drawn to men with property or money. Americans are no exception.

These male/females appetites are probably innate. It is to a male's ge- 34 netic advantage to fall in love with a women who will produce viable offspring; it is to a woman's biological advantage to become captivated by a man who can help support her young. As Montaigne, the 16th-century French essayist, summed it up, "We do not marry for ourselves, whatever we say; we marry just as much or more for our posterity."

LOVE AT FIRST SIGHT

Could this human ability to adore another within moments of meeting 35 come out of nature? I think it does. In fact, love at first sight may have a critical adaptive function among animals. During the mating season a female squirrel, for example, needs to breed. It is not to her advantage to copulate with a porcupine. But if she sees a healthy squirrel, she should waste no time. She should size him up. And if he looks suitable, she should grab her chance to copulate. Perhaps love at first sight is no more than an inborn tendency in many creatures that evolved to spur the mating process. Then among our human ancestors what had been animal attraction evolved into the human sensation of infatuation at a glance.

INFATUATION FADES

Alas, infatuation fades. As Emerson put it, "Love is strongest in pursuit, 36 friendship in possession." At some point, that old black magic wanes. Yet there does seem to be a general length to this condition. [Psychologist Dorothy] Tennov measured the duration of romantic love, from the moment infatuation hit to when a "feeling of neutrality" for one's love object began. She concluded, "The most frequent interval, as well as the average, is between approximately 18 months and three years." John Money agrees, proposing that once you begin to see your sweetheart regularly the passion lasts two to three years.

[Psychiatrist Michael] Liebowitz suspects that the end of infatuation is 37 also grounded in brain physiology. He theorizes that the brain cannot eternally maintain the revved-up site of romantic bliss. As he sums it up, "If you want a situation where you and your long-term partner can still get very excited about each other, you will have to work on it, because in some ways you are bucking a biological tide."

HAREM BUILDING

Only 16 percent of the 853 cultures on record actually prescribe   38
monogyny, in which a man is permitted only one wife at a time. Western cultures are among them. We are in the minority, however. A whopping 84 percent of all human societies permit a man to take more than one wife at
once—polygyny.

Men seek polygyny to spread their genes, while women join harems to   39
acquire resources and ensure the survival of their young. If you ask a man
why he wants a second bride, he might say he is attracted to her wit, her
business acumen, her vivacious spirit, or splendid thighs. If you ask a
women why she is willing to "share" a man, she might tell you that she loves
the way he looks or laughs or takes her to fancy vacation spots.

But no matter what reasons people offer, polygny enables men to have   40
more children; under the right conditions women also reap reproductive
benefits. So long ago ancestral men who sought polygyny and ancestral
women who acquiesced to harem life disproportionately survived.

MAN IS MONOGAMOUS

Because of the genetic advantages of ploygyny for men and because   41
so many societies permit polygyny, many anthropologists think that harem
building is a badge of the human animal. But in the vast majority of societies
where polygyny is permitted, only about five to 10 percent of men actually
have several wives simultaneously. Although polygyny is widely discussed,
it is much less practiced.

Whereas gorillas, horses, and animals of many other species *always*   42
form harems, among human beings polygyny and polyandry seem to be optional opportunistic exceptions; monogamy is the rule. Human beings almost never have to be cajoled into pairing. Instead, we do this naturally. We
flirt. We feel infatuation. We fall in love. We marry. And the vast majority of
us marry only one person at a time.

Pair-bonding is a trademark of the human animal.   43

UNFAITHFULLY YOURS

Although we flirt, fall in love, and marry, human beings also tend to be   44
sexually unfaithful to a spouse. Americans are no exception. Despite our attitude that philandering is immoral, regardless of our sense of guilt when we
engage in trysts, in spite of the risks to family, friends, and livelihood that
adultery entails, we indulge in extramarital affairs with avid regularity.

A survey of 106,000 readers of *Cosmopolitan* magazine in the early   45
1980s indicated that 54 percent of the married women had participated in at
least one affair, and a poll of 7,239 men reported that 72 percent of those
married over two years had been adulterous.

Why? From a Darwinian perspective, it is easy to explain. If a man has 46
two children by one woman, he has, genetically speaking, "reproduced" himself. But if he also engages in dalliances with more women and, by chance,
sires two more young, he doubles his contribution to the next generation.
Those men who seek variety also tend to have more children. These young
survive and pass to subsequent generations whatever it is in the male genetic makeup that seeks "fresh features," as Byron said of men's need for
sexual novelty.

Unlike a man, a woman cannot breed every time she copulates. In 47
fact, anthropologist Donald Symons has argued that, because the number
of children a woman can bear is limited, women are biologically less motivated to seek fresh features.

SEXUAL VARIETY

Are women really less interested in sexual variety? My own modest 48
proposal is that during our long evolutionary history most males pursued
trysts to spread their genes, while females evolved two *alternative* strategies
to acquire resources: some women elected to be faithful to a single man in
order to reap a lot of benefits from him; others engaged in clandestine sex
with many men to acquire resources from each. This scenario roughly coincides with common beliefs: man, the natural playboy; women, madonna or
whore.

In a recent study by Donald Symons and Bruce Ellis, for example, 415 49
college students were asked whether they would have sex with an anonymous student of the opposite sex. In this imaginary scenario, participants
were told that all risk of pregnancy, discovery, and disease was absent. The
results were those you would expect. Males were consistently more likely to
say yes, leading these researchers once again to conclude that men are
more interested in sexual variety than women are.

But here's the glitch. This study takes into consideration the primary 50
genetic motive for male philandering (to fertilize young women). But not the
primary motive for female philandering—the acquisition of resources.

There is no evidence whatsoever that women are sexually shy or that 51
they shun clandestine sexual adventures. Instead, both men and women
seem to exhibit a mixed reproductive strategy: monogamy *and* adultery are
our fare.

PARTING

We all have our share of troubles. But probably one of the hardest 52
things we do is leave a spouse. From the tundras of Siberia to the jungles of
Amazonia, people accept divorce as regrettable—although sometimes necessary. They have specific social or legal procedures for divorce. And they
do divorce. Moreover, unlike many Westerners, traditional peoples do not

make divorce a moral issue. The Mongols of Siberia sum up a common worldwide attitude, "If two individuals cannot get along harmoniously together, they had better live apart."

Why do people divorce? Bitter quarrels, insensitive remarks, lack of   53 humor, watching too much television, inability to listen, drunkenness, sexual rejection—the reasons men or women give for why they leave a marriage are as varied as their motives for having wedded in the first place.

Overt adultery heads the list. Sterility and barrenness come next. Cru-   54 elty, particularly by the husband, ranks third among worldwide reasons for divorce. I am not surprised that adultery and infertility are paramount. Darwin theorized that people marry primarily to breed.

THE FOUR-YEAR ITCH

Hoping to get some insight into the nature of divorce, I turned to the   55 demographic yearbooks of the United Nations. Divorce generally occurs early in marriage—peaking in or around the fourth year after wedding— followed by a gradual decline in divorce as more years of marriage go by. The American divorce peak hovers somewhat below the common four-year peak. Purely as a guess, I would say that this may have something to do with American attitudes toward marriage itself. We tend not to marry for economic, political, or family reasons. Instead, as anthropologist Paul Bohannen once said, "Americans marry to enhance their inner, largely secret selves."

I find this remark fascinating—and correct. We marry for love *and to*   56 *accentuate, balance out, or mask parts of our private selves.* This is why you sometimes see a reserved accountant married to a blond bombshell or a scientist married to a poet. Perhaps it is no coincidence that the American divorce peak corresponds perfectly with the normal duration of infatuation— two to three years. If partners are not satisfied with the match, they bail out soon after the infatuation wears off. So there are exceptions to the four-year itch.

DIVORCE IS FOR THE YOUNG

[Another] pattern to emerge from the United Nations data regard "di-   57 vorce with dependent children." Among the hundreds of millions of people recorded in 45 societies between 1950 and 1989, 39 percent of all divorces occurred among couples with no dependent children, 26 percent among those with one dependent child, 19 percent among couples with two "issue," 7 percent among those with three children, 3 percent among couples with four young, and couples with five or more dependent young rarely split. Hence, it appears that the more children a couple bear, the less likely they are to divorce.

This pattern is less conclusively demonstrated by the U.N. data than 58
the first two. Yet it is strongly suggested and it makes genetic sense. From a
Darwinian perspective, couples with no children should break up; both individuals will mate again and probably go on to bear young—ensuring their
genetic futures. As couples bear more children they become less economically able to abandon their growing family. And it is genetically logical that
they remain together to raise their flock.

PLANNED OBSOLESCENCE OF THE PAIR BOND

Marriage clearly shows several general patterns of decay. Divorce 59
counts peak among couples married about four years. And the longer a couple remain together, the older the partners get, and probably the more offspring they produce, the less likely spouses are to leave each other.

This is not to say that everybody fits this mold. George Bush, for ex- 60
ample, does not. But Shakespeare did. Etched in Shakespeare's marriage
and in all these other divorces recorded from around the world is a blue
print, a primitive design. The human animal seems built to court, to fall in
love, and to marry one person at a time; then, at the height of our reproductive years, often with single child, we divorce; then, a few years later, we remarry once again. ©

CRITICAL READING

1. Explain Fisher's points about the relative advantages and disadvantages of men
   having multiple wives (polygyny), engaging in serial monogamy (a series of
   monogamous relationship), and staying in monogamous, lifelong marriages.
2. What does Fisher mean when, in the second paragraph, she says that she makes
   no effort to be politically correct? What is it about her subject matter that impels
   her to say this?
3. If these points about relationships are true, why do you think marriage—as a life
   commitment—exists in so many cultures? What cultural purpose might be
   served by this monogamous version of marriage? Are these purposes still relevant?

CLASS DISCUSSION

1. As a class, examine how Fisher uses evidence to support her points and where
   certain pieces of evidence seem more reliable than others. Are there points that
   seem inadequately supported? How persuasive is this piece overall, and why?
2. Discuss the possible ways that biological findings about love and sex could
   change the cultural institution of marriage in mainstream American. If we accepted these kinds of ideas about our innate qualities and decided not to try to
   fight or change them, while at the same time, we wanted to retain the institution
   of marriage, what might marriage look like, and how might it be set up?

DIRECTED FREEWRITE

After reading Fisher's article, write a detailed account of two potential mates encountering each other for the first time at a party. As you imagine the scenario, write down all the subtle behaviors that the participants in this situation might exhibit, on the basis of your own experiences. When your description is complete, go back and underline or circle all the details that seem to you to be standard flirting behaviors. Then reread the section titled "At the Bar" in Fisher's article, and note which of your details match hers, and which don't.

BIOCHEMISTRY UNIT WRITING ASSIGNMENTS

1. If we view love and relationships as largely matters of chemistry and biology, what kinds of changes could this view bring about in our beliefs about such seemingly mystical (or at least mysterious, since they involve the human heart) things like falling in love, physical attraction, courtship, and the like? Even more important, in what ways could such changes in beliefs affect our behavior, our cultural traditions, and institutions? Write an essay exploring these questions, ultimately settling on what you believe to be a likely answer or set of answers to them. For more discussion of exploratory writing, see assignment 2 on page 137 in the Computer Science unit of Chapter 2.

2. Surveys are a very important kind of instrument of research in the social sciences, and sometimes in the sciences as well. Depending on how they are designed, surveys can produce data that are quantifiable—that is, capable of being rendered as numerical percentages and other kinds of statistical representations. This kind of quantitative data is typically viewed as more scientific than the more subjective qualitative data that are often produced by in-depth interviews or some forms of observation. Surveys can also produce qualitative data, since surveys can contain what are called *open-ended* questions. These kinds of questions leave answers totally up to the participant filling out the survey; the amount of variation in the ways in which people often respond to these questions can make numerical tabulation difficult or impossible, and the responses can lead to more interpretive, qualitative findings. *Closed-ended* questions are those that specifically elicit set responses that can be quantified; these are essentially multiple-choice questions, structured in different ways for different purposes. Some kinds of information require categories to be checked, such as questions about age, gender, race, and income-level. Other questions require yes/no responses, and others require levels of response, measured in scales such as ratings of "excellent" to "poor," or "strongly agree" to "strongly disagree."

   Survey design is more difficult than it might seem at first, since questions have to be carefully designed so as to elicit the exact kinds of information that truly addresses the researcher's concern(s), and so that people responding to the survey fully understand and can thus respond appropriately to the questions.

   Design a one- to two-page closed-ended survey to test one of Fisher's assertions about people's own courtship behavior when pursuing a potential romantic/sexual partner, and/or people's experience of the courtship behavior directed at them by others. First, you will have to form a clearly worded and thought-out research question, and you should do this in response to one of Fisher's specific points. The formulation of a clear research question is essential to designing survey questions. Think about the ways that different questions could help to answer your research question or different parts of your question. Draft preliminary questions, and then decide what kinds of responses should be allowed for the questions, making sure that all responses are closed-ended and thus more easily quantifiable. Which questions require simple yes or no responses? Which questions are best answered with a set of options for selection? What sorts of options should you choose? Do these cover all the bases, or if not, should you include a category labeled "other"? Make sure that your options don't overlap; for example, if providing age-group categories, list these as 18–20, 21–23, rather than 18–20, 20–23. Some questions will best be answered by providing a scale for degrees of response. Formulate both your questions and your response choices carefully. Avoid what are called "double-barreled" questions, in which two separate things are being asked. Such questions as "Do you feel nervous or clumsy in the presence of a person to whom you are sexually attracted? Yes or No," are problematic, because respondents who feel nervous but not clumsy will be unsure of their response. Think carefully about the logical order of your questions. Decide what kinds of directions you should provide at the beginning of your survey, and word these clearly and concisely.

One last note. This survey method will not measure people's actual courtship behavior; to do that, one would need to design a more detailed observational study or experiment. Rather, this survey will measure your respondents' *perceptions* of their own or others' behaviors, and even more specifically, the ways that your respondents wish to represent their own or others' behaviors. Keep this fact in mind as you design your questions; sometimes, to try to encourage honesty, it is a good idea to include a couple of questions that are set up differently but that ask for the same or very similar information in order to identify discrepancies in peoples' self-reported behavior. Unless your instructor decides otherwise, you won't actually distribute the surveys, although you might want to test out the clarity of your questions on some of your fellow students to make sure a respondent would understand what you're asking for.

3. Locate a science report dealing with the issue of brain chemistry and love/sex, for example, an article on pheromones and their effect on sexual desire. Make sure that the article is one written by a scientist or scientists for an academic audience—look in scholarly science journals such as the *Journal of Sex Research.* You will have to spend some time choosing an article, since you want it to be academic, but you also want to be able to understand it. Then write an essay reporting on the findings of this study, but doing so for a nonacademic audience, similar to the kinds of audiences addressed by Brownlee and Fisher.

Unit 2:
Zoology—Animal Anomalies

GENDER-BENDING HYENAS: BERKELEY PROJECT STUDIES THE ANIMALS' UNUSUAL PHYSIOLOGICAL MAKE-UP

Liz McMillen

In this short description of an ongoing project at the University of California at Berkeley, McMillen reports that researchers are studying causes for the seemingly hermaphroditic (that is, having both male and female reproductive organs) physiology and behavior of hyenas. Apparently, both male and female hyenas are exposed to large amounts of male hormones while in the womb. This finding helps to explain the aggressive behavior of the females. Scientists think that this phenomenon may be an evolutionary response to competition for food. This article first appeared in *The Chronicle of Higher Education,* which is directed at an academic, but not specifically scientific, audience; therefore, as you read, notice the details of McMillen's writing style that distinguish this report from the report that the Berkeley researchers themselves might write for a specifically scientific audience, when reporting the results of their study. Where and how does McMillen deviate from the "just the facts" approach taken in most academic science reporting?

Liz McMillen is editorial manager of The Chronicle of Higher Education's Career Network, *a Web site about the academic job market. She was a Michigan Journalism Fellow at the University of Michigan in 1997–98 and was senior editor in charge of research and publishing for five years prior to that appointment. A staff member at* The Chronicle *since 1984, she has written for* The Washington Post, *the* Washingtonian, *and several university publications. McMillen is a graduate of the University of Pennsylvania.*

Boys may be boys and girls may be girls, but for the spotted hyena, things are not so simple.   1

Crocuta Crocuta has long puzzled scientists. At times, the hyena has 2
been thought to change sex, or to be a hermaphrodite. Writers throughout
history have described the animals as "dirty brutes," scavengers, or seductive witches.

But a research project at the University of California at Berkeley has 3
cleared up much of the mystery. In a series of studies, researchers produced findings that not only explain the behavior of hyenas, but also may
change how we think about gender, aggression, and the role of hormones.

MEETING CEREMONIES

High above the campus, in the Berkeley Hills, the university's Hyena 4
Project houses a colony of 38 spotted hyenas, the only such group outside
of Africa. In a series of indoor and outdoor pens, the animals feed, mate,
and enact their "meeting ceremonies" and other complicated social rituals
under the eyes of the Berkeley scientists.

The focus of their interest is the female spotted hyena, a true oddity of 5
nature. In the womb, both male and female cubs are exposed to large
amounts of male hormones—so much so that the female's genitals become
masculinized. What appears indistinguishable from a fully formed penis is
actually an enlarged clitoris, through which the female urinates, mates, and
gives birth in a extraordinary but highly inefficient process. Females have no
vagina (their labia are fused to form a pseudoscrotum), but internally they
do have a standard female reproductive system.

As a result of their elevated hormones, female hyenas rule the roost. 6
Clans are dominated by networks of females, which are larger and more aggressive than males. Female cubs inherit their mother's rank, and even the
smallest or lowest-ranking female will push around the males. One can often
tell a hyena's station in life by checking its back and neck for bite wounds.

What's more, hyena cubs are fighting machines as soon as they leave 7
the womb. Usually born in pairs, they emerge fully mobile, with eyes open
and a fully erupted set of teeth. Hours, even minutes after birth, a hyena cub
will bite and fight with its twin, sometimes to death. This behavior had rarely
been observed before the Berkeley colony was established, and it is believed to be linked to the hormone bath in the womb.

Their aggressiveness and unusual physiology make hyenas a "power- 8
ful natural experiment," says Stephen Glickman, a professor of psychology
at Berkeley and director of the Hyena Project. "This project allows us to test
our current understanding of the process of sexual differentiation. The basic
thing we're after is, how do males become males and females become females?"

The Berkeley scientists believe that the female's aggression and mas- 9
culinization are an evolutionary response to intense competition for food.
These traits increase her fitness to survive, but they also have costs, in mating

and birthing difficulties. Because of the female's genitalia and long birth canal, more than half of first-born cubs die during birth.

Mr. Glickman and this colleagues caution against drawing too many   10
conclusions about hormones and aggression from their studies, however. "You have to understand that discovering some of these things doesn't mean that people are condemned to live out their hormones," he says. "Even with hyenas, if you change the social context, you change what happens very dramatically."

The project began in 1984, when 10 infant hyenas were captured in   11
southwest Kenya and brought to Berkeley. Another 10 were brought the following year. Since then, several of the original hyenas have mated and given birth, and some of the cubs have been donated to zoos.

COMPLEX ANIMALS

Laurence Frank, an animal behaviorist and a research associate at the   12
project, had been studying hyenas in the wild for several years when he collaborated with Mr. Glickman on setting up the colony. Financial support has been provided by the university and the National Institute of Mental Health, which is interested in hormones and aggression.

When Mr. Frank began his research, hyenas didn't have "cachet," he   13
says. He believed that they were complex and intelligent animals, worthy of study. "My work was to figure out the long-term relations among individuals. Their social interaction is similar to monkeys and just as complex."

Many of the hyenas that were raised at Berkeley regard the re-   14
searchers as parents, he says. "It's been very unusual to raise wild animals and have them be relatively tame, cuddly animals as adults. These guys are totally reliable."

The same cannot be said for hyenas in the wild. And nearly everyone   15
who works closely with the Berkeley hyenas has sustained a bite or two. Still, Mr. Frank likes to say that if hyenas had been domesticated, they may have made more-intelligent pets than dogs.

KENYA AND CALIFORNIA

The project combines long-term field studies of hyena behavior at the   16
Masai Mara National Reserve in Kenya with laboratory research conducted in Berkeley on the animals' biochemical makeup. Several other researchers and graduate students have joined in the project, including Paul Licht, an endocrinologist and dean of the division of biological sciences at Berkeley; Jean Wilson, an endocrinologist at the University of Texas Southwestern Medical School at Dallas; Nancy Forger, a psychologist at the University of Massachusetts at Amherst; and Pentti K. Siiteri, a chemist retired from the University of California at San Francisco.

Although the hyenas at Berkeley resemble dogs in size and in tame-   17
ness, they are actually closer to the cat family. (The spotted hyena is one of

four species of hyenas.) They have large, round heads and curved ears, black snouts, and grayish coats with brown spots. Their back legs are shorter than their front legs, an arrangement that gives them an awkward lope but also allows them to cover large distances.

The spotted hyena is also known as the laughing hyena, because of its [18] high-pitched laugh. But a laughing hyena is not a happy hyena, since it tends to "giggle" at times of distress. It can also make a range of whoops, growls, and grunts.

Hyenas have remarkably strong jaws, and a group can reduce a zebra [19] to a stain on the ground in a half-hour, the researchers say. The animals are fond of munching on bones, and the project keeps a supply on hand, along with a specially prepared diet of horse meat. "Bones are like potato chips to them," notes Mr. Frank.

AN IMAGE PROBLEM

Despite their reputation as cowardly scavengers, Mr. Glickman main- [20] tains that to know hyenas is to love them. (As far as their notorious smell goes, it appears to be a myth.) He would like to see greater interest and respect for the animals, since their public-relations problems may harm preservation efforts. But rehabilitating the hyena may be difficult, since human societies have uniformly regarded the animals with disgust.

Aristotle warned that hyenas will readily attack people and will burrow [21] in graveyards for food. In *Green Hills of Africa,* Hemingway seized upon their confusing sexuality in a general indictment of the "hermaphroditic self-eating devourer of the dead."

Even in *The Lion King,* the trio of spotted hyenas were connivers who [22] skulked around the jungle. When the Disney studio began working on the movie, several artists visited the Berkeley colony to observe the animals. Although the script was already written, the artists promised that they would make the hyena characters comical, not evil. Nevertheless, Mr. Glickman is not a big fan of the movie.

The "scavenger" rap that has hounded the hyena is not accurate, ac- [23] cording to the researchers. Too often, people have observed a lion feasting on prey, surrounded by hyenas, and assumed that the hyenas were scavenging. More likely, Mr. Glickman points out, the lion has stolen the kill from the hyenas. Hyenas most often kill their own prey—typically giraffes, zebras, and wildebeests.

WHERE THE PROJECT BEGINS

A better understanding of the hyena's anatomy came about in the late [24] 1930s, when a British zoologist explained their reproductive organs and determined that individual hyenas were either male or female, not hermaphroditic. How and why the females were masculinized would emerge later.

"The fact that you have a female hyena who has basically a penis-like   25
structure is where the project begins," says Mr. Glickman. "The only way of
making this is to have androgens circulating in fetal life—or there's another
way of making male-like genitalia that we've never known before."

Conventional wisdom has it that the chromosomes contributed by a   26
male mammal's sperm determine whether or not the fetus's gonad will develop into testes, which in turn secrete androgens, the male hormones that
masculinize the genitals. In the absence of those chromosomes, the gonad
will develop into ovaries.

But in a paper published in 1993, the Berkeley researchers reported   27
that pregnant hyenas have significantly elevated levels of androstenedione,
a male hormone that had been dismissed by scientists as insignificant. The
researchers discovered that androstenedione was produced in the mother's
ovaries, and that the placenta changed it into testosterone.

Generally, the adrenal gland—not the ovaries—was thought to be re-   28
sponsible for androgens in female mammals, while the placenta was
thought to protect the female fetus from androgens. In effect, this study
showed that sexual differentiation in the hyena was being controlled not by
the chromosomes or hormones of the individual, but by hormones produced
by the mother, a departure from the standard model.

TESTS ON PREGNANT HYENAS

In the current phase of the project, the researchers are attempting to   29
test their ideas about hormones by administering drugs to pregnant hyenas
that will block the effects of the androgens. Theoretically, such drugs should
halt the masculinization of the females. Mr. Glickman will say only that the
drugs have had an effect, but that it is subtle. The group plans to publish the
results of this study soon.

Mr. Licht, who is studying the hyena's biochemistry, believes that the   30
project's work may have implications for understanding human sexual differentiation and such conditions as genital abnormalities or infertility in women
caused by excess androgens.

"Mammals are clearly related to one another," he says. "They share   31
many basic features. If you find this very unusual condition in one, there's a
very good chance that it is an abnormal condition in another. It says that the
basic equipment of the mammal is capable of evolving in this condition."

Mr. Glickman agrees. "In fact, we don't prove something in a hyena   32
about a human. But if you were to go into medical textbooks on sexual differentiation written as late as last year, as far as I know there is no mention
of the placenta's playing a role. Once you begin thinking about it, then you
begin looking at these human conditions in new ways.

"That's the primary thing this project does," he says. "It calls people's   33
attention to things they neglected."   ©

CRITICAL READING

1. The last sentence of McMillen's piece quotes Glickman, who says that the hyena project "calls people's attention to things they neglected," such as the role of the placenta in sexual differentiation. Explain how the project does capture people's attention.
2. In addition to the neglected things mentioned in the previous question, the study of hyenas has itself been neglected. According to the article, why haven't scientists been interested in studying hyenas? After explaining this disregard, discuss how such neglect relates to the notion of scientific objectivity.
3. Explain what Glickman means when he says, in the tenth paragraph, that "discovering some of these things doesn't mean that people are condemned to live out their hormones . . . Even with hyenas, if you change the social context, you change what happens very dramatically." How does the project itself seem to demonstrate this last point?
4. Discuss your reaction to the descriptions of female hyena behavior and physiology. Why do think that you react the way you do?

CLASS DISCUSSION

1. What observations have you made or what knowledge do you have of other animals that seems to break our "rules for appropriate gender behavior? For example, have you observed any other female animals acting aggressively, and if so, under what circumstances? What do you think about physiological differences between male and female animals that are contrary to current Western standards of masculinity and femininity, for example, the fact that most male birds display much more colorful plumage than do their rather drab female counterparts. As a class, discuss these different animal behaviors, and then move on to discuss why the hyenas seem to be regarded as more "abnormal" in their gender behavior than these other animals.
2. The article describes some of the reactions to the behavior of "gender-bending" female hyenas; as a class, compare these reactions with typical human reactions to human females who seem to bend or break the conventions for female gender roles. How do different kinds of behaviors on the part of human females (such as aggression) elicit different reactions, and why do you think this behavior is so?

DIRECTED FREEWRITE

We know that scientists study different aspects of the physical, natural world. Regardless of whether science interests you, if you were going to study some element within the natural world, what would that be? In other words, what questions about the natural world are most interesting to you—and don't limit yourself to zoology's focus on animals; think about anything that a scientist, such as an astronomer or a chemist or whatever, might study. Describe such an interest in detail, clearly articulating what you would want to know about this thing. Then explore what this interest says about you or how your own personality and general interests relates to the topic/question you have chosen; in other words, examine the role that your subjectivity plays in the things you might choose to study objectively.

SEX ROLES, PARENTAL EXPERIENCE AND REPRODUCTIVE SUCCESS OF EASTERN KINGBIRDS, *TYRANNUS TYRANNUS*

Jason D. Woodward and Michael T. Murphy

In this article, Woodward and Murphy report the results of their study on the parental investment exerted by experienced and inexperienced male and female eastern kingbirds during the incubation and the nestling periods of their young offspring. Because this article is structured in the standard scientific report format and is addressed to an audience of the writers' scholarly peers, the language may be difficult at times. Don't expect to understand all of what is discussed here, since much of the material is technical; rather, make sure that you get a general sense of what the authors were looking for and what they found. Read the abstract and the introduction that follows it, skim the Methods and Results sections, and read the Discussion section. As you read, notice the kinds of explanations that the authors offer for *why* the animal behavior on which they're focusing occurs.

> *Michael Murphy received his M.A. in 1981 and his Ph.D. in 1985 from Kansas University at Lawrence. He has been working on kingbirds for 17 years in both Kansas and New York. Murphy has published dozens of papers including nearly twenty papers on the biology of kingbirds. He is a recipient of the Hartwick College Trustees Research Grant and the National Science Foundation, Research Opportunity Award. Additionally, he is a member of the American Ornithologists' Union, the British Ecological Society, the Cooper Ornithological Society, the Ecological Society of America, Sigma Xi, The International Society of Behavioral Ecology, The Wilson Ornithological Society and he is an associate editor of the Auk. Murphy taught at Hartwick College in Oneonta, NY for twelve years and is now an assistant professor in the Department of Organismal Biology at Portland State University.*

Source: "Sex Roles, Parental Experiences and Reproductive Success of Eastern Kingbirds, *Tyrannus tyrannus*" by Jason D. Woodard and Michael T. Murphy in *Animal Behaviour,* 1999, 57. Copyright © 1999 by The Association for the Study of Animal Behaviour. Reprinted with permission of the publisher, Academic Press.

Jason D. Woodward attended Hartwick College, where in 1997, he grad-
uated Summa Cum Laude with departmental distinction honors and received
a B.A. in biology. He worked as a laboratory analyst for an environmental con-
sulting firm in Burlington, VT during 1997–1998 and entered into a Master's of
Science program at Colorado State University in the fall of 1998. He is cur-
rently working towards the completion of his M.A. The focus of his research is
documenting the role of habitat and disturbance on the nesting success of the
burrowing owl, a declining species of the Great Plains.

We quantified parental behavior of eastern kingbirds during the incu- 1
bation and nestling periods to determine parental roles, and to examine the
impact of previous breeding experience (defined as having bred on the territory in the past) on behaviour and reproductive success. Females performed all incubation, while males spent more than 60% of their time in
vigilant or nest guarding behaviour during incubation. Parental roles were
not defined as sharply during the nestling periods. Females spent more time
vigilant, but males provisioned young at only 54% of the rate of females.
Vigilance and nest watching were still primarily male duties. Male and female behaviour did not vary with the pair's combination of experience (e.g.
experienced–experienced versus inexperienced–inexperienced in previous–current breeding season, respectively) during either phase of reproduction, but experienced males were more vigilant during incubation and fed
young relatively more than inexperienced males. Experienced females were
also more efficient foragers. Although behaviour did not differ among the
four combinations of pair experience, inexperienced pairs none the less lost
the most young to starvation and predation. Consequently, inexperienced
pairs fledged one less nestling per nesting attempt than did pairs with at
least one experienced breeder. Our results suggest that having at least one
experienced breeder substantially improved a pair's reproductive success.
We propose that female site fidelity is a safeguard to avoid the lower breeding success a female would incur if she were to move to a new territory and
breed with an inexperienced male.   .

Parental behaviour is generally thought to be costly because it may re- 2
duce adult survivorship (Lessels 1991), reduce future reproductive success
(Gustafsson & Sutherland 1988), or limit opportunities to seek additional
mates. The sexes often come into conflict over levels of parental investment
(Trivers 1972), and only one sex generally cares for young among most vertebrates. Females bear the greatest load in mammals (Kleiman & Malcom
1981) and amphibians (Wells 1981), but in fish it may often be either sex
(Gittleman 1981; Gross & Sargent 1985). Among most birds, biparental care
is the norm (Lack 1968; Silver et al. 1985) and the traditional explanation for
this pattern has been that single parents cannot adequately care for a full
brood of dependent young (Lack 1968). However, removal experiments
suggest that male help is often unnecessary for successful reproduction

(Gowaty 1983, reviewed by Bart & Tornes 1989). Biparental care may have instead evolved because fertilizable females are limited (Maynard Smith 1977), and in lieu of attracting additional mates, males profit by investing time and energy in raising young.

Despite the prevalence of biparental care in birds, selection often 3 favours different levels of male and female investment, due presumably to greater initial investment in gametes by females and the existence of additional reproductive opportunities for males (e.g. Hartley et al. 1995; Dunn & Cockburn 1996). Males defend territories and guard mates (Westneat 1994), but females usually build nests and incubate alone (Verner & Willson 1969; Maynard Smith 1977). Cooperation appears to peak during the nestling period as theory predicts (Winkler 1987; Whittingham et al. 1992; Yamamura & Tsuji 1993) and empirical research has shown that males and females usually share equally in the care of young (see Discussion). Reduced male parental care might be expected, however, if other reproductive opportunities exist (Westneat & Sherman 1993) or males frequently lose paternity (Xia 1992; Westneat & Sherman 1993). In the latter case, males may facultatively adjust their effort to their perceived level of paternity at each breeding event (Westneat & Sherman 1993; e.g. Dixon et al. 1994), or show nonfacultative (i.e. evolved and relatively fixed reductions in effort when losses of paternity occur regularly (e.g. Westneat 1988).

Another factor that might account for variation in male and female 4 parental care that has received very little attention is the level of experience and the duration of pair bonds. Most migrants and short-lived residents do not maintain pair bonds between breeding seasons (see Murphy 1996a), but among many species, individuals appear to prefer experienced and/or older breeders as mates. Reid (1988) showed that active mate choice underlies the positive assortative mating for age/experience among species for which data exist, possibly because reproductive success is often higher among pairs with experienced breeders (e.g. Nol & Smith 1987; Reid 1988; Saether 1990; Smith 1993). Greater success of experienced pairs may be related to the pair bond itself (Scott 1988; Black & Owens 1995), improved feeding efficiency and/or predator avoidance (Crawford 1977), greater parental effort as reproductive value declines among older breeders (Pugesek 1981, 1983), or a product of an extrinsic factor such as territory quality (e.g. Holmes et al. 1996) that increases the probability of pair reformation and high reproductive success. Although we expect experience to be an important source of variation in parental behaviour in most species, we for the most part do not know whether a pair's history with each other or their territory affects their quality of parental care and reproductive success.

Here we present data on parental care in eastern kingbirds to describe 5 male and female parental roles, and to asses whether or not experience level of the pair affects parental behaviour and reproductive success. Kingbirds are medium-sized, long-distance Neotropical migrants that maintain socially monogamous pair bonds while they raise their single annual brood of three to four young (Murphy 1996b). Males show very high site fidelity and relatively high survivorship (70%), and if both former partners return to breed, pair bonds reform nearly 90% of the time (Murphy 1996a). The high frequency with which former partners remate suggests that females benefit by pairing with former mates. We thus also attempted to determine whether the benefits of mating with a former mate underlie female site fidelity.

METHODS

Study Area

We conducted behavioural studies during June and July, 1996 and 6 1997 on a population of colour-banded kingbirds breeding in Delaware and Otsego Counties, New York (42°78'N, 74°53'W; see Murphy 1996a for a detailed description of the area and general field methods). In brief, kingbirds build open-cup nests 3–5 m above the ground in trees situated along hedgerows, in pastures and in riparian habitats (Murphy 1996b). We located 90 and 82 nests in 1996 and 1997, respectively, and recorded laying date, clutch size, brood size, hatching success, losses to predators, starvation of young and number of young fledged.

We determined the experience level of all pairs with each other and their 7 territory based on the identification of individuals that were colour-banded over the previous 7–8 years (Murphy 1996a). Pairs that had previously bred with one another on the same territory were classified as experienced (E–E = experienced–experienced). Conversely, a pair that had no breeding experience together and in which neither bird used the territory in the past year was labelled inexperienced (I–I = inexperienced–inexperienced). In making the latter classification we assumed that the presence of two unbanded birds on a territory, which in the past year had two banded birds, did not result from the dispersal of an existing pair together to this site. As this has been observed only once over the previous 7 years (<1% of returning pairs), it is a safe assumption. We also identified two other pair combinations. For territories in which both members were banded the previous year but only one individual returned to breed with a new mate, there were two situations: experienced female with inexperienced male (EM–IF), and experienced female and inexperienced male (EF–IM). Because of the low breeding-site dispersal of females, and especially males (Murphy 1996a), we had little opportunity to observe the behaviour of experienced breeders on new territories.

We made instantaneous recordings every 60 s during 1-h observa- 8 tions of pairs at nests during the incubation and the nestling period. We classified behaviours into discrete categories, and observed all nests two to four times. We observed nests during incubation ($N = 20$) in 1996 only, but made observations during the nestling period in both 1996 ($N = 25$) and

1997 (N = 17). Due to the demands of other activities, we made observations (primarily by J.D.W.) mainly between 1000 and 1500 hours Eastern Standard Time (EST) using 10 × 25 binoculars and a spotting scope at a distance of about 25–50 m from a roadside automobile or from behind naturally occurring cover. We used a mixture of colour-band combinations and physical appearance to separate males from females. At least on individual was banded in most pairs (28 of 36 in the nestling period), and although the sexes have virtually identical plumages, past experience and observations of banded pairs showed that males tend to raise their crown feathers into a slight crest and maintain a more vertical posture when perched than do females. Our behavioural categories included (1) absent: bird not visible and thus absent from the immediate nest area, (2) foraging, (3) chasing intruders (hetero- or conspecifics), (4) vocalizing, (5) vigilant, (6) watching nest (see below), or (7) incubating eggs. Male vigilance and nest watching, both classified as nest-guarding behaviours, were differentiated by the proximity of the bird to the nest and the presence of the female. Vigilant birds (male or female) perched in a tree near the nest tree and maintained an alert posture. Nest watching was a male behaviour that occurred only in the female's absence and required that the male relocate and perch in the nest tree near the nest. We recorded the same seven variables (as above) during the nestling period except we replaced incubation with brooding of young, and we added feeding of the young as a behaviour during which we made continuous recordings of the number of feeding trips. We also derived two additional variables: (1) the combined number of male and female feeding trips and (2) the difference between the number of female and male trips.

Data Analysis

During 1996, we observed each nest an average of 2 and 2.5 times during incubation and nestling periods, respectively. In 1997, we observed all nests twice. To avoid problems of pseudoreplication, we used the average number of times a behaviour was observed during the two to four 1-h observation periods as an indication of the amount of time devoted to that behaviour. Most behaviours were mutually exclusive (e.g. feeding and chasing), but vocalizing could be performed simultaneously with other behaviours.

First, we compared male and female behaviour without regard to experience level (using t tests) during both phases of reproduction. We then separated pairs into the experienced–experienced (E–E), experienced male–inexperienced female (EM–IF), experienced female–inexperienced male (EF–IM), and inexperienced–inexperienced (I–I) combinations and compared males and females (separately) across all four pair types using analysis of variance (ANOVA), or the Kruskal–Wallis test when variances were heteroscedastic. Because average nestling age varied slightly among pair types during the nestling period (due to losses of nests to predators), we used multiple regression analysis to remove the effects of nestling age before making comparisons of parental behaviour among the four pair combinations.

Finally, we also measured the reproductive consequences of reuniting [11] with a former mate or breeding with a new bird on the same or different territory by comparing the following variables (using ANOVA) for initial nests of the 1995, 1996 and 1997 seasons among all four pair combinations: (1) timing of breeding, (2) clutch size, (3) brood size, (4) number of addled eggs (for pairs that reached hatching), (5) number of eggs and nestlings lost to predators, (6) number of young that starved, (7) fledging success (number of young/nest), and (8) seasonal output. The latter variable included the number of young to fledge from any renesting attempts made by pairs that failed initially. Sample sizes vary because of incomplete data (e.g. some nests failed before the clutch was complete). Additional tests are described in the Results. Unless otherwise stated, we used $P \leq 0.05$ for establishing statistical significance.

RESULTS

Male and Female Parental Roles

Male and female kingbirds spent equal amounts of time chasing in- [12] truders and vocalizing, but otherwise engaged in different behaviours during incubation (Fig. 1). Males were absent from the nest area and foraged more than females, and not surprisingly, females spent most of their time incubating eggs (70%; Fig. 1). Males were vigilant near the nest 57% of each hour and spent an additional 5% of their time closely watching the nest. Males spent 62% (vigilance + watching) and females spent 92% (incubation + vigilance) of their time at the nest. As a result, nests were unattended less than 3% of each hour, suggesting that pairs coordinated incubation and nest-guarding behaviour. Female absence was correlated with the time the female spent foraging ($r_{18} = 0.838$, $P<0.001$) and chasing intruders ($r_{18} = 0.615$, $P = 0.004$). Male vigilance, the main male behaviour, was independent of female absence, female foraging time and all other female behaviours (maximum $r_{18} = 0.257$, $P = 0.27$). However, male nest watching was correlated strongly with female foraging time ($r_{18} = 0.868$, $P<0.001$), and the total time the female was away from the nest (foraging + chasing + absent; $r_{18} = 0.788$, $P<0.001$). Males thus increased nest watching in direct response to female absence, whereas vigilance was a routine male behaviour that was performed independently of the female's presence or absence.

During the nestling period, females spent less time away from the [13] nest, less time chasing intruders, but more time feeding the young than males (Fig. 2), and averaged ($\pm$ SD) 5.7 ± 2.97 feeding trips/h ($N = 42$) compared with 3.1 ± 2.38 feeding trips ($N = 42$) for males. There were positive correlations between male and female foraging time ($r_{40} = 0.690$, $P<0.0001$),

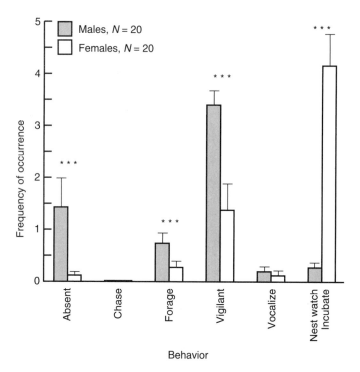

Figure 1 Male and female behaviour during incubation. Frequency of occurrence is the number of 1-min intervals in which the behaviour occurred during a 1-h observation period. ***$P<0.001$.

feeding time (r_{40} = 0.467, P = 0.002), and feeding trips (r_{40} = 0.656, $P<0.0001$), but on average, males made only 0.54 trips for every female trip to the nest. There were no differences between the sexes in the amount of time spent foraging, vigilant or vocalizing (Fig. 2). Males did not brood young, but instead watched the nest closely during the female's absence. Consequently, male nest guarding (vigilance + watch) comprised 50.2% of the male's time, which was nearly identical to the total time females were attendant at the nest (vigilance + brood = 51.5%, t_{82} = 0.29, P = 0.77). The pair's combined activities left the nest unguarded for 11% of each hour.

The lower feeding rates, greater time spent chasing intruders (nestling 14 period) and substantial commitment of time to vigilance and nest guarding during both incubation and nestling periods ($\geq$ 50%) suggested that nest defense was the male's primary role. To identify the proximate causes of variation in male vigilance during the nestling period, we tested for relationships between vigilance and nestling age, brood size and all female and male behaviours using stepwise regression analyses. The four variables selected by

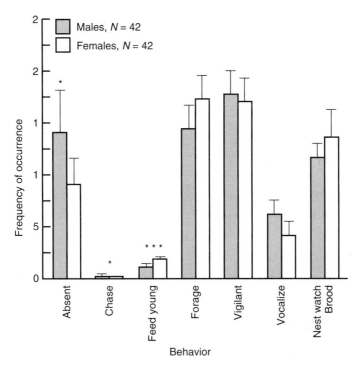

Figure 2 Male and female behaviour during the nestling period. Frequency of occurrence is the number of 1-min intervals in which the behaviour occurred during a 1-h observation period. *P<0.05, ***P<0.001.

the stepwise regression explained 97% of the variation in male vigilance, and indicated that vigilance decreased as males spent more time absent, foraging for and feeding young, and nest watching (all four P values<0.0001).

Females expended equal amounts of time on foraging and vigilance (Fig. 2), and we performed similar stepwise regression procedures on both variables to understand the basis for individual variation. The stepwise regression of female foraging time failed to select any female behaviours, suggesting that variation in time spent foraging was more strongly associated with the behaviour of the female's mate. The three male behaviours that were selected indicated that female foraging time increased when male foraging time increased (P<0.0001; an effect of nestling age), as males spent more time watching the nest (P = 0.0002), and as the difference between the number of female and male trips increased (P = 0.004; model $r^2 = 69.6\%$). In other words, females spent more time foraging when males watched the nest for long periods without feeding the young. Female vigilance correlated negatively with every female behaviour (all P values ≤ 0.04) except time spent vocalizing (NS) and number of feeding trips (NS). Interestingly, female

15

vigilance varied positively with male absence ($P = 0.03$). The stepwise regression accounted for 99% of the variation in female vigilance, and suggested that, just as in males, vigilance only occurred when time spent in other activities (except feeding young) was reduced, but that females also spent more time vigilant when males were absent for long periods.

Pair Experience and Parental Behaviour

The six incubation and seven nestling period behaviours that we recorded for both males and females (Figs 1 and 2) yielded 26 possible comparisons among the four levels of pair experience (E–E, EM–IF, EF–IM and I–I). Three of the 26 comparisons differed significantly among the four groups (male vocalizations during incubation: $P = 0.05$; male foraging time during incubation: $P = 0.05$; female foraging time during incubation: $P = 0.04$). Assuming a 5% probability of error, up to two significant comparisons would be expected to appear by chance, which was close to the observed number. All three significant comparisons became nonsignificant after we applied a Bonferroni adjustment for the large number of comparisons. In addition, neither the total number of male ($F_{3,32} = 0.51$, $P = 0.68$) nor female ($F_{3,32} = 0.91$, $P = 0.45$) feeding trips, or the total time that the nest was left unattended ($F_{3,32} = 0.93$, $P = 0.44$) varied among groups. 16

Although none of the four combinations of male–female experience significantly influenced parental behaviour during incubation or the nestling period, this did not preclude the possibility that male and/or female experience had important influences on parental behaviour. Assuming that experienced males were better mates, we predicted that experienced males would (1) be absent from the nest less, (2) feed the young more, and spend more time (3) vigilant, and/or (4) watching the nest than inexperienced males. To test these predictions, we ignored female experience level and compared experienced and inexperienced males. Contrary to our predictions, we found no difference in the amount of time that experienced and inexperienced males were absent or watched the nest during either the incubation or the nestling period (Table 1). Time spent vigilant also did not differ between experienced and inexperienced males during the nestling period, but during incubation, experienced males spent 36% more time ($P = 0.03$) vigilant at the nest (Table 1). The total number of feeding trips (male + female) did not vary with male experience (Table 1). And, although experienced males did not make significantly more feeding trips, the difference between the number of female and male trips was significantly lower in pairs in which the male was experienced (Table 1). The latter difference was especially pronounced in comparisons between E–E pairs and all other pairs ($t_{34} = 2.50$, $P = 0.017$). Given that the total number of trips did not differ ($t_{34} = 0.27$, $P = 0.78$), a smaller difference between the sexes in the number of feeding trips among pairs with an experienced male indicated that experienced males contributed 17

Table 1.   Parental behaviour of experienced and inexperienced males during the incubation and nestling periods.

Behaviour	Stage	Experienced males X̄ (SD, N)	Inexperienced males X̄ (SD, N)	t (P)
Absent from territory	Incubation	11.6 (10.74, 12)	18.6 (15.48, 8)	1.21 (0.24)
	Nestling	9.0 (7.45, 17)	13.8 (14.87, 19)	1.23 (0.23)
Watch nest	Incubation	2.7 (2.90, 12)	3.6 (3.54, 8)	0.63 (0.53)
	Nestling	11.8 (5.72, 17)	12.6 (8.24, 19)	0.33 (0.74)
Vigilant at nest	Incubation	38.4 (9.40, 12)	28.2 (9.68, 8)	2.36 (0.03)
	Nestling	20.1 (8.29, 17)	18.0 (10.16, 19)	1.67 (0.51)
Number of feeding trips	Nestling	3.6 (2.89, 17)	2.6 (1.89, 19)	1.26 (0.22)
Difference in feeding trips	Nestling	1.7 (1.94, 17)	3.3 (2.32, 19)	2.24 (0.03)

With the exception of the number of feeding trips and the difference in feeding trips (female feeding trips–male feeding trips), values in the table represent the number of 1-min intervals in which the behaviour occurred during a 1-h observation. Sample sizes refer to the number of pairs observed. Statistical comparisons were made using t tests.

relatively more to the feeding of young. Our results are consistent with the hypothesis that experienced males provided more parental care.

Given that females are primarily responsible for feeding the young, we predicted that experienced females would spend more time foraging and feeding the young than inexperienced females. Assuming also that trade-offs exist, we expected that experienced females would be absent from the nest more. Our final prediction was that vigilance would not vary with experience because males take the lead in nest defence. Only our final prediction was supported. Experienced and inexperienced females showed similar levels of vigilance and were absent equally often during the incubation and the nestling period (Table 2). Inexperienced females also fed their young at the same rate as experienced females. However, inexperienced females spent significantly more time foraging (Table 2). Controlling for possible confounding effects of brood size did not change this result. Experienced females thus appeared to be more efficient foragers than inexperienced females.

Reproductive Performance

Our results to this point indicated that experienced males were more vigilant during incubation and that they fed the nestlings relatively more than inexperienced males. Experienced females also appeared to be more efficient

Table 2.   Parental behaviour of experienced and inexperienced females during the incubation and nestling periods

Behaviour	Stage	Experienced females X̄ (SD, N)	Inexperienced females X̄ (SD, N)	t (P)
Absent from territory	Incubation	1.5 (2.14, 12)	1.4 (1.63, 8)	0.12 (0.91)
	Nestling	6.1 (7.70, 17)	7.3 (7.74, 19)	0.45 (0.66)
Vigilant at nest	Incubation	14.4 (12.70, 12)	9.6 (10.84, 8)	0.88 (0.39)
	Nestling	20.0 (11.04, 17)	16.6 (8.34, 19)	1.06 (0.30)
Number of feeding trips	Nestling	5.3 (2.66, 17)	5.9 (3.12, 19)	0.58 (0.78)
Time spent foraging	nestling	15.0 (7.87, 17)	22.6 (7.79, 19)	2.91 (0.01)

Table designations as outlined in Table 1, except for the exclusion of nest watching (a male behaviour) and the inclusion of time spent foraging for females (which did not significantly differ between experienced and inexperienced males).

foragers. Based on these findings, we predicted that reproductive success would be highest among E–E pairs and lowest for I–I pairs. Among the four pair combinations of male and female experience, there were differences for five of the 11 reproductive variables (Table 3). Females in the E–E combination initiated clutches before both categories of inexperienced females, and EF–IM females began breeding before females in the I–I combination, which produced the smallest clutches (Table 3). Failure of eggs to hatch, loss of eggs to predators, and the total loss of eggs (failure to hatch + predation), however, did not vary with pair type (Table 3). Sample sizes were smaller during the nestling period due to losses of nests to predators. Within this subset of nests, females in the E–E combination had the largest broods. Neither loss of nestlings to predators nor total clutch and brood loss varied among the four pair combinations (Table 3). While nestling starvation did not differ by type, losses tended to be greater in the I–I pair combination than in pairs in which at least one individual had previous breeding experience on the territory (t_{65} = 1.96, P = 0.067). In combination with smaller clutch and brood size, pairs with inexperienced females fledged the fewest young. Pairs in which both the female and male lacked previous breeding experience with the territory and one another (I–I pairs) showed particularly low success when compared to pairs with at least one experienced breeder ($X \pm$ SD = 0.9 ± 1.15, N = 27 versus 2.0 ± 1.66, N = 68). Renesting following the failure of a first nest potentially allowed pairs to produce some young before the breeding season ended. However, even after taking renesting into account, pairs with inexperienced females (and I–I pairs in particular) fledged fewer young over the course of the season than pairs in which one of the adults was experienced (Table 3).

Table 3. Reproductive performance of kingbirds in 1995, 1996 and 1997 based on the combination of male and female breeding experience with the territory

Reproductive variable	Experienced males		Inexperienced males		F (P)
	Experienced females X̄ (SD, N)	Inexperienced females X̄ (SD, N)	Experienced females X̄ (SD, N)	Inexperienced females X̄ (SD, N)	
Breeding date	6 June (3.52, 23)A	9 June (3.39, 25)BC	7 June (5.55, 18)AB	12 June (4.76, 21)C	8.10 (0.000)
Clutch size*	3.5 (0.59, 23)AB	3.2 (0.61, 22)AB	3.6 (0.49, 23)A	3.1 (0.76, 23)B	3.30 (0.024)
Added eggs†	0.1 (0.33, 17)	0.2 (0.41, 20)	0.2 (0.43, 18)	0.3 (0.59, 17)	0.45 (0.722)
Depredated eggs‡	0.7 (1.40, 23)	0.4 (1.18, 22)	0.6 (1.35, 20)	1.0 (1.60, 23)	0.81 (0.497)
Total egg losses§	0.8 (1.38, 23)	0.5 (1.18, 22)	0.8 (1.32, 20)	1.2 (1.54, 23)	0.95 (0.423)
Brood size**	3.5 (0.63, 16)A	2.9 (0.62, 21)B	3.4 (0.78, 17)AB	2.9 (0.88, 15)B	2.89 (0.041)
Depredated nestlings‡	0.2 (1.00, 16)	0.2 (0.62, 21)	0.5 (1.06,17)	0.1 (0.52, 15)	2.56 (0.464)^{b}
Depredated eggs and nestlings	0.9 (1.57, 22)	0.6 (1.26, 22)	1.0 (1.60, 20)	1.0 (1.57, 23)	0.38 (0.772)
Nestlings that starved	0.2 (1.00, 16)	0.4 (0.99, 20)	0.4 (1.00, 17)	1.1 (1.41, 14)	1.97 (0.130)
Fledged young††	2.2 (1.76, 22)A	1.8 (1.52, 26)AB	2.1 (1.77, 20)A	0.9 (1.15, 27)B	3.72 (0.014)
Seasonal production‡‡	2.6 (1.43, 22)A	2.0 (1.52, 26)AB	2.4 (1.54, 20)A	1.3 (1.29, 27)B	4.44 (0.006)

Sample sizes (N) refer to the number of pairs for which data were available. Variables were compared among the four groups using analysis of variance. Group means were compared using Tukey's test when the analysis of variance detected significant differences. Groups that share an upper case letter (e.g. A or B) did not differ significantly ($P<0.05$) from one another based on the a posteriori comparisons.

*Mean number of eggs laid per nest.

†Number of eggs that survived incubation but failed to hatch.

‡Number of eggs or young that were eaten by predators.

§The sum of addled and depredated eggs.

**Number of eggs that hatched and the number of young that were fed by the parents.

††Number of young that survived to leave the nest.

‡‡The total number of young produced in a season, including renesting attempts following the failure of an initial nest.

DISCUSSION

Male and female eastern kingbird showed distinctly different parental   20
roles. Females were the sole incubators and brooders, and provided most of
the food to young. Males fed at 50–55% the rate of females, but spent
50–60% of each hour guarding the nest. Daily energy expenditure (DEE) of
free-living birds is highly correlated with flight time (Tatner & Bryant 1986),
and because feeding young requires far more flight time than nest vigilance
and nest watching, females no doubt had a higher DEE than males during
the nestling period. Male and female behaviour did not vary either with the
pair's experience with one another or with the territory, but certain behaviours were affected by either male or female experience. For instance, experienced males were more vigilant during incubation and provided a more
nearly equal share of the food for nestlings. The relatively higher feeding effort of experienced males was especially pronounced when they were
paired with a former mate. Because adult males rarely disperse (Murphy
1996a), most of the inexperienced males were probably first-time breeders,
suggesting that the differences between experienced and inexperienced
males in nest vigilance during incubation and provisioning rates of nestlings
might be age related.

For both sexes, there were substantial trade-offs between vigilance   21
and most other behaviours. The main function of vigilance in kingbirds
seems to be the early detection of nest predators, which then permits the
birds to mount an attack before the predator reaches the nest. Given that
nest predation is the primary cause of nest failure in kingbirds (Blancher &
Robertson 1985; Murphy 1996b), and that nest success has been linked to
aggressive nest defence in this species (Blancher & Robertson 1982; Murphy et al. 1997), it is not surprising that vigilance is such a dominant behaviour. Increases in feeding time, chasing intruders and other behaviours
apparently came only at the expense of nest vigilance. Male nest watching
involved much less time than vigilance, but it also served an important defensive function, especially during incubation.

Although parental behaviour did not vary among the four combinations   22
of male and female experience, there were differences in reproductive success, most of which appeared to be associated with female experience. Experienced females breeding with experienced males bred the earliest, laid
large clutches, lost few young to starvation, and fledged the most young.
Conversely, inexperienced females with an inexperienced male bred the latest, laid the fewest eggs, lost the most young to starvation, and fledged the
fewest young. The other two pair combinations were intermediate in seasonal fledging success, but did not differ from the E–E pair. Given that we
found no behavioural differences between I–I pairs and pairs with intermediate combinations of experience, yet the former had lower reproductive success, differences in territory quality probably contributed heavily to the poor

success of inexperienced pairs. The lower foraging efficiency of inexperienced females and the greater loss of nestlings to starvation among I–I pairs are consistent with this interpretation.

Male and Female Parental Care

In comparison to other socially monogamous songbirds, the different feeding rates (or parental investment, PI) of male and female kingbirds seemed pronounced. We have considerable confidence in our finding because we obtained identical patterns in both years. Moreover, Hayes & Robertson (1989) removed male kingbirds and found that unassisted females were able to match the feeding effort of control pairs without the unassisted female having to double her number of feeding trips, suggesting that males fed the young less than females. Theory predicts (Winkler 1987, among others), and our review of empirical studies of songbirds showed that males and females in most species contribute nearly equally to the feeding of young (Fig. 3). Of a random sample of 39 monogamous, 10 primarily monogamous (≥ 95% monogamy) and five polygynous passerines,

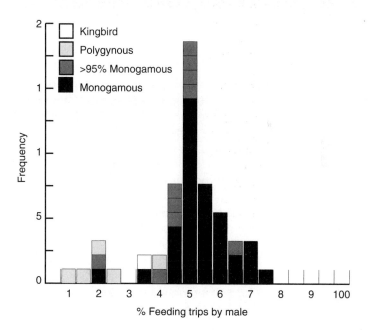

Figure 3 A comparison of the proportion of nestling feeding trips that were made by the male parent for 54 species of passerines. Data are separated according to whether the mating system was strictly monogamous, mainly monogamous (≤5% of males polygynous) or regularly polygynous. See Appendix for a list of sources.

males of 51.0% of the nonploygynous species made 46–55% of the feeding trips to the nest, while an additional 24.5% of the species contributed even more (Appendix, Fig. 3). Although males of polygynous species make (on average) only 21% of the feeding trips to the nest, males of most other species contribute at least half of the feeding trips. The only monogamous species in which males contribute less than roughly half are the reed bunting, *Emberiza schoeniclus,* common chaffinch, *Fringilla coelebs,* and eastern kingbird, all three of which fell midway between what is typical of most polygynous and monogamous species.

One explanation for the low feeding effort of male kingbirds is that 24 equal male–female effort may be unnecessary if a female on a high-quality territory can feed the young alone. Gowaty (1983) argued that male parental care in eastern bluebirds, *Sialia sialis,* may only be beneficial in poor or highly variable environments. This surely does not apply to kingbirds because young starve (Table 3) and the fledging mass of nestlings normally varies inversely with brood size (Murphy 1983; unpublished data). More likely, males may be forced to guard the nest. Kingbirds generally lose over 50% of nests to predation (Murphy 1996b), but aggressive nest defence has been shown to reduce kingbird nest losses (Blancher & Robertson 1982). Having a sentinel may more than counteract the costs of reduced male feeding effort. Hayes & Robertson's (1989) removal experiment also showed that assisted females were more likely to fledge entire broods than were unassisted females, and the principal reason seemed to be that the absence of the male increased loses of entire broods to predators.

Another reason for reduced male feeding effort may be that losses of 25 paternity are common. DNA fingerprinting studies of this population indicate that extra pair parentage occurs frequently: 41% of young at 12 or 20 nests were not sired by the presumptive father (D. L. Rowe, M. T. Murphy, R. C. Fleischer & P. Wolf, unpublished data). In response to suspected cuckoldry, males might facultatively reduce their effort by decreasing the number of feeding trips to either the entire brood or specific nestlings. We find the latter unlikely, however, because there is no evidence that male birds can identify offspring that they have not sired (Kempenaers & Sheldon 1997). We suspect that kingbirds also lack this ability because males readily feed broods that have been enlarged by the addition of up to two foster young. We find it more likely that the low feeding rates of male kingbirds result from either a general facultative adjustment downward when confidence of paternity in the present broods is low, or that it represents a relatively inflexible, nonfacultative response (sensu Westneat & Sherman 1993) to consistently high levels of cuckoldry. Further work will be required to distinguish between these two hypotheses, but in either case, selection should favour males that withhold effort when parental care is costly and the probability of losing paternity can change through time (Winkler 1987; Westneat & Sherman 1993; Yamamura & Tsuji 1993; Houston 1995). The advantages of maintaining a sentinel at the nest probably also reinforces selection for low male feeding effort. Instead of investing in the costly behaviour of feeding young, male kingbirds that maintain high levels of vigilance provide an important nondepreciable form of parental care that can be shared equally by young that they have and have not sired. A male can thus provide an essential component of parental care to all young without incurring increased risks of reduced survivorship due to the costs of feeding young (Maigret & Murphy 1997). Male kingbirds may be making the 'best of a bad situation' by cooperating with females, yet withholding the most expensive form of parental care.

Persistence of Pair Bonds

The question of why kingbird pair bonds remain intact for up to 4–5 26 years (M. T. Murphy, unpublished data), despite frequent cuckoldry (D. L. Rowe, M. T. Murphy, R. C. Fleischer & P. Wolf, unpublished data) and relatively low male feeding effort (this study) seems better understood from the female than the male perspective. Female kingbirds that return to breed on their previous territory lay earlier than other females, regardless of whether or not their mate is experienced (this study), but unlike great tits, *Parus major* (Perrins & McCleery 1985) and marsh tits, *P. palustris* (Smith 1993), experienced female kingbirds in this study that remated with a former mate did not lay larger clutches than experienced females that paired with a new male. Laying date and clutch size thus appear to be purely female traits that are not influenced by the experience of the female's mate. Apparent benefits that females derive from renesting with a former mate include significantly more male vigilance during incubation, and relatively higher male feeding effort. E–E pairs tended to lose the fewest young to starvation, but fledging success did not vary between groups in which at least one bird had experience on the territory.

Given that males arrive before females and show nearly life-long site 27 fidelity (Murphy 1996a), females must often choose between mating with a former mate on her old territory, or moving to a new territory where the male may or may not have experience. Because the probability that an experienced bird will breed on the territory is 1.0 every time a female reuses her former territory, but only 0.7 (average male survivorship; Murphy 1996a) when a female moves to a new territory, female site fidelity will virtually always be favoured over dispersal because if will guarantee that an experienced bird is present. Our results are consistent with evidence from other studies suggesting that divorce should not occur unless it leads to an increase in reproductive success (Choudhury 1995). Moreover, like female splendid fairy wrens, *Malurus splendens* (Brooker & Rowley 1995), female kingbirds that remate with former partners on former territories benefit by gaining (1) access to known resource sites, (2) a reliable assistant for raising young, and (3) knowledge of neighbouring males from whom to solicit extrapair copulations. Consequently, we believe that female kingbirds re-establish pair bonds with former mates mainly because of reproductive advantages associated with reuse of a former territory rather than benefits of remating with a former mate (contra Murphy 1996a).

Acknowledgments

        Funding for our research was provided by a Trustees Research Grant 28 from Hartwick College, and in part by NSF grant BSR 9106854 to M.T.M. We would like to thank the numerous residents of Delaware and Otsego Co. for providing access to critical study areas. D. L. Rowe, Drs Peter O. Dunn, David F. Sherry, David F. Westneat and an anonymous referee provided especially important comments on early versions of the manuscript. Permission to colour-band kingbirds was granted to MTM by the Bird Banding Laboratory of the U.S. Fish and Wildlife Service. Permission to conduct this research was not required by the Animal Care and Use Committee of Hartwick College because animals were observed under natural conditions.

Appendix

Species	Proportion of trips by male	Mating system	Reference
Microrhopias quixensis	0.55	M	Greenberg & Gradwohl 1983
Sayornis phoebe	0.43	M	Conrad & Robertson 1993
Tyrannus tyrannus	0.35	M	This study
Progne subis	0.48	M	Wagner et al. 1996
Tachycineta bicolor	0.48	M	Leffelaar & Robertson 1986
Hirundo rustica	0.47	M	Moller & Birkhead 1993
Aphelocoma coerulescens	0.59	M	Moller & Birkhead 1993
Pica pica	0.62	M	Buitron 1988
Corvus monedula	0.69	M	Moller & Birkhead 1993
Parus major	0.69	M	Smith et al. 1988; Moller & Birkhead 1993
Parus caeruleus	0.57	M	Moller & Birkhead 1993
Parus gambeli	0.54	M	Grundel 1987
Troglodytes aedon	0.25	P	Moller & Birkhead 1993
Phylloscopus sibilatrix	0.63	95%M	Moller & Birkhead 1993
Phylloscopus trochilus	0.50	95%M	Moller & Birkhead 1993
Ficedula hypoleuca	0.44	95%M	Moller & Birkhead 1993

Species	Proportion of trips by male	Mating system	Reference
Ficedula albicollis	0.44	M	Moller & Birkhead 1993
Oenanthe oenanthe	0.50	95%M	Moreno 1987
Sialia sialis	0.46	95%M	Moller & Birkhead 1993
Sialia currucoides	0.55	M	Power 1980
Dumetella carolinensis	0.67	M	Johnson & Best 1982
Mimus polyglottos	0.47	M	Breitwisch et al. 1986
Toxostoma rufum	0.59	M	Heagy & Best 1983
Sturnus vulgaris	0.46	95%M	Wright & Cuthill 1989; Moller & Birkhead 1993
Vermivora ruficapilla	0.43	M	Knapton 1984
Dendroica petechia	0.52	M	Biermann & Sealy 1982; Studd & Robertson 1985
Dendroica caerulescens	0.47	M	Goodbred & Holmes 1996
Dendroica discolor	0.45	95%M	Nolan 1978
Setophaga ruticilla	0.53	M	Omland & Sherry 1994
Protonotaria citrea	0.58	M	Petit 1991
Acrocephalus arundinaceous	0.49	M	Moller & Birkhead 1993
Nectarinia osea	0.46	M	Markman et al. 1995
Prunella modularis	0.50	M	Hatchwell & Davies 1990
Taeniopygia guttata	0.43	M	Moller & Birkhead 1993
Passer domesticus	0.45	95%M	Moller & Birkhead 1993
Geospiza conirostris	0.50	M	Moller & Birkhead 1993
Geospiza fortis	0.61	M	Moller & Birkhead 1993
Cardinalis cardinalis	0.57	M	Fiiliater & Breitwisch 1997
Passerina cyanea	0.10	P	Moller & Birkhead 1993
Aimophila aestivalis	0.55	M	Haggerty 1992
Spizella pusilla	0.48	M	Best 1977; Carey 1990
Passerculus sandwichensis	0.48	M	Bedard & Meunier 1983
Melospiza melodia	0.71	M	Moller & Birkhead 1993
Zonotrichia leucophrys	0.40	95%M	Moller & Birkhead 1993
Junco hyemalis	0.55	M	Wolf et al. 1990
Emberiza schoeniclus	0.16	M	Moller & Birkhead 1993
Emberiza calandra	0.17	95%M	Moller & Birkhead 1993

(continued)

Appendix (*continued*)			
Species	Proportion of trips by male	Mating system	Reference
Plectrophenax nivalis	0.47	M	Lyon et al. 1987
Dolichonyx oryzivorus	0.40	P	Moller & Birkhead 1993
Agelaius phoeniceus	0.15	P	Muldal et al. 1986; Moller & Birkhead 1993
Xanthocephalus xanthocephalus	0.16	P	Willson 1966
Euphagus cyanocephalus	0.46	M	Patterson et al. 1980
Fringilla coelebs	0.34	M	Moller & Birkhead 1993
Carpodacus mexicanu	0.50	M	Moller & Birkhead 1993

The proportion of trips to feed nestlings that were made by the male for 54 passerine species. Data were obtained from Moller & Birkhead (1993) and original literature sources. The mean value was calculated when data from more than one source were located. Species were classified as to whether the mating system was strictly monogamous (M), primarily monogamous (95% of males monogamous; 95%M) or regularly polygynous (P) based on the original sources, Verner & Willson (1969), and Moller (1991). Data for *Prunella modularis* limited pairs in monogamous relationships.

CRITICAL READING

1. On the basis of the report's abstract and introduction, sum up in your own words the specific research question, or set of questions, these researchers were investigating. Did they ultimately answer their questions?
2. Discuss a few places in the text where the writers report facts and where they (or some other researcher cited by them) interpret facts. What theoretical lens do the authors and their sources typically use for examining why certain behaviors occur?
3. Look at Table 3, and describe why exactly this information is presented in the form of a table rather than being described in prose form.

CLASS DISCUSSION

1. Discuss what the commonsense expectations might be when considering the effect of experience on the birds' parental behavior and on the reproductive success of their efforts. Then discuss what the researchers found in relation to this expectation. How do they account for their findings?
2. Discuss how the parental behavior that the researchers observed in kingbirds relates to typical male and female parental behavior in humans.
3. Discuss what role monogamy and polygyny seem to play in the parental investment of birds.

DIRECTED FREEWRITE

Since sciences such as zoology require the ability to observe as objectively as possible and then to report observations in clear and objective language, describe some natural, inanimate object in as much objective detail as possible. As you write, notice the points at which you are tempted to insert subjective evaluations or descriptions. After writing this description, write a totally subjective description that is consciously infused with your own belief, experiences, and judgments as these relate to the object under study.

THE GAY SIDE OF NATURE

Jeffrey Kluger

In this short piece from *Time* magazine, Jeffrey Kluger discusses findings on the homosexual behavior of nonhuman animals reported in a book entitled *Biological Exuberance,* by Bruce Bahemihl.

Jeffrey Kluger is a senior writer at Time *magazine. Prior to working with* Time, *Kluger was a columnist for* Discover *magazine, a health editor at* Family Circle *magazine, a story editor at* The New York Times Business World Magazine, *and an associate editor at* Science Digest *magazine. His features and columns have appeared in a number of publications, including* The New York Times Magazine, Gentlemen's Quarterly, The Wall Street Journal, Cosmopolitan, Omni, McCall's, *and* Time. *Kluger is an adjunct instructor in the graduate journalism program at New York University and a licensed but non-practicing, attorney. He is the co-author, along with astronaut Jim Lovell, of* Lost Moon, *the book on which the 1995 movie,* Apollo 13 *is based. He is currently writing a new book for Simon & Schuster about the unmanned space program and the exploration of the solar system.*

Giraffes do it, goats do it, birds and bonobos and dolphins do it. Humans beings—a lot of them anyway—like to do it too, but of all the planet's species, they're the only ones who are oppressed when they try.   1

What humans share with so many other animals, it now appears, is freewheeling homosexuality. For centuries opponents of gay rights have seen same-gender sex as a uniquely human phenomenon, one of the many ways our famously corruptible species flouts the laws of nature. But nature's   2 morality, it seems, may be remarkably flexible, at least if the new book *Biological Exuberance* (St. Martin's Press), by linguist and cognitive scientist Bruce Bagemihl, is to be believed. According to Bagemihl, the animal kingdom is a more sexually complex place than most people know—one where couplings routinely take place not just between male-female pairs but also between male-male and female-female ones. What's more, same-sex partners don't meet merely for brief encounters, but may form long-term bonds, sometimes mating for years or even for life.

Bagemihl's ideas have caused a stir in the higher, human community, 3 especially among scientists who find it simplistic to equate any animal behavior with human behavior. But Bagemihl stands behind the findings, arguing that if homosexuality comes naturally to other creatures, perhaps it's time to quit getting into such a lather over the fact that it comes naturally to humans too. "Animal sexuality is more complex than we imagined," says Bagemihl. "That diversity is part of human heritage."

For a love that long dared not speak its name, animal homosexuality is 4 astonishingly common. Scouring zoological journals and conducting extensive interviews with scientists, Bagemihl found same-sex pairings documented in more than 450 different species. In a world teeming with more than 1 million species, that may not seem like much. Animals however, can be surprisingly prim about when and under whose prying eye they engage in sexual activity; as few as 2,000 species have thus been observed closely enough to reveal their full range of coupling behavior. Within such a small sampling, 450 represents more than 20%.

That 20% may spend its time lustily or quite tenderly. Among bonobos, 5 a chimplike ape, homosexual pairings account for as much as 50% of all sexual activity. Females especially engage in repeated acts of same-sex sex, spending far more than the 12 or so seconds the whole transaction can take when a randy male is involved. Male giraffes practice necking—literally—in a very big way, entwining their long bodies until both partners become sexually aroused. Heterosexual and homosexual dolphin pairs engage in face-to-face sexual encounters that look altogether human. Animals as diverse as elephants and rodents practice same-sex mounting, and macaques raise that affection ante further, often kissing while assuming a coital position. Same-gender sexual activity, says Bagemihl, "encompasses a wide range of forms."

What struck Bagemihl most is those forms that go beyond mere sexual 6 gratification. Humboldt penguins may have homosexual unions that last six years; male greylag geese may stay paired for 15 years—a lifetime commitment when you've got the lifespan of a goose. Bears and some other mammals may bring their young into homosexual unions, raising them with their same-sex partner just as they would with a member of the opposite sex.

But witnessing same-sex activity and understanding it are two different   7
things, and some experts believe observers like Bagemihl are misreading
the evidence. In species that lack sophisticated language—which is to say
all species but ours—sex serves many nonsexual purposes, including establishing alliances and appeasing enemies, all things animals must do with
members of both sexes. "Sexuality helps animals maneuver around each
other before making real contact," says Martin Daly, an evolutionary psychologist at McMaster University in Ontario. "Putting all that into a homosexual category seems simplistic."

Even if some animals do engage in homosexual activity purely for   8
pleasure, their behavior still serves as an incomplete model—and an incomplete explanation—for human behavior. "In our society homosexuality
means a principal or exclusive orientation," says psychology professor
Frans de Waal of the Yerkes Primate Center in Atlanta. "Among animals it's
just nonreproductive sexual behavior."

Whether any of this turns out to be good for the gay and lesbian com-   9
munity is unclear. While the new findings seem to support the idea that homosexuality is merely a natural form of sexual expression. Bagemihl
believes such political questions may be beside the point. "We shouldn't
have to look to the animal world to see what's normal or ethical," he says.
Indeed, when it comes to answering those questions. Mother Nature seems
to be keeping an open mind.

CRITICAL READING

1. Describe the animal behaviors discussed here that seem most surprising to the
   writer of the article. What language and tone does he use to indicate such surprise? Are these behaviors surprising to you, as well?
2. Explain why reports of homosexual sex in animals might be useful to advocates
   of gay rights.
3. Critics of these findings point out in the seventh paragraph that "sex serves many
   non-sexual purposes" for animals, "including establishing alliances and appeasing enemies," thus, as one critic says, "putting all that into a homosexual category seems simplistic." What nonsexual purposes might be served by
   homosexual behavior in humans? Discuss the ways that we tend to define homosexuality itself in overly simplistic terms.

CLASS DISCUSSION

1. Discuss how ideas about what is "natural" are used in discussions of homosexuality, as well as in discussions of other kinds of human behavior. Further, discuss
   the paradoxical way in which the concept of "nature" can be used to justify as
   well as to condemn certain behaviors.

2. Although it may be overly simplistic to draw direct parallels between animal and human behavior, nonetheless, we do so all the time. Discuss some of the ways that animals are compared with humans, and vice versa—in science as well as in daily life. What purposes are served by such comparisons?

DIRECTED FREEWRITE

Brainstorm the ways in which the sex and coupling between animals of the same sex, as reported here by Kluger, could be used to support arguments in favor of acceptance of homosexuality as a viable, natural orientation. Then brainstorm the rebuttal points that someone vehemently opposed to acceptance of homosexuality might raise to your points.

ZOOLOGY UNIT WRITING ASSIGNMENTS

1. Humans, with our massive egos, have a tendency to anthropomorphize animals; that is, we tend to interpret the behavior of animals, especially our pets, in human terms. Our dog jumps around and licks us when we arrive home from a trip, and we assume that she is happy to see us, that she missed us. In reality, the dog's behavior could mean any number of things having more to do with wolves' social behavior in packs than with any humanlike feelings. Similarly, we find a dead baby bird on the sidewalk and feel sad about this loss of life, imagining the bird's mother morning her lost chick. The reality might be that the mother bird pushed the baby out of the nest because she had too many babies to feed.

   In this piece of writing, a variety of autobiographical narrative, we ask that you tell the story of some incident or experience you have had with an animal of any kind, but an incident in which you engaged in this kind of projecting—where you interpreted the animal's behavior from a human perspective. Then propose alternate interpretations, one that might go completely counter to what we expect from human behavior, as the story of the mother bird does.

   The first stage in the writing process for this paper involves a bit of prewriting in whatever form is comfortable for you. Think back through your life, and write about any special incidents that involved animals—your first pet, an animal that captured your attention in a zoo, a squirrel to whom you fed nuts in the park, and so on. Don't necessarily filter out those incidents that seem tangentially related to the topic; sometimes seemingly unimportant events can turn out to be the most special and illuminating. Also, unless you want to write a ten-page paper, keep your listed or clustered incidents brief—a few hours or at most a single day. Remember to focus on the human interpretations you gave to animal behavior, and be creative in imagining other, perhaps less human, interpretations.

2. Writing assignment 3 in this chapter's Evolutionary Psychology unit (page 302) introduced the genre of the research design; after reading this assignment, please refer back to that unit for more instruction. In as much detail as you can, design a study that could be conducted on humans, that, like Woodward and Murphy's experiment, measures parental investment and its relation to experience and

reproductive success. Then write a research design that describes the various procedures entailed in such a study. Feel free to imagine something grandiose; your study could be a long-term, very expensive and complicated study, if you wish.

3. Write a short research report on animal gender or sexual behavior, based on material you gather from the library. Your report should focus on a particular pattern that you notice in the ways the topic has been approached by biologists or on a particular pattern of behavior that you notice in the animals themselves. For example, you could focus on the parental behavior of a variety of animals, comparing them, but focusing on a feature or on several features that are common to most of them. You are thus being asked here to synthesize different sources on a similar topic, and out of that synthesis to arrive at a point or set of points that will serve as the focal point of your essay.

CHAPTER FOUR

CAPITAL ECONOMIES

INTRODUCTION

Capitalism is the prevailing economic system of the postindustrial world. In capital economies, private and corporate entities make products or provide services to people; they trade these goods and services through an intricate web of markets. Capital markets are usually based on some token of exchange, which in our culture we call money. Most of us like to have some money, because we use it to buy food, shelter, medicine, along with certain nonessentials, such as electronic bug zappers and clothing with designer labels.

Although the beginnings of capitalism can be traced back to antiquity and can be found in cultures worldwide, capitalism—in the form we know and practice today—is a relatively recent Western phenomenon, having reached its height in nineteenth-century Europe. Capitalism spread throughout the world and remained the predominant economic and social system until Marxism emerged as a dynamic competing system; in fact, the term "capitalism" was first introduced in the mid-nineteenth century by Karl Marx, the founder of communism.

The word capitalism carries with it a great deal of emotional and intellectual baggage. Reading articles about capitalism, one will observe that people are either fiercely loyal to this economic philosophy or doggedly opposed to it, and that both camps argue their cases loudly and persuasively. On the pro-capital side, for instance, philosopher Ayn Rand, says:

> The moral justification for capitalism lies in the fact that it is the only system consonant with man's rational nature, that it protects man's survival qua man, and that its ruling principle is: justice.

According to Rand, free enterprise—unregulated economic competition—represents the best way to achieve the "common good." In a similar tone, the website of a large and national organization proclaims that "Capitalism is a social system based on the principle of (individual) rights" and is "the most rational and moral, political system man has even known."

In stark contrast, however, another website condemns capitalism as being responsible for a raft of social ills:

> The crisis of capitalism is systemic; it is insatiable greed, corporate drive for maximum profits. And the results are the millions of unemployed, underemployed and homeless. And the crisis of capitalism is racism. It is the terrible infant mortality rate. It is in the fact that there are more African-American young men in jail than there are in college. It is drug-infested, crime-infested ghettoes and barrios of our country, where hope and future are two words never heard . . . The Republicans and the Democrats are all responsible for this crisis, but the Republican Right is totally out of touch with reality. The party of Lincoln has become the party of open racism, male supremacy and antilabor capitalist greed.

Following the same logic, if in a more academic tone, economist George Soros makes this statement: "Wealth does accumulate in the hands of its owners, and if there is no mechanism for redistribution, the inequities can become intolerable." If these few examples are any indication (and they are), a terrible divisiveness exists in people's opinions of capital-based economies, and this chapter reflects this polarity, providing discussions on related topics from a range of disciplinary perspectives. In between the two extremes of pro-capital sentiment on one side and Marxism/socialism on the other, lies a wide range of related economic philosophies, social opinions, and scientific practices, and this chapter will explore some middle-of-the-road views of capital economies as well as the more extreme.

There has traditionally existed a division between economics and the humanities. As Michael Novak, holder of the George Frederick Jewett Chair in Religion and Public Policy at the American Enterprise Institute, notes,

> From Adam Smith's *Inquiry into the Nature and the Causes of the Wealth of Nations* in 1776 until well after the publication of John Stuart Mill's *Principles of Political Economy* in 1848, economics was viewed as a branch of moral philosophy astonishingly underdeveloped by earlier philosophers . . . The problems of political order and rule of law were of such importance—neither person nor property being safe from marauders, brigands, and feuding princes, whether in Europe or in other places on the planet—that the development of economics required the prior development of politics and law.

In other words, the necessities of economic survival have prevented people from looking at economics from a humanistic philosophical perspective as, in

Novak's example, a branch of moral philosophy. One outcome of this phenomenon has been that the humanities and economics have often had a stormy relationship with one another. Some governmental agencies, for instance, have slashed or even eliminated public monies to support the arts, because music, theater, photography, and sculpture are seen to have marginal utility in terms of human "necessities": transportation, housing, medical care, and so forth. This movement, many artists and social observers believe, has had dire consequences for the state of the arts in modern America, with some critics arguing that aesthetics are a necessity, that a society without grounding in the arts is destined to collapse. Within the Popular Music Studies unit of the humanities section of this chapter, two articles point out ways in which economics and popular music intersect, perhaps to the detriment of pure artistic expression.

However, if art and economics do not always go philosophically hand in hand, certain practitioners within humanities-based academic disciplines do make use of economic principles and theories to examine artistic products such as paintings, popular songs, and literature, so that in this way, economics and humanities make a happy and productive union. Literary critics within the humanities examine an abundantly wide array of artifacts, with fascinating results. Anne L. Bower, for example, has examined cookbooks as literary works and as representations of their authors' preoccupations with fortifying their economic and social achievements and building their community. Similarly, English literary critic Gerhard Joseph has examined nineteenth-century British poet Alfred Lord Tennyson's use of financial metaphors in depicting grief; by rendering melancholy in tangible literary descriptions, says the critic, Tennyson indicates that the act of mourning is "real" and worldly, in keeping with the Victorian materialist economic perspective. Following this model, the Literature unit of this chapter's humanities section features an article that points out economic themes in a modern American novel, whereas a short story satirizes the effects of corporate culture on the average American male and his family.

There is no question in people's minds that the social sciences and economics are inextricably bound together, especially since economics as an academic discipline is usually placed under the broad umbrella of the social sciences. The overlap between economic theory and the study of human interaction—generally the province of the social sciences—is broad and far-reaching, providing fertile ground for addressing issues of survival, standard of living, and prosperity, and for proposing solutions to real problems such as poverty. For example, much recent social welfare policy research has concentrated on economic transformations and cyclical processes to examine the work experiences and prospects of the poor, with the goal of producing some productive poverty and welfare discourse, the ultimate goal of which, naturally, would be the reduction of economics-based suffering in the United States and in the world. Likewise, working from the social/economic perspectives of welfare theory and neighborhood theory, researcher Thomas P. Vartanian has used data from the U.S. Census to examine how adolescent conditions affect the labor market and economic outcomes, indicating that adolescents living in the most economically disadvantaged neighborhoods have had far lower levels of positive "outcome variables" than adolescents living in only slightly more advantaged neighborhoods. Once a researcher, such as Vartanian, can identify such variables, it becomes much more possible for reformers to propose solutions to these economic inequities. In the same way, two articles in the History unit of this text's social science section study the way that past economic forces have shaped our culture and economy, whereas articles in the Ethnic Studies unit discuss ways in which Hispanics and African Americans attempt to cope with inequalities in our country's economic fabric.

Although many individuals outside the field of economics might not necessarily make the connection, for more than a century, economics has been advanced and practiced as a science, largely on mathematical models. Economics borrows (or, perhaps more accurately, shares) theories, tools, and techniques from the fields of probability, advanced mathematics, physics, and computer programming; and if you think such disciplinary overlap occurs only in the rarified, scholarly air of the academy, you need look no farther than Microsoft Corporation's multimillionaire Senior Vice President, Nathan Myhrvold, who holds master's degrees in physics and mathematical economics, along with a Ph.D. in theoretical/mathematical physics.

As further evidence of the connection between economics and the hard sciences, several economists have won the Nobel Prize since 1985 for mathematical studies on the ways in which investors set stock prices. In fact, many contemporary economists go so far as to insist that mathematically ignorant economists have an overly limited and constraining view of the ways in which financial markets operate, both on the micro- and macroeconomic scales. The science section of this chapter explores this assertion, examining closely the connection between hard science and economics. Two articles within the Computer Science unit focus on ways in which new technology is radically changing the methods that economists use to interpret financial data, whereas the Mathematics unit illuminates ways in which the disciplines of mathematics and economics combine to enable researchers to make bold financial predictions and to teach students more effectively.

Before embarking on intensive study within this chapter on capital economics, you might want to consider the notion of money from both the personal and the social perspectives. On the personal level, what is your relationship to the "almighty dollar"; are you indifferent to money; do you have only passing, superficial interest in personal finance; or are you highly driven to make a financial success of yourself, in the mold of the Microsoft executive described earlier? Where did you derive these personal feelings about money—from personal experiences of your own financial situation as a child, from observing other people's financial situations, or from ideas delivered by parents, teachers, and the media?

From a broader social perspective, to what prevailing economic/political philosophy do you tend to adhere? Do you consider yourself a fiscal conservative: do you believe that certain existing economic inequalities are tolerable or at least unavoidable, and that the existing order is about as close to ideal as is practically attainable; do you have strong commitment to free markets and economic "survival of the fittest"? Or do you consider yourself a liberal when it comes to economics: do you support a stronger role for government in regulating and manipulating the private economy and providing public support for the economically and socially disadvantaged? Or are you perhaps a socialist, insisting that the government must in principle reflect the will of the masses of the population (or at least their "true" best interests) and favoring an economic system in which all or most productive resources are the property of the government (i.e., the people), in which the production and distribution of goods and services are administered primarily by the government rather than by private enterprise, and in which any remaining private production and distribution is heavily regulated by the government rather than by market processes? Or do you fall somewhere between (or outside) the scope of these ideologies?

Thinking about your relationship to money, both on the personal and the social levels, will assist you in critically approaching the articles contained in this chapter. As you read each article, attempt to discern its underlying assumptions, methodologies, and ideologies, and—perhaps most important—notice whether the authors' assertions "ring true" in terms of your own conceptions of capitalism and personal finance. At the same time, keep your mind open to modifying your own economic preconceptions, based on your having encountered some economic philosophies, perspectives, and methodologies that you may never have encountered before.

THINKING AND WRITING IN THE HUMANITIES

Unit 1
Literary Studies—The Book and the Buck

THORSTEIN VEBLEN AND *THE GREAT GATSBY*

E. Ray Canterbury

Numerous contemporary novels portray American culture as rife with vulgar displays of wealth and opulence. Books such as Tom Wolfe's *Bonfire of the Vanities* or Martin Amis's *Money* depict the modern individual as being money- and power-obsessed, and in the process overindulging in every other vice imaginable, including gluttony, lust, greed, covetousness, and homicide. However, such fictional characterizations are not restricted to the second half of the twentieth century and afterward. In this article, one literary critic—E. Ray Canterbury, a professor at Florida State University—argues that F. Scott Fitzgerald's famous novel *The Great Gatsby,* which was published in 1925, exhibits a satirical account of early American socioeconomic conditions. In the author's opinion, Fitzgerald's economic themes may have been lifted from the theories of an economist named Thorstein Veblen. As you read, notice the specific ways in which literary critics make connections between theoretical constructs, such as Veblen's theories, and literary texts, drawing connections—both explicit and inferred—between the two.

E. Ray Canterbury received his Ph.D. in Economics from Washington University in 1966. He has published several articles on economics that have appeared in a range of journals including Southern Economic Journal, Journal of Economic History, *and* Journal of Economic Issues. *Canterbury has served on the Board of Directors for The International Trade and Finance Association and is a member emeritus of the Board of Directors for the Eastern Economic Association. Additionally, he has contributed chapters to several economic texts and is the author of* The Literate Economist.

Source: "Thorstein Veblen and the Great Gatsby" by E. Ray Canterbury in *Journal of Economic Issues,* vol. 33, no. 2, June 1999. Copyright © 1999 by The Association for Evolutionary Economics. Reprinted with permission of the Association for Evolutionary Economics, Bucknell University.

Canterbury is currently a professor of economics at the University of Florida where his areas of specialty include economic theory (macro, micro, trade, finance), and the history of economic thought.

F. Scott Fitzgerald's short novel *The Great Gatsby* is set in the 1920s; like its author, it is strongly identified with the Jazz Age—that temporal slice of self-indulgence sandwiched between the Great War and the Great Depression. Yet Fitzgerald's original setting for Gatsby was the middle of the Gilded Age (1885), and the theme of the novel is widely recognized as an indictment not so much of the Roaring Twenties as of the "American Dream," which had attained an honored place in American mythology well before the opening of the twentieth century. It is my contention in this paper that much of the socioeconomic satire informing The Great Gatsby is not original with Fitzgerald, but reflects the influence, both directly and indirectly, of that earlier adversary of conspicuous consumption and pecuniary emulation, Thorstein Veblen.

THE DOMINANCE OF SOCIAL DARWINISM DURING THE GILDED AGE

During the Gilded Age (1870–1910), when cutthroat competition and unbridled capitalism led to the accumulation of wealth and capital in a few hands, a need arose to justify the excesses of the newly rich and their corrupt business practices. Thus emerged the "American Dream"—a blend of the Newtonian belief in a beneficent, finely tuned universe and the American versions of Calvinism and Puritanism, which condoned and encouraged the accumulation of wealth as a way of doing God's work.

Since the rich of the Gilded Age chose to display their great wealth in vulgar ways, their continued respectability required some blend of science with religion to make their wealth appear not only just, but inevitable. American Social Darwinism served this purpose, particularly as set forth in Horatio Alger, Jr.'s popular fiction for boys, which injects into the Protestant ethic an element from Newtonian science, the idea of a universe that rewards.

In the view of Herbert Spencer (1820–1903), the English founder of sociology, the fact that the rich get richer and the poor get poorer is just nature's way of improving the species and the economy at the same time. Spencer's books sold by the hundreds of thousands, and his reception in New York in 1882, two years before Gatsby originally was to arrive there, would have been the envy of Madonna's press agent.

Though a generation of scholars wallowed in Spencer's wake, the most eminent of the American Social Darwinists was William Graham Sumner (1840–1910), Veblen's professor at Yale. Sumner was direct, proclaiming that "the millionaires are a product of natural selection . . . the naturally selected agents of society for certain work. They get high wages and live in luxury, but the bargain is a good one for society." Thus, while Horatio

Alger's heroes could achieve in fiction the American Dream of rising to the top, the doctrines of the Social Darwinists helped to preserve a social process that made sure such successes were infrequent.

Sumner ingeniously put Newtonian natural law, the Protestant ethic, and a misunderstanding of Darwinian natural selection all on the side of classical economics. Evoking both Calvin and science, his sociology equated the hard-working, thrifty person of the Protestant ethic with the "fittest" in the struggle for survival. Monetary success in the capitalistic society was the fulfillment of an automatically benevolent, free competitive order. In the competitive struggle, people went from natural selection to social selection of fitter persons and from "organic forms with superior adaptability to citizens with a greater store of economic virtues." Not surprisingly, Andrew Carnegie and John D. Rockefeller became disciples.

VEBLEN'S COUNTERPOINT: *THE THEORY OF THE LEISURE CLASS* (TLC)

Social Darwinism met its antithesis in *The Theory of the Leisure Class*. When Veblen applied the law of natural selection to human institutions (broadly defined to include ideas and habits of thought), he found not progress, but regression. Human institutions (environment) perpetually lagged behind material change. Still, the successful individuals are those who can best adapt to changing institutions—more a Lamarkian than a Darwinian process. Because people are also creatures of habit, changes are made reluctantly and rarely. Because the leisure class is sheltered from pressures of subsistence, its members have no urgency to change and so retain their old habits of living. The social or cultural environment makes the survival of some characteristics more likely than others.

A state of savagery requires people to be community-centered for survival. When technology advances sufficiently to create surpluses, predation and barbarism emerge, as do classes distinguished by wealth holdings. Barbarism promotes not only selfishness and emulation, but brutality. Though such characteristics assure survival in an economy of surpluses, they are neither noble nor progressive. Aggressive behavior is rewarded; the most cunning and competitive of the leisure class have the upper hand. If Veblen is correct, it is neither surprising that the "American Dream" is to become even more affluent nor that the affluent promote exclusive institutions. Since pecuniary emulation is an individual's strongest motive, the standard of living shared by a particular class determines the "accepted standard of expenditure." As Veblen put it,

> To accept and practise the standard of living which is in vogue is both agreeable and expedient, commonly to the point of being indispensable to personal comfort and to success in life. The standard of living of any class, so far as concerns the element of conspicuous waste, is commonly

as high as the earning capacity of the class will permit—
with a constant tendency to go higher.

Emulation dominates Veblen's chapter "Dress as an Expression of the   9
Pecuniary Culture," where he writes that "admitted expenditure for display is
more universally practised in the matter of dress than in any other line of
consumption." Sharpening the edge of his sarcasm, Veblen writes, "the
woman's shoe adds the so-called French heel to the evidence of enforced
leisure afforded by its polish; because this high heel obviously makes any,
even the simplest and most necessary manual work extremely difficult." Of
course, much more complex and subtle sociology is at work in TLC, including the woman's service as a "chief ornament" around the house and an adequately adorned "trophy" for her husband. Women indeed comprise an
abused class in TLC.

Taboos also play roles in consumption. Ceremonial consumption such   10
as "choice articles of food, and . . . rare articles of adornment, becomes tabu
to the women and children; and if there is a base (servile) class of men, the
tabu holds also for them." Certain intoxicating beverages and narcotics are
reserved for the use of men. Such taboos separate one class from another;
members of the "superior class" identify themselves not only by what they
consume, but by their power to prevent the consumption of the same items
by others. The taboo is a way of preventing emulation of the upper classes
by the lower classes.

PARALLELS BETWEEN *THE THEORY OF THE LEISURE CLASS* AND *THE GREAT GATSBY*

All of which brings us to Fitzgerald's *The Great Gatsby*. Fitzgerald's   11
masterpiece is the supreme Veblenian parable of conspicuous consumption,
of conspicuous emulation, of pecuniary culture, and of vicarious consumption—even of waste and the leisure class itself. Jay Gatsby wants to live with
Daisy Buchanan because she is a member of the established American aristocracy of wealth. Gatsby lacks the maturity to realize that Daisy cannot be obtained by money alone and in a vulgar display of conspicuous consumption,
he flaunts his nouveau wealth. Despite Daisy's infinite price (perhaps "price-
less"), Gatsby is most attracted to Daisy's voice (not the supra-price), which
he describes as "full of money," a voice fostering an illusion he considers real.
Fitzgerald here has put on display Veblen's "secondary utility," based on emulation that "seized upon the consumption of goods as a means to an invidious
comparison, . . . as evidence of relative ability to pay." The "evidence" of ability to pay, however, is not the same as the actual ability to pay, especially in
the instance of "purchasing" Daisy whose price in infinite. Gatsby attempted to
display a purchasing ability that was out of his reach.

Surpluses, so essential to Veblenian economics, allow ostentatious   12
display; they also promote advertising. During the Gilded Age, of course, the

rich engaged in self-advertisement. By the 1920s, advertising had become an important allied industry. (Not accidentally, Fitzgerald's first post–Great War job was writing for the Barron Collier advertising agency in New York City.) Daisy, in her turn, is attracted to Gatsby because he reminds her of "an advertisement," the superficial illusion he represents. She sobs when she sees "such beautiful shirts." As Veblen would predict, for Fitzgerald's central characters the cultural illusions are more important than wealth.

The first dust jacket for Gatsby depicted the painted eyes of an oculist's 13 billboard advertisement, the source of symbolism for a business dedicated to persuasion through fallacies and exaggerations. But the eyes look out over a wasteland. George Wilson, after his wife Myrtle's death (from the careless driving of Daisy), mistakes the "eyes" on such a sign for the all-seeing of God and cannot believe that they are "just an advertisement."

As to snobbery, Fitzgerald's Gatsby again provides instruction. Tom 14 and Daisy Buchanan live in a Georgian colonial mansion representing established wealth. Gatsby, not unlike the robber barons at the turn of the century, has purchased a pretentious, vulgar imitation of a European mansion in East Egg. Even Gatsby's ivy is nouveau and not in the same league as the Buchanans'. The establishment sees clearly that Gatsby, having no sense of tradition, simply copies the style of others, much as an American university will pattern its library on a medieval Gothic chapel. Worse, Gatsby's sartorial choice, a pink suit, is as vulgar and nouveau as his gaudy, cream-colored car, his mansion, and his lavish parties.

Daisy could never leave Tom for Gatsby because she and Tom are 15 partners in a "secret society" of wealth, one that Gatsby cannot recognize, much less join. Daisy cannot leave the trappings of the old aristocracy. Tom, having originally "bought" Daisy with the gift of a $350,000 necklace, deploys brutality to keep her—even at the far greater cost to Gatsby of his (American) dreams and his life. Though Gatsby does not know it, no matter how great his acquisitive spirits as a bootlegger, the acquisition of Daisy is taboo.

Members of the upper-middle class or even middle-class who want to 16 emulate the rich leisure class must do so by buying cheap imitations or by borrowing, even at the risk of bankruptcy or worse, which I have called the "Gatsby effect." The Gatsby effect, of course, intimates disasters beyond bankruptcy from which recovery is possible. After all, Jay Gatsby died for the sins of his own emulation, a conspicuous waste.

Before Fitzgerald, only Veblen seems to have captured this cultural 17 richness and the culture of the rich with just the proper subtle balance, mixing satire, irony, and realism to expose the false values and social waste of the upper classes. At the center of the American dream, as well as Gatsby's own, is the belief that sufficient wealth can recapture and fix everything, even the ephemeral, illusory qualities of youth and beauty. It was the same kind of "beauty" satirized by Veblen.

In Gatsby, both new wealth (Jay Gatsby's) and old wealth (Daisy's)   18
lead to human failings, though the failings are manifested differently. Early
in the novel, Jay Gatsby is observed in the attitude of a worshipper, alone,
stretching his arms toward a single, faraway green light at the end of the
Buchanans' dock across the water—the visible symbol of his aspirations.
Green is the color of promise, of hope and renewal, and, of course, of
money. For Gatsby, ideals are wrapped up with wealth, and so the means
corrupt the ends. But it turns out that Daisy Buchanan is unworthy of his vision of her, and her "vulgar, meretricious beauty," her pretentiousness, is a
snare. Gatsby dies disillusioned, while Daisy lives on, oblivious. So much for
Gatsby-like hope, so much for the shallow end of the American Dream.

ULTIMATELY, WAS FITZGERALD INFLUENCED BY VEBLEN?

The Theory of the Leisure Class was a scholarly yet satirical protest   19
against the false values and social waste of the upper classes during the
Gilded Age. The Great Gatsby was the exemplary novel of the Jazz Age in
which Fitzgerald's sharp social sense enabled him to vividly depict the excesses and false values of the upper class at a time when gin was the national drink and sex the national obsession. The two works share not only a
set of themes and a moral stance, they also exhibit many of the same writing qualities—humor, satire, teasing, exaggeration, poetic imagery, symbolism, allegory, and folklore. Nevertheless, the parallels might be dismissed
as coincidental, were it not for two pieces of evidence directly linking the two
writers.

THE DIRECT EVIDENCE

Fitzgerald first described an East Egg type of society in a March 30,   20
1924, syndicated article originally titled "Our Irresponsible Rich." Although
Fitzgerald does not refer to Veblen in the article itself, his notes relating to
the article make clear that he was consciously documenting Veblen's theme
of conspicuous consumption and waste. In May of the same year, Fitzgerald, with three chapters of Gatsby in manuscript, abandoned Long Island's
lavish parties and escaped with Zelda to the more sedate Riviera, where he
completed the draft. It is thus plausible to assume that the Veblenian sentiments explored in the article were much on Fitzgerald's mind as he wrote
and rewrote the novel.

One paragraph of the syndicated article is especially revealing. In it   21
Fitzgerald writes: "Here we come to something that sets the American
'leisure class' off from the leisure class of all other nations—and makes it
probably the most shallow, most hollow, most pernicious leisure class in the
world."

Fitzgerald continues in high Veblenian style: "At no period in the   22
world's history, perhaps, has a larger proportion of the family income been

spent upon display . . ." And the waste goes on: "All that leisure—for nothing! All that wealth—it has begotten waste and destruction and dissipation and snobbery—nothing more. . . . He [the young man of inherited wealth] stocks his cellar with liquor and then votes righteously for prohibition 'for the good of the masses'."

Fitzgerald even appears to update Veblen's view of rich, oppressed 23 women: "The boy watches his mother's almost insane striving toward a social position commensurate with her money. He sees her change her accent, her clothes, her friends, her very soul, as she pushes her way up in life, pulling her busy husband with her."

Overall, Fitzgerald's theme is that the American upper class had no 24 sense of stewardship of society so that corruption, such as the Teapot Dome scandal (then afflicting the Harding administration), was to be expected, given the premises of the American Dream associating money with success. The status of the upper class is at once gracious in its advantages and privileges but not worthy of aspiration and vision in its callous treatment of those below. The inherited rich are families in decay.

An earlier direct reference to Veblen appeared in a paragraph in- 25 tended for a published review of a 1921 book by H. L. Mencken. "It seems cruel," wrote Fitzgerald, "that the privilege [of reviewing Mencken] could not have gone to Thorstein Veblen." The paragraph, deleted by a party unknown, was apparently a Fitzgerald joke, given the fact that Mencken had earlier published an assault on Veblen's critique of capitalism as a "wraith of balderdash."

THE INDIRECT EVIDENCE

While Fitzgerald (who considered himself not only a good historian, but 26 a practicing socialist) often refers to Karl Marx's *Das Kapital* and other socialist writers such as Upton Sinclair, none of his published writings cite or even mention Veblen. And when Fitzgerald designed "courses" for the education of Sheilah Graham, he did not list any of Veblen's books, though he included Marx. Nonetheless, the class distinctions made in *The Great Gatsby* are clearly Veblenian, not Marxist. We can only speculate about the motives for Fitzgerald's failure to acknowledge fully his debt to Veblen. It may be simply a matter of ego. Though he was generous in attributions, Fitzgerald prided himself in his originality. The parallels between his depiction of class, especially in *The Great Gatsby,* and Veblen's sharpest satire may have been too close for comfort, providing a motive for distancing himself from Veblen. Alternatively, Veblen's influence may have been more subliminal by the time Fitzgerald wrote *Gatsby.*

Other evidence of the Veblen-Fitzgerald connection may be lost to 27 history. Fitzgerald had no secretary until 1932; thereafter, he retained carbon copies of his correspondence. Out of a total of 6,000 known letters, an estimated 3,000 were written prior to 1932, Fitzgerald's pre-carbon age. Thus, much of the missing correspondence covers the *Gatsby* period. We may never know the extent of Fitzgerald's debt to Veblen.   ©

CRITICAL READING

1. Describe the "American Dream" as it arose during the Gilded Age (1870–1910), according to this article's author. What philosophical and social ideologies does the "American Dream" bring together, in Canterbury's view?

2. Canterbury says that the continuing respectability of the Gilded Age rich required a blend of science and religion to make their wealth appear not only just but also inevitable. According to Canterbury, "American Social Darwinism served this purpose, particularly as set forth in Horatio Alger, Jr.'s popular fiction for boys, which injects into the Protestant ethic an element from Newtonian science, the idea of a universe that rewards." Explain each of the elements of this question: What does Social Darwinism mean; who is Horatio Alger; what is the Protestant ethic; and what is Newtonian science? How do all these elements combine to justify the "vulgarity" of the rich?

3. What is the "Gatsby effect," a term coined by the author? Related to this term, what does the author mean when he says, "Jay Gatsby died for the sins of his own emulation, a conspicuous waste"?

CLASS DISCUSSION

1. Explain the main tenets of Thorstein Veblen's economic philosophy, along with that of his precursors. How does *The Great Gatsby* reflect Veblen's theories, in the view of this article's author?

2. List the specific pieces of evidence, both direct and indirect, that Canterbury provides to make a connection between Veblen and Fitzgerald. In a class discussion, examine this evidence critically, to determine whether or not you find it convincing.

DIRECTED FREEWRITE

In an extended freewrite, apply Veblen's theories to any cultural artifact(s) with which you're familiar: explain the ways in which your chosen artifact—whether novel, movie, comic strip, advertising campaign, magazine series, televised cartoon—satirizes or otherwise critiques that phenomenon known as the "American Dream."

THE UNLUCKIEST CONSUMER IN THE WORLD

Michael Petracca

Creative writers find the germ of their inspiration in many places. For some, a beautiful sunset might inspire a sonnet about the glories of the natural world. For others, a flea bite might cause lyrical flights of fancy involving metaphors of human sexuality. In this short story by novelist and popular culture critic Michael Petracca, the author finds the inspiration for his fictional account in the most unlikely of places: the Product Recalls section of *Consumer Reports.* Every month, that magazine includes a section devoted to the various consumer items that for some reason have been determined to be defective and potentially dangerous, and that have therefore been recalled by their manufacturers. In this story, Petracca imagines a nightmarish scenario in which one individual—the "unluckiest consumer" in the title—happens to purchase all the recalled items that are listed in one issue of *Consumer Reports,* and with predictably disastrous results. As you read this story, note the childlike tone and style the author chooses to imply, and consider why he made such an artistic choice. Consider also the underlying economic theme of this story: what message is the author slyly making about the relationship of corporate America to us, the faithful and trusting consumers?

Michael Petracca was conceived in Brooklyn and born in Los Angeles. After moving to Santa Barbara in pursuit of advanced degrees, Petracca became a full-time lecturer in the Writing Program at the University of California, Santa Barbara, where he has taught for the past seventeen years. Petracca teaches fiction and writing workshops at Antioch University and the UCLA Writers' Program as well. As a youngster, Michael enjoyed watching sudsy clothes tumble in the laundry room. This unnatural behavior evolved into a passion for surfing during his high school and college years. In addition to teaching and surfing, Petracca also dedicates himself to writing. His publications include novels, such as Doctor Syntax *and* Captain Zzyzx, *college-level writing texts, short stories, and articles on interpreting the products of popular culture.*

> You can have binding repaired by manufacturer or authorized dealer—or, if you make repair yourself, you will get free corduroy hat.
> —*Consumer Reports*

It had been a hard year for Mary Grace, and she didn't understand   1
much of it. First her mommy went to heaven in January, when the electrical

Source: "The Unluckiest Consumer in the World" by Michael Petracca, *Turnstile,* Winter 1991.

circuitry in the center console of the family's 1988 Saab 9000—the one her father bought Mommy as an anniversary surprise—overheated and then caught fire. That made Mommy take her eyes off the road for a second because she thought there was a big bumblebee in the driving compartment, but it was really an ash from her burning Fiesta City street map which had been sitting on the console when it overheated. In that moment a bicycle rider came around a corner, and when Mary Grace's mommy saw the man frantically waving and then turning his bike over onto the pavement, she swerved to miss him and slammed the automatic-transmission Saab 9000 into a parked pickup truck. Mary Grace was in ballerina class when Mommy died behind the wheel of the Saab. For months after the funeral, Mary Grace imagined Mommy coming through her bedroom door with cool, dry goodnight kisses and her scent like peach soda and jasmine blooms, but she never did.

That was hard, and then Daddy had to go to the hospital after his 1988   2 Volkswagen Jetta's brake line leaked, causing partial brake failure. Daddy couldn't steer the car very well with the brakes malfunctioning like that, so he bumped into a tree and wrenched his neck so badly that he had to be in traction for a number of days. Mary Grace stayed with Aunt Rose but got to visit her father. Aunt Rose dropped Mary Grace off at the front of the hospital and the doors opened all by themselves. A nice lady in a pink-striped dress accompanied her up the elevator and showed Mary Grace where her daddy was, and he was happy to see her. He said he would be out of the hospital soon and they would go to Kiddieland to ride the ponies and the little boats that went around in a circular trough of water. The day after he got out of the hospital, and with every intention of making good his promise, he buckled her into the back seat of a rented 1990 Geo Storm—he had learned from a TV show that children are safer in the back seat—but when he used the release lever to tip his seatback forward, he caught his finger in the hinge mechanism and had to drive to the emergency room for X-rays. Luckily the finger wasn't broken, so the doctor, whose white plastic lapel tag said, "Jack D. Hobbs, M.D.," bandaged it up. Mary Grace thought her daddy's finger looked like a big white lollipop with a fudge center. It was too late to go to Kiddieland, though, so they went home.

His finger still throbbing a little and his neck surrounded by a cloth-   3 covered polyfoam brace, Clark Spataro derived pleasure from imagining how he was going to make Mary Grace happy. It had been a heartbreaking year for Clark, too, and sometimes he felt as though Mary Grace was the only thing in his life that kept him going. Saturday was her seventh birthday, and he was planning a party to which all her friends would come, the best party ever. He was listening affectionately to his daughter play Barbie-house on the floor of her bedroom, when he smelled smoke coming from his Aqua Hex one-gallon aquarium. The fish were swimming around as though nothing were going on, but Clark could see that the electric light mounted inside the metal top of the aquarium had gone out. He turned off the light, which made the aquarium stop smoking, and then reached into the water to make sure the Aqua Clear Power Head aquarium pump, model 200, was still working properly—the fish would quickly die without it—and received an electrical jolt of such amplitude that it threw him back, halfway across the dining room, where he lay stunned on his deep-loop Berber remnant for several moments before regaining full consciousness. When Clark got up and inspected the aquarium, all the fish were floating inertly on the top of the water, from which a cloud of steam rose and then evanesced into the air. Clark was sad for his fish but cheered himself by listening to Mary Grace, who was still holding pretend conversations between Barbie and Ken and one of their friends whose name he couldn't remember. He thought it might be Whitney.

The next day Clark, who held a middle-management position at a 4 major airborne delivery service, called in sick. He used his burned hand as an excuse, but really he wanted to spend the day buying prizes for Mary Grace's birthday. Driving the rented Geo Storm all around town, he was so filled with the spirit of celebratory promise that he didn't even notice the traffic or mind the lines at the stores. At the K Mart in the Fairplex Plaza he bought Mary Grace a Ceramic Potpourri House, item #32-67-47, with a special electrical "Tealight Candle" that he knew his daughter would like, because it would go with her Barbie House. While he was there, he also bought several seven-ounce cans of It's Fun Tyme! String Confetti, taking care to select product cans marked, "Safe for the environment, fluorocarbon free," because he knew from another TV show that spray cans were doing something bad to the ozone layer around the earth: either putting more ozone there, or displacing the ozone with aerosol gases, he couldn't remember which. At the Toys R Us store in the new Paseo Tranquillo mall with its conquistador-theme architecture and red-tile roofing, Clark bought Mary Grace a bright red "Musical Ice Cream Car," model D13/3, which had a rear crank for winding up the music box feature. The ice cream decals on the front, sides, back and top of the Ice-Cream car reminded Clark of his childhood, when he used to chase the Good-Humor man down the street on hot summer days, and it made him feel good to think about those carefree times. Before leaving the Toys R Us store, Clark also bought eight Siren Whistles by Lucky Star Enterprises, model #69096 (SKNO81825) in a variety of colors—yellow, white, red, blue, orange, green, pink, and black—so that all the children at Mary Grace's party would have their own special noisemakers and nobody would feel left out of the fun.

Clark made sure to arrive home before the school bus dropped Mary 5 Grace off, in order that he'd have time to closet his purchased treasures behind a collection of dusty wing-tipped oxfords and calf-high side-zipped boots that he never wore. When Mary Grace came in the back door and set her metal Jetsons lunch pail on the kitchen counter, Clark gave her a kiss and said, "Honey, I need you to stay out of here for a little while, because

I'm going to be making a surprise for you. Can you do that for Daddy?" Clark wanted to bake Mary Grace's birthday cake himself, the way his deceased wife, Carin, used to. At first Mary Grace was a bit wounded that her father was sending her away, but she knew that Daddy was doing something for her birthday, so she shouted, "Priiiiizes!" and bounded out the spring-loaded kitchen door, which swung back and forth several times and came to rest in its closed position, leaving Clark alone in the kitchen.

Clark had never baked a cake before, but he had Carin's wooden   6
recipe box, its flip-top painted with enamel designs of flowers. The box was packed tightly with blue-lined flashcards and scraps of paper separated by alphabetical dividers. Under "G" Clark had found "Grandma Comstock's Chocolate Cake," a stained and spotted recipe card which called for sugar, real Vermont maple syrup, baker's chocolate, margarine, baking powder, eggs, flour, and milk, all of which Clark had purchased at the store on the way home from the bicycle store. The first instruction, written in his dead wife's loopy hand (it always made Clark nostalgic and weepy to see his wife's handwriting), was: "Pulp the margarine in the blender to bring it to soft consistency, like tapioca pudding." Clark had never heard pulp used as a verb before, but he knew how to put things in the blender, so he took their La Machine III, model LM5, food processor out of the cabinet below the electric range console and set it on the counter next to Mary Grace's lunch pail. He plugged it into the wall socket and removed the smoke-tinted plastic bowl cover in preparation for mixing ingredients in the processor's cylindrical bowl. Unfortunately, moving the bowl cover also overrode the machine's safety interlock mechanism, and the processor whirred unexpectedly into activity while Clark's hand was inside. He was merely startled at first by the motor sound and felt a kind of pulling sensation, but when he saw fine droplets of red liquid misting out of the top of the rotating bowl, he comprehended that he must have cut himself and withdrew his hand. To his horror, the tip of his right index finger was no longer there, and blood was pouring forth from the laceration and running down his hand and wrist. Clark was moved to shout, "I cut off my finger!" at the top of his lungs, but he didn't want to alarm Mary Grace, so he hoarsely whispered, "Ahh, my finger, my finger," over and over while he covered the gushing wound with paper towels to stanch the blood flow.

After the shock of having partially amputated his finger subsided a bit,   7
Clark ran his hand under warm tap water to inspect the damage. It wasn't as bad as he had imagined. True, his finger terminated abruptly and flatly where before it had been rounder and more elongate, and blood was seeping from several exposed capillaries, but the processor blades had missed the bone and sliced off only a cross-section of flesh, leaving the nail intact. Surprisingly, the cut didn't hurt very much, either. Clark remembered having heard about people who had whole appendages sewed back on after getting them severed in industrial accidents, so he looked inside La Machine

for the rest of his finger. Sure enough, there inside the red-spattered mixing bowl was the missing tip, which looked something like a blanched almond that had been dipped in shrimp cocktail sauce. Although Clark felt somewhat queasy at handling his own mutilated appendage, he picked up the fingertip with his better hand—the one that had the bandaged finger—and put it inside a Glad sandwich bag, which he secured tightly by pressing its two flaps together at the interlocking Ziploc ridges. Taking care to compose himself so as not to frighten Mary Grace, Clark peeked his head inside his daughter's bedroom door and told her, "Daddy got a little owwie on his finger, honey. Let's go see the doctor at the hospital."

"The hostiple?" Mary Grace whined. "Do we have to go there, Daddy?"   8

"Yes, honey, Daddy cut his finger."   9

"Again?"   10

"Last time Daddy pinched it. This time I cut a different one in La Machine," Clark explained, adding, "You can bring Barbie and Whitney along if you want to."   11

"Kimberley," Mary Grace corrected him.   12

At the emergency room, Clark left Mary Grace, Barbie and Kimberley in the waiting area that had a children's annex well-stocked with storybooks and rag dolls and colorful wooden blocks. Doctor Hobbs, a squat, muscular man with a gray-streaked beard and long black hair combed straight back, joked with Clark, "Back again so soon? Maybe you should rent a room here," while slipping on a pair of rubber gloves and gesturing for Clark to extend his hand, which he did. "Let's have a look," said Doctor Hobbs. "Mm-hm, ah-yess," he intoned, turning Clark's hand over several times in his own gloved hands. "I'm afraid there's not much we can do to save the tip," he told Clark, explaining the reasons in medical terms that Clark didn't comprehend completely. As he stitched up the wound, Doctor Hobbs went on to predict that Clark might have some permanent loss of feeling in his finger, but that the wound would otherwise heal just fine. "It might even be a plus, if you plan to go into certain areas of crime, like burglary," Doctor Hobbs appended.   13

"Burglary?" asked Clark, still shocky from the food processor incident and therefore not quick to pick up less-than-explicit meanings.   14

"Sure," quipped the doctor. "No fingerprints."   15

Saturday morning, while Mary Grace played with her extensive collection of plastic horses in the TV room, Clark set about making preparations. From his shoe-closet Clark retrieved a flat brown paper bag that contained party favors he had picked up from the Hallmark store during one of his errand runs. He blew up some Maeno-Ma "Happy Party Balloons," item #B91, tied short lengths of ribbon to the knotted-off valves of the remaining balloons and taped them up all over the dining area and front room. In the kitchen he stuck nine bud-shaped plastic candle holders into the prepackaged devil's food cake he had picked up on the way home from the doctor's, placed an equal number of pastel colored, helical-twisty candles into the   16 holders, and then put the cake in the icebox. As he overspread the dining table with a blue polythene tablecloth and laid it out with matching paper plates and cups, Mary Grace came in, a plastic chestnut-brown mare in one hand and a grayish foal in the other. Clark, glancing up at the clock, asked, "Don't you think you ought to start getting ready, lambie?"

"For my party?" she asked in a tone of coy expectancy.   17

"Your friends will be here pretty soon," said Clark, adding a musical lilt   18
to the last two words.

"Oh-kaay," enthused Mary Grace and ran off, only to return several   19
minutes later, curtseying and twirling theatrically in a pink taffeta dress and shiny black pumps. Clark told Mary Grace she was just about the cutest thing he had ever seen, and she jetted off to play horses some more.

The first party guests began to arrive just after noon. Marcy Bratton   20
came first, and then Kotsya Nikitin and Ronnette McCullough and Diane Moreling, all bearing gaily wrapped gifts. Nan Carmody and Toni Moniz showed up next, and right behind them Mary Grace's best friend, Emily Wrightson, in a red jumper and black party shoes. Emily's little sister, Carly, came along too, toddling and clutching her "Kensington Bears" stuffed grizzly cub which was wearing a maroon print frock with pink and blue ribbon trimming at the bottom, white lace bloomers and a straw hat with a pink bow. The bear's dress had little heart-shaped buttons. Emily explained that her parents had to go to some kind of brunch, but that they would be back before the end of the party, to take care of Carly and help cleaning up. Clark liked the part about cleaning up.

Several of the kids immediately moved to Mary Grace's room, where   21
they pretended Ken was a cowboy riding plastic horses, while Marcy and Kotsya sat at the spinet and produced a passable four-handed version of "Heart and Soul." Clark meanwhile arranged his stackable Virco chairs, series 890, around the table and then announced, "All right, children, let's all sit down." The kids took a while to drift into the dining room, but eventually they seated themselves, still chattering, around the table. Clark remained standing. "I'm glad you could all come," Clark orated, pouring a waxed-paper cup of apple juice and handing it to Kotsya, who passed it on to Marcy, and so on. As Clark poured juice for all the kids, he told them that it meant so much that they could be here on Mary Grace's special day, and then he took a seat away from the table, remembering that as a child he didn't enjoy having his parents nearby when his friends were around. He moved one of his Virco chairs next to the patio sliding glass window, and when he sat on it, the Virco 890's leg collapsed. Luckily, it was a front leg that buckled, so Clark didn't fall backwards through the plate glass window and sever an artery. All the girls laughed because they thought Clark was clowning for their benefit.

Standing up and brushing off his slacks even though there was no dirt   22
or house dust on them—he had vacuumed earlier—Clark told the kids it

might be a good time to open presents, and everyone cheered in agreement. Mary Grace opened her gifts one by one, commenting briefly on each
and thanking its donor, just as her parents had drilled her over the past
seven years. The Ceramic Potpourri House was her favorite; when Clark
plugged it into the wall and switched on the electrical "Tealight Candle," all
the girls said, "Oooh!" and "Pretty!"

"And now," Clark paused to sustain the dramatic effect already created 23
by the candle, "it's time for cake."

"Yumm," said Nan Carmody. 24

"It's chocolate," Mary Grace said. 25

"Chocolate. Num-nummies," said Kotsya Nikitin. 26

"Yes, but before I bring out the cake, I have a little present for each of 27
you, too." Clark reached into a brown paper sack while the children sat
open-mouthed with anticipation. When Clark passed around the Siren Whistles by Lucky Star Enterprises, the kids seemed a bit disappointed, and he
even thought he heard Diane Moreling mutter, "I'll say it's little," but they
started blowing through the Siren Whistles anyway, so that the dining room
sounded like a congress of asthmatics in pollen season. Clark didn't mind
the noise, though; if Mary Grace was having a good time, then he was
happy.

While the children were wheezing away on their sirens, Clark went into 28
the kitchen and got the cake out of the refrigerator. After lighting the candles
one by one, he pushed open the swinging door and made a grand entrance,
singing, "Happy Birthday to youuu!" with all the girls joining in merry discord.
Clark set the cake down on the table, and Nan Carmody told Mary Grace,
"Go ahead, make a wish." While Mary Grace closed her eyes solemnly, in
the manner of a saint receiving a beatitude, Clark produced the can of It's
Fun Tyme! String Confetti from the brown paper bag, and at the precise moment when Mary Grace opened her eyes and took a big breath in preparation for blowing out the candle, Clark began spraying aerosol party
streamers from the can and shouting, "Happy birthday!" Multi-colored
streamers jetted from the can's nozzle, twisting and sprawling and looping in
the air, draping themselves on the hanging light fixture over the table. The
girls all Oohed again, and Clark let fly another blast of It's Fun Tyme!, this
one aimed a bit lower than the previous.

A big mistake, lowering the can: The still-lit birthday candles ignited the 29
aerosol propellant, causing the can to become a sort of blow-torch that set
fire to Marcy Bratton's gingham dress. Marcy began screaming and slapping
at her right shoulder and bouncing up and down, which caused her Virco
stackable chair to collapse. All the partiers were paying horrified attention to
Marcy's distress, so nobody noticed that the "Tealight" candle on the Ceramic Potpourri House had meanwhile shorted or overheated, thereby starting a small fire on the other end of the table, beginning with the Ceramic
Potpourri House itself, and then spreading to the paper tablecloth, which

began smouldering and then flaming, so that the hem of Kotsya Nikitin's dress and petticoat burst into flame and she, too, started shrieking and slapping at herself and rolling on the floor. Ronnette McCullough and Diane Moreling and Nan Carmody were so shocked by the sight of their good friends' clothing being incinerated that they breathed in a collective sigh of horror and inhaled several small parts from their Siren Whistles, which lodged in their windpipes. They clutched at their throats and attempted futilely to expel the intrusive whistle-parts by coughing. Toni Moniz, who had been playing with the Musical Ice-Cream Car, was moved to help her stricken friends, but her initial horror at witnessing the escalating birthday carnage caused Toni to squeeze the toy car tightly; it broke into several pieces with sharp points that lacerated Toni's hand, so that a rivulet of blood began running down her forearm and she, too began shrieking. Little Carly Wrightson, who had been playing on the floor with the JA-RU "Play to Learn" furniture, had the plastic boy in her mouth and swallowed it when Nan Carmody fell out of her collapsed Virco chair and onto Carly's back, and little Carly started gagging, a look of panic frozen on her reddening face.

Clark had no idea what to do with so many choking, burning, gagging,   30
bleeding, and panicking children, but as fortune would have it, Bill and Carol Wrightson arrived from their brunch. When they came upon the scene, Bill and Carol reacted first by stunned disbelief, then with hasty paramedical action. Trying to calm the terrified children as best they could with soothing words, the Wrightsons helped Clark load all the kids into their 1989 Chrysler LeBaron GTS van with nonturbo 4, and Bill, pale, shaky and aghast, asked Clark where the nearest emergency facility was. Clark told him, and Bill gunned the van down the residential streets and onto the coast highway toward Schooner Valley General, but on the way some engine oil leaked from the faulty valve-cover gasket, causing a fire in the van's engine compartment. The fire produced so much smoke, and so quickly, that Bill Wrightson was momentarily unable to see well enough to steer. Instead of turning the wheel so that the van might follow the big bend in the coastline at Castellamare, he kept the LeBaron going straight. Realizing his error, Bill hit the brakes hard, but his Hercules Tires, no. UPHFKE 179, failed, causing the van to lose traction. When the van went airborne after hitting the canted asphalt shoulder, Mary Grace looked out the window and saw a bird flying by at the same speed that the van was flying. She imagined for a moment she was a bird, too, flying heavenward to visit her mommy. Clark shouted something, possibly the name of his deceased wife, Carin, but it was scarcely decipherable because other people started shouting just before the LeBaron hit the granite-scrapple seawall embankment and tumbled all the way down into the Pacific, its waters gray and craggy as crumpled sheet metal. The Wrightsons' recall notice arrived from Chrysler some days later, but nobody was home to read it.   ©

CRITICAL READING

1. What kind of man is Clark, the story's protagonist? What kinds of things happen to him in the course of the story? Is Clark at fault for the mishaps in the story, or do external forces play a more important role?
2. Why does the author choose to include small details, such as the serial numbers of the recalled items from *Consumer Reports?* Why does he include actual products from the "real" world in an otherwise fictional story?
3. Describe the narrative structure of this story. How does the author deliver background information about his characters? How does he keep the reader's interest? How does he build narrative tension? Where would you say that the story's major climax occurs?

CLASS DISCUSSION

1. How would you describe the tone of this piece? How does the story end? Why does the author choose to have the story end in this way? What thematic points are suggested by this short story's resolution? Discuss some "alternative" endings for this story; how would the substitute endings alter Petracca's intended message(s)?
2. Some movies are criticized for being "one-joke wonders"—that is, they repeat the same basic motif throughout, and as a result, the piece becomes boring for many viewers. From your experience with movies, provide some examples of this phenomenon, and then discuss "The Unluckiest Consumer in the World" in light of this concept. Does this story fail artistically because it relies on a singular motif—people get hurt by faulty consumer items—or is it actually strengthened by such repetition?

DIRECTED FREEWRITE

Freewrite a brief narrative (a sequence of events in some kind of chronological order) involving a traumatic encounter between yourself (or a loved one, a friend, or an acquaintance) and some product of corporate America: a car accident, a snowboarding mishap in which your bindings broke, a fall from atop a pair of platform shoes. For the purposes of this freewrite, feel free to use the same ironic tone as Petracca uses in "The Unluckiest Consumer in the World," or if you wish, you might make your story more darkly tragic than Petracca's, for example.

LITERARY STUDIES UNIT WRITING ASSIGNMENTS

1. Write an analytical essay in which you focus on contemporary "texts" to demonstrate ways in which corporate America has appropriated the youthful spirit of rebellion or individuality to market its wares, and, ironically, to homogenize young people in the process. For the purposes of this essay, you can interpret "text" broadly to include words (or even nonverbal images) delivered through

contemporary books, magazines, websites, popular song lyrics (including rap
and hip-hop), advertisements, television programs, and so forth.

   Use specific examples from several of these broad areas to illustrate ways in
which the identity of young people might be constructed by these texts or artifacts. Also, feel free to adopt a contrary thesis: that you and your peers are not
homogenized by media-generated texts and that young people manage to retain
their individuality and rebelliousness in the face of this media onslaught.
2. Here's a poem written by contemporary author Tom Wayman:

Unemployment

The chrome lid of the coffee pot
twists off, and the glass knob rinsed.
Lift out the assembly, dump
the grounds out. Wash the pot and
fill the water, put everything back with
fresh grounds and snap the top down.
Plug in again and wait.

Unemployment is also
a great snow deep around the house
choking the street, and the City.
Nothing moves. Newspaper photographs
show the traffic backed up for miles.
Going out to shovel the walk
I think how in a few days the sun will clear this.
No one will know I worked here.

This like whatever I do.
How strange that so magnificent a thing as a body
with its twinges, its aches
should have all that chemistry, that bulk
the intricate electrical brain
subjected to something as tiny
as buying a postage stamp
Or selling it.
Or waiting.

From *Living on the Ground* by Tom Wayman. Published in 1980 by McClelland & Stewart,
Inc. Reprinted by permission of Harbour Publishing Co. Ltd. and Tom Wayman.

   Based on your having read and understood Canterbury's discussion of economic themes in *The Great Gatsby,* write an explication/analysis of "Unemployment," pointing out any economic themes you see playing out in the poem, along
with any other ideas that the poem suggests.

An explication/analysis essay looks at a textual artifact on two broad levels, the literal (explication) and the implied (analysis). In the explication portion of the essay, you will do a close reading of a text to determine what the words mean and how they are arranged to create meaning. Explication concerns itself with surface elements, such as character; point of view (omniscient, intrusive, first person, etc.); setting (when and where); tone (the attitude of the speaker toward subject and/or characters); and diction (the author's choice of words for persuasive or emotive effect). By contrast, the analysis portion of the essay will discuss the poem's underlying meaning(s) or theme(s). Analysis concerns itself with figurative language, such as image (an appeal to one of the five senses, a mental "picture" evoked by the poem); symbol (something concrete that stands for and embodies something abstract, such as the billboard eyeglasses in *Gatsby,* which might represent God looking down on the characters); metaphor (an indirect comparison or renaming of something or someone); simile (a direct comparison using "like" or "as"); and personification (giving human characteristics to something that is not human).

Read the Wayman poem carefully, explaining how its words work together to convey meaning on the literal level, and then go on to discuss the thematic elements contained in the poem.

3. Most (if not all) of the writing assignments in this textbook ask you to engage in some kind of academic writing: a research essay, an argumentative piece, a summary, and so forth. By way of imaginative relief, this writing assignment asks you to come up with something nonacademic, for the sheer joy of indulging your creative muse and for practice in writing concretely and evocatively, which will lend interest to your academic writing. Building on the freewrite at the end of "The Unluckiest Consumer" piece in this unit, create a story that involves a traumatic encounter between a character of your actual acquaintance (or a character of your invention) and a corporate product.

The freewrite suggests some possibilities—an automobile accident, a snowboarding mishap, a fall from atop a pair of platform shoes—but you can undoubtedly come up with highly charged and narratively effective encounters of your own. As you construct your story, try to be conscious of avoiding the very pointed focus that you want to stress in academic essays. Whereas most modes of academic discourse build from a singular and assertive thesis statement, short stories do just the opposite: they imply many possible themes and usually take great care not to "hit the reader over the head" with a social message. In other words, just tell your story with as much sense detail as you can, and let your readers derive their own meaning(s) from it.

Unit 2
Popular Music Studies— Corporations and Creativity

WHO CONTROLS THE MUSIC?

Mark Crispin Miller

It has been a common—and, to many observers, alarming—fact of the late-twentieth and early-twenty-first century that large multinational corporations have purchased many of the traditional manufacturers and purveyors of popular art. Whereas once small publishers used to take risks on beginning writers, now the large conglomerates, attuned to bottom-line economics, are less likely to take such risks. Likewise in Hollywood, where the corporate movie studios are more likely to make carbon-copy facsimiles of successful movies than to take chances on new and groundbreaking scripts. In this article, a social commentator observes the same phenomenon taking place in the popular music industry, which, as with movies and books, is more than ever driven by profits. Miller, a member of the Department of Culture and Communications at New York University and the author of the recent *Mad Scientists* (a study of United States propaganda), notes some problems with the ways in which the six major corporations dominating the music industry—Capitol-EMI, CBS, MCA, PolyGram, RCA, and Warner—conduct their business. As you read this article, notice Miller's tone and rhetorical stance: while he works in an academic setting, he takes care to appeal to a broader, magazine-reading audience by establishing a more conversational (and less rigorously academic) tone ("Wouldn't it be nice . . .") and a less objective ("sadly," "sublime") point of view. Think also about his persuasive position: although Miller presents his thesis eloquently and convincingly, how might corporate executives and/or certain artists defend the pop-musical status quo?

Mark Crispin Miller received his B.A. from Northwestern University and his M.A. and Ph.D. in English from Johns Hopkins University. Miller is a professor of media studies at New York University and is known for his

Source: "Who Controls the Music?" by Mark Crispin Miller in *The Nation,* August 25, 1997. Reprinted by permission of *The Nation.*

*writings on film, television, advertising and rock music which have ap-
peared in numerous journals and newspapers, including* The Nation *and*
The New York Times. *Additionally, he has written several books including*
Boxed In: The Culture of TV; Mad Scientists: The Secret History of Modern
Propaganda *and he is currently working on* Spectacle: Operation Desert
Storm and the Triumph of Illusion. *Miller also directs the Project on Media
Ownership (PROMO) which raises public awareness as to the problem of
a few American culture industries controlling too much of our media.*

Wouldn't it be nice if rock and roll was once a good time pure and sim- 1
ple—and not a cutthroat business, too? Sadly, that sweet music always had
the Man behind it, counting the receipts and yelling "Shake your money-
maker!" At first, there were crafty profiteers like Leonard Chess, who stiffed
Chuck Berry and Bo Diddley; Roulette Records' Morris Levy, whose broad
influence on early rock—*Variety* dubbed him "the Octopus" in 1957—owed
plenty to his mob connections; and "Col." Tom Parker, who kept as much as
50 cents out of every dollar Elvis made from the end of 1955 until his death
(and after it).

But the biggest beneficiaries of pop's commercialism, finally, were no 2
lone goniffs, but the major record companies, which really cleaned up in the
sixties. Though they'd been slow to spot the gold in rock and roll (because
their people hated it), the majors soon caught on, then prevailed: Warner,
CBS, PolyGram, RCA, MCA and Capitol-EMI had 81 percent of U.S. market
share by 1974. (By the early eighties, the Six had also taken over distribution, driving out the many independent firms that had long supplied the
record stores.) The profits were immense—high enough to lay the basis of
the national entertainment state: Warner Bros. could not have gone on to
become the largest media corporation in the world without that awesome income from electric blues and acid rock.

The Six went global in the eighties. After a calamitous post-disco crash 3
in 1979, the industry bounced back, thanks mainly to the compact disc. As
millions chucked their vinyl for the pricier CDs, the business surged again;
and several media giants, hot to rock the whole wide world, came courting.
Thus were the Six sucked into the transnational behemoth that now the
whole world sing (and which is outlined in our latest gatefold chart): CBS
went to electronics giant Sony of Japan in 1985, then RCA went to Bertelsmann of Germany, PolyGram (owned by the Dutch electronics giant Philips)
bought Chrysalis, then Virgin; and MCA (now owned by the Canadian booze
giant Seagram, and renamed Universal) bought Geffen Records. And so the
Warner empire (Time Warner as of 1990) was the only major U.S.-owned
purveyor of the great forms of American music—rock, r&b, blues, country,
jazz—while Bruce Springsteen was making product for the Japanese, and
Elvis Presley had become a German asset.

Today, this international cartel is striking out—a crisis that's the ner-   4
vous buzz of all the industry, and a frequent topic in the business press. The
slump began in 1994, when the rush on CDs ended. With our vinyl oldies all
replaced, "sales of tried-and-true catalog titles, from Sinatra to the Stones,
have dried up," Forbes reports. Meanwhile, the new stuff isn't selling. Sales
of rock have been going down—from 46 percent of the total U.S. market in
1987 to 33 percent last year—and pop has also slipped (from 14 to 10 percent). R&b and country have each jumped a bit (to 11 and 16 percent, respectively), and rap has jumped three points (to 9 percent). Yet even that
bold, booming genre may be headed for a downswing, according to some
close observers. ("Hip-hop's market probably peaked in '93 or '94," says rap
label manager Jeff Chang. "Nobody wants to admit it, but it's true.") In any
case, overall unit sales are flat, so such slight generic increases don't make
much difference.

Typically, the business is now trying to save its bacon by promoting yet   5
another costly format: the digital versatile disc (DVD), a six-track gizmo that
promises extreme fidelity—and whose coming would force us all to buy new
discs and a new thing to play them on. But no high-tech fix will solve the
problem, because it's not the hardware that's unpopular. There is "a general
lack of enthusiasm for current product," as one Smith Barney observes. The
business now is so commercial it's turning people off. Quoting a study by
two industry associations, she notes that "consumers generally perceive the
music industry as 'focused on profit' and 'unoriginal.' As a result, follow-up
albums that are rushed to market have received a cold reception from consumers."

Surely that big chill has many causes, some larger than the current   6
practices within the business. First of all, rock's definitive outrageousness
may finally be impossible, now that everyone has seen it all already. "To
me, that's what rock and roll should always come down—the unallowed,"
says punk band manager Lee Black Childers, noting a theatrical faux-
terrorism that has clearly run its course, leaving us with big bad circus acts
like Marilyn Manson. More important, the rise of MTV et al. has taken some
intensity out of the sound—by lessening the impact of live shows, by favoring hot bodies over talent and by forcing every tune to take a back seat to
those hypnotic, easy visuals.

Artists can and do resist such deadening trends, although it's getting   7
harder all the time—which is where the music business is to blame. Although clearly out to make big bucks, the majors of the sixties also had the
sense to listen to the musical advice of their "house freaks"—hip young producers who would freely cruise the scene in search of genius that the majors might invest in for the long term. That's all over, now that the industry
belongs to tone-deaf giants that want only quick returns. Thus today's "general lack of enthusiasm" is a mass response to the industry's refusal to seek
out and nurture acts that might build up a loyal following. "The shortsighted,

slash-and-burn policies of the '90s," writes Michael Greene in Billboard, "have virtually eradicated any kind of sound, coherent approach to the development of new talent." Instead, those working for the Six seek only blockbusters, just like their counterparts within the giants' book and movie units—whose output has also received "a cold reception from consumers."

On the one hand, the Six spend tons on elder stars, through mammoth "megadeals" that have yielded many duds. "Since 1991, Michael Jackson, Janet Jackson, Aerosmith, Motley Crue, The Artist Formerly Known as Prince, ZZ Top and the Stones have all signed megadeals," reports Keith Moerer. "Stars who sign megadeals," as he notes, "never seem to produce great albums musically," nor do such works earn out those vast advances— money that will not be spent on several artists just as good, and still unknown. 8

Meanwhile, the Six are also overspending in their scramble for the Next Hot Thing—which, by the time it hits the stores, won't even be lukewarm. "EMI Records is looking for its own 'Macarena'—but with a Far Eastern flavor," began a recent article in Billboard. Likewise, since the relative success of Philips' Hanson, a just-pubescent trio of Nordic siblings out of Oklahoma, there's been a run on other little kids with talent; last year Ben Kweller, 16, had more than a dozen labels fighting to sign Radish, the child's band. Such "copycat signing," says Billboard's Melinda Newman, is "one of the biggest problems in the industry," freezing out musicians who don't fit an image set by someone else. 9

That conformist pressure has affected every genre. "Now how many women rockers do we have?" asks Georges Sulmers, owner of the independent hip-hop label Rawshack. "It's not because all these people came out of the woodwork. It's because it's like, 'Maybe we can tap into that Alanis Morissette thing!' And now we're going to see a lot more ska bands because [Seagram's] No Doubt has sold however many records." Rap too has been homogenized—as well as brutalized—by the copycat disease. It's mainly gangsta rap that the giants want, says Sulmers, "because lyrics about guns and women sell." 10

Thus the Six will often sign young performers not for their musicianship but because they're so derivative. That impulse is, of course, not new (Dick Clark got very rich off pallid types like Fabian and Chubby Checker), but today it drives the industry from top to bottom, Greene observes: "A&R folks [talent scouts] run in packs, desperate to sign flavor-of-the-month acts, many of whom are just learning how to tune their instruments." Even those with talent don't have too much time to rise. "Years ago, artists were given a much longer shot at making it. You're no longer guaranteed that chance," says Newman. Today, she notes, an act is lucky to be carried for a year or two, until its CD finally sells—as with Jewel, or the Gin Blossoms. Although it's striking nowadays, such a wait would not have been remarkable some thirty years ago, when your label would have stuck with you through several albums, not just one. 11

And if you do break through, that corporate pressure never to be differ-   12
ent can be as stifling as rejection. "Once an act succeeds, their attitude is
'Don't change.'" says Sulmers of the major labels. "It halts the normal progression of what people do musically." "They had very narrow expectations
of what I should do," Michelle Shocked said recently of Mercury (i.e.,
Philips), whom she had sued to break her contract. Even huge success
does not insure artistic freedom; on the contrary. What the giants want most
today is not, say, ten CDs that may each gross $12 million, but one monster
album that will gross ten times as much: Michael Jackson's *Thriller,* Springsteen's *Born in the U.S.A.,* Alanis Morissette's *Jagged Little Pill* (which has
to date earned $200 million for Time Warner). If it works, that strategy—
called "going deep" into an album—makes a major's chiefs feel very good.
("That was a great marketing experience," Al Teller, former head of CBS
Records, reminisces fondly about Springsteen's album.) But that protracted
blowout, although lucrative, may stall the artist, who will now spend roughly
two years dedicating all his or her energies to what Fred Goodman calls "the
industry's new holy trinity: videos, touring and label promotion." That means
two years of playing the same old song(s)—and then a different singer will
replace you, because your follow-up will surely be a letdown (even if it sells
"only," say, 7 million copies).

Such aesthetic stasis, and those inflated expectations, cannot do an   13
artist any good; but that bad influence doesn't matter to the Six, who are no
more interested in powerful songs than in good novels or hard-hitting magazines. What matters to them, rather, is the media machine itself; and so they
concentrate on "product" they can stretch into as many forms as possible—
soundtrack albums, cover stories, TV shows and videos, ads, T-shirts, hats,
whatever. It is that synergistic strain that's turning off "consumers," who are
right to think they're being hustled, and that they've heard it all before.

In prior times of pop ennui—the early fifties, the age of arena rock and   14
disco—the independents ultimately shook things up. Such renewal is less
likely now, because within the seeming universe of "independent" labels,
there's a whole lotta fakin' goin' on (see Janine Jaquet's "Media Matters").
"There's a lot of ignorance about what's actually independent and what's
not," says rock band manager and lawyer Jamie Kitman. "Often record companies that appear independent are actually funded by major labels." It may
be part or total ownership that puts the majors in control or it might be the
all-important vehicle of distribution. Although there are still some true maver-
icks such as Profile, Rykodisc and Righteous Babe (although not Maverick,
which is co-owned by Time Warner), most indies now are tiny start-ups with
no audience. Disney is now the lion king of "independents," and the source
not only of the merry soundtrack albums for, say, Hercules but also of, for
example, the Suicide Machines' *Destruction Definition,* a tight blast of suburban ska ("I don't give a shit about you stupid motherfuckers!").

The rough graphics of punk rock, and the def posturing of gangsta rap,   15
obscure many CDs' corporate provenance. Along with Michael Jackson,

Celine Dion and Neil Diamond, Sony also brings us Rage Against the Machine ("Fuck the norm"), owns Ruthless/Relativity (Bone Thugs-n-Harmony) and Ruffhouse (the Fugees), and distributes Bag, Risky Business, Slamm Dunk, Outburst and Hard Hands. Bertelsmann—publisher of *Fitness, Child* and *Family Circle,* and owner of BMG Christian Music Service also distributes Time Bomb, Deconstruction Radikal and Sick Wid It, and co-owns Bad Boy Entertainment (the Notorious B.I.G.) and Loud Records (WuTang Clan).

This grand ingestion of the independents is recent corporate policy, 16 says rock historian David Sanjek. The majors started buying up the indies in the nineties as a way to "maximize all means of generating income." A giant will now snap up whole labels rather than mere acts because such ownership permits it to exploit the songs and the musicians throughout its other media.

Moreover, the apparent gritty "independence" is itself a salable mys- 17 tique—an attitude that often replaces musical invention. Kids won't shell out for an act that doesn't seem authentic: "Your cultural capital loses credibility," as Sanjek puts it. (According to New York deejay Bobbito Garcia, owner of rap label Fondle 'Em, the giants try to imitate the raw look of the indie discs.) And so, however carefully you scan that shrink-wrapped "underground" CD—the one you bought at Borders or Sam Goody—you may not know that you've just given several dollars to a multinational that also makes HARM missiles, say, or floods the inner cities with cheap wine.

And yet there is a world of music out there—still crazy, precious, free, 18 sublime. Turn the radio off (to quote the title of the new CD from ska band Reel Big Fish) and, if you go looking for them, you will find a scattered multitude of excellent musicians ready, willing and quite able to (as Little Richard shouted) rip it up—the great American expression of a spirit that no league of suits can ever quite suppress, however grimly they keep looking for more ways to make the music pay. In that spirit, and for the sake of those musicians, we should look closely, and critically, at what the Six are up to because the music has always fought back, and has been the better for it. ©

CRITICAL READING

1. Explain the statement, "The business now is so commercial it's turning people off." What are the specific "commercial" qualities of contemporary popular music that are causing people to take less interest in new releases?
2. The phrase "going deep" into a record album refers to what preoccupation on the part of producers? How might the drive to "go deep" into albums contribute to musical stagnation?
3. What is meant by the term "house freaks" in the music business? In the past, what role did house freaks play in the success of certain record labels? Why do the current music industry executives have less interest in the house freaks, and what has been the result, in the author's opinion?

4. How has the corporate "monopoly" of the music industry compromised the originality of independent artists and record labels, in Miller's estimation?

CLASS DISCUSSION

1. What is the cause for the recent slump in music sales, according to Miller? What steps is the music industry taking to combat this slump? What other steps might you propose to revitalize the music industry?
2. Outline the history of commercialism in popular music, as set out by Miller. What are the roots of today's corporate interest in rock, hip-hop, and so forth? On the basis of your own knowledge of pop musical forms, what other examples can you cite for the pervasive influence of corporate interest in musical artistry?

DIRECTED FREEWRITE

Miller ends his article with the statement that "we should look closely, and critically, at what the Six are up to because the music has always fought back, and has been the better for it." In a focused freewrite, note the ways that musicians past and present have resisted the corporate pressure for homogeneity, and brainstorm some ways in which musicians of the present and future can "fight back" to counter this numbing corporate influence.

WORLD CITIES AND WORLD BEAT: LOW-WAGE LABOR AND TRANSNATIONAL CULTURE

George Lipsitz

In many university music programs, one will find students majoring or minoring in a subdiscipline called ethnomusicology: the study of music as it reflects and helps shape cultures around the world, both historically and in the present. One facet of ethnomusicology focuses on our own contemporary culture and on the ways in which the pop music of the United States helps define who we are. In this essay, author George Lipsitz, a professor at the University of California, San Diego, looks at the way popular music serves as a sensitive register of economic changes in black and Latino communities. As you read, notice the ways in which the author combines three major disciplinary threads—popular musicology, economic theory, and contemporary ethnography—into one focused argument.

George Lipsitz earned his A.B. from Washington University in 1968 and his M.A. from the University of Missouri, St. Louis in 1975. In 1979, he was awarded a Ph.D. in history from Washington University. In the course of his career, Lipsitz has taught at several universities including the University of Minnesota, Mount Holyoke College, the University of Houston at Clear Lake City, and the University of Missouri, St. Louis. Currently, he is a professor and Department Chair in Ethnic Studies at the University of California, San Diego. His primary areas of interest are 20th Century African American History, Cultural Theory, and Race and Ethnicity in Mass Media. Lipsitz has used his background to write several texts including The Possessive Investment in Whiteness: How White People Profit From Identity Politics; Dangerous Crossroads: Postmodernism, Politics, and the Poetics of Place; Rainbow At Midnight: Labor and Culture in the 1940s; The Sidewalks of St. Louis; Time Passages: Collective Memory and American Popular Culture; *and* A Life in the Struggle: Ivory Perry and the Culture of Opposition.

The grass-roots realities of everyday life for residents of global cities like Miami and Los Angeles rarely find expression in public pronouncements by politicians or in the public relations-oriented journalism of commercial, electronic, and print media. The ways in which people make meaning for themselves in the context of dramatic social change can be discerned, however, through critical interpretation of the links between changes in popular music and the demographic and social life of the city. Popular music in Miami and Los Angeles serves as an especially sensitive register of recent changes in black and Latino identities under the press of massive immigration, the rise of low-wage labor, the evisceration of the welfare state, and the disturbances in sexuality and gender roles provoked by new social relations. The emergence of hip hop, dancehall reggae, and banda music reflects new trends in commercial culture in these two cities, as well as emerging social identities and social relations.

Los Angeles and Miami have experienced parallel periods of growth as centers of metropolitan, regional, and national economic activity. Both cities have exploited their oceanfront locations and mild climates to attract tourists, migrants, and federal spending for infrastructure development and improvement. Yet the imperatives of industrial urbanization that once shaped Miami and Los Angeles no longer determine their cultural configurations or directions of economic development. With the rise of satellite, fiber optic, and computer chip technologies, the attendant globalization of management, marketing, and investment, and the migration of refugees and immigrants fleeing austerity conditions in the Southern Hemisphere to pursue low-wage jobs in the previously industrialized countries, cities like Los Angeles and Miami have become global rather than national or regional centers. Every aspect of urban life—from the costs of child care to the price of drugs on the streets, from the identities of clerks in convenience stores to the quantity of capital available for investment—reflects the increasing integration of global cities into international networks.

Immigrant capital and immigrant labor have played vital roles in trans-   3
forming Miami and Los Angeles into global cities. Cuban American investors and entrepreneurs positioned Miami to fill a leadership role in the economies of the Caribbean and South America through the formation of banks, import-export companies, transportation, and service companies. At the same time, low-wage labor by Cuban American men and especially Cuban American women generates high profits for investors and low prices for consumers in the city's construction and apparel industries. Every month some 200 cargo ships and 5,000 cargo planes transport commercial goods through Miami. The city's airport and seaport account for 70 percent of the trade conducted between the United States and Latin America. Trade-related businesses employ 98,000 workers and net more than $13 billion annually in Miami. The city boasts more foreign-owned banks than any other U.S. city except New York. Similarly, the emergence of Los Angeles as the busiest customs district in the nation has depended in no small measure on the presence in the city of people of Asian and Latino origin with the language skills, personal connections, and cultural sensitivity conducive to conducting trade in Asia and Latin America. At the low-wage end of the economic spectrum, exploitation of immigrant labor has benefited agribusiness, construction, tourist, and service industries. For example, the transformation of drywall work in home construction from a unionized high-wage job into a low-wage job performed mostly by immigrants forced down wages for that trade from eight cents per square foot in 1980 to four cents per square foot by the 1990s. This decline in wages imposed severe hardships on immigrant drywall workers in Los Angeles, but it lowered the costs of construction and increased profits for developers, contractors, and realtors.

Because of immigration to cities like Miami and Los Angeles, the   4
United States is now the fifth-largest Spanish-speaking nation in the world. If present population trends continue in Argentina and Columbia, the United States will have the third-largest population of Spanish speakers within the next decade. Forty percent of all persons of Puerto Rican ancestry now live on the North American mainland. More than 300,000 people from the Dominican Republic now dwell in New York City, while anywhere from 300,000 to 500,000 Salvadorans reside in Los Angeles. The number of Caribbean-born residents of New York City exceeds the combined populations of San Juan, Puerto Rico, Port-of-Spain, Trinidad, and Port-au-Prince, Haiti. New York contains what would be the second-largest Jamaican, Haitian, and Guyanese cities in the world. More people from the Caribbean island of Nevis live in New York City than live on Nevis itself. Likewise, Los Angeles

contains the second-largest urban concentrations of Mexicans, Salvadorans, and Guatemalans in the world, as well as one of the greatest concentrations of Iranians outside of Iran, Koreans outside of Korea, and Armenians outside of Armenia. The Samoan population of Los Angeles is larger than the population of American Samoa. Nearly 50 percent of the residents of Miami and Dade County are Latino, and nearly 20 percent are black. As early as 1980 foreign-born individuals accounted for 20 percent of Miami's black population, including 70,000 Haitians, 8,000 Jamaicans, 4,000 Bahamians, and 17,000 immigrants from other Caribbean, South American, and African countries. Under these circumstances, "local" life and culture in Miami and Los Angeles have decidedly international dimensions.

Miami maintains traces of its past as a national tourist destination and regional economic center, but it has also become an important crossroads for the entire hemisphere. The city is marked in distinctive and lasting ways by its Cuban, Haitian, Puerto Rican, Jamaican, and Nicaraguan populations, by its commercial links with Central and South America, and by the transformations these connections enact on the meaning of race, class, citizenship, and cultural franchise in the metropolis. The physical contours of Los Angeles remain visibly marked by decades of development and growth in the industrial era, most notably through the presence of dangerous toxic hazards and pollutants in residential neighborhoods. Traces of the industrial past also permeate Los Angeles culture through the enduring presence of recreational practices that originated in the technologies central to industrial production, like fiberglass for surf boards and hydraulic lifts for low rider automobiles—technologies that emerged in the auto and aerospace industries during the late industrial era. Yet Los Angeles today is also a prime port of entry and an ultimate destination for an astounding proportion of new immigrants, ranging from highly educated skilled workers from Korea to displaced peasants from remote areas in Guatemala. Links to Latin America and the Pacific Rim have transformed the physical spaces of Los Angeles— from the downtown office buildings owned by Asian investors to the street-level vending carts pushed by Central American immigrants in the Pico-Union section. 5

Globalization has changed social identities in Los Angeles as well; the influx of 600,000 Central Americans changes what it means to be Chicano for the nearly 3,000,000 people of Mexican origin in the city, while the migration of nearly 200,000 Koreans dramatically reconfigures the contours of the area's Asian American population. Indeed, demographic changes emanating from immigration change the meaning of all racial identities in Los Angeles by changing cultural networks, transforming the color of low-wage jobs, promoting new forms of entrepreneurial activity, and increasing competition for scarce resources. 6

While globalization affects nearly every aspect of urban life, the grass-roots realities of global cities rarely register in public pronouncements by politicians or in the public-relations oriented journalism of commercially 7 supported electronic and print media. Political competition among groups for scarce resources, as well as organized campaigns against immigrants and against bilingualism, may offer temporary visibility to globalization as a problem, but they occlude the important issue of how people make meaning for themselves in the context of dramatic social change, and they discourage understanding of the world that is emerging all around us. These attacks divert attention from the realities of low-wage labor, the hardships faced by workers (and the benefits that others derive from their exploitation), the shake-up in social identities engendered by migration, economic restructuring, and new communications media, and the creative adaptations and unlikely affiliations (and antagonisms) that emerge under current conditions.

Some of these new realities of global cities find representation through commercial culture, especially popular music. It is often the case that realities not yet possible in political life appear first within popular culture. Consequently, the world that is emerging all around us can be understood in part through analysis of the ways in which popular music in Miami and Los Angeles registers the changes in black and Latino identities enacted by massive immigration, as well as the ways in which these changes represent disturbances in gender roles and sexuality provoked by the new social relations in global cities. 8

Latinos and African Americans in Miami understandably enough view each other as competitors for political power and wealth. Nevertheless, the potential for coalitions appears often in cultural products, and the worlds of the two groups merge in different ways in popular music. Puerto Rican rapper Lisa M won a following among African Americans and in diverse immigrant communities with her song "Jarican Jive." Her recording mixed English and Spanish lyrics in celebrating the benefits of mixing Jamaican and Puerto Rican music. Similarly, African American rapper Luther Campbell's production of an interlingual Spanish-English hip hop song by his group, 2 Live Crew, features Debbie Bennett, the group's Honduran-born publicity director, rapping (obscenely) in Spanish. 9

Likewise, at a time when political rivalries and economic competition between organized African American and Latino groups in Los Angeles had reached an all-time high, African American hip hop artist Ice-T's half-Bolivian manager assisted Chicano rapper Kid Frost's attempts to secure a recording contract. Kid Frost, in turn, joined forces with Ice-T and with "Godfather" (from the Los Angeles Samoan rap group Boo Yaa Tribe) in public appearances where the three rap artists condemned censorship and gang violence while affirming the importance of interethnic unity. 10

African Americans in Miami share many cultural and political affinities with African Americans in other U.S. cities, but waves of migration from Caribbean countries give a unique cultural inflection to the local black culture. The musical components of Luther Campbell's "Miami Bass" sound and the similarity of his song lyrics to the sexual imagery in Jamaican 11 "dancehall" reggae demonstrate this Caribbean connection in clear and distinct ways. Mexican Americans in Los Angeles share a history of struggle against Anglo domination with their compatriots in New Mexico, Texas, and the upper Midwest, but continuing immigration from Mexico and Central America, combined with extraordinary ethnic and racial diversity in immigrant neighborhoods, has given rise to distinct new cultural identities evident in the popularity of banda music and Latin hip hop.

The emergence of 2 Live Crew in the early 1990s as an economically 12 successful hip hop group makes little sense on purely aesthetic grounds, given the members' limited talents as rappers and mixers. But as a social phenomenon, 2 Live Crew made sense as an expression of diverse currents attendant to the hip hop culture uniquely visible in Miami. The group's success came after it hired Joseph Kolsky as manager in the late 1980s. A former senior executive of Roulette Records in New York, the label featuring one of the first African American/Puerto Rican groups—Frankie Lymon and the Teenagers—Kolsky moved to Florida with the intention of playing golf and listening to big band tunes. Aware of his successful track record with rhythm and blues and disco artists in New York, Luther Campbell of 2 Live Crew coaxed Kolsky out of retirement. Under the guidance of Kolsky, an elderly Jewish American man described by his son as a conservative and prudish person, 2 Live Crew recordings made by Campbell's Luke Records secured gold and platinum status, with sales of 500,000 and 1,000,000 respectively, for songs titled "Me So Horny" and "Pop My Pussy."

Campbell and 2 Live Crew describe themselves as a "comedy act" 13 rather than a hip hop group. Yet the stylistic features they incorporate into their music reveal a good understanding of some aspects of hip hop, most especially its affinities for contemporary immigrant music, such as Jamaican "slackness" dancehall music and the Afro-Latin hip hop of the Caribbean and Central America. 2 Live Crew rose to prominence because of the group's sexually explicit lyrics, but the vehicle for delivering these words was a distinctive bass-oriented sound influenced by the Latino presence in Miami.

Campbell grew up in Miami's Liberty City ghetto and saw his first 14 turntable artists and rappers in African Square Park and at local radio station WEDR. He quickly sized up the profit-making potential in commercialized leisure. Even as a teenager, he leased a Pac-Man video game from a distributor and made money by inviting friends to his house to play (with their quarters). He refused to perform for free in the park like the other rappers in his neighborhood but secured paying jobs instead at skating rinks and school dances. Discussions of hip hop as an artistic form that realistically depicts many aspects of ghetto life often neglect its economic significance as one of the very few sites in our society where the knowledge and talents of innercity youth have value, where they can translate their skills into opportunities for economic upward mobility. For ghetto youths like Campbell, hip hop is about reality and a salary.

Many hip hop artists have surpassed Campbell artistically, but few 15 have displayed his ability to succeed financially or to attract lawsuits because of that success. The sheriff of Broward County sued him for performing obscene lyrics. George Lucas sued him for taking the stage name Luke Skywalker from *Star Wars* without permission. The Nashville publishing house Acuff-Rose sued him for an unauthorized parody of Roy Orbison's "Pretty Woman." Eventually, Campbell was vindicated in these actions, except the case involving Lucas, who forced him to change his label name to Luke Records instead of Luke Skywalker. Most critics have seen Campbell's repeated contests in the courts as deliberate publicity stunts that play important roles in his astute business strategy. It is also likely, however, that he has been targeted for attack because of his role in voter registration drives and his support for Janet Reno in her campaign for Prosecuting Attorney of Dade County against right-wing attorney Jack Thompson.

In addition to Campbell's flair for self-promotion and his run-ins with 16 political opponents, the Caribbean aspects of his music lead to yet another explanation of why he has had so many tangles with the law. Like Shabba Ranks, Buju Banton, Bounti Killer, Beenie Man, and other West Indian dancehall artists—or, for that matter, Jamaican-born Richard Shaw (a.k.a. Bushwick Bill) of the Houston rap group the Geto Boys, also known for their frank lyrics—Campbell's misogynistic "toasting" illustrates a more generalized hostility between men and women from aggrieved Caribbean communities at a time of extraordinary economic austerity. The frank discussion of sexuality in this music embarrasses some members of the community, making the music seem irredeemably sexist to some and pornographic to others. But all of these forms of moral evaluation evade the prior question of why these expressions have emerged at this time and what they mean for the people producing and consuming them.

Louis Chude-Sokei charges that dismissals of "slackness" lyrics as either sexist or pornographic miss the point. He notes the ways in which the sexuality of black women stands at the center of dancehall reggae's world. Chude-Sokei detects a strong strain of female self-affirmation in women's responses to the lyrics of male dancehall artists on the dance floor, as well as in the lyrics of women artists who take to the microphone themselves. Chude-Sokei explains that women buy more of these recordings than do men and that women control the dance floor in Jamaican dancehalls. Conceding that dancehall lyrics are offensive to Euroamerican feminist sensibilities, Chude-Sokei nonetheless argues that women dancehall fans "find both affirmation and power in the fear that their sexuality creates in the men. It allows them the freedom and security to navigate in and around a world of brutality, violence, and economic privation."

Like Chude-Sokei, Carolyn Cooper argues that sexual topics in dance- 18 hall lyrics provide an alternative to the denial of women's sexuality in most popular music. Music and cultural critic Andrew Ross endorses Cooper's claims, citing the overt and uninhibited demands for sexual pleasure by women in dancehall music as a positive alternative to gangsta rap's demonization of women as "ball breakers" and "gold diggers." Cooper also argues that the sex-affirmative songs by women in dancehall music need to be understood as a reaction against the masculinist and patriarchal politics of reggae with its biblically inspired Rastafarianism. The visionary black nationalism of 1970s Jamaican reggae proved tremendously appealing to political radicals in North America and Europe, many of whom failed to notice that reggae and Rastafarianism privileged male perspectives, advocated the subordination of women, and preached an asceticism that associates the female body with impurity. Reggae fans around the world have tended to see the rise of dancehall music as a degeneration from the morally and politically superior "conscious" reggae of the Bob Marley years. But these critics living outside the Caribbean have not had to confront the failures of 1970s radicalism, the costs of the economic austerity programs that followed, or the social disintegration and changes in gender roles imposed on Caribbean society over the past two decades.

Like Dominican merengue and bachata, Mexican banda, and West 19 Coast gangsta rap, "slackness" dancehall reggae reveals that one of the ways that men react to a global economy increasingly organized around the low-wage labor of women is through affirmations of masculine privilege and denigrations of female independence. Yen Le Espiritu points out that, in the current global economy, men generally lose social and economic status through migration while women secure advances in their status. Immigrant men of color suffer additional assaults on their dignity because of the racism in U.S. society. Similarly, Pierrette Hondagneu-Sotelo's brilliant research on Mexican immigrants indicates that, although immigrant men maintain more status and enjoy more mobility than immigrant women, immigrant men nonetheless lose power and status because migration undermines their authority within the family. Misogyny is an understandable if counterproductive response to this status anxiety.

In Jamaica over 60 percent of women worked full-time even before the 20 structural adjustment policies advocated by the International Monetary Fund (IMF) and the World Bank in the late 1970s. Efforts by global finance to restructure the Jamaican economy revolved around attracting capital with the lure of low-wage female labor for garment, textile, light assembly, data processing, and electronics work. Constituting more than 45 percent of their nation's labor force, Jamaican women already in the work force were well positioned to avail themselves of the opportunities for work as domestics, nurses, and child-care workers that opened up in global cities like New York and Miami in the 1980s and 1990s. Women also recognized quickly the ways in which migration from Jamaica to the United States could provide favorable opportunities for social independence through separation or divorce, and for economic upward mobility through the pursuit of professional credentials.

One manifestation of the misogyny exacerbated by new social rela- 20
tions comes through the symbolic value given to male perspectives in immigrant music, especially bachata, merengue, and dancehall reggae and rap.
In addition, the same loss of male self-respect that can lead to incisive critiques of racialized capitalism in popular music can also lead to a vicious homophobia. Slackness dancehall performer Buju Banton connects declining
educational opportunities and the rise of drug use in inner-city ghettos to a
plot by the rich who "no want see ghetto youth elevate out a the slum" and
consequently "give we all type a things [drugs], try turn we down." Nonetheless, in 1992, Banton also recorded "Boom Bye Bye," a song inciting anti-
gay violence. Similarly, Afro-Panamanian dancehall reggaespanol artist
Rude Girl (La Atrevida) attacks lesbians in "Lesbiana" because she thinks
they "harass woman" and refuse "procreation."

The important scholarship of Jacqui Alexander explains how postcolo- 21
nial economic and political elites have used heterosexuality, nuclear families, and traditional roles for women as key symbols of national
independence and integrity. Originally intended to displace slurs by colonial-
ists that stereotyped Third World men as hypersexualized rapists while portraying Third World women as sexually aggressive "Jezebels," this
discourse of sexual respectability has become the last refuge of neocolonial
scoundrels as they sell out the political and economic autonomy of their nations to global capital. They attempt to portray their own nations as modern,
safe, and appealing to outsiders by persecuting homosexuals, suppressing
women, extolling the nuclear family, and policing sexuality. In this context,
as Andrew Ross argues, the homophobia of dancehall reggae plays into
the hands of neocolonial cultural elites, while at the same time the sex-
affirmative pro-pleasure politics of Lady Saw, Patra, Lady Apache, and
Shelly Thunder create cultural and social spaces with distinct counter-
hegemonic possibilities.

Consequently, the "obscene" lyrics of 2 Live Crew need to be seen, at 22
least in part, as a result of their connections in Miami to ragamuffin "slackness" dancehall and to dancehall reggaespanol. At Luther Campbell's obscenity trial, Harvard professor Henry Louis Gates correctly noted the long
history of misogynist and sexually explicit rhymes within African American
oral traditions like playing the "dozens." Yet part of Campbell's significance
comes as well from his blending of African American and Caribbean traditions. In Hallandale and other Miami suburbs and neighborhoods, West Indian dancehall music by Bounti Killer, Beenie Man, and Buju Banton
provides a focal point for a vibrant immigrant dancehall subculture. Miami
has become, in fact, the second-largest dancehall market outside the West
Indies, trailing only New York City. Jamaican-born Miami DJ Waggy Tee
has drawn huge audiences to his weekly dances at the Cameo Theater
where he specializes in hip hop–style mixing and scratching. Dancehall in
Miami is not just another immigrant subcultural music but rather an import

that blends perfectly with hip hop in a fusion that leaves both musical styles transformed. One of Miami's leading DJs, Rory of Stone Love, explains, "Hip-hop and dancehall have the same beats. You can mix the records, and they will groove."

Andrew Ross points out that the emergence of dancehall reggae reflected two political changes: first, the demise of the political project announced by the appropriation of reggae by Michael Manley during his first term in office as Jamaica's president, and second, the victory of the IMF and the World Bank over efforts to correct the nation's maldistribution of wealth. The subsequent Edward Seaga and Manley regimes implemented the austerity demanded by the U.S. government and the international financial community with devastating results. These measures increased internal pressures to migrate to the United States, transforming not only Jamaican society but African American life and culture as well. At a time when large numbers of African Americans are now immigrants from the West Indies, any project aimed at racial unity needs to acknowledge and recruit those African Americans of Caribbean origin. 23

Chude-Sokei notes that dancehall has re-envisioned the African diaspora, moving beyond the Rastafarian vision in reggae that portrays the African past and future as the center of the diasporic imagination. Dancehall replaces attention to the African past and future with relentless attention to the here and now, to the documentary realities of poverty and racism and the suppression of pleasure and desire confronting Africans around the world. Chude-Sokei also notes that this vision is one that dancehall shares with hip hop. The two forms share a sexual hedonism that involves both large doses of sexism and profound commitments to sexual pleasure as an emotional and physical antidote to the aching muscles, frayed nerves, and psychic insults of lives oriented around low-wage labor. These affinities can be seen in many ways, such as the collaborations between hip hop artists and dancehall stars: Salt-n-Pepa with Patra, KRS-1 with Shabba Ranks, Special Ed's hip hop remix of Beenie Man's "slam," and Bounti Killer's 1996 album *Xperience* with guest appearances by Busta Rhymes, Rae-kwon, Jeru the Damaja, and the Fugees, themselves a fusion of Haitian American and African American music. 24

The backgrounds of the members of 2 Live Crew reveal the intercultural connections that link mainland North American hip hop to the Caribbean. DJ David Hobbs (Fresh Kid Ice) hails from California, Mark Ross (Brother Marquis) from New York, Chris Wong Won from Trinidad, and Campbell from Miami. In his autobiography, copublished in Jamaica by Kingston Publishers, Campbell identified Jamaican immigrants to New York as the originators of turntable mixing and scratching. Campbell's music testifies to Miami's important long-standing relationship with the anglophone Caribbean. Miami-based clear channel AM radio stations played a key role in alerting Bob Marley to the possibilities of fusing Jamaican music with 25

North American black music via broadcasts of Southern rhythm and blues and Motown "soul" music in the early 1960s. Jamaican musicians like Marley blended the music they heard broadcast by U.S. radio stations with Jamaican Burru, Kumina, Pocomania, and Nyabinghi rhythms. At the same time, reggae rhythmic patterns and chord progressions have long formed an important subtext of soul music from Miami. Campbell has attributed his trials for obscenity to the local political ramifications of this cultural mixing, especially to fear by whites and Cubans that Campbell's artistic and business success might prefigure political and economic cooperation between U.S.-born blacks and their Caribbean and West Indian cousins.

Just as migration from the hispanophone and anglophone Caribbean 26 has transformed the meaning of ethnic identities in Miami, the movement to Los Angeles of low-wage workers from Sinaloa, Jalisco, and Colima to clean pools, trim trees, prepare food, and provide child care for affluent families in Los Angeles has transformed the meaning of ethnic and racial identities in that city as well. These workers have little protection from employer mistreatment, Immigration and Naturalization Service harassment, or even vigilante violence. They find few politicians willing to speak out for their interests but many eager to seek advancement by demonizing hard-working and productive immigrants as parasites and interlopers. But while these workers lack power as citizens and as workers, they do have market power as consumers, as a target audience for advertisers. It is in that realm that new forms of Mexican American identity first became visible to the broader society in the early 1990s.

Largely because of an influx of immigrants from Mexico and Central 27 America, the Los Angeles Spanish-language daily newspaper, *La Opinion,* expanded its circulation by 155 percent between 1981 and 1991. Advertising revenue at the newspaper increased by 600 percent during the same ten-year period. In 1986 only six radio stations in Los Angeles broadcast Spanish-language programs, but by 1997 seventeen of the region's eighty-two stations broadcast Spanish programming exclusively. People of Mexican origin in Los Angeles have experienced great difficulty turning their demographic power into political power, but they have succeeded in turning the strength of their numbers into market visibility—especially through Latin hip hop and banda music, genres that represent for Los Angeles the same degree of interethnic dialogue and sense of sexual crisis that dancehall and Campbell's hip hop registered in Miami.

Deindustrialization, capital flight, and economic restructuring devastated black and Latino neighborhoods in Los Angeles during the 1980s. By the time of the 1992 insurrection, almost 20 percent of the city's young people between the ages of sixteen and nineteen did not have jobs and were not in school. Vicious police initiatives like "Operation Hammer," ostensibly aimed at "gang" members, led to the arrest and creation of criminal records for more than 50,000 minority youths. The shift from manufacturing to service jobs, rampant employer violations of minimum wage and other labor laws, and migration motivated by even more desperate conditions in Mexico and Central America left young Latinos as the poorest of the poor in the 1990s. At the same time, African American outmigration and Latino immigration, coupled with widespread discrimination in housing, left Latinos and blacks increasingly aligned as neighbors in inner-city areas stripped of opportunities and resources. As once nearly all-black South Central Los Angeles became 50 percent Latino, African American–based hip hop music became the preferred form of expression for many inner-city Latinos.

An early promotional video for Chicano rap artist Kid Frost featured a 29 group of very dark-skinned musicians in mariachi outfits as well as an African American interlocutor who originally mis-hears "Ya Estuvo" ("That's It for You") as "That's Stupid" but who gets corrected (and converted) to Spanish by Frost. Afro Cuban rapper Mellow Man Ace presented deft interlingual rhymes such as "I said, 'Hey, ya me voy' 'cause you ain't treating me like I'm some sucker toy," while in another song Kid Frost claimed, "I'm a chingon ese, like Al Capone ese." African American rapper Anthony Smith took the stage name "Tone Loc" from the nickname given to him by Spanish-speaking friends who referred to him as "Antonio Loco."

At a time when competition for scarce resources and the racial ten- 30 sions fomented within the state prison system increasingly pit aggrieved racialized minorities against one another, Latin hip hop groups Aztlan Underground, DarkRoom Family, Funky Aztecs, Cali Life Style, Proper Dos, Lighter Shade of Brown, and Delinquent Habits reference Chicano history in English and in Spanish, but they also acknowledge longstanding interactions among blacks and Latinos as well as other minority populations. The three members of Cypress Hill, a "Chicano" group from South Gate, include B Real (son of a Mexican American father and an Afro Cuban mother), Sen Dog (a Cuban), and Muggs (an Italian American). Cypress Hill proteges Funkdoobiest consist of a Mexican, a Native American, and a Puerto Rican who refer to themselves as a coalition of Aztec, Sioux, and Arawak origin.

Utopian desires for interracial reconciliation are not uncommon within popular culture, but the performers of Latin hip hop reflect the actual experiences of differentially racialized populations, not just abstract desires for transformation and transcendence. Yet if Latin hip hop helped build unity across racial lines, it often did so by expressing a shared masculine contempt for women. From the bikini-clad models "decorating" Kid Frost's vision of Chicano nationalism in "La Raza" to Mellow Man Ace's put-down of his girl friend as a "skeezer" and a liar in "Mentirosa," Los Angeles Latin hip hop expressed the same uneasy relations between the genders seen in Miami dancehall and hip hop productions.

If Latin hip hop has become the key venue in Los Angeles for express- 31 ing the things that different groups in the city have in common, banda music has come to represent the specific experiences and aspirations of recent immigrants from Mexico. In 1992 Spanish-language radio station KLAX-FM (La Equis) became the most popular radio station in Los Angeles—the world's most lucrative and competitive local radio market—by changing its format to banda music, a form aimed primarily at new immigrants from Mexico. This horn-heavy dance music from the west coast of Mexico, and the acrobatic quebradita dance craze associated with it, seemed like an unlikely candidate for commercial success in the Los Angeles market, but its emergence as an emblem of identity among new immigrants has given it an unexpected influence and prestige.

One key to banda's popularity derives from its connection to issues of immigrant identity. Banda artists and audiences flaunted their rural Mexican roots by wearing vaquero (cowboy) styles: stetson hats (called Tejanos), fringe jackets, leather boots, and tight jeans. Song titles referenced ranch life and rodeos, while dancers characteristically carried cuartos (small horsewhips). Males most often wore button fly jeans, fringed leather vests, felt or straw cowboy hats, and shiny boots. Women tended to wear tight-fitting jeans or western skirts, belts with big buckles, black stretch tops, and cowboy boots. Banda's dance rhythms, characteristic sounds, and the styles of its fans all signaled a distinctly rural and Mexican identity, one that made no move to assimilate into U.S. culture but also did not exist in the same form in any location in Mexico. The banda craze was a product of migration, an expression of immigrant consciousness, and a strategic and symbolic source of unity in the face of outside attacks.   32

Like dancehall music, banda music often met with disapproval from respected community leaders who saw it as a dangerous expression of exuberant sexuality among low-wage workers. The close dancing encouraged by the quebradita and the tight outfits favored by banda dancers displayed desires for pleasure more openly than many traditional Mexican Americans deemed acceptable. As migration changed the power realities between Mexican men and women at home and at the workplace, a resurgent hypermasculinity came to the fore within banda music, nowhere more evident than in the name of the genre's first superstar group, Banda Machos.   33

Sexism and homophobia are not the sole content of dancehall reggae, Miami hip hop, Latin hip hop, or banda. Each genre now seems to have moved beyond the sexism that it once represented. Slackness artists have moved past homophobia (in part because protests and boycotts limited their profit-making potential in North America and Europe) and turned to more spiritual and politically conscious themes. Luther Campbell has turned his efforts away from music altogether, toward a peculiar combination of philanthropy and pornography—he sponsors the annual children's Easter egg hunt in Liberty City while raising capital for a "black" alternative to *Penthouse* and *Playboy*. Latin hip hop no longer displays much of the cultural nationalist and masculinist bravado of Kid Frost's big hit "La Raza," and banda has crested as a musical form and a social force, becoming one   34 genre within a broader constellation on Spanish-language radio stations, dances, weddings, Quinceneras, and other social occasions. Yet dancehall reggae in English or Spanish, hip hop, and banda remain important sites for entrepreneurial activities and employment. They continue to arbitrate the contradictions low-wage workers face in their class, racial, gender, and sexual identities.

Music can be a sensitive register of changes in social relations that re- 35 main obscured when examined through other lenses. Popular music in Miami and Los Angeles at the present moment offers useful insights into the nature of globalization, its implications for racial and national identities, and the inescapable importance of gender and sexuality as the sites where some of the most important changes of our era are being experienced.

CRITICAL READING

1. Explain the author's statement that "every aspect of urban life—from the costs of child care to the price of drugs on the streets, from the identities of clerks in convenience stores to the quantity of capital available for investment—reflects the increasing integration of global cities into international networks." How do those individual details of urban life factor into an economics-based network that transcends cultural and geographic boundaries, in Lipsitz's view?
2. What specific financial evidence does Lipsitz provide to support his assertion that "immigrant capital and immigrant labor have played vital roles in transforming Miami and Los Angeles into global cities"?
3. Why does the author mention pop-culture-based technologies such as "fiberglass for surf boards and hydraulic lifts for low rider automobiles" as relevant to his discussion of Los Angeles's industrial past?
4. From an economic point of view, the author notes that Latinos and African Americans view each other as competitors for wealth. However, he also observes that "the potential for coalitions appears often in cultural products, and the worlds of the two groups merge in different ways in popular music." How do these two ethnic groups find common economic ground in the world of popular music, in Lipsitz's opinion?

CLASS DISCUSSION

1. Lipsitz sums up his essay's thesis this way: "Consequently, the world that is emerging all around us can be understood in part through analysis of the ways in which popular music in Miami and Los Angeles registers the changes in black and Latino identities enacted by massive immigration, as well as the ways in which these changes represent disturbances in gender roles and sexuality provoked by the new social relations in global cities." Discuss the way in which he organizes his supporting points to develop this argument. As you bring up each supporting point, discuss its merits on the basis of your own political/economic views and your knowledge of popular music.

2. Discuss the ways in which the author merges three different disciplinary approaches—popular musicology, economic theory, and contemporary ethnography—to develop his argument. What features of this article resemble popular music criticism, and how does Lipsitz merge his discussions of Miami-based and Los Angeles-based musical forms with an awareness of economic and cultural forces?

DIRECTED FREEWRITE

In an extended freewrite, explain the ways in which certain critics defend the sexuality and gender stereotyping in hip-hop and dance hall music, and then go on to discuss your own take on this defense of certain attitudes toward women as expressed in popular music. Do you agree with critics, for instance, that women "find both affirmation and power in the fear that their sexuality [as expressed in popular music] creates in . . . men," or do you have a different opinion on this score?

POPULAR MUSIC STUDIES UNIT WRITING ASSIGNMENTS

1. Critic Sheila Whiteley, in her new book *Sexing the Groove: Popular Music and Gender,* states "There is nothing 'natural,' permanent or immovable about the regime of sexual difference which governs society and culture," and she goes on to describe a "regime of sexual difference" that she believes to be perpetuated, at least in part, by popular music. In an argumentation essay, take a position on the issue of sexism and/or gender stereotyping in contemporary popular music, and support it with evidence derived from your own experience with music. Do you agree that women are generally degraded and objectified by popular music, or do you have a contrary opinion on this phenomenon—that popular music is, perhaps, a source of empowerment for members of both genders? As much as possible, use quotations from actual song lyrics to support the assertions you make in your essay's body paragraphs. Refer back to our discussion of argumentation in assignment 2 of the Social Psychology unit on page 60 of Chapter 2.
2. Write a recommendation essay focusing on the problem of large corporations controlling the music industry. A recommendation essay[1] is a form of argumentation in which the author convinces the reader that a certain problem exists, explains a number of alternatives to solving the problem, proposes a specific solution to the problem, and then concludes by discussing the feasibility of the proposed solution. Therefore, for the first portion of this essay, discuss Miller's thesis that the music industry—namely, the six major corporations that dominate the music industry, Capitol-EMI, CBS, MCA, PolyGram, RCA, and Warner—is in trouble because these large corporations will not allow new acts to become popular over a period of time. Draw on Miller's essay, and perhaps a bit of addi-

---

[1] A recommendation essay is similar to a position paper, which is typically written in political science. Although the focus and structure of both essays is almost identical, we don't call our assignment here a position paper because you will be discussing a somewhat more abstract problem and solution than is usually dealt with in position papers.

tional World Wide Web and library research, to develop this portion of your essay. Then, go on to discuss a number of possible alternative solutions to this problem, and, finally, select the solution that seems the most reasonable to you. In the conclusion of your essay, you might explain to the reader why your proposed solution would be feasible, given today's economic climate.

3. Both of the articles in this unit discuss the relationship between economics and contemporary popular music, suggesting that music—and musicians—cannot exist in a creative vacuum, separate from the demands and pressures of corporate capitalism. One such pressure you may not have considered is the copying of recorded music by consumers. Most of us at some point have engaged in this practice, considering it essentially harmless; yet the creative community would, for the most part, insist that when you copy a CD that you haven't paid for, you're stealing. Write a miniresearch/argumentation essay, in which you explore the World Wide Web and your school's library to determine whether there exists a need to find ways to protect the work of creative artists from being duplicated without fair compensation. Having completed a bit of research, go on to argue a specific thesis. You may end up believing, and therefore arguing, that if technology permits an activity such as music duplication, such activity must be permissable. However, you may also conclude that criminal penalties for violating a copyright should extend to individuals who copy CDs for their personal use. Whatever position you finally take, make sure that you back up your supporting arguments with evidence from your secondary sources, as well as from your own experience.

THINKING AND WRITING
IN THE SOCIAL SCIENCES

Unit 1
History—Financial Influences
Past and Present

TWO CHEERS FOR MATERIALISM

James Twitchell

Materialism—the belief that one's physical possessions constitute the greatest value in one's life—has been around since prehistoric humans began crafting (and presumably trading and hoarding) artifacts, yet it remains one of the most misunderstood personality traits. According to this article, adapted from James B. Twitchell's book *Lead Us Into Temptation: The Triumph of American Materialism,* although materialism may lead to certain social ills such as gender inequalities and poverty, it may also serve more positive functions in the modern world. As you read this piece, consider whether Twitchell—who is an English professor and not a history professor—has interpreted history correctly or whether he may be off the mark, on the basis of your own experiences with the consumer lifestyle.

James B. Twitchell received his Ph.D. from the University of North Carolina-Chapel Hill. He has been a professor at the University of Florida for almost thirty years and his areas of interest include commercialism and culture. He has written numerous books including The Living Dead: The Vampire in Romantic Literature; Romantic Horizons: Aspects of the Sublime in English Poetry and Painting 1770–1850; Dreadful Pleasures: An Anatomy of Modern Horror; Forbidden Partners: The Incest Taboo in Modern Culture; Preposterous Violence: Fables of Aggression in Modern Culture; Carnival Culture: The Trashing of Taste in America; Adcult USA: The Triumph of Advertising in America; For Shame: The Loss of Common Decency in American Culture; *and the forthcoming* Lead Us Into Temptation: Advertising Packaging, Branding Fashion and the Triumph of American Materialism.

Source: "Two Cheers for Materialism" by James Twitchell in *Wilson Quarterly,* vol. 23, no. 2 (Spring 1999). Copyright © 1999 by Woodrow Wilson International Center for Scholars. Reprinted by permission of Professor James Twitchell, University of Florida.

It's the thing that everybody loves to hate. But let's face it . . . material-   1
ism—getting and spending—is a vital source of meaning and happiness in
the modern world.

Of all the strange beasts that have come slouching into the 20th cen-   2
tury, none has been more misunderstood, more criticized, and more important than materialism. Who but fools, toadies, hacks, and occasional loopy
libertarians have ever risen to its defense? Yet the fact remains that while
materialism may be the most shallow of the 20th century's various -isms, it
has been the one that has ultimately triumphed. The world of commodities
appears so antithetical to the world of ideas that it seems almost heresy to
point out the obvious: most of the world most of the time spends most of its
energy producing and consuming more and more stuff. The really interesting question may be not why we are so materialistic, but why we are so unwilling to acknowledge and explore what seems the central characteristic of
modern life.

When the French wished to disparage the English in the 19th century,   3
they called them a nation of shopkeepers. When the rest of the world now
wishes to disparage Americans, they call us a nation of consumers. And
they are right. We are developing and rapidly exporting a new material culture, a mallcondo culture. To the rest of the world we do indeed seem not
just born to shop, but alive to shop. Americans spend more time tooling
around the mall—three to four times as many hours as our European counterparts—and we have more stuff to show for it. According to some estimates, we have about four times as many things as Middle Europeans, and
who knows how much more than people in the less developed parts of the
world? The quantity and disparity are increasing daily, even though, as we
see in Russia and China, the "emerging nations" are playing a frantic game
of catch-up.

This burst of mallcondo commercialism has happened recently—in my   4
lifetime—and it is spreading around the world at the speed of television. The
average American consumes twice as many goods and services as in 1950;
in fact, the poorest fifth of the current population buys more than the average fifth did in 1955. Little wonder that the average new home of today is
twice as large as the average house built in the early years after World War
II. We have to put that stuff somewhere—quick!—before it turns to junk.

Sooner or later we are going to have to acknowledge the uncomfort-   5
able fact that this amoral consumerama has proved potent because human
beings love things. In fact, to a considerable degree we live for things. In all
cultures we buy things, steal things, exchange things, and horde things.
From time to time, some of us collect vast amounts of things, from tulip
bulbs to paint drippings on canvasses to matchbook covers. Often these objects have no observable use.

We live through things. We create ourselves through things. And we   6
change ourselves by changing our things. In the West, we have even

developed the elaborate algebra of commercial law to decide how things are exchanged, divested, and recaptured. Remember, we call these things "goods," as in "goods and services." We don't—unless we are academic critics—call them "bads." This sounds simplistic, but it is crucial to understanding the powerful allure of materialism.

Our commercial culture has been blamed for the rise of eating disorders, the spread of "affluenza," the epidemic of depression, the despoliation of cultural icons, the corruption of politics, the carnivalization of holy times like Christmas, and the gnat-life attention span of our youth. All of this is true. Commercialism contributes. But it is by no means the whole truth. Commercialism is more a mirror than a lamp. In demonizing it, in seeing ourselves as helpless and innocent victims of its overpowering force, in making it the scapegoat du jour, we reveal far more about our own eagerness to be passive in the face of complexity than about the thing itself.   7

Anthropologists tell us that consumption habits are gender-specific. Men seem to want stuff in the latent and post-midlife years. That's when the male collecting impulse seems to be felt. Boys amass playing marbles first, Elgin marbles later. Women seem to gain potency as consumers after childbirth, almost as if getting and spending is part of a nesting impulse.   8

Historians, however, tell us to be careful about such stereotyping. Although women are the primary consumers of commercial objects today, they have enjoyed this status only since the Industrial Revolution. Certainly in the pre-industrial world men were the chief hunter-gatherers. If we can trust works of art to accurately portray how booty was split (and cultural historians such as John Berger and Simon Schama think we can), then males were the prime consumers of fine clothes, heavily decorated furniture, gold and silver articles, and of course, paintings in which they could be shown displaying their stuff.   9

Once a surplus was created, in the 19th century, women joined the fray in earnest. They were not duped. The hegemonic phallocentric patriarchy did not brainwish them into thinking goods mattered. The Industrial Revolution produced more and more things not simply because it had the machines to do so, and not because nasty producers twisted their handlebar mustaches and whispered, "We can talk women into buying anything," but because both sexes are powerfully attracted to the world of things.   10

Karl Marx understood the magnetism of things better than anyone else. In *The Communist Manifesto* (1848), he wrote: 11

> The bourgeoisie, by the rapid improvement of all instruments of production, by the immensely facilitated means of communication, draws all, even the most barbarian nations into civilization. The cheap prices of its commodities are the heavy artillery with which it batters down all Chinese walls. . . . It compels all nations on pain of extinction, to

adopt the bourgeois mode of production; it compels them to introduce what it calls civilization into their midst, i.e. to become bourgeois themselves. In one word, it creates a world after its own image.

Marx used this insight to motivate the heroic struggle against capital- 12
ism. But the struggle should not be to deter capitalism and its mad consumptive ways, but to appreciate how it works so its furious energy may be understood and exploited.

Don't turn to today's middle-aged academic critic for any help on that 13
score. Driving about in his totemic Volvo (unattractive and built to stay that way), he can certainly criticize the bourgeois afflictions of others, but he is unable to provide much actual insight into their consumption practices, much less his own. Ask him to explain the difference between "Hilfiger" inscribed on an oversize shirt hanging nearly to the knees and his rear-window university decal (My child goes to Yale, sorry about yours), and you will be met with a blank stare. If you were then to suggest that what that decal and automotive nameplate represent is as overpriced as Calvin Klein's initials on a plain white T-shirt, he would pout that you can't compare apples and whatever. If you were to say next that aspiration and affiliation are at the heart of both displays, he would say that you just don't get it, just don't get it at all.

If you want to understand the potency of American consumer culture, 14
ask any group of teenagers what democracy means to them. You will hear an extraordinary response. Democracy is the right to buy anything you want. Freedom's just another word for lots of things to buy. Appalling perhaps, but there is something to their answer. Being able to buy what you want when and where you want it was, after all, the right that made 1989 a watershed year in Eastern Europe.

Recall as well that freedom to shop was another way to describe the 15
right to be served in a restaurant that provided one focus for the early civil rights movement. Go back further. It was the right to consume freely which sparked the fires of separation of this country from England. The freedom to buy what you want (even if you can't pay for it) is what most foreigners immediately spot as what they like about our culture, even though in the next breath they will understandably criticize it.

The pressure to commercialize—to turn things into commodities and 16
then market them as charms—has always been particularly Western. As Max Weber first argued in *The Protestant Ethic and the Spirit of Capitalism* (1905), much of the Protestant Reformation was geared toward denying the holiness of many things that the Catholic church had endowed with meanings. From the inviolable priesthood to the sacrificial holy water, this deconstructive movement systematically unloaded meaning. Soon the marketplace would capture this off-loaded meaning and apply it to secular

things. Buy this, you'll be saved. You deserve a break today. You, you're the one. We are the company that cares about you. You're worth it. You are in good hands. We care. Trust in us. We are here for you.

Materialism, it's important to note, does not crowd out spiritualism;   17
spiritualism is more likely a substitute when objects are scarce. When we have few things we make the next world holy. When we have plenty we enchant the objects around us. The hereafter becomes the here and now.

We have not grown weaker but stronger by accepting the self-   18
evidently ridiculous myths that sacramentalize mass-produced objects; we have not wasted away but have proved inordinately powerful; have not devolved and been rebarbarized, but seem to have marginally improved. Dreaded affluenza notwithstanding, commercialism has lessened pain. Most of us have more pleasure and less discomfort in our lives than most of the people most of the time in all of history.

As Stanley Lebergott, an economist at Wesleyan University, argues in   19
Pursuing Happiness (1993), most Americans have "spent their way to happiness." Lest this sound overly Panglossian, what Lebergott means is that while consumption by the rich has remained relatively steady, the rest of us—the intractable poor (about four percent of the population) are the exception—have now had a go of it. If the rich really are different, as F. Scott Fitzgerald said, and the difference is that they have longer shopping lists and are happier for it, then we have, in the last two generations, substantially caught up.

The most interesting part of the book is the second half. Here Leber-   20
gott unloads reams of government statistics and calculations to chart the path that American consumption has taken in a wide range of products and services: food, tobacco, clothing, fuel, domestic service, and medicine—to name only a few. Two themes emerge strongly from these data. The first, not surprisingly, is that Americans were far better off by 1990 than they were in 1900. And the second is that academic critics—from Robert Heilbroner, Tibor Scitovsky, Robert and Helen Lynd, and Christopher Lasch to Juliet Schor, Robert Frank, and legions of others—who've censured the waste and tastelessness of much of American consumerism have simply missed the point. Okay, okay, money can't buy happiness, but you stand a better chance than with penury.

The cultural pessimists counter that it may be true that materialism   21
offers a temporary palliative against the anxiety of emptiness, but we still must burst joy's grape. Consumption will turn sour because so much of it is based on the chimera of debt. Easy credit = overbuying = disappointment = increased anxiety.

This is not just patronizing, it is wrongheaded. As another economist,   22
Lendol Calder, has argued in *Financing the American Dream* (1999), debt has been an important part of families' financial planning since the time of Washington and Jefferson. And although consumer debt has consistently

risen in recent times, the default rate has remained remarkably stable. More than 95.5 percent of consumer debt gets paid, usually on time. In fact, the increased availability of credit to a growing share of the population, particularly to lower-income individuals and families, has allowed many more "have nots" to enter the economic mainstream.

There is, in fact, a special crippling quality to poverty in the modern 23 Western world. For the penalty of intractable, transgenerational destitution is not just the absence of things; it is also the absence of meaning, the exclusion from participating in the essential socializing events of modern life. When you hear that some ghetto kid has killed one of his peers for a pair of branded sneakers or a monogrammed athletic jacket you realize that chronically unemployed poor youths are indeed living the absurdist life proclaimed by existentialists. The poor are the truly the self-less ones in commercial culture.

Clearly what the poor are after is what we all want: association, affilia- 24 tion, inclusion, magical purpose. While they are bombarded, as we all are, by the commercial imprecations of being cool, of experimenting with various presentations of disposable self, they lack the wherewithal to even enter the loop.

The grandfather of today's academic scolds is Thorstein Veblen 25 (1857–1929), the eccentric Minnesotan who coined the phrase "conspicuous consumption" and has become almost a cult figure among critics of consumption. All of his books (save for his translation of the *Lexdaela Saga*) are still in print. His most famous, *The Theory of the Leisure Class,* has never been out of print since it was first published in 1899.

Veblen claimed that the leisure class set the standards for conspicu- 26 ous consumption. Without sumptuary laws to protect their markers of distinction, the rest of us could soon make their styles into our own—the Industrial Revolution saw to that. But since objects lose their status distinctions when consumed by the hoi polloi, the leisure class must eternally be finding newer and more wasteful markers. Waste is not just inevitable, it is always increasing as the foolish hounds chase the wily fox.

Veblen lumped conspicuous consumption with sports and games, "de- 27 vout observances," and aesthetic display. They were all reducible, he insisted, to "pecuniary emulation," his characteristically inflated term for getting in with the in-crowd. Veblen fancied himself a socialist looking forward to the day when "the discipline of the machine" would be turned around to promote stringent rationality among the entire population instead of wasted dispersion. If only we had fewer choices we would be happier, there would be less waste, and we would accept each other as equals.

The key to Veblen's argumentative power is that like Hercules cleaning 28 the Augean stables, he felt no responsibility to explain what happens next. True, if we all purchased the same toothpaste things would be more efficient and less wasteful. Logically we should all read *Consumer Reports,* find out the best brand, and then all be happy using the same product. But we aren't. Procter & Gamble markets 36 sizes and shapes of Crest. There are 41 versions of Tylenol. Is this because we are dolts afflicted with "pecuniary emulation," obsessed with making invidious distinctions, or is the answer more complex? Veblen never considered that consumers might have other reasons for exercising choice in the marketplace. He never considered, for example, that along with "keeping up with the Joneses" runs "keeping away from the Joneses."

Remember in *King Lear* when the two nasty daughters want to strip   29
Lear of his last remaining trappings of majesty? He has moved in with them, and they don't think he needs so many expensive guards. They whittle away at his retinue until only one is left. "What needs one?" they say. Rather like governments attempting to redistribute wealth or like academics criticizing consumption, they conclude that Lear's needs are excessive. They are false needs. Lear, however, knows otherwise. Terrified and suddenly bereft of purpose, he bellows from his innermost soul, "Reason not the need."

Lear knows that possessions are definitions—superficial meanings,   30
perhaps, but meanings nonetheless. And unlike Veblen, he knows those meanings are worth having. Without soldiers he is no king. Without a BMW there can be no yuppie, without tattoos no adolescent rebel, without big hair no Southwestern glamor-puss, without Volvos no academic intellectual, and well, you know the rest. Meaning is what we are after, what we need, especially when we are young.

What kind of meaning? In the standard academic view, growing out of   31
the work of the Frankfurt school theorists of the 1950s and '60s (such as Antonio Gramsci, Theodor Adorno, and Max Horkheimer) and later those of the Center for Contemporary Cultural Studies at the University of Birmingham, it is meaning supplied by capitalist manipulators. What we see in popular culture, in this view, is the result of the manipulation of the many for the profit of the few.

For an analogy, take watching television. In academic circles, we as-   32
sume that youngsters are being reified (to borrow a bit of the vast lexicon of jargon that accompanies this view) by passively consuming pixels in the dark. Meaning supposedly resides in the shows and is transferred to the sponge-like viewers. So boys, for example, see flickering scenes of violence, internalize these scenes, and willy-nilly are soon out jimmying open your car. This is the famous Twinkie interpretation of human behavior—consuming too much sugar leads to violent actions. Would listening to Barry Manilow five hours a day make adolescents into loving, caring people?

Watch kids watching television and you see something quite different   33
from what is seen by the critics. Most consumption, whether it be of entertainment or in the grocery store, is active. We are engaged. Here is how I watch television. I almost never turn the set on to see a particular show. I am near the machine and think I'll see what's happening. I know all the channels; any eight-year-old does. I am not a passive viewer. I use the remote

control to pass through various programs, not searching for a final destination but making up a shopping basket, as it were, of entertainment.

But the academic critic doesn't see this. He sees a passive observer   34
who sits quietly in front of the set letting the phosphorescent glow of mindless infotainment pour over his consciousness. In the hypodermic analogy
beloved by critics, the potent dope of desire is pumped into the bleary dupe.
This paradigm of passive observer and active supplier, a receptive moron
and smart manipulator, is easily transported to the marketplace. One can
see why such a system would appeal to the critic. After all, since the critic is
not being duped, he should be empowered to protect the young, the female,
the foreign, the uneducated, and the helpless from the onslaught of dreck.

In the last decade or so, however, a number of scholars in the humani-   35
ties and social sciences have been challenging many of the academy's assumptions. What distinguishes the newer thinking is that scholars have left
the office to actually observe and question their subjects. Just one example:
Mihaly Csikszentmihalyi, a psychology professor at the University of
Chicago, interviewed 315 Chicagoans from 82 families, asking them what
objects in the home they cherished most. The adult members of the five
happiest families picked things that reminded them of other people and
good times they'd had together. They mentioned a memento (such as an
old toy) from their childhood 30 percent of the time. Adults in the five most
dissatisfied families cited such objects only six percent of the time.

In explaining why they liked something, happy family members often   36
described, for example, the times their family had spent on a favorite couch,
rather than its style or color. Their gloomier counterparts tended to focus on
the merely physical qualities of things. What was clear was that both happy
and unhappy families derived great meaning from the consumption and interchange of manufactured things. The thesis, reflected in the title of his co-
authored 1981 book, *The Meaning of Things: Domestic Symbols and the
Self,* is that most of the "work" of consumption occurs after the act of purchase. Things do not come complete; they are forever being assembled.

Twentieth-century French sociologists have taken the argument even   37
further. Two of the most important are Pierre Bourdieu, author of *Distinction:
A Social Critique of the Judgment of Taste* (1984), and Jean Baudrillard,
whose books include *The Mirror of Production* (1983) and *Simulacra and
Simulation* (1994). In the spirit of reader-response theory in literary criticism,
they see meaning not as a single thing that producers affix to consumer
goods, but as something created by the user, who jumbles various interpretations simultaneously. Essentially, beneath the jargon, this means that the
Budweiser you drink is not the same as the one I drink. The meaning tastes
different. The fashion you consider stylish, I think is ugly. If we buy the package not the contents, it is because the package means more.

The process of consumption is creative and even emancipating. In an   38
open market, we consume the real and the imaginary meanings, fusing

objects, symbols, and images together to end up with "a little world made cunningly." Rather than lives, individuals since midcentury have had lifestyles. For better or worse, lifestyles are secular religions, coherent patterns of valued things. Your lifestyle is not related to what you do for a living but to what you buy. One of the chief aims of the way we live now is the enjoyment of affiliating with those who share the same clusters of objects as we do.

Mallcondo culture is so powerful in part because it frees us from the 39 strictures of social class. The outcome of material life is no longer preordained by coat of arms, pew seat, or trust fund. Instead, it evolves from a never-ending shifting of individual choice. No one wants to be middle class, for instance. You want to be cool, hip, with it, with the "in" crowd, instead.

One of the reasons terms like Yuppie, Baby Boomer, and GenX have 40 elbowed aside such older designations as "upper middle class" is that we no longer understand social class as well as we do lifestyle, or what marketing firms call "consumption communities." Observing stuff is the way we understand each other. Even if no one knows exactly how much money it takes to be a yuppie, or how young you have to be, or how upwardly aspiring, everybody knows where yuppies gather, how they dress, what they play, what they drive, what they eat, and why they hate to be called yuppies.

For better or worse, American culture is well on its way to becoming 41 world culture. The Soviets have fallen. Only quixotic French intellectuals and anxious Islamic fundamentalists are trying to stand up to it. By no means am I sanguine about such a material culture. It has many problems that I have glossed over. Consumerism is wasteful, it is devoid of otherworldly concerns, it lives for today and celebrates the body, and it overindulges and spoils the young with impossible promises.

"Getting and spending" has eclipsed family, ethnicity, even religion as a 42 defining matrix. That doesn't mean that those other defining systems have disappeared, but that an increasing number of young people around the world will give more of their loyalty to Nike than to creeds of blood, race, or belief. This is not entirely a bad thing, since a lust for upscale branding isn't likely to drive many people to war, but it is, to say the least, far from inspiring.

It would be nice to think that materialism could be heroic, self-abnegat- 43 ing, and redemptive. It would be nice to think that greater material comforts will release us from racism, sexism, and ethnocentrism, and that the apocalypse will come as it did at the end of romanticism in Shelley's *Prometheus Unbound,* leaving us "Scepterless, free, uncircumscribed . . . Equal, unclassed, tribeless, and nationless."

But it is more likely that the globalization of capitalism will result in the 44 banalities of an ever-increasing worldwide consumerist culture. The French don't stand a chance. The untranscendent, repetitive, sensational, democratic, immediate, tribalizing and unifying force of what Irving Kristol calls the American Imperium need not necessarily result in a Bronze Age of culture. But it certainly will not produce what Shelley had in mind.

We have not been led into his world of material closeness against our 45
better judgment. For many of us, especially when young, consumerism is
our better judgment. We have not just asked to go this way, we have demanded. Now most of the world is lining up, pushing and shoving, eager to
elbow into the mall. Getting and spending has become the most passionate,
and often the most imaginative, endeavor of modern life. While this is dreary
and depressing to some, as doubtless it should be, it is liberating and democratic to many more.

CRITICAL READING

1. In the author's opinion, what psychological, sociological, and/or historical factors account for our culture's rampant materialism?
2. What does history teach us about the consumerism of men and women in past
   eras, according to the author of this article?
3. Who was Thorstein Veblen, as described by Twitchell in this piece? What are
   the key features of Veblen's theory of socioeconomics? How does this theory
   fall short, in the opinion of the author?

CLASS DISCUSSION

1. According to Karl Marx in 1848, "The bourgeoisie, by the rapid improvement of
   all instruments of production, by the immensely facilitated means of communication, draws all . . . nations into civilization. The cheap prices of its commodities are the heavy artillery with which it batters down all Chinese walls. . . . It
   compels all nations on pain of extinction, to adopt the bourgeois mode of production; it compels them to introduce what it calls civilization into their midst,
   i.e. to become bourgeois themselves." What does the word "bourgeois" mean in
   this context? How does making and selling of material "commodities" result in
   the spread of bourgeois culture, according to Marx? Argue for or against this
   Marxist/historical view of materialism's social effect.
2. Why, according to the author, should we not "demonize" materialism; what
   are his reasons for asserting, "The process of consumption is creative and
   even emancipating"? Argue in support of or in opposition to Twitchell's central
   thesis.

DIRECTED FREEWRITE

Do a twenty-minute freewrite in which you explore the materialism of yourself and
your close personal circle. Do you consider yourself a materialist? Do you have
other values that you place higher than the material ones? What about your friends
and family: cite as many concrete examples as you can as evidence for the materialism—or relative lack of it—in yourself, your friends, and your family.

THE MAKING OF AN UNDERGROUND MARKET: DRUG SELLING IN CHICAGO, 1900–1940

Joseph Spillane

Economic "historians understand marketplaces to be the kinds of 'space' " in which both social and economic relationships can be studied. It is interesting that the same appears to be true for illicit drug marketplaces, which have been highly visible centers of economic exchange in twentieth-century United States cities. This article examines the evolution of drug distribution in Chicago between 1890 and 1940, during which time a collection of independent "entrepreneurs" created underground drug distribution networks serving customers from throughout the city. Later, with the closing of Chicago's "Levee" district and the end of sanctioned vice, the drug trade moved into the "Black Belt" neighborhoods of the South Side. According to the author of this article, the concentration of drug selling in the Black Belt was not inevitable. Rather, it "had much to do with choices made by law enforcement and city government that implicitly endorsed a containment policy for drug marketplaces" within African American neighborhoods. As you read, notice the way that the author—like historians in general—relies on stories of bygone times to develop his points. What is the function of such extended narrative in the writing produced by historians?

Joseph F. Spillane received his Ph.D. from Carnegie-Mellon University in 1994. He is an assistant professor of criminology and history at the Center for Studies in Criminology and Law at the University of Florida. Spillane is the author of several articles and texts on drugs including Cocaine: From Medical Marvel to Modern Menace in the United States, 1884–1920.

Historians understand marketplaces to be the kinds of "space" which illuminate social and economic relationships. Taken together, the diverse transactions of the marketplace show how terms such as "community" and "neighborhood" are given meaning through daily activity. Studies from diverse settings have also demonstrated that marketplaces are institutions which bring into focus the relationship of one part of a city to the larger whole. This article suggests that the same appears to be true for illicit drug marketplaces, which have been highly visible centers of economic exchange in twentieth-century United States' cities. Although contemporary

1

Source: "The Making of an Underground Market: Drug Selling in Chicago, 1900–1940" by Joseph Spillane in Journal of Social History, vol. 32, no. 1 (Fall 1998). Copyright © 1998 by Joseph Spillane. Reprinted by permission of the publisher.

drug markets sometimes appear to be defining features of modern urban life, the identification of drug selling with particular city neighborhoods is a phenomenon as old as legal prohibitions on specific substances.

Despite the obvious importance of drug marketplaces, the social scientific literature of the twentieth century paid insufficient attention to drug selling as work, or as economic enterprise. Instead, scholars have employed several traditional analytical frameworks, including: the sociological view of drug selling as deviant behavior; participation in the drug market as a manifestation of addiction and the addict's "hustling" lifestyle; or drug marketplaces as a reflection of individual and community pathology, or more recently, of "underclass" formation. In each instance, drug marketplaces are meaningful only as extensions of certain moral, social, or ecological conditions. Even when the organization of drug distribution has been the object of historical investigation, prominent organized crime figures responsible for large-scale importation and wholesale distribution rather than retail level sellers have drawn the most attention.

Recent scholarly work from a number of disciplines suggests a new framework for historical analysis. One line of contemporary research employs a "market approach" which incorporates social and cultural context, and the ways they change over time. Vincenzo Ruggerio and Nigel South prefaced their 1995 study of European drug markets by describing illicit drugs "simply as commodities" which "shape and are shaped by demand and supply, exchange and consumption." Another line of contemporary research takes an ethnographic approach to the participants in drug markets. Representative studies include Patricia Adler's work on upper-level drug dealers in California, and Terry Williams' more recent ethnographic study of street-level cocaine sellers in New York City. Historical research into other forms of illicit enterprise also suggest ways in which drug markets might be apprehended. As Mark Haller observed, "in order to understand such activities . . . it is necessary to ask the same sorts of questions that would be asked concerning any other retail business activity."

This article examines the evolution of drug distribution in Chicago between 1890 and 1940. Few legal restrictions on the drug supply existed at the start of this period, but growing concerns over the popular use of opiates and cocaine led to efforts at limiting access. By the first decade of the twentieth century, a broad coalition of Progressive reformers in Chicago were able to curtail sharply the legal supply of "dangerous" drugs. As the legal supply of opiates and cocaine shrank, public pressure and law enforcement drove the drug marketplace into Chicago's well-known vice districts. Here, a collection of independent entrepreneurs created underground drug distribution networks serving customers from throughout the city. For a few, drug selling yielded enormous rewards and a measure of status in underground Chicago. For most drug sellers, their occupation brought a small measure of economic reward, always tempered by the risk of victimization or arrest.

With the closing of Chicago's "Levee" district, and the end of sanctioned vice, the drug trade moved into the Black Belt neighborhoods of the South Side. The concentration of drug selling in the Black Belt was not inevitable, but had much to do with choices made by law enforcement and city government that implicitly endorsed a containment policy for drug marketplaces.

PROTECTING NEIGHBORHOODS: THE ORIGINS
OF THE ILLICIT MARKETPLACE

Cities have long housed concentrations of "underground" trades in   5
sex, drink, gambling, or bawdy entertainment. Most large cities of the nineteenth-century United States had clearly defined vice districts, such as New Orleans' Storyville or New York City's Tenderloin, formally or informally protected by public policy which aimed to contain and isolate illicit activity. Until the twentieth century, however, drug selling was only marginally related to these enterprises. The primary exceptions were the opium dens which flourished in most vice districts in the last quarter of the nineteenth century. The social sanction on the use of opium for pleasure, its association with Chinese immigrants, and the desire of smokers themselves for close association outside of conventional society, combined to keep opium dens isolated. The other important link between drug selling and vice was the high prevalence of opiate use and addiction among female prostitutes.

In general, however, few or no formal legal controls constrained drug   6
distribution. Retail druggists were therefore free to dispense drug products to their customers, although a prescription requirement was increasingly common by the turn of the century. Over-the-counter medicines were widely available, any number of which might contain morphine or cocaine as a key ingredient. These same drugs were even available through the mail in some instances. Quite simply, the absence of formal or informal controls made specific underground markets unnecessary.

Underground drug selling did not appear overnight. The rise of "recre-   7
ational" usage of cocaine and opiates at the end of the nineteenth century, especially among socially and economically marginal groups, created a sense of public crisis. Attacking health and safety concerns both real and imagined, a powerful coalition of forces sought to close off legal access to certain drugs. The old legal market gradually faded away, the victim of informal pressure and formal legal restrictions, and was slowly replaced by an underground market bearing most of the characteristic features of the contemporary illicit drug trade.

Events in Chicago mirrored these national trends. By 1890, the city had   8
already developed well-defined vice districts, including the soon-to-be-famous "Levee" on the South Side. Herbert Asbury once wrote of the Levee that "the most disreputable superlative that could be imagined would fail to do it justice." Yet, with the exception of a vigorous campaign against opium

smoking in the 1880's, Chicago authorities still defined drug use as a private concern. Sensational stories of prominent individuals brought down by drug addiction emphasized the individual nature of the drug problem. Dr. Charles D. Bradley's story was representative: a compulsive cocaine user who initiated cocaine use at the height of his medical career, advanced to the use of one gram each day, subsequently lost his marriage, children, property and career, and was finally arrested for trying to kill a drugstore clerk who refused to sell him cocaine. Bradley's story may have been shocking, but it was not frightening. The unfortunate doctor was, at worst, a pitiable "victim of cocaine."

After 1890, two trends came together in Chicago (and elsewhere) to   9
redefine drug use as a public issue. First, the use of opiates and cocaine expanded among the residents of working-class, immigrant neighborhoods. Where drug use had once appeared to be a problem among the "respectable" classes, it now appeared to be prevalent among the socially and economically marginal. Second, Chicago's drug users were increasingly likely to be consuming for non-medical reasons, without much pretense of therapeutic necessity. Thus, the concerns over the characteristics of the city's drug-using population were joined by an equally strong distaste for their self-consciously pleasure-seeking behavior.

Cocaine was the first drug to become a major public concern. As in the   10
rest of the United States, the popular use of cocaine in Chicago grew tremendously at the turn of the century. Readily available in pure form or in a variety of over-the-counter medicines, cocaine attracted many new consumers. In the immigrant neighborhoods of Chicago's West Side, young boys discovered the pleasures of cocaine's stimulant and euphoriant effects. As one youth described it, cocaine made him feel "as if I was going up in a flying machine" or "as if I was a millionaire and could do anything I pleased." Concerned with their children's cocaine use, mothers brought the issue of drug sales from neighborhood pharmacists to the attention of Hull House. The Juvenile Court Committee reported a "restlessness and disposition to run away" among delinquent boys on parole from the John Worthy School which were "found to have their cause in the almost universal habit, among this class of boys, of using cocaine." Officers of juvenile courts also observed a number of children whose parents used cocaine, and concluded that chronic use of the drug could lead to parental neglect. By 1908 the phrase "as crazy as a West Side dope fiend" had entered the lexicon of city residents.

In 1904 Jessie Binford, who would later become the long-time head of   11
the Juvenile Protective Association, had just moved to Chicago and taken up residence at Hull House. For her first project, Binford was assigned the task of investigating the cocaine problem, identifying the source of sales, and eliminating those sales. Over the next several years, Binford organized a remarkable coalition of public and private Progressive reform interests. The attendees of a 1904 Hull House conference on the cocaine question highlighted the breadth of Binford's coalition: Binford, Jane Addams, Julia

Lathrop, public health pioneer Dr. Alice Hamilton, an attorney from the State Board of Pharmacy, several mothers of young cocaine users, local physicians, and representatives from the Chicago Bureau of Charities, the Chicago Police Department, and the Juvenile Court Committee. Binford was later joined by Municipal Court Judge Frank Sadler, and House of Corrections Superintendent John Whitman.

The efforts of the Hull House coalition must be distinguished from the activities of the many moral entrepreneurs who crowded into Chicago decrying the evils of drugs and drink. While evangelists and temperance advocates marched through the streets, the Hull House reformers introduced two distinct and important dimensions to the anti-drug movement. For the first time, public and private interests worked together to limit the legal supply of opiates and cocaine in the city. In addition, the anti-cocaine movement emphasized the traditional Progressive critique of corporate and business interests profiting at the expense of the public. As *The Commons* observed regarding the Hull House campaign, "greed for profits has led to crimes of every description, on the part of individuals and large corporation interests, but few have been more diabolical than the deliberate and designing plot to enslave young boys in the horrible toils of the cocaine habit." Finally, the Hull House coalition helped to define the drug problem as a public health issue. The cocaine campaign, for instance, immediately followed the efforts of Dr. Hamilton and others to reduce the incidence of tuberculosis and typhoid and to improve housing conditions on the West Side. Like the unsanitary tenements which produced disease and degeneracy, cocaine seemed to produce its own kind of degeneracy. The process was poorly understood, but the results seemed clear enough, as the Juvenile Court Committee observed: "quickly and surely the brain cells are destroyed, and victim is left a mental, moral, and physical wreck." [12]

To deal with the drug threat, the Hull House coalition sought to control the legal distribution system through passage of restrictive legislation. The result was a trial-and-error process of creating new state and local regulations. As early as 1893 the Illinois legislature had attempted to limit the popular use of opiates by imposing labeling requirements on patent medicine manufacturers. The preamble to this proposed legislation stressed the links between drug control and public health: "In the public health the necessity of guarding against contagious diseases, the indiscriminate practicing of medicine, pharmacy, and dentistry, has been recognized in nearly every state of the union. But amid all this restriction and supervision . . . stalks a specter of death and destruction, claiming its victims from the babe in the cradle to the octogenarian." Opposition from the drug trade and the health professions delayed passage of any state legislation until 1897, and even this law was widely regarded as ineffective and unenforceable. In 1903, the State Board of Pharmacy secured the passage of a new state law which prohibited the [13] sale of cocaine except upon the prescription of a physician. Shortly there-after, the board sent twenty-five Chicago druggists the following letter:

> Report on credible authority has been made that, in spite of public attention in the press and pharmaceutical journals, you still sell cocaine contrary to law. You are hereby noti-fied, by registered letter . . . that I have given you due warn-ing. To sell cocaine in any way, shape or manner, no matter under what name and in what compound, without a pre-scription from a licensed physician, is contrary to the crimi-nal code, and subjects you to a heavy fine; and on second offense to fine and imprisonment. . . . If after receipt of the registered notice you still persist in this violation, you, and you alone, are responsible for the trouble that comes to you.

Despite the severity of the board's language, a number of "loopholes" 14 immediately presented themselves: the law failed to mention any of co-caine's close chemical cousins, contained no prohibition on multiple refilling of prescriptions, and did not cover sales by wholesale drug firms. Moreover, the 1903 state law only provided for a fine of between 25 and 200 dollars and the possibility of up to six months in jail, and repeated offenses were punishable only by the fine. In 1905, Chicago passed a local anti-cocaine ordinance which required cocaine to be sold in packages no smaller than the smallest of original packages sold by wholesalers. This measure was designed to "stop the sale of cocaine and morphine for other than legitimate purposes." In 1907, the state legislature modified the 1903 legislation and raised the penalties for violations, largely at the urging of several Chicago Municipal Court judges, Hull House, and the Superintendent of the House of Correction.

In the West Side neighborhoods where the concerns over cocaine use 15 first emerged, there was always some ambivalence about the reformers' ef-forts. Neighborhood residents may well have been troubled by the easy availability of opiates and cocaine. Parents who sought assistance through Hull House or the juvenile court demonstrated by their actions concern over drug selling. Most importantly, the expense of a cocaine habit strained the fi-nances of many working-class and unemployed users. Even under the best of circumstances, where retailers did not inflate their prices, dilute their product, or otherwise take advantage of their customers, a habitual user would have spent thirty cents a day to purchase ten grains of cocaine; some habitual users purchased between twenty and sixty grains a day. Adding to the burden, buyers rarely found cocaine for only three cents a grain. David Musto has shown that the retail price of a "deck" (1.3 grains) of cocaine in New York after 1908 was twenty-five cents.

On the other hand, as Lizabeth Cohen and others have observed, resi-   16
dents of Chicago's working-class immigrant neighborhoods could be deeply
suspicious of state intervention in private life. The retail druggists charged
with selling cocaine and opiates could be viewed sympathetically as honest
businessmen engaged in legitimate trade. As Dr. Hamilton herself recounted, one the strongest strategies for defendants in criminal cases was
to call for a jury trial: "The defendant druggists in our cases always demanded a jury trial and their lawyers always intimated that we from Hull-
House were meddling, high-brow reformers, trying to keep an honest man
from earning his living." Jane Addams remembered neighborhood reaction
in a similar fashion: "I recall an Italian druggist living on the edge of the
neighborhood, who finally came with a committee of his fellow countrymen
to see what Hull-House wanted on him, thoroughly convinced that no such
efforts could be distinterested. . . . Through all this the Italian druggist, who
had greatly profited by the sale of cocaine to boys, only felt outraged and
abused." Similar sentiments also turned some pharmacists against the state
pharmaceutical organization, which was widely (and correctly) thought to be
dominated by middle-class druggists suspicious of their immigrant brethren.

In spite of the mixed reaction of some West Side neighborhood resi-   17
dents, the campaign against drug selling between 1904 and 1909 achieved
much of what it intended. In a narrow sense, their efforts succeeded in subjecting West Side pharmacists and drug sellers to repeated arrest and prosecution, forcing them to move or close their business. Prosecution of
cocaine-selling druggists was a difficult affair, as Jessie Binford related to
the Legal Aid Society, which funded some of her work at Hull House:

> In the prosecution of cases we have to have someone wit-
> ness the sale of the "dope," as they call it, then an analysis
> made, as they sell other substances closely resembling co-
> caine, whenever they are at all suspicious of the purchase.
> If it proves to be cocaine, we then have the man who owns
> the drug store arrested, as well as the clerk who made the
> sale. Under the city ordinance they can be fined to the ex-
> tent of $200. Mr. Dudley, attorney for the State Board of
> Pharmacy, will proceed in each case we get, under the
> State law, under which a fine of $200 can be imposed for
> the first offense and $1,000 for the second conviction, as
> well as the revocation of the license.

As Binford's report made clear, the regulations limiting cocaine sales   18
were worthless without a great deal of effort on the part of interested parties
to pursue investigations and convictions. Between 1904 and 1908, the Hull
House anti-cocaine movement invested enormous time and energy to the
cause, and they achieved much of what they intended. The annual report of
the Juvenile Court Committee observed that "one druggist told our officer

that there were sixty-one druggists selling cocaine in the city; that he did not intend to stop selling unless everyone else did the same. However, after being brought into Court and fined five times, he changed his mind and said he would cease selling the drug."

Two years later, the annual report of the Juvenile Court Committee proudly announced that the cocaine problem in the city was over. The committee failed to note, however, that drug selling had not disappeared, despite their success in narrowing the legal market in opiates and cocaine. Rather, underground drug marketplaces emerged in Chicago's three flourishing vice districts: first, the eighth police district on the Near North Side of the city, especially along N. Clark Street; second, a portion of the West Side along Madison Street just to the north of the Hull House neighborhoods; and third, the South Side "Levee" whose vital center was the area between 18th and 22nd streets and between Wabash and S. Clark Streets, and which also included the city's Chinatown. The concentration of illicit activity in these areas was as much a matter of policy as personal choice; Chicago's civic leaders and law enforcement officials maintained that there was an ongoing need to contain and isolate illicit trades in "red-light" districts. Reinforcing this view, Chief of Police Shippy posed a series of pointed rhetorical questions to the city's resident in 1908: "we can drive out every occupant of the 22nd Street district in forty-eight hours. But do you want us to drive them into the lake, as has been suggested? Do you want them driven to the resident districts? What do you want done with them? Isn't it better to keep them corralled in one spot with their names and histories tabulated?" 19

INTO THE LEVEE: THE ORGANIZATION
OF THE DRUG MARKETPLACE

Drug selling in Chicago constituted a "market," in the simple sense that individuals were engaged in buying and selling a specific commodity. That drug selling constituted a "marketplace"—at least in the traditional sense of the term as an open and public area of exchange operating under legal approval—is less certain. An examination of the organization of drug selling and the relationship of sellers to their community, however, suggests that the distribution of opiates and cocaine can be understood as both market and marketplace. 20

Specific locations where drugs were bought and sold defined part of the underground marketplace. In Chicago, as elsewhere, two types of retail settings predominated. The first were those locations where drugs were both sold and consumed. The most obvious examples were the opium dens which concentrated near the South Side Levee and Madison Street on the West Side. Opium smoking establishments in twentieth-century Chicago were not the public "dens" prominent in other cities in the nineteenth century. Instead, opium smokers gathered in private residences, cheap hotels, 21 and retail shops. Alongside the opium smokers' hangouts were the "hop joints" and "snow pads" where morphine, heroin, or cocaine were available. When investigators for the Chicago Civil Service Commission examined illegal drug sales in the city, they found 43 of the 44 identified outlets located in or around the three vice districts—8 on the Near North Side, 27 in the Levee precincts, and 8 in the West Side district.

The more prevalent type of exchange involved the purchase of drugs   22 for use elsewhere. Sellers conducted business from fixed locations throughout the levee, including hotels, saloons, brothels, cigar stores, newsstands, drugstores and pool halls, private homes, apartments, street corners and alleys. While retail sales took place in diverse settings, long-time customers always seemed to know where and how to find their connection. In the course of one hour in the summer of 1914, investigators from Charles Merriam's City Council Committee on Crime observed thirty-seven people "of all classes, both white and black" knock on the back door of one South Side residence and purchase small packages of cocaine. As the investigators noted, "some of the men and women could not wait until they got out of sight and snuffed the cocaine in the alley back of this place," where some of the users sat for hours drinking beer and sniffing cocaine, periodically going back to the building for more. This system of distribution may have seemed wide open, but it was closed in important ways—one investigator approached the back door three times without it opening, apparently because he was unaware of the correct knock.

The experience of Merriam's investigator hints at a still more important   23 defining characteristic of the marketplace in opiates and cocaine—the networks of relationships between sellers and their customers. The Chicago experience does not strongly support the traditional image of retail drug dealers actively seeking to recruit purchasers and initiate the unsuspecting. To be sure, the local press occasionally reported stories of drug sellers marketing reduced-cost drugs to younger customers in order to "hook" them, and some retailers did in fact employ "route builders" who peddled to young boys in neighborhood pool rooms. In general, however, sellers operated a distribution system closed to those without connections. The drug trade relied on trust and long-term relationships, a reciprocal arrangement in which sellers demanded the discretion and loyalty of buyers, and buyers rewarded those sellers with a reputation for providing a product of consistent quality and avoiding police entanglements. Bingham Dai observed in 1936 that "It is generally denied by drug addicts, most of whom are petty peddlers at one time or another, that they ever try to make proselytes. On the whole, this denial is borne out by our limited experience with drug users."

Contacts between buyer and seller involved a variety of signals and   24 codes, all designed to protect the distribution system from detection. On the West Side, customers entering one laundry and asking for a "liverwurst sandwich" received a roll with a packet of smoking opium inside. The

Record-Herald marveled at the "free masonry of drug users" which protected the trade: "a stranger who tried to buy cocaine from them would have his trouble for his pains, but the regular cocaine fiend has no trouble. He knows that if he goes to certain sections of the city in which the peddlers make their headquarters he can get all the 'dope' he wants, if he has the money, even though he could not buy it at a reputable drug store . . . the usual way of doing it is easy. Without a word the one who wants cocaine, knowing the ropes, places the exact change in the hands of a man who has it to sell. He knows better than to ask for it; he wouldn't get it if he did." Sellers also employed intermediaries (both formally and informally) to screen potential customers. In such an apparently public distribution system, the importance of long-term relationships, trust, and reliability is striking.

The use of such intermediaries suggests the complexity of distribution 25 roles in the underground drug market. At the very top of the retail distribution system were those figures who combined wholesale and retail functions. Individuals who reached this level in Chicago before 1920 usually had some connection to the legitimate drug industry, either as retail druggists or through contacts with legitimate wholesale drug firms. The Vice Commission of Chicago observed that it was "practically impossible to ascertain exactly how much cocaine or morphine any particular [drug]store buys in spite of the fact that wholesale houses keep a record" because some drugstores turned in written orders for small amounts, but asked for and received larger amounts. After 1920, diversion of the legal supply was largely replaced by international smuggling operations. J. H. Montgomery, a pharmacist who operated a South Side drugstore, exemplifies the wholesaler-retailer role. Montgomery supplied smoking opium, morphine, heroin, and cocaine to numerous lower-level distributors, including the owners of the above-mentioned cocaine distribution center observed by Merriam's investigators. When the investigators approached Montgomery seeking to purchase opium, he replied that he was willing, but that "it is better for you buy it by the pound so that you will not have to come so often."

Only a few Chicago retailers attained this level, but those who did were 26 well known, and reaped enormous profits from the business. Among the high profile sellers in the city before 1920: Montgomery; Adolph Brendecke, who owned two West Side drugstores targeted by Hull House; Eugene Hustion, an African-American cocaine distributor in the South Side levee; a man known only as "Omaha" or the "King Cocaine Dealer" who reportedly employed twenty-five to thirty men and women, selling drugs "on a 20% basis"; and Jim Hing, popularly known as the "Rockefeller of Dope." When police raided Hing's laundry, they discovered a dazzling array of personal articles which testified to both the profitability to sellers and the high costs of a drug habit. Among Hing's cache were clocks, vases, rugs, furniture and jewelry (including twenty wedding rings). Eugene Hustion and his college-educated wife Lottie began their operations in 1904, and were still actively in business in 1914. The Hustions obtained his supply through the wholesale drug firm of Knox, Greene, and Company, operated several "subagencies" throughout the South Side, stocked over thirty pounds of cocaine at their Dearborn Street location, and sent runners nightly to some of the most famous houses of prostitution in the city. According to Hustion, he had "gross daily sales as high as $200, of which $160 was profit."

At the next level in the distribution system were the full-time retailers, the "men who sell cocaine all day long for a living" as one Chicago newspaper put it. As noted, wholesalers like Montgomery sold to a number of these full-time retailers, such as Cato Stevens. Stevens bought smoking opium by the pound at Montgomery's drugstore, and then supplied a number of smaller retail locations, such as the Monroe Hotel, home of a black "hop-joint" operated by a man named "Allen" and protected by two police officers who smoked opium there each night. Another example of the distribution chain: a retailer named "Little Montie" purchased large quantities of smoking opium at a South Side saloon, and operated his own route, which included customers like Eddie Creeley and Jock Ross, owners of a rear apartment at 2217 Wabash Avenue "where the mob comes to smoke any time they feel like it." 27

The operations of these full-time dealers also required numerous part-time employees to carry out various functions, including soliciting business and running drugs to customers. Merriam's Committee on Crime estimated (somewhat conservatively) that there were between 75 and 100 runners engaged in retail drug sales in the city. Walter Manson worked for a drug retailer in the early 1920s in Chicago, and described his role as follows: "the addicts would call on the phone for me to meet them and then I would find out how much they wanted, and would then take these to them. This was the job I had and it was easy. All I had to do was watch for the officers and not get caught." Sellers at this level were paid to take the risks of conducting highly visible street sales. 28

At this level, a kind of sub-market operated. These sellers were often users themselves, working for a full-time retailer in exchange for a steady supply of drugs for personal use. These user-sellers frequently bargained with other users who lacked the same connections, stole from their employers when they could, and generally engaged in the kind of "hustling" lifestyle observed among heroin users in several notable post–World War Two studies. Walter Manson, for example, would provide female addicts with heroin in exchange for sex. Manson also employed a variety of cons, such as claiming to have been robbed, in order to extract more of his employer's supply for personal use; when his stealing became too obvious, he simply "disappeared" for a while. Full-time retailers, for their part, treated the problems caused by their part-time distributors as part of the regular expense of doing business. 29

To further develop the profile of the participants in Chicago's retail drug markets, ninety-nine drug sellers have been identified through newspaper accounts and the reports of Merriam's investigators. All ninety-nine were 30 active in the early underground drug market between 1903 and 1915. Neither the investigators nor the newspapers provided a consistent range of seller characteristics, yet the data do begin to suggest some commonalities. First, many sellers operated in their own neighborhoods, living in close proximity to where they sold. Racial segregation, of course, meant that even high-level African-American sellers such as the Hustions were forced to stay relatively close to the drug marketplace. Still other sellers conducted business directly from their own residences. Second, the business of drug selling was the only reported vice interest of retailers. In only four of ninety-nine cases were retailers explicitly identified as participants in organized prostitution or gambling. Retailers clearly had other proprietary interests (at least ten owned the retail establishments from which drugs were sold), but there seems to have been little direct proprietary overlap among the underground trades. Third, the business was overwhelmingly male. Of the ninety-nine sellers identified, eighty-seven were male. Of the twelve female sellers, at least four were in business with their husbands. Fourth, most sellers were linked to small distribution networks, although these combinations of sellers do not appear to have been very extensive or fixed. Among the thirty-five retailers whose operations were based in or around the Levee, twenty-one were reported to be operating in connection with at least one other retailer.

Another defining feature of the underground drug marketplace was the extent to which it was connected to the other institutions of the neighborhood. Messenger boys delivered drugs, hotel employees arranged purchases for customers, and bartenders acted as part-time distributors. The Vice Commission of Chicago recorded some of these distribution networks in operation, observing that a levee madam "is in the habit of calling up Mr.———— and ordering a certain quantity of cocaine, who in turn calls this messenger boy and sends it out to her residence." In this way, "the messenger becomes an important link in the system whereby cocaine and various other drugs used by habitues are secured by them." Another prostitute determined that messenger boys "talked too much and cannot be trusted," and instead commissioned a newsboy to purchase cocaine for her. Inevitably, these extensive distribution networks strengthened the connections between the drug market and other levee institutions, including the abundant cheap hotels, saloons, brothels, pool halls, drugstores, cigar stores, and clubs. 31

Finally, the police were a daily part of the drug trade in the city, although their role was hardly consistent. At times, political pressure to "clean up" certain areas of the city forced the Chicago police into their role as active agents of the government. The ensuing police sweeps were always well publicized, as reporters tipped off in advance watched the police send both buyers and sellers scrambling. In the confusion of Christmas raids on the West Side in 1911, reporters covering the action watched young Walter McKendrick dive head first from the third story window of Hector Mariner's cocaine flat. In between the periodic roundups, police activity targeted the 32 small-time sellers who operated in the most visible ways, and could not afford to pay substantial protection money. Sellers on the street were constantly on the watch for being "pinched" by the police, sometimes developing a habit of selling and walking at the same time to avoid attracting too many addicts at once and drawing unwanted attention to themselves. Because the earliest laws dealt with sales, not possession, sellers caught with drugs would often be charged with disorderly conduct or some other offense. In this way, an arresting officer could take a seller into custody without having to prove that a sale had taken place. As a consequence, only twenty-five criminal cases for cocaine selling were disposed of in the Municipal Court of Chicago between 1908 and 1913, despite the reported arrest of a far greater number of sellers.

At other times, the Chicago police operated as independent agents 33 whose loyalty was for sale to the highest bidder. The evidence is overwhelming that most sellers paid police for protection as a routine part of their business, with payoffs varying according to the rank of the officer and the size of the seller's business. West Side opium dens paid patrolmen from the Desplaines Street station one dollar a week, while Eugene Hustion paid over $3,000 dollars a year to continue his operations in the Levee. The payoffs and corruption continued even after passage of the federal Harrison Narcotic Act in 1914 brought federal agents to Chicago. Federal agents took payoffs from dealers, and confiscated drug supplies promptly disappeared from government warehouses. Even when local police and federal agents were not on the take, they seldom made much difference to the operation of retail drug markets. The real problem, according to one federal agent, was a reluctance to "lock horns with the higher ups," as officials "simply meet with stool pigeons and knock off the petty peddlers that they turned in."

In sum, the underground drug marketplace in Chicago was an impor- 34 tant part of the neighborhoods in which it thrived. Forced out of many of the city's residential neighborhoods, drug sellers took refuge in the complex network of vice interests which dominated the South Side Levee district, Madison Street on the West Side, and North Clark Street on the Near North Side. Operating a visible but closed system of distribution, sellers relied on relationships with each other, with their employees, customers, other vice interests, neighborhood businesses, and the police to maintain their trade.

"THE GHOST OF THE LEVEE": DRUG DEALING MOVES TO THE BLACK BELT

The campaign to limit legal sales of opiates and cocaine achieved 35 much of what it had intended. These drugs were no longer legally available without a physician's prescription, most city drugstores exercised careful scrutiny over sales, and the patent medicines which had thrived on their opiate or cocaine content were rapidly disappearing from the market. As the legal supply shrank, an important new underground drug trade developed within the traditional geographic centers of Chicago's underground economy. In the Levee, drug sellers had created a new distribution system which drew customers from throughout the city. Almost immediately, however, the forces of Progressive reform instigated another shift in the location of drug selling, this time towards the South Side Black Belt, the segregated residential area housing the majority of the city's African-American population. By 1920, the drug selling which had been concentrated around the Levee between 18th and 22nd streets (which already bounded the northern edge of the Black Belt) had sifted further south to the area between 31st and 35th streets, into the heart of Chicago's rapidly growing African-American neighborhoods.

The impetus for the shift was the highly successful campaign, waged between 1910 and 1914, to end "wide-open" vice in the Levee. Propelling the effort was a succession of public and private organizations, which included: the Chicago Service Commission, Vice Commission, Law and Order League, Committee of Fifteen, and Charles Merriam's City Council Commission. In a remarkable series of investigations and reports, these groups exposed the political corruption which sustained the Levee, and roundly condemned the continued existence of segregated vice districts. The fate of the Levee was sealed when the city government turned slightly but significantly toward the reform forces, with the grudging support of Mayor Carter Harrison II. The Chicago Police Department created a highly effective Morals Division, replaced the notoriously corrupt captain of the 22nd Street police station, and closed down brothels and dives by the dozen. The days of segregated vice in the Levee were largely over by the end of 1914. Expecting this crackdown to be as temporary as all the others which had preceded, the leaders of the Levee's underground economy confidently proclaimed they would soon be back in business. 36

As the leaders of the Levee predicted, the vice trades, including drug selling, revived fairly quickly, but in new locations under the control of new interests. As with the earlier anti-cocaine campaign on the West Side, the ultimate effect of the crackdown was a shift of the center of operations for the underground markets. Now, the drug trade moved further south, into Chicago's Black Belt. As in many cities, the vice districts in Chicago had always been in fairly close proximity to African-American neighborhoods. Drug selling continued to thrive around Madison Street on the West Side, and to some extent on North Clark Street, but the heart of the drug trade was now the Black Belt. The Herald and Examiner had this to say of the new underground markets at 31st Street: "They say the levee is dead. Perhaps it is, but the ghost of the levee is stalking about the streets and alleys of the South Side, manifesting unmistakable desires for resurrection." 37

By the 1920s, the 31st Street area was the heart of the Black Belt's night life, with an entertainment district featuring the cabarets and dance halls that nurtured Chicago's emergent jazz scene. When Louis Armstrong 38 arrived in Chicago from New Orleans in the summer of 1922, he headed straight for the Lincoln Gardens dance hall at 459 East 31st Street. The Lincoln Gardens, Dreamland Dance Hall, Entertainers Cafe, Pekin Cafe and many others drew musicians from across the country, and supported a notoriously wild and rowdy night life. The city's underground trades flourished among these legal entertainment venues. The traditional gambling, drug and sex trades moved into the area, along with a vast new underground liquor distribution system which appeared with the advent of national alcohol prohibition. Much as the old Levee had, the Black Belt entertainment and vice district drew people from all over the city, something which the *Chicago News* noted in disapproving remarks in 1922: "the lawless days of the famous 'red light' district when the demimonde and the professional gambler, under the appraising eye of the police, were once more restored in the South Side negro belt . . . without a doubt this district is the foulest spot in Chicago. Black and tan cabarets, buffet flats, soft drink saloons, and every form of vice are flourishing."

Indeed, of all the features of the 31st and 35th Street entertainment and vice districts, the most objectionable seemed to be its attractiveness to Chicagoans of every class and race. The purported evil effects of this kind of interaction, particularly at the "black and tan" cabarets, received much mention in the wake of the city's deadly race riot of 1919. Following days of violence in which much property was destroyed, hundreds were injured, and at least thirty-eight people died, many critics observed that the worst violence had occurred in the heart of the entertainment district, and concluded that solution would be to end the "intermingling of races" in the Black Belt. Throughout the 1920s, Chicago officials made periodic attempts to shut down the clubs that newly elected Mayor William Dever called "vile in the last degree." 39

It was in the volatile atmosphere of the Black Belt vice district that the drug trade established a new center. During the first two terms of Mayor William Hale Thompson, between 1915 and 1923, the new vice districts of the Black Belt operated in much the same fashion as had the old segregated districts. The Thompson administration, it was well-known, stood for the "open town" and a low-key approach to vice suppression. Drug sellers continued the tradition of operating out of fixed locations, including many clubs and retail establishments in the area. The Iowa Club, for example, was a black-owned business whose manager and entertainers were drug consumers as well as distributors, paying protection money to police officers who frequented the club. Along 31st Street, a pool room drew a dozen or more "snow fiends" regularly, and cocaine and heroin were available at a massage parlor for 25 cents a shot. Marijuana selling in particular seemed to echo the wide-open spirit of the early years of drug selling; the popularity of "tea pads" and "reefer dens" highlighted the social nature of marijuana distribution. 40

Despite some continuities, drug selling in the South Side Black Belt   41
after 1920 was a different kind of enterprise in some important respects.
First, although fixed locations were still important to the business, they appear to have been less permanent than before, and were more likely to be
rooms in apartment buildings or cheap hotels. Second, street selling became more central to retail activities. When Bingham Dai looked for the
"centers of illicit drug traffic in the city" he found that South Side street corners such as 31st and State, 31st and Wabash, 26th and State, 22nd and
Wabash, and 22nd and Michigan as "being some of the favorite street corners for the meeting of drug addicts and peddlers." Third, legal prohibitions
on opiates and cocaine probably drove buyers and sellers into greater proximity than ever before. Although drug selling became an underground trade
well before the federal Harrison Narcotic Act ushered in national drug prohibition, tighter legal controls meant that many users found it easier to simply
stay close to their source of supply. Fourth, organized criminal syndicates
were now in control of drug importation and wholesaling. As federal control
measures restricted the legal production system from which most drug supplies had been diverted, the syndicate stepped in to manage the complicated task of delivering narcotics into Chicago. As one dealer informed
federal drug agent Maurice Helbrandt in the early 1930's, "The Syndicate
will take away all the dope a man's got if they find he brought it in from out of
town and is selling here in Chicago. You got to buy from them." Most profits,
of course, went to the syndicate interests, and the importance of independent entrepreneurs such as Eugene Hustion waned.

Despite changing circumstances for drug sellers, one constant was the   42
importance of Black Belt neighborhoods as a center for the trade. Bingham
Dai's doctoral dissertation at the University of Chicago identified the centers
of drug selling in the city based on 1,591 cases from the federal Bureau of
Narcotics and the Narcotic Division of the Chicago Police Department gathered between 1929 and 1934. Of 120 "sub-communities," the highest number of arrests was in the old West Side vice district, along Chicago's bleak
Skid Row and "Hobohemia." Seven of the next eight districts with the highest arrests totals, however, were either wholly or partly within the Black Belt,
accounting for 678 arrests.

Contemporary accounts seldom emphasized the role of public policy in   43
creating the Black Belt drug market. Observers frequently attributed the
prominence of drug selling to the degeneracy of the residents themselves,
or to the lure of the immoral city to newcomers from the South. Even many
long-time residents, as James R. Grossman has observed, were quick to
find fault with the new migrants who crowded into the emerging ghetto side-
by-side with the underground trades. This view grew into what many
Chicagoans viewed as a kind of conventional wisdom, of the kind offered by
Jack Lait and Lee Mortimer in their sensationalistic book *Chicago Confidential:* "During the war, when the Chicago labor shortage was more severe

than in most places because of the diversity of her plants and her un-equaled transportation setup, it was not unique for a farmhand who had never owned $10 at one time to earn $200 a week with overtime. This started the Bronzeville boom, with its drinking and doping and the resultant laxities that blossomed into flagrant vice." Sociologists refined this argument into one of social disorganization, as Dai did in the 1930s: "here the control of traditional mores and of what are ordinarily called primary-group associa-tions, such as the family and local community, is practically nil, and the indi-vidual's life, thereby, often lacks organization or direction."

Subsequent generations of scholars rejected the social disorganization   44 argument in favor of one which defined participation in the underground trades as an adaptive form of niche employment (or even as an empowering choice among narrowly restricted work opportunities). As Mark Haller con-cluded, "In ways that were both destructive and productive, the black experi-ence in the city was linked to the opportunities that lay in the vice resorts, cabarets and dance halls of the teeming slums." Haller's conclusions echoed St. Clair Drake and Horace R. Cayton's 1945 sociological study, *Black Metropolis: A Study of Negro Life in a Northern City.* Drake and Cay-ton described the importance of "policy"—illegal lottery gaming—to the eco-nomic and social life of the African American community in Chicago, and underscored the prominence of the "policy kings" who ran the operations.

Like policy and other illicit enterprise, drug selling was undeniably prof-   45 itable for some Black Belt residents, and provided one kind of opportunity. But drug selling never achieved the "status" of policy, as Drake and Cayton observed. Even in the run-down neighborhoods of the northern Black Belt, where most of the trade concentrated, most residents objected to the easy access to opiates and cocaine the sellers brought. The congregations of ad-dicts on street corners, the unwanted police attention, the affronts to moral sentiment, and the feeling that the ultimate profit went elsewhere all worked to keep popular sentiment against the drug trade. It seems clear that drug selling thrived in the Black Belt despite the wishes of most residents, and for reasons beyond their control. Thomas Philpott's conclusion that "Black peo-ple were helpless to prevent the authorities from locating the red-light district where they lived, just as they were unable to stop whites from segregating them" may ignore some of the ways in which the drug trade may have served useful purposes, but it does suggest that historians must consider those outside forces which helped keep the drug marketplaces in the Black Belt.

Perhaps the most visible of these forces were the city officials and po-   46 lice who adopted a policy of vice containment. In the tradition of formal vice segregation, most Chicagoans never rejected the idea that underground trades would always exist, and that their isolation was a more reasonable goal than elimination. The 1922 report of the Chicago Commission on Race Relations strongly emphasized the double standard of vice regulation for the city's black neighborhoods: "little consideration is given to the desire of Negroes to live in untainted districts, and they have not been able to make effective protest." The report spoke of "roistering saloons . . . a kind which would not be tolerated in any other part of the city since the old Twenty-Second Street levee was broken up." The report emphasized the importance of outside interests to the operation of Black Belt vice trades: "White proprietors have brought them into the district, and many of them are patronized by crowds from other parts of the city. The resorts are forced on the colored people. Many white owners of real estate who speak in horrified whispers of vice dangers view such dangers with complacency when these are thrust among colored families."

The emergence of syndicate control of high-level drug distribution also   47 reinforced the location of drug retailing. In the run-down areas of the northern Black Belt, the syndicate found a useful base of operations. As Walter Reckless observed, "the vice syndicates often let the slum families—specially Negroes on the Near South Side—use their houses or buildings for residence or store front churches. Sometimes there is a poor Negro family or store front church on the ground floor and quarters for a vice assignment on the second or third floor." Reckless noted that the ability of underground trades to avoid detection depended in part upon "the use of a great deal of slum property—more or less vacated buildings and houses . . . bought up by vice syndicates in large numbers." Former Levee operators moving south toward Thirty-First Street found new properties in the Black Belt where they could renew operations, and "they could afford to pay high rents. . . . numbers of real estate owners profited greatly by dealing with them." The dilapidated housing nearby attracted many of the worst drug addicts, who could afford little better for their residences. One such building on Wabash Avenue housed twenty-one drug users.

The geographic concentration of drug selling proved to be one of the   48 most enduring features of Chicago's underground enterprise, a legacy of Progressive-era anti-drug crusades and ghetto containment of vice. In the summer of 1950, with heroin use on the rise among Chicago's youths, the *Sun-Times* ran a series of articles detailing the city's drug problem. Jessie Binford, who had first dealt with drug selling upon her arrival in the city in 1904, determined that the Juvenile Protective Association would reprint the series under the title *Dope—And Chicago's Children.* In the publication's foreword, Binford wrote: "the sale of 'dope' to minors and their addiction to this devastating, consuming habit now presents one of the most menacing and destructive conditions this Association has ever faced." If Binford echoed many of the themes of 1904 in her 1950 work, so did the report's conclusion about the patterns of drug sales in the city. "The great majority" of addicts, the report observed, bought their drugs in the South Side ghetto. In what the *Sun-Times* called the "social jungle" of the ghetto, drug peddlers sold from "their own flats or hotel rooms . . . pool halls, saloons, cheap night clubs, and elevated railroad stations." "You walk along 43rd any old night," an addict recounted, "and just say to one of them pool room bums, 'Seen the swing man?' and pretty soon you can get what you need."

To explain the enduring presence of illicit drug marketplaces in the "social jungle" of the twentieth-century city, generations of social scientific studies defined participation in the underground trade as a by-product of ghetto life, or of urban decay. This study, however, employs a social historical approach in treating drug selling as a form of enterprise defined by the daily exchanges between buyers, sellers, neighborhood residents, and police. With a few notable exceptions, Chicago's underground drug sellers never achieved great financial rewards. Most drug retailers simply sought to exploit the limited opportunities to make some money, exchange drugs for favors or sex, or simply to support their own drug habits. Even these limited rewards, however, were sufficient to attract hundreds of Chicagoans into the illicit drug business in the early twentieth century. Above all, sellers constantly looked for ways to minimize the risks they faced in carrying out their public transactions. The result was a highly visible marketplace in illicit drugs that was essentially closed to outsiders. By maintaining strong networks of personal associations with buyers and other sellers, individuals in the retail drug trade established reputations for reliability critical to maintaining their enterprise.

The Chicago experience also highlights the importance of neighborhoods to the retail drug trade. At least as much as legitimate business, the city's underground trades needed to adjust to the social and spatial dimensions of the surrounding community. The Levee offered drug sellers a fairly stable network of neighborhood institutions, from brothels to cigar stores, from which to operate. The regulated vice district also allowed the most social aspects of the drug business, from opium dens to snow pads, to flourish in long-term fixed locations. The closure of the Levee sent the trade further south, into the Black Belt, where for a time the entertainment district offered an echo of the old Levee. By the early 1930s, drug sellers conducted a street-corner trade, no longer able to rely on long-term fixed locations, and more dependent on a series of flophouses and cheap apartments. The sellers' constant process of adaptation to changing community conditions reveals how closely the retail drug trade integrated itself into neighborhood structures.

Finally, although this study emphasizes the ways in which the exchanges between buyers and sellers defined the character of the drug marketplace, its location was also the product of constant external pressures. While drug marketplaces brought a measure of opportunity for some, they were never really a welcome part of any Chicago neighborhood. Where sufficient time, resources, and political power could be mobilized and brought to bear, a community might rid itself of an unwanted drug trade, as the efforts of the Hull House coalition suggest. Anti-drug legislation was useless without the kind of coordinated public/private effort which drove the West Side druggists out of business. Where either resources or cooperation were lacking, as in the case of the South Side Black Belt, city policy settled comfortably into a policy of vice containment. City government took little sustained action, real estate interests profited from the use of dilapidated housing, and organized crime syndicates took most of the earnings. Law enforcement, in the meantime, pursued a policy of frequent arrests of drug retailers and their customers, without seriously confronting the conditions that allowed the trade to thrive in the first place.   ©

CRITICAL READING

1. In this article, the author says that, despite the importance of drug marketplaces, the social scientific literature of the twentieth century "has paid insufficient attention to drug selling as work, or as economic enterprise." In what ways have scholars examined drug marketplaces, according to Spillane? What are the deficiencies of such approaches, in the author's opinion?
2. According to this article, what social and/or economic factors accounted for the rise in "underground drug selling" in Chicago and elsewhere throughout the United States during the historical period under discussion?
3. Briefly summarize the history of cocaine abuse, legislation, and the illegal economic activity surrounding the drug, as outlined in this article.
4. In what ways does the illegal drug trade in Chicago mirror more mainstream market economies? In what ways (other than the obvious fact that it's illegal) does that drug trade differ?

CLASS DISCUSSION

1. Explain the author's statement, "In sum, the underground drug marketplace in Chicago was an important part of the neighborhoods in which it thrived." Considering your knowledge of the contemporary urban drug trade, how might this statement be applicable to certain neighborhoods in the American cities of today?
2. Considering the information given in this article, what do you think the relationship is between racial attitudes and drug policy in this country's history? On the basis of your own experience and observation, do you think that this relationship has disappeared or that it has continued into present-day urban America?

DIRECTED FREEWRITE

A fair amount of this piece consists of historical narrative: the author recounts Chicago drug trade-related events in chronological sequence. Why do historians engage in such detailed retelling of happenings that may seem ancient to modern readers: is it just to tell an interesting story, or do they believe there is something to be learned from these narratives? If the answer is "yes" to the latter point, what "lessons" can the modern reader glean from this detailed overview of the drug trade in the Chicago of a bygone era?

HISTORY UNIT WRITING ASSIGNMENTS

1. On the basis of a close reading of the Twitchell article in this unit, write a comparison/contrast essay in which you explore the effects of materialism on contemporary American culture. Twitchell's main point—unlike that of many of the social critics you have encountered in this book and probably elsewhere—seems to be that although materialism may promote certain gender-specific habits and poverty, it also promotes a number of positive product offerings and services and as such may ultimately serve as a major source of meaning and happiness in the modern world. Discuss the specific positive effects of materialism, as suggested by Twitchell, and then go on to explain some of the drawbacks with the ultimate goal of arriving at a clear statement of your own position relative to materialism's social effects.

2. Using Spillane's essay in this unit as a model, research and write a seven-page history of some socioeconomic aspect of your own home town. If you come from Los Angeles, for example, you might study and write about the ways in which water, diverted from the Colorado River, helped shape that city, both for good (plenty of cheap water for personal and agricultural use) and ill (scandals, political graft, ecological problems and so on). Similarly, if you come from New York, you might write about issues of labor or sweatshops, attitudes toward immigration, or the emergence of an urban ethnic "melting pot"; feel free to use Ric Burns's recent multipart PBS miniseries as secondary source material. Don't be merely "encyclopedic" in relating historical events here; along with presenting historical facts, interpret their effect on the social fabric of the city, just as Spillane does in his piece.

3. In a recent speech delivered at the University of North Carolina by Professor E. M. Adams, Professor of Philosophy, the speaker presented a brief history of capitalism. For the past hundred and fifty years, he said, capitalism has been under severe moral, political, and economic challenge, but recently that has changed. Pointing to the "collapse" of communism in the former Soviet Union and Eastern Europe and with China's moves towards market-based economics, many seem to think that not only communism but also all forms of socialism and even the regulative/welfare state have been discredited and that capitalism has been vindicated and cleared of moral criticism. However, Adams said,

> Its current reputation and undeniable beneficial achievements notwithstanding, I contend that a capitalist economy as we know it is not fit for human beings for several reasons. It undermines our moral/civic/religious culture that underwrites our identity and the meaning of our existence, and grounds the norms and values by which we should live our lives and order the society; the offices or positions in our economic institutions tend to be morally corrupting or dehumanizing for those who hold them, and, with the dominance of the

economy, the one-value rationality of our economic institutions tend to invade and to pervert other institutions.

After explaining these points in detail, Adams concluded his speech by sketching some of the main features of an "alternative economy" and culture that will afford future commentators on American history more grounds for praise. On the basis of your understanding of the two economics-focused historical articles in this unit, along with your general understanding of this country's history and economic foundations, write an essay in which you address Adams's thesis—that history has proved American capitalism unfit for civilized human beings. As you develop your argument, point to at least three specific historical phenomena that prove your thesis, whether it be pro- or anti-capitalism (or something in between).

Unit 2

Ethnic Studies—
"I Have a(n American) Dream"

THE ECONOMICS OF BEING HISPANIC

John Maggs

According to the author of the next piece, although there is relatively
little wide-ranging and specific data on the economic status of Hispanics, statistics demonstrate that "Hispanics are increasingly stuck on the
lowest rung of the economic ladder" in contemporary American society. Maggs examines what he believes are the causes for the economic
position of most American Hispanics and proposes a simple but challenging solution to the problem. As you read, consider the credibility of
the author's conclusions about the status of Hispanic persons in this culture. Consider, too, the practicability of the author's proposed solution:
How likely is the government to implement the kinds of measures prescribed in this article? What kinds of changes would be required for
such measures to be effected?

*John Maggs, who graduated from Columbia College in 1984, has been a
writer at the* National Journal *since June 1998. He principally writes about
economics and foreign affairs, specializing in Latin America and Hispanic
issues. Maggs spent 11 years at the* Journal of Commerce, *a daily business newspaper, where he covered international economics out of Washington. He's written for the* New Republic, *the* Chicago Tribune, *and has
had his newspaper work syndicated in several newspapers. He has
served on the Board of Governors of the National Press Club and received
a three-star "excellent" rating on the Forbes list of the best print journalists.*

Are Hispanics the new underclass of a prosperous America? Broad   1
and detailed statistics on the economic status of Hispanics are in short supply, but what numbers there are indicate that Hispanics are increasingly
stuck on the lowest rung of the economic ladder. And although this status is
partly due to a steady stream of recent immigrants who lack the basic tools
to succeed in an Information Age America, the relative position of Latinos

economically seems to be dropping even as native-born Hispanics are making up a larger share of the Hispanic population.

The causes of this disparity are many, but chief among them are lower   2
high school and college graduation rates for Hispanic-Americans, and a changing economy that marginalizes low-skilled, low-education workers. Despite this bad news for Latinos, new research shows that successive generations of Hispanics can overcome many of the disadvantages faced by their parents and grandparents. And, despite popular suspicions that Hispanic immigrants are taking away jobs, depressing wages, and draining tax dollars, the evidence suggests otherwise.

THE NUMBERS

Over the past two decades, a period of unprecedented Hispanic immi-   3
gration, the relative economic status of Hispanics in America has been dropping steadily. According to the U.S. Department of Labor, median weekly earnings in 1998 for a full-time worker 16 years of age or older were $572, or about $30,000 a year. The median for a Hispanic worker, in contrast, was $398, or about $21,000 per year, just 69.5 percent of the median for all workers. This percentage has been falling steadily since 1980. That year, when workers were taking home weekly earnings of $292, Hispanics were earning $230, or 78.7 percent of the median. In 1985, when median weekly earnings were up to $378 for all workers, Hispanic earnings were only $292, or 77.2 percent of the median. The relative earnings of Hispanic workers have been declining ever since, to last year's 69.5 percent level.

That's an 11 percent drop in the earning power of Hispanics, relative to   4
all Americans, in 18 years. The depth of that decline seems even more dramatic when compared with the relative earning power of another minority group—blacks. Over the same 18-year period, when the relative earning power of Hispanics was falling steadily, the relative earnings of black workers were virtually unchanged, and hardly fluctuated in any year.

In 1980, black workers had median weekly earnings of $232, amount-   5
ing to 79.4 percent of the $292 earned by all workers. Fast-forward to 1998, and the relative amount of black earnings has barely changed, rising slightly to 79.7 percent of that for all workers. Throughout that period, the ratio of black earnings to the national average never changed by more than a few tenths of a percentage point.

But consider how Hispanics did compared with blacks. In 1980, black   6
and Hispanic workers had almost exactly the same median weekly earnings—$232 for blacks and $230 for Hispanics. By 1985, a small gap had appeared—blacks earned $300 and Hispanics earned $292, or 97.3 percent of black earnings. The gap widened. In 1990, Hispanic earnings were 94 percent of blacks'; in 1998, they were 87 percent. That change, 12 percent over

18 years, is almost exactly the same amount by which Hispanic earnings declined compared with the national average during the same period.

So during a generation of great economic turmoil and growth for the   7
United States, although Hispanics emerged as the ascendant ethnic minority, they also steadily lost ground economically, compared with other Americans and with those previously stuck in that low rank. Americans have prospered in those nearly 20 years, but some more than others: Earnings by all Americans and by blacks nearly doubled in that generation. Hispanic earnings rose too, but 20 percent less than that of whites and blacks.

EDUCATION LAGS

There are no easy answers for this phenomenon. It is tempting to con-   8
clude that recent waves of immigration, both legal and illegal, are responsible, because recent Hispanic immigrants are mostly poor and take the lowest-paying jobs when they arrive. But against this backdrop of rising Hispanic immigration in the 1990s has been a much larger increase in the overall population of native-born Hispanics. At current birthrates and levels of legal and illegal immigration, more than three times as many Hispanics are born in the United States each year as are added from immigration. Simply blaming the lagging earnings of Hispanics on the disadvantages of recent immigrants is not enough of an explanation.

A major factor seems to be education, or the lack of it. According to a   9
study in the December 1998 *Population and Development Review,* a New York–based academic journal, the proportion of adult immigrants without a high school education has been rising since 1980; by 1994, they numbered about a third of all immigrants in the United States, or 5.1 million workers. That's a small proportion of the total U.S. work force of well over 100 million people, but immigrants represent 30 percent of all U.S. workers without a high school diploma.

Another factor hurting Hispanic earnings is the changing economy,   10
which demands that workers have more education if they are to get ahead. Although some immigrants are foreign-born doctors or computer programmers bringing their skills to U.S. shores, most new arrivals are part of the low-skilled work force—indeed, they have come to dominate it. Between 1980 and 1994, the number of native-born low-skilled workers dropped from 20 million to 13 million.

And as improved living standards become more dependent on educa-   11
tion and skills in an information-based economy, immigrants (half of them Hispanic) are falling further and further behind. In 1980, the poverty rate for immigrants was 15.6 percent, not much more than the 12.2 percent poverty rate for native-born Americans. By 1994, the poverty rates for immigrants had grown to 22.7 percent compared to 13.9 percent for natives. Here's why: For immigrants without a high school diploma, the poverty rate rock-

eted from 20 percent in 1980 to 36 percent in 1994. Changes in the U.S. economy have made education and English-language skills more vital than ever. The lack of English proficiency tends to work against low-skilled workers in the Information Age more than it did in previous generations, when manufacturing jobs didn't necessarily require much in the way of language skills. Those immigrants without education and English are more likely to be trapped in poverty.

It is impossible to say exactly how much of the low-skilled work force is   12
made up of recent Hispanic immigrants, but new research by Jeffrey S. Passel of the Urban Institute in Washington indicates that Hispanics are much more likely to lack basic education than the next-largest immigrant ethnic group—Asians.

Passel said that sharp differences between Asian and Hispanic immi-   13
grants' earnings are due almost entirely to disparities in educational attainment. Hispanic immigrants earn about two-thirds of what is earned by "third-generation" white workers, whom Passel defines as those whose parents were born in the United States. But Asian immigrants earn much more—95 percent of what whites earn. The source of this disparity is clear: Only 41 percent of Hispanic immigrant workers are high school graduates, vs. 84 percent of Asian immigrants. Among third-generation whites, 92 percent complete high school.

The gulf is even more dramatic among the college-educated. Asian im-   14
migrants have an even higher college graduation rate—42 percent—than third-generation whites' 30 percent. Only 5 percent of Hispanic immigrants graduate from college, all but shutting out millions of other Hispanics from the credentials and skills that are increasingly the means for escaping poverty in America.

Passel said there is some good news for Hispanics in his research,   15
however. The disadvantages that plague Hispanic immigrants recede sharply for their children and grandchildren. For U.S.-born children of Hispanic immigrants, or for children who were less than 10 years old when they arrived, the benefits of an American education close the wage gap to 90 percent of the earnings of third-generation whites. Unfortunately, third-generation Hispanics don't make further progress, earning the same 90 percent achieved by their parents, he said.

This is again mainly due to the lag in the college graduation rate for   16
Hispanics, which is only 19 percent for second-generation Hispanics and 13 percent for third-generation Hispanics. The wage gap reflects the education gap—third-generation whites are more than twice as likely to graduate from college, and third-generation Asians three times as likely. This huge difference seems to point to a continued lag and perhaps even a widening of the earning gap for Hispanics unless more of them can graduate from high school and college. Passel's research will be detailed in a study to be published this fall by the Urban Institute.

THE BIGGER PICTURE

A question separate from how well Hispanics are doing is what impact   17
Hispanic immigrants have on the U.S. economy. Some Americans view immigrants as a pool of cheap and conscientious workers in a tight labor market—one in which arduous or distasteful jobs are especially hard to fill.
Others see immigrants taking away jobs from American-born workers, depressing wages, and becoming a burden for federal and local governments.

An influential work on this debate is *The New Americans,* a 1997 study   18
by the government's National Research Council. The study argues that immigration provides clear benefits to the U.S. economy. First, by boosting the
supply of labor, immigration adds to U.S. output, providing more wealth for
all Americans to share. Also, a larger labor pool allows workers to specialize
and be used more productively, the study says. Overall, the actual gain from
immigrant labor in an $8 trillion economy is minuscule—between $1 billion
and $10 billion a year—but a clear plus.

There are winners and losers from immigrant labor, however. The win-   19
ners include business owners and higher-skilled workers whose pay is
boosted, since low-wage immigrants allow capital to be used more productively. More generally, benefits are extended to all consumers who buy
goods and services that are cheaper because of immigrant labor. The losers
are less-skilled workers who compete with immigrants for jobs and wages.

However, empirical research indicates that the damage to the losers is   20
very slight, and is overwhelmed by the benefits to others. The NRC study
estimates that immigrants depressed the wages of other lower-skilled workers by only 1 percent to 2 percent in the 1980s, while boosting wages for
high-skilled workers and benefiting consumers by a much larger amount.

Even in those areas where large numbers of immigrants compete with   21
other lower-skilled workers—in Los Angeles, for example—research shows
little impact on native-born workers. Although some observers have argued
that blacks suffer disproportionately from competition with immigrants, this is
not true, according to the council's study. In fact, the main victims are earlier
waves of immigrants.

Despite suspicions that immigrants are a fiscal burden on government,   22
they are actually a net revenue generator, through the taxes they pay on
their income and spending. The revenue produced by immigrants in two
immigrant-rich states—New Jersey and California—reduced federal taxes
by $2 to $4 a year for each American household nationwide, the study
found, even allowing for the cost of education and welfare payments.

Gary Burtless, an economist at the Brookings Institution, a think tank in   23
Washington, says he tends to think that the disadvantages Hispanics face—
even after several generations in the United States—will diminish over time.
The United States, almost alone among developed nations, confers one advantage that tends to reduce the disadvantages faced by immigrant

groups—full citizenship for anyone born here. "It is a powerful force," said Burtless. ©

CRITICAL READING

1. The author suggests that Hispanics may be "the new underclass of a prosperous America." What specific causes does Maggs cite for the economic disparity between Latinos and other groups, including whites and African Americans?
2. How does the author refute the argument that recent waves of immigration, both legal and illegal, are responsible for the relatively low earning rates of Hispanic workers?
3. In what specific ways does education—or the relative lack of it—factor into the lower socioeconomic status of Hispanics in this culture, according to Maggs? How, in the author's view, is education responsible for the marked differences between Asian and Hispanic immigrants' earnings?
4. Summarize the findings of *The New Americans,* a 1997 study by the government's National Research Council: how, according to the study, does immigration provide benefits to the U.S. economy?

CLASS DISCUSSION

1. The author paints an alarming picture of the socioeconomic state of Hispanics in contemporary America, but not an entirely bleak one: he says that there is also "some good news for Hispanics" suggested by recent research. What causes for guarded optimism does he cite? On the basis of your observation or experience, what other causes do you find for optimism (or pessimism) regarding the status of Hispanics and other disadvantaged minority groups in this country?
2. This essay concludes with a brief discussion of Gary Burtless, a Brookings Institution economist, who believes that the disadvantages will diminish over time, because of the effects of full citizenship for anyone born here. In what specific ways is citizenship a "powerful force" for economic enfranchisement in this country?

DIRECTED FREEWRITE

The author, in a later section of this piece, addresses the impact that Hispanic immigrants have on the U.S. economy. In this view, certain Americans view immigrants as a source of inexpensive labor, whereas others see immigrants as taking away jobs from American-born workers, resulting in a number of negative economic impacts. Into which of these camps would you place yourself? Try to come up with as many concrete reasons as you can for your adherence to either (or neither) of these conflicting positions.

ETHNIC STUDIES UNIT WRITING ASSIGNMENTS

1. The Maggs article in this unit focuses on the impact that Hispanic immigrants have on the U.S. economy. He points out that some Americans consider Hispanic immigrants to be an exploitable pool of cheap labor, whereas others believe that immigrants take jobs away from American-born workers, resulting in a number of negative economic impacts, whereas still others, presumably, hold a more benevolent view of immigrants, knowing that almost everybody in this country is descended from an immigrant. For the purposes of this assignment, conduct research into the impact of another (non-Hispanic) ethnic subgroup—Armenians, African Americans, Jews, Koreans, Italians, Native Americans, Irish, Persians, and so forth—on the American economy. As Maggs does, make sure that you avoid the noxious pitfall of ethnic stereotyping by educating yourself well in the complex cultural traditions of your chosen group, before you attempt to write about it. Consult both primary and secondary sources, if you can. For example, as a primary source, you could interview members of your chosen group about their experiences working in the United States. Consult secondary historical sources as well. If you don't have the time or the inclination to immerse yourself thoroughly in the customs of another culture, feel free to write about the ethnic group of your origin (since you probably know more about it), analyzing the effects this group has had—and continues to have—on the American economic fabric.

2. A case study is a qualitative, in-depth, structured observation and analysis of some social unit, such as a political party, a business, or a church, or an in-depth investigation of a particular individual, usually as part of the individual's clinical treatment for a physical, psychological, or social problem. Thus psychologists often use case studies to support or refute a particular theory. Political scientists use what are called administrative case studies to explain some aspect of a government agency's operation. Sociologists use the case study to describe and draw conclusions about a wide variety of subjects, such as labor unions, police departments, medical schools, gangs, public and private bureaucracies, and many other social units.

   The article in this chapter discusses issues challenging the economic success of Hispanics in this country, and it also proposes some means of remedying financial inequities facing members of this group. There are a number of organizations whose primary goals are to increase educational, economic, and employment opportunities for Hispanics as well as for other economically disadvantaged minority groups. For example, the NAACP (National Association for the Advancement of Colored People) has traditionally championed economic rights for African Americans and is currently monitoring American corporations to hold them accountable on minority employment, vending, and executive management. This assignment asks you to write a case study about one of these kinds of organizations. Include in your case study a description and an analysis of the "case"—the organization—you have selected.

If we were to ask you to conduct empirical research, by joining and/or observing the actual functioning of a specific organization, this study could be termed an ethnographic case study, because it would involve an in-depth examination over time of people in an organization or a group. However, with limited time and resources, we ask that instead of such empirical research, you conduct library and Internet research in order to present a full picture of the organization under examination. Describe the organization in detail, explaining the problems it proposes to redress and the means by which it attempts to redress them. Then analyze the effectiveness of the organization's approach, using points from Maggs's essay as analytical tools, comparing the organization's functioning with the kinds of things the authors argue for.

Just as there are many different kinds of case studies in different disciplines, there is also a lot of variation in the ways in which writers in different fields structure their case studies. As an overarching kind of format, many case studies contain introductions, descriptive sections, analytical sections, and a conclusion or discussion section. Your case study should follow this very loose structure, and you should come up with your own topical or thematic headings to characterize the subsections of your descriptive and analytical sections.

Your introduction ought to provide general background information about the organization and the problems your case study seeks to address. Then provide a more detailed description of different elements of the organization, grouping these elements into categories that you label with subheadings, such as internal structure of the organization, different problems the case study addresses, typical methods for addressing problems, and the like. Your analysis section then evaluates these elements of the organization in relation to points from this unit's readings; again, you should use subheadings for different parts of your analysis. As a conclusion, sum up your overall evaluation of the group, and perhaps even make recommendations for improvement.

THINKING AND WRITING
IN THE SCIENCES

Unit 1
Computer Science—
Brave New Economic World

WALL STREET'S KING QUANT:
DAVID SHAW'S SECRET FORMULAS
PILE UP MONEY

James Aley

In the world of computer-aided finance, there has emerged a phenomenon called statistical arbitrage—a "financial black art," in the words of a recent *Fortune* magazine article. In general, the article suggests, "arbitrage is the closest thing that exists in finance and economics to getting a free lunch." The savvy trader begins by noticing a price discrepancy—that shares of Caterpillar Tractor, for example, are selling for $59.50 in New York and $60 in Tokyo. The trader exploits this small difference, by buying in New York and selling simultaneously in Tokyo, guaranteeing the trader a profit of fifty cents per share, minus transaction costs. The following article describes the life and economic practice of one such trader, D. E. Shaw, who has spent approximately $100 million researching and developing statistical arbitrage software. Armed with this computer expertise and experience, Shaw's firm has managed to uncover enough of these price discrepancies to produce average annual returns to investors of 18 percent. As you read, note the tone and style of this article: it's written for the popular financial press and not for a scholarly computer science journal; therefore, it has a more accessible tone and diction, and a more narrative voice, while still imparting a great deal of information about the relationship between computers and finance.

James Aley graduated from the University of Michigan in 1988. In 1992, he worked briefly as a computer programmer at Morgan Stanley and then joined the staff of Fortune *as a reporter where he helped create its front-of-the-book section, "First:." While at* Fortune, *his writing centered on business-related issues, specifically economics and technology. He is currently the Managing Editor of the San Francisco-based business magazine* Company Now.

Way up atop a Manhattan skyscraper, inside the investment banking firm of D. E. Shaw & Co., is a tiny hexagonal room staffed by six people who look fresh out of college. They stare at computer screens that cover the walls, clicking their mice, occasionally talking calmly to one another or into their phones. It is utterly unlike the typical Wall Street trading floor (where scores of shouting, sweating Mylanta chuggers raise a Dantesque din). In fact, it is utterly unimpressive—except for the fact that Shaw's trading volume is sometimes equal to 5% of the total volume of the New York Stock Exchange.   1

D. E. Shaw & Co. is the most intriguing and mysterious force on Wall Street today. It's the ultimate quant shop, a nest of scientists and other devotees of quantitative analysis who use their arcane sciences to monitor the world's financial markets and squeeze profits out of places most people would never think of looking. It's the answer you'll get if you ask the question, What's the most technologically sophisticated firm on the Street? Many investment banks and trading firms, of course, have stocked their ranks with hot-rod quants plying their Ph.D.s to figure out the markets. But D. E. Shaw doesn't just have lots of "rocket scientists." This place is run by rocket scientists, starting with the 44-year-old chief executive and founder, David Shaw, Ph.D., a former Columbia University computer science professor who used to design and build supercomputers for a living.   2

Few people outside the world of finance have ever heard of D. E. Shaw, and until recently that suited him just fine. The firm's primary business—quantitative trading, using techniques like statistical arbitrage—is very esoteric stuff, as we'll see, and its other investment banking activities are done in obscure markets. But now Shaw and his computer scientists are pursuing a hugely ambitious plan to venture far beyond Wall Street. If they succeed—anything but a sure thing—D. E. Shaw could become as well known as Charles Schwab, if not Bill Gates. Shaw envisions nothing less than using his firm's computational muscle to offer free E-mail to every man, woman, and dweeb on the Internet, and later to add online personal financial services, including home banking. He sounds more like the academic he used to be than the mogul he's become when he talks about his business plan. What he's aiming to do, he says, is "to identify ways in which technology has the potential to fundamentally transform our world, and to play a significant role in bringing about that transformation."   3

Shaw formed his company eight years ago as a hedge fund—an investment partnership designed to use everything from derivatives to short selling to make money in any market environment—with $28 million in startup capital. The most prominent of the handful of original investors were   4

Donald Sussman of Paloma Partners, another hedge fund, and Continental Casualty Co., owned by Loews Corp. Shaw started with six employees and leased his first office space in a loft near Greenwich Village. ("We have the distinction," he notes, "of being the only investment bank to be started above a communist bookstore.") The company made its first trade about six months after startup, turned a profit, and has been making money ever since. Today, D. E. Shaw & Co. has about 300 employees and more than $600 million in gross capital, ranking it among the top 25 securities companies in the country.

How has the company performed? Very nicely. According to one person familiar with his operations, D. E. Shaw has been averaging 18% annual returns since its inception. Numbers like that put Shaw well above the average, if not into the stratosphere, of money managers. But what really attracts hedge fund investors to Shaw is the fund's low volatility relative to the broader market. Last year, through December 1, the take was around 16%, well behind the S&P 500. But in 1994, a year when most hedge funds either lost money or barely broke even, Shaw delivered a 26% return.

Getting this kind of hard information about D. E. Shaw isn't easy. In fact, getting practically any information about the company is difficult. The paragraph you just read may well be the most detailed account of Shaw's finances that's ever been published. Shaw's penchant for secrecy is legendary; his attitude toward the press has been indifferent. The company not only refuses to discuss specifics of its investment performance—it even declines to reveal simple facts such as the names of all of its original partners, though they are listed on a publicly available document. (True, you have to track down the limited partnership papers at the Secretary of State's Office in Albany, New York.)

To make sure nothing gets out that isn't supposed to get out, Shaw has all his employees sign nondisclosure agreements, and these gag orders do their job well. Two former employees who initially agreed to be interviewed by *Fortune* changed their minds after sleeping on the decision, both citing the nondisclosure agreements. Only one would say anything at all, to wit: "I only have positive things to say anyway."

The secrecy is understandable when it comes to the firm's proprietary technology—what Shaw calls "our life's blood." Shaw's market-beating algorithms are so secret, even limited partners such as Morgan Miller (one of Shaw's earliest investors and an executive at National Spinning Co.) aren't entirely sure what's going on behind the curtain. "With most of the investments I have, I understand exactly what's going on. I don't with David," says Miller. "It does bother me in a way. But it's something I can live with." Shaw himself will give only a coarse description of the statistical-arbitrage trading strategies his mathematicians have invented, which are designed to exploit tiny pricing mismatches, taking a little profit here and a little more there, in the hope that by the time you add it all up, you come out well ahead. Shaw is quick to point out that this strategy is "market neutral," meaning the goal is finding these little profit pockets without actually betting on the direction of the market. "Although to be fair," he says, "if we did know how to do that, we would."

Given his reputation as an amalgam of Einstein, Midas, and Rasputin, 9
Shaw in person turns out to be surprisingly unpretentious. Consider the unassuming way he explains himself and his firm. "Our goal," he says, carefully picking his words to get it right the first time, "is to look at the intersection of computers and capital, and find as many interesting and profitable things to do in that intersection as we can." He doesn't live extravagantly, either. A favorite restaurant is a Brazilian buffet joint across the street from his offices—"The last time I was here a cockroach was walking across the floor," he tells a dinner companion.

Shaw got a computer science Ph.D. from Stanford in 1980, very close— 10
temporally and geographically—to the epicenter of the computer revolution. It took him eight years to earn his doctorate because he took a few years off to start and run a successful computer software company. He wasn't the only wallah-in-training at Stanford in those days. Leonard Bosack and Andreas Bechtolsheim, co-founders of Cisco Systems and Sun Microsystems, respectively, and Jim Clark, founder of Silicon Graphics and now chairman of Netscape—all were either faculty members or fellow students. "It was a fascinating time to be at Stanford, absolutely incredible," says Jerry Kaplan, a prominent Silicon Valley entrepreneur who was a research associate there at the same time. Although Shaw didn't have a reputation as a superstar, Kaplan recalls, "he was considered one of the core, competent people."

Fresh from Stanford, Shaw got a job as an assistant professor of com- 11
puter science at Columbia, where he did research on massively parallel supercomputing. In 1986, Morgan Stanley lured him into its analytical and proprietary trading technology group, offering him six times his professor's salary and an environment where there were much greater financial resources at his disposal than he'd ever see in academia. The shift to Wall Street was a natural, says Shaw. "Finance is really a wonderfully pure information-processing business," he says. But he soon started coming up with his own ideas about applying computer technology to financial markets, and although he speaks admiringly of Morgan today, he found the place too restrictive. He wanted to build his own company, as he puts it, "designed from the beginning from a computer science perspective." A year and a half after joining Morgan, he quit to form D. E. Shaw & Co.

Despite all his success as a pathbreaker in these arcane forms of pro- 12
prietary trading, Shaw—incredibly—says that if he were starting out today, he'd probably stay out of the business altogether, simply because it's gotten so much harder to break into. As competition has increased, profit opportunities have gotten ever tinier. Over the past eight years, D. E. Shaw has spent roughly $100 million developing its technology and uncovering new

ways to beat the market. State-of-the-art computer hardware is everywhere, but the real soul of the operation is the software. Trying to re-create the systems it has come up with would cost much more today than the original investment. "For us, proprietary trading is still very important and very good," Shaw says, "but that's partly because we lucked out." In other words, they got into the statistical arbitrage game early, when it cost only $100 million to play.

The company already devotes two-thirds of its personnel to newer services aimed at outside customers, unlike proprietary trading, which is all for its own account. For the past couple of years, Shaw has been using his $100 million technological toolbox to build a financial services division. Among other functions, this new client-seeking enterprise specializes as a market maker for obscure, complex securities like Japanese warrants and convertible bonds. One reason these issues are attractive to Shaw is that they're hard for most people to figure out—that is, those without his computational firepower find them more trouble than they're worth. Perhaps a more important reason, says Andrew Schwaeber, a trader of Asian securities at Highbridge Capital who has experience dealing with D. E. Shaw both as customer and broker, is that Shaw got into the Japanese warrant and convertible business at a time when the business was declining and other securities firms were scaling back because they weren't making enough money. The market opened up, Shaw jumped in, and now, says Schwaeber, "they're doing it better than anybody." 13

Okay, so Shaw built his firm into the quant shop other quant shops dream about, and since then has blazed a path toward bona fide investment bankdom. Then what's a smart outfit like D. E. Shaw doing flirting with that crowded no-profit zone, the Internet? "I'm embarrassed to tell anybody, just because everything in the newspaper seems to have the word Internet," Shaw admits. But, media drenching notwithstanding, he thinks cyberspace really is a place where he can do business—and where he can compete with the likes of Microsoft, Sun Microsystems, MCI, and every other high-tech company frantically trying to capture a market no one can even measure yet. 14

The first Net project is a spinoff called Juno, a free E-mail service. The simple, sensible pitch of Juno is right there in its advertising material, scheduled for direct mail, broadcast, and print onslaught in March: "E-mail was meant to be free." Users of the service don't pay a dime—not if they just want to send and receive E-mail to or from anyone anywhere on the Internet. "It has a huge potential," says Phoebe Simpson, an online analyst at Jupiter Communications. "There's a huge market for people who want to simplify the E-mail process, who go online just for their E-mail." The profits in this scheme will theoretically come through ads displayed onscreen as people use the software. "It's like network TV," says Charles Ardai, Juno president—a former pulp mystery writer with a background in marketing. "You want to watch Seinfeld? You get a few ads." Optional fee-based services may be added later, like online shopping or the ability to attach 15 graphics or spreadsheet files to your E-mail. "If you want to send pictures of your kids, God bless you, but it may not be free," says Ardai.

Even more audacious than Juno is the second venture, called Farsight. 16 Essentially, Farsight's ambition is to become your online banker, broker, insurance salesman—whatever you do with your money, they want you to do it with them on their Web page. The service isn't ready for outsiders to test, although the prototype Shaw demonstrated for *Fortune* looks slick and easy to use. Shaw says he's lined up some partners; he's also talking to commercial banks and mutual fund companies, but (there's that secretiveness again) he won't say who. Will it succeed? Remember, a successful online personal finance enterprise has been the elusive dream of the entire banking industry for more than a decade. It's something no one from Citibank to Microsoft has figured out how to do yet. D. E. Shaw's Farsight could be the online personal finance breakthrough everyone's been waiting for. Or not.

On a recent evening, Shaw whirls into his lobby, apologizing profusely. 17 He's a half-hour late for an appointment because of an urgent phone call from Richard Gephardt. The House minority leader wanted to ask a fellow liberal Democrat what would really happen on Wall Street if the government defaulted on its debts. ("I told him it wouldn't be good," says Shaw.) Shaw is also an acquaintance of President Clinton's—they met while Clinton was still governor of Arkansas—and has served on presidential advisory bodies. Back in college he was an early anti-Vietnam protester.

Yet another persona. Could this quant among quants, with his mas- 18 sively parallel business ambitions, also have an incipient case of Potomac fever? Shaw laughs at the suggestion. He can't imagine going into politics. Or leaving the private sector, period. Or being bought out. "The most fun I've ever had has been serving as CEO of this company," he says. More he won't say, just as he's not about to tell anyone how he beats the market. ©

CRITICAL READING

1. Why does James Aley, the author of this piece, choose to use descriptive phrases such as "sweating Mylanta chuggers" and "free E-mail to every man, woman, and dweeb" in an article about economics, which is sometimes called the dismal science? In what ways might the style of this article differ from an article in a computer science journal?
2. In characterizing the financier Shaw, the author says he has a reputation "as an amalgam of Einstein, Midas, and Rasputin." Identify those three individuals, and explain how each illustrates certain aspects of Shaw's personality and economic practice.
3. Shaw says that his goal "is to look at the intersection of computers and capital, and find as many interesting and profitable things to do in that intersection as we can." What "things" in particular does Shaw do to profit on the intersection between computers and capital?

CLASS DISCUSSION

1. Why, according to this article's author, is Shaw devoting so much time and attention to the Internet—thus far in history a relatively profitless area for companies, despite all the hype—when his "quant" activities are generating such respectable income? What specific Internet-related activities does he plan to undertake? On the basis of your own experience of the Internet, evaluate the potential success (or lack thereof) of these Internet ventures.

2. According to Aley, this article's author, Shaw wants "to identify ways in which technology has the potential to fundamentally transform our world, and to play a significant role in bringing about that transformation." How, in Shaw's mind, will technology fundamentally transform the world of finance? In addition to Shaw's ideas, in what other ways can you imagine technology's dramatically affecting the economic realm?

DIRECTED FREEWRITE

Toward the end of this article, Aley says, "Farsight's ambition is to become your online banker, broker, insurance salesman—whatever you do with your money, they want you to do it with them on their Web page . . . Will it succeed?" In an extended freewrite, explore the ramifications of this computer-based economic venture—what specific services such a website might provide for consumers—and then to go on to answer the question, Will it succeed? In answering the latter, use your imagination and experience with websites, both successful and unsuccessful, as evidence and/or inspiration.

POLITICS FOR THE REALLY COOL

Josh McHugh

According to a recent government report, new technologies and new applications for existing technologies will continue raising living standards in the United States over the next quarter century. By one estimate, more than half the entire store of human knowledge has been produced over the past fifty years—thanks in large part to the invention of the computer and of the microprocessor—and such growth is expected to accelerate over time, as technologies become increasingly sophisticated. However, as this store of knowledge increases, new technologies arise to challenge traditionally accepted ways of thinking, organizing and analyzing infor-

Source: "Politics for the Really Cool" by James McHugh in *Forbes,* vol. 160, no. 5 (September 8, 1997). Copyright © 1997 by Forbes, Inc. Reprinted by permission of Forbes Magazine.

mation, and doing business. This article describes one such techno-challenge: namely, cryptographic software that is emerging to thwart the governmental restrictions of strong encryption software. According to this article, the founder of a company called C2Net is committed to uniting a libertarian political philosophy with computer science, in order to facilitate a government revolution in which national economies are compromised by the power of innovative cryptographic software. As you read, notice the dispassionate stance that McHugh adopts toward his anti-establishment protagonist; although the author probably has some feelings—even strong ones—toward the revolutionary whom he describes here, he takes great care to make his written piece relatively nonjudgmental: a hallmark of "responsible" reportage, which aims to deliver fact and let readers, such as yourself, come to their own conclusions.

Forbes, *founded in 1918, is one of the leading business magazines. It features predictive reporting, bold opinions and tough-minded analysis of companies and their leaders. Each issue anticipates major trends, indentifies new opportunities and offers clear business lessons. The coverage ranges from companies' management strategies and technology to investing and gobal economics. Overall,* Forbes *offers a unique perspective in the business world where it boasts the most affluent and influential readership of any business magazine.* Forbes *also produces* Forbes Global, *an English-language international edition of* Forbes, Forbes ASAP, *a specialized magazine dealing with the convergence of business and technology,* Forbes Special Interest Publication, Inc., *a group that produces a wide range of special interest magazines for highly targeted niche markets, and* Forbes.com, *a website that offers an online version of the magazine as well as an array of interactive tools, calculators, and databases.*

"This is a cool holiday," says Sameer Parekh over a July 4 breakfast in   1
a cafe near the University of California at Berkeley. "It's the day we celebrate overthrowing the government."

A disheveled 22-year-old, 135 pounds, shirttails down to the knees of   2
his jeans, with a 4-inch black goatee hanging from a cherubic face, Parekh is no violent revolutionary out to establish a dictatorship of the proletariat. Parekh is a libertarian of a new sort. His weapon: software.

Parekh traffics in a substance known among his peers as "strong   3
crypto," cryptographic software massively stronger than the stuff American companies are allowed to exort. Cryptography is the science of scrambling messages so they cannot be read by prying eyes. It is the lifeblood of telephone commerce—credit card verifications, bank teller machine transactions, wire transfers. It is useful to crooks. And it is magnificently antiauthoritarian.

Encrypted with a sufficiently powerful code, a cellular phone conversa-   4
tion becomes untappable, a written message or computer file indecipherable. Federal authorities are attempting to limit the spread of this technology abroad. But they are no match for Parekh and other rebels with his programming skills.

For the last three years Parekh has been mixing sophisticated com-   5
puter science with libertarian philosophy, selling a cryptographic product
made in an undisclosed foreign country through an Anguillan subsidiary. His
company, C2Net, thereby skirts U.S. export restrictions.

Looking further out, cryptography's challenge to Washington's author-   6
ity—indeed, to that of all governments—is daunting. Even if the federal government can somehow keep strong crypto out of the hands of Muammar
Qaddafi—extremely doubtful at this point—it would still have all manner of
domestic users to worry about.

Cryptography is very useful to anyone who can't afford to leave behind   7
a paper trail. That could be someone running an illegal gambling business
or doing insider trading or distributing child pornography or arranging the details of a cocaine shipment. It could also be someone who is a perfectly legitimate business operator except that he doesn't want to pay income taxes
or otherwise submit his transaction to the prying eyes of increasingly intrusive governments.

Parekh envisions a revolution in which federal buildings don't burn to   8
the ground but rather just run out of money. There would still be a government, but it would not be the expansive welfare state we have today. It
would be a minimalist version of the sort seen in a place like Hong Kong—
strong on law and order, sanctity of contract and minimal social security but
that's about it.

Walter Wriston, former chairman of Citibank, devoted a chapter of his   9
brilliant 1992 book *The Twilight of Sovereignty* to the history of cryptography. Wriston foresaw the weakening of national governments through the
power of technology and recognized that cryptography would play a key
role. He knew something about it from personal experience. During World
War II he was responsible for the electromechanical devices used by the Allies to encrypt their messages. Wriston sees encryption technology as a key
ingredient in the transfer of social and economic power from the governments of nation-states to the PC-packing populace. Since the success of Internet commerce depends on strong cryptography, its proliferation is
inevitable. "The government can't do much about it," says Wriston. "It's another thing slipping through their fingers."

Rejoice, libertarians. Lament, Hillary Clinton and partisans of the nanny   10
state. If you want to participate in the cryptographic revolution against Big
Government, you don't have to traffic with an arms merchant in a dark alley.
Go to the Internet. Pretty Good Privacy (pgP), from $99 to $249, is a popular
program. Another one is SynCrypt, by SynData Technologies Inc., just out.

Using this off-the-shelf stuff you can transact business in total privacy.   11
Don't worry about spies. With what is presently known about code cracking,
it would take a supercomputer a billion years to divine your message.

There is another dimension to the spread of crypto. The same mathe-   12
matical tricks used to encode a message can be run in reverse, to generate

a so-called digital signature. This is a computer stamp of authenticity. It can be used to prove that an electronic document originated with a particular sender, such as a bank depositor or a bank officer. Assemble a few digital signatures in a clever fashion and you have created a mechanism for digital cash—a system of electronic payments akin to Visa or MasterCard but with the added feature that it can be made anonymous.

Think about that. Money transfers that are genuine but untraceable. 13 Anonymous, secure E-cash could give rise to a blossoming of commerce on the Internet and a reduction in the billions of dollars spent annually processing paper checks and paper credit-card chits.

Bad news, of course, for the Internal Revenue Service and its 3,570– 14 page maze of a tax code. And what happens to the Fed's control of the money supply when more and more money takes the form of digital blips on a satellite in the sky? How do you stop money laundering once cash is invisible and leaves no paper trail? How do you catch tax dodgers?

The IRS figures that it is already losing $120 billion a year on income 15 that goes unreported. When E-cash becomes commonplace, that number is going to get larger. The underground economy, after all, does surface at times. Dogs can sniff the traces of cocaine in a satchel of bills. In the ionosphere economy there is no odor for dogs to sniff.

For the libertarian set, today's encryption technology is the best thing 16 to come along since the right to bear arms. After all, why risk getting arrested for dumping tea into the harbor when you can just order the tea from a tax-free jurisdiction over the Net, encrypt the purchase order and pay with anonymous digital currency? Libertarians see encryption technology as the weaponry for a bloodless grassroots revolution in which revenue streams replace street barricades as the fields of battle.

"We are looking at kidnappers, we are looking at terrorists, we are 17 looking at banking integrity, we are looking at propriety interests and economic secrets," Louis Freeh, director of the Federal Bureau of Investigation, told members of the International Cryptography Institute two years ago. Freeh has been stumping for tougher government controls on encryption technology. He wants a "key escrow" bureaucracy that would hold cryptographic keys that could, if law enforcement deemed it necessary, be used to unscramble any encrypted message.

But do we want to put that much power in the hands of bureaucrats? 18 "Back in England, when the king wanted to smoke out people we'd call terrorists today—the people we see in retrospect as patriots—he wanted to steam open envelopes," scoffs Wriston. "Nothing has changed—now governments want to steam open your E-mail. If I were the national drug czar, I'd want to, too. The problem is, none of us trust the government to limit that interception to those particular messages."

If the FBI is threatened, that doesn't entirely dismay the libertarian 19 crowd that seems to be overrepresented in the hacker community. "With the

Internet being ubiquitous and crypto being cheap and easy to get, it's going to be more and more difficult for governments to control transactions between people," declares Adam Shostack, a 24-year-old cryptography consultant whose clients include Fidelity Investments. In February he instructed attendees at a financial cryptography conference in the finer points of using encryption to protect large networks from attackers and con men. Site of the conference: the Caribbean tax haven of Anguilla.

It's too early to give it a name, but computer technology and modern   20 communications are at the threshold of creating a new kind of political movement. Talk to David Friedman, a professor of economics at the University of California at Santa Clara. Friedman espouses an anti-big-government philosophy a little stronger even than that of his famous father, Milton Friedman. He calls the set of questions raised by encryption "easily the most important privacy issue of the decade, and perhaps the most important policy issue." He concedes the downside to a technology that will be useful to lawbreakers. But he says the advantages of pervasive privacy outweigh the disadvantages: "On the whole, it'll be a change to a freer and more interesting society."

Cryptography, the craft of secret writing, has been around almost as   21 long as writing itself. Bad guys have always used it. So have rebels. Its better-known applications through the ages have been in making secure military plans and espionage communiques. Today's biggest user is, if not the government, the bank industry. Encryption safeguards the more than $1 trillion a day that flows over the Fedwire and the Chips systems.

Modern cryptography was born two decades ago at Stanford Univer-   22 sity with the invention of so-called public key encryption by Whitfield Diffie and Martin Hellman. In classic cryptography, keys were kept private. The sender would use a key, or formula, to encode a document; the receiver would use a closely related formula to decode. To communicate, the sender and receiver would have to share a key. This was usually the weak spot. A messenger sent to transfer the key could be intercepted or compromised.

With public-key encryption, this problem is finessed. The receiver of   23 confidential messages simultaneously creates an encoding and a decoding key. The peculiar arithmetic of these keys, perfected by a trio of MIT mathematicians, is such that the one cannot be divined from the other: Knowing the encrypting formula tells you absolutely nothing about how to unscramble a message. So the receiver need not be particular about his choice of messenger to deliver the encrypting key. Indeed, he can afford to publish the key for all the world to see. Modern-day practice is to dump the key onto an Internet home page or server.

What makes encryption a killer application just now? The MIT algo-   24 rithm requires that both sender and receiver do several billion calculations on each message, a practical impossibility not too long ago. Moore's Law to the rescue. The doubling of computing power every 18 months has placed the ability to process virtually unbreakable cryptographic algorithms within reach of anyone with a 166-megahertz Pentium.

Legitimate users? Any company planning on doing business on-line. 25 When you send an order over the Internet, the contents of your message pass through a series of network routers and servers before reaching their final destination. Anyone who gains control of one of the machines along the way could intercept your credit card information. You're not going to send in the order unless you know it is secure.

Illegitimate ones? This is an imaginary scenario. You work at Apple 26 and know, two days before it is to be announced, that Microsoft is going to pump in some cash and probably give a kick to the stock price. You're going to tip off your brother-in-law, who is going to feed the tip to a third party, an active trader in technology stocks. Do this with phone calls and you stand a fairly high risk of being caught, even though you have never met the trader.

So you encrypt the stock tip with your brother-in-law's public key and publish it on the Internet, perhaps in the middle of a chat room that lots of people visit. Your brother-in-law does the same, using the trader's public key. Both of these messages look like meaningless garbles to an outsider. They betray nothing about whose key was used to encrypt them.

Convicted insider trader Dennis Levine used a secret account in the 27 Caribbean. But how do you use an offshore account without going through customs or making tappable phone calls? Given the power of encryption and digital signatures, a modern-day Levine could do anonymous E-trading from the comfort of his home PC, without making any suspicious phone calls or getting on a plane. Might the government have to throw up its hands someday, accepting the libertarian view that laws against insider trading just impede the efficiency of the marketplace?

Someday it might. In the meantime, the government is trying to put the 28 crypto genie back into the bottle. The current export controls permit the sale of weak crypto (the sort that could be cracked by the National Security Agency) but not crypto that would take the NSA a trillion years to crack.

The problem is that the basic tricks are widely known; indeed, the 29 equation that drives these public key systems was published by a Swiss mathematician in the 1760s. Any reasonably competent Russian programmer can reinvent the software from scratch, and that is just what is happening. At this point, trying to regulate cryptography is like trying to cut the murder rate by regulating the sale of kitchen knives.

The next battleground will be fought over digital cash. One system, 30 Mondex, has been adopted by an international consortium of banks led by National Westminister. The system, however, includes a digital trail that could be subpoenaed.

Not good enough, says cryptographer David Chaum, whose rival prod- 31 uct is anonymous and untraceable—except to the spender. Customers want anonymity, he says—that's why 2.6 billion $100 bills are in circulation.

Chaum distances himself from the libertarian crowd, but his preaching 32 about getting snoops off our backs is music to their ears. His invention may very well lead to the society espoused by Friedman and Parekh, in which widespread encryption forces the government to accept a less intrusive role in information flow.

Now the government polices what can be claimed about a prescription 33 drug, what can be said in a real estate ad, who can talk about a publicly traded stock and when, and who can finance a political ad. Is all this necessary to preserve the union and insure domestic tranquility? The answer depends on your politics. If you are a Big Government liberal or Big Government right-winger, the answer is yes. But not everyone thinks we need as much government as we currently have.

When he was a 16-year-old high-school student in Libertyville, Ill., 34 Sameer Parekh typed Henry David Thoreau's 9,000-word essay "Civil Disobedience" into an Apple II GS computer and posted it to an electronic bulletin board. The treatise begins: "I heartily accept the motto 'That government is best which governs least,' and should like to see it acted up to more rapidly and systematically. Carried out, it finally amounts to this, which also I believe,—'That government is best which governs not at all.'"

Look Thoreau's "Civil Disobedience" up on the World Wide Web and 35 chances are you'll see "typed by: Sameer Parekh. . . . 1/12/1991" at the end of the text. Over the years, scores of people have made copies of the document and posted them, complete with Parekh's name and typos, on their own Web sites.

Thoreau's essay paraphrases another hero of Parekh's, Thomas Jef- 36 ferson. It happens that one of Jefferson's many passions, along with fighting to keep the fledgling U.S. government as small as possible, was cryptography. In the 1790s he invented an elegant, handheld rotary cipher machine. What could he have done with a laptop!

There is something about the Internet that brings out resistance to au- 37 thority. "Libertarianism is much more important in cyberspace than in real space," says David Friedman. "Nearly all political discussion on-line is pro- or antilibertarian. Libertarianism is the central axis."

Libertarianism as a central axis? Perhaps. The cyberheads have al- 38 ways been defiant of authority, going back to the Phone Phreaks of the 1970s, who used their knowledge of electronics to beat Ma Bell out of long-distance charges. Some of the phone acrobats evolved into today's self-styled "cypherpunks," a term combining the science fiction genre cyberpunk with the British spelling of "cipher." The cypherpunk clan (check out the Internet newsgroup "alt.cypherpunks") includes John Gilmore, one of the first employees at Sun Microsystems and an early member of the Electronic Frontier Foundation. The libertarian axis is particularly strong in the EFF, which defends hackers and cryptographers against their federal adversaries.

At Berkeley, Parekh programmed E-mail servers to allow subscribers 39
to send and receive E-mails anonymously or under pseudonyms, and to surf
the Web through a specially programmed "anonymizer" server without leaving the electronic trail that could let the Web site operators—or an enforcer
for the Securities & Exchange Commission—know who visited and when.
After dropping out of Berkeley in 1995, he went full time into the business of
protecting Web surfers' identities.

Realizing that his subscribers' privacy was only as secure as the 40
servers their accounts sat in, Parekh invited his friends in the hacker community to try to break into Web servers sold by Microsoft and Netscape.
Successful break-ins were rewarded with T shirts. The results ("I had to stop
giving T shirts out") convinced him that the real money to be made was in
selling crackproof, Web-server software.

With Microsoft and Netscape restrained by U.S. law from exporting 41
sever software with strong encryption, Parekh saw an opportunity. He took a
copy of Apache, a popular server software package available free on the Internet, and set about the arduous task of weaving heavy-duty encryption
programs into the server software. Once he had figured out how to do that,
Parekh contracted with programmers in a country he won't name (lest the
U.S. lean on the country to tighten up its cryptography export laws) to write
the software and formed a sister corporation in the Caribbean tax haven of
Anguilla to sell it to the rest of the world.

If you don't like the tax rate or export laws in your native country, set 42
up a Web server in a Caribbean tax haven, on the Isle of Man or on Vanu-
atu, incorporate there and run your business from anywhere over the Internet. Countries like those use low taxes and secrecy protection to compete
for corporate custom.

As the world economy becomes less land- and factory-based and 43
increasingly server-based, expect more nations to welcome boundary-
jumping business. Encryption provides two essential functions in this sort of
economy: It keeps transactions secure as they course along the world's networks, and it makes the nature of the transactions invisible to the prying
eyes of border guards and tax collectors.

After less than a year, C2Net's encryption-studded software is running 44
on about 30,000 domains—more than any other commercial software outside
of the stuff sold by Netscape and Microsoft. In the process, the U.S. lost a few
high-tech jobs, not to mention the taxes on the sales of the software.

As more and more business transactions are hidden from the IRS by 45
encryption, Parekh predicts, tax revenues will decrease. Declining tax revenues will lead to the privatization of many of the government's present
functions, and people will be more free to choose what services to spend
their money on. They will even be free to choose what kind of money they
will use.

Maybe it won't be the Federal Reserve's notes. Curiously enough, Fed   46
Chairman Alan Greenspan is not entirely unsympathetic to the libertarian
aim of taking money out of the exclusive control of the federal government.
Greenspan was a libertarian in his youth—a regular in the salon of Ayn
Rand (1905–1982). Greenspan predicts that electronic commerce will give
rise to private currencies.

"As the international financial system becomes ever more complex,"   47
Greenspan said at a Treasury conference last year, "we, in our regulatory
roles, are being driven increasingly toward reliance on private market self-
regulation similar to what emerged in more primitive forms in the 1850s in
the United States."

Greenspan made it clear that he did not think the government should   48
seek to stem the tide, even though it will undermine the authority of organizations like his Federal Reserve Board. "I am especially concerned," he
went on, "that we not attempt to impede unduly our newest innovation, electronic money, or, more generally, our increasingly broad electronic payments system."

Ian Goldberg is working on that very innovation, folding encryption   49
schemes together to create a universal digital currency that will incorporate
all the disparate forms of digital cash in the electronic marketplace. Goldberg, 24, a Canadian graduate student at Berkeley, spends most of his time
tinkering with and poking into cryptosystems.

In September 1995 Goldberg sent a chill down Netscape's spine   50
(and a ripple through its stock price) when he announced that he and a
colleague, David Wagner, had found a major vulnerability in the security
layer of the Navigator Web browser. Sixteen months later, in response to
a challenge by security software company RSA, Inc., Goldberg devised a
program that harnessed the spare computing cycles of about 250 as-
sorted workstations in Berkeley's computer science department to attack
a message encrypted with a 40-bit key, the government's limit on un-
registered encryption software for export. Trying 100 billion keys an
hour, Goldberg's gang broke the cipher in 3½ hours. The experiment got
noticed.

Where does all this end? Goldberg predicts that tax laws and commer-   51
cial regulations will need to change to adapt to the world of encrypted online business. The FBI will have to go after bombers by keeping an eye on
ammonium nitrate rather than its ear on phone lines. "Taxes will have to be
based more on physical things like land—assuming one believes in taxation
at all," he says. "With encryption, not only can you hide your transactions,
but your assets as well. Intellectual property can be hidden easily."

As for governmental restrictions on encryption, Goldberg finds them   52
more ridiculous than pernicious. "I don't think terrorists will say, 'Since
there's a law against strong cryptography, we won't use it.'"

Against all this governments are fighting a battle they have no prayer   53
of winning, says Walter Wriston. Fortified with strong cryptography and
growing exponentially, Wriston says, the Internet will irrevocably weaken
governments as we know them. "They haven't got a chance in hell with that
thing," he chuckles. "There's no way anybody can control it."

We do not know where all this will end, and neither does anyone else,   54
but for better or worse, the implications for politics, for economics and for
human freedom are enormous. The 20th century was the century of Big
Wars and Big Governments—fascist, communist, welfare state. The 21st
century is going to be something quite different.   ©

CRITICAL READING

1. According to Walter Wriston in his 1992 book *The Twilight of Sovereignty,* how
   might the power of technology contribute to the weakening of national governments? How might encryption technology be a "key ingredient" in this weakening?
2. The author says, "Dogs can sniff the traces of cocaine in a satchel of bills. In the
   ionosophere economy there is no odor for dogs to sniff." Explain how an underground ("ionosphere") economy might be generated by individuals' having access to strong cryptography, and what effect that underground economy might
   have on the national (and international) financial picture.
3. What is the relationship between Sameer Parekh and author Henry David
   Thoreau, as represented by this article? What philosophies/political stances
   might the two have in common? In what ways might the two differ?

CLASS DISCUSSION

1. According to Parekh's vision, how do computer technology and economics combine to undermine governmental power, and possibly even to topple governments? Consulting your own knowledge of computers, finance, and government,
   argue the merits of Sameer's "libertarian" vision.
2. Explain, in your most understandable layman's terms, what the phrase "strong
   crypto" means. How, according to Parekh, might having access to strong crypto
   give the user certain advantages over the mass populace, and even over the government? What additional advantages can you imagine strong crypto's bestow-
   ing on the user?

DIRECT FREEWRITE

In a two-page freewrite, explore where you stand on the libertarian/governmental
control issue. At one end of the spectrum, where Sameer Parekh claims to reside,
are individuals who believe that all governmental control should be stripped away,
leaving individuals free to engineer their own destinies; at the other end of the

spectrum are individuals who believe that human beings need to have their drives, desires, and impulses reined in—that the anarchy that would result from no governmental controls would be a highly undesirable state. Where do you situate yourself along this continuum?

COMPUTER SCIENCE UNIT WRITING ASSIGNMENTS

1. On the basis of the freewrite you produced in response to the McHugh article in this unit, write a persuasive essay in which you present both sides of the libertarian/governmental control issue as discussed in the essay, and then argue for one side or the other. In structuring this essay, try to remain as judgment-free as possible as you summarize the main arguments of Sameer Parekh and "libertarians" like him, along with the arguments of those who favor stronger governmental controls, especially in the area of the Internet, the World Wide Web, and computer encryption. Having objectively summarized these arguments, go on to argue in favor of one of the positions (or some compromise between the two), citing evidence from the article and from your own experience to support whatever persuasive points you raise.

2. On the basis of the Aley article in this unit, write an imaginative process essay in which you tell the reader how to construct some sort of computer-aided economic venture: a hip-hop music Website, an Internet start-up company, a Web-based essay writing service, whatever strikes your fancy. A process essay either tells the reader how to do something or describes how something is done, and an imaginative process essay asks you to make up some elements of the process (since, in this case, you probably have little practical experience as a professional designer of Web pages). As you write this process essay, you might consider any or all of the following: What specific process are you trying to explain, and why should it be important to readers? Are there different ways of doing the process, and if so, what are they? Who are your readers, and what skills or special knowledge do they need to understand this process? What equipment will be needed, and how long will the process take? How many individual steps are there in the process, and why is each step essential to the successful completion of the project? What difficulties might be encountered, and how might these difficulties be overcome? Do similar processes exist that might shed light on the process you're writing about? Although process papers are often written in the second person ("First you need to . . ."), some teachers prefer that you remain in the third person ("It is essential that the Web designer first . . ."), as you maintain in most academic essays; check with your teacher on this consideration before proceeding. See our earlier discussion of process essays in assignment 2 on page 110 of the Neuroscience unit, in Chapter 2.

3. Both of the articles in this unit describe a close relationship between computer-aided skills and economic life. In a research or "I-search" essay, explore some potential career paths open to computer science majors. Traditionally, as college

graduates, computer scientists have expected to be employed in a variety of positions, such as hardware design, system analysis and design, network and communications engineering, database design and development, artificial intelligence, graphics and image processing, and technical consulting and marketing. Beyond these relatively obvious pursuits, are there other areas in which computer scientists might find work, as suggested by the two articles in this unit or by your own experience? Alternatively, if you're not a budding computer scientist or economist yourself, you might discuss ways in which computer expertise might enhance the pursuit of your discipline, whether it be art history, anthropology, speech therapy, or sports coaching.

Unit 2
Mathematics—Finance by the Numbers

THE NEW SCIENCE OF FINANCE
Don M. Chance and Pamela P. Peterson

In recent years, finance has developed into an academic discipline, thanks to borrowed elements, tools, and techniques from mathematics—specifically the fields of probability and advanced mathematics—and also from economics and physics. The growing academic reputation of finance can be gleaned from the fact that six economists have won the Nobel Prize since 1985 for their work on how investors set prices. This *American Scientist* article by Don M. Chance, a First Union professor of financial risk management at Virginia Polytechnic and State University, and Pamela P. Peterson, a professor of finance at Florida State University and a specialist in corporate finance and empirical methods, illustrates that the ways in which people acquire and invest money have a number of intriguing links with the more traditional scientific disciplines, especially mathematics. The authors demonstrate that the increasing use and refinement of risk-management tools has corresponded with the increasing complexity of mathematical instruments—derivatives, for example—to study complex financial phenomena, such as the movement of stock prices. As you read, observe the ways in which academic disciplines converge, overlap, and sometimes split off to form entirely new disciplines, as finance did in recent times.

Don M. Chance holds a Ph.D. in finance from Louisiana State University. He is a professor of financial risk management at Virginia Polytechnic and State University where his research, teaching, and consulting are concentrated in the area of financial derivatives and risk management. He has addressed these topics extensively in two of his books: An Introduction to Derivatives, 4/e *and* Essays on Derivatives.

Pamela P. Peterson earned a Ph.D. from the University of North Carolina at Chapel Hill. She is currently a professor of finance at Florida State University, where she has taught for almost twenty years. Her research and teaching are concentrated primarily in corporate finance and empirical methods. She has written two textbooks on finance: Starry Starry Night: Provincetown's Response to the AIDS Epidemic; *and* Company Performance and Measures of Value Added: Financial Management and Analysis. *She is currently an editor of* Contemporary Finance Digest.

Money fascinates most people. And whether endowed with a little or a lot, we all tend to want more. This common desire has produced a seemingly insatiable demand for popular books on money and investing, which shows that people with limited financial training are in awe of those who know—or profess to know—a great deal about the subject. Yet finance (the study of how money is acquired and invested) is a relatively young field, having emerged out of the shadows of economics after World War II. Since then, finance has evolved into a critically important pursuit, as evidenced by the influence it has had on so many people and institutions. 1

Although finance has only recently become a recognized academic discipline, its roots go back centuries. From the days when bankers were called moneychangers, financiers have had to perform tricky computations, borrowing frequently from higher mathematics. In recent years, they have also begun to embrace some elements of physics. To many scientists this marriage of quantitative fields has brought lucrative new jobs. For bankers and investors, it has spawned opportunities to expand the products they offer and to carry out previously intractable calculations. 2

The scientific character of finance arises largely from its preoccupation with risk. Since the time when sailing the high seas meant subjecting one's life and fortune to great dangers and uncertainties, people have sought to analyze, understand and control the various hazards they face. The development of probability theory, which began in earnest during the 16th and 17th centuries with the works of Italian scholar Girolamo Cardano and the French mathematicians Blaise Pascal and Pierre de Fermat, has allowed risk to be studied, understood and if not reduced, at least faced with greater confidence and awareness. 3

Over the past half century, economists studying finance have taken the body of knowledge about how human beings behave when faced with uncertainty and translated it into mathematical descriptions of the way people obtain and invest funds. With the advances in computers and the development of increasingly powerful statistical techniques, finance has become a truly empirical science, demanding that its various experiments be as objective, accurate and repeatable as those in particle physics or microbiology. This evolution has not been confined to the hallowed halls of academe: Financial theories and tests are now as likely to be formulated at major financial institutions as at universities. 4

The importance of such research has not gone unnoticed. Since 1985 Nobel prizes in economics have gone to Robert Merton, Myron Scholes, 5

William Sharpe, Franco Modigliani, Merton Miller and Harry Markowitz for their influential research on how investors set prices. Indeed, making such determinations, a process called valuation, is one of the central tasks of finance.

THE PRICE IS RIGHT

Valuation is the science, and sometimes the art, of estimating what something in the future is worth today. The underlying principles involved are not new. For example, Alfred Marshall, a professor of political economy at the University of Cambridge, published a textbook in 1890 in which he discussed how the present value of an anticipated future benefit could be ascertained. His reasoning began with something that every schoolchild learns: Money in the bank grows considerably faster when the interest is compounded. More precisely, it multiplies by a factor of $[(1 + r).sup.t]$, where r represents the interest earned during one period and t is the number of elapsed periods. Translating future values to the present day requires only that $[(1 + r).sup.t]$ be placed in the denominator to give the correct multiplicative factor.   6

Similar calculations apply to the price of stocks. As long ago as 1938, the economist John Burr Williams of Harvard University argued that the appropriate price for a stock is the present value of all future dividends paid to its owner. In 1959, Myron Gordon (then at the University of Rochester) took this notion further, assuming that dividends increase gradually at a constant rate, which is indeed the pattern for many mature companies. Some elementary mathematical manipulations of infinite series will show that this assumption implies that the price of a stock today (denoted by P) equals the ratio of the next period's dividend (call it $[D.sub.1]$) to the difference between the rate of return investors demand from the company ("the cost of capital" or "discount rate," k) and the expected growth rate of dividends (g). That is, $P = [D.sub.1]/(k - g)$. This formulation, sometimes called the Gordon model, can be widely applied because g is almost always smaller than k.   7

Financial analysts still use the Gordon model or one of its many variants to determine the value of certain stocks—although it is clearly not appropriate for those many publicly traded companies that have not yet paid any dividends. Formulations like the Gordon model use the discount rate to account both for the time value of money and for the fact that the returns earned on securities also depend on the amount of risk involved—a connection that holds for many types of investments. For example, owning stock in small, upstart companies typically subjects investors to more variation from year to year—higher volatility—than owning stock in large, stable corporations, but the small companies generally provide higher returns.   8

The analysis of how the price of various assets reflects volatility has occupied many economists since Gordon first introduced his model. William   9

Sharpe (then at the University of Washington) and John Lintner (then at Harvard University) independently developed the first formulation specifically to address this problem during the 1960s. Called the capital asset pricing model, their theory describes the returns on securities as comprising compensation for the time value of money and for the risk associated with overall movements of the stock market. In 1976, Stephen Ross (then at the University of Pennsylvania) published a more general method, which he named the arbitrage pricing theory. His approach is based on the idea that if the prices of equivalent assets become unbalanced, there will always be clever investors ready to take advantage of the misalignment.

Both the capital asset pricing model and arbitrage pricing theory are   10
difficult to test definitively, so the theoretical foundation for establishing the price of stocks is far from solid. But the valuation of options—agreements that grant the purchaser the right to buy or sell something at a fixed price for a predetermined period of time—is the area where the science of finance is better equipped to handle risk.

AN OPTIONAL ASIDE

Most of the progress in calculating the price of options has been quite   11
recent, even though the need has long been present. Indeed, options have been traded for centuries. They served, in essence, as insurance policies for firms that needed to assure themselves that the future price of a commodity they bought or sold regularly would not rise or fall too dramatically. Yet it was not until the turn of the last century that Louis Bachelier, a student at the Sorbonne studying under the renowned mathematician Henri Poincare, first addressed the problem of assigning prices to options. Poincare was not impressed with such an applied dissertation topic, and, though approving the research, he gave Bachelier a mark of less than the highest distinction, thereby condemning the young scholar to teach at one of France's lesser-known institutions, where little was heard from him for the rest of his career.

Bachelier's model was unrealistic (his theory allowed the fluctuating   12
cost of commodities sometimes to become negative), and so his methods for determining the value of options were not reliable. Still, Bachelier's mathematical description of erratically shifting commodity prices holds the distinction of having anticipated the formulation Einstein used in 1905 to describe Brownian motion, the jittering of small particles suspended in liquid that the Scottish botanist Robert Brown observed in 1827. Norbert Wiener subsequently refined the mathematics of Brownian motion at the Massachusetts Institute of Technology during the 1920s.

The equation of Brownian motion that plays so important a role in op-   13
tion pricing relates the shift in price (δP) that occurs over a small interval of time (δt) to the expected rate of rise or fall of the price (symbolized by μ) and

its inherent volality (σ). The equation also involves the variable δZ, which is a random process characterized by a normal, bell-shaped distribution with a mean of zero and a dispersion proportional to δt. Specifically, the equation states that $\delta p = \mu\, P\delta t + \sigma\, P\delta Z$, where μ and σ can be functions of both time and price.

Physicists recognize the variable P as describing generalized Brown-   14
ian motion, a formulation that is widely applicable to a variety of physical and financial phenomena. This mathematical description of Brownian motion belongs to the family of stochastic differential equations, which are characterized by extremely rapid oscillations that decrease in magnitude as the time interval, δt, shrinks. Ordinary derivatives and their corresponding integrals do not exist for these functions, necessitating the invention of something called stochastic calculus.

This new branch of mathematics blossomed in the period immediately   15
following World War II from the pioneering work of the Japanese mathematician Kiyosi Ito. Probably his most influential contribution was the development of an equation that describes the evolution of a random variable driven by Brownian motion. Ito's Lemma, as mathematicians now call it, is a series expansion of a stochastic function giving the total differential. Just as Taylor's theorem leads to the total differential of ordinary calculus and is considered "the fundamental theorem of calculus," Ito's Lemma has become known as the fundamental theorem of stochastic calculus.

Although these mathematical abstractions may seem far removed   16
from the nitty-gritty world of finance, they are in fact intimately linked. And it was M. F. M. Osborne, a physicist in the U.S. Navy, who first realized in 1959 that financial market prices followed the equations of Brownian motion that Einstein and Wiener had forged decades earlier.

Soon after Osborne's observation, mathematical techniques for ana-   17
lyzing Brownian motion reached business schools and economics departments, where scholars applied them to one of the perennial problems of finance: the valuation of options. Economists then created various new pricing schemes, but all of these prescriptions either required knowledge of expected changes in the price of the underlying asset or other measures that were equally hard to quantify, such as how investors react to uncertainty.

A tractable solution emerged only after Fischer Black, then an em-   18
ployee of the consulting company Arthur D. Little, and Myron Scholes, a young professor of finance at MIT, applied the concept of arbitrage to the problem. Arbitrage relies on the fact that two financial instruments (or combinations of financial instruments) that produce the same return in every situation should, logically, sell for the same price—and clever investors will quickly take advantage of cases where this premise is violated. The arbitrageur purchases the security or portfolio where the price is low, sells it where the price is high and profits at no risk. If financial markets are working properly, such opportunities should not exist.

Black and Scholes applied this principle to the strategy of purchasing 19
some stock and simultaneously selling someone else an option to buy that
stock at a fixed price. They showed that the risk in owning the stock can be
eliminated by continually revising the ratio of options sold to stock owned.
The resulting combination should therefore earn the equivalent of the return
offered by buying risk-free bonds. From there Black and Scholes backed out
the option price from a parabolic partial-differential equation based on the
premise that stock prices exhibit Brownian motion. Black held a bachelor's
in physics and a doctorate in applied mathematics, but he was not a specialist in differential equations and only later learned that the equation he solved
could be transformed into the heat-diffusion equation of thermodynamics,
for which the solution was already known.

Although it is now called the Black-Scholes model, Robert C. Merton, a 20
young economist also at MIT (working independently but in contact with
Black and Scholes), derived the same solution at around the same time.
Merton graciously delayed publication of his article in deference to Black
and Scholes, whom he felt deserved primary recognition. After some difficulty convincing journal editors of its merits, their article appeared in *The
Journal of Political Economy* in the spring of 1973—timed, coincidentally,
with the opening of the Chicago Board Options Exchange, the first organized facility for trading options in the U.S.

The Black-Scholes model found its way into finance textbooks over the 21
next decade, and by the middle of the 1980s, Black was busy putting his
theories to work at the New York investment firm of Goldman Sachs. Many
other economists followed Black from academe to investment banking and
brokerage houses. And when the next generation of business school graduates reached the working world filled with knowledge of the Black-Scholes
modal, a revolution ensued. Corporations and investment fund managers
were barraged with new products, such as swaps, structured notes, asset-
backed securities and exotic kinds of options, which integrated well with the
array of forward contracts, futures contracts and the standard options that
had been trading for many years. These instruments collectively came to be
known as derivatives, their values being derived from the values of stocks,
bonds, currencies or commodities.

Derivatives have become increasingly elaborate, owing not just to the 22
ingenious scheming of high-tech financiers but also to a recognition that risk
is both complicated and pervasive. The new instruments allow the buying
and selling of financial uncertainty in its many incarnations, so that firms
needing to reduce risk can transfer it to firms willing to bear it. The theories
of Black and Scholes laid the groundwork for this complex edifice, which
came to be called financial engineering. And in 1997 the Nobel committee
awarded its prize in economics to Merton and Scholes. Black had died two
years earlier and thus could not be named for the prize that he, too, clearly
deserved.

For many scientists, the burgeoning market in derivatives and the   23
quantitative nature of their pricing has brought a bonanza. Mathematicians,
physicists, systems engineers and computer scientists—"quants" in the parlance of the trades—are now widely employed at brokerage firms and large
corporations.

WANNA SWAP?

Much of the quantitative work in finance seeks to establish the value of   24
new and oftentimes complex derivatives. One of us (Chance), for example,
has recently studied equity swaps, transactions between two parties in
which the first agrees to make a series of payments to the second and the
second agrees to make a series of payments to the first, where at least one
of the two sets of payments depends on the course of a stock price or stock
index.

People make equity swaps to lessen the financial hazards associated   25
with the ups and downs of the stock market. Some executives, for example,
use these swaps to rid themselves of the risk of being heavily invested in
their own companies—while maintaining voting rights on the shares they,
technically, still hold. For example, an executive owning 30 percent of the
shares of her firm, which are worth perhaps many millions, might enter into
an agreement to pay a bank on a quarterly basis the return on her stock
plus dividends. The bank in turn gives the executive a fixed interest rate.
How can the bank decide what rate to offer without knowing the future returns to expect from the stock?

Working with Donald Rich of Northeastern University, Chance realized   26
that no definitive system for pricing these instruments had been published
and, after some study, concluded that what at first glance seems a thorny
problem is really no problem at all. The solution is merely an extension of
the brilliant insight that Merton, Black and Scholes brought to the problem of
pricing options a quarter century ago: Risk premiums do not need to be explicitly predicted if one applies the principle of arbitrage.

This conclusion is most obvious for a swap that involves only one pay-   27
ment (which, technically, would be considered a forward contract). For example, suppose the firm of Goldman Sachs agrees to pay an executive of
Microsoft a fixed rate of interest, r, and the executive agrees to pay the firm
the return on Microsoft stock, which (because this stock pays no dividends)
is simply the percentage change in the stock price. The two parties agree to
make the transaction at the end of a year, paid on the basis of the assumption that $100,000 is invested. Assume also that the rate of interest on a
one-year loan from a bank is also exactly r.

If the return on the Microsoft stock over the year turns out to be x, the   28
net cash flow to the executive will be $100,000(r − x), which could be posi-
tive or negative. For the firm, it is the same amount with an opposite sign,

$100,000(x − r). An alternative way to accomplish the same thing would be for Goldman Sachs to borrow $100,000 from a bank and purchase that much worth of Microsoft stock. After a year, the firm can sell the Microsoft stock and pay off the loan. Goldman Sachs earns $100,000(x) from the stock but loses $100,000(r) from paying interest on the loan. In total it earns $100,000(x − r)—generating the same cash flow as a swap for which the rate of fixed payment is equal to the going rate of interest at the bank.

For realistic equity swaps, which involve a series of payments spaced over time, the algebra becomes considerably more involved. But this simple example nevertheless illustrates the principle behind the calculation: The price of an equivalent portfolio determines the price of the derivative. 29

One might ask whether the underlying assumption—that the market operates so well that opportunities for arbitrage are few and far between—is valid. The answer, in short, is that modern financial markets do even out prices rapidly when they get out of kilter. In fact, real markets act in ways that fit closely (though not exactly) with the ideals of economic theory. 30

A WELL-OILED MACHINE

Many economists have mounted studies of market efficiency and found that the prices of the assets being traded quickly reflect the news available to all investors. This line of research has roots that go back several decades, but it began to mature with the work of Eugene Fama, who published an influential paper on market efficiency in 1970 while he was at the University of Chicago. 31

Fama classified efficiency according to how traders react to various types of information. If the values of the assets being bought and sold take into account all past prices and other market-generated figures (such as the number of transactions), the market would be, in Fama's terminology, weak-form efficient. If values also mirror all publicly available knowledge, the market would be semi-strong-form efficient. In that case, trading on the basis of information available to all investors does not help any of them earn abnormal returns—profits in excess of what one expects given returns on the market and the inherent volatility of the stock being traded. (That is, performing financial analyses of companies will not help you beat the market—other investors have already done so, and the prices of the stocks have adjusted immediately in response.) If the values already reflect not only all publicly available information but also all private or "insider" knowledge, Fama classified the market as strong-form efficient. 32

The bulk of the evidence indicates that U.S. stock markets are at least weak-form efficient. But as with much of the analytical work in economics and finance, conclusions sometimes differ. For example, some controversial studies purport to show regular annual patterns (for example, a rising "January effect") in the prices of some stocks. 33

One of us (Peterson) has recently examined whether the stock market 34 exhibits Fama's semi-strong form of market efficiency. The investigation involved how the U.S. stock markets respond to announcements of earnings that are higher or lower than expected. If the profits of a company are better than forecast, the price of its stock generally rises; if earnings are worse, the stock price usually plummets. In either case, the stock should quickly reach a new equilibrium if the market is efficient.

Several studies conducted over the past two decades have indicated 35 that after the public declaration that earnings that are higher than expected, savvy investors may be able to obtain abnormal returns for as long as 40 days before the news filters through the market and the rising stock price for the prospering company reaches a plateau. But such analyses are questionable. Because investors receive countless reports about the economy, financial markets and individual companies, stock prices bounce up and down constantly in response to the continual bombardment of information. It thus proves difficult to judge just when an upward jog in price after a report of surprisingly robust earnings is truly a reaction to that statement. And even if the cause-and-effect relation is obvious, it may be hard to determine exactly when the stock attains the new level of equilibrium.

One solution is to look at many companies, aligning the records of re- 36 turns on their stock by the date of their earnings announcements and averaging over the complete set. The results of that exercise demonstrate semi-strong market efficiency, with stock prices typically responding to new information within about 15 minutes. Interestingly, buying stocks within one or two days following the announcement of earnings that are better than expected sometimes provides abnormal profits—although it is not clear whether the modest gains that can be garnered in this way would compensate for the various fees brokers charge for making the transaction.

There is limited formal research on whether markets qualify as strong- 37 form efficient. But the general suspicion—confirmed by many well-publicized prosecutions—is that there are hefty profits to be made if investors trade illegally using insider information.

EXPERT ATTENTION

Financial markets are indeed vulnerable to the ills of insider trading, 38 but they are for the most part fair to investors. And although many of these people feel compelled to learn the nuances of financial engineering, few truly need to be able to manipulate infinite series or solve parabolic partial-differential equations. Nor do they need to become experts in chaos theory, Benoit Mandelbrot's now-famous factual geometry (which, ironically, he had first considered in a financial context before applying it to the natural sciences) or neural network programming—all hot areas of research for the many quantitatively minded professionals now studying finance in academic settings and on Wall Street.   ©

CRITICAL READING

1. What is finance, in relation to the authors' definition of the emerging discipline/practice? In what ways is finance similar to the traditional discipline of economics, and in what ways might it differ?
2. How did finance become a recognized academic discipline, as described by the authors? Explain their statement, "The scientific character of finance arises largely from its preoccupation with risk." What role does probability theory, a mathematical concept, play in the discipline of finance?
3. What is meant by the financial term "valuation," and how does it relate to equities (stocks)? What are stock options, and how does the new discipline of finance affect the way in which individuals study and trade them?

CLASS DISCUSSION

1. Even if you don't understand all the mathematical calculations presented in "The Price Is Right" section of this article, discuss the significance of those concrete mathematical examples to the author's thesis that the new discipline of finance incorporates elements of other, more traditional academic disciplines, especially mathematics?
2. The authors conclude their article as follows:

> Financial markets are indeed vulnerable to the ills of insider trading, but they are for the most part fair to investors. And although many of these people feel compelled to learn the nuances of financial engineering, few truly need to be able to manipulate infinite series or solve parabolic partial-differential equations. Nor do they need to become experts in chaos theory, Benoit Mandelbrot's now-famous fractal geometry (which, ironically, he had first considered in a financial context before applying it to the natural sciences) or neural network programming—all hot areas of research for the many quantitatively minded professionals now studying finance in academic settings and on Wall Street.

What do you take this statement to mean? In class discussion, explore the ways in which an understanding of a variety of disciplines and theories might help one gain a better understanding of the movements of stocks on Wall Street.

DIRECTED FREEWRITE

Do an extended freewrite on the emergence of the discipline described in this article as finance. How did it come about? What were the social/economic/technological changes that might have enabled practitioners of this discipline to carve out a niche for themselves in the world of the academy?

ALGEBRA AND SOCIAL SECURITY: A PERFECT FIT

Arthur C. Mead

Economists who teach in universities frequently ask themselves some key pedagogical questions, namely, "What is it that economists can contribute to their students?" and "What do economists want students to take away from their experiences in economics—a discipline that's sometimes called 'the dismal science,' because it deals in such relatively unsexy areas as unemployment, recessions, and marginal utilities?" In this article, Arthur C. Mead, professor of economics at the University of Rhode Island, asserts that although economists have been known more for their ability to disagree, they would probably agree that the skill of mathematical modeling is crucial in the teaching of economics to university students. Mead discusses the Social Security system as a case in point, indicating ways in which this economic phenomenon might be approached from a mathematical perspective. As you read, notice the way in which the author systematically goes about identifying crucial economic variables that must be included in the mathematical model he proposes, and the ways in which he attempts to make these sophisticated mathematical concepts available to mainstream college students.

Arthur C. Mead attended Boston College where he received his Ph.D. in 1978. Mead has worked at the National Bureau of Economic Research and is currently a professor of economics at the University of Rhode Island. His research interests are in the areas of regional economic performance, demographics, and the economics of higher education. Professor Mead has also spent time as a department advisor and department director for student internships. His articles have appeared in the Providence Journal, Providence Business News Public Productivity & Management Review, and The Journal of Economic Education.

Economists have a long heritage of working with abstract models designed to help us sort through the complexities of a situation. Because these models are so often designed to explain the behavior of quantifiable phenomena, we have developed significant quantitative skills and often choose to express our models mathematically. For proof of how pervasive mathematics has become, we need look no further than the staples of our introductory courses, the graphs of the supply-demand model of price determination.   1

Source: "Algebra and Social Security: A Perfect Fit" by Arthur C. Mead in *Journal of Economic Education*, vol. 29, no. 1 (Winter 1998). Copyright © 1998 by Heldref Publications. Reprinted with the permission of the Helen Dwight Reid Educational Foundation. Published by Heldref Publications, 1319 Eighteenth Street NW, Washington, DC 29936-1802.

Can students build their own mathematical models? If we expect them 2
to master the skill of model building, they need practice building models.
However, we now have a new problem. Where do we find examples of real-
world issues that can be modeled, issues that lend themselves to a rather
straightforward mathematical representation and capture students' attention? The importance of the latter has been pointed out by Lillydahl and supported by Strober and Cook, who concluded, after reviewing videotapes of
their students doing economics, that "economic educators need to do more
to relate economic models to the experiences of students."

One issue that has worked for me, in both my introductory and quanti- 3
tative skills courses, is Social Security. This topic has four distinct advantages. First, discussions of Social Security invariably revolve around
demographics, a forgotten topic in most economics classes. Economics
textbooks have very little to say about demographic factors despite the fact
that they have been recognized in the professional literature as having potential impact on many aspects of the economy, including economic growth,
saving rates, and housing prices. The popular business press, which I encourage my students to read, is also filled with articles on the impact that
demographic change has on business decisions and on the performances
of markets. For example, Bennet described the impact of the aging of the
baby boom on the design of automobiles, Mantell looked at the type size in
books, and Schonfeld examined the performance of the stock market.
Hamish McRae took the importance of demographics one step further and
identified demographic change as one of the two primary determinants of
long-term economic growth. Before we are done with the Social Security
issue, students have discussed four important demographic "stylized facts"
that exert a significant influence on the U.S. economy: increasing life expectancies, changing family structures, immigration, and the aging of the
baby boomers.

Social Security is also an issue that students can relate to personally, 4
either because they have grandparents receiving benefits or because they
at least have heard it discussed outside the classroom. Social Security,
thanks to the heated debate over the balanced budget amendment, has
moved from the op-ed and business sections of the newspapers to the front
page; from those Sunday morning news/education shows to a major story
on the nightly news. Students have listened to "experts" talk about an
emerging intergenerational conflict over resources and about how their generation, Generation X, will be the first generation not to achieve the standard
of living set by their parents. They need little encouragement to talk about
intergenerational equity.

Social Security's third advantage is that it is an issue that lends itself to 5
a rather straightforward algebraic representation. With a very simple algebraic model, one can show that the Social Security system, which has been
quite successful at helping to alleviate poverty among the nation's elderly,

has structural flaws that will produce severe fiscal strain on the federal budget in the near future. Finally, by focusing on the future implications of the system's structure, the example provides students with the opportunity to produce their own forecast and to see firsthand how economic forecasting can be an important input into public policy debates. It also has provided me with a number of satisfying moments when I see that glimmer of excitement in some students who "discover" the nature of the structural flaw and identify potential solutions after working through the logic themselves.

THE MODEL

The Social Security exercise begins, in all my courses, with a brief description of the heated debate surrounding the passage of the Social Security legislation during the Depression, with a focus on how the debate has come full circle since that time. It then shifts to a description of a set of assumptions that capture the essentials of the system's structure. For my quantitative skills and small introductory seminar classes, I begin by dividing the class into small groups and assign them two sets of tasks. On the first night, each group is asked to transform the assumptions into a structural model and then to derive the reduced form equation for the tax rate, which they must bring to the next class. They are also responsible for tracking down the historical data on the key variables specified in one of the assumptions and then generating appropriate graphs. This gets students into the government publications area in the library and/or on the Internet to find the data and provides them with some valuable practice using spreadsheet software.

Students in all classes are provided with the reduced form equation, historical information on all of the economic and demographic variables, and some current data relating to income, population in millions, participation rates, tax rate and so forth. In my small classes, the groups are then asked to find the population projection data and to write a brief memo in which they forecast the tax rate and identify some policy decisions that could alter their forecast for the tax rate. In the large classes, students are given the population projections and are asked to come to class prepared to describe the bases for their forecasts of each right-hand side variable and their policy proposals to offset the impact of the projected demographic changes on the tax rate.

THE DISCUSSION

Once the class reassembles, our attention turns to the problem of forecasting the tax rate. We begin with a brief discussion of Keynes's assertion that a prerequisite for forecasting is a thorough understanding of the present, well-grounded in a knowledge of the past. This invariably leads to a discussion of a number of important demographic and economic trends highlighted by the students' graphs in the small classes and my graphs in the large class. A brief summary of some of their findings appears below:

- Size of elderly and working age populations. The elderly population, as a result of the aging of the baby boomers and increasing life expectancies, is projected to grow upward of 10 times faster than the nonelderly population in upcoming years. The leading edge of the baby boomers, a cohort that represents approximately one-third of the U.S. population, will reach age 60 within a decade. And they will live longer. In 1940, when the Social Security system was taking form, an American could expect to live to about 60, but by 1990, life expectancy had risen to more than 72 years.
- Retirement rate. Not only are Americans aging, they are also retiring earlier, which reduces the pool of taxpayers and increases the pool of benefit recipients. In 1940, approximately four out of every six men over the age of 65 were in the labor force, but by 1990, the rate had fallen to less than one in six.
- Labor force participation rates. In the post–World War II era, the pool of taxpaying workers had been swelled by the substantial increase in the number of women entering the work force. Unfortunately, after years of convergence in the participation rates of males and females, there is little room for additional labor force growth from this source, and we should expect to see a slowdown in the growth of workers in upcoming years.
- Average benefits. Average monthly Social Security benefits in the past 20 years have increased nearly a third faster than median family income. If inflation-adjusted wages continue to stagnate while Social Security benefits continue to be pegged to inflation, this differential will continue to grow.
- Average income. The growing financial burden of Social Security on the taxpayers caused by slower labor force growth will be further exacerbated by slower income growth as American workers continue to struggle with the structural changes associated with the Information Revolution and the emergence of a single, global labor market.

After completing the discussion of the historical data and the demographic projections, our attention turns to the structural flaws in the system. To help focus the discussion, I present a forecast of the tax rate under the assumption that the only thing that changes between 1992 and 2020 is the age composition of the population. The tax rate nearly doubles (97 percent increase) by 2020, and after I point out what this will mean to their paychecks, they are ready to talk seriously about public policy and what can be done to avoid this situation.

Once the class has seen how the tax rate can be affected by changes   10
in certain variables, we begin some serious discussions of policy proposals.
A few proposed suggestions follow:

- Altering the composition of the population. It does not take long for my
  students to identify this option, which leads to a discussion of rationing
  health care and immigration.
- Lowering the retirement rate/raising the retirement age. We may not
  be able to coax retired workers back into the labor force, but we can
  move to extend the worklife of those still in the work force. A 65-year-
  old can expect to live approximately 17 more years. Can we expect
  America's workers to support someone for this long? My students do
  not think that they should and advocate higher retirement ages.
- Lowering benefit levels. Questions concerning the appropriate inflation
  measure to be used in adjusting Social Security benefits have sur-
  faced in recent months, and we invariably touch on the question of an
  appropriate benchmark for yearly increases. Some suggest that it may
  be time to explore the possibility of some measure of average income
  as a benchmark rather than a measure based on the price level, while
  others suggest a move toward means testing where Social Security
  benefits would be reduced for those who make over a certain income
  level.
- Raising taxable earnings. Recognizing that there is no Social Security
  saving fund and that all surpluses are simply used to pay the government's existing bills, we explore the possibility of eliminating the upper
  limit on taxable income.

CONCLUSION

At some point, I am forced to invoke my authoritative powers and re-   11
luctantly close debate, a debate that often becomes quite heated. What
started out as a simple application of algebraic modeling invariably turns
into much more. During the course of our work, students have had an opportunity to see how algebra can help them structure their ideas on issues
that they are hearing about in the news; to rummage around in the government publications sections of the library and on the Internet for information
that adds substance to the algebraic skeleton; to transform historical data
into a story with demographic, economic, and policy chapters; to take their
first tentative steps toward developing skills that venture into upper-division
econometrics classes; and to see how economic policies can be based in
economic theory. If your experiences are similar to mine, you will find that
the dismal science seems a bit less dismal to the students and that many
students will enjoy doing economics, which increases the odds that they will
continue to do it as they grapple with new issues long after they have left
their economics course.   ©

CRITICAL READING

1. List at least three important demographic and economic trends pertaining to Social Security, as outlined by the author in the Discussion section of this essay, and briefly summarize each trend.
2. The author says, "Once the class has seen how the tax rate can be affected by changes in certain variables, we begin some serious discussions of policy proposals." Summarize at least three of the proposed changes to the current Social Security system, discussing the ways in which these changes would improve the system in the future.
3. The author concludes this piece by telling his colleagues, "If your experiences are similar to mine, you will find that the dismal science seems a bit less dismal . . . and that many students will enjoy doing economics . . ." How, in the author's opinion, will the method described in this essay help students to enjoy economics, which is too often referred to as "the dismal science"?

CLASS DISCUSSION

1. List the "four advantages" of using the Social Security system as a model of study for introductory and quantitative skills courses, in the view of this article's author, and discuss your reaction to each advantage. Do you agree that, based on these advantages, studying the Social Security system might be relatively interesting? Why or why not?
2. Discuss why, according to the author, the elderly population is projected to grow more than ten times faster than the nonelderly population in upcoming years. What effect will this phenomenon have on the Social Security system in this country, as projected by statistical models?

DIRECTED FREEWRITE

According to the author, "The growing financial burden of Social Security on the taxpayers caused by slower labor force growth will be further exacerbated by slower income growth as American workers continue to struggle with the structural changes associated with the Information Revolution and the emergence of a single, global labormarket." Do an extended freewrite in which you discuss the ways in which the advent of the World Wide Web and other mass media, along with the globalization of capital economies, may burden this country's financial system(s) in general, and the Social Security system in particular.

MATHEMATICS UNIT WRITING ASSIGNMENTS

1. In reading, discussing, and thinking about the Mead article in this unit, you considered, among other things, the numerous factors contributing to a growing financial burden that the Social Security system is placing on American taxpayers. Write a formal recommendation essay in which you examine this problem and propose some solutions to it. In a recommendation essay—a rhetorical form that falls within

the broad category of argumentative essays—the writer defines a problem, proposes several alternatives to solving the problem, arrives at a concrete solution to the problem, and discusses the feasibility of that solution. For the purposes of this essay, therefore, you will want to reread the Mead article, and perhaps do a bit of additional research on the Web or on your school library's computerized database, to uncover specific ways in which the Social Security system might place increased economic burdens on American citizens in the future. Having defined this problem, then present a broad palette of suggestions to solve this problem, as suggested by Mead and others. Next, from this list of possible solutions, propose a solution that you think will best address this problem. Finally, explain why you think your proposed solution will be feasible in the American economy of this millennium.

2. The Chance and Petersen article in this unit describes the emergence of the discipline (some would call it an economic subdiscipline) known as finance. Since the chances (no pun intended) are high that you are not a finance major, it might therefore be interesting for you to explore the origins of an academic area with which you are presumably more familiar, namely, your own major. In a brief research essay, explain to the reader how your discipline of anthropology, or computer science, or engineering—or whatever your major happens to be—came about. In developing this chronology, try to incorporate as many diverse sources as you can: a book or two, an academic journal essay, an article from the popular press, some Web-based material, and even a personal interview from a professor in your major area. Try as much as possible to present a range of opinions regarding your major discipline's origins, rather than merely presenting a one-sided, "encyclopedic" version of this disciplinary chronology.

3. Both articles in this unit, and the writings elsewhere in this chapter, suggest that this decade has seen a wave of mathematicians migrating to Wall Street and apparently making enormous sums of money there. Mathematicians, one would gather from the reading, have been at the forefront of a revolution in finance, applying sophisticated mathematical and statistical formulas to the endless river of data pouring out of the world's financial markets. The success of these mathematicians suggests that the market is predictable—not the hit-or-miss "crapshoot" that many analysts previously assumed stock picking to be. For the purposes of this essay, write a case study of two stocks, one picked at random and one picked through the application of a mathematical model that you discover while reading this chapter's articles and/or through poking around the Internet or your library's database a bit. For your random pick, you can close your eyes and point to a stock listing in your local newspaper's financial section. For your mathematically selected stock, attempt to pick one that appears to have the potential of a quick profit, since you don't have the luxury of waiting years for its valuation to increase. Having selected your stocks, track them carefully for one month, and create a line graph that compares their relative movements. At the end of the month, write a statistical analysis of your stocks' performance. Did the mathematically selected one outperform the randomly selected one, and why did it do so (or why not)? In writing your statistical analysis, try to find as many concrete and quantifiable reasons as possible to account for your securities' performance.

CHAPTER FIVE

T**HE** E**NVIRONMENT**

INTRODUCTION

In the last decade or two, researchers have observed a number of changes in the environment, on both the local and global scales. Higher levels of potentially carcinogenic chemicals in the water—the result of industrial disposal and spillage—have been posited as being responsible for the increasing incidence of certain types of cancer in recent years. Researchers predict that the numbers of people dying of such malignancies will continue to escalate, if industries' waste disposal practices are not stringently controlled. Similarly, clear-cutting of the rain forests in the equatorial regions of the world has resulted in lower production of life-sustaining oxygen and a concomitant rise in carbon dioxide in the atmosphere. These changes are believed to cause a phenomenon known as global warming, in which the temperature of the earth is predicted to rise gradually in the next century, unless the emission of greenhouse gases, such as the aforementioned carbon dioxide—along with carbon monoxide from automobile exhausts, chlorofluorocarbons from aerosol cans, and freon from refrigeration systems—is reduced.

People meet such predictions with a variety of responses. In the popular media, some observers agree with these predictions and insist that humans need to be more proactive in reversing the dire effects of industrialization on the environment. For example, Niles Eldredge, a paleontologist at the American Museum of Natural History, says in a recent *Time* magazine article,

> We can stabilize our numbers and temper our patterns of consumption.
> We can work to stem the tide of ecosystem destruction and species
> loss. We can, in short, see ourselves for what we have become: the first
> global economic entity, a fascinating state arrived at through no end of

cleverness but a state that is ultimately limited to the health and productivity of the natural system in which we live.

However, other media commentators present a different slant on this issue. Conservative social critic Tyrrell R. Emmett, Jr., in an *American Spectator* article, criticizes environmentalists for portraying nature as a fragile system—environments are highly resilient over time, he notes, looking at the earth's geological record—and he decries the way members of the environmental camp demand that populations and governmental agencies comply with ecologically minded regulations. Author Jonathan H. Adler, in his recent book entitled *Eco-Scam,* likewise criticizes environmental researchers as being "false prophets of ecological doom."

If members of the media are so polarized on this issue, it should come as no surprise that similar differences of opinion occur in the academic world as well. Still focusing on global warming as a case in point, climatologist Norman J. Rosenberg and others, in an article written this year for the journal *Climatic Change,* assessed the possible impacts of global warming on the hydrology of the high plains aquifer region of the United States, which provides water for about 20 percent of this country's irrigated land. On the basis of several intensive long-range studies, Rosenberg et al. predict sharply decreased precipitation and, hence, reduced water yields in this area, with potentially dire consequences to a large portion of this country's food-producing geography.

By contrast, Thomas G. Moore, writing in the scholarly journal *Public Interest,* suggests that global warming may not be entirely unfavorable, especially to industrialized countries. In fact, says Moore, despite dire predictions of many scientists, a significant change in global temperature would be beneficial to mankind, although some agriculturally dependent societies may have difficulty adjusting to warmer periods. Citing organisms' tendency to flourish in warmth, Moore concludes that "global change is inevitable—warmer is better, richer is healthier."

Whatever position they take on this controversial subject, most—if not all—observers agree that the environment is in a state of accelerating change and that this change may not represent an entirely healthy trend for the planet and its inhabitants. For the purposes of this chapter, we therefore make the assumption that everyone—whether defining oneself as an environmentalist or not—has some degree of concern with the environment, with changes that are taking place within ecosystems—whether they be fragile or resilient—and with the future of the spheroid space vessel on which we all live. As you will discover, the environment is an unusually rich topic for study, one that can be approached in a myriad of ways from literally any discipline.

The sciences, of course, have always been concerned with this topic; after all, the overarching object of study in the sciences is "the natural world," and from the earliest days of human scientific inquiry, the workings of the cosmos and of the earth have been of utmost concern to scientists. From a practical standpoint, the revolutionary transition early humans made from nomadic hunting and gathering societies, to the agrarian lifestyle that made possible the formation of human "civilization" as we define it, relied on increased human understanding of the changing seasons, weather patterns, plant and animal biology, and so forth. Much later in human history, the Age of Enlightenment in the West saw a great florescence of scientific inquiry, as Western thinkers came to believe that humans could, through exercising their reason, "master" nature. This way of thinking, and the discoveries and inventions that followed, are a remarkable testament to the power of human imagination and ingenuity. The industrial revolution that followed on the heels of this philosophical shift in Western thinking permanently altered our way of life, our economic systems, our class structures and governments.

As we all know by now, however, such achievement was not without cost, and in harnessing the wind, we may have reaped a whirlwind, so to speak. Our progress, our use of nature, is now catching up to us, as we confront both pollution and the outright loss of natural resources. Today, many scientists from different disciplines study the loss of species, the conditions of air, the chemical content of water, and the quality of our soil. In addition to understanding the changes we've effected in the natural environment, many scientists are involved in finding ways to correct damage we have done and to prevent our doing any more damage to the world that is our home.

Of course we haven't abandoned efforts to shape and alter nature. In fact, our efforts have become far more dramatic than ever as we learn more about the genetic makeup of living things. The Human Genome Project is currently working to map our entire genetic code. The locations of certain genetic diseases have been discovered, and we will soon have the capacity to screen human fetuses for particular congenital diseases, as well as other inherited qualities such as gender, height, intelligence, and perhaps sexual orientation as well. Increasingly, the food we eat is genetically engineered; our agricultural practices today would be completely baffling to a farmer from earlier centuries. Scientists have now cloned sheep, and the capabilities for human cloning are on the horizon. All of these advances are raising moral and ethical questions, some of which are inspired by our awareness of earlier mistakes we've made in altering the natural landscape and its inhabitants. We'll no doubt be wrestling with these issues for years to come.

Social scientists, with their primary focus on the world of human societies and interactions between people, engage environmentally related topics in a number of different ways. Our relationship to the land we live on has enormous influence over the kinds of human cultures we develop. Historians and anthropologists have documented a wide variety of cultural attitudes toward nature, as well as religious and ritual practices that embody these attitudes. It has almost become a cliché that many Native American cultures developed religious and philosophical traditions closely tied to the earth and to the belief that a spiritual energy runs through all living things. Some anthropologists are now disputing some earlier, romanticist accounts of indigenous Americans' naturalism, but nonetheless, evidence does suggest that these people possessed a different attitude toward nature (and toward their place within it) than many Western cultures have had.

Today, with increased consensus that the earth needs some protections and that our behavior toward it has to change in some ways, sociologists are concerned with the ways in which people respond to these realizations. From studies of protest methods used by radical environmentalist groups, to research into average American ecologically minded practices—the recent surge in the popularity of recycling practices, for example—we have learned about the degrees to which Americans will go to address environmental problems and the limits to such willingness. When economic realities confront environmental realities, a predictable conflict arises; scholars in political science and in economics are concerned with finding ways of mediating these conflicts.

We may not immediately associate the humanities as readily with environmental issues as we do with the sciences and the social sciences, yet ecology appears everywhere in this field. The most obvious way in which the environment figures into humanities disciplines is in artistic depictions of nature. Given that our natural surroundings are inescapable and that they inspire so much wonderment, it follows that artists—working in every medium, from every historic period and every conceivable culture—have focused their attentions on representing different elements of the natural world. In some ways, we might characterize artists as the first environmentalists. In portraying the exquisite and even terrifying beauty of nature (see van Gogh's painting *Landscape at St. Remy*), in singing the praises of nature's awesome grandeur (read Wordsworth's poem *The Prelude*), or in characterizing its terrible dangers (read Melville's whale-hunting novel *Moby Dick*), artists have helped to keep human attention on nature—an entity most people would like to preserve in all its wildness and beauty.

Recently, not only artists, but critics of the arts as well, have declared an allegiance to the environment. Calling themselves ecocritics or green theorists, these individuals argue that their emerging field of study actually benefits from interdisciplinary relations with the sciences, promoting ecological awareness through the study of artistic texts—paintings, pieces of popular and classical music, poems, novels, statues, architectural structures, and so forth. Believing that criticism of the arts should carry with it a strong social and public role, green theory has spawned a number of subspecialties, such as ecofeminism, which sees the main contradiction in the world economy as the undervalued reproductive work of women, along with the traditionally unequal power relationships between men and both nature and women.

As you can see from the preceding examples, there is a profusion of ways in which writers in the "hard" sciences, the social sciences, and the humanities approach the subject of the environment. In this chapter, we start with the sciences, and our first unit is organized around the broad, interdisciplinary field of environmental science. The latter is a discipline whose range and influence—and importance—has grown tremendously in the last twenty or so years, influenced by, and enhancing our increasing awareness of changes to our natural environment effected by human civilization. Whereas scholars in environmental science take a number of different approaches to their study and, of course, focus on a number of different environmental issues, our unit focuses on one important area of research—and also of much public controversy, as we noted earlier: the problem of global warming. We present two readings on this issue. The first depicts a mock trial in which two opposing positions on global warming are presented; in the second reading, a noted physician and environmental activist both explains causes of global warming and proposes some possible solutions.

Our second science unit focuses on the discipline of engineering, which is intimately involved in addressing environmental issues from a practical standpoint. Engineers devise strategies for dealing with current environmental problems such as toxic waste and air quality, and perhaps of even more importance, developing technologies to decrease outputs of pollution in the first place. Water pollution is a key issue of concern to both chemical and mechanical engineers, who are engaged in finding solutions to water shortages, removal of surface water contaminants, odor problems in sanitation, corrosion in municipal water system piping, and the like. Our engineering unit thus focuses on the problem of ensuring clean drinking water, through changing the ways we deal with water runoff, and through improving methods of wastewater treatment. With our worldwide growth in population and its resultant demands on water, engineers and scientists face daunting challenges as they devise ways to preserve water resources and find new sources of clean water—the stuff on which all life depends.

The social science section of this chapter opens with a unit from social ecology: a relatively new, interdisciplinary field that addresses problems affecting regional and global communities, problems of individual behavior and motivation, social influence and power, community dynamics, and governmental policy initiatives. According to the website of the Institute for Social Ecology,

> social ecology integrates the study of human and natural ecosystems through understanding the interrelationships of culture and nature. It advances a critical, holistic worldview and suggests that creative human enterprise can construct an alternative future, reharmonizing people's relationship to the natural world by reharmonizing their relationship with each other. This interdisciplinary approach draws on studies in the natural sciences, feminism, anthropology and philosophy to provide a coherent radical critique of current anti-ecological trends, and to offer a reconstructive, communitarian and ethical approach to social life.

As one can imagine, this discipline unfurls a very large umbrella, under which many different kinds of work may fit; we've chosen readings that address the moral dimension of environmental awareness and change, as well as describing some of the social practices of modern American society and examining their impact on environments.

Political economy, as the name implies, is a combination of political science and economics, and this discipline comprises the focus of the second unit in this section. Academics in the field of political economy analyze and explain the interrelationships between political and economic processes, policies, and institutions.

Clearly, the interrelationships here are many, as the policies and laws implemented by governments typically affect—to different degrees depending on the type of government and its overall role in its country's affairs—economic functioning in many ways. Conversely, political economy is also concerned with the ways in which economic systems and people's economic behavior within these systems affect governmental policies and laws. The relationship between economics, politics, and the environment in today's world is often rife with conflict; the two readings from this section examine this complicated relationship and explore ways that we can try to resolve some of the conflict inherent in the intersections of these areas of human life.

The humanities section, with which we end this chapter, starts with a cultural studies unit. Cultural studies—another relatively new discipline—involves looking out into the society at large and analyzing the cultural productions that permeate modern life. Such productions are instructive for the ways in which they both reflect and influence our beliefs, ideals, cultural practices, and identities. Cultural critics treat all cultural products—from newspaper articles to deodorant cans—as "texts" that can be read and interpreted. Cultural critics use textual analysis—in which they describe, take apart, and note the meanings of cultural product—to argue for an overall interpretation. At the same time, they note the differing interpretations that different kinds of viewers or readers might have of the artifact, on the basis of the viewers' own group memberships, interests, identities, knowledge, and so on. For example, since movies such as *The Birdcage* or *In and Out* contain codes and symbols that might resonate differently with gay and heterosexual audiences, a cultural critic might analyze the textual features of these films, point out the differing meanings received by these different audiences, and construct an argument about the most prominent meanings the critic identifies within the movie.

Although the cultural landscape provides many fields of inquiry for cultural critics who are interested in environmental issues—television, music, graffiti "tags," film, billboards, magazines, advertising, popular fiction, and video games, for instance—we have focused our cultural studies unit on a particular theoretical position that has come out of environmental thought within cultural studies. A recent article by reporter Gregory McNamee in the *UTNE Reader* describes a new type of literary critic: "a '60s survivor who, having transferred his or her idealism from politics to the realm of nature, has been teaching Thoreau's *Walden,* Rachel Carson's *Silent Spring,* and perhaps Annie Dillard's *Pilgrim at Tinker Creek* to likeminded undergraduates." Basing their critical approach on an appreciation of the environment, these ecocritics have, according to McNamee, "carved a niche for ecologically based literature in the English curriculum, territory once hotly contested by devotees of deconstructionism, postmodernism, feminism, structuralism, and psychoanalytical criticism." Naming the theoretical underpinnings of environmentally focused literary criticism "green theory," the new ecocritics are regularly offering seminars and survey courses on environmental literature and nature writing, and they are publishing their critical insights in well-respected journals within the disciplines of English and environmental studies. This unit will present two readings: one, from the *UTNE Reader,* will explain how environmental literature and nature writing are fast gaining acceptance in academic circles, while academies and universities are increasing their recognition of the subject. The second reading looks at ecothemes in a contemporary pop-cultural artifact: cereal boxes.

Next to the subject of love, nature is perhaps the most common topic explored and celebrated by poets. The second humanities unit contains two nature poems, "The Windhover," by British poet Gerard Manley Hopkins, and "Song at Sunset," by the American Walt Whitman. Although traditionally in literary studies, English literature and American literature have been grouped and studied separately, the fact that these two poets were both innovators of poetic traditions and the fact that they wrote during the same era make for an interesting linkage. Following the poems themselves, the unit ends with an essay in which a literary critic discusses the links between Hopkins and Whitman.

As you read these poems—and, in fact, all of the readings in this chapter—pay attention to your reactions: not only your intellectual ones, but your "gut" reactions as well. A well-crafted nature poem should be so evocative that it "puts you there," evoking your senses in such a way that you feel moved in some way—by the dizzying beauty of a cliffside verge or by the threat of death by drowning. Likewise, a persuasively written science or social science article will undoubtedly provoke a response in you—perhaps one of gratified agreement or of outraged contradiction. As we have exhorted you in previous chapters, be as aware as possible of your own political/ethical feelings about the environment as you embark on these readings, and keep an open mind to having your beliefs altered or reinforced by the material you encounter here.

THINKING AND WRITING IN THE SCIENCES

Unit 1

Environmental Science— The Global Hothouse

GLOBAL WARMING ON TRIAL

Wallace S. Broecker

Wallace S. Broecker is an atmospheric scientist who describes, in this piece, a mock trial, presenting the two opposing sides in a debate over global warming. Using actual public figures to represent both sides of the issue, Broecker's essay helps to lay out some of the key issues that need to be resolved if we are to come to any kind of consensus on the reality and the extent of this atmospheric phenomenon. As you read, pay attention to the rhetorical strategies Broecker uses to clearly reveal his own position in this debate, while also noting the weaknesses in the position that global warming is occurring as a result of industrialization.

Wallace S. Broecker is a geochemist who received his Ph.D. from Columbia University. He is currently the Newberry Professor of Earth and Environmental Sciences at Columbia University's Lamont-Doherty Earth Observatory. His articles have appeared in various publications including Scientific American *and* Oceanography. *Among his various awards, Broecker has received the 1979 Ewing Medal, the 1996 National Medal of Science, and the Desert Research Institute's 1999 Nevada Medal. His research is directed toward the role of the oceans in climate change.*

Jim Hansen, a climatologist at NASA's Goddard Space Institute, is   1
convinced that the earth's temperature is rising and places the blame on the buildup of greenhouse gases in the atmosphere. Unconvinced, John Sununu, former White House chief of staff, doubts that the warming will be great enough to produce a serious threat and fears that measures to reduce the emissions would throw a wrench into the gears that drive the United States' troubled economy. During his three years at the White House,

---

Sununu's view prevailed, and although his role in the debate has diminished, others continue to cast doubt on the reality of global warming. A new lobbying group called the Climate Council has been created to do just this.

The stakes in this debate are extremely high, for it pits society's short-term well-being against the future of all the planet's inhabitants. Our past transgressions have altered major portions of the earth's surface, but the effects have been limited. Now we can foresee the possibility that to satisfy the energy needs of an expanding human population, we will rapidly change the climate of the entire planet, with consequences for even the most remote and unspoiled regions of the globe. 2

The notion that certain gases could warm the planet is not new. In 1896 Svante Arrhenius, a Swedish chemist, resolved the longstanding question of how the earth's atmosphere could maintain the planet's relatively warm temperature when the oxygen and nitrogen that make up 99 percent of the atmosphere do not absorb any of the heat escaping as infrared radiation from the earth's surface into space. He discovered that even the small amounts of carbon dioxide in the atmosphere could absorb large amounts of heat. Furthermore, he reasoned that the burning of coal, oil, and natural gas could eventually release enough carbon dioxide to warm the earth. 3

Hansen and most other climatologists agree that enough greenhouse gases have accumulated in the atmosphere to make Arrhenius's prediction come true. Burning fossil fuels is not the only problem; a fifth of our emissions of carbon dioxide now come from clearing and burning forests. Scientists are also tracking a host of other greenhouse gases that emanate from a variety of human activities; the warming effect of methane, chlorofluorocarbons, and nitrous oxide combined equals that of carbon dioxide. Although the current warming from these gases may be difficult to detect against the background noise of natural climate variation, most climatologists are certain that as the gases continue to accumulate, increases in the earth's temperature will become evident even to skeptics. 4

The issue under debate has implications for our political and social behavior. It raises the question of whether we should renew efforts to curb population growth and reliance on fossil fuels. In other words, should the age of exponential growth initiated by the Industrial Revolution be brought to a close? 5

The battle lines for this particular skirmish are surprisingly well-balanced. Those with concerns about global warming point to the recent report from the United Nations' Intergovernmental Plan on Climate Change, which suggests that with "business as usual," emissions of carbon dioxide by the year 2025 will be 25 percent greater than previously estimated. On the other side, the George C. Marshall Institute, a conservative think tank, published a report warning that without greenhouse gases to warm things up, the world would become cool in the next century. Stephen Schneider, a leading computer modeler of future climate change, accused Sununu of "brandishing the [Marshall] report as if he were holding a crucifix to repel a vampire." 6

If the reality of global warming were put on trial, each side would   7
have trouble making its case. Jim Hansen's side could not prove beyond a
reasonable doubt that carbon dioxide and the other greenhouse gases have
warmed the planet. But neither could John Sununu's side prove beyond a reasonable doubt that the warming expected from greenhouse gases has not occurred.

To see why each side would have difficulty proving its case, let us re-   8
view the arguments that might be presented at such a hearing. The primary
evidence would be the temperature records that have been kept by meteorologists since the 1850s. A number of independent analyses of these measurements have reached the same basic conclusions. Over the last century
the planet has warmed about one degree. This warming was especially pronounced during the last decade, which had eight of the warmest years on
record, with 1990 being the hottest. While Sununu's group might question
the adequacy of the geographic coverage of weather stations during the
early part of the record and bicker a bit about whether the local warming
produced by the growth of cities has biased some of the records, in the end
they would concede that this record provides a reasonably good picture of
the trend in the earth's temperature. Sununu's advocate would then counter
by asking, "Isn't it strange that between about 1940 and 1975 no warming
occurred?" The Hansen group would have to admit that there is no widely
accepted explanation for this leveling. Sununu's advocate would continue.
"Isn't it true that roughly half the warming occurred before 1940, even
though almost all the emissions of carbon dioxide and other greenhouse
gases have taken place after this date?" Again the Hansen group would
have to admit this to be the case.

At this point, a wise judge might pose the following question to both   9
sides: "What do we know about the temperature fluctuations that occurred
prior to the Industrial Revolution?" The aim of this question would be to determine what course the earth's temperature might have taken if the atmosphere had not been polluted with greenhouse gases. The answer by both
sides would have to be that instead of remaining the same as it was in 1850,
the planet's temprature would have undergone natural fluctuations, which
could have been as large as the changes measured over the last one hundred years. Neither side, however, would be able to supply the judge with
an acceptable estimate of what would have happened to the earth's temperature without the release of greenhouse gases.

Perhaps a longer record of the earth's climate would shed light on its   10
natural variability. The climate prior to 1850 can be reconstructed from historical records of changing ice cover on mountaintops and on the sea. The
earliest evidence of this type dates from the end of the tenth century A.D.,
when Eric the Red first sailed from Iceland to Greenland. Ship logs written
between that time and 1190 indicate that sea ice was rarely seen along the
Viking sailing routes. The temperature was warm enough that grain could
be grown in Iceland. At the end of the twelfth century, however, conditions

deteriorated, and sea ice appeared along the Viking sailing routes during the winters. By the mid-fourteenth century, these routes were forced far to the south because of the ice, and sometime in the late fifteenth century, ships were cut off altogether from Greenland and Iceland because of severe ice conditions. As temperatures dropped, people could no longer grow grain in Iceland. The Medieval Warm had given way to the Little Ice Age.

After 1600 records of sea-ice coverage around Iceland and of the extent   11
of mountain glaciers in the Alps improved, giving us an even better idea of recent climate change. The glaciers attracted the attention of seventeenth-century tourists, including artists whose drawings and paintings document the position of a number of major Alpine glaciers. Modern measurements show that the leading edges of these glaciers fluctuated with temperature changes over the last century. Assuming that this correlation held true through the Little Ice Age, the historical evidence shows a long interval of glacier expansion, and thus cold climate, lasting until 1860. During the late 1800s, a widespread recession of Alpine glaciers heralded the end of the Little Ice Age. Ridges of rock and earth bulldozed into position by the advancing ice still mark the point of maximum glacial progress into the valleys. (The glaciers are still shrinking; less than half of their 1860 volume remains.) The mild conditions that prevailed during the Medieval Warm did not return until this century.

The problem with all this evidence is that it represents only one region   12
of the earth and is, in a sense, anecdotal. An informed judge might also challenge this evidence by pointing out that the northern Atlantic Ocean and its surrounding lands are warmed by powerful ocean currents, collectively known as the Great Conveyor, that transport heat away from the equator (see "The Biggest Chill," *Natural History,* October 1987). A temporary shutdown of this circulation eleven thousand years ago brought about an eight-hundred-year cold period called the Younger Dryas, during which northern Europe was chilled by a whopping 12°F. Could the Little Ice Age have been brought about by a similar weakening of the Great Conveyor? If heat release from the northern Atlantic was the key factor, the Little Ice Age would have been restricted to the surrounding region, and the historical evidence from Iceland and the Alps could not be taken as an index of global temperatures.

Although records of similar duration and quality are not available from   13
other parts of the world, we do have firm evidence that by 1850, mountain glaciers in some regions, such as New Zealand and the Andes, reached down into valleys as far as they had at any time during the last eight thousand years. Furthermore, by 1870 these glaciers had also begun their retreat. This suggests that the Little Ice Age was indeed global in extent.

The global warming that caused the demise of the Little Ice Age con-   14
fuses attempts to estimate how much of the last century's warming is natural and how much has been caused by pumping greenhouse gases into the atmosphere. The Sununu side would pin as much of the blame as possible on the natural warming trend that ended the Little Ice Age, while Hansen's side would emphasize the role of the greenhouse gases. What is

needed to resolve this dispute is a detailed, continuous temperature record that extends back beyond the Medieval Warm to see if cycles could be identified. By extending these cycles into the present century, scientists could estimate the course the earth's temperature would have taken in the absence of the Industrial Revolution.

I made such an attempt in 1975, at a time when the earth's temperature   15
seemed to have remained almost constant since the mid-1940s. Puzzled scientists were asking, "Where's the expected greenhouse warming?" I looked for the answer in the only detailed long-term record then available, which came from a deep hole bored into northern Greenland's icecap at a place called Camp Century. In the 1950s, Willi Dansgaard, a Danish geochemist, had demonstrated that the ratio of heavy to light oxygen isotopes (eighteen neutrons to sixteen neutrons per atom, respectively) in the snow falling in polar regions reflected the air temperature. Dansgaard made measurements of oxygen isotopes in different layers of the ice core; each represented the compressed snowfall of an arctic year. His results served as a proxy for the changes in the mean annual temperature. Dansgaard and his colleagues analyzed the record to see if the temperature fluctuations were cyclic. They found indications of two cycles, one operating on an eighty-year time scale and a weaker one operating on a 180-year time scale. (The Milankovitch cycles, caused by changes in the earth's orbit around the sun, operate on a much longer time scale. Ranging from twenty thousand years upward, these cycles are thought to control the large swings between glacial and interglacial climates.)

I took Dansgaard's analysis a step further by extending his cyclic pat-   16
tern into the future. When combined with the expected greenhouse warming, a most interesting result appeared. Temperatures leveled off during the 1940s and 1950s and dropped somewhat during the 1960s and 1970s. Then, in the 1980s, they began to rise sharply. If there is a natural eighty-year cycle and it was acting in conjunction with a greenhouse effect, I would explain the leveling of temperature after 1940 as follows: Dansgaard's eighty-year cycle would have produced a natural warming between 1895 and 1935 and a natural cooling from 1935 to 1975. The cooling in the second half of the cycle might have counterbalanced the fledgling greenhouse warming. After 1975, when the natural cycle turned once again, its warming effect would have been augmented by the ever stronger greenhouse phenomenon, producing a sharp upturn in temperature in the 1980s.

My exercise showed that the lack of warming between 1940 and 1975   17
could not be used to discount the possibility that the pollution we are pumping into the atmosphere will ultimately warm the globe. We cannot rule out this possibility until that time in the future when the predicted warming is so great that it can no longer be masked by natural temperature fluctuations. My projection suggested that a firm answer will not be available until the first decade of the next century.

While the Camp Century record seemed to provide a good method of   18
determining how natural variations and increasing greenhouse gases were

working in concert to produce the measured global temperatures, additional ice core data only created confusion. Oxygen isotope records from ice cores extracted from the Antarctica icecap and mountain glaciers in China and Peru do not follow the Camp Century ice core pattern. Even worse, oxygen isotope records from three additional Greenland ice cores differ significantly from one another and from the original Camp Century record. Perhaps the most disconcerting feature of these ice core records is that the Medieval Warm and Little Ice Age do not even stand out as major features. Local temperature variations could account for these discrepancies, but oxygen isotope ratios also depend on the season the snow falls and the source of the moisture. For these reasons, ice cores may provide good records of large changes, but the smaller ones we are looking for over the last several hundred years are obscured.

At this point, the judge would likely lose his patience and call a halt to this line of argument, saying, "while regional climate changes certainly occurred during the centuries preceding the Industrial Revolution, firm evidence for a coherent global pattern in these natural fluctuations is lacking." The judge might then suggest a different approach to settle the question of whether we are causing the earth to warm. What drives the natural changes? If we could pin down the villain, then perhaps we could say more about how temperature would have changed in the absence of the Industrial Revolution. Witnesses would point to three such mechanisms. First, the sun's energy output may have changed. Second, large volcanic eruptions may have injected enough material into the stratosphere to reflect a substantial amount of solar radiation back into space, cooling the planet. Third, the operation of the ocean-atmosphere system may have changed internally, causing the earth's temperature to wander. 19

For several centuries astronomers have been observing the cycles of the sun and trying to link them with climate patterns on earth. Sunspots, caused by knots in the sun's magnetic field, undergo cyclic change, alternating between a maximum of spots in the Northern Hemisphere and then a maximum in the Southern Hemisphere. Between these peaks, the number of sunspots drops almost to zero. A complete solar cycle takes twenty-two years. With satellites, astronomers have been able to directly monitor the sun's energy output over the last cycles. Although the energy seems to dip slightly when sunspots disappear, the change seems too small to greatly alter the earth's temperature. 20

An intriguing proposal was recently made in this regard. Two Danish meteorologists, Eigil Friss-Christensen and Knud Lassen, point out that over the last 130 years for which observations are available, the sunspot cycle has lengthened and shortened with a periodicity of about eighty years, and that these changes closely parallel the earth's temperature. The Danes suggest that during intervals when the sunspot cycle is longer than average, the sun's energy output is a bit lower, and that when the cycle is shorter, the energy output is higher. Could it be that Dansgaard was correct in thinking that the earth's temperature changes on an eighty-year time scale and that these 21 changes are driven by the sun? Most scientists remain skeptical because no physical mechanism has been proposed tying solar output to the length of the sunspot cycle. Others say that the strong similarity between the length of the sunspot cycle and the earth's temperature could be a coincidence.

In addition to the twenty-two-year solar cycle, however, change on a longer time scale has been documented. Between 1660 and 1720, sunspots disappeared altogether. Auroras, which are created when charged particles driven out from the sunspots enter the earth's upper atmosphere, were also absent from the skies during this period. Further, we know from measurements of carbon 14 in tree rings that this radioactive element, produced by cosmic rays bombarding the atmosphere, increased substantially during this time. Normally, charged particles streaming outward from sunspots create a magnetic shield that deflects cosmic rays away from the earth and the inner planets. From 1660 to 1720, this magnetic shield failed, permitting a larger number of cosmic rays to strike our atmosphere and form an unusually large number of radioactive carbon atoms. 22

From the record of radiocarbon locked up in tree rings, we can identify two even earlier periods of reduced sunspot activity: the Wolf sunspot minimum, from about 1260 to about 1320, and the Spörer sunspot minimum, from about 1400 to 1540. These three periods span a major portion of the Little Ice Age, but the last ended more than a hundred years before the Little Ice Age did—too long a time lag. This mismatch in timing and the small change in the sun's energy output (as measured by satellites over the last solar cycle) make a link between the Little Ice Age and the absence of sunspots unlikely. But the partial match prevents a firm rejection of the sun as a cause of the earth's natural temperature changes. 23

What about volcanic eruptions? Major volcanic eruptions occur roughly once per decade. Most have little effect on the climate, but occasionally an eruption blasts a large volume of sulfur dioxide high into the stratosphere. Within a month or two, the sulfur dioxide is transformed into droplets of sulfuric acid, which remain aloft in the stratosphere for a year or more. These tiny spheres reflect sunlight away from the earth, cooling the planet. Hansen and his colleagues predict that the recent eruption of Mount Pinatubo in the Philippines (which shot more sulfur dioxide into the upper atmosphere than any other eruption this century) will cool the planet about one degree Fahrenheit over the next two years. 24

Could the Little Ice Age have been caused by five hundred years of intense volcanism releasing copious amounts of sulfur dioxide? This seems implausible, as the world's one hundred or so major volcanoes erupt independently of one another and no mechanism exists that could cause them all to erupt with great frequency. Therefore, the chance is slim that one long interval would be followed by a similar period of lesser activity. 25

Fortunately, a record is available in ice cores to check this assumption. When the droplets of sulfuric acid from a volcanic eruption drift down from the stratosphere, they are quickly incorporated into raindrops and snowflakes and 26 carried to the earth's surface. So, in the years immediately following a major volcanic eruption, snow layers rich in sulfuric acid are deposited on all the world's icecaps. An ice core taken from the Dye 3 site in southern Greenland reveals that at about the time of the transition from the Medieval Warm to the Little Ice Age the acid content in the ice doubled. On the other hand, low acidity from 1750 to 1780 (during a time of cold weather) and the relatively high acidity from 1870 to 1920 (when the climate was warming) do not fit the pattern of climate change. Therefore, no strong correlation exists between the trends in volcanic sulfur dioxide and the trend in the earth's temperature.

The last of the three mechanisms that might account for the natural 27 variations in the earth's temperature is a dramatic shift in the way the planet's ocean and wind currents operate. Of the three mechanisms, this one is the hardest to build a case around because we have only a rudimentary understanding of how the interacting elements of the earth's climate system might cause natural fluctuations in temperature. The only well-documented example of such a mechanism is the El Niño cycle, in which winds and ocean currents cause the temperatures of the surface waters of the eastern equatorial Pacific to alternate between warm and cold. The cycle was first noticed because of the severe drops in fish production along the west coast of South America during the warm episodes. Since the timing between these disruptive events ranges from three to seven years, scientists became interested in predicting their arrival. What emerged from these studies is that El Niño cycles are the product of a complex interaction between winds and ocean currents. The importance of this discovery to the global warming debate is that it raises the possibility that cycles involving larger-scale interactions between the atmosphere and oceans—over longer periods—may play an important role. If the earth's temperature is being pushed up and down by such an internal cycle, our chances of determining what would have happened in the absence of the extra greenhouse gases are indeed slim.

Again the judge would become restive and call a halt to this line of evidence as well. At this point he would likely dismiss the case and suggest that the litigants return a decade from now when additional evidence regarding the warming trend has accumulated.

Sununu would deem this decision a victory, for it would provide an excuse to delay actions directed toward reductions in carbon dioxide emissions. On the other hand, Hansen could surely maintain that in the absence of proof that the world is not warming at the rate predicted by computer simulations, we should follow the standard applied to other environmental threats and rule on the side of caution. Instead of placing the burden of proof on the environmentalists, the proponents of "business as usual" should be obliged to prove that the unfettered release of greenhouse gases will *not* significantly warm the planet. And such proof does not exist; the balance of scientific opinion is that business as usual will alter the climate.

The debate over global warming is merely a small skirmish that marks 30 the beginning of a far broader war. Many of the things that we could do to curb the buildup of greenhouse gases—such as conserving energy, switching to renewable energy sources, or increasing our use of nuclear power—will be stopgap measures if the underlying problem of population growth is not addressed. World population is now 5.5 billion and growing by about 1.8 percent every year. If this rate is not substantially reduced, world population will double by the year 2030. If by that time the rate of population growth has not been greatly reduced, we run the risk that the population will skyrocket to 20 billion or more before it finally levels off. Each additional person adds to the pressure to increase the use of fossil fuels, pumping ever larger amounts of carbon dioxide into the atmosphere. In countries such as the United States and Canada, where per-capita energy consumption is the highest in the world, each person, on average, adds twenty tons of carbon dioxide a year to the atmosphere. In developing countries, where most of the population growth will occur, per-capita energy consumption is much smaller, with less than three tons of carbon dioxide emitted per person. But as these countries strive to better the lot of their citizens through industrialization, their energy demands will climb. Most of the increase will be met by burning fossil fuels, particularly coal, which releases more carbon dioxide per unit of energy produced than oil or gas. Therefore, annual emissions of greenhouse gases are likely to increase.

We are rapidly approaching a limit beyond which we cannot maintain   31
our numbers without long-term damage to our planet's environment and its remaining wildlife and to the quality of life of its human populations. While Sununu may be particularly shortsighted with regard to the effects of greenhouse gases on the climate, most of the world's leaders are shortsighted with regard to the population problem. They seem to ignore it completely. I hope the concern about global warming will force us to develop a broader perspective of our planet's future—one that will include the reality of the population bomb. Only then will we be able to begin the extraordinarily difficult task of defusing it.   ©

CRITICAL READING

1. What aspects of our short-term well-being are at stake in this debate? Can you envision some sort of compromise between maintaining this well-being and "protecting the future of all the world's inhabitants," as Broecker puts it in his second paragraph?

2. Describe the different kinds of evidence used by Broecker in this debate. Which kinds of evidence are more persuasive than others? Why?

3. Describe all the energy-consuming behaviors in which you engage on a daily basis. Estimate the duration of time you spend doing each thing. Which of these behaviors are necessary and which aren't? How do you define necessary? Are there any of these behaviors—necessary or not—that you would be willing to cut out or to cut down if asked to, or if required to, in order to decrease carbon dioxide emissions?

CLASS DISCUSSION

1. Should government delay action on reducing carbon dioxide emissions, since, as Broecker notes, we don't yet have clear evidence supporting either side? Or should we "rule on the side of caution," as Hansen suggests in the third paragraph from the end, and proceed as if we had absolute proof that global warming is occurring? Have class members take sides and address this specific issue. What measures might someone like Hansen suggest? And how might someone like Sununu respond?

2. As a class, make a master list of energy consumption on the board. Discuss the purposes served by these behaviors, and separate essential from nonessential practices, discussing where consumption of energy could be cut, how such cuts might be accomplished, whether students (and the rest of the American public) would be willing to cut down in any of these areas, or what it might take to get us as a society to cut down our energy consumption.

DIRECTED FREEWRITE

Discuss other problems besides the greenhouse effect that you believe are a threat to the earth's environment. Which of these seem the most pressing? Which problems do you think would be easier, and which more difficult, to fix? Which problems do you think the American public in general is likely to be most concerned about, and why?

THE GREENHOUSE EFFECT

Helen Caldicott

A physician and activist, Dr. Caldicott is perhaps best known for her work in the 1970s and 1980s protesting and arguing against the use of nuclear energy. In this essay, Caldicott cites a number of sources to assert the reality of the greenhouse effect, and she offers critiques of our high energy consumption. Within her critiques, she often mentions possible solutions as well. As you read, notice the kinds of language Caldicott uses to indicate the likelihood of her predictions.

*Dr. Helen Caldicott is a physician, humanist, and advocate for nuclear disar-
mament. She has received numerous awards including a Nobel Peace Prize
nomination, seventeen honorary degrees, the Peace Medal Award (United
Nations Association of Australia), the Integrity Award (John-Roger Foundation), the Peace Award (American Association of University Women); the
SANE Peace Award; and the Ghandi Peace Prize. Caldicott has founded
and headed several organizations including the Cystic Fibrosis Clinic at the
Adelaide Children's Hospital, Physicians For Social Responsibility, and
Women's Action For Nuclear Disarmament (WAND). She has written articles
for nearly every major newspaper and magazine and has authored four
books:* Nuclear Madness, Missile Envy, If You Love This Planet: A Plan to
Heal the Earth, *and* A Desperate Passion: An Autobiography.

The earth is heating up, and the chief culprit is a gas called carbon   1
dioxide. Since the late nineteenth century, the content of carbon dioxide
(CO_2) in the air has increased by 25 percent. Although this gas makes up
less than 1 percent of the earth's atmosphere, it promises to have devastating effects on the global climate over the next twenty-five to fifty years. Carbon dioxide is produced when fossil fuels—coal, oil, and natural gas—burn,
when trees burn, and when organic matter decays. We also exhale carbon
dioxide as a waste product from our lungs, as do all other animals. Plants,
on the other hand, absorb carbon dioxide through their leaves and transpire
oxygen into the air.

Carbon dioxide, along with other rare man-made gases, tends to hover   2
in the lower atmosphere, or troposphere, covering the earth like a blanket.
This layer of artificial gases behaves rather like glass in a glasshouse. It allows visible white light from the sun to enter and heat up the interior, but the
resultant heat or infrared radiation cannot pass back through the glass or
blanket of terrestrial gases. Thus the glasshouse and the earth heat up.

In one year, 1988, humankind added 5.66 billion tons of carbon to the   3
atmosphere by the burning of fossil fuels, and another 1 to 2 billion tons by
deforestation and the burning of trees. Each ton of carbon produces 3.7
tons of carbon dioxide.

But carbon dioxide accounts for only of the greenhouse effect. Other   4
gases, the so-called trace gases, which are present in minute concentrations, are much more efficient heat trappers. Chlorofluorocarbons (CFCs)
are ten to twenty thousand times more efficient than carbon dioxide.
Methane is also very efficient (twenty times more effective than carbon dioxide) and is released at the rate of 100 liters per day from the intestine of a
single cow. For example, Australia's cows make an annual contribution to
global heating equivalent to the burning of thirteen million tons of black coal
(about half the coal used in Australia per year). The scientists Ralph Laby
and Ruth Ellis, from the Australian Commonwealth Institute and Research
Organization, have developed a slow-release capsule that diminishes by 20

percent the production of methane by bacteria in the rumen of cows. (Methane is also a wonderful gas for heating and lighting houses; for example, Laby and Ellis estimated that two cows produce enough methane to heat and light an average house!) Further sources of methane are garbage dumps, rice paddies, and termites. Nitrous oxide is another greenhouse gas, a component of car and power plant exhausts, of chemical nitrogenous fertilizers, and of bacterial action in heated, denuded soil. Nitrous oxide has increased by 19 percent over preindustrial levels and methane by 100 percent. A report from the World Wide Fund for Nature published in August 1991 stated that carbon dioxide emissions from aircraft flying at altitudes of ten to twelve kilometers account for 1.3 percent of the global warming. However, the nitrous oxide that aircraft also emit is an extremely efficient heat trapper at that height and may increase global warming by 5 to 40 percent.

Within fifty years, the "effective carbon dioxide concentration" (CO_2 5 and trace gases) will probably be twice that of preindustrial levels, raising global temperatures 1.5° to 5.5°C (2.7° to 10°F). Because many scientific variables—heat trapping by clouds, change in radiation over melting ice caps, and so on—are not well understood, this rise in temperature could be as high as 10°C (18°F). Other scientists say the earth could cool several degrees. But all agree that we are in trouble.

Such a rapid change in climatic conditions has never occurred in 6 human history. If global heating were at the lower predicted level, it would match 5°C warming associated with the end of the last ice age, eighteen thousand years ago. But this change would take place ten to a hundred times faster. And at present temperatures, a 5°C increase would cause global temperatures to be higher than at any other time during the last two million years.

What will happen to the earth? Let us look at a worst-case scenario. 7 Changes of climate could have devastating consequences in the tropical forests and food-growing areas of the world, causing extinction of many plant and animal species over a few years, in evolutionary terms. Dust bowls could develop in the wheat belt of the United States, creating a situation like that described in *The Grapes of Wrath,* and the productive corn and wheat belt might migrate north into Canada and into the Soviet Union.

Already the futures markets are speculating that productive banana 8 and pineapple plantations will develop in the middle of arid Australia. Cyclones, tidal waves, and floods will almost certainly affect temperate areas of the world, which were previously immune to such catastrophes.

Sea levels will probably rise as the warming oceans expand, and great 9 areas of land will be flooded, particularly during storms. Rivers, lakes, and estuaries will have their courses and boundaries changed forever. This will disturb the hatching habitats of millions of fish.

Because about one-third of the human population lives within sixty 10 kilometers of the sea, millions, or even billions, of people will either be killed by floods or storms or be forced to migrate to higher levels, thereby severely dislocating other urban and rural populations. These refugees will create chaos as they move into established rural areas, towns, and cities. Food production will already have been disrupted by the change in climate, and a redistribution of the scarce remaining resources will probably not happen.

As sea levels rise, beautiful cities, including Venice and Leningrad, will   11
be submerged, and even Westminster Abbey and the houses of Parliament, in London, will be threatened. Many beautiful, exotic Pacific islands will be underwater. Sea levels could rise seven feet (2.2 meters) by the year 2100, according to the U.S. Environmental Protection Agency.

It is possible that the polar ice caps will melt; alternatively, the Antarc-   12
tic snow cover might increase in volume as warm air induces a buildup of snow-forming clouds over the South Pole. (Warm air promotes the evaporation of water from the earth's surface, thereby thickening the cloud cover.)

The aquatic food chain will be threatened because the base of the   13
pyramid of the ocean food chain—algae and plankton—will be seriously affected. These ubiquitous single-celled plants are food for primitive life forms and are themselves consumed by more evolved species of fish. Some forms of algae and plankton will be threatened by rising sea temperatures, and many are extremely sensitive to UV light. . . . Therefore, as the temperature rises and as the ozone diminishes, this essential element of the food chain will be jeopardized.

Moreover, plankton and algae, together with trees and plants, are na-   14
ture's biological traps for elemental carbon from atmospheric carbon dioxide, 41 percent being trapped in sea plants and 59 percent in land plants. Higher concentrations of atmospheric carbon dioxide will promote the growth of algae. But if algae are threatened by global warming and ozone depletion, this hypothetical fertilizer effect will become irrelevant. By increasing the atmospheric concentration of carbon dioxide from man-made sources, we are thus also threatening the survival of trees, plants, algae, and plankton.

Forests, too, are terribly vulnerable to climatic change and ozone de-   15
struction. Because temperature changes will be relatively sudden, specific tree species will not have thousands of years to migrate to latitudes better suited to their survival, as they did at the end of the last ice age. When the ice cap slowly retreated northward, the spruce and fir forests moved from the area of the United States into Canada at the rate of one kilometer per year. Although some plants that adapt rapidly will thrive under changed circumstances, most forests will die, and along with them many animal and bird species.

Interestingly, although sudden global warming will kill large numbers of   16
trees, increased carbon dioxide concentrations will actually stimulate the growth of those that remain, because the gas is a plant food during photosynthesis and thus acts as a fertilizer. Therefore, as forests become extinct

in the unusually hot climate, some food crops and surviving trees will grow bigger and taller. Unfortunately, many weeds are even more responsive to high carbon dioxide levels that crop plants are, and they will almost certainly create adverse competition.

Another factor to consider in this rather dire biological scenario is that 17 faster-growing crops utilize more soil nutrients. Hence more artificial fertilizer will be needed, and, since electricity is required for its production, more carbon dioxide will be added to the air. But nitrogen-containing fertilizers themselves release the greenhouse gas nitrous oxide into the air. In addition, as soil heats, vegetable matter decays faster, releasing more carbon dioxide. These are just a few of the interdependent and variable effects of global warming that are so difficult to calculate.

When forests are destroyed by greenhouse and ozone deforestation, 18 or by chainsaw and bulldozer deforestation, massive quantities of rich topsoil will be lost forever as floods and erosion wash it out to sea. Downstream waterways will overflow their banks as rain pours off the denuded high ground, and when the floods subside, the once deep rivers will be silted up from the eroded topsoil. Large dams designed for predictable rainfalls could collapse and drown downstream populations, and associated hydroelectric facilities would then be destroyed.

Decreased rainfall in other parts of the world will reduce stream runoff. 19 For example, a rise of several degrees Celsius could deplete water levels in the Colorado River, causing severe distress for all communities that depend upon the river for irrigation, gardening, drinking water, and so forth. The water quality will also suffer, because decreased volumes will not adequately dilute toxic wastes, urban runoff, and sewage from towns and industry. Until April 1991, when rain began to fall again in some quantity, California experienced a severe five-year drought, whose impact was rapidly becoming critical. After this April rainfall, the California drought continued unabated. That may be an omen of worse to come.

Cities will be like heat traps. For instance, Washington, D.C., at pres- 20 ent suffers one day per year over 38°C and thirty-five days over 32°C (100°F and 90°F). By the year 2050, these days could number twelve and eighty-five, respectively. In that case, many very young and many old and infirm persons would die from heat stress, and there would be a general temptation to turn on air conditioners, which . . . use CFCs and electricity, whose generation produces more carbon dioxide. People will thus be in a catch-22 situation—damned if they do and damned if they don't. . . .

How did the problem of atmospheric degradation become so alarming, 21 and what are the solutions?

When CFC was first concocted, in 1928, nobody understood the com- 22 plexities of atmospheric chemistry, and during subsequent decades scientists really believed that chlorofluorocarbons were ideal for refrigeration, air conditioners, plastic expanders, spray cans, and cleaners for silicon chips. Industry became so heavily invested in its production that it now finds it very difficult to cut back, even though the environmental consequences of not doing so will be severe. . . .

In the early years of the Industrial Revolution, no person could have   23 predicted the atmospheric havoc that the internal-combustion engine and coal-fired plants would wreak. Even during the 1930s and 1940s, when General Motors, Standard Oil, Phillips Petroleum, Firestone Tire and Rubber, and Mack Manufacturing (the big-truck maker) bought up and destroyed the excellent mass transit systems of Los Angeles, San Francisco, and most other large U.S. cities in order to induce total societal dependence on the automobile, global warming was a vague future threat. These companies were subsequently indicted and convicted of violating the Sherman Antitrust Act.

But now that we understand the coming disaster, we are in a position   24 to act. In order to act, we must be willing to face several unpleasant facts.

FACT NUMBER ONE

The United States, constituting only 5 percent of the earth's popula-   25 tion, is responsible for 25 percent of the world's output of carbon dioxide. It uses 35 percent of the world's transport energy, and an average-size tank of gasoline produces between 300 and 400 pounds of carbon dioxide when burned. Together, the United States and the Soviet Union consume 44 percent of the world's commercial energy.

In China, by contrast, there are 300 million bicycles, and only one per-   26 son in 74,000 owns a car. Each year three times more bicycles than cars are produced. Domestic bicycle sales in 1987 came to 37 million—more than all the cars bought worldwide. Motor vehicles globally produce one-quarter of the world's carbon dioxide, and in the United States transportation (cars, buses, trains, and trams [streetcars]) produces 30 percent of all the carbon dioxide. Transport consumes about one-third of all the energy consumed globally. The United States also produces 70 percent of the carbon monoxide gas (which leads to deoxygenation of the human blood), 45 percent of the nitrous oxides (which cause acid rain), and 34 percent of the hydrocarbon chemicals (many of which are carcinogenic).

In 1985, there were 500 million motor vehicles in the world, 400 million   27 of them cars. Europeans and North Americans owned one-third of these.

FACT NUMBER TWO

In order to reduce carbon dioxide production, cars must be made ex-   28 tremely fuel efficient, and some computer models and prototype automobiles can indeed achieve 60 to 120 miles per gallon (mpg) by means of lightweight materials and better design. But these techniques are not being employed. In 1987, U.S. car manufacturers dropped most of their research on fuel-efficient cars, and in 1986 the fuel-efficient standard, or minimum mpg, in the States was only 26 mpg. In 1991, it was still only 27.5 mpg, and the Bush administration has resisted any move to increase fuel efficiency in cars. In fact, the president's new energy plan of 1991 barely deals with these issues, and does not deal at all with mass transportation. It is more efficient to transport hundreds of bodies in one train than hundreds of single bodies in hundreds of cars. Furthermore, the construction of sleek state-of-the-art trains would constructively reemploy the one in eight people in California who currently are employed producing weapons of mass destruction. Far more people will work in this wonderful new civilian industry than in the obsolete weapons industry, because the military sector is capital intensive, whereas the civilian sector is labor intensive. The corporation that first accepts that challenge could become the world's leading producer of global mass transit systems and could earn huge profits while saving the planet.

Cars can be fueled with solar energy. In 1990, an international solar   29
car race across Australia was held. The cars achieved the acceptable speed of approximately 60 mph. They were slow to accelerate, but who needs cars that go from 0 to 90 mph in a matter of seconds? Cars can also be fueled with natural gas, which generates less carbon dioxide than gasoline does, and with alcohol. By investing heavily in this form of energy, Brazil has been helped to become somewhat energy independent. In 1988, alcohol provided 62 percent of Brazil's automotive fuel. Although alcohol is relatively expensive, it gives off 63 percent less carbon emission than gasoline. This excellent form of energy production is renewable, and marginal land can be used to grow crops that can be converted into alcohol. The United States already produces twenty million barrels of alcohol by the fermentation of corn. As oil prices climb, alcohol will obviously become a viable fuel alternative.

Cars can also be fueled with hydrogen; the technology is available.   30
One can drink the exhaust of a car powered by hydrogen, because when hydrogen burns it produces pure water. Unfortunately, major U.S. auto companies seem resistant to being inventive and creative. They stick to old, outdated designs and have been resorted to copying the latest Japanese designs—a rather sorry setback for an industry that once led the world in automobile technology. It could overtake the Japanese industry by manufacturing solar-, hydrogen-, and alcohol-powered cars, while helping to save the planet.

FACT NUMBER THREE

Bicycles use human energy and save global energy. They are clean,   31
efficient, and healthful for human bodies. Roads must give way to bicycle tracks. In China, special bicycle avenues with five or six lanes are separated from motorized traffic and pedestrians. This sort of planning is required by a large percentage of the population of the United States and of the Western

world. The arrangement is simple, easy, cheap, and clean. Distant, large-scale supermarkets and shopping malls accessible only by car will become obsolete as people demand small, convenient shops within walking distance of their homes. We can reestablish small community shopping centers, where people meet each other and socialize and where the emphasis is on the community rather than on consumerism. What a healthy, exciting prospect!

FACT NUMBER FOUR

Buildings can be made extremely energy efficient. Improved designs for stoves, refrigerators, and electric hot-water heaters can increase energy efficiency by between 5 and 87 percent. The sealing of air leaks in houses can cut annual fuel bills by 30 percent, and double-paned insulated windows greatly reduce energy loss. Superinsulated houses can be heated for one-tenth of the average cost of heating a conventional home. In the United States, 20 percent of the electricity generated is used for lighting, but new fluorescent globes are 75 percent more efficient than conventional globes. Theoretically, then, the country could reduce its electricity usage for lighting to 5 percent of the total. This, together with other conservation measures, would cause the closing down and mothballing of all nuclear reactors in the States, because 20 percent of all the electricity used there is generated by nuclear power. 32

I lived in the beautiful city of Boston for fourteen years and grew to love the old New England houses. But now that I am more aware of the fate of the earth, I realize that these are totally inappropriate dwellings. They are big, rambling, leaky, and inefficient. The vast quantities of oil required to heat these large volumes of enclosed air through a long Boston winter adds to carbon dioxide greenhouse warming. When these handsome houses were built, in the last century, no one imagined that the earth would someday be in jeopardy. Fuel supplies seemed endless, and the air was relatively clean. 33

Houses of that kind can be made somewhat fuel efficient by the insulation of walls, ceilings, and windows and by the sealing of all leaks. To encourage such reform, the federal government must legislate adequate tax incentives, for in the long run these will provide insurance for our children's future. 34

Actually, solar buildings are now in an advanced stage of design and development. The need is for legislation that requires all new buildings, residential and office, to be solar designed—with large heat-trapping windows oriented toward the south and with floors made of tiles and cement, which trap the sun's heat during the day, and appropriate window insulation, which retains the heat at night. Solar hot-water panels and solar electricity generation are relatively cheap and state-of-the-art. Firms that manufactured such equipment would make large profits. Householders would benefit because they would become independent of the utilities; they could even sell back 35 electricity to the local utility at off-peak hours. Indeed, some Americans are already vendors of electricity.

Solar technology would then become highly efficient and cheap, and a huge market would open up in the Third World. The industrialized countries could assist billions of people to bypass the fossil-fuel era, so they could generate electricity from solar and wind power and use solar cookers and solar hot-water generators. This is a signal solution to the problem of ongoing global warming. The First World must help the Third World bypass the fossil-fuel era if the earth is to survive. 36

Attention should also be given to the strange high-rise buildings covered in tinted glass that seem to be in vogue in many U.S. cities. These are not solar buildings. The windows cannot be opened to allow ventilation during the summer, and they must be cooled with air conditioners, which use ozone-destroying CFCs and carbon dioxide–producing electricity. In the winter, heat leaks from the windows like water through a sieve. And these buildings are generally lit up like Christmas trees at night, for no apparent purpose, by energy-inefficient lighting. Dallas, Houston, and Los Angeles boast numerous of these monstrosities, many of which now sit empty and idle, built by speculators who cashed in on the savings and loan scandal. (I used to wonder as I traveled through the United States in the 1980s why the Sun Belt was thriving. Now we know! This prosperity was a by-product of the deregulation of the savings and loan industry by the Reagan administration.) 37

We all must become acutely conscious of the way we live. Every time we turn on a switch to light a room, power a hair dryer, or toast a piece of bread, we are adding to global warming. We should never have more than one light bulb burning at night in our house unless there are two people in the house in different rooms—then two bulbs. Lights must not be left on overnight in houses or gardens for show, and all lights must be extinguished in office buildings at night. 38

Clothes dryers are ubiquitous and unnecessary. In Australia, we dry our clothes outside in the sun, hung by pegs from a line. Americans can do the same in the summer, and in the colder climes, like Boston's, clothes can be hung on lines in the cellars in the winter. In some American cities there are laws prohibiting people from hanging clothes on lines outside, on grounds that it is not aesthetically pleasing. This method of drying offers, in fact, an easy and efficient step toward the reduction of atmospheric carbon dioxide and radioactive waste. Clothes dryers use over 10 percent of the electricity generated in the States, a large fraction of that generated by nuclear power. And bear in mind that electrically operated doors, escalators, and elevators all contribute to global warming. . . . 39

Renewable energy sources (wind, solar, geothermal, and so on) could theoretically provide a total energy output equal to the current global energy consumption. Today these sources already provide approximately 21 per- 40 cent of the energy consumed worldwide and are freely available to be developed further.

Solar power will soon yield electricity as cheap as coal-fired electricity.   41
In fact, scientists at the U.S. Solar Energy Research Institute estimate that photovoltaic solar systems could supply over half the U.S. electricity within forty to fifty years. This technology will decrease in price as it is mass produced, modified, refined, and made more efficient. Solar water and household heating is already widespread in Australia, Greece, and the Middle East.

Wind power offers an obvious and benign technique that is being used   42
to generate electricity in many countries, including Greece, China, Australia, Israel, Belgium, Italy, Germany, Britain, the United States, and Denmark. Since 1974, fifty thousand wind machines have been built, mainly in California and Denmark. Wind "farms" cover areas of the desert between Los Angeles and Palm Springs, and by the year 2030 wind power could provide 10 percent of the world's energy.

Geothermal power, which taps into the intrinsic heat and lava trapped   43
below the earth's crust, is already being used to good advantage in New Zealand, Iceland, and Hawaii, and there is much potential for its use in the United States, Soviet Union, and Central America. Output is increasing by 15 percent per year.

Tidal power utilizes the twice daily changes in sea levels to generate   44
electricity. It is suitable only for certain coastlines, but it certainly offers great possibilities in places where the tides vary twenty to a hundred feet per day. Wave power is another dynamic area awaiting development.

Hydropower has been expanding by 4 percent annually worldwide, and   45
the potential for further expansion is vast. Hydroelectric and geothermal power provides over 21 percent of the world's electricity. Electricity generated at dams and waterfalls crosses borders and can be used in other countries; for instance, New England uses Canadian hydroelectricity. Hydroelectric dams that flood large areas of natural forests are ecologically dangerous, and careful planning is essential before and during their construction.

Cogeneration is a wonderful method for harnessing heat usually   46
wasted in factories. One technique, used extensively in the Soviet Union and in Scandinavia, is to heat water and pipe it to warm whole towns and cities. Another is to use waste steam to drive electricity-generating turbines, to run refrigerators, and to power industrial machinery. An ordinary power plant is 32 percent efficient, but a cogenerator consuming the same amount of fuel is 80 percent efficient.

Conservation can save large quantities of energy. Society must invest   47
in highly efficient light bulbs, refrigerators, stoves, cars, and street lighting. Energy-efficient equipment uses one-third to one-half less energy than does conventional technology. Much of it has already been invented, but monopolistic corporations tend to encourage distribution of inefficient equipment, thus leading to increased electricity consumption. For example, General Electric manufactures not only nuclear reactors but also hair dryers, toasters,

stoves, and refrigerators. Is it not therefore in GE's best interests to encourage people to use more electricity with less efficient appliances and to use electric brooms, electric hedge clippers, and electric lawn mowers instead of ones operated by muscle power?

But energy-efficient investments are much cheaper financially and 48 ecologically than the building and operating of coal or nuclear plants. Patents for wonderful energy-saving inventions abound, but most inventors lack the money to develop their product. And corporations seem uninterested in pursuing or financing such inventions.

Not least, utilities hide enormous government subsidies that they re- 49 ceive for fossil fuels and nuclear power. This deception makes renewable energy appear to be more expensive. Because utilities enjoy an almost total monopoly in energy advertising and technologies of energy production, it is very hard to understand and dissect their propaganda. Solar-heating systems and photovoltaic cells endow people with energy self-reliance, but clearly such self-sufficiency is not and will not be seen to be in the best interests of the utilities.

Trees and other plants (biomass) are sources of energy mainly in the 50 developing world. In India, people even burn pats of cow dung for cooking. But inhabitants of these countries often decimate their forests for short-term survival. I have seen Indian women spend a whole day walking to a patch of trees, gather the wood, and walk home for another day in order to cook food for their families. The burning of wood adds to atmospheric carbon dioxide.

Deforestation is leading to desertification in many countries—to creep- 51 ing deserts and utter destruction of the land. Brazil is even using parts of the Amazon forest to fuel iron ore smelters. So wood is not necessarily a good fuel and needs to be replaced by solar, wind, and other kinds of power. Still, garbage and agricultural wastes can be used to produce methane, an excellent gas for cooking and heating. Biomass supplies 12 percent of the energy worldwide and up to 50 percent in some poor countries.

Industrial efficiency has been shown to have enormous potential. It 52 must be developed on a massive scale, for industry uses 40 to 60 percent of the available energy in the developed countries and 10 to 40 percent in the developing countries.

If all fossil fuels were taxed to avoid climate change, the ecosphere 53 could be brought into a relatively stable equilibrium. In the United States, this tax would raise the price of electricity by 28 percent and that of a gallon of gasoline by seventeen cents, but it would produce $60 billion in revenue, and this money could then be earmarked for alternative-energy facilities and conservation. In India, the tax would raise $17.5 billion. The international community within the United Nations must endorse this tax proposal. According to the Worldwatch Institute report of 1990, in order to stabilize atmospheric greenhouse gas concentrations by 2050, net carbon emissions will need to be reduced by two billion tons per year. So, given a probable global population of eight billion by then, all people will require levels of net carbon emissions similar to India's today, which is only one-eighth of the current levels in Western Europe. Furthermore, 20 percent of the global carbon tax could be diverted to Third World reforestation, benign energy production, and renewable energy sources.

A 12 percent reduction in global greenhouse gas emissions by 2000 54
seems an appropriate interim goal if we are to achieve a stabilization of carbon dioxide concentrations by 2050. This means that the United States and the Soviet Union would have to reduce carbon dioxide production by 35 percent over the next ten years. To be fair, though, Kenya and India could actually increase carbon dioxide emissions, because they produce so little at present. If we fail to make these important decisions and if the industrial countries maintain present-day emission levels, the Third World, by emulating the First World, could increase the quantity of carbon dioxide by some 20 to 30 percent by the year 2000 and by 50 to 70 percent by 2010, as its fuel use and population base expand.

I don't think we have any choice in these matters, and the sooner we 55
knuckle down to the task, the sooner we can reassure our children that they
will inherit a viable future.   ©

CRITICAL READING

1. In describing the possible effects of global warming, what factors, according to Caldicott, make these effects so difficult to predict?
2. In the twentieth paragraph on page 499, Caldicott discusses how rising temperatures in American cities would lead to increased use of air conditioners. She calls this result a "catch-22" because air conditioners release harmful gases and use a lot of electricity. Looking over her discussion of the possible deleterious greenhouse effects that she describes, what other catch-22 situations can you identify as possibilities arising out of our responses to global warming?
3. Summarize Caldicott's "Fact Number Three," and discuss what our urban and suburban landscapes might look like if her ideas were put into practice.

CLASS DISCUSSION

1. During the 1970s and early 1980s we, as a nation, seemed concerned about fuel efficiency in cars, but in the last decade, that concern appears to have diminished. This trend is evident when one examines the number of SUVs and other large cars on the road, vehicles that get very low mileage per gallon of gas. Discuss all the reasons Caldicott notes that we should be concerned about, and theorize regarding why Americans in general don't seem concerned. Then speculate about ways we could change this situation, or debate whether we should change it.

2. If it's true, as Caldicott asserts, that if a corporation produced energy-efficient global mass transit systems, it would "earn huge profits while saving the planet" (twenty-eighth paragraph on page 501), why do you think that nobody seems to be making this effort?

DIRECTED FREEWRITE

Make a list of all the electric-powered appliances that are convenient but not necessary, such as clothes dryers. Discuss the relative usefulness of these, and explain whether you would be willing to give up using any of these appliances, noting why or why not.

ENVIRONMENTAL SCIENCE UNIT WRITING ASSIGNMENTS

1. Write a summary of Caldicott's essay. Summarizing is an important skill for writers in all disciplines, at all levels, and we discuss it in detail on page 109 in assignment 1 in the Neuroscience unit in Chapter 2. In preparing your summary, don't present a chronological summary that is based in structure around that of Caldicott's essay ("first she talks about this, then she moves to this other point, etc."); rather, reformulate her ideas, and structure them according to the importance you think they should have. By doing this, you will organize your summary around the points that she makes and that you have selected as being key to developing the essay's overall purpose.

2. Write a critique of a recent global warming-related article that you select from an academic journal. You will need to exercise care in choosing an article that is suitably "scholarly" and scientific, yet is not too far above your current level of knowledge. For a discussion of the typical format of these articles, take a look at assignment 3 on page 90 in the Chapter 2 Religious Studies unit.

   Read the piece carefully, and take detailed notes; you will need to reread the essay a number of times. Your critique should contain the following information:

   A. *The article's thesis.* Sometimes the thesis or main point of an article is fairly easy to find; however, at other times, the writer may not state a thesis in one place but may build points ultimately to construct a main point.

   B. *The methods used by the article's author(s) to investigate the topic.* Remember that you are critiquing here, so in addition to noting briefly what method was used, you need to indicate whether this method was appropriate to the task and whether the author employed the method correctly.

   C. *The kinds of evidence used by the author(s) to support the thesis.* Did the author adequately support his or her thesis?

   D. *The contribution to the literature on this specific topic that this article makes.* Usually these kinds of journal articles contain an introduction (sometimes called a literature review) in which the author notes how his or her work fits into the preexisting work that has been done on the topic under discussion. For this assignment, you can rely to some extent on the information presented here. To take the evaluation further, you will need to do some

library research to get a sense of the other related work being done or conducted in the past on the topic.

E. *Your overall evaluation of the article.* Essentially, this last section of your
critique is where your paper's thesis is located, since it is here that you will
sum up your evaluation. You ought to indicate for whom the article would be
most useful, in what way the article would be useful, and what the extent of
that usefulness would be.

You may not have enough knowledge yet to evaluate the methods used in an
environmental sciences article, and if this is the case, you can leave out item B.

3. Write a short argumentative essay in which you attempt to convince readers to
stop using appliances that are convenient but not essential. Use points from
Caldicott's essay to develop and support your points. Alternatively, write a short
essay arguing that your congressional representative should propose a bill inspired by Caldicott's essay. For example, you might suggest that Congress legislate that all new buildings in the United States must be equipped for solar energy,
as Caldicott suggests, or use Caldicott's predictions and list of "facts" to inspire
more drastic legislation to address the kinds of problems she discusses. Refer to
assignment 2 on page 60 in the Social Psychology unit of Chapter 2 for more discussion of argument.

4. After conducting library research examining the ways in which the debate over
global warming has taken place in newspaper columns and editorials, write an
essay synthesizing the dominant arguments used by each side in this debate. As
you examine the articles—and you may want to limit yourself to one major
newspaper such as the *New York Times* or the *Los Angeles Times,* as well as limiting yourself to a specific time period—you should be able to identify patterns
in the arguments used. Identifying such patterns could then help you to decide on
an overall category that seems to characterize the kinds of arguments made by
each side. For example, do the contending sides fall into liberal/conservative
camps, or skeptics/true believers, and so forth? To what extent are scientists engaged in the public debate, and which side do they tend to favor? Identifying
these kinds of overall categories can help to unify this kind of essay, but if you
find that you can't divide the two sides into neat little categories, then this kind
of observation can also provide the starting point for an argument around which
to structure your essay.

We introduced the explanatory synthesis mode of writing in the Evolutionary
Psychology unit of Chapter 3; for this assignment, we ask you to try an argument
synthesis. In addition to simply summing up the overall parameters of the global
warming debate as represented in newspapers, go further and state a conclusion
about this debate. This conclusion will serve as the thesis statement of your
essay, an arguable assertion about what you see going on in the ways that this
issue is addressed by writers in the news. You might argue about the level of scientific evidence used by either side or both sides, the partisan character of the debate, underlying assumptions that you can identify operating on either side or
both sides of the issue, and so on.

Unit 2

Engineering—Cleaning Up Our Mess

HOW SAFE IS YOUR TAP WATER?

Julie Miller

In this piece from the periodical *California Engineer,* Miller examines the quality of tap water, explaining some of the standards required by the Environmental Protection Agency, and comparing the quality of tap water with that of the much more expensive bottled water. While noting that people in general are concerned about the quality of drinking water, she ends up concluding that we have less to worry about than many seem to think. As you read, pay attention to the approach Miller takes to answering the question posed in the article's title. What concrete evidence does she use to support her ultimate evaluation of tap water safety? Does she leave any important issues out, do you think?

Started in 1920, the California Engineer *is a non-profit quarterly magazine featuring technical articles written by students of the University of California.*

Have you ever turned on the faucet to get a drink of water, but hesi- 1
tated before drinking it? Water often comes out of the tap bubbly, discolored, or even with a slight odor. Frequently, we hear complaints that our drinking water is unsafe from people who sell home filtration devices or benefit financially from the public's fear of drinking water. One such person is Cheryl Watson, who sells purification devices. She states that "dissolved in a supposedly pure glass of water is a plethora of bacteria, waste products that didn't quite get removed, industrial contaminants, lead, chlorine, and a lot of other nasty stuff besides." She comments that water companies can't get it all out and that "there's some stuff, like chlorine, that they put in to try to kill the bacteria, then don't bother to take it out when they're done." Are these rumors true? Do all of these pollutants actually exist in our drinking water, and if so, can they be removed? How safe is our drinking water?

Source: "How Safe Is Your Tap Water?" by Julie Miller from *California Engineer,* January 1997. Reprinted by permission of the author.

SOURCES AND TREATMENT

To understand drinking water's safety, we first need to know where the   2
water originates. The two major sources of drinking water are ground water
and surface water. Ground water is pumped from wells that water suppliers
drill into aquifers, or geologic formations made with sand, gravel, or other
like materials which filter water when it flows through the medium. Local well
water is ground water that comes from deep within the ground and is free of
bacteria and other natural contamination. Over fifty percent of the nation's
ground water is distributed untreated. The water suppliers rely on the "natural filtration" that is provided by mother nature to purify the water.

Surface water comes from rivers, lakes, and reservoirs. Since this   3
water flows over the land, it can easily be contaminated and must be
treated. Most surface water is treated by adding chemicals called coagu-
lants that combine with dirt particles. The dirt particles are then filtered out,
which makes the water clear. This filtering stage is also important because it
removes many tiny organisms called microbes (bacteria, viruses, protozoa)
that are hard to kill. Finally, the remaining microbes are removed by disinfecting.

Chlorine is the most common chemical that is used for disinfecting   4
water. It is used by 75% of large water suppliers and 95% of small ones.
The remaining water suppliers use chloramine, which is similar to chlorine,
or more exotic disinfectants such as ozone or chlorine dioxide. All of these

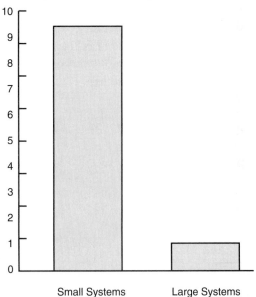

Percentage and Size of Water Systems with Violations

Smaller water systems usually have larger problems keeping their water up to par with EPA standards.

chemicals are beneficial to use for disinfecting because they kill disease-causing microbes without directly harming humans. After disinfecting, the water is distributed to the consumers and is now safe to drink.

IS TAP WATER SAFE?

Many people wonder how water is determined to be safe. In the United States, every municipal water supplier must meet strict standards. Occasionally, a water supplier will fail to meet the requirements and must alert consumers to the problem, even though some violations do not necessarily pose a health hazard. If a water supplier does not test the water as frequently as required by the Environmental Protection Agency (EPA), that constitutes a violation and consumers must be notified immediately. This does not mean that the water quality is poor, but that not enough is known about the quality of the water. 5

One of the most serious violations occurs when the water supplier fails to meet microbial removal requirements. *Giardia* and *Cryptosporidium* are two common microbes that cause waterborne illness in humans. For normal healthy individuals, symptoms usually disappear in one to two weeks and include severe diarrhea or vomiting. In severely immuno-compromised people, the infection can continue and can even cause death. Since these microbes are not easily killed by the disinfecting process, the filtration step in water treatment is crucial. The majority of sicknesses directly traced to drinking water occurred because of improper disinfecting or no disinfecting at all. Each year, there are about 7,700 cases of gastrointestinal sickness in the United States that result directly from inadequate treatment which does not meet the EPA's requirements. Usually, small water systems (fewer than 3300 customers) have more trouble meeting these standards. 6

HOW SAFE ARE THE EPA'S STANDARDS?

A common fear among the public is that the EPA's standards are not stringent enough. The standards are determined by risk assessment, the process whereby the EPA determines the nature and magnitude of the risks that are associated with constituents in drinking water. Risk assessment is controversial because it is not an exact process. It is based upon the concept of "reasonable risk," not "risk free." Nobody knows the definite long term risks from exposure to chemicals or microbes. Chlorine is added to water to kill harmful microbes that pose a significant health hazard to humans. Therefore, adding chlorine to drinking water is beneficial. On the other hand, the health risks associated with ingesting chlorine have not been defined completely. Thus, the EPA must decide what levels of chlorine will not cause any adverse health effects. 7

Dr. James M. Symons explains that "for cancer-causing chemicals, reasonable risk is defined as follows: if one million people drank water for a 8 period of seventy years with the amount of chemical in it equal to the standard, one person would probably get cancer from the drinking water." Thus, levels are set so that very small health risks result from drinking water that meets the standards. Each of these levels of risk can be converted into a maximum contaminant level in drinking water. Exceeding the maximum contaminant level results in a violation of which the public must be notified; otherwise, one can assume that the water is safe to drink.

BOTTLED VS MUNICIPAL WATER

Though municipal water that meets the standards is safe, a large portion of the population chooses to buy bottled water. In fact, from 1988 to 1989, bottled water sales increased 10.6 percent to become a $2.4 billion business. Some people buy bottled water because they think it is more pure, while others buy it because it tastes better. The main reason to buy bottled water should be personal taste, not a concern about water safety. Bottled water must meet the same quality standards as tap water, but it is 250 to 7000 times more expensive than tap water, and the main difference is the taste. Refrigerating tap water usually eliminates most of the bad taste and makes it nearly indistinguishable from bottled water.

The Santa Clara Valley Water District (SCVWD) performed a laboratory test of tap water versus bottled water in 1985. This test showed that SCVWD's tap water surpassed many of the bottled waters. The most important contaminant in drinking water is bacteria, which is virtually nonexistent in treated tap water. SCVWD's tap water contained higher levels of chloride and sodium than bottled water; however, neither are harmful to humans at these levels.

A few reasons to buy bottled water should be noted. Since some tap water contains high levels of sodium, people who are on sodium-restricted diets may choose to buy bottled water. However, these consumers must check because many bottled waters also contain high levels of sodium. Another important reason for buying bottled water is high nitrate levels. In agricultural areas, some water suppliers are having trouble meeting nitrate standards. High nitrate levels are bad for small children because the nitrates bond with hemoglobin in the blood, thereby decreasing the blood's capacity to carry oxygen. When this occurs it is called "blue baby syndrome." Water suppliers are required to notify their customers if nitrate levels exceed the Safe Drinking Water Standard. It is important to read the labels on bottled water to see what is in it before buying it. After all, it may have higher levels of contaminants than the inexpensive water at home.

One contaminant that may be present at harmful levels in selected homes is lead. In the past, lead was used in some pipes and soldered connections. While the water is not moving, the lead can dissolve into it and cause contamination. Though lead has now been banned in the use of pipes and solder, it may still exist in older plumbing. Since lead contamination occurs after the water is distributed to the consumer, there is little that the water supplier can do about it. Water utilities with corrosive water (i.e., low pH, low alkalinity, and low hardness) usually have increased the alkalinity and pH to minimize corrosion of pipes. This significantly reduces the amount of lead that leaches into the water. The best way to lessen tap water's lead content is to allow the water to run for a few minutes before use. If in doubt, call the water supplier to find out how to get tap water tested, or ask a plumber to look at the pipes.

13   Despite the high quality of municipal drinking water, there are many who distrust the safety of their tap water and buy home filtration devices. There are a variety of home filtration units that remove many different contaminants. Common types of home filtration devices include carbon filters, reverse osmosis, ozonation, and ultraviolet light.

14   Often, a customer is sold a filtration device that does not remove the contaminant that he is concerned about. Carbon filters, for example, are good at removing taste and odor in water as well as organic compounds such as pesticides and chloroform. However, the carbon filter has no effect on lowering lead levels. On the other hand, if a reverse osmosis filtration unit is purchased, it may remove the lead content but may not have the desired effect on certain organic compounds. Thus, if contaminant levels are a concern, one should test one's water to see which contaminants need to be removed. Then the appropriate filtration device may be purchased. Be skeptical about taking the advice of a salesman. It is always safer to consult with a water quality expert from the water supplier. These experts can tell you what is in the water and the best treatment process, if any that will remove the contaminants.

15   Aside from lead, nitrates, and sodium restrictions, there is virtually no reason to worry about the quality of tap water if it meets the EPA's standards. In fact, California has "among the most stringent drinking water standards in the nation." As more and more contamination of ground and surface water occurs, technological improvements allow water suppliers to meet the strict guidelines set by the EPA so that tap water is safe for the public to drink.

16   From time to time, we hear media reports of disease outbreaks or sicknesses caused by contaminated drinking water. However, it is important for the general public not to panic because the majority of these outbreaks are due to inadequately treated or untreated water, such as from private wells. Properly treated tap water presents an extremely small risk to the customer. Before buying bottled water or home filtration devices, consult your water supplier and find out whether water concerns are legitimate. When properly treated, tap water is very safe.

CRITICAL READING

1. Discuss the method that the Environmental Protection Agency uses to set safety standards for water. Why is this method controversial?
2. Miller doesn't address engineering issues explicitly; discuss why this article appears in *California Engineer*. Aside from the fact that they drink water, just like the rest of us, how does the issue of water safety concern engineers?
3. Describe the evidence Miller uses to support her ultimate assertion that tap water is very safe "when properly treated."

CLASS DISCUSSION

1. Miller notes that ground water is an important source for regional water supplies and describes the natural filtration process that occurs with such water. As a class, discuss the differences between ground water and surface water: How safe is each? How is each treated, and why? How might increased pollution affect the quality of both kinds of water?
2. As a group, explore the role that engineers—both chemical engineers and mechanical engineers—might play in ensuring the safety of drinking water.

DIRECTED FREEWRITE

Reflect on and write about your personal experiences with drinking water. Do you freely drink tap water, or are you one of the millions of people who prefer the supposed safety of Evian and Pellegrino? Was there a particular point in your life—a bout of the runs, perhaps—when you stopped drinking tap water? If so, why? What does the tap water in your hometown taste like? Smell like? Do you feel safe drinking any kind of water? Perhaps you've never thought about the issue of drinking water quality—if not, what do you think about it after reading this article? Are you reassured, or are you alarmed, and why?

POLYMER COST
AND PERFORMANCE EVALUATION

Anthony J. Tarquin, Gregg B. Haan, and Douglas Rittmann

After delineating some of the problems and concerns about water quality, we now present a piece that is more explicitly positioned within the discipline of engineering. Engineers create chemical and mechanical solutions to specific problems, and the challenges of environmental pollution have led to a high demand for environmental engineers. These engineers work to devise methods for cleaning up existing pollution, as well as creating new technologies for decreasing or even eliminating our output of pollution. Since new technologies must be tested and evaluated extensively, a lot of writing in engineering consists of the kind of evaluative report that we present here. As you read the report, don't worry about any of the unfamiliar jargon (although it will be helpful for you to know that turbid water is cloudy and nontransparent); instead, focus on the ways that this report is useful, and to whom.

One last note: a polymer is a compound of high molecular weight derived either by the addition of many smaller molecules, as in polyethylene (a kind of plastic), or by the condensation of many smaller molecules with the elimination of water, alcohol, or the like, as in nylon.

Anthony Tarquin received his Ph.D. in Environmental Engineering from West Virginia University in 1969. He has published numerous articles and written three books: Engineering Economy: A Behavioral Approach, Introduction to Engineering, *and* Career Opportunities in Engineering and Technology. *In Environmental Engineering, Dr. Tarquin's main interest is in water and wastewater treatment. He has completed several projects in this area, most of them related to industrial wastewater treatment, some related to domestic wastewater treatment, and a few related to small waste flows. Dr. Tarquin has recently been involved in projects pertaining to water treatment, particularly the economic aspects of alternative treatment processes.*

Gregg Haan graduated from the University of Texas at El Paso with a B.S. in Civil Engineering in May 1995. He received his M.S. in Environmental Engineering from the University of Texas at El Paso in August 1997. He is currently employed as a Field Representative with the Texas Water Development Board, Inspection and Field Support Services Division, Houston Field Office.

Douglas Rittmann is now retired. He was formerly the El Paso Water Utilities' Water Systems Division Manager and assisted on this article by providing laboratory space and materials in addition to his expertise in water chemistry.

Source: "Polymer Cost and Performance Evaluation" by Anthony J. Tarquin, Gregg B. Haan, and Douglas Rittmann in *Water/Engineering & Management,* January 1998. Reprinted by permission from Scranton-Gillette Communications.

Under the Safe Drinking Water Act (SDWA) Amendments of 1996, ex- 1
otic compounds and trace heavy metals receive second priority to microbiological contaminants, such as *Cryptosporidium* and *Giardia lambia.* As
sources of uncontaminated water become scarce, and as treated wastewater
effluents are discharged into surface waters, the removal of microbiological
contaminants becomes a major concern. One method of removing the larger
microbiological contaminants from potable water is through filtration.

One goal of the EPA that may be accomplished is to have a value of 2
0.10 nephelometric turbidity units (NTU) for finished water, with a settled
water turbidity prior to filtration of 1.0 NTU. Currently, finished water is required to be less than 0.5 NTU and there is no standard for settled water. It
is believed that a finished water turbidity of 0.10 NTU or less indicates that
Cryptosporidium and *Giardia* cysts have been removed. High turbidity loading on filters reduces the filter run and increases the chance of breakthrough, leading to system contamination. One method of reducing the
turbidity of prefiltered settled water is through the use of polymers.

An evaluation was undertaken on the performance and cost of 23 dif- 3
ferent synthetic organic polyelectrolyte coagulation aids (polymers). The aim
was to identify the polymer that reduces filter loading to an extent that the
saved cost of the reduction in backwash water is greater than the cost of
polymer. The study took place at the 40 MGD Jonathan Rogers Water
Treatment Plant in El Paso, Texas.

PROCEDURE

Jar Test Set Up

To accurately simulate the plant, jar tests were "calibrated" with similar 4
plant conditions. In the first part of the calibration process, the settling curve
of the flocculation basin effluent (turbidity vs. time) was plotted. This was
completed by collecting samples from the flocculation basin and measuring
the turbidity as a function of settling time. The samples were collected and
allowed to settle in two-liter Hach rectangular batch containers. Turbidity
readings were taken every 15 minutes for two hours. The settling curve for
the plant was then created by plotting the turbidity readings vs. time. This
curve represented the removal rate for solids entering the secondary settling
tanks.

The second part of the calibration process was to get the settling curve 5
obtained in the lab to match that obtained in the plant. This was essentially
achieved through a trial and error flash mix, flocculation process. In this
case, the flash mix was simulated by lowering the blades to mid depth and
adding the chemicals, ferric chloride ($FeCl_3$), and lime (CaO) at 7mg/L and
2mg/L, respectively. The lime was added first with the rpm set at 68 and allowed to mix for 3.21 minutes. The ferric chloride was added next and was
mixed at 83 rpm for 30 seconds.

For the flocculation process, the mixing blades were dropped to the   6
bottom of the container and rotated at 4 rpm, 3 rpm and 2 rpm, progressively lowered in ten minute intervals.

The mixing was stopped at the end of the 30 minute flocculation period   7
and the sample was allowed to settle with turbidity readings taken every 15
minutes for two hours. The curves from the plant and simulation are plotted
in Figure 1.

Polymer Testing

To evaluate the polymers, the lime and ferric sulfate were added and   8
flashed mixed as described above, after which the polymer to be tested was
added at 0.5 ppm and mixed at 103 rpm for 30 seconds.

The flocculation process was the same as described above, with the   9
mixing blades dropped to the bottom of the container, and the mixing
speeds of 4 rpm, 3 rpm and 2 rpm progressively lowered in ten minute intervals. The mixing was stopped at the end of the 30 minute flocculation period
and turbidity readings were taken as before.

The removal percentage for each polymer was found by determining   10
the additional turbidity removal that a specific polymer yielded over the
standard conditions (i.e., if the final turbidity when using a polymer was 2.45

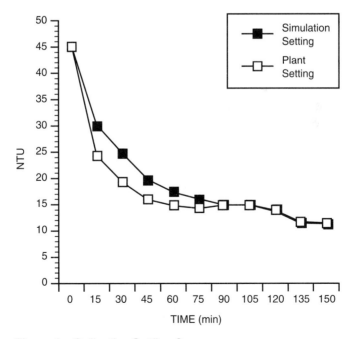

Figure 1   Calibration Settling Curves

NTU while the control [without polymer] for the same conditions yielded a turbidity of 4.0 NTU, the removal percentage was calculated as 38.8 percent).

Data Collection

All jar tests were performed in duplicate on a six-container apparatus 11 with two containers representing the plant standard (no polymer), and the four others containing polymers at a concentration of 0.5 ppm. If the two samples of an individual polymer differed by more than 5 percent in removal percentages, the test was rerun until a difference of less than 5 percent was obtained.

Since all polymers could not be tested on the same day and at the same initial turbidity, several of the samples were tested at different initial turbidities. Polymer D was initially tested at 104 NTU and yielded a removal percentage of 35.9 percent. The second time it was tested at 61.4 NTU and the removal percentage was 35.9. In the case of polymer D, the difference in the removal percentages at different initial turbidities was less than one percent. The removal percentages for all 23 of the polymers were found to be within three percent, regardless of where the initial turbidity fell in the study turbidity range of 60–120 NTU. The results from four representative polymers are shown graphically in Figure 2.

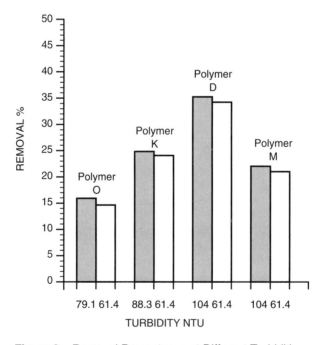

Figure 2   Removal Percentages at Different Turbidities

The polymers tested are not identified by name since individual results 12 are obviously site-specific. However, the procedures used here should be applicable anywhere.

RESULTS AND DISCUSSION

Performance Analysis

One of the key topics of this study was to identify the polymer that re- 13 duced filter loading. A reduction in filter loading would presumably result from the increased turbidity removal associated with each polymer. The ranking of the polymers based on their removal percentages was the first step in evaluating their overall performance (Table 1). The removal percent-

Table 1. Removal Percentages

Polymer	Percent Removal
A	38.8
B	37.9
C	37.0
D	36.1
E	33.6
F	33.3
G	32.0
H	31.6
I	28.6
J	27.6
K	24.6
L	21.4
M	20.7
N	18.7
O	15.5
P	15.5
Q	13.8
R	12.8
S	11.5
T	10.3
U	5.8
V	5.8
W	+2.9

ages had a large range (i.e., from 38.8 percent removal of turbidity to 2.9 percent gain in turbidity).

Cost Analysis

Since the aim of this study was to identify the polymer that is the most 14
cost effective, the cost analysis process is more than just pricing each polymer and ranking them by cost because their performances differed. To accurately determine the true benefit of each polymer, the cost of the water
saved due to the reduction of backwashing frequency had to be determined,
and the savings, if any, would be compared to the cost of the polymer.

To determine the amount of backwash water that was saved by the re- 15
duction of filter loading, a history of filter loading and backwash logs was
used to create a backwash rate vs. filter loading curve. Once the equation of
the curve was generated, using Microsoft Excel ($y = 43.3 \times^{-12}$), the curve
was used to determine the filter run time for a specified filter loading rate.

For example, if the standard conditions yielded a filter loading of 4.0 16
NTU, the filter run time would be 24.9 hours. By using Polymer A, the filter
loading would be reduced by 38.8 percent, to a 2.45 NTU, increasing the filter run time to 30.3 hours, for a net increase of 5.4 hours. This 5.4 hours of
increased filter run reduces the amount of water required for backwashing
the filter and, therefore, the backwash water cost as shown below.

The determination of the monetary saving resulting from the reduction 17
in backwash water per million gallons of treated water was obtained using
Equation 1.

If the filter run increases when a polymer is used, the gallons of back- 18
wash water used per MG of water produced are obviously decreased. In this
case, the 5.4 hour increase of filter run time would decrease the amount of
backwash water used per MG of water produced from 48,533 gallons to
39,894 gallons. In 1997 dollars, the cost of producing water was $0.54 per
1000 gallons; therefore, the savings of the backwash water would be $4.32
in 1997 dollars.

Equation 1
Reduction in Backwash Water Per Million Gallons of Treated Water

$$\frac{\text{Backwash Water Used}}{\text{MG of Water Produced}} = \frac{\text{Length of Backwash} \times \text{Backwash Flow Rate}}{\text{MG of Water Produced Per Day} \times \text{Filter Run}}$$

where:

Length of Backwash = 24 Min   MG of Water Produced Per Day Per
                                             Filter = 3.33 MG
Backwash Flow Rate = 7000 gal/min   Filter Run Time = 24.95 hours (stan-
                                             dard with no polymer)

Table 2. Cost Analysis

Polymer	Cost per Barrel	Percent Reduction	Filter Run without Polymer	Filter Run with Polymer	Gallons of Backwash Water per MG Water Produced (No Polymer)	Gallons of Backwash Water Saved per MG	Cost of Backwash Water Saved per MG	Cost of Polymer per MG	Net Savings per MG
A	$239.25	38.8	24.76	30.18	48900	8775	$4.74	$2.18	$2.56
B	$329.99	37.9	24.76	30.00	48900	8539	$4.61	$3.00	$1.61
C	$399.50	37	24.76	29.83	48900	8304	$4.48	$3.63	$0.85
D	$215.32	36.1	24.76	29.66	48900	8071	$4.36	$1.96	$2.40
E	$399.50	33.6	24.76	29.20	48900	7435	$4.02	$3.63	$0.38
F	$323.23	33.3	24.76	29.15	48900	7360	$3.97	$2.94	$1.04
G	$400.00	32	24.76	28.92	48900	7036	$3.80	$3.64	$0.16
H	$400.00	31.6	24.76	28.85	48900	6937	$3.75	$3.64	$0.11
I	$211.50	28.6	24.76	28.36	48900	6205	$3.35	$1.92	$1.43
J	$220.50	27.6	24.76	28.20	48900	5965	$3.22	$2.00	$1.22
K	$342.50	24.6	24.76	27.74	48900	5257	$2.84	$3.11	-$0.27
L	$391.50	21.4	24.76	27.28	48900	4520	$2.44	$3.56	-$1.12
M	$211.50	20.7	24.76	27.19	48900	4361	$2.36	$1.92	$0.43
N	$389.50	18.7	24.76	26.91	48900	3912	$2.11	$3.54	-$1.43
O	$161.55	15.5	24.76	26.50	48900	3207	$1.73	$1.47	$0.26
P	$318.25	15.5	24.76	26.50	48900	3207	$1.73	$2.89	-$1.16

(*Continued*)

Table 2. Cost Analysis (Continued)

Polymer	Cost per Barrel	Percent Reduction	Filter Run without Polymer	Filter Run with Polymer	Gallons of Backwash Water per MG Water Produced (No Polymer)	Gallons of Backwash Water Saved per MG	Cost of Backwash Water Saved per MG	Cost of Polymer per MG	Net Savings per MG
Q	$365.89	13.8	24.76	26.29	48900	2839	$1.53	$3.33	–$1.79
R	$318.25	12.8	24.76	26.17	48900	2625	$1.42	$2.89	–$1.48
S	$365.89	11.5	24.76	26.01	48900	2348	$1.27	$3.33	–$2.06
T	$202.10	10.3	24.76	25.87	48900	2095	$1.13	$1.84	–$0.71
U	$380.80	5.8	24.76	25.36	48900	1163	$0.63	$3.46	–$2.83
V	$199.50	5.8	24.76	25.36	48900	1163	$0.63	$1.81	–$1.19
W	$318.00	–2.9	24.76	24.48	48900	–566	–$0.31	$2.89	–$3.20

The costs of the polymers were obtained from bid submittals. Since [19] the concentration of the polymer was 0.5 ppm, or 0.5 gallons per million gallons, the cost of the polymer used per MG of water treated was found by dividing the cost per 55 gallon drum by 110. Results of the cost analysis ranking can be seen in Table 2.

To determine whether the use of any of the polymers would be cost ef- [20] fective, the net saving was determined by subtracting the cost of the polymer from the saving in backwash water cost. For example, the saving due to reduced backwash water when using Polymer A was $4.74 per million

Table 3. Overall Cost Analysis

Rank	Polymer	Overall Savings in 1997 $ per MG	Savings for 1996 Season (in 1997 $)
1	A	$2.56	$19,020.71
2	D	$2.40	$17,831.92
3	B	$1.61	$11,962.25
4	I	$1.43	$10,624.85
5	J	$1.22	$9,064.56
6	C	$0.85	$6,315.47
7	F	$0.46	$3,417.78
8	M	$0.44	$3,269.19
9	E	$0.39	$2,897.69
10	O	$0.26	$1,931.79
11	G	$0.16	$1,188.79
12	H	$0.11	$817.30
13	K	−$0.27	−$2,006.09
14	T	−$0.71	−$5,275.28
15	L	−$1.12	−$8,321.56
16	P	−$1.16	−$8,618.76
17	V	−$1.18	−$8,767.36
18	N	−$1.43	−$10,624.85
19	R	−$1.47	−$10,922.05
20	Q	−$1.80	−$13,373.94
21	S	−$2.06	−$15,305.73
22	U	−$2.83	−$21,026.80
23	W	−$3.20	−$23,775.89

gallons of water produced. The cost of the polymer was $2.18 per million gallons of water produced, yielding a saving of $2.56 per million gallons.

FINAL RANKINGS

Initially, the goal was to identify the polymer that reduced filter loading   21
to an extent that the use of the polymer would save money. In that respect, the performance and the cost must both be considered before deciding which polymer is the best in a given plant. The polymers rankings according to net cost of each polymer (i.e., saving in backwash water cost minus the cost of the polymer) are shown in Table 3.

It should be pointed out that the two most cost effective polymers did   22
not have the lowest cost per barrel. In fact, they were ranked 6th and 7th, respectively. If the evaluation process was based on bid price per barrel alone, these two polymers would not have been recognized as the best.

The polymers also were tested at 0.25 and 1.0 ppm concentrations. At   23
a polymer concentration of 0.25 ppm, for all polymers, the removal percentage was so small that it was obvious that the saving due to the reduction of backwash water would not cover the cost of the polymer. Similarly, at a polymer concentration of 1.0 ppm, the removal percentages changed so slightly (increased or decreased) that no economic analyses were required for these data.

CONCLUSIONS

This study has shown that when the costs of the polymer and the   24
backwash water are taken into account, the most cost effective polymer for a given plant is not likely to be the one with either the highest or lowest cost per barrel. Rather, a procedure similar to the one used here must be followed to identify the polymer that would be most cost effective in a particular water treatment plant situation.   ©

CRITICAL READING

1. What specific problem in water treatment is the present study meant to address?
2. What assumptions do the authors make that influence their interpretation of the study's results?
3. This study appeared in a periodical entitled *WATER/Engineering and Management.* Basing your response on that title and on the focus and language used in the essay, whom in addition to engineers is this essay meant to address?

CLASS DISCUSSION

1. As a group, explore some specific reasons why the authors don't identify by name the polymers that were tested. Does their omission of that information affect the usefulness of their study in any ways?

2. Even though this study focuses on cost effectiveness rather than on environmental concerns, discuss how the authors' findings could be environmentally as well as economically useful. In what ways are the two areas related?

DIRECTED FREEWRITE

Speculate about other environmental problems with water, or discuss any problems you are aware of. Then brainstorm some ways in which engineers might be called on to address some of these problems. You don't need to get too specific about these solutions; just describe in general terms how chemical, mechanical, or computer technologies might relate to the world's need for abundant and clean water supplies.

ENGINEERING UNIT WRITING ASSIGNMENTS

1. The abstract is an important genre of writing in the sciences and the social sciences. Abstracts are summaries that serve a very specific purpose and adhere to certain guidelines. Most science and social science journals require the authors of articles—especially those reporting the results of empirical studies—to supply an abstract with their articles. The abstract appears at the beginning of an article, usually set off from the rest of the text by its placement between the title and the introduction of the article; abstracts are also often recorded in electronic databases to facilitate the research process. Aiding scholars in their research is the purpose of abstracts: an abstract succinctly sums up all the important elements of an article, and thus a researcher can know at a glance whether an article is applicable to his or her research.

   Two common types of documents that typically feature abstracts are the experimental report and the theoretical essay. As you may know (if you've ever written one), the experimental report consists of four standard sections: introduction, methods, results, and discussion; therefore, the abstract accompanying this kind of article should contain one or two sentences summing up the key points contained in each of these sections. These key points usually consist of the research question and/or the hypothesis of the article; the procedures of and the participants in the study; the results; and the significance of the results. Abstracts are almost always written in one paragraph, and although they appear first in an article, they are prepared last, after all the key points have been worked out and written. Further, abstracts should contain key words of the study so that searches conducted on electronic databases are more likely to turn up relevant abstracts. Even though this description sounds pretty straightforward, it can be challenging to distill the report of a complex study into such a brief format. For examples of abstracts in this textbook, take a look in Chapter 3: the article by West and Zimmerman in the Communications unit and the article by Woodard and Murphy in the Zoology unit both contain abstracts—one in a social science report, and the other in a science report.

Theoretical essays and review essays also sometimes start off with abstracts. These kinds of abstracts need to sum up—again, in one or two sentences—the specific topic engaged by the essay; the writer's thesis; the kinds of evidence used to support the thesis; and a summation of the overall conclusion or significance of the piece.

You may have noticed that the experimental report by Tarquin, Haan, and Rittmann, although following the typical experimental report format, does not contain an abstract. Your job in this assignment is to write one for the article, to be based on the information contained within. Isolate the key points of each section, use the terminology employed by the authors, and provide a one-paragraph abstract that would fit this piece.

2. Based on the issues raised in this unit, design a survey measuring student awareness of a specific water-related environmental issue of your choosing. Unless your instructor desires otherwise, you won't distribute the survey; rather, the assignment is meant as practice in the survey genre, which in turn provides practice in constructing clear, concise sentences. You may refer to the more extensive discussion of surveys provided in assignment 2 on page 320 in the Biochemistry unit of Chapter 3.

3. One major source of water pollution is called "polluted run-off." Water used in farming, industry, and individual households is often polluted with chemicals such as fertilizers and cleaning agents, and if it's allowed to run into the ground or water systems, it carries toxins into the environment. Although legislation such as the Clean Water act has helped mitigate the problem, it hasn't solved it.

Imagine that an engineering firm has designed a simple device for collecting and purifying wastewater produced by farms and industry. However, the process is somewhat costly and time-comsuming, and industries and farmers aren't interested in the device. In order to create a market for their product, the engineering company lobbies Congress to require more stringent enforcement of existing clean water laws. Imagine you are hired by the engineering company to contact congresspersons about the problems of polluted runoff, its threats to water supplies, and the need for industries and farms to clean their wastewater more stringently. Research the issue and draft a document detailing the problem— especially focusing on the role played by industries and farms in producing contaminated water—and arguing that more needs to be done to prevent water pollution. You might start your research by reading materials contained on the National Wildlife Federation website (**http://www.nwf.org**), then move on from there.

THINKING AND WRITING IN THE SOCIAL SCIENCES

Unit 1:

Social Ecology—A Planet for the People

TOWARD A LAND ETHIC

Aldo Leopold

As an advocate for wildlife management, founding the Wilderness Society in 1934, Aldo Leopold is one of our earliest environmentalists. In this excerpt from his book *A Sand County Almanac,* published in 1949, Leopold articulates ideas that have had a significant impact on the environmental movement. His theories represent early formulations of the kinds of ideas inherent in social ecology, since he focuses on the interrelation and interdependence between humans and the rest of the natural world. Leopold's notion of a "land ethic" would require some radical changes in our attitudes toward the environment; since this piece was written in the late 1940s, notice, as you read, whether points in Leopold's argument seem outdated.

> *Aldo Leopold (1887–1948) was born near Burlington, Iowa. He attended Yale where he received a degree in forestry. After Yale, Leopold joined the U.S. Forest Service and was assigned to the Arizona Territories. In 1924 he served as associate director at the U.S. Forest Products Laboratory in Madison. Later, he began teaching at the University of Wisconsin where he was the first chair of the Department of Game Management. He has published various books including* The Almanac, Game Management, *and his best-selling text* A Sand County Almanac.

When god-like Odysseus returned from the wars in Troy, he hanged all 1 on one rope a dozen slave-girls of his household whom he suspected of misbehaving during his absence.

This hanging involved no question of propriety. The girls were prop- 2 erty. The disposal of property was then, as now, a matter of expediency, not of right and wrong.

Concepts of right and wrong were not lacking from Odysseus' Greece: 3
witness the fidelity of his wife through the long years before at last his black-
prowed galleys clove the wine-dark seas for home. The ethical structure of
that day covered wives, but had not yet been extended to human chattels.
During the three thousand years which have since elapsed, ethical criteria
have been extended to many fields of conduct, with corresponding shrink-
ages in those judged by expediency only. . . .

The first ethics dealt with the relation between individuals; the Mosaic   4
Decalogue is an example. Later accretions dealt with the relation between
the individual and society. The Golden Rule tries to integrate the individual
to society; democracy to integrate social organization to the individual.

There is as yet no ethic dealing with man's relation to land and to the   5
animals and plants which grow upon it. Land, like Odysseus' slave-girls, is
still property. The land-relation is still strictly economic, entailing privileges
but not obligations. . . .

THE COMMUNITY CONCEPT

All ethics so far evolved rest upon a single premise: that the individual   6
is a member of a community of interdependent parts. His instincts prompt
him to compete for his place in the community, but his ethics prompt him also
to cooperate (perhaps in order that there may be a place to compete for).

The land ethic simply enlarges the boundaries of the community to in-   7
clude soils, waters, plants, and animals, or collectively: the land.

This sounds simple: do we not already sing our love for and obligation   8
to the land of the free and the home of the brave? Yes, but just what and
whom do we love? Certainly not the soil, which we are sending helter-
skelter downriver. Certainly not the waters, which we assume have no function except to turn turbines, float barges, and carry off sewage. Certainly not
the plants, of which we exterminate whole communities without batting an
eye. Certainly not the animals, of which we have already extirpated many of
the largest and most beautiful species. A land ethic of course cannot prevent the alteration, management, and use of these "resources," but it does
affirm their right to continued existence, and, at least in spots, their continued existence in a natural state.

In short, a land ethic changes the role of *Homo sapiens* from con-   9
queror of the land-community to plain member and citizen of it. It implies respect for his fellow members, and also respect for the community as such.

In human history, we have learned (I hope) that the conqueror role is   10
eventually self-defeating. Why? Because it is implicit in such a role that the
conqueror knows, *ex cathedra,* just what makes the community clock tick,
and just what and who is valuable, and what and who is worthless, in community life. It always turns out that he knows neither, and this is why his con-
quests eventually defeat themselves. . . .

SUBSTITUTES FOR A LAND ETHIC

. . . One basic weakness in a conservation system based wholly on 11 economic motives is that most members of the land community have no economic value. Wildflowers and songbirds are examples. Of the 22,000 higher plants and animals native to Wisconsin, it is doubtful whether more than 5 percent can be sold, fed, eaten, or otherwise put to economic use. Yet these creatures are members of the biotic community, and if (as I believe) its stability depends on its integrity, they are entitled to continuance.

When one of these noneconomic categories is threatened, and if we 12 happen to love it, we invent subterfuges to give it economic importance. At the beginning of the century songbirds were supposed to be disappearing. Ornithologists jumped to the rescue with some distinctly shaky evidence to the effect that insects would eat us up if birds failed to control them. The evidence had to be economic in order to be valid.

It is painful to read these circumlocutions today. We have no land ethic 13 yet, but we have at least drawn nearer the point of admitting that birds should continue as a matter of biotic right, regardless of the presence or absence of economic advantage to us.

A parallel situation exists in respect of predatory mammals, raptorial 14 birds, and fish-eating birds. Time was when biologists somewhat overworked the evidence that these creatures preserve the health of game by killing weaklings, or that they control rodents for the farmer, or that they prey only on "worthless" species. Here again, the evidence had to be economic in order to be valid. It is only in recent years that we hear the more honest argument that predators are members of the community, and that no special interest has the right to exterminate them for the sake of a benefit, real or fancied, to itself. Unfortunately this enlightened view is still in the talk stage. In the field the extermination of predators goes merrily on. . . .

Some species of trees have been "read out of the party" by economics- 15 minded foresters because they grow too slowly, or have too low a sale value to pay as timber crops: white cedar, tamarack, cypress, beech, and hemlock are examples. In Europe, where forestry is ecologically more advanced, the noncommercial tree species are recognized as members of the native forest community, to be preserved as such, within reason. Moreover some (like beech) have been found to have a valuable function in building up soil fertility. The interdependence of the forest and its constituent tree species, ground flora, and fauna is taken for granted.

Lack of economic value is sometimes a character not only of species 16 or groups, but of entire biotic communities: marshes, bogs, dunes, and "deserts" are examples. Our formula in such cases is to relegate their conservation to government as refuges, monuments, or parks. The difficulty is that these communities are usually interspersed with more valuable private lands; the government cannot possibly own or control such scattered parcels. The net effect is that we have relegated some of them to ultimate extinction over large areas. If the private owner were ecologically minded, he would be proud to be the custodian of a reasonable proportion of such areas, which add diversity and beauty to his farm and to his community.

In some instances, the assumed lack of profit in these "waste" areas   17
has proved to be wrong, but only after most of them had been done away with. The present scramble to reflood muskrat marshes is a case in point. . . .

To sum up: a system of conservation based solely on economic self-   18
interest is hopelessly lopsided. It tends to ignore, and thus eventually to eliminate, many elements in the land community that lack commercial value, but that are (as far as we know) essential to its healthy functioning. It assumes, falsely, I think, that the economic parts of the biotic clock will function without the uneconomic parts. It tends to relegate to government many functions eventually too large, too complex, or too widely dispersed to be performed by government.

An ethical obligation on the part of the private owner is the only visible   29
remedy for these situations.

THE LAND PYRAMID

An ethic to supplement and guide the economic relation to land pre-   20
supposes the existence of some mental image of land as a biotic mechanism. We can be ethical only in relation to something we can see, feel, understand, love, or otherwise have faith in.

The image commonly employed in conservation education is "the bal-   21
ance of nature." For reasons too lengthy to detail here, this figure of speech fails to describe accurately what little we know about the land mechanism. A much truer image is the one employed in ecology: the biotic pyramid. I shall first sketch the pyramid as a symbol of land, and later develop some of its implications in terms of land-use.

Plants absorb energy from the sun. This energy flows through a circuit   22
called the biota, which may be represented by a pyramid consisting of layers. The bottom layer is the soil. A plant layer rests on the soil, an insect layer on the plants, a bird and rodent layer on the insects, and so on up through various animal groups to the apex layer, which consists of the larger carnivores.

The species of a layer are alike not in where they came from, or in   23
what they look like, but rather in what they eat. Each successive layer depends on those below it for food and often for other services, and each in turn furnishes food and services to those above. Proceeding upward, each successive layer decreases in numerical abundance. Thus, for every carnivore there are hundreds of his prey, thousands of their prey, millions of insects, uncountable plants. The pyramidal form of the system reflects this

numerical progression from apex to base. Man shares an intermediate layer with the bears, raccoons, and squirrels which eat both meat and vegetables.

The lines of dependency for food and other services are called food chains. Thus soil-oak-deer-Indian is a chain that has now been largely converted to soil-corn-cow-farmer. Each species, including ourselves, is a link in many chains. The deer eats a hundred plants other than oak, and the cow a hundred plants other than corn. Both, then, are links in a hundred chains. The pyramid is a tangle of chains so complex as to seem disorderly, yet the stability of the system proves it to be a highly organized structure. Its functioning depends on the cooperation and competition of its diverse parts. 24

In the beginning, the pyramid of life was low and squat; the food chains short and simple. Evolution has added layer after layer, link after link. Man is one of thousands of accretions to the height and complexity of the pyramid. Science has given us many doubts, but it has given us at least one certainty: the trend of evolution is to elaborate and diversify the biota. 25

Land, then, is not merely soil; it is a fountain of energy flowing through a circuit of soils, plants, and animals. Food chains are the living channels which conduct energy upward; death and decay return it to the soil. The circuit is not closed; some energy is dissipated in decay, some is added by absorption from the air, some is stored in soils, peats, and long-lived forests; but it is a sustained circuit, like a slowly augmented revolving fund of life. There is always a net loss by downhill wash, but this is normally small and offset by the decay of rocks. It is deposited in the ocean and, in the course of geological time, raised to form new lands and new pyramids. 26

The velocity and character of the upward flow of energy depend on the complex structure of the plant and animal community, much as the upward flow of sap in a tree depends on its complex cellular organization. Without this complexity, normal circulation would presumably not occur. Structure means the characteristic numbers, as well as the characteristic kinds and functions, of the component species. This interdependence between the complex structure of the land and its smooth functioning as an energy unit is one of its basic attributes. 27

When a change occurs in one part of the circuit, many other parts must adjust themselves to it. Change does not necessarily obstruct or divert the flow of energy; evolution is a long series of self-induced changes, the net result of which has been to elaborate the flow mechanism and to lengthen the circuit. Evolutionary changes, however, are usually slow and local. Man's invention of tools has enabled him to make changes of unprecedented violence, rapidity, and scope. 28

One change is in the composition of floras and faunas. The larger predators are lopped off the apex of the pyramid; food chains, for the first time in history, become shorter rather than longer. Domesticated species from other lands are substituted for wild ones, and wild ones are moved to new habitats. In this world-wide pooling of faunas and floras, some species 29 get out of bounds as pests and diseases, others are extinguished. Such effects are seldom intended or foreseen; they represent unpredicted and often untraceable readjustments in the structure. Agricultural science is largely a race between the emergence of new pests and the emergence of new techniques for their control.

Another change touches the flow of energy through plants and animals 30 and its return to the soil. Fertility is the ability of soil to receive, store, and release energy. Agriculture, by overdrafts on the soil, or by too radical a substitution of domestic for native species in the superstructure, may derange the channels of flow or deplete storage. Soils depleted of their storage, or of the organic matter which anchors it, wash away faster than they form. This is erosion.

Waters, like soil, are part of the energy circuit. Industry, by polluting 31 waters or obstructing them with dams, may exclude the plants and animals necessary to keep energy in circulation.

Transportation brings about another basic change: the plants or ani- 32 mals grown in one region are now consumed and returned to the soil in another. Transportation taps the energy stored in rocks, and in the air, and uses it elsewhere; thus we fertilize the garden with nitrogen gleaned by the guano birds from the fishes of seas on the other side of the equator. Thus the formerly localized and self-contained circuits are pooled on a world-wide scale.

The process of altering the pyramid for human occupation releases 33 stored energy, and this often gives rise, during the pioneering period, to a deceptive exuberance of plant and animal life, both wild and tame. These releases of biotic capital tend to becloud or postpone the penalties of violence.

This thumbnail sketch of land as an energy circuit conveys three basic 34 ideas:

1. That land is not merely soil.
2. That the native plants and animals kept the energy circuit open; others may or may not.
3. That man-made changes are of a different order than evolutionary changes, and have effects more comprehensive than is intended or foreseen. . . .

LAND HEALTH AND THE A-B CLEAVAGE

A land ethic, then, reflects the existence of an ecological conscience, 35 and this in turn reflects a conviction of individual responsibility for the health of the land. Health is the capacity of the land for self-renewal. Conservation is our effort to understand and preserve this capacity.

Conservationists are notorious for their dissensions. Superficially 36
these seem to add up to mere confusion, but a more careful scrutiny reveals
a single plane of cleavage common to many specialized fields. In each field
one group (A) regards the land as soil, and its function as commodity-
production; another group (B) regards the land as a biota, and its function
as something broader. How much broader is admittedly in a state of doubt
and confusion.

In my own field, forestry, Group A is quite content to grow trees like 37
cabbages, with cellulose as the basic forest commodity. It feels no inhibition
against violence; its ideology is agronomic. Group B, on the other hand, sees
forestry as fundamentally different from agronomy because it employs natural species, and manages a natural environment rather than creating an artificial one. Group B prefers natural reproduction on principle. It worries on
biotic as well as economic grounds about the loss of species like chestnut,
and the threatened loss of the white pines. It worries about a whole series of
secondary forest functions: wildlife, recreation, watersheds, wilderness
areas. To my mind, Group B feels the stirrings of an ecological conscience.

In the wildlife field, a parallel cleavage exists. For Group A the basic 38
commodities are sport and meat; the yardsticks of production are ciphers of
take in pheasants and trout. Artificial propagation is acceptable as a permanent as well as a temporary recourse—if its unit costs permit. Group B, on
the other hand, worries about a whole series of biotic side-issues. What is
the cost in predators of producing a game crop? Should we have further recourse to exotics? How can management restore the shrinking species, like
prairie grouse, already hopeless as shootable game? How can management restore the threatened rarities, like trumpeter swan and whooping
crane? Can management principles be extended to wildflowers? Here again
it is clear to me that we have the same A-B cleavage as in forestry. . . .

In all of these cleavages, we see repeated the same basic paradoxes: 39
man the conqueror versus man the biotic citizen; science the sharpener of
his sword versus science the searchlight on his universe; land the slave and
servant versus land the collective organism. . . .

THE OUTLOOK

It is inconceivable to me that an ethical relation to land can exist with- 40
out love, respect, and admiration for land, and a high regard for its value. By
value, I of course mean something far broader than mere economic value; I
mean value in the philosophical sense.

Perhaps the most serious obstacle impeding the evolution of a land 41
ethic is the fact that our educational and economic system is headed away
from, rather than toward, an intense consciousness of land. Your true modern is separated from the land by many middlemen, and by innumerable
physical gadgets. He has no vital relation to it; to him it is the space between

cities on which crops grow. Turn him loose for a day on the land, and if the spot does not happen to be a golf links or a "scenic" area, he is bored stiff. If crops could be raised by hydroponics instead of farming, it would suit him very well. Synthetic substitutes for wood, leather, wool, and other natural land products suit him better than the originals. In short, land is something he has "outgrown."

Almost equally serious as an obstacle to a land ethic is the attitude of 42 the farmer for whom the land is still an adversary, or a taskmaster that keeps him in slavery. Theoretically, the mechanization of farming ought to cut the farmer's chains, but whether it really does is debatable. . . .

The "key-log" which must be moved to release the evolutionary 43 process for an ethic is simply this: quit thinking about decent land-use as solely an economic problem. Examine each question in terms of what is ethically and esthetically right, as well as what is economically expedient. A thing is right when it tends to preserve the integrity, stability, and beauty of the biotic community. It is wrong when it tends otherwise.

It of course goes without saying that economic feasibility limits the 44 tether of what can or cannot be done for land. It always has and it always will. The fallacy the economic determinists have tied around our collective neck, and which we now need to cast off, is the belief that economics determines *all* land-use. This is simply not true. An innumerable host of actions and attitudes, comprising perhaps the bulk of all land relations, is determined by the land-users' tastes and predilections, rather than by his purse. The bulk of all land relations hinges on investments of time, forethought, skill, and faith rather than on investments of cash. As a land-user thinketh, so is he. . . .

The evolution of a land ethic is an intellectual as well as emotional 45 process. Conservation is paved with good intentions which prove to be futile, or even dangerous, because they are devoid of critical understanding either of the land, or of economic land-use. I think it is a truism that as the ethical frontier advances from the individual to the community, its intellectual content increases.

The mechanism of operation is the same for any ethic: social approba- 46 tion for right actions: social disapproval for wrong actions.

By and large, our present problem is one of attitudes and implements. 47 We are remodeling the Alhambra with a steam shovel, and we are proud of our yardage. We shall hardly relinquish the shovel, which after all has many good points, but we are in need of gentler and more objective criteria for its successful use. ©

CRITICAL READING

1. Throughout his essay, Leopold gradually constructs what he believes are the necessary components of a "land ethic." Summarize the qualities inherent in this kind of ethical position.

2. Leopold discusses the ways in which conservation has traditionally been framed in economic terms in order to be accepted, and he states that we have "drawn nearer the point of admitting that birds should continue as a matter of biotic right, regardless of the presence or absence of economic advantage to us" in the second and third paragraphs of the "Substitutes for a Land Ethics Program" section. If you've read the environmental sciences global warming unit in this chapter, look over Helen Caldicott's essay, and discuss to what extent she includes economic incentives in her arguments for changing our practices that increase global warming. Alternatively (or additionally), describe what an argument in favor of protecting a particular species would look like if it were based solely on the right of a particular species to exist, that is, based on the kinds of points made by Leopold.
3. Describe the features of the "biotic pyramid" that Leopold outlines. Why is this pyramid a better model for understanding the interdependence of all living things than is the more widely known "balance of nature" paradigm?

CLASS DISCUSSION

1. In the fifth paragraph of the article, Leopold asserts that we as a society haven't as yet developed an ethic "dealing with man's relation to land and to the animals and plants which grow upon it." As a class, explore the following questions: Have we developed such an ethic since this piece was written? If so, in what ways, and if not, why not?
2. Discuss in whole-group format Leopold's assertion that the development of a "land ethic is an intellectual as well as emotional process" from the third from last paragraph in the article. How does emotion figure into this? In what ways might this emotional element serve as one of the obstacles to our approaching the environment from an ethical viewpoint?

DIRECTED FREEWRITE

Explore your own attitudes about and experiences both with the natural environment and with ecologically minded ideals. Do your attitudes and experiences seem to support or to refute the argument that we still haven't developed an ethical approach to the environment? Or does it seem that we have partially begun to do so? Are there behaviors in relation to the environment that receive social disapproval or social approbation in our culture in general?

LONG ON THINGS, SHORT ON TIME

Alan Thein Durning

Alan Durning is a senior researcher at the Worldwatch Institute, which, according to its Web page, is a nonprofit public policy research organization that works to "inform policymakers and the public about emerging global problems and trends and the complex links between the world economy and its environmental support systems." Durning has written a number of books and articles exploring our consumer society and its relation to the environment. Another writer and thinker interested in these kinds of social/ecological issues, Murray Bookchin, has written that "either ecology action is revolutionary action or it is nothing at all." Bookchin believes that small-scale reforms in our habits or legislation will never be enough to halt the degradation of the earth, that only a profound change in our social structures will save us from ourselves. As you read Durning's essay, notice to what degree Durning's argument is revolutionary and to what extent it is reformist. How does Durning compare with Leopold in this regard?

Alan Thein Durning began his environmental career as a researcher assistant and later a senior researcher with the Worldwatch Institute in Washington, D.C. In 1993, Durning founded Northwest Environment Watch, a wholly independent, not-for-profit research and publishing organization modeled after Worldwatch. As the executive director, Durning has made it Northwest Environment Watch's mission to foster an environmentally sound economy and way of life in the Pacific Northwest. Durning has written several books including How Much Is Enough? The Consumer Society and the Future of the Earth; This Place of Earth; The Car and the City; *and* Green-Collar Jobs. *He has also co-authored* Stuff: The Secret Lives of Everyday Things *with John Ryan;* Misplaced Blame: The Real Roots of Population Growth *with Christopher Crowther; and* Tax Shift: How to Help the Economy, Improve the Environment, and Get the Tax Man Off Our Backs *with Yoram Bauman. Durning often speaks at conferences nationwide, provides commentary for NPR, and holds readings at Northwest bookstores.*

The consumer society was born in the United States in the 1920s. Economists and business executives, concerned that the output of mass production might go unsold when people's natural desires for food, clothing, and shelter were satisfied, began pushing mass consumption as the key to continued economic expansion. As brand names became household words, packaged and processed foods made their widespread debut, and the automobile   1

Source: "Long on Things, Short on Time" by Alan Thein Durning in *How Much Is Enough?* Reprinted by permission of Worldwatch Institute.

assumed its place at the center of the culture, the "democratization of consumption" became the unspoken goal of American economic policy.

Since then, the consumer society has moved far beyond U.S. borders, expanding to Western Europe and Japan by the 1960s. Yet far outpacing growth of the consumer class itself—the 20 percent of the world's people who earn 64 percent of world income—is the spread of its underlying cultural orientation, consumerism. That term, writes British economist Paul Ekins, refers to the belief that "the possession and use of an increasing number and variety of goods and services is the principal cultural aspiration and the surest perceived route to personal happiness, social status and national success." But even as, over a few short generations, more than a billion of the world's people have become car drivers, television watchers, mall shoppers, and throwaway buyers, social scientists have found striking evidence that high-consumption societies have not achieved satisfaction. The consumer society fails to deliver on its promise of fulfillment through material comforts because human desires are insatiable, human needs are socially defined, and (perhaps most critically) the real sources of personal happiness are elsewhere. "The conditions of life which really make a difference to happiness," writes psychologist Michael Argyle, "are . . . social relations, work, and leisure. And the establishment of a satisfying state of affairs in these spheres does not depend much on wealth, either absolute of relative." The consumer society, it seems, has succeeded mostly in impoverishing us. This impoverishment is profoundly spiritual, but it is also demonstrably environmental. Our way of life entails an enormous and continuous dependence on the very commodities that are most damaging to the earth to produce: energy, chemicals, metals, and paper. By drawing on resources far and near, we consumers—though our numbers are concentrated primarily in North America, Western Europe, Japan, Australia, Hong Kong, Singapore, and the oil sheikdoms of the Middle East—cast an ecological shadow over wide regions of the world. Our appetite for wood and minerals, for example, motivates the road-builders who open tropical rainforests to poor settlers, resulting in the slash-and-burn forest clearing that is condemning countless species to extinction. A blouse in a Japanese boutique may come from Indonesian oil wells by way of petrochemical plants and textile mills in Singapore and assembly factories in Bangladesh. Likewise, an automobile in a German showroom bearing the logo of an American-owned corporation typically contains parts manufactured in a dozen or more countries, and raw materials that originated in a dozen others. From global warming to species extinction, we consumers bear a huge responsibility for the ills of the earth.

Yet our consumption too seldom receives the attention of those concerned about the fate of the planet. Technological change and population stabilization—as reasonable as it is to emphasize their importance—must be complemented by a reduction of our material wants. Human desires will still overrun the biosphere unless they shift from material to nonmaterial ends. The ability of the earth to support billions of human beings depends on whether we continue to equate consumption with fulfillment. At the same time, we need to challenge the received wisdom that consumption must be pursued—regardless of its human and environmental effects—as a matter of national policy in order to keep ourselves employed.

The latter assumption runs deep. Broadcast news programs cover retail districts in the holiday season as if they were scenes of national significance, offering commentary on shoppers' readiness to buy. When recession hit the United States in mid-1990, everyone from the president on down began begging loyal Americans to spend.   4

The reasoning behind such entreaties sounds impeccable: if no one buys, no one sells, and if no one sells, no one works. Thus, in the consumer economy—where two-thirds of gross national product consists of consumer expenditures—everything from fortunes on the stock market to national economic policies hinges on surveys of "consumer confidence" and "intentions to buy." If this consume-or-decline view is right, then lowering our consumption on purpose, individually and collectively, would be self-destructive. Cutting our driving in half, for example, would throw half the gasoline station attendants out of work, along with half the car mechanics, auto workers, auto-insurance agents, and car-financing specialists. The shock of those layoffs would cause a chain reaction of additional job losses that could end in a repeat of the Great Depression.   5

Mainstream economists paint a similarly nightmarish scenario for developing countries. The industrial countries, they solemnly intone, are the locomotive of the world economy. Contracting demand in industrial countries would leave the citizens of impoverished lands stranded in destitution. Having gambled everything on consumers' endlessly growing appetite for their exported raw materials, developing nations would fall into irreversible decline. In this view, failing to increase consumer-class intake of raw materials is a crime against the 42 poorest nations what the United Nations calls the least-developed countries—because they depend on commodity exports for more than 60 percent of their foreign earnings.   6

The consume-or-decline argument contains a grain of truth. The global economy is indeed structured primarily to feed the consumer lifestyle of the world's affluent fifth, and shifting from high to low consumption would shake that structure to its core. It would require legions of workers to change jobs, entire continents to reconfigure their industrial bases, and enterprises of all scales to transform their operations. It would, worst of all, entail painful dislocation for thousands of families and communities.   7

But consider the alternative: continuing to pillage and poison the earth would guarantee not only the same misfortunes but worse. Fishers will be left idle if water pollution and overharvesting decimate fisheries. Farmers will abandon their fields if recurrent drought kills their crops and animals.   8

Loggers will have little to do if the forests are destroyed by air pollution, acid rain, clearcutting, and shifting climatic zones. Carmakers and homebuilders will not find many buyers if people must spend most of their earnings on scarce food supplies. Business, in short, will not do well on a dying planet. In this light, the admittedly unsettling changes to the global economy so gloomily defended against by the consume-or-decline school are no more an argument against lowering consumption than job losses in the weapons industry are an argument against peace.

The contention that the world's poor cannot afford for us consumers to 9 live on less is debatable at best. Although many developing countries are integrated into the world economy as suppliers of raw materials, this situation puts them in a dependent status that their leaders have decried for decades. Furthermore, the trickle-down effects of the growing consumer economy have proved a disappointing source of economic stimulus. Indeed, the most notable consequence so far has been to create enclaves of world-class consumers in every nation. These elites profit mightily from the exports of natural resources from the global South to the global North. But the world's poor have gained little beyond devastated homelands. Ending poverty, as innumerable experts confirm, depends on aggressive national campaigns for basic health, education, and family planning, on broad-based, labor-intensive development schemes in rural areas, on the mobilizing efforts of grassroots organizations, and on the existence of responsive local and national governments. To finance all these, economic policies must promote innovation, reward success, and allow markets to work efficiently. Ending poverty does not necessarily depend on the production of bulky, low-value goods destined for export to the consumer class. More beneficial by far would be world-trade rules written to make commodity prices reflect more of the ecological costs of production.

The transition to an economy of permanence will be challenging, but 10 perhaps less so than the consume-or-decline argument suggests, because that line of thought rests on three arguable assumptions: that consumption of economic services is immutably bonded to consumption of physical resources in the economy; that employment is equally bonded to flows of physical resources; and that only one model of employment—40 hours a week, all year round—is viable, even though that model requires more hours devoted to work than have been committed by most civilizations in history.

Physical flows of natural resources would slow radically in an economy 11 of permanence, while the money value of the services that people enjoy might fall little. The crucial distinction is between commodities and the services people use those commodities to get. For example, nobody wants telephone books or newspapers for their own sake; rather, we want access to the information they contain. In an economy of permanence, that information might be available to us for much the same price on electronic readers.

That would enable us to consult the same texts but eliminate most paper manufacturing and the associated pollution.

Likewise, people do not want cars as such; they buy them to gain   12
ready access to a variety of facilities and locations. Good town planning and public transportation could provide that access equally well. In every sector of the economy, from housing to food, this distinction between means (physical goods) and ends (services) helps lay bare the vast opportunities to disconnect high resource consumption from the quality of life.

The total amount of work done in an economy of permanence may de-   13
crease little, because the most ecologically damaging products and forms of consumption also usually generate the fewest jobs. Indeed, there is a striking correspondence between high labor intensity and low environmental impact. Repairing existing products, for example, uses more labor and fewer resources than manufacturing new ones. Railway systems employ more people but fewer natural resources than comparable fleets of cars do. Improving energy efficiency would employ more people than would boosting energy production. And recycling programs employ more people than waste incinerators or landfills do.

Were the consumer class to substitute local foods for grain-fed meat   14
and packaged fare, to switch from cars to bikes and buses, and to replace throwaways with durable goods, labor-intensive industries would benefit greatly. Still, on balance, the amount of paid work done might decrease, because low-impact industries would probably expand less than high-impact industries contracted. To cope fairly with slackening job markets, societies in transition to low consumption would (among other initiatives) have to provide laborers in high-impact fields with sufficient job retraining, offer adequate unemployment compensation to smooth the process, and reduce the number of hours each person works. Fortunately, as far as this last-named strategy is concerned, most of us consumers work more than we wish to anyway—a topic we will examine in greater depth shortly.

Governments will also find themselves addressing the employment   15
question when they tackle—as they must—a radical reorientation of their prevailing tax and subsidy policies, many of which promote the worst kinds of consumption. Most nations favor their auto, energy, mining, timber, and grain-fed livestock industries with a long list of tax write offs and direct subsidies. The United States virtually gives away minerals on federal land, builds logging roads into national forests at taxpayer expense, and sells irrigation water in the arid West at a loss. France massively subsidizes its nuclear-power complex, Russia its oil industry, the United Kingdom its auto drivers, the Canadian province of Quebec its aluminum smelters, and Japan its feed-grain growers. Beyond financial transfers and biased policies are the implicit subsidies of the nature-blind economic accounting systems that governments use. Coal and oil are not priced to reflect the damage their production and combustion cause to human health and natural ecosystems.

Pulp and paper are not priced to reflect the habitat destroyed and water poisoned in their production. Scores of products—from toxic chemicals to excessive packaging—cost the earth more than their price tags reveal.

If goods were priced to reflect something closer to their full environ- 16 mental costs, the market would help guide consumers toward lower resource consumption. Disposables and packaging, for instance, would rise in price relative to less-packaged goods; local unprocessed food would fall in price relative to prepared products trucked from far away. If legislators shifted the tax burden from labor to resources, companies would swiftly move to trim resource use as environmental taxes rose, and hire more people as income taxes fell.

Already environmental and taxpayer groups in many nations single out 17 egregious subsidies and tax shelters as targets for reform. But they commonly lose the big battles, overwhelmed by the political clout of the billion-dollar industries that doggedly defend the status quo. Every battle lost demonstrates the difficulty and the urgency of mobilizing more members of the consumer class in support of prices that tell the ecological truth.

As previously suggested, an important approach to a low-consump- 18 tion, sustainable future is for us consumers to release ourselves from the strictures of full-time work. Many of us find ourselves agreeing with American industrial designer William Stumpf, who says, "We've got enough stuff . . . We need more time."

Although fulfilling work and adequate leisure are both key determi- 19 nants of human contentment, the balance in the consumer society tilts too far toward work. Working hours in industrial societies, although far below their peak during the Industrial Revolution, remain high by historical standards. Japanese and Americans are especially overworked. Europeans have been trading part of their pay raises for additional leisure time since 1950, but Americans and Japanese have not. In Germany and France, the average hours worked per week have gone from 44 and 38 hours respectively in 1950 to 31 hours in 1980, with much of the decline reflecting annual vacation leaves spanning four to eight weeks. In Japan, weekly hours have gone from 44 to 41. In the United States, meanwhile, the workweek declined slightly from 1950 to 1970, but has actually increased since then. Americans work 38 hours a week, on average, and have added an entire month's worth of work to their schedule since 1970.

Harvard University economist Juliet Schor writes in *The Overworked* 20 *American:* "Since 1948, the level of productivity of the U.S. worker has more than doubled. In other words, we could now produce our 1948 standard of living in less than half the time. Every time productivity increases, we are presented with the possibility of either more free time or more money. We could have chosen the four-hour day. Or a working year of six months. Or every worker in the United States could now be taking every other year off from work with pay." Instead, Americans work the same hours and earn twice the money. To check whether that choice reflected the will of American workers, Schor delved into the arcane field of labor-market economics and, having surveyed dozens of studies, concluded that it did not. Workers in all the core regions of the consumer society express—either in opinion surveys or in collective-bargaining positions—a strong desire for additional leisure time and a willingness to trade pay increases for it. They also report that they do not have that option: They can take a job or leave it, but they cannot take it for fewer hours a day. Part-time work, furthermore, is in general less skilled, less interesting, and less well paid because it lacks fringe benefits such as retirement and insurance plans. So most of us are left with the choice of good fulltime jobs or bad part-time ones.

In an earlier era, cynics said workers would squander free time on   21
drinking and gambling. But when the W. K. Kellogg Company shortened its workday from eight hours to six during the Great Depression, community initiatives proliferated. Contemporary observer Henry Goddard Leach noticed "a lot of gardening and community beautification. . . . Athletics and hobbies were booming. . . . Libraries [were] well patronized . . . and the mental background of these fortunate workers . . . [was] becoming richer."

Mounting pressure for more time instead of more money is evident in   22
things like the campaign of some 240 U.S. labor, women's, and children's organizations for the right to take time off for family and medical purposes. The coalition, chaired by the Women's Legal Defense Fund, pushed a bill through Congress in 1991 that was vetoed twice by President Bush. Similarly, for two decades unions such as Service Employees International have been supporting voluntary work-time reduction programs for workers who want free time instead of money. The Service Employees won such a program temporarily for California state government workers in the 1970s, and later prevailed permanently for New York state government employees.

More recently, interest has surged in flexible work arrangements such   23
as job sharing, particularly among women stretched thin by the "double day" of career and family. So far, unfortunately, American men have not joined women in pushing for flexible or reduced hours, perhaps because our culture disapproves of men who don't want to work full-time. Meanwhile, in Japan, where karoshi (death from overwork) kill perhaps 10,000 people a year, young workers are displaying a newly disapproving attitude toward overtime, pressuring colleagues to leave the office at the end of the scheduled day. The Japanese government plans to switch the country from a six-day workweek to a five-day one by early in the next century. In Europe, too, unions continue to press for additional time off.

No one can say yet how strong this preference for free time over extra   24
consumption is. In theory, if everyone consistently chose free time over additional money, normal gains in labor productivity would cut consumer-class working hours in half by 2020, giving us abundant time for personal development and for family and community activities.

A culture of permanence will not come quickly. Much depends on 25
whether we, among the richest fifth of the world's people, having fully met
our material needs, can turn to nonmaterial sources of fulfillment. Can we—
who have defined the tangible goals of world development—now craft a new
way of life at once simpler and more satisfying? Having invented the automobile and airplane, can we return to bicycles, buses, and trains? Having
introduced the junk-food diet, can we nourish ourselves on wholesome fare
that is locally produced? Having pioneered sprawl and malls, can we recre-
ate human-scale settlements where commerce is an adjunct to civic life
rather than its purpose?

If our grandchildren are to inherit a planet as bounteous and beautiful 26
as we have enjoyed, we in the consumer class must without surrendering
the quest for advanced, clean technology—eat, travel, and use energy and
materials more like those on the middle rung of the world's economic ladder.
If we can learn to do so, we might find ourselves happier as well.

Accepting and living by sufficiency rather than excess offers a return to 27
what is, culturally speaking, the human home: to the ancient order of family,
community, good work, and good life; to a reverence for skill, creativity, and
creation; to a daily cadence slow enough to let us watch the sunset and stroll
by the water's edge; to communities worth spending a lifetime in; and to
places pregnant with the memories of generations. Perhaps Henry David
Thoreau had it right when he scribbled in his notebook beside Walden Pond,
"A man is rich in proportion to the things he can afford to let alone."   ©

CRITICAL READING

1. Explain Durning's point about the distinction between means and ends, and the
   way that this distinction helps us conceive of a society in which we are less re-
   liant on physical things (means) to meet our needs (ends).
2. Respond to the point that Durning quotes from William Stumpf, who says,
   "We've got enough stuff . . . We need more time." Then discuss whose interest
   is served by giving workers more money instead of more time off.
3. Describe what Durning means by the term "a culture of permanence."

CLASS DISCUSSION

1. Discuss the features of our consumer society. In what ways are class members
   "good consumers"? How has this identity been formed? How might this be
   changed, on an individual as well as a societal scale? How do students feel about
   changing this identity? What do class members like and not like about being participants in this consumer society?
2. If we worked less, what kinds of endeavors does Durning suggest that we would
   engage in during our extra time? Assuming that Durning is correct, discuss as a
   group the benefits that would accrue from these endeavors. What other ways can
   you imagine that people might spend their time?

DIRECTED FREEWRITE

1. Let your mind go and muse on the issues raised by Durning. How possible are his ideas, how desirable are they, and what are the obstacles faced by individuals who might want to implement his ideals? Write in response to questions such as these, and just see what ideas you come up with.

SOCIAL ECOLOGY UNIT WRITING ASSIGNMENTS

1. Write a short essay arguing against Leopold's land ethic, and making a case for the economic view of the natural environment. In your prewriting for this essay, make a list of all the possible arguments that one could bring to support such a position, drawing from Leopold's essay as well as from your own imagination, experiences, and observations. See the discussion of argument in assignment 2 on page 60 of the Social Psychology unit of Chapter 2.
2. Write a short essay explaining the Thoreau quotation with which Durning ends his essay. Use points from Durning's article to explain the point Thoreau makes. You might, if you are familiar with Thoreau's *Walden,* bring in others of Thoreau's ideas to flesh out your discussion.
3. Write an essay comparing and contrasting Leopold's land ethic approach to addressing environmental problems with Durning's points about changing our economic and social structures rather than (or in addition to) our belief systems. Ultimately, your comparison and contrast should arrive at a conclusion about which, if any, of these ideals is most workable, and why. For more discussion of comparison and contrast as a mode of writing, see assignment 2 on page 165 of the Philosophy unit in Chapter 2.
4. In assignment 2 on page 526 of the Engineering unit of this chapter, we introduced the form of writing known as the abstract. Read the description provided there, and then add these instructions.

    Imagine an empirical study into some environmental issue, and write an abstract for the imagined report that a researcher would write. This will be an abstract for an experimental report, rather than for a theoretical essay or review essay. Be creative, and focus on the key elements that the imagined report would contain, since these are what comprise the abstract. Take a scientific or a social scientific approach, depending on what interests you and on what you feel most comfortable imagining and writing about. For example, you might imagine yourself a chemist who is trying to construct a biodegradable material that would work as an alternative to plastic. Imagine the basic outlines of an experiment in which a certain chemical formula for this material is tested in some way. Or imagine that the material has been produced and that you are putting it through various tests to match its performance with that of plastic. Or, as a sociologist, you might imagine a study into the recycling behavior of individuals in a certain region, perhaps testing peoples' claims about the extent of their recycling against their actual handling of recyclable trash.

Alternatively, find an empirical study on some environmental topic, and after reading the abstract for it once, cover or cut out the abstract, and write your own, on the basis of the key points you discern from the report. Your job will be much easier if you don't fudge and look at the article's actual abstract after you have read the article; sometimes when we read others' words, we have more difficulty coming up with original wording of our own.

Unit 2

Political Science/Political Economy—
Politics, Money, and the Environment

GOVERNMENT AND THE ECONOMICS
OF THE ENVIRONMENT

Frances Cairncross

Frances Cairncross, a British writer with degrees in history and in economics, has written for such publications as *The Economist* magazine in London, the *Observer,* and the *Guardian.* She's written a number of books on economics, and this piece is excerpted from the introduction to her 1991 book *Costing the Earth,* which discusses at length the environmental challenge for governments and the ecology-based opportunities for business. As you read, notice the interplay between economic issues, government intervention, and business practices that Cairncross advocates.

Frances Cairncross was educated at Oxford University and Brown University, RI. She is a senior editor on The Economist *magazine where she covers topics as diverse as media and communication as well as economics and the environment. She is a regular presenter of the BBC's "Analysis" program, a governor of the National Institute of Economic and Social Research and on the council of the Institute for Fiscal Studies. Her previous books include* Costing the Earth: The Challenge for Governments, the Opportunities for Business *and* Green, Inc.

Environmentalism involves dangerous issues for politicians. [Former British Prime Minister] Margaret Thatcher can hardly have thought through the telling metaphor she used in her speech to the Conservative party conference in October 1988 that marked her transition from Iron Lady to Green Goddess. "No generation has a freehold on the earth," she said. "All we have is a life tendency—with a full repairing lease." The implications are enormous. For up to now, no generation has carried out its fair share of   1

---

planetary repairs. Each has ignored the costs that accrue to future generations. To demand that this generation should undertake repairs means making people pay for something that they have previously regarded as free. Yet only government can ultimately set the terms of that "full repairing lease."

Environmental policy is inevitably interventionist. Without government   2
intervention, the environment cannot be fully protected. That was clearly anticipated over a century ago by John Stuart Mill. "Is there not the earth itself, its forests and waters, above and below the surface?" he asked in his *Principles of Political Economy.* "These are the inheritance of the human race. . . . What rights, and under what conditions, a person shall be allowed to exercise over any portion of this common inheritance cannot be left undecided. No function of government is less optional than the regulation of these things, or more completely involved in the idea of a civilized society."

This intrinsic need for intervention makes environmentalism difficult for   3
political radicals to accept, especially after the 1980s' fashion for deregulation. An eloquent exposition of the free-marketer's case for environmental intervention was made by one of Mrs. Thatcher's closest political allies, Nicholas Ridley, while he was British environment secretary:

> Pollution, like fraud, is something you impose on others against their will so that you can perhaps gain financial advantage. It is an ill for which the operation of the free market provides no automatic cure. Like the prevention of violence and fraud, pollution control is essentially an activity which the State, as protector of the public interest against particular interests, has to regulate and police.

Harder yet for many governments to accept, environmental issues are   4
frequently about justice, too. Allocating rights and determining conditions drags government, willy-nilly, into nasty questions of winners and losers that politicians usually prefer to avoid. The winners and losers may live in the same town. But the gainers may be rich and powerful, the losers poor and weak. The losers may even be foreigners, if one country's environmental damage harms the citizens of another. Or they may be the weakest of the weak: generations yet unborn. "Why should I care about posterity?" Groucho Marx is supposed to have said. "What's posterity ever done for me?" Posterity has no votes; yet caring for the environment is often a matter of changing the habits of today's voters for the benefit of future generations. Heating our homes would cost far more if we used only wind power and solar energy, in order to avoid putting into the atmosphere the carbon dioxide that may well cause global warming. Why should politicians ask us to bear such costs? After all, alarming though the speed of global warming may be in terms of the history of evolution, by the time today's politicians retire, its results will still be barely noticeable.

Even within a country, environmental issues may raise awkward ques- 5
tions of justice and rights which only government can protect. For it is only
government that can decide how much society should value the environment, and how that value should be inserted into economic transactions.
The market, that mechanism that so marvelously directs human activity to
supply human needs, often has no way of putting a proper price on environmental resources. "Free as the air" is all very well, but it means that factories pay nothing to belch smoke from their stacks. It is easy to put a price on
a tree as timber. But that price will take no account of its value as a mechanism for preventing soil erosion, or as a home for rare birds or insects, or as
a store of carbon dioxide that might otherwise add to the greenhouse gases
in the atmosphere.

To talk of trees in the language of economics seems odd to many envi- 6
ronmentalists. The very idea that values can be attached to natural beauty
is an affront to those who think that it is beyond price. Yet to think of the environment in economic terms is a useful way of understanding environmental problems. In particular, it is a helpful approach for politicians and
mangers who are familiar with using economic concepts to analyze policy
decisions. Some environmentalists have grasped this, and realize that governments and companies may become more concerned with environmental
issues if they see them as benefiting their economic interest.

Because the market does not set prices on environmental resources, 7
the economy is skewed in favor of those things that can be developed and
marketed and against those that cannot. A developer who wants to put up a
factory in a beauty spot can easily calculate the gain in terms of jobs and
production. Those who want to protect the beauty spot have no such numbers. The undeveloped spot has no "output" to set against the products of
the factory. It is never easy to argue that the gain to those generations who
can enjoy its views will be greater, over the years, than the hard cash that
the developer thinks can be earned.

Why are environmental goods so often unpriced or underpriced? 8
Sometimes the reason is cultural: in Muslim countries, many of which are
dangerously short of water, people have strong religious objections to paying for a gift from God. More often, the reason is that the resource is owned
by everybody and therefore by nobody. People take less care of what is
theirs than of what is owned collectively; and the ozone layer, the oceans,
and the atmosphere are all common property.

This point was made by Joan Robinson, a distinguished British econo- 9
mist, in a famous question: "Why," she asked, "is there litter in the public
park, but no litter in my backyard?" In primitive societies, people frequently
have long-established customs for ensuring that common property is managed to the maximum benefit of all. Herdsmen accept limits on the number
of cattle they can graze on a common field. Yet such traditions are vulnera-

ble. An individual herdsman can always do better by grazing more cattle on the land. Once the common restraint goes, all will be tempted to overgraze until the common field is bare and all are worse off than before. This dilemma was described as "The Tragedy of the Commons" in a famous article by Garret Hardin. In fact, property owned in common is more likely to escape tragedy than property that is accessible to all. That is the position of most environmental resources.

No one owns the sea or the sky; therefore no one charges those who   10
overfish the sea or fill the air with ozone smog. Nobody owns quietness; therefore nobody can set a price on nasty noises. Where no one owns an environmental resource, the market will not give its usual warning signals as that resource is used up. In the early 1970s, some environmentalists fretted terribly about the imminent exhaustion of oil, iron, and copper, which, they rightly pointed out, were nonrenewable. Once all the oil was burned, that was that. They reckoned without the oil-exporting countries, which behaved like any cartel with limited supplies of a product in great demand and jacked up the price. Result: much investment went into energy conservation and into searching for oil in places like the North Sea and Alaska where it would not previously have been profitable.

We will never pump the last barrel of oil. We may well, however, kill the   11
last elephant, for as that mammal becomes more scarce, so the rewards for catching it increase. In fact the true limits to growth are not the earth's stocks of natural resources such as coal, oil, and iron, which are bought and sold at prices that will rise to reflect their increasing scarcity. The limits are the capacity of the environment to deal with waste in all its forms and with the "critical" resources—such as the ozone layer, the carbon cycle, and the Amazon forest—that play no direct part in world commerce but that serve the most basic economic function of all, which is to enable human beings to survive. It is these two kinds of resources, long treated as free goods, that have been most dangerously overexploited.

MAKING MARKETS WORK

Because the forces of unfettered markets can destroy the environ-   12
ment, environmental lobbyists have wanted to replace markets with government. If private enterprise chops down forests, the argument runs, put the forests in the hands of the state. This extreme faith in the benign green role of the state has faded, thanks in part to growing realization of the scope of environmental catastrophe in the state-run lands of Eastern Europe. Many examples show that bad government policies may make even more of a mess of the environment than the unfettered market.

A better starting point is to look for ways to improve markets. Clear   13
rights of ownership for natural resources may sometimes improve the way

they are managed. If ownership of environmental assets is clearly established, then polluters and the polluted will be able to bargain over a reasonable price for allowing pollution to take place. Sometimes such solutions
work. If people have fishing rights in a river that they can rent out to others,
they will have a strong interest in seeing that their bit of the river is not over-
fished. They will also be able to bargain with other owners to prevent the
whole river from being overexploited. But often—think of the ozone layer—it
is simply not possible to use private enterprise in this way. Establishing
ownership is too difficult; the number of polluters and of those affected by
pollution is too great for bargaining to be practical.

Another way to improve the working of the market is to make sure con- 14
sumers and producers pay the true costs of the environmental damage they
cause. Markets work best when prices reflect as accurately as possible the
costs of production. So the price of a gallon of gas ought to reflect the damage caused by exhaust gases, while the cost of running a bath should incorporate the environmental harm caused by water extraction and sewage
disposal. The main ways in which economists urge politicians to pass such
information into pricing is through taxation.

But making polluters pay is easier advocated than done. Once a politi- 15
cian pauses and wonders, "Right: but how much?" another set of problems
appears. It is impossible to estimate exactly the price that a green government
should exact from polluters. If the developer who wanted to build a factory in a
beauty spot had wanted, instead, to build it where a housing estate now
stands, the price of the site would have reflected the price at which houses
are bought and sold. There is a housing market, but there is no beauty market. So if government is to make sure that the beauty spot is properly valued,
it has to put a price on loveliness. Economists have thought up ways to do
this, such as asking people what they would be willing to pay to keep the spot
undeveloped. But none has the real-world quality of the price of a house. Besides, faced with a powerful developer, only a very rash politician would become involved in a fight over the social value of undeveloped land.

Simply because environmental costs are so hard to estimate is no ar- 16
gument for abandoning the effort, for two reasons. First, setting a rough
value may be a better basis for policy than none at all. Only by groping for
values for environmental resources can governments think sensibly about
costs and benefits. Scientists who are alarmed by the prospect of global
warming tend to argue that carbon emissions must be halted at any price.
Wise governments will first ask what the costs of global warming are likely to
be, and then will want an estimate of the costs of slowing the buildup of
greenhouse gases. Both figures will be wobbly and widely disputed. But
without some grasp of costs and benefits, governments are likely to do either too much or—worse—too little.

Most governments, far from making polluters carry the costs of envi- 17
ronmental damage, do precisely the opposite. So a second reason for trying

to put values on environmental goods is to discourage such perversity. Many governments subsidize polluting activities. In particular, many third world countries hold down electricity prices. That drives up demand. Generating electricity to supply this demand produces more gases, sulphur dioxide and carbon dioxide, both harmful in different ways. It may mean building more dams for hydropower. It may encourage a country to develop polluting industries.

18   Such folly is not confined to the poor world. Most rich countries subsidize agriculture. That encourages monoculture—usually more polluting than mixed cropping—and increases the demand for fertilizer and pesticides. America subsidizes the logging of its ancient forests. Britain subsidizes company cars. Germany subsidizes coal mining. Each country has its green madness, often as economically perverse as it is environmentally damaging. Such perversities survive because powerful lobbies back them. Governments, in democracies at least, can rarely do more than their electors want. If this generation of electors is not prepared to foot the bill for that "full repairing lease," governments will find it hard to make them.

19   To rely exclusively on the force of the market, however ingeniously harnessed, to clean the environment is as naive as relying solely on government intervention. For one thing, markets need information. If polluters are to pay, governments will need to measure pollution. Government will need to punish polluters who cheat. Monitoring, measurement, and enforcement are all jobs that cannot be done voluntarily. They require a legal framework and the sanction of the state.

20   Governments may sometimes need to make the market work better in other, more subtle ways. If a market does not exist in the first place, giving it green signals will be pointless. The countries of Eastern Europe had elaborate systems of fines and charges to discourage pollution; but, as the fines were rarely collected and the charges were carried by monopolies, pollution simply continued unabated. It is important to worry about creating a market in the first place—getting, say, someone in the Soviet Union to worry about leaks of natural gas or someone in America to care about water lost from pipes—before building elaborate schemes to ensure that polluters carry the full costs of environmental damage.

21   This is important because a characteristic of many of the activities that most affect the environment—energy supply, the provision of water, transport—is that they are highly regulated by the state. Power lines, sewage works, roads, and airports are frequently monopolies or near-monopolies. It may therefore be difficult to rely on pricing alone, or on market forces harnessed in other ways, to influence the supply of and demand for these services. Raising the price of electricity may encourage consumers to turn off their lights, or it may simply leave them with less cash to spend on other things. Only gradually will it encourage them to buy more efficient central heating or to install double glazing. It may be faster and less painful—and

politically easier—if governments also boost conservation in more direct ways. . . .

Many people hope that economic growth can be made environmentally benign. It never truly can. Most economic activity involves using up energy and raw materials; this, in turn, creates waste that the planet has to absorb. Green growth is therefore a chimera. But green*er* growth is possible. The history of technology has been about squeezing more output from the same volume of raw materials. Governments can dramatically reduce the environmental harm done by growth if they create incentives for companies to use raw material more frugally. That means harnessing the inventive energy of industry. 22

If effective environmental policies are to be combined with vigorous economic growth, policies must be designed with an eye to their cost-effectiveness. As people grow richer, and want higher environmental standards, the cost of attaining them will rise. Compliance with federal environmental laws and regulations in the United States already costs over $100 billion a year. Almost two-thirds of that bill falls on private business. That has made politicians pause, when lobbied by environmentalists, and wonder who will pick up the tab. At the same time, it is increasingly clear in the richest countries that well-run companies are now reaching a stage where becoming cleaner will cost much more. The first steps in pollution control are inevitably the cheapest. The best companies have already taken most of these. Subsequent measures will cost more with each succeeding step. Diminishing returns will set in. 23

Plenty remains to be done, of course, to bring the worst companies up to the standards of the best. But further advances in pollution control may involve changing not what companies do, but how individuals behave. To take just one example, for the same number of dollars far more could be achieved to remove nitrous oxides from California's air by changing the cars individuals drive and the ways they drive them than by fitting more exotic bits of machinery to the smokestacks of the state's electricity utilities. . . . 24

. . . Sound economics and sound environmental policies go hand in hand. Inflation, subsidies, and a failure to charge people the true costs of their activities all breed weak economies; they also breed environmental damage. Similarly, sound economics dictates that policies should put as little burden as possible on society to achieve their goal. Environmental policies that harness market forces meet that test. . . . 25

. . . Beyond the requirements of policy [are] the implications for companies. . . . Only by enlisting the help of companies . . . can governments hope to combine economic growth with good environmental stewardship. Electors will not welcome greener policies if those deliver what they perceive to be a lower standard of living. Government will be able to pursue better environmental policies only if companies find ways to give people the level of comfort to which they have become accustomed, in less environmentally 26 damaging ways. Companies are more likely to help politicians if politicians take their proper responsibilities seriously.

Government must establish environmental priorities and determine 27 what information (as a minimum) needs to be put before the public. It needs to set clear rules and work out how true environmental costs are to be reflected in costs of production. These are not responsibilities for companies. Their role is to respond, energetically and inventively, to the framework that government sets out. The better that framework is designed, and the more imaginatively companies use it, the more electors will support environmental policies.

There is an important lesson here for environmental lobbyists. Many 28 of them feel uncomfortable when companies approach them, as now sometimes happens, asking them to put down their placards, abandon their boycotts, and come into the boardroom with constructive advice. If environmentalists are to campaign effectively for a cleaner world, they need to understand how companies can help. If they talk the language of wealth creation, of incentives, of efficiency, of market opportunities, they are more likely to be listened to by politicians and by managers. To say "We want a green world and to hell with who pays for it" may be good television, but it is ultimately bad politics. By harnessing technology through the deft application of market forces, companies, governments, and environmentalists stand the best chance of jointly building a cleaner environment.   ©

CRITICAL READING

1. Describe the distinction that Cairncross makes between property that is accessible to all and property that is owned in common. How is each of these usually treated by people?
2. What is the problem, according to Cairncross, with charging governments to own, manage, and preserve environmental resources? On what evidence does she base this point? Describe the alternatives she proposes.
3. Cairncross's economic approach to environmental protection is interesting when compared with approaches discussed in earlier units, such as that of Aldo Leopold in his piece, "Toward a Land Ethic." If you've read Leopold's essay about developing an ethical approach to the environment, discuss how Cairncross's points compare and contrast to Leopold's.

CLASS DISCUSSION

1. Since 1991, when Cairncross wrote this piece, the economic world has become increasingly globalized (interconnected and interdependent at a global level as a result of advances in technology). As a class, explore the problems that this circumstance might pose with regard to the kinds of governmental roles in environmental protection that the author discusses.

2. Discuss, in group format, Cairncross's assertion in the third paragraph from the end that "Government will be able to pursue better environmental policies only if companies find ways to give people the level of comfort to which they have become accustomed, in less environmentally damaging ways." Do you agree? Is this change possible?

DIRECTED FREEWRITE

Describe some environmental problems of which you are aware; you either may have firsthand experience with these or may have heard or read about them. Describe several examples of some kind of pollution or spoliation, and explore to what extent these problems seem to be perpetrated by individuals, businesses, and/or the government.

DONNA DOGOOD/
JOSE HOLISTIC DIALOGUE

Navroz K. Dubash

In this piece, Navroz Dubash, a former staff member of the Environmental Defense Fund, uses a fictional dialogue to lay out some of the conflicting concerns of environmental activists. Donna Dogood represents the traditional, liberal American environmentalist, and Jose Holistic serves as the more radical voice of local, grassroots environmental movements. Although this piece doesn't explicitly lay out specific political and economic issues, it does address some of the concerns that lie behind such specific issues; therefore, as you read, think about how the points raised by each speaker would translate into political economic policy.

Navroz Dubash holds his M.A. and Ph.D. degrees in Energy and Resources from the University of California, Berkeley, and an A.B. in public policy from Princeton University. He is a Senior Associate in the Institutions and Governance Program at the World Resources Institute. Prior to joining WRI, he served as coordinator of the international Climate Action Network with the Environmental Defense Fund. Dr. Dubash is an Indian national with research and work experience in India where he has worked on local institutions for management of groundwater resources as well as on international policy levels. Most recently, he co-authored The Right Conditions: The World Bank, Structural Adjustment, and Forest Policy Reform Leverage for the Environment: A Guide to the Private Financial Services Industry.

Overheard at a bar at the "Earth Summit" . . .   1

Person 1: Beautiful city, isn't it?   2

Person 2: Yes. Too bad about all the street children.   3

Person 1: Isn't it terrible? Natural riches side-by-side with human   4
poverty. Well, it is a good thing we are finally beginning to recognize these problems at the international level. It makes me very happy to finally witness an event like the Earth Summit—where wasteful and short-sighted destruction of our environment is finally given the attention it deserves. By the way, my name is Donna Dogood, I used to be with the U.S. Environmental Protection Agency but now work for the Global Organization for Nature, Everywhere (GONE), a non-governmental organization (NGO) based in Washington, DC. We work on all issues of environmental destruction worldwide and have chapters around the globe—even in some developing countries.

Person 2: I am pleased to meet you. I am Jose Holistic, and my NGO is   5
called Local Organization for Community Awareness (LOCA). I am from Brazil, and my organization works with local community-based peoples' groups on low-income enhancement and resource conservation projects. We assist local groups in their fight for legal and historic rights over resources when they are threatened by government or private sector appropriation. I am afraid I am not as positive about this jamboree as you seem to be. I find it hard to understand how all these speeches, press conferences and negotiations about the placement of punctuation in official documents will make any difference to the people with whom we work. And where it does make a difference, I am afraid my country and the other poorer nations are being pushed into deals and arrangements that will further impoverish us.

Dogood: Surely that judgement is too harsh. I see the Earth Summit as   6
a vindication of my organization's work. From our early years advocating wilderness preservation, we have moved on to encouraging sustainable and efficient energy and water use and the effective disposal of waste. We have also recently begun looking at how all these problems, combined with the population explosion, lead to potentially catastrophic global environmental problems. Admittedly, the conference does not go nearly far enough in terms of setting out concrete and enforceable actions for all countries to take. However, the process of developing national plans has forced bureaucracies to grapple with environmental issues, and the presence of world leaders has a not insignificant symbolic value. The Earth Summit has raised environment and development issues to the fore in the post cold war era. In

addition, there are concrete gains: the international convention on the preservation of biological diversity represents the first step to stem the tide of species loss. The climate change treaty acknowledges—implicitly, at least—that our current consumption pattern and lifestyle is fraying the very fabric of . . .

Holistic (interrupts): Excuse me. Whose lifestyle? Not mine nor that of the people I work with. Some people in my country, yes,—those that benefit from close contact with the North. But they are very few. The rest are too busy worrying about food, clothing and shelter to care about wilderness preservation, marginal health risks from industrial pollutants, or half-baked ideas of global destruction wrought by ultra-violet rays or global warming. Let me be honest. Your concerns are valid, but they are far in the future for me. My organization was created to empower local people, to organize for the fight for control over local resources. You are only now beginning to broaden your environmentalism to include development. I have never been an "environmentalist" and never will be if it means putting nature before people. Environmentalism is the battle over sensible natural resource use for development. It is a battle that must occur within our own countries. I am here largely because the people in power in my country now listen more to your government than to its own people, and so this battle is out of our control. Our government is in the hands of capitalists who want cheap labor and cheap raw materials. Our patterns of production are changed to suit you and our elites. For example, food crops are increasingly being replaced by cash crops for export, and most of the benefits accrue to the North. Does it make sense that for every $10 of Brazilian coffee sold in your country, my country gets only $1? The rest goes to transportation, storage, processing and retailing in your country. And the work of the farmer, the value of the soil depleted and the water used are all together assessed at only 25–50 cents—less than one twentieth what the coffee is sold for! Forgive me if I sound angry, but for me the Earth Summit is not about efficiency and global objectives, it is about inequality and local problems, and the perpetuation of these problems by existing international power structures.

Dogood: You are talking of changing existing power structures. I am far more modest than that. I am guided by immediate problems on which I can have a positive impact. For example, I know that promoting energy efficiency—in my country and in developing countries—is cheaper than building economically wasteful and environmentally destructive new thermal power plants. I focus on using the technical tools and political influences I have to convince governments to implement energy efficiency measures. We could spend all our time complaining about unequal power but I prefer to use sound analysis and take practical measures to solve pieces of the problem.

Holistic: You are only looking at a few pieces of the puzzle, those pieces that your analytical methods are suited to. There are many things we cannot price and cannot value economically. Moreover, prices assigned to goods and services reflect social values, and since these may differ between groups, prices currently reflect only the values of the socially dominant. No, I do not subscribe to the new orthodoxy of global economic efficiency and materialism. Besides, even if the international pie of material goods grows as promised, most of the extra pieces are siphoned off to your country.

Dogood: I agree with much of what you say about economic methods. 10 But we cannot throw up our hands and say that some things do not have a price. The market system, like it or not, is the system within which we must operate, and we must find a way of incorporating our values into the market framework. For example, I agree with you that undervaluing natural resources—as with your example of coffee production—encourages wasteful use of these resources. My organization is researching ways of factoring natural resource depletion into national income-accounting methods. In the short term, this is the best way of ensuring economically and environmentally efficient use of natural resources.

Holistic: There are values other than economic values that cannot be 11 ignored. Your approach deifies materialism; equates it with happiness. It assumes a common set of values irrespective of geography, history, socioeconomic status and culture. My approach would return control over natural resources to local communities. This would enable collective decision-making on resource use based on the values of the local community, who would factor in the impact of those decisions on future generations. Decisions on natural resource use must be de-centralized, which is why I am very suspicious of declarations of global solidarity such as those I hear here.

Dogood: But surely there are global dimensions to all these problems 12 that you are ignoring. Unsustainable resource use at local levels has a global impact. Destruction of the Amazonian rainforest deprives future generations the aesthetic and medical benefits of biological diversity. Rapid population growth puts pressures on the globe's resource base and waste processing capabilities.

Holistic: Concern about global population growth is the best illustration 13 of the distorted perspective of this conference. When a Bangladeshi consumes less than one percent of the energy consumed by one American, what does it matter to you if many more Bangladeshis are born than Americans? It is an important problem for the Bangladeshis who have to feed those people. I have repeatedly heard northern delegates say that your attempts to curb greenhouse gas emissions will be in vain because of the rising tide of brown, black and yellow people who will demand your style of development and hence emit increasing amounts of greenhouse gases. Let us look at the facts. At the moment, New York City uses more electricity than all of Sub-Saharan Africa (excluding South Africa)! Currently, the 25% of global population in the industrialized nations are responsible for 75% of global emissions, and that does not count historical emissions since the industrial revolution, which would be an appropriate measure of responsibility. It will be a long time before the Third World approaches the total level of northern emissions—on the order of a century. We have many more pressing problems to occupy us until 2092. The concerns about population growth are not of global nature. The problems, and the solutions, lie at the local level.

Dogood: You keep talking about the local level, but, once again, I think   14
pragmatism dictates we look beyond a romantic vision of ecologically sustainable communities living off the land. The social structure in my country is concentrated around urban areas—we cannot go back to idyllic rural communities. I also wonder whether you romanticize local communities in your countries. I am sure many such communities over-exploit natural resources for short term gain. Their attitude of responsible stewardship, if it ever existed, is breaking apart as social structures break down and are replaced by those suited to increased access to markets—particularly international markets—and opportunities for trade. Many people in rural communities now also desire television sets and cars—they won't get those by returning to a Gandhian vision of self-reliance.

Holistic: I, too, worry about these questions. But, in my own way, I am   15
also a pragmatist. My pragmatism involves pushing these questions to the background, and, in the short term, fighting against logging rights for timber corporations, fighting for local people to have access to fodder and firewood from forests, training local people to build efficient wood-stoves from local materials, recovering and restoring ancient agricultural and irrigation practices, and arguing against fertilizer-intensive, single strain, multi-cropping. All these actions will help in the short run. In the long-run, I am not sure where I am going; but I am sure that I do not wish it to be where your country is now.

Dogood: That I can sympathize with. I do not like my country's devel-   16
opment path either. And I worry that the people in power in your country wish to follow us blindly. At the very least, the Earth Summit will send the message that our path is unsustainable, and maybe your country will try it a different way. That is the message I hope to send to my government, aid agencies and, through the media, to our people.

Holistic: Please also send the message that the different way is to be   17
designed by us. It is not for you to tell us, on the basis of an analysis of what went wrong in your country, which new path we should forge. In the meantime, I should like to hear about how you address the problems in your country; some of the methods you discover may be appropriate. And I will be happy to let you know how we progress, so that you can try some of the ways we have found to be useful.

(A muffled beeping noise emerges from Dogood's jacket).   18

Dogood: Excuse me, that is my cellular phone. (Into the phone.) An in- 19
terview with the *Wall Street Journal?* Now? Yes, I'll be right there.

(To Holistic.) Excuse me, but this is a rare opportunity . . . 20
Holistic: Please go ahead. I must leave too. I must attend a meeting of 21
NGO to draft an alternative non-governmental Convention on Poverty Eradi-
cation (COPE). ©

CRITICAL READING

1. What does the very first exchange between person 1 and person 2—where Dogood exclaims about the beauty of the surroundings while Holistic mentions the
street children—tell you about each?
2. Discuss the specific ways in which Dogood views worldwide environmental
problems from her perspective as an American, not taking regional and cultural
differences into account. Holistic objects to this biased view; to what other
points or positions of Dogood does he object?
3. Clearly the writer agrees more with one side of the debate over the other. Identify elements in this piece that make Dubash's position clear. Do you think that
Dubash is too hard on the person he doesn't favor here?
4. If you've read the social ecology unit, discuss the points in this dialogue when
the revolution versus reform dichotomy is present.

CLASS DISCUSSION

1. In group format, discuss the various points Holistic makes to support his position
that environmental issues should be dealt with on a local, not a global, level.
2. Engage in a class discussion about ways in which Dubash gets his ideas across:
is his imagined dialogue format effective or not? How might a reader's reaction
to the ideas change if they were presented as an argumentative essay?

DIRECTED FREEWRITE

Write your own dialogue between two people on two opposite sides on some environmental issue that is different from the one represented by Dubash. For example,
you could imagine a corporate CEO who has been fined several times by the EPA
for pollution, engaged in a discussion with a radical environmental activist or with a
person who recycles her or his waste could discuss recycling with someone who
never bothers to recycle.

POLITICAL SCIENCE UNIT WRITING ASSIGNMENTS

1. Write an essay comparing and contrasting the ethical approach to solving environmental problems, such as that of Aldo Leopold in the Social Ecology unit, to
the kind of economic approach Cairncross advocates. Ultimately, use your discussion of similarities and differences to arrive at a conclusion about which

approach, or which elements of one of the approaches, would work best to remedy past environmental destruction and to minimize future degradation of the earth. Assignment 2 on page 165 in the Philosophy unit of Chapter 2 gives more details about the comparison and contrast mode of writing.

2. The World Trade Organization is a governing body charged with overseeing the facilitation and expansion of global trade by setting policies. You may recall that when the WTO met in Seattle, Washington, way back in November 1999, a record number of protesters, who were representing diverse interests such as human rights, workers' rights, and environmental protection, converged on Seattle, attempting to interfere with the WTO's meetings and to publicize the causes represented by the protesters. Since the WTO is an important element of today's economy and since its policies bear directly on environmental issues, conduct some library research into this organization and into the grounds on which it is criticized by environmentalists. Rely on newspaper accounts and on World Wide Web sources in order to provide a reader with an overview of the relationship between the WTO and environmental issues.

   Alternatively, you might use the same kinds of sources to write an essay examining the ways in which the scope of the WTO's policies provides a site for the often competing interests of environmentalists and trade unions representing the rights of workers to converge. You might bring in some of the points raised in Dubash's article and discuss how a coalition of workers' rights groups and environmentalists might work to solve particular problems concerning both groups.

3. Write a position paper advocating an approach to one particular environmental issue with both global and local implications, using a combination of Donna Dogood's and Jose Holistic's approaches. You will be arguing for a way in which international environmental policies could be formulated so that local control and decision making are preserved. Examples of particular environmental problems with issues at stake at both the global and local levels might be air pollution from factories manufacturing American products in a developing nation, or clear-cutting or burning the rain forests in South America to provide land for cattle to supply Americans with beef.

   The position paper is a genre of writing that is commonly used in political science. Position papers are typically written to influence policy makers to adopt particular solutions to specific problems. You might think of this kind of essay as a problem-solution piece, with the writer taking a position regarding a certain solution. There are three things that a writer typically needs to cover in a position paper: (1) define a specific problem that policies, laws, or particular organizations might address; (2) evaluate different methods for solving the problem; (3) out of those methods, recommend one, and describe how it would translate into a specific policy, followed by a description of how that policy would be implemented.

   That's the general overview of the components of a position paper, but this assignment asks you to complete a scaled-back version, since we are working with limited sources. You will be working with Dubash's piece, and using the points that the speakers make about the problem, you will use the solutions that are implied by the speakers as the different solutions to be evaluated and then will recommend an approach that combines ideas from the two speakers. You don't need to go so far as to describe how this approach would be implemented, however.

Alternatively, the assignment could be completed in a more detailed form if you conduct some library research on a specific environmental problem. For example, you might propose a solution to a particular problem of enforcing car emission standards or to a particular town's need to reduce the garbage that goes into a landfill.

THINKING AND WRITING IN THE HUMANITIES

Unit 1

Cultural Studies—It's Not Easy Being Green

AN EXPERIMENT IN ECOCRITICISM

William Rueckert

The following article by William Rueckert, an avowed ecocritic, describes the origins of green theory and proposes ecocriticism as a literary practice more grounded in a "principle of relevance" than are other fields of literary study, because it has as its aim the protection of the natural environment. As you read this article, consider the merits of Rueckert's arguments while noting the "organic" and nonacademic shape that the "essay" takes, the ways in which the form of this essay mirrors the things of nature that Rueckert hopes to protect.

William Rueckert has been an English professor, avowed ecocritic, and Burkean scholar. His last teaching position was at the State University of New York at Geneseo where he taught English and American literature and from which he retired in 1988. He is the author of a study of Glenway Wescott; three books on Kenneth Burke (Kenneth Burke and the Drama of Human Relations; Critical Responses to Kenneth Burke, 1924–1966, and Encounters with Kenneth Burke) *and he has written several essays on American criticism and culture.*

"It is the business of those who direct the activities that will shape tomorrow's world to think beyond today's well being and provide for tomorrow."

—Raymond Dasmann, *Planet in Peril*

"Any living thing that hopes to live on earth must fit into the ecosphere or perish."

—Barry Commoner, *The Closing Circle*

". . . the function of poetry . . . is to nourish the spirit of man by giving him the cosmos to suckle. We have only to lower our standard of dominating

---

Source: "Literature and Ecology: An Experiment in Ecocriticism" by William Rueckert in *Iowa Review,* 9.1 (Winter 1978). Reprinted by permission of the author.

nature and to raise our standard of participating in it in order to make the reconciliation take place. When man becomes proud to be not just the site where ideas and feelings are produced, but also the crossroad where they divide and mingle, he will be ready to be saved. Hope therefore lies in a poetry through which the world so invades the spirit of man that he becomes almost speechless, and later reinvents language."

—Francis Ponge, *The Voice of Things*

SHIFTING OUR LOCUS OF MOTIVATION

Where have we been in literary criticism in my time? Well, like Count 1 Mippipopolus in *The Sun Also Rises,* we seem to have been everywhere, seen and done everything. Here are just some of the positions and battles which many of us have been into and through: formalism, neoformalism, and contextualism; biographical, historical, and textual criticism; mythic, archetypal, and psychological criticism; structuralism and phenomenology; spatial, ontological, and—well, and so forth, and so forth. Individually and collectively, we have been through so many great and original minds, that one wonders what could possibly be left for experimental criticism to experiment with just now. . . .

Furthermore, there are so many resourceful and energetic minds 2 working out from even the merest suggestion of a new position, that the permutations of even the most complex new theory or methodology are exhausted very quickly these days. If you do not get in on the very beginning of a new theory, it is all over with before you can even think it through, apply it, write it up, and send it out for publication. The incredible storehouse of existing theories and methods, coupled with the rapid aging (almost pre-aging, it seems) of new critical theories and methods, has made for a somewhat curious critical environment. For those who are happy with it, a fabulously resourceful, seemingly limitless, pluralism is available: there is something for everybody and almost anything can be done with it. But for those whose need and bent is to go where others have not yet been, no matter how remote that territory may be, there are some problems: the compulsion toward newness acts like a forcing house to produce theories which are evermore elegant, more baroque, more scholastic, even, sometimes, somewhat hysterical . . .

I don't mean to ridicule this motive; in fact, I have recently defended 3 it rather energetically. I'm really reminding myself of how things can go in endeavors such as this one, so that I can, if possible, avoid the freakism and exploitation latent in the experimental motive. Pluralism, a necessary and valuable position, which is not really a position at all, has certain obvious limitations because one always tries to keep up with what's new but must still work always with what has already been done and is already known. So what is to be done if one wants to do something that is worth doing, that is significant; if one is suffering from the pricks of historical conscience and consciousness; wanting to be "original," to add something new, but wanting to avoid the straining and posturing that often goes with this motive, and above all, wanting to avoid the Detroit syndrome, in which the new model is confused with the better or the intrinsically valuable. Whatever experimental criticism is about, the senseless creation of new models just to displace or replace old ones, or to beat out a competitor in the intellectual marketplace should not be the result. To confuse the life of the mind with the insane economy of the American automobile industry would be the worst thing we could do.

The more I have thought about the problem, the more it has seemed to me that for those of us who still wish to move forward out of critical pluralism, there must be a shift in our locus of motivation from newness, or theoretical elegance, or even coherence, to a principle of relevance. I am aware that there are certain obvious hazards inherent in any attempt to generate a critical position out of a concept of relevance, but that is what experiments are for. The most obvious and disastrous hazard is that of rigid doctrinal relevance—the old party-line syndrome. I have tried to avoid that. Specifically, I am going to experiment with the application of ecology and ecological concepts to the study of literature, because ecology (as a science, as a discipline, as the basis for a human vision) has the greatest relevance to the present and future of the world we all live in of anything that I have studied in recent years. Experimenting a bit with the title of this paper, I could say that I am going to try to discover something about the ecology of literature, or try to develop an ecological poetics by applying ecological concepts to the reading, teaching, and writing about literature. To borrow a splendid phrase from Kenneth Burke, one of our great experimental critics, I am going to experiment with the conceptual and practical possibilities of an apparent perspective by incongruity. Forward then. Perhaps that old pair of antagonists, science and poetry, can be persuaded to lie down together and be generative after all. 4

LITERATURE AND THE BIOSPHERE

What follows can be understood as a contribution to human ecology, specifically, literary ecology, though I use (and transform) a considerable number of concepts from pure, biological ecology. 5

The problem now, as most ecologists agree, is to find ways of keeping the human community from destroying the natural community, and with it the human community. This is what ecologists like to call the self-destructive or suicidal motive that is inherent in our prevailing and paradoxical attitude toward nature. The conceptual and practical problem is to find the grounds upon which the two communities—the human, the natural—can coexist, cooperate, and flourish in the biosphere. All of the most serious and thoughtful ecologists (such as Aldo Leopold, Ian McHarg, Barry Commoner, and 6

Garret Hardin) have tried to develop ecological visions which can be translated into social, economic, political, and individual programs of action. Ecology has been called, accurately, a subversive science because all these ecological visions are radical ones and attempt to subvert the continued-growth economy which dominates all emerging and most developed industrial states. A steady or sustainable state economy, with an entirely new concept of growth, is central to all ecological visions. All this may seem rather remote from creating, reading, teaching, and writing about literature; but in fact, it is not. I invoke here (to be spelled out in detail later) the first Law of Ecology: "Everything is connected to everything else." This is Commoner's phrasing, but the law is common to all ecologists and all ecological visions. This need to see even the smallest, most remote part in relation to a very large whole is the central intellectual action required by ecology and of an ecological vision. It is not mind-bending or mind-blowing or mind-boggling; it is mind-expanding. As absurd as this may sound, the paper is about literature and the biosphere. This is no more absurd, of course, than the idea that man does not have the right to do anything he wants with nature. The idea that nature should also be protected by human laws, that trees (dolphins and whales, hawks and whooping cranes) should have lawyers to articulate and defend their rights is one of the most marvelous and characteristic parts of the ecological vision.

ENERGY PATHWAYS WHICH SUSTAIN LIFE

I'm going to begin with some ecological concepts taken from a great   7
variety of sources more or less randomly arranged and somewhat poetically
commented upon.

A poem is stored energy, a formal turbulence, a living thing, a swirl in   8
the flow.

Poems are part of the energy pathways which sustain life.   9

Poems are a verbal equivalent of fossil fuel (stored energy), but they   10
are a renewable source of energy, coming, as they do, from those ever generative twin matrices, language and imagination.

Some poems—say *King Lear, Moby Dick, Song of Myself*—seem to   11
be, in themselves, ever-living, inexhaustible sources of stored energy,
whose relevance does not derive solely from their meaning, but from their
capacity to remain active in any language and to go on with the work of energy transfer, to continue to function as an energy pathway that sustains life
and the human community. Unlike fossil fuels, they cannot be used up. The
more one thinks about this, the more one realizes that here one encounters
a great mystery; here is a radical differential between the ways in which the
human world and the natural world sustain life and communities.

Reading, teaching, and critical discourse all release the energy and   12
power stored in poetry so that it may flow through the human community; all
energy in nature comes, ultimately, from the sun, and life in the biosphere

depends upon a continuous flow of sunlight. In nature, this solar "energy is used once by a given organism or population; some of it is stored and the rest is converted into heat, and is soon lost" from a given ecosystem. The "one-way flow of energy" is a universal phenomenon of nature, where, according to the laws of thermodynamics, energy is never created or destroyed: it is only transformed, degraded, or dispersed, flowing always from a concentrated form into a dispersed (entropic) form. One of the basic formulations of ecology is that there is a one-way flow of energy through a system but that materials circulate or are recycled and can be used over and over. Now, without oversimplifying these enormously complex matters, it would seem that once one moves out of the purely biological community and into the human community, where language and symbol-systems are present, things are not quite the same with regard to energy. The matter is so complex one hesitates to take it on, but one must begin, even hypothetically, somewhere, and try to avoid victimage or neutralization by simple-minded analogical thinking. In literature, all energy comes from the creative imagination. It does not come from language, because language is only one (among many) vehicles for the storing of creative energy. A painting and a symphony are also stored energy. And clearly, this stored energy is not just used once, converted, and lost from the human community. It is perhaps true that the life of the human community depends upon the continuous flow of creative energy (in all its forms) from the creative imagination and intelligence, and that this flow could be considered the sun upon which life in the human community depends; but it is not true that energy stored in a poem—*Song of Myself*—is used once, converted, and then lost from the ecosystem. It is used over and over again as a renewable resource by the same individual. Unlike nature, which has a single ultimate source of energy, the human community would seem to have many suns, resources, renewable and otherwise, to out-sun the sun itself. Literature in general and individual works in particular are one among many human suns. We need to discover ways of using this renewable energy-source to keep that other ultimate energy-source (upon which all life in the natural biosphere, and human communities, including human life, depends) flowing into the biosphere. We need to make some connections between literature and the sun, between teaching literature and the health of the biosphere.

Energy flows from the poet's language centers and creative imagina- 13 tion into the poem and thence, from the poem (which converts and stores this energy) into the reader. Reading is clearly an energy transfer as the energy stored in the poem is released and flows back into the language centers and creative imaginations of the readers. Various human hungers, including word hunger, are satisfied by this energy flow along this particular energy pathway. The concept of a poem as stored energy (as active, alive, and generative, rather than as inert, as a kind of corpse upon which one performs an autopsy, or as an art object one takes possession of, or as an antagonist—a knot of meanings—one must overcome) frees one from a variety of critical tyrannies, most notably, perhaps, that of pure hermeneutics, the transformation of this stored creative energy directly into a set of coherent meanings. What a poem is saying is probably always less important than what it is doing and how—in the deep sense—it coheres. Properly understood, poems can be studied as models for energy flow, community building, and ecosystems. The first Law of Ecology—that everything is connected to everything else—applies to poems as well as to nature. The concept of the interactive field was operative in nature, ecology, and poetry long before it ever appeared in criticism.

Reading, teaching, and critical discourse are enactments of the poem 14
which release the stored energy so that it can flow into the reader—sometimes with such intensity that one is conscious of an actual inflow; or, if it is in the classroom, one becomes conscious of the extent to which this one source of stored energy is flowing around through a community, and of how "feedback," negative or positive, is working.

Kenneth Burke was right—as usual—to argue that drama should be 15
our model or paradigm for literature because a drama, enacted upon the stage, before a live audience, releases its energy into the human community assembled in the theater and raises all the energy levels. Burke did not want us to treat novels and poems as plays; he wanted us to become aware of what they were doing as creative verbal actions in the human community. He was one of our first critical ecologists.

Coming together in the classroom, in the lecture hall, in the seminar 16
room (anywhere, really) to discuss or read or study literature, is to gather energy centers around a matrix of stored poetic/verbal energy. In some ways, this is the true interactive field because the energy flow is not just a two-way flow from poem to person as it would be in reading; the flow is along many energy pathways from poem to person, from person to person. The process is triangulated, quadrangulated, multiangulated; and there is, ideally, a raising of the energy levels which makes it possible for the highest motives of literature to accomplish themselves. These motives are not pleasure and truth, but creativity and community.

POEMS AS GREEN PLANTS

Ian McHarg—one of the most profound thinkers I have read who has 17
tried to design a new model of reality based upon ecology—says that "perhaps the greatest conceptual contribution of the ecological view is the perception of the world and evolution as a creative process." He defines creation as the raising of matter from lower to higher order. In nature, he says, this occurs when some of the sun's energy is entrapped on its path to entropy. This process of entrapment and creation, he calls—somewhat cacophonously—negentropy, since it negates the negative process of entropy

and allows energy to be saved from random dispersal and put to creative ends. Green plants, for example, are among the most creative organisms on earth. They are nature's poets. There is no end to the ways in which this concept can be applied to the human community, but let me stay close to the topic at hand. Poems are green plants among us; if poets are suns, then poems are green plants among us for they clearly arrest energy on its path to entropy and in so doing, not only raise matter from lower to higher order, but help to create a self-perpetuating and evolving system. That is, they help to create creativity and community, and when their energy is released and flows out into others, to again raise matter from lower to higher order (to use one of the most common descriptions of what culture is). One of the reasons why teaching and the classroom are so important (for literature, anyway) is that they intensify and continue this process by providing the environment in which the stored energy of poetry can be released to carry on its work of creation and community. The greatest teachers (the best ecologists of the classroom) are those who can generate and release the greatest amount of collective creative energy; they are the ones who understand that the classroom is a community, a true interactive field. Though few of us—maybe none of us—understand precisely how this idea can be used to the ends of biospheric health, its exploration would be one of the central problems which an ecological poetics would have to address.

THE REMORSELESS INEVITABLENESS OF THINGS

As a classic textbook by E. Odum on the subject tells us, ecology is always concerned with "levels beyond that of the individual organism. It is concerned with populations, communities, ecosystems, and the biosphere." By its very nature it is concerned with complex interactions and with the largest sets of interrelationships. We must remember Commoner's first Law of Ecology: "Everything is connected to everything else." The biosphere (or ecosphere) is the home that life has built for itself on the planet's outer surface. In that ecosphere there is a reciprocal interdependence of one life process upon another, and there is a mutual interconnected development of all of the earth's life systems. If we continue to teach, write, and write about poetry without acknowledging and trying to act upon the fact that—to cite a single example—all the oceans of our home are slowly being contaminated by all the pollutants disposed of in modern communities—even what we try to send up in smoke—then we will soon lose the environment in which we write and teach. All the creative processes of the biosphere, including the human ones, may well come to an end if we cannot find a way to determine the limits of human destruction and intrusion which the biosphere can tolerate, and learn how to creatively manage the biosphere. McHarg and others say that this is our unique creative role, but that as yet we have neither the vision nor the knowledge to carry it out, and that we do not have much more time to acquire both. This somewhat hysterical proposition is why I tried to write this paper and why, true to the experimental motive intrinsic to me as a human being, I have taken on the question of how reading, teaching, and writing about literature might function creatively in the biosphere, to the ends of biospheric purgation, redemption from human intrusions, and health.

As a reader and teacher and critic of literature, I have asked the largest, most important and relevant question about literature that I know how to ask . . . It is interesting, to me anyway, that eight years ago, trying to define my position, I was asking questions about the visionary fifth dimension and about how man is *released from the necessities of nature into this realm of pure being by means of literature.* Four years ago, attempting to do the same thing, I was writing about history as a symbol and about being boxed in the void, convinced that there were no viable concepts of or possibilities for the future, and about literary criticism as a necessary, endlessly dialectical process which helps to keep culture healthy and viable throughout history. Nothing about nature and the biosphere in all this. Now, . . . here I am back on earth (from my heady space trips, from the rigors and pleasures of dialectic, from the histrionic metaphor of being boxed in the void) trying to learn something about what the ecologists variously call the laws of nature, the "body of inescapable natural laws," the "impotence principles" which are beyond our ability to alter or escape, the remorseless inevitableness of things, the laws of nature which are "decrees of fate." I have been trying to learn something by contemplating (from my vantage point in literature) one of ecology's basic maxims: "We are not free to violate the laws of nature." The view we get of humans in the biosphere from the ecologists these days is a tragic one, as pure and classic as the Greek or Shakespearean views: in partial knowledge or often in total ignorance (the basic postulate of ecology and tragedy is that humans precipitate tragic consequences by acting either in ignorance of or without properly understanding the true consequences of their actions), we are violating the laws of nature, and the retribution from the biosphere will be more terrible than any inflicted on humans by the gods. In ecology, man's tragic flaw is his anthropocentric (as opposed to biocentric) vision, and his compulsion to conquer, humanize, domesticate, violate, and exploit every natural thing. The ecological nightmare (as one gets it in Brunner's *The Sheep Look Up*) is of a monstrously overpopulated, almost completely polluted, all but totally humanized planet. These nightmares are all if/then projections: *if* everything continues as is, *then* this will happen. A common form of this nightmare is Garrett Hardin's ironic population projection: if we continue our present 2% growth rate indefinitely, then in only 615 years there will be standing room only on all the land areas of the world. 19

To simply absorb this tragic ecological view of our present and possible futures (if nothing occurs to alter our anthropocentric vision) into the doomsday syndrome is a comforting but specious intellectual, critical, and historical 20

response: it dissipates action into the platitudes of purely archetypal and intellectual connections. Better to bring Shakespearean and Greek tragedy to bear
upon our own biosphere's tragedy as a program for action than this—any day.
I will not attempt to deal here with the responses to the tragic/doomsday ecological view generated by a commitment to the economic growth spiral or the
national interest. Others have done it better than I ever could. Let me say here
that the evidence is so overwhelming and terrifying that I can no longer even
imagine (using any vision) the possibility of ignoring Ian McHarg's mandate in
his sobering and brilliant book, *Design With Nature:*

> Each individual has a responsibility for the entire biosphere
> and is required to engage in creative and cooperative activi-
> ties.

As readers, teachers, and critics of literature, we are used to asking ourselves questions—often very complex and sophisticated ones—about the
nature of literature, critical discourse, language, curriculum, liberal arts, literature and society, literature and history; but McHarg has proposed new concepts of creativity and community so radical that it is even hard to
comprehend them. As readers, teachers and critics of literature, how do we
become responsible planet stewards? How do we ask questions about literature and the biosphere? What do we even ask? These are overwhelming
questions. They fill one with a sense of futility and absurdity and provoke
one's self-irony at the first faint soundings of the still largely ignorant,
preaching, pontificating voice. How does one engage in responsible creative
and cooperative biospheric action as a reader, teacher (especially this), and
critic of literature? I think that we have to begin answering this question and
that we should do what we have always done: turn to the poets. And then to
the ecologists. We must formulate an ecological poetics. We must promote
an ecological vision. At best, I can only begin here. Following McHarg and
rephrasing a fine old adage, we can say that "where there is no ecological
vision, the people will perish." And this ecological vision must penetrate the
economic, political, social, and technological visions of our time, and radical-
ize them. The problem is not national, but global, planetary. It will not stop
here. As Arthur Boughey points out, "There is no population, community, or
ecosystem left on earth completely independent of the effects of human cultural behavior. Now [this human] influence has begun to spread beyond the
globe to the rest of our planetary system and even to the universe itself."

THE CENTRAL PARADOX: POWERLESS VISIONS

One has to begin somewhere. Since literature is our business, let us   21
begin with the poets or creators in this field and see if we can move toward
a generative poetics by connecting poetry to ecology. As should be clear by
now, I am not just interested in transferring ecological concepts to the study

of literature, but in attempting to see literature inside the context of an eco-logical vision in ways which restrict neither and do not lead merely to prose-lytizing based upon a few simple generalizations and perceptions which have been common to American literature (at least) since Cooper, and are central to the whole transcendental vision as one gets it in Emerson, Thoreau, Whitman, and Melville. As Barry Commoner points out, "The com-plex web in which all life is enmeshed, and man's place in it, are clearly—and beautifully—described in the poems of Walt Whitman," in Melville's *Moby Dick* and everywhere in Emerson and Thoreau. "Unfortunately," he says, with a kind of unintentional, but terrible understatement for literary people, "this literary heritage has not been enough to save us from ecologi-cal disaster." And here we are back again, before we even start, to the para-doxes which confront us as readers, teachers, and critics of literature—and perhaps as just plain citizens: the separation of vision and action; the futility of vision and knowledge without power.

THE HARSHEST, CRUELEST REALITIES OF OUR PROFESSION

Bringing literature and ecology together is a lesson in the harshest, cruelest realities which permeate our profession: we live by the word, and by the power of the word, but are increasingly powerless to act upon the word. Real power in our time is political, economic, and technological; real knowledge is increasingly scientific. Are we not here at the center of it all? We can race our verbal motors, spin our dialectical wheels, build more and more sophisticated systems, recycle dazzling ideas through the elite of the profession. We can keep going by charging ourselves back up in the class-room. In the end, we wonder what it all comes down to. Reading Com-moner's (or almost any other serious ecologists's) statements, knowing they come from a formidable scientific knowledge, from direct involvement with the problems and issue from a deeply committed human being, can we help but wonder what we are doing teaching students to love poetry, to take liter-ature seriously, to write good papers about literature:

> Because the global ecosystem is a connected whole, in which nothing can be gained or lost and which is not sub-ject to overall improvement, anything extracted from it by human effort must be replaced. Payment of this price can-not be avoided; it can only be delayed. The present envi-ronmental crisis is a warning that we have delayed nearly too long.
>
> . . . we are in an environmental crisis because the means by which we use the ecosphere to produce wealth are destructive of the ecosystem itself. The present system of production is self-destructive. The present course of human civilization is suicidal. In our unwitting march toward

ecological suicide we have run out of options. Human beings have broken out of the circle of life, driven not by biological need, but by social organization which they have
devised to conquer nature . . .

All my literary training tells me that this is not merely rhetoric, and that no
amount of rhetoric or manipulation of the language to political, economic,
technological, or other ends will make it go away. It is a substantive,
biosphere-wide reality we must confront and attempt to do something about.

THE GENEROSITY OF THE POETS

I will use what I know best and begin with the poets. If we begin with   23
the poets (who have never had any doubts about the seriousness and relevance of what they are doing), they teach us that literature is an enormous,
ever increasing, wonderfully diverse storehouse of creative and cooperative
energy which can never be used up. It is like the gene-pool, like the best
ecosystems. Literature is a true cornucopia, thanks to the continuous generosity of the poets, who generate this energy out of themselves, requiring,
and usually receiving, very little in return over and above the feedback from
the creative act itself.

This is probably nowhere more evident than in a book such as Gary   24
Snyder's *Turtle Island;* or, to take quite a different kind of text, in Adrienne
Rich's *Diving into the Wreck.* What the poets do is "Hold it close" and then
"give it all away." What Snyder holds close and gives away in *Turtle Island* is
a complete ecological vision which has worked down into every detail of his
personal life and is the result of many years of intellectual and personal
wandering. Every poem is an action which comes from a finely developed
and refined ecological conscience and consciousness. The book enacts a
whole program of ecological action; it is offered (like *Walden*) as a guide
book. It has in it one of the most useful and complete concepts of renewable, creative human energy which can be put to creative and cooperative
biospheric ends that I know of. Its relevance for this paper is probably so obvious that I should not pursue it any longer.

The Generosity of Adrienne Rich's *Diving Into the Wreck*

Things are very different in this book of poems, and not immediately   25
applicable to the topic of this paper. But this book is the epitome—for me—
of the ways in which poets are generous with themselves and can be used
as models for creative, cooperative action. Without exception, the poems in
this book are about the ecology of the female self, and they impinge upon
the concerns of this paper in their treatment of men as destroyers (here of
women rather than of the biosphere, but for remarkably similar reasons). As
Margaret Atwood's profound ecological novel, *Surfacing,* makes clear, there

is a demonstrable relationship between the ways in which men treat and destroy women and the ways in which men treat and destroy nature. Many of
the poems—and in particular a poem such as "The Phenomenology of
Anger"—are about how one woman changed and brought this destruction
and suppression to an end, and about what changes must occur to bring the
whole process to an end. A mind familiar with ecology cannot avoid the
many profound and disturbing connections to be made here between
women and western history, nature and western history.

The Deconstructive Wisdom of W. S. Merwin's *Lice*

One of the most continuously shattering experiences of my intellectual 26
life has been the reading, teaching, and thenceforth re-reading and re-
teaching of this book of poems. This is one of the most profound books of
poems written in our time and one of the great ecological texts of any time.
Whatever has been argued from factual, scientific, historical, and intellectual
evidence in the ecology books that I read is confirmed (and more) by the
imaginative evidence of this book of poems. Merwin's generosity consists in
the extraordinary efforts he made to deconstruct the cumulative wisdom of
western culture and then imaginatively project himself into an almost un-
bearable future. Again, as with Adrienne Rich, these poems are about the
deep inner changes which must occur if we are to keep from destroying the
world and survive as human beings. I know of no other book of poems so
aware of the biosphere and what humans have done to destroy it as this
one. Reading this book of poems requires one to unmake and remake one's
mind. It is the most painfully constructive book of poems I think I have ever
read. What these poems affirm over and over is that if a new ecological vision is to emerge, the old destructive western one must be deconstructed
and abandoned. This is exactly what Rich's poems say about men and
women.

The Energy of Love in Walt Whitman's *Song of Myself*

This energy flows out of Whitman into the world (all the things of the 27
world) and back into Whitman from the things of the world in one of the most
marvelous ontological interchanges one can find anywhere in poetry. This
ontological interchange between Whitman and the biosphere is the energy
pathway that sustains life in Whitman and, so far as he is concerned, in the
biosphere. There is a complete ecological vision in this poem, just as there
is in Whitman's conception of a poetry cycle which resembles the water
cycle within the biosphere. Whitman says that poems come out of the poets,
go up into the atmosphere to create a kind of poetic atmosphere, come
down upon us in the from of poetic rain, nourish us and make us creative
and then are recycled. Without this poetic atmosphere and cultural cycle, he
says, we would die as human beings. A lovely concept, and true for some of

us, but it has not yet resolved the disjunction (as Commoner points out) between vision and action, knowledge and power.

The Biocentric Vision of Faulkner's *Absalom, Absalom!*

Can we not study this great fiction, and its central character, Thomas 28 Sutpen, in relation to one of the most fundamental of all ecological principles: "That nature is an interacting process, a seamless web, that it [nature] is responsive to laws, that it constitutes a value system with intrinsic opportunities and constraints upon human use." There is an ecological lesson for all of us in the ferocious destructiveness of human and natural things brought about by Thomas Sutpen.

Looking upon the World, Listening and Learning with Henry David Thoreau

Does he not tell us that this planet, and the creatures who inhabit it, in- 29 cluding men and women, were, have been, are now, and are in the process of becoming? A beautiful and true concept of the biosphere. His model of reality was so new, so radical even in the mid-nineteenth century, that we have still not been able to absorb and act upon it more than a hundred years later.

Entropy and Negentropy in Theodore Roethke's "Greenhouse," "Lost Son," and "North American Sequence"

Was there ever a greater ecological, evolutionary poet of the self than 30 Roethke, one who really believed that ontology recapitulates phylogeny, one so close to his evolutionary predecessors that he experiences an interchange of being with them and never demeans them with personification and seldom with metaphor. Kenneth Burke's brilliant phrase—vegetal radicalism—still takes us to the ecological centers of Roethke, self-absorbed, self-obsessed as he was.

But enough of this. The poets have always been generous. I mean 31 only to suggest a few ecological readings of texts I know well. Teaching and criticism are the central issues here, so let me move on toward some conclusions.

TEACHING AND CRITICAL DISCOURSE AS FORMS OF SYMBIOSIS

"Creativeness is a universal prerequisite which man shares with all 32 creatures." The central, modern idea of the poet, of literature, and of literary criticism is based upon the postulate that humans are capable of genuine creation and that literature is one of the enactments of this creative principle. Taking literature to ecology by way of McHarg's statement joins two principles of creativity so that humans are acting in concert with the rest of the biosphere, but not necessarily to the ends of biospheric health. That has always been the problem. Some of our most amazing creative achievements—say in chemistry and physics—have been our most destructive. Culture—one of our great achievements wherever we have gone—has often fed like a great predator and parasite upon nature and never entered into a reciprocating energy-transfer, into a recycling relationship with the biosphere. In fact, one of the most common antinomies in the human mind is between culture/civilization and nature/wilderness. As Kenneth Burke pointed out some time ago, man's tendency is to become rotten with perfection. As Burke ironically formulated it, man's entelechy is technology. Perceiving and teaching (even writing about) human creativity in this larger ecological context could be done in all literature courses and especially in all creative writing courses. It could only have a salutary effect. It would make the poet and the green plants brothers and sisters; it would charge creative writing and literature with ecological purpose.

Symbiosis, according to McHarg, is the "cooperative arrangement that 33 permits increase in the levels of order"; it is this cooperative arrangement that permits the use of energy in raising the levels of matter. McHarg says that symbiosis makes negentropy possible; he identifies negentropy as the creative principle and process at work in the biosphere which keeps everything moving in the evolutionary direction which has characterized the development of all life in the biosphere. Where humans are involved and where literature provides the energy source within the symbiotic arrangement, McHarg says that a very complex process occurs in which energy is transmuted into information and thence into meaning by means of a process he calls apperception. As McHarg demonstrated in his book, both the process of apperception and the meaning which results from it can be used to creative, cooperative ends in our management of the biosphere. The central endeavor, then, of any ecological poetics would have to be a working model for the processes of transformation which occur as one moves from the stored creative energy of the poem, to its release by reading, teaching, or writing, to its transmutation into meaning, and finally to its application, in an ecological value system, to what McHarg variously calls "fitness and fitting," and to "health"—which he defines as "creative fitting" and by which he means to suggest our creation of a fit environment. This work could transform culture and help bring our destruction of the biosphere to an end.

Now there is no question that literature can do all this, but there are a 34 lot of questions as to whether it does in fact do it, how, and how effectively. All these concerns might well be central for teachers and critics of literature these days. We tend to over-refine our conceptual frameworks so that they can only be used by a corps of elitist experts and gradually lose their practical *relevance* as they increase their theoretical *elegance*. I am reminded here of the stridently practical questions Burke asked all through the thirties and early forties and of the scorn with which they were so often greeted by literary critics and historians of his time. But none of these questions is anti-thetical to literature and there is a certain splendid resonance which comes from thinking of poets and green plants being engaged in the same creative, life-sustaining activities, and of teachers and literary critics as creative medi-ators between literature and the biosphere whose tasks include the encour-agement of, the discovery, training, and development of creative biospheric apperceptions, attitudes, and actions. To charge the classroom with ecologi-cal purpose one has only to begin to think of it in symbiotic terms as a coop-erative arrangement which makes it possible to release the stream of energy which flows out of the poet and into the poem, out of the poem and into the readers, out of the readers and into the classroom, and then back into the readers and out of the classroom with them, and finally back into the other larger community in a never ending circuit of life.

BUT . . .

I stop here, short of action, halfway between literature and ecology, the   35
energy pathways obscured, the circuits of life broken between words and actions, vision and action, the verbal domain and the non-verbal domain, between literature and the biosphere—because I can't go any further. The desire to join literature to ecology originates out of and is sustained by a Merwin-like condition and question: how can we apply the energy, the cre-ativity, the knowledge, the vision we know to be in literature to the human-made problems ecology tells us are destroying the biosphere which is our home? How can we translate literature into purgative-redemptive biospheric action; how can we resolve the fundamental paradox of this profession and get out of our heads? How can we turn words into something other than more words (poems, rhetoric, lectures, talks, position papers—the very sub-stance of an MLA meeting: millions and millions of words; endlessly recircu-lating among those of us in the profession); how can we do something more than recycle WORDS?

Let experimental criticism address itself to this dilemma.   36

How can we move from the community of literature to the larger bios-   37
pheric community which ecology tells us (correctly, I think) we belong to even as we are destroying it?

. . . *Free us from false figures of speech.*   © 38

CRITICAL READING

1. After describing the origins of ecocriticism, Rueckert says that "there must be a shift in our locus of motivation from newness . . . to a principle of relevance." Against the backdrop of what other kinds of criticism is the author proposing this new field of literary study? Why is ecocriticism more grounded in the "principle of relevance" than are other theoretical approaches, in Rueckert's view?

2. Why has ecology been called a "subversive science," according to the author? What arguments does the author use to defend ecology as "marvelous" and worthy of defense by articulate lawyers and others?
3. What does the term "symbiosis" mean in the natural world? How does this term apply to literary criticism, in the author's view?

CLASS DISCUSSION

1. Proposing to unite science and poetry under the umbrella of green theory, Rueckert says, "I am going to experiment with the conceptual and practical possibilities of an apparent perspective by incongruity." In what ways have science and the arts traditionally been considered to be incompatible? Consider areas other than ecocriticism in which science and the arts have recently come together.
2. Why are poems worthy of study from an ecological perspective, according to the author? In what ways do poems resemble green plants? As a class, discuss the relative merits of Rueckert's "subversive" points, such as his statement, "Poems are a verbal equivalent of fossil fuel."

DIRECTED FREEWRITE

In a freewrite, describe the form of this "essay." In what ways does Rueckert's piece resemble that of traditional academic writing? In what ways is it different? How do the differences between this article and traditional pieces of academic writing underline Rueckert's points about the relationship between literature and the natural world?

CORNYPHONES AND CARDBOARD FLAMINGOS: A GREEN CONSUMER READS HIS BREAKFAST

Michael Petracca

According to proactive members of the ecological movement, the forces behind America's capitalist machine—specifically manufacturers, advertisers, and media giants—have a responsibility to portray environments as complex arrangements of interrelated parts in a constant state of change. One of the criticisms that ecocritics often level at advertisers, for instance, is the way that they "construct" the general public's perception of the natural world as nothing more than a resource to be used up, commodified, and subjected to humans' whims and drives. In this essay, the author levels a similar kind of criticism at the makers of prepackaged cereal, such as Kix. Cereal cartons—and the "literature" printed on them, Petracca notes, are being used in an apparent attempt to increase environmental awareness, but they make unfortunate generalizations that actually end up subverting this "ecoconscious" intent. As you read, note the author's tone, which swings from serious to humorous and almost parodic; what is his intention in using this treatment? Note also that he ends the piece with a footnote in which he confesses, "In order to stave off charges of academic impropriety, I must confess that this is a bogus citation. . . ." Whereas you, as a college student would undoubtedly get thrown out of school for making up sources for a research paper, this author—who's earned his reputation as a fiction writer as well as a cultural critic—gets away with it, because it serves a rhetorical purpose in this subversive essay. Consider, therefore, your reaction to this creative "cheating" that flaunts academic convention. Is it fair that he can do so, whereas you can't?

Michael Petracca was conceived in Brooklyn and born in Los Angeles. After moving to Santa Barbara in pursuit of advanced degrees, Petracca became a full-time lecturer in the Writing Program at the University of California, Santa Barbara, where he has taught for the past seventeen years. Petracca teaches fiction and writing workshops at Antioch University and the UCLA Writers' Program as well. As a youngster, Michael enjoyed watching sudsy clothes tumble in the laundry room. This unnatural behavior evolved into a passion for surfing during his high school and college years. In addition to teaching and surfing, Petracca also dedicates himself to writing. His publications include novels, such as Doctor Syntax *and* Cap-

Source: "Cornyphones and Cardboard Flamingoes: A Green Consumer Reads His Breakfast," by Michael Petracca in *Journal of American Culture,* vol. 19, no. 2 (Summer 1996). Reprinted by permission of the publisher.

tain Zzyzx, *college-level writing texts, short stories, and articles on interpreting the products of popular culture.*

Recent figures released by the Cereal Action Council of America   1
suggest that on any morning, approximately sixty million Americans are "enjoying a lovely bowl of cereal." The rich diversity of breakfast products—hyper-sweetened Count Chocula, staid and venerable Shredded Wheat, along with the trusty, regularity-inducing All-Bran—signifies the multicultural stewpot that is America. Despite the variety of breakfast products available at the market, however, there is one element almost all of them have in common: cartons featuring words and attendant illustration. Unlike that of other processed foods, cereal's packaging doubles as a source of entertainment. We don't read a burrito's wrapper after taking it out of the microwave, for instance, nor do we spend more than several seconds assimilating the valuable lessons on a box of Saltines. Cold cereal differs from other products in that it's the one packaged foodstuff we bring to the table, where we place the box before us and gaze at it with a sometimes trancelike fixity, thereby rendering ourselves captive audiences to messages that may be insidious in their rhetorical effect. This essay will focus on one "traditional" corn cereal product from a green perspective, to discover ways in which cereal literature—whether intentionally or not—is put as a cultural text of considerable authority, one whose pervasive presence at the table may contribute to people's view of themselves as superior to the land and therefore free to plunder it immoderately.

While growing up I never thought about rhetoric, and I certainly didn't   2
consider cereal insidious. I liked cereal. It tasted good and gave me energy to walk the several blocks to Brockton Avenue school, where I would collapse in a species of hypoglycemic coma until the mid-morning sweet roll revived me. Furthermore, besides the dubious nutrition afforded by their contents, cereal boxes provided me with reasons for living, dangling before me a panoply of indispensable playthings unavailable at local retail outlets. For countless boom-babies, Battle Creek, Michigan was the Holy Land, promising exotic playthings aplenty for a quarter and a proof-of-purchase. I rushed daily to the mailbox until that cardboard-encased novelty arrived: a frogman who alternately floated and submerged by some arcane interaction between bathwater and baking soda; a genuine Kellogg's Corn Flake Cornyphone that turned out to be an out-of-tune harmonica in yellow polythene molded to resemble an ear of corn. Despite the shameful cheapness of these wares, I was never disappointed and continued to read cereal boxes avidly, scouring them for the next geegaw on which I might squander my allowance. Nowadays, although I can get excited by Rice Krispies' offer of an "Exciting, Full-Color Poster Featuring World Series Tickets Throughout History," I must also take a more dispassionate view of things pop, in order

to consider the rhetorical purpose and potential psychological effects in messages disseminated by the purveyors of mass consumables. To be honest, I never considered cereal literature a worthy subject of study—my area of academic expertise being the hydrological seduction and betrayal encoded in water theme-parks—not, that is, until I faced my Kix the other day and found myself captivated, then horrified by the box's superficially innocent text.

In most ways, this Kix box looks like every other thirteen-ounce Kix box that's ever been produced. The familiar canteloupe-orange background features the prominent **K₋ᵢX** logo in blue, its oversized lower-case "i" dropped in jaunty subscript between two capital letters, thereby adding a touch of childlike wackiness to the presentation's overall spirit. As a concession to modern parents' health concerns, a band of red across the middle of the front panel bugles the promise, "Low in Sugar! Kids Love it!" and a blue box in the bottom right-hand corner contains a rider: "No added colors/No added flavors/No preservatives." Finally, the front of the box features a glass bowl brimming with larger-than-life Kix, several plump red strawberries, and frothy milk . . . as unsubtle a signifier of bourgeois plenitude as ever existed outside the Playboy mansion.

While the front of the box is a slightly updated version of a well-established graphic, the rear is novel and eccentric. Across the top of the rear panel there are two horizontal red stripes, between which a blue banner head proclaims, "America's Regions!" along with a smaller, all-cap subhead, also in light blue: "EXPLORE THIS GREAT LAND OF OURS!" In the middle of the panel sits a crudely outlined map of a United States notably disconnected from the rest of the North American continent. Mexico and Canada have drifted away, as have the oceans, leaving the U.S. to float insularly in a clear ether of negative space. The map is divided into eleven color-regions—Pacific Coast, Mountain, Heartland, Southwest, Great Lakes, Southeast, Appalachian Highlands, Mid-Atlantic, New England, Alaska and Hawaii—and each region has four or five of its most significant characteristics listed. For instance, the Pacific Coast region—the one in which I live—is credited with featuring:

- REDWOOD TREES
- GRAPES • SALMON
- HYDROELECTRICITY

Nowhere on the panel do the words "Kix" or "cereal" appear, although the Heartland region (color-coded a tired sienna-brown, perhaps to emblematize the depleted soil of the plains) is given credit for producing corn—Kix's main ingredient—along with farming, oats, wheat, and walleyed pike. Accompanying each list of regional characteristics is a grouping of small icons painted in a jejune style of water-coloring, each icon corresponding to one of the characteristics listed for a particular region. For instance, the icon-grouping for the Pacific Coast depicts an impressionistic waterscape with two spiky redwoods incongruously growing out of it, a massive concrete dam in its spillover phase, and a jumping or flying salmon trying futilely to devour a clump of wine-grapes that's nearly as large as the redwood trees. Each region features a similar grouping of icons, each more surreal than the next. The Southeast, to select another example, has a pink flamingo towering over a pine tree that seems to be growing out of a peanut. Thus the peruser of this text, on arising in the morning, finds herself confronted with a rendering of nature that is at best whimsical, at worst nightmarish and disorienting, depending on how much sleep that reader has gotten the night before. In any case, the individual reader's experience of nature is mediated by these unnatural and consumption-skewed texts, and the reader's view of the environment must be reconstructed to some degree by each instance of such contact.

In their defense, the anonymous artists and designers who conceived   5 and executed this pop artifact probably didn't intend for it to be a piece of accurate geography. More likely, General Mills gave them a small budget to kill some space on the back of a cereal box, perhaps with the suggestion that they wax patriotic in a bland, inoffensive way. Unfortunately, the result of their effort falls squarely under the heading of what the humanistic geographer Edward Relph calls "a geography of violence," since it unwittingly exhibits "the twin geographical bleakness of inexorable environmental degradation and the potential for total place destruction." The text is, in fact, a veritable paean to environmental degradation. The initial exhortation, "Explore this great land of ours," sets the tone for the entire piece, suggesting that "this land"—namely, that portion of the earth lying within the arbitrary geographic borders of the United States—literally belongs to us. As such, it echoes the sort of language a possessive husband might use in referring to "my" little woman: "She's quite a catch, ain't she?" This possessory tone continues in the regional lists, each of which contains at least one resource to be exploited. Alaska's main feature, according to Kix, is "OIL;" the Heartland has "FARMING;" the Great Lakes are best known for "MINING;" New England yields consumers its bounty of "MAPLE TREES" and "LOBSTER;" the Mid-Atlantic gives us "OYSTERS;" the Southeast, following its proud plantation heritage, has "COTTON;" the Appalachian Highlands have "HOGS" and "MINING;" the Southwest hands over several exploitable resources, including "WHEAT," "OIL," and "LONGHORN CATTLE;" and Hawaii gladly donates its dwindling supply of "SUGAR CANE" and "PINEAPPLE" to the cause of corporate-driven mass consumption.

Further, the very act of separating "America" from the rest of the conti-   6 nent, and of dividing it into eleven "regions," is a perfect example of a process which I have elsewhere termed *ecomandering*—that is, "generalizing from one element of a local terrain to assume that a broader geographic region contains that same element, and creating a language to perpetuate that illusion." When one overlooks the unique geographic characteristics of different bio-enclaves—scrub-oak forests, pine ridges, Mojave flora, the Willammette valley and Cascadia subduction zones—and comes to see all of Washington, Oregon and California as a single "region," this is concrete evidence that one has internalized the values of the Developer Class to such a degree that one has become blinded to the *oikos*—the place, the "real" world of a given ecosystem. Not only are one's perceptions compromised by this process, but one's very language is rewritten by repeated exposure to texts such as that of the Kix carton, and the resulting passive "subjectification" leads people to consider themselves as apart from their objectified surroundings.

The catastrophic effects of this subject/object split need not be catalogued here, as every rainbow warrior, deep ecologist, geofeminist, humanistic geographer, green theorist, NPR and PBS commentator has padded the literature with sadly credible lists of environmental disasters with human causes, from Valdez to the equatorial rain forests, to McDonald's wrappers at the south pole. While nobody who places herself under the broad umbrella of environmentalism would dispute the existence of a dire global problem requiring immediate and radical attention, there is heated—and too frequently acrimonious—debate about the sociopolitical forces that have brought this problem to its present calamitous proportions, and about ways of solving it. In fact, the multiplicity of ecological viewpoints and recommendations for "healing the planet" raises a crucial question, not only about the Kix carton presently under scrutiny, but about environmentalism and ecocriticism generally: *can* we heal the planet by attacking the problem at the pop-cultural level, where language—specifically the language people use to talk about nature—is constructed and reconstructed daily on a mass scale? 7

To answer this question, one must have at least a rudimentary understanding of green theory's origins and current status as a field of discourse, if not as a discipline with a well-defined ideology and critical methodology. Until quite recently, green was another color in Junior's crayola box, carrying with it numerous denotations—leafy, gullible, naive, juvenile—and even more associative baggage, from jealousy to alcoholic nausea. Ecology itself evolved as a discipline less than a century ago, when individuals such as George Perkins Marsh began exploring the relationship between physical geography and "human action." Although he never used the word "ecology," Marsh's interest was irrefutably ecological, since he moved away from scientific taxonomy, focusing instead on the dynamics of habitat and species. Following Marsh, other naturalists began discussing relationships between social formation and ecology, leading to Aldo Leopold's oft-quoted position statement that informed the worldview of subsequent generations—"A thing is right when it contributes to the lasting harmony of a system"—and a body of work supporting his belief that human behavior has a direct ethical connection to natural history. A branch of the Leopold-influenced school 8 developed later into what one might call the history of environmental ideas, the most prominent figure in that area being the editor of Leopold's journals, Roderick Nash, who hypothesized a dynamic interaction between the history of ideas and naturalism, and as such formulated a kind of proto-ecology.

Meanwhile, following in the theoretical footsteps of Habermas, who fo-   9
cused on practices that facilitate the development of public communication, a cultural-critical brand of social ecology began to develop. Lewis Mumford, for example, wrote in *The Culture of Cities* and *The City in History* that building structures should serve the psychological and practical needs of people by encouraging social interaction. Mumford's interest was perhaps more sociological than purely ecological, focusing as it did on the dynamics of human population and the ways in which human beings engineer and design relationships via a reshaping of the environment—specifically, their urban centers. Nevertheless, these ideas represent one more step in researchers' considering the human/habitat relationship, and in their making pro-ecological recommendations founded in Marxist critical theory. When Bookchin described the decline of "citizenship" that has accompanied the rise of urban centers and proposed a Marxist-based dialectical naturalism as the foundation of his "ecology of freedom," he became (as many have argued) the foundational theorist of what later became the Green political movement in Europe. Thus, by the early seventies, a politically-based green theory was firmly in place, as represented by Bookchin's theories of society and its dynamic interactions with nature, and by manifestoes of the various Green parties that formed in Europe and other areas during that period. Although differing frequently in the specific methods of implementing ecological change, most members of the nascent Green movement shared an underlying belief that *political* unity and action are the most effective means of reversing damage to the environment.

In the early '70's one strand of environmentalism took a decidedly liter-   10
ary twist, when Joseph Meeker's *Comedy of Survival* introduced the term "literary ecology" to describe any textual inquiry after factors—whether phenomenological, semiotic, linguistic, or psychoanalytic—that contribute to environmental perceptions, values and attitudes. William Rueckert, best known as a Kenneth Burke scholar, is generally credited with coining the term "eco-criticism" several years later, and subsequent scholars, while debating whether this relatively new criticism need be directly connected to environmental activism, began examining literary artifacts, from Sir Gawain to General Mills cartons . . . which brings us back to the container presently under consideration, and to the multiplicity of theoretical perspectives from which modern eco-critics might consider Kix's ambiguous textual significations.

At this point in its relatively brief evolution, eco-criticism appears to be   11
more a dialogue than a discipline, since it encompasses so many apparently

conflicting perspectives. In fact, if one member of each theoretical subgroup were to tackle our Kix carton, each would most likely produce a reading that differs to some degree from the next. A deep ecologist would probably point out the ways in which the General Mills text overlooks the negative consequences of industrialization-effected resource depletion, and—depending on that critic's degree of biocentrism—might recommend anything from the substitution of ecologically responsible packaging literature to the wholesale abolition of processed cereals, packaging for mass consumption, or even the eradication of the entire human population of the earth . . . which would certainly solve the problem of environmentally irresponsible cereal boxes once and for all. By contrast, a post-Lacanian eco-feminist might point to the eradication of all oceans by the Kix writers, who in so doing have constructed a phallocentric "language" (i.e. text and graphics) to quash readers' sense of sublime oceanic unity. The Kix carton thus tames healthy vital instincts, perverting them into a greedy orgy during which the "big boys" collectively gulp, swallow and subsequently excrete the environment. By way of solution, such a critic might suggest replacing the present text with a presentation featuring natural language that has no specific cognitive appeal but instead creates sympathetic states through rhythmic patterns, thus restoring to the reader a sense of unity with the chora, the mother-body, and therefore the sense of harmonized place-being that precedes psychic individuation. Meanwhile, a red-green Marxist eco-critic might use the Kix carton's ecomandered regional America as an example of ways in which the profit motive drives individuals to "greenwash" the natural landscape—that is, to commodify nature with the expressed goal of producing capital, and such a critic might envision some form of resistance (using tools ranging from word processors to AK-47's) to challenge the dominance of capitalist hegemony, and to promote environmental protection in ways that corporate capitalism clearly has not.

As for myself—a marxist (small m) pop-cultural critic who also considers himself an environmentalist—I enter the eco-debate late and therefore have the luxury of reflecting on it from a somewhat distanced perspective, as do many contemporary environmental "meta-critics" who attempt to forge a feasible theory and praxis from the current dialectic. Janet Biehl, for example, argues that ecofeminism, in the hands of some critics, seems to have become "a force for irrationalism, most obviously in its embrace of goddess worship, its glorification of the early Neolithic, and its emphasis on metaphors and myths." What Biehl proposes is a move—some might call it retrogressive—in the direction of social ecology, which, "with its eco-anarchist, anti-hierarchical approach, argues for the need to raise once again the social and intellectual questions that the early radical feminist movement raised—including women's need to go beyond the domestic realm into a new politics for radical social change." Similarly, Martin Lewis comments on some of the near-hysterical posturings by adherents to certain extreme positions. He asserts that "only a capitalist economy can generate the resources necessary for the development of a technologically sophisticated, ecologically sustainable global economy." Attempting (unsuccessfully, I would guess) to appease the cultural-critical left, Lewis qualifies this position by adding that, "in embracing capitalism I do not thereby advocate the laissez-faire approach of the Republican right," but he makes it clear that the future of the planet lies not in abandoning technology altogether, as a deep-ecological Marxist might insight, but in "harmonizing it to a new environmental vision." Lewis goes on to propose a "Promethean environmentalism" which takes the products of the corporate machine and applies them toward progressive, ecological ends. While the term "Promethean" seems ill-chosen—it sounds suspiciously like a sexist counterpart to the already-suspect Gaia hypothesis—and while it seems doubtful to me that elected heads-of-capitalist-state might ever be enlightened enough to give anything but condescending lip-service to green issues, Lewis' suggestion that we can heal the environment through science and rationalist philosophy is appealing and even believable—especially were governments to move toward a humane brand of socialism.

Given our current political climate, it seems unlikely that the world will 13 embrace a humane socialism within the next six months. Until such radical social change does occur, it goes without saying—at least to a predominately pro-ecological readership—that we need to protect and preserve the natural environment in whatever ways we can, however local and circumscribed those ways might be. One area in which we can have some immediate effect is that of language: specifically, the language with which people describe nature, since such diction necessarily constructs readers' attitude toward the environment; change the language, and you begin to change people's eco-attitudes. Cereal box packaging is a small component in such a strategy but an important one, since—as has been demonstrated—the typical consumer is most open to suggestion during the morning hours, when he is likely to be enjoying (or at least forcing down) that "lovely bowl of cereal" and simultaneously reading the carton.

Some breakfast food manufacturers have already begun to modify 14 their packaging literature. In fact, I have before me a box of Nature's Haven All-Organic Wheat Flakes, which contains, "All-Natural, All-Organic Products of the Earth," and whose carton is made from "100 percent Recycled Materials." While this is a step in the right—i.e. eco-conscious—direction, such a text still engages the reader in cognitive activity which the Bourdieu would criticize as creating an embodied memory of distinctions between "man" and "nature" that is echoed in daily behavior until it forms a *habitus*. Within such a critical context, cereal-box language—even such consciously "environmental" language as Nature's Haven—becomes not merely a means of communication but also a medium of power, habituating the eating/reading public into a exploitative attitude vis-a-vis the natural landscape and its "products." What I envision for future cereal boxes is something more radical: a new packaging model that, building on a Kristeva-based non-representational approach to language, uses ambiguous signifiers to overturn intellection, thus generating in the reader certain transcendent states of harmony, resonance and union. Cereal manufacturers have an opportunity—no, a responsibility—to impart to readers a sense that, as French surrealist author Michel Leiris' works suggest, things exist not in disunified fragments, but as parts of a whole which is in a constant state of organic unfolding. Like Leiris and other contemporary transformational poets of the land, carton authors must adopt a style that invokes in readers an inventory of their dreams, childhood memories and erotic experiences—all of which trace their roots back to a primal earth-body connection. With such a model in mind, I issue this challenge to any fabulously wealthy left-wing social democrat who wishes to share the wealth and save the planet: form a cereal company devoted to printing transformative writing on the backs of your cartons. Invite poets, cyberpunk fictionalists, post-absurdist playwrights, virtual designers and magical hypertext scriptographers to participate in this brave venture. I will even volunteer to serve as editor, *pro bono,* so strongly do I feel about this. If such a program isn't enacted, we may soon find ourselves trapped on an America that is regionalized and commodified, surrounded by extinct, negatively spatial oceans and bereft of all but the waste products of consumer culture: Cornyphones, peanut husks, and cardboard pink flamingos.   ©

CRITICAL READING

1. Why, according to the author, do people read the backs of cereal boxes? What effect might the exposure to cereal box "literature" have on its captive audiences, according to Petracca?
2. The author makes this statement about the Kix cereal box: "In their defense, the anonymous artists and designers who conceived and executed this pop artifact probably didn't intend for it to be a piece of accurate geography. More likely, General Mills gave them a small budget to kill some space on the back of a cereal box, perhaps with the suggestion that they wax patriotic in a bland, inoffensive way." Despite this lack of antiecological intention, what are the potentially negative effects of the Kix box's printed material, in the author's view?
3. What are the social and philosophical origins of green theory, as described in this article? Where does the word "ecology" come from?

CLASS DISCUSSION

1. In this article, the author poses a central question to the reader: "Can we heal the planet by attacking the problem at the pop-cultural level, where language—specifically the language people use to talk about nature—is constructed and reconstructed daily on a mass scale?" In a class discussion, debate this question: do

you believe that paying attention to the media's portrayal of nature—and, by extension, gender, race, and so on—is an important step in changing the ways people deal with nature, women, and minorities?
2. This article's author notes that the Kix carton "tames healthy vital instincts, perverting them into a greedy orgy during which the 'big boys' collectively gulp, swallow and subsequently excrete the environment." Think of some other popculture artifacts, such as advertisements, music videos, movies, and television programs, that similarly degrade the environment, portraying it as a disposable commodity.

DIRECTED FREEWRITE

At the end of the article, the author issues a challenge "to any fabulously wealthy left-wing social democrat who wishes to share the wealth and save the planet: form a cereal company devoted to printing transformative writing on the backs of your cartons. Invite poets, cyberpunk fictionalists, post-absurdist playwrights, virtual designers and magical hypertext scriptographers to participate in this brave venture." Imagine yourself a writer who has been given a sixty-thousand-dollar grant to produce some original, creative, and ultimately ecological writing for the back of a cereal box, and freewrite enough text to fill the back of a cereal box; imagine the average breakfast-food eater as your audience. For extra credit, you can fill the box's side panels with text as well.

CULTURAL STUDIES UNIT WRITING ASSIGNMENTS

1. Referring to the theories proposed by Rueckert and following the model of the Petracca article in this unit, write a summary/analysis of an advertisement that portrays the environment in some way. In your summary portion of the assignment, describe your advertisement in as much detail as you can, just as Petracca describes the Kix box objectively and exhaustively before commenting on it. Having given a reader a detailed picture of your advertisement, go on to analyze the specific means by which your advertisement degrades the environment. In writing your analysis, you might also discuss the impact of the advertisers' awareness of their respective audiences: how does the intended audience of each advertisement affect its portrayal of nature?
2. Write a historical critique of the theoretical movement known as green theory. Using the two articles in this unit as your main sources of information (feel free to add additional paraphrases and/or quotations gleaned from websites or journal articles as well), write a detailed history of the evolution of green theory, and then move into a section in which you comment on this movement. What, if anything, do you find meritorious in this theoretical movement? What specific points of view or methodologies do you find excessive, annoying, and/or off base? There is no right or wrong answer to this question; the main requirement is that you be entirely honest and forthright in articulating your thoughts and opinions about green theory and its adjunct literary activity, ecocriticism.

3. Keeping firmly in mind that you will never, NEVER make up sources for real academic papers, this assignment gives you license to have a bit of harmless fun by writing an environmental-based "research" essay in which you explore some ecological problem or catastrophe—a waste dump that's too near the city, an ever-shrinking hole in the ozone layer, an oil spill in Lake Erie—and in which you use nothing but bogus, made-up secondary sources for your quotations and paraphrases. Such an article may seem liberating or downright frivolous, if not scandalous; however, it has a somewhat more serious intent: to make you aware of the way secondary research is incorporated as evidence for assertions that you make in supporting paragraph, as well as to underline the grave dangers of plagiarism. Beyond officially sanctioned activities such as this one, this kind of invention will not sit well with professors and disciplinary review panels!

Unit 2
Literary Studies—Natural High

THE WINDHOVER[1]: TO CHRIST OUR LORD
Gerard Manley Hopkins

A Jesuit priest whose works were not made public until twenty-nine years after his death, Gerard Manley Hopkins has been celebrated as an innovative and adventurous poet because of his bold experiments with meter. Most of his poetry celebrates the wonders of God's creation, often focusing on nature and the creatures in it. Hopkins was born in Britain in 1844 and died in 1889. His poetry was published in 1918, however, and because of this date—and his bold style—Hopkins has consequently been compared with the modern poets of that later time rather than with the Victorians of his own. We present just one of his many poems here, one that has often been called his best.

> *Gerard Manley Hopkins (1844–1889) was born in Stratford, London. He attended Highgate School and Balliol College, Oxford. In 1866, he converted to Catholicism and was eventually ordained a priest in 1877. In 1884, Hopkins was appointed to the chair of Greek at University College, Dublin. None of his poems were published during his lifetime, but a full edition, edited by his friend and Poet Laureate Robert Bridges, was published posthumously in 1918. His first, and most famous poem, "The Wreck of the Deutschland" used what he called 'sprung rhythm,' which gave extraordinary freshness to his best-loved poetry including "Pied Beauty" and "The Windhover."*

I caught this morning morning's minion,[2]
   king-dom of daylight's dauphin,[3] dapple-dawn-drawn Falcon, in his riding
   Of the rolling level underneath him steady air, and striding
High there, how he rung upon the rein of a wimpling[4] wing

---

[1]A small falcon.
[2]Darling.
[3]A prince who is heir to the French throne.
[4]Rippling. "Rung upon the rein": circled at the end of a rein.

Source: Public domain.

In his ecstasy! then off, off forth on swing, 5
    As a skate's heel sweeps smooth on a bow-bend: the hurl and gliding
    Rebuffed the big wind. My heart in hiding
Stirred for a bird,—the achieve of, the mastery of the thing!

Brute beauty and valour and act, oh, air, pride, plume, here
    Buckle![5] AND the fire that breaks from thee then, a billion 10
Times told lovelier, more dangerous, O my chevalier![6]

    No wonder of it: shéer plód makes plough down sillion[7]
Shine, and blue-bleak embers, ah my dear,
    Fall, gall[8] themselves, and gash gold-vermilion.

---

[5]The verb can be read as imperative or indicative. All three meanings of "buckle" are relevant: to prepare for action, to fasten together, to collapse.
[6]Knight.
[7]The ridge between two furrows of a ploughed field.
[8]Break the surface of.

SONG AT SUNSET[1]

Walt Whitman

Walt Whitman is an important nineteenth-Century American poet, and his work is as innovative and bold as that of Hopkins, although in different ways. Born in 1819, and dead in 1892, Whitman lived through an exciting time in American history and contributed some interesting views of the events of that time. In 1855, Whitman published his book of poems *Leaves of Grass* at his own expense. The first, and perhaps best-known, poem of that volume is "Song of Myself" in which Whitman

---

[1]SUNSET] This brilliant paean, first printed in *LG* 1860 as "Chants Democratic" No. 8, received its present title in *LG* 1867 in the supplement, "Songs Before Parting," p. 29, and was transferred to the "Songs of Parting" cluster in *LG* 1871. In MS (Barrett) the title reads, "A Sunset Carol"; In WW's 1860 "Blue Copy" revisions is the same title with two words in the margin opposite—"finale" and "religious." The poem received but little revision. The poet Rilke called poetry "the past that breaks out in our hearts." This poem is the poet's joyous affirmation of his whole life.

Source: Public domain.

celebrates himself, his body, the bodies of all men and women, the physicality of nature, and the connections between all living things. Lacking rhyme or meter, Whitman's poetic structure was very unconventional, but his subject matter and highly personal focus were perhaps the elements that most shocked readers of that time. Although *Leaves of Grass* was not a financial success by any means, throughout the rest of his life, Whitman continued to add poems to the book and to reissue revised versions. His influence on American letters has been keenly felt throughout the twentieth century.

Even though some of the unfamiliar language and poetic structure in these poems might seem alien—and therefore intimidating—at first, let the footnotes help you with the language. As you read and reread the poems, try to work out as much of the literal meaning as you can, so that you'll be better able to move on to the underlying meanings.

Walter Whitman (1819–1892) was born in West Hills, Long Island, New York and was raised in Brooklyn. He worked as a printer and journalist in the New York City area where he wrote articles on everything from civics to politics. During the Civil War, he was a volunteer assistant in military hospitals in Washington, DC. After the war, he worked in several government departments until he suffered a stroke in 1873. He spent the rest of his life in Camden, New Jersey where he continued to write poems and articles. Whitman is best known for his collection of poems, Leaves of Grass, *which features many of his best-known poems including "Song of Myself," "When Lilacs Last in the Dooryard Bloom'd," and "O Captain! My Captain!"*

Splendor of ended day floating and filling me,
Hour prophetic, hour resuming the past,
Inflating my throat, you divine average,
You earth and life till the last ray gleams I sing.

Open mouth of my soul uttering gladness,   5
Eyes of my soul seeing perfection,
Natural life of me faithfully praising things,
Corroborating forever the triumph of things.

Illustrious every one!
Illustrious what we name space, sphere of unnumber'd spirits,   10
Illustrious the mystery of motion in all beings, even the tiniest insect,
Illustrious the attribute of speech, the senses, the body,
Illustrious the passing light—illustrious the pale reflection on the new moon
   in the western sky,
Illustrious whatever I see or hear or touch, to the last.

Good in all,   15
In the satisfaction and aplomb of animals,

In the annual return of the seasons,
In the hilarity of youth,
In the strength and flush of manhood,
In the grandeur and exquisiteness of old age,   20
In the superb vistas of death.

Wonderful to depart!
Wonderful to be here!
The heart, to jet the all-alike and innocent blood!
To breathe the air, how delicious!   25
To speak—to walk—to seize something by the hand!
To prepare for sleep, for bed, to look on my rose-color'd flesh!
To be conscious of my body, so satisfied, so large!
To be this incredible God I am!
To have gone forth among other Gods, these men and women I love.   30

Wonderful how I celebrate you and myself!
How my thoughts play subtly at the spectacles around!
How the clouds pass silently overhead!
How the earth darts on and on! and how the sun, moon, stars, dart on and
    on!
How the water sports and sings! (surely it is alive!)   35
How the trees rise and stand up, with strong trunks, with branches and leaves!
(Surely there is something more in each of the trees, some living soul.)
O amazement of things—even the least particle!
O spirituality of things!
O strain musical flowing through ages and continents, now reaching me and
    America!
I take your strong chords, intersperse them, and cheerfully pass them forward. 40

I too carol the sun, usher'd or at noon, or as now, setting,
I too throb to the brain and beauty of the earth and of all the growths of the
    earth,
I too have felt the resistless call of myself.

As I steam'd down the Mississippi,   45
As I wander'd over the prairies,
As I have lived, as I have look'd through my windows my eyes,
As I went forth in the morning, as I beheld the light breaking in the east,
As I bathed on the beach of the Eastern Sea, and again on the beach of the
    Western Sea,[2]

---

[2]Western Sea] WW never reached the Pacific in his travels, but from the times of the Greek navigators the "western sea" has been in the common stock of poetry as a symbol for the far-off or unattainable. Cf. Tennyson's "Stars of the western sea" in a song of *The Princess* (1847), familiar to WW.

As I roam'd the streets of inland Chicago, whatever streets I have roam'd,   50
Or cities or silent woods, or even amid the sights of war,
Wherever I have been I have charged myself with contentment and triumph.

I sing to the last the equalities modern or old,
I sing the endless finalés of things,
I say Nature continues, glory continues,   55
I praise with electric voice,
For I do not see one imperfection in the universe,
And I do not see one cause or result lamentable at last in the universe.
O setting sun! though the time has come,
I still warble under you, if none else does, unmitigated adoration.   60

CRITICAL READING

1. Discuss how each poem makes you feel. Did your feelings change from your first reading of each poem to subsequent readings? Do the poems convey feelings to you even without your fully understanding them (feelings, that is, other than, or in addition to, frustration)? What is it in the poems that conveys emotion, do you think? Or what is it in you that leads to your emotional responses?
2. Discuss what literal meanings you glean from each poem—in other words, what is happening in the poems, and what are the obvious things that each poem says? Then explore what you think the "deeper" meanings are in each poem. Why does Hopkins discuss the ordinary and mundane things such as "shéer plód" and the furrows of a plowed field, especially after he's been describing a more majestic subject for the bulk of the poem? Why, in a poem ostensibly celebrating a specific event—the beauty of a sunset—does Whitman discuss abstract and vast things such as wandering over the prairies, "the equalities modern or old," and the universe?
3. What is the tone of each poem, and how is the tone conveyed? What do you make of the religious or spiritual elements in each poem?

CLASS DISCUSSION

1. Both poems feature a speaker who observes and comments on the natural elements the poets are celebrating. Discuss both how the persona of these two speakers is similar and how each persona is different. How do these differing personae relate to the different emphases and concerns that each poet seems to focus on?
2. A dramatic shift in tone occurs in Hopkins's poem at the beginning of the third stanza. Discuss what effect this shift has on the meaning of the poem or on the emotional "feel" of the poem. Discuss whether any such shifts are evident in Whitman's poem, and if so, how these affect his meaning and how these compare with Hopkins's shift.

DIRECTED FREEWRITE

Brainstorm about all the similarities and differences you notice between these two poems. We've already hinted at several differences, such as the ways in which the speaker functions in each, the way religion or spirituality is evident in each, and the way the tone in each poem shifts or not. There are numerous other comparisons and contrasts between these poems; see how many you can come up with in your writing.

WHITMAN, HOPKINS, AND THE WORLD'S SPLENDOR

Christopher Clausen

In this essay, Clausen starts off by noting an interesting admission by Hopkins about his connection to Whitman's mind, and Clausen continues on to explore the relationship between these two poets' work. Ironically, Hopkins had the opportunity to read the older Whitman's work, whereas Whitman would not have read Hopkins, since the latter's work was published well after both poets' deaths. As you read this piece of literary criticism and analysis, notice how Clausen uses various literary references to compare and contrast Hopkins and Whitman to each other and to other nineteenth-century writers and thinkers. What points do these references ultimately help him to make?

Christopher Clausen received his B.A. from Earlham College, his M.A. from the University of Chicago and a Ph.D. from Queen's University. He is an English professor at Penn State University and the author of many articles on literature and culture in the 19th and 20th centuries. He has also written several texts including My Life With President Kennedy; The Moral Imagination: Essays on Literature and Ethics; *and* The Place of Poetry: Two Centuries of an Art in Crisis.

"I always knew in my heart Walt Whitman's mind to be more like my   1
own than any other man's living," Gerard Manley Hopkins wrote to Robert
Bridges in 1882. "As he is a very great scoundrel this is not a pleasant

Source: "Whitman, Hopkins, and the World's Splendor" by Christopher Clausen in *The Sewanee Review,* vol. 105, no. 2 (Spring 1997). Copyright © 1997 by Christopher Clausen. Reprinted by permission of the editor and the author.

confession." Beyond surmising that Hopkins had Whitman's homosexual tendencies in mind, and sometimes briefly comparing their styles, scholars have rarely taken up the implications of this seemingly improbable admission. One reason is its obscurity: what else did the fastidious, classically educated Jesuit think he had in common with the rowdy self-educated democrat? Another, no doubt, is the academic dogma that American and British literature are entirely separate realms. Yet, unlike most Victorian poets, Whitman and Hopkins have been widely admired in the twentieth century—and for reasons that are at least partly identical. Their work seems fresher than that of their contemporaries, both because of their attitudes toward the world and because they restored life to the art of poetry by radical technical innovation.

In his letter to Bridges, Hopkins was defending himself against a   2
charge of having imitated Whitman in his recent poem "The Leaden Echo and the Golden Echo." According to Paul Mariani, Hopkins, almost a generation younger than Whitman, had begun to read the older poet no later than 1874. In 1882 he claimed to have read only a few poems. It is nonetheless rash to minimize the significance of his "confession." Between them Whitman and Hopkins illuminate not only the central problem of nineteenth-century poetry—how to revive an art whose forms had gone stale—but also the most important nineteenth-century philosophical problem, which entails the relation between the natural and human worlds.

Whitman's view of the world, which was spelled out in the first edition   3
of *Leaves of Grass* (1855), never essentially changed. As he wrote many years later in "A Backward Glance O'er Travel'd Roads," "One main contrast of the ideas behind every page of my verses, compared with establish'd poems, is their different relative attitude towards God, towards the objective universe, and still more (by reflection, confession, assumption, &c.) the quite changed attitude of the ego, the one chanting or talking, towards himself and towards his fellow-humanity." In contrast it was Hopkins, in a poetic career that lasted (apart from juvenilia) only thirteen years, whose views changed radically—from an affirmation of nature recognizably similar to Whitman's toward an extreme suspicion of the natural world.

Although Victorian poets on both sides of the Atlantic were in obvious   4
respects the spiritual children of romanticism, most of them held sentiments towards the natural world that were qualified and sometimes pessimistic. External nature remained seductive but not altogether trustworthy. The estrangement from nature, encapsulated in Tennyson's phrase "nature red in tooth and claw" from *In Memoriam* (1850) and Matthew Arnold's "darkling plain" from "Dover Beach" (1867), is usually attributed to a growing awareness of the grim processes of biological evolution. But the roots of this ambivalence can be found as early as Wordsworth and Coleridge and antedate not only Darwin (whose *Origin of Species* was not published until 1859) but also the geologists whose research distressed Tennyson. What one finds

increasingly from Wordsworth on is a new tendency to apply moral judgments to natural processes. In *In Memoriam* this tendency reaches some of its most memorable formulations, culminating in this traumatic question: "Are God and nature then at strife?" Although Tennyson's answer was ultimately negative, his misgivings lingered.

One might summarize these uncertainties with some exaggeration by saying the nineteenth century noticed for the first time that nature sooner or later kills everyone. That century's relative tender-heartedness, in comparison with previous centuries, is evident in numerous aspects of culture, from legislation protecting child laborers to the medical emphasis on perfecting anesthetics and other pain-killers. Because pain and death are natural processes, nature—despite its beauty and, for English writers, an increasing sense as the century progressed of ecological fragility—came to be seen ambiguously even by poets who regarded themselves as Wordsworth's heirs. The emphasis on cruelty in popularizations of Darwinian evolution was a consequence of a widespread moral queasiness about nature that preceded rather than followed the theory of natural selection. Both Victorian religion and Victorian irreligion were highly moralistic ways of viewing the world. 5

If, at its most negative, nature is the mindless torturer it appears to be in the early sections of *In Memoriam,* then moral progress carries us away from the natural world, not more deeply into it. Living in harmony with nature like the noble savage of myth involves accepting of ignoring too many evils. Most poets found ways to circumvent a conclusion so offensive to their residual romanticism, but John Stuart Mill, whose outlook long preceded the theory of evolution, and Thomas Henry Huxley, Darwin's chief scientific advocate, expressed it without evasion. In his posthumously published essay "Nature," Mill declared roundly: "The order of nature, in so far as unmodified by man, is such as no being, whose attributes are justice and benevolence, would have made, with the intention that his rational creatures should follow it as an example. . . . In sober truth, nearly all the things which men are hanged or imprisoned for doing to one another, are nature's every day performances. Killing, the most criminal act recognized by human laws, Nature does once to every being that lives; and in a large proportion of cases, after protracted tortures such as only the greatest monsters whom we read of ever purposely inflicted on their living fellow-creatures." 6

One is not surprised that Mill concluded that "the duty of man is the same in respect to his own nature as in respect to the nature of all other things, namely not to follow but to amend it." Huxley echoed these sentiments decades later in his lecture "Evolution and Ethics" (1893): "Let us understand, once for all, that the ethical progress of society depends, not on imitating the cosmic process, still less in running away from it, but in combating it." Really following nature, after all, would then mean abandoning the search for a cure for tuberculosis—or, today, AIDS. 7

Among nineteenth-century writers in English, Whitman constitutes the   8
most important exception to this whole line of thought. His acceptance of all
that happens in the world, including death, is uniquely consistent. In effect
he short-circuits the whole problem by refusing to accept that there *is* a
problem. If one denies, as Whitman does, that death or any other occurrence in the natural world calls for disapproval, then no gap exists between
nature and human aspirations, no moral or intellectual difficulty to be solved.
"I will show you," he wrote in "Starting from Paumanok" (1856), "that there is
no imperfection in the present, and can be none in the future,/And I will
show that whatever happens to anybody it may be turn'd to beautiful results,/And I will show that nothing can happen more beautiful than death,
. . . /And that all the things of the universe are perfect miracles, each as profound as any."

To contrast these lines with Tennyson's "O yet we hope that somehow   9
good/Will be the final goal of ill" is to enter a different spiritual world. If nature offers no check to our moral sense, then the universe becomes available for unlimited aesthetic enjoyment. For Whitman that universe
intermingles nature and human life, even urban, industrial human life, without distinction. One of the finest passages in one of his best poems, "Crossing Brooklyn Ferry," describes the whole visible scene at length, paying
equal tribute to "the gladness of the river and the bright flow" (an image that
might be found in any romantic poet) and "the fires from the foundry chim-
neys burning high and glaringly into the night" (which, as a positive image, is
Whitman's alone).

Such a point of view immediately raises the question whether human   10
life stands apart from nature in a different sense. That is, if one applies standards of right and wrong to human behavior but not to the natural world, is
one not again positing a gulf between the two? Whitman avoids this problem
by refusing, with an impressive degree of consistency, to judge human beings or their actions. His salute to a prostitute in "To a Common Prostitute" is
often quoted with approval in our time. His even-handedness towards
slaves and slaveowners in "Song of Myself" finds fewer enthusiasts. It
clearly troubles his most recent biographer, David S. Reynolds. Many modern people mistakenly think they repudiate the whole concept of objective
moral standards when in fact they only deny the validity of particular rules.
Here again Whitman, as a visionary poet, is an exception:

> What blurt is this about virtue and about vice?
> Evil propels me and reform of evil propels me, I stand
>   indifferent,
> My gait is no fault-finder's or rejecter's gait,
> I moisten the roots of all that has grown.

Whitman the reforming journalist was a different story, as Gay Wilson Allen
and a succession of other commentators have pointed out. But, in his poetry,

the refusal to choose between one thing and another, the denial that any constituent of the world calls for censure, rises to a universal principle. Body and soul, slave and master, pioneer and Indian, the natural environment and human threats to it—all have equal standing, all are beautiful. In an uncommonly fault-finding century, nothing at all cries out for protest.

The key to such undiscriminating affirmation, as Whitman repeatedly 11 emphasized, is the embracing of death. "Has anyone supposed it lucky to be born?" he asks in "Song of Myself." "I hasten to inform him or her it is just as lucky to die, and I know it." In "Out of the Cradle Endlessly Rocking" (1859) he presents his whole art as springing from the sea's gift to him in childhood of "the low and delicious word death." After middle age, illness, and the Civil War have tested his convictions, he reaffirms this outlook in "When Lilacs Last in the Dooryard Bloom'd (1866): *"Come lovely and soothing death,/Undulate round the world, serenely arriving, arriving."* Only the poet, "the true son of God," he declares in "Passage to India" (1871), by revealing the world in its proper light can answer the nagging question, "What is this earth to our affections? (unloving earth, without a throb to answer ours,/Cold earth, the place of graves)." If one can happily accept death for oneself and others, the acceptance of anything else becomes much less difficult. Thus Whitman could say more convincingly than any other nineteenth-century writer:

> A word of the faith that never balks,
> Here or henceforward it is all the same to me, I accept Time
>   absolutely. . . .
> I accept Reality and dare not question it,
> Materialism first and last imbuing.

For Whitman, then, the relations among God, nature, and humanity 12 that obsessed other writers of his time did not need to be precisely defined because they raised no moral problems. One consequence was that, again unlike Tennyson, Whitman needed no God as a guarantor of nature's ultimate beneficence. If no divine being hidden behind the world of appearances could be more marvelous than the least object in that world when rightly seen, there is no need to look for comfort beyond the veil. This point of view is nearly impossible to maintain consistently for a lifetime, and the post–Civil War Whitman sometimes falters. For the poet of "Song of Myself," however, all discrimination between the sacred and the profane is unreal:

> And I say to mankind, Be not curious about God,
> For I who am curious about each am not curious about
>   God,
> (No array of terms can say how much I am at peace about
>   God and about death.)

> I hear and behold God in every object, yet understand God
>   not in the least,
> Nor do I understand who there can be more wonderful than
>   myself.

There are, for the bard who embraces every imaginable experience, no pressing questions to which God would be the answer.

As a Catholic convert who became a priest, Hopkins could hardly have 13 started from a more drastically different set of assumptions about the world. Yet he too began his career as a poet who celebrated death. "The Wreck of the Deutschland" (completed in 1876 but, like nearly all Hopkins's poems, not published in his lifetime) is dedicated to the "happy memory" of five Franciscan nuns who drowned after the ship on which they were emigrating to America struck a sand bar in the mouth of the Thames. A shipwreck that takes place during a snowstorm and kills a quarter of the passengers would seem to present nature in an inhospitable guise, to say the least—hardly promising material for a poet who wishes to show harmony between the human and nonhuman worlds.

Appearances to the contrary, however, nature even at its most hostile 14 mirrors the divine purpose of salvation. Because the chief nun recognized Christ's hand in the storm and welcomed her death, the poet's own acceptance of the natural world is—at this stage of his life—as enthusiastic as Whitman's. Just as for Whitman, the poet is the indispensable figure who grasps and enunciates the true meaning of the event, in this case that God is "throned behind/Death with a sovereignty that heeds but hides, bodes but abides." The seemingly murderous processes of nature constitute no problem, either moral or (for any who "Read the unshapeable shock night" with the single eye of faith) epistemological. If those who died were saved, the circumstances of their passing are grounds for praise.

Hopkins's rationale for affirming the world of experience differs radi- 15 cally from Whitman's, but the result often looks the same. The conviction that whatever happens is God's will leads to the same destination by a different route. "The Wreck of the Deutschland" sets a pattern for the first stage of Hopkins's brief career in which some aspect of nature is celebrated with an enthusiasm unusual among either Victorian poets or most Christian poets of any period, and then a theological moral is drawn. At least to a secular reader, the moral, though undoubtedly sincere, often seems less impassioned than the natural description that preceded it. The genuineness of Hopkins's Catholic faith is not worth disputing or demonstrating, but there are many passages in which he sounds more like Whitman than like other nineteenth-century Christians. One stanza shows, in style and substance, both his affinity for the older poet and his differences:

> I kiss my hand
>   To the stars, lovely-asunder
>   Starlight, wafting him out of it; and
>   Glow, glory in thunder;
> Kiss my hand to the dappled-with-damson west:
> Since, though he is under the world's splendour
>   and wonder,
>   His mystery must be instressed, stressed;
> For I greet him the days I meet him, and bless when I
>   understand.

In the careful patterning of its lines, this passage shows a tighter disci- 16
pline than Whitman's verse (a letter in 1882 to Bridges defensively dismissed Whitman's style as "irregular rhythmic prose"). While Whitman on
some days might have referred to "wafting" God out of nature, Hopkins's
complex theory of instress and inscape would have struck him as forced
and unnecessary. Yet a Whitmanesque exuberance finds its way into the
passage. In the Old Testament, kissing one's hand to heavenly bodies dis-
approvingly suggested a pagan worship of nature. For the Hopkins of 1876,
as for Whitman, there was no reason to emphasize the distinction between
the natural and supernatural realms. God and nature were emphatically not
at strife. The only caveat one might emphasize here is the implication in the
last line that there are days when the poet does not meet God and does not
understand.

The embracing of nature and death paradoxically involves, for both 17
Whitman and Hopkins, the assertion of the self. Whitman's longest poem
begins with this famous line: "I celebrate myself, and sing myself." "The
Wreck of the Deutschland," Hopkins's longest poem, might seem to make a
dramatic contrast: its opening lines are "Thou mastering me,/God! giver of
breath and bread." The word *me,* however, occupies the most emphatic position at the end of the line. Furthermore the mysterious uniqueness and
supreme value of individual selves is as important a doctrine for Hopkins as
it is for Whitman. In verse and prose, he hails the irreplaceable distinctive-
ness of each created being, human or natural. "As kingfishers catch fire"
(1877) coins a new verb to proclaim

> Each mortal thing does one thing and the same:
>   Deals out that being indoors each one dwells;
>   Selves—goes its self; *myself* it speaks and spells,
> Crying *What I do is me: for that I came.*

To be what one inherently is: perhaps nothing more is required. In "Pied 18
Beauty" this possibility leads to an abbreviated but otherwise Whitmanlike catalogue of praise

> For skies of couple-colour as a brinded cow;
> For rose-moles all in stipple upon trout that swim;
> Fresh-firecoal chestnut-falls; finches' wings;
> Landscape plotted and pieced—fold, fallow, and plough;
> And all trades, their gear and tackle and trim.

Had Hopkins been a full-time poet instead of an overworked priest, he might have written longer poems in this vein. Instead he composed a series of sonnets in 1876 and 1877, including "God's Grandeur," "The Starlight Night," "As kingfishers catch fire," "Spring," "The Windhover," and others, that proclaimed the harmony of human, natural, and supernatural purposes. Norman MacKenzie, editor of the definitive text of Hopkins's work, points out that residence among the beauties of rural North Wales during his theological training affected his poetry decisively. For whatever combination of biographical reasons, this harmony seen at the heart of his poems began to break down soon after his ordination. [19]

The first step toward disharmony was a nagging awareness of human destructiveness toward nature. This theme becomes significant in the poems with "The Sea and the Skylark" (1877), a sonnet that pointedly contrasts natural beauty with the burgeoning seaside resort of Rhyl. The tawdriness of "this shallow and frail town" reflects the urbanization and commercialism that characterize "our sordid turbid time," which in turn leads to reflections on the decline of humanity—a consequence both of original sin and of historical changes in the nineteenth century. As Hopkins spent more time ministering to Catholic congregations in urban areas, the theme of ecological destruction as a symptom of human depravity became common in his poems. "Duns Scotus's Oxford" (1879) refers to the "base and brickish skirt"—the new suburbs—of the town where Hopkins had spent happy undergraduate years and, once again, treats them as a sign of a rift between human beings and the natural world. In "Binsey Poplars" (1879) he mourns a vanished row of aspens, lamenting the thoughtless environmental destruction in which "Strokes of havoc unselve/The sweet especial scene"; the result is a form of human self-blinding. (In a journal entry of 1873, Hopkins had described the effect on him when another favorite tree was cut down: "there came at that moment a great pang and I wished to die and not to see the inscapes of the world destroyed any more.") Note the coinage *unselve,* negative counterpart of the earlier *selve:* once again the emphasis is on the uniqueness of something nonhuman, but this time it has been wantonly destroyed. [20]

Asserting the incomparable value of selves militates strongly against the undiscriminating acceptance of whatever happens in the world, for many things happen that frustrate the aspirations any self may have, and eventually like the trees it dies. The romantic emphasis on the self brings us back [21] to the very problem with which we began. Hopkins's most frequently anthologized poem, "Spring and Fall: To a Young Child" (1880), uses trees to parallel the human self in a different way. Here the trees' autumnal loss of their leaves foreshadows the eventual death of every human, even that of the child who weeps without knowing why. Original sin, a concept wholly alien to Whitman and romanticism in general, is the ultimate cause of death. The idea of happy death that Hopkins had shared with Whitman a few years earlier makes no appearance in this poem, whose tone is wholly of grief:

> Now no matter, child, the name:
> Sorrow's springs are the same.
> Nor mouth had, no nor mind, expressed
> What heart heard of, ghost guessed:
> It is the blight man was born for,
> It is Margaret you mourn for.

Nature shares in the human fall and has altogether lost any independent selfhood. The only self that matters is the fatally flawed human one. Similarly, in the Sonnets of Desolation, composed during the last few years of Hopkins's life, natural description is used entirely as a metaphor for mental processes. Powerful lines like "O the mind, mind has mountains; cliffs of fall/Frightful, sheer, no-man-fathomed" have a purely psychological meaning: natural features no longer retain any interest in their own right.

In all these late poems, the suffering and death of the self become 22 once again problems to be solved—or at least endured. Whitman had avoided this predicament by identifying the self with all of its actual and possible experiences. In Hopkins's last period the human self is overwhelmed by the consciousness of its isolation in a hostile cosmos. It is odd that, as Hopkins's view of the world veers away from that of Whitman, his rhythms become more like those of the older poet—hence Bridges's presumption of influence. Whitmanlike echoing cadences are put to increasingly sombre uses. Hopkins accurately described his verse as "oratorical, that is the rhythm is so," a comment that, as F. O. Matthiessen pointed out, applies equally to Whitman. (Matthiessen also found political similarities between the two poets that perhaps looked more convincing in 1941 than they do today.) Despite their increasingly eccentric coinages, the long lines when read aloud remind the hearer of no other nineteenth-century poet. "Earnest, earthless, equal, attuneable, vaulty, voluminous, stupendous/Evening strains to be time's vast, womb-of-all, home-of-all, hearse-of-all night," begins "Spelt from Sibyl's Leaves" (1886). "Epithalamion" (1888) begins with the Whitmanesque line "Hearer, hearer, hear what I do; lend a thought now, make believe."

"That Nature is a Heraclitean Fire and of the comfort of the Resurrec- 23 tion" (1888) is Hopkins's most striking late statement of the relations between mankind and the two worlds, natural and supernatural, with which we have dealings. Written in the last year of his life, it marks a final break with the optimism expressed in the Welsh poems. Heraclitus was perhaps the most obscure of Greek philosophers; rightly or wrongly, he has usually been associated with the doctrine that change, symbolized by fire, is the ultimate reality. In Hopkins's poem Heraclitean fire, the ever-changing natural world, offers no encouragement to either human aspirations or divine purposes—a total contrast with the harmonious relationship among these three entities in the major poem of his early career, "The Wreck of the Deutschland." The scene again involves a storm, though this time only a summer rain. In its aftermath sun, breeze, and puffy clouds reappear; the sodden ground begins to dry. What sounds like an attractive picture, however, immediately takes on overtones of endless, fickle changeableness empty of human or divine meaning: "Million fuelèd, nature's bonfire burns on." Viewed philosophically, the once precious natural world is nothing but a conflagration interminable devouring leaves and other dead matter.

Worse is yet to come: part of its fuel is the highest form of creation, 24 man himself with all his works. For killing human beings and reducing their achievements to obscurity, nature (of which time is an aspect) becomes unforgivable. Once again, as in "The Wreck," drowning is used as a general metaphor for death, but this time with wholly negative implications:

> O pity and indignation! Manshape, that shone
> Sheer off, disseveral, a star, death blots black out; nor mark
>   Is any of him so stark
> But vastness blurs and time beats level.

Such a sweeping rejection of nature is nearly unprecedented in nineteenth-century poetry. Nothing remains to fall back on except a supernatural order that now, instead of using nature to reveal itself, has become an escape from nature. "Enough!" says the poet after contemplating a scene that offers only faded romantic illusions. "The Resurrection,/A heart's clarion!" God and man alike disown the natural world. The poet, like the nun of "The Wreck," finds himself on a "foundering deck," but this time he offers no hope that any part of creation is redeemable besides the human soul. The image is of divine rescue from a universe finally recognized for what it is:

> Flesh fade, and mortal trash
> Fall to the residuary worm; world's wildfire, leave but ash:
>   In a flash, at a trumpet crash,
> I am all at once what Christ is, since he was what I am, and
> This Jack, joke, poor potsherd, patch, matchwood, immortal
>   diamond,
>   Is immortal diamond.

The residuary worm who inherits the shards of a fallen world is a 25 far cry from anything in Whitman (though he might have liked "immortal diamond" as a metaphor for the human self), and stands equally remote from the poet who a dozen years earlier had wafted God out of the loveliness of nature. The world's splendor and wonder have deliquesced into the world's wildfire, a sadder and, one presumes, wiser image. It would be hard to imagine this Hopkins worrying much about the environment, let alone kissing his hand to the stars. Unlike such thinkers as Mill and Huxley, Hopkins had orthodox Christianity to offer solace and direction—an enormous difference; but his indictment of the order of nature is similar to theirs.

"Wales set me up for a while," he wrote to Bridges in 1887; "but the effect is now past." Under the pressure of ill health and many discouragements, the moralist in Hopkins finally overcame the visionary. A comparison with Whitman may make the younger man, who died at the age of forty-four, seem a reactionary figure. The two most original poets in English between Wordsworth and the modernists, however, have much more in common than the ambiguous sexuality they shared. Both struggled against the literary grain of their times for a recognition and influence that eluded them until the twentieth century. More systematically and with less evasion than any of their poetic contemporaries, they confronted the same questions about what kind of world we live in and how poems should be written. Though in the end they came to opposite conclusions about the world, their minds were more alike than anyone but Hopkins has noticed. ◎ 26

CRITICAL READING

1. What important nineteenth-century philosophical problem does Clausen believe Hopkins and Whitman helped to illuminate? What are their ultimate answers to the question inherent in that problem, according to Clausen?
2. Describe Clausen's view of Whitman's treatment of God. Where is this treatment evident in "Song at Sunset"? If not evident, what different treatment of the spiritual or divine do you see in this poem?
3. How does "The Windhover," written by Hopkins in 1877, fit in with the assertions Clausen makes about Hopkins's early and later treatment of nature?

CLASS DISCUSSION

1. Discuss the different nineteenth-century attitudes towards nature and humankind's relation to it that Clausen elaborates. How are these attitudes related to our own? Further, how might any of these attitudes help to inspire or to hinder environmental movements in our time?
2. Having read this essay on Whitman and Hopkins, go back to the poems in this unit. Reread them, and then discuss what elements in the poems relate to Clausen's points, and how. Does having read the critical essay change your reading of the poems in any way? If so, how? If not, why not?

DIRECTED FREEWRITE

One of Clausen's points concerns the ways in which the poets deal with the individual or the self and its relation to nature and to God (in the fifteenth and sixteenth paragraphs). In relation to these points, explore your own thoughts on the self; the importance of the individual; and the way that you feel that you as an individual fit into the larger scheme of nature, the universe, and, if you like, the spiritual realm. How do your thoughts relate to those of Whitman and Hopkins?

LITERARY STUDIES UNIT WRITING ASSIGNMENTS

1. An autobiographical narrative is one of the most basic rhetorical forms, in that it focuses on one specific event or grouping of events from your life and seeks to derive meaning from those events. This assignment invites you to describe—or to tell the story of—a specific encounter you have had with or in nature, an encounter that somehow shaped your attitude toward the natural world. Thus, your relation of the story will culminate in an articulation of your view of nature and either your or humankind's relation to it. This viewpoint might be one you still hold, or it might be one you have since modified. If they are relevant, you might want to refer to ideas or points in Clausen's essay and/or in either of the poems in the unit in order to help articulate the view of nature your narrative ends up asserting.

2. Write an essay in which you compare and contrast the "The Windhover" and "Song at Sunset." Rather than cataloging all the ways in which the poems are similar or different, focus your discussion on one or several (related) sites of comparison, for example, the poems' apparent stance toward nature and the rest of the human world, or the kinds of spirituality represented in the poems.

   An alternative comparison and contrast essay assignment might be to locate a poem about nature written by another Victorian poet, such as William Wordsworth, and compare that poem's depiction of nature with that of either Whitman's or Hopkins's in the poems of this unit. Refer to assignment 2 on page 165 in the Philosophy unit of Chapter 2 for more discussion of comparison and contrast.

3. Choose one of Hopkins's later poems (see those mentioned by Clausen). Write an interpretive analysis of the ways in which this poem approaches the relationships between human beings, nature, and God or spirituality, using Clausen's points about this subject and arguing for the ways the poem relates to Clausen's ideas. You might dispute Clausen's reading, support it, or modify it in some way, using a careful reading of the poem to support your position. Assignment 3 on page 200 in the Art History unit of Chapter 2 contains more details about critical interpretation essays.

4. Use the ecocritical approach outlined in the Cultural Studies unit of this chapter to interpret a poem or set of poems by Hopkins, Whitman, or some contemporary "nature poet" of your choosing.

DOCUMENTATION OF SOURCES

Whenever you use source material to support your arguments in academic papers, you have to document that material. You do this by using footnotes and/or parenthetical in-text citations, along with works cited or references pages. Such documentation serves both to acknowledge your having borrowed ideas and/or actual phrases from outside source material, while at the same time enabling readers to verify the sources used. Furthermore, documentation allows readers to explore a paper's topic further, should they find the issues raised thought-provoking and worthy of pursuit.

All systems of documentation share certain fundamental characteristics. They provide uniform information about quoted or paraphrased material from books, journals, newspapers, Web sites, and so forth. Unfortunately for students (and the people who teach them), there are several major documentation formats, such as MLA, APA, CBE, and each system has different features and requirements. Part of learning to navigate the terrain of the multidisciplinary university is to learn to follow the guidelines for citation appropriate in each discipline. Such guidelines help to insure consistency, so that scholars within that field understand precisely the nature of source references within written texts.

Students in multidisciplinary writing classes sometimes wonder, "Why do we have to learn all these different documentation styles?" It seems unnatural, obnoxious, and illogical that there should exist so many different ways to do the same thing: namely, to document the sources that one uses to write an academic essay. The cynical (and not wholly incorrect) answer to that reasonable student question would be: "There are many different documentation styles, just as there are many different types of deodorant soap in the supermarket: free market competition." While the academic world is perceived by many as existing outside (or above, as in the "ivory tower" metaphor) the "real" world of corporate enterprise, the fact is that competition exists within universities, just as it does in the outside world. Departments and disciplinary communities compete for grant money, tax revenues, prestige and recognition; they establish and guard their academic territory in a variety of ways, such as setting up their own documentation conventions (APA, MLA, CBE) to "mark" their territory within the academy.

While there may be some truth to this scenario, it would be a simplistic argument if left to rest solely upon its own merits. Another—and more generous—way of looking at the multi-format documentation problem might be to note that APA, MLA, and CBE styles exist for reasons that are intrinsic to the goals and activities of each discipline. According to this view, the different documentation styles support the unique needs and preferences of certain academic communities. For instance, in the social sciences, sources are cited by author and date far more often than by page number because in that area of inquiry, intellectual conclusions are frequently more important than individual quotations. Writers in the humanities use direct quotations far more frequently than do writers in the social sciences, and therefore the MLA format evolved to provide page numbers instead of dates—whether these sources are quoted directly or simply paraphrased.

Since, during your university career, you will undoubtedly be writing papers in all these disciplinary areas, you would be well advised to learn the rudiments of documenting within each discipline. A student who follows the exacting routines for citing sources in a particular essay distinguishes him or herself from the mass of students who don't bother to get all the aspects of the citation recorded correctly. In your work as an undergraduate writer, showing that you understand and can follow the different formats for citing sources within the different disciplinary systems demonstrates to professors and teaching assistants that you're one of those rare and prized students who values (or at least is attentive to) the specialized language practices within the academy.

On the other hand, you may know right now that you will be spending the majority of your time within a particular discipline, such as English literature or psychology. If this is the case, then you might want to familiarize yourself with the rudiments of all the major citation formats, while learning, memorizing and practicing the specific documentation requirements of the area in which you will be majoring. If you already know you're going to major in English, then concentrate on learning MLA citation style, and learn it inside and out; if you've already decided on a psychology career, then take special care to learn everything there is to know about APA format, because you'll be relying on it extensively throughout your career as an undergraduate, and perhaps beyond.

THE MAJOR DOCUMENTATION STYLES

The major systems for documentation arise out of the different fields of academic inquiry. Professional organizations within those fields, such as the Modern Language Association (MLA) and the American Psychological Association (APA) standardize the ways in which source materials—quotes and paraphrases from print materials, television programs, Web sites, personal interviews, and so forth—are acknowledged within essays and other forms of academic writing. Within the humanities, the MLA, a nationwide organization of scholars in the humanities, sets the rules for citation in humanities texts and studies. For social scientists, the APA largely dictates the rules for dealing with sources in the work of social science, and like the MLA, sets the rules for consistency in the ways supporting information is presented. In the sciences, many researchers and writers use the documentation method outlined by the Council of Biology Editors (CBE).

While these three are generally recognized as the most important and widely accepted methods of documentation, it's important to keep in mind that absolute standardization does not exist. Variations in citation practice occur in different regions of the country; you will soon discover that some professors have devised their own, preferred systems for documentation; different academic journals require different variations of standard documentation styles; and the MLA, APA and CBE are dynamic organizations that occasionally change certain rules to accommodate the fluid nature of source material. For example, as computer-based media have become widely recognized as valid research resources, the professional organizations are scrambling to standardize the ways in which student and professional researchers can document material gathered from Web sites, e-mail, chat rooms, and so forth.

Documentation is evidently a fluid medium, and it's therefore important to keep up with the changes that occur in the documentation styles of the various disciplines. Each of the major professional organizations periodically issues revised printings of their citation guidelines. If you're interested in staying on top of the current fine points of these conventions, you might invest in the latest editions of the following:

MLA Handbook for Writers of Research Papers, (5th edition, 1999)

The Publication Manual of the American Psychological Association, (4th edition, 1994)

Scientific Style and Format: The CBE [Council of Biology Editors] *Manual of Authors, Editors, and Publishers* (6th Edition, 1994)

The Chicago Manual of Style (14th ed., 1993)

However, if you're not interested in spending your hard-earned cash on these manuals, we herewith provide you with the most important details of these documentation formats.

MODERN LANGUAGE ASSOCIATION (MLA) DOCUMENTATION STYLE

The main features of MLA format are these:

- All sources are cited within parentheses (known in the academic world as "in-text parenthetical citations,"), using the author's name and the number of the page from which the source was derived.
- Sources are listed alphabetically at the end of the paper, on a sheet of sheets with the heading "Works Cited."
- Footnotes or endnotes are used sparingly, for explanations of special terms or ideas, or for more in-depth bibliographic information.

In-Text Citations

In-text citations occur whenever you reference somebody else's ideas within the body of your essay, either by direct quotation or by paraphrase. In either case you must include two pieces of information: the author's name and the page(s) on which the idea was found, and this information is typically recorded in parentheses at the end of the sentence or phrase in which the reference appears.

There are several ways to incorporate this citation information into your text. The information about who provided the quote or the original idea can be stated in what's called a "signal phrase" that contains the author's name to introduce the quotation, or paraphrase, then the sentence is followed by a parenthetical citation listing the page number on which the quotation or paraphrase appeared. For example,

> Contemporary fiction writer Doris Lessing commented, "As you start to write at once the question begins to insist: Why do you remember this and not that? Why do you remember in every detail a whole week, month, more, of a long ago year, but then complete dark, a blank?" (12)

or

> Freud argued that dreams occur predominantly as visual images, but not exclusively; they occur as auditory images as well, and to a lesser extent as impressions belonging to other senses (82).

Since we already identified the author in the signal phrase (Lessing commented, Freud argued), we don't need to repeat that information in the parenthetical citation. However, in a differently worded sentence, the citation would look different:

> One modern author notes, "As you start to write at once the question begins to insist: Why do you remember this and not that? Why do you remember in every detail a whole week, month, more, of a long ago year, but then complete dark, a blank?" (Lessing 12)

or:

> Traditional psychology posits dreams as occurring mainly in visual imagery, but also as auditory impressions and occasionally as impressions belonging to the other senses (Freud 82).

In the latter cases, the author's name occurs within the parentheses, because each author's name was not introduced within the signal phrase. Note also that the parenthetical citation includes only the author's last name—the reader can locate the full name in the Works Cited list if necessary—and that there's no need to place a "p." notation before the page number, since in this context, most readers will know that the number refers to a page within a certain source.

Full Citations

At the end of an essay using the MLA documentation format, authors collect all the sources actually cited in the paper (this does *not* include works consulted but not cited) and lists them alphabetically in a section titled "Works Cited." While a large number of complexities and idiosyncrasies are listed within the *MLA Handbook,* the main rules for setting up Works Cited pages are these:

- All full citations contain basic information: the author's name, the title of the work, and the publication information which includes the place of publication, the publisher's name, and the date published. This information is formatted slightly differently for different kinds of sources.
- List sources alphabetically by author's last name followed by a comma and the author's first name and middle name if provided.
- For sources with multiple authors, list all authors' full names linked by commas and "and" before the last name listed.
- Double-space all entries on your works cited page, as well as double-spacing between entries.
- Use a hanging indentation for each entry, whereby you indent (by the usual half-inch tab) all lines following the first one.

Here are some specific formats for the most commonly cited sources.

Books:

List book derived citations using the following information, in order: the author's name exactly as it appears on the book's title page, last name first; the title of the book in underlining or italics; the place of publication followed by a colon; the publisher, followed by a comma; and the data of publication. A typical MLA-formatted book listing will look like this:

> Lessing, Doris. *African Laughter: Four Visits to Zimbabwe.* New York: HarperCollins, 1992.

Journal Articles:

Journals are specialized publications, usually academic in content and tone. A typical MLA journal citation will contain six pieces of information: the author; the article's title listed in quotation marks; the journal's title underlined or italicized; the volume number; the date of publication; and the article's page numbers. A typical MLA-formatted journal listing will look like this:

> Scanlan, Margaret. "From the Margins of Empire: Christina Stead, Doris Lessing, Nadine Gordimer." *Modern Fiction Studies* 45 (1999): 1056–9.

Magazines:

Popular magazines tend to be less formal and academic in tone than journals, and they often appear more frequently—weekly, monthly, or bimonthly. The MLA format for a magazine listing in a works cited page provides the same information as the journal citation, but it omits the volume number, as in the following:

> Gray, Paul. "The Fifth Child." *Time* 14 March 1988: 86.

Newspapers:

Newspaper-derived source materials receive treatment similar to that of journals, but—since newspapers are often divided into sections—a works cited entry regarding a newsprint-derived source provides the section number/letter along with the page number, as in the following:

> Disch, Thomas M. "The New Age Meets an Ice Age." *Wall Street Journal* 15 Jan. 1999): 10E–11E.

Electronic Citation:

Since this is such a rapidly evolving area of information presentation and gathering, the major professional organizations are working hard to adapt their documentation styles to accommodate information acquired from Web sites. To cite files acquired by viewing/downloading via the World Wide Web, give the author's name (if known), the full title of the work in quotation marks, the title of the complete work if applicable in italics, the date of publication or of the latest update, the date of access, and the full URL or http address. For example,

> DeBertodano, Helena. "Life is Stranger Than Fiction—at 76, Doris Lessing Wants to be Alone." *Edmonton Journal Extra.* (11 April 2000). 23 May 2000 <http://www.edmontonjournal.com/sens/0411two.html>.

If the author's name isn't found anywhere on the Web site, then list the Web page alphabetically, by the first word in the title bar above the browser window. Likewise, if you can't find a date or a complete work within the site, provide as much information as you can within the citation:

> "Doris Lessing, a Retrospective." 24 May 2000 <http://lessing.redmood .com/>

Of course, there are many other categories of source material that might be listed in an MLA-formatted works cited page, far too numerous to mention here. If you want specific information on citing material derived from sources such as personal interviews, specific types of Internet sources such as online newspapers, television programs, videos, and so forth, consult the MLA Handbook, or one of the many research texts available in your school's library; these contain detailed information on every facet of correct documentation.

AMERICAN PSYCHOLOGICAL ASSOCIATION (APA) DOCUMENTATION STYLE

The main features of APA format are these:

- All sources are cited within parentheses (known in the academic world as "in-text parenthetical citations,"), using the author's last name and the year of publication. The number of the page from which the source was derived is only listed for direct quotations, although you may list page numbers for paraphrased ideas.

- Sources are listed alphabetically at the end of the paper, on a sheet or sheets with the heading "References."
- Footnotes or endnotes are used sparingly, for explanations of special terms or ideas, or for more in-depth bibliographic information such as copyright permission information.

In-Text Citations

In-text citations occur whenever you reference somebody else's ideas within the body of your essay, either by direct quotation or by paraphrase. When including direct quotations, you include the author's name, year of publication, and the page number. For paraphrased ideas, page numbers are not required, although they are encouraged, since they are helpful to your readers for locating ideas used in your writing. Author's last name and the year of publication are the only required information for documentation of paraphrased ideas. In all cases, the information is typically recorded in parentheses at the end of the sentence or at the end of the phrase in which the reference appears.

There are several ways to incorporate this citation information into your text. The information about who provided the quote or the original idea can be stated in what's called a "signal phrase" that contains the author's name to introduce the quotation, or paraphrase, then the sentence is followed by a parenthetical citation listing the year in which the quotation or paraphrase appeared, followed by the page number if quoting directly. For example,

> While Lopez found that "respondents indicated a preference for the first set of terms" (1998, p. 177), her findings are based on a relatively small sample.

or:

> Their critique of identity politics rests on Fabin and Jackson's argument that such approaches "have effectively reinforced the status-quo by limiting the formation of cross-racial, cross-cultural coalitions" (1993, p. 45).

APA rules also allow the placement of the year immediately following the author's name; applied to the Lopez example above, this version would appear as follows:

> While Lopez (1998) found that "respondents indicated a preference for the first set of terms" (p. 177), her findings are based on a relatively small sample.

In all these cases, we identified the author in the signal phrase (Lopez found), or simply in the sentence's wording (Fabin and Jackson critiqued and argued); thus, we don't need to repeat that information in the parentheses. Also, note here that the placement of the parenthetical citation differs based on where the outside source's idea appears in the sentence.

In a sentence worded without the signal phrase, the citation would look different:

> Since human beings are selfish, morality depends upon interdependent social relations under which people are forced to "take account of other people," to fashion norms and laws that require them to regulate themselves by something other than their "own egoism" (Durkheim, 1893, p. 331).

or:

> Social-psychology has traditionally focused upon environment, or a "social constructivist paradigm for explaining human behavior," and evolutionary psychologists question that approach, seeking casual factors for complex social behavior in nature, or our "genetic make-up, which serves our species' evolutionary adaptation" (Baxter and Oldman, 1994, p. 1134).

or:

> The researcher found "at least 27 serious problems with previous studies' findings" (Swift, 1991, p. 140).

In the latter cases, the author's names occur within the parentheses, because their names were not introduced within the sentence.

When citing a work in your text that was written by two authors, link the last names with "and"; in citations of works written by more than two but fewer than six authors, list the entire group of authors the first time you refer to their work, and in subsequent references, include the last name of the first author followed by "et al." and the year of publication, as usual. For example, your first in-text citation of a collaborative study would look like the following:

> Haley, Greenly, Mateo, and Ryan (1999) reported . . .

In subsequent citations of this work:

> Haley et al. (1999) reported . . .

If you refer to this study repeatedly in the same paragraph, you only include the year in the first citation. Thus, subsequent references to this study in the same paragraph would look like this:

> Haley et al. also found . . .

With six or more authors, the first as well as all subsequent citations contain only the last name of the first author followed by "et al." and the year.

Full Citations

At the end of an essay using the APA documentation format, authors collect all the sources actually cited in the paper (this *does not* include works consulted but not cited) and list them alphabetically in a section titled "References." While a large number of complexities and idiosyncrasies are listed within the *APA Publication Manual,* the main rules for setting up References pages are these:

- All full citations contain basic information: the author's name, the year of publication, the title of the work, and the publication information. Specifics regarding how this information is presented vary according to the kind of sources listed.
- List sources alphabetically by author's last name; use initials for first names (and middle names, if provided)
- For sources with multiple authors, list all authors' names. For two authors, link the last names with an ampersand (&) rather than the word "and." Separate all multiple author names with commas.
- Follow the author or authors' names with the date of publication in parentheses.
- Underline book and periodical titles, and only capitalize the first words of your titles.
- Double-space all entries on your references page, as well as double-spacing between entries.
- Use a hanging indentation for each entry, whereby you indent, by the usual half-inch tab) all lines following the first one.

Here are some specific formats for the most commonly cited sources.

Books:

List book-derived citations using the following information, in order: the author's last name and initials for first name (and middle name if given), last name first; the year of publication in parentheses; the title of the book in underlining, with only the first word of the title capitalized; the place of publication followed by a colon; and the publisher, followed by a period. A typical APA-formatted book listing will look like this:

> Hunt, M. (1985). *Profiles of social research: The scientific study of human interactions.* New York: Russell Sage.

Usually you list cities and states, or countries, for the place of publication; however, with well-known cities such as New York and Boston, you need only list the city name.

Journal Articles:

Journals are specialized publications, usually academic in content and tone. A typical APA journal citation will contain six pieces of information: the author's name; the date of publication; the article's title; the journal's title, underlined along with

the volume number; and the article's page numbers. A typical APA-formatted journal listing will look like this:

> Rank M. (1992). A view from the inside out: Recipients' perceptions of wel-
> fare. *Journal of Sociology and Social Welfare,* 45 (2), 27–47.

Magazines:

Popular magazines tend to be less formal and academic in tone than journals, and
they often appear more frequently—weekly, monthly, or bimonthly. The APA version of a magazine listing in a references page provides the same information as the
journal citation, but usually has more than the year included for the date, as in the
following:

> Gray, Paul. (1988, March 14). The fifth child. *Time,* 131 (11), 86.

Newspapers:

Newspaper-derived source materials receive treatment similar to that of journals,
but—since newspapers are often divided into sections—a references entry regarding a newsprint-derived source provides the section number/letter along with the
page number, as in the following:

> Disch, Thomas M. (1999, January 15). The new age meets an ice age. *Wall
> Street Journal,* 10E–11E.

Electronic Citation:

Since this is such a rapidly evolving area of information presentation and gathering,
the major professional organizations are working hard to adapt their documentation
styles to accommodate information acquired from Web sites. To cite files acquired
by viewing/downloading via the World Wide Web, give the author's name (in
known), the date of publication or of the latest update, the full title of the work, a
note in brackets identifying the source as one that is online, then a sentence starting
with the word "Available" followed by a colon and the source's URL or http address. For example,

> Blais, E. (1996, August). O brave new net! *CMC Magazine* [Online serial].
> Available: http://www.dcember.com/cmc/mag/1996/aug/last.html.

If the author's name isn't found anywhere on the Web site, then list the Web
page alphabetically, by the first word in the title bar above the browser window.
Likewise, if you can't find a date or a complete work within the site, provides as
much information as you can within the citation:

> Hayward, D. (1999). Romance on the net. [Personal webpage]. Available:
> http://www.soft.net.uk/pinevalley/hayward/iromance/olymp.htm.

Of course, there are many other categories of source material that might be
listed in an APA-formatted references page, far too numerous to mention here. If

you want specific information on citing material derived from sources such as unpublished dissertations, television programs, videos, and so forth, consult the *APA Publication Manual,* or one of the many research texts available in your school's library; these contained detailed information on every facet of correct documentation.

Council of Biology Editors (CBE) Documentation Style

The main features of CBE format are these:

- All sources are cited in your text using one of two accepted methods. Following any reference to a source, writers use either a sequential numbering system keyed to a list of endnotes, or use parenthetical citations containing an author's last name and year of publication.
- Sources are listed at the end of the paper, on a sheet or sheets with the heading "References." Endnotes are listed in the order in which they appear, while if you use parenthetical citations, you list your references in alphabetical order according to authors' last names.

In-Text Citations

In-text citations occur whenever you reference somebody else's ideas within the body of your essay, either by direct quotation or by paraphrase. When quoting or paraphrasing in CBE style, authors are referenced in your text either through sequential numbering or in parenthetical citations containing author's last name and date of publication. In either case information is typically recorded at the end of the sentence, or at the end of the phrase in which the reference appears.

There are several ways to incorporate this citation information into your text. The information about who provided the quote or the original idea can be stated in what's called a "signal phrase" containing the author's name to introduce the quotation, or paraphrase, then the sentence is followed by a parenthetical citation listing the year in which the quotation or paraphrase appeared, followed by the page number if quoting directly. For example,

Santos[1] reports the most recent data on this phenomenon.

or:

Santos reports the most recent data on this phenomenon (Santos 1999).

or:

The most recent data on this phenomenon (Santos 1999) suggest that a correlation does exist between the species' neurological activity and the presence of large amounts of the amino acids.

When citing a work written by two authors, link the last names with "and"; in citations of works written by more than two authors, list the last name of the first author followed by the phrase "and others" and the date, as in the following:

In later studies, the amino acids were found in even larger quantities (Santos and Vaughn 2000).

Multiple sources for one idea are listed in parenthetical citations separated by semicolons. For example,

Drawing upon earlier work on amino acids (Chandler 1987; Cain and Fargate 1991; Lavery and others 1997), the research was designed to measure amino acid concentration (Santos 1999).

Full Citations

At the end of an essay using the CBE documentation format, authors collect all the sources actually cited in the paper (this *does not* include works consulted but not cited) and list them in a section titled "References." While a large number of complexities and idiosyncrasies are listed within the *CBE Manual,* the main rules for setting up References pages are these:

- All full citations contain basic information: the author's last name and first initial, the date of publication, the title of the work, and the publication information. Specifics regarding how this information is presented vary according to the kind of sources listed, as well as whether the sequential numbering system or the parenthetical citation method has been used.
- List sources in the numerical order in which they appeared if using the sequenced numbering method, and alphabetically by author's last name when using parenthetical citations.
- For sources with two or more authors, list all authors' names and separate them with a comma.
- The placement of the publication date varies; in the sequential numbering system, you place the date at the end of the citation, right before the page number, and with parenthetical citations, you put the date immediately following the author's name.
- Titles of books, periodicals, or articles are typically not underlined or placed in quotation marks; only capitalize the first words of your book and article titles.
- Double-space all entries on your references page, as well as double-spacing between entries.
- Use a hanging indentation for each entry only when using the parenthetical name-year method of in-text citation.

Here are some specific formats for the most commonly cited sources.

Books:

A. Sequenced numbering:

[7]Hanski I, Cambefort Y. Dung beetle ecology. New Haven, CT: Princeton University Press; 1991. 201 p.

B. Parenthetical citations:

> Hanski I, Cambefort Y. 1991. Dung beetle ecology. New Haven, CT: Princeton University Press. 201 p.

Journal Articles:

Journals are specialized publications, usually academic in content and tone. A typical CBE journal citation will contain six pieces of information: the author's name; the date of publication; the article's title; the journal's title; and the article's page numbers. A typical CBE-formatted journal listing will look like this:

A. Sequenced numbering:

> [10]Lawrence JF, Newton Jr. AF Evolution and classification of beetles. Annual Review of Ecology and Systematics, 1982; 13: 261–290.

B. Parenthetical citations:

> Lawrence JF, Newton Jr. AF. 1982. Evolution and classification of beetles. Annual Review of Ecology and Systematics 13: 261–290.

Magazines:

Popular magazines tend to be less formal and academic in tone than journals, and they often appear more frequently—weekly, monthly, or bimonthly. The CBE version of a magazine listing in a reference page provides the same information as the journal citation, but usually has more than the year included for the date, as in the following:

A. Sequenced numbering:

> [4]Gladwell M. John Rock's error: what the co-inventor of the Pill didn't know: menstruation can endanger women's health. New Yorker 2000 Mar 13; 76 (3): 52–63.

B. Parenthetical citations:

> Gladwell M. 2000 Mar 13. John Rock's error: what the co-inventor of the Pill didn't know: menstruation can endanger women's health. New Yorker 76 (3): 52–63.

Newspapers:

Newspaper-derived source materials receive treatment similar to that of journals, but—since newspapers are often divided into sections—a references entry regarding a newsprint-derived source provides the section number/letter along with the page number, as in the following:

A. Sequenced numbering:

> [22]Saltus R. Scientists report discarded tissue can yield insulin. Boston Globe 2000 July 4; SectA: 9 (col 1).

B. Parenthetical citations:

> Saltus R. 2000 July 4. Scientists report discarded tissue can yield insulin. Boston Globe; SectA: 9 (col 1).

Electronic Citation:

Since this is such a rapidly evolving area of information-presentation and -gathering, the major professional organizations are working hard to adapt their documentation styles to accommodate information acquired from Web sites. To cite files acquired by viewing/downloading via the World Wide Web, give the author's name (if known); the title of the source; the organization responsible for hosting or posting the information; the type of source you're citing—in brackets; the date of publication or last updating; and the URL, telling the reader where the source is available. For example,

> The Rhinoceros and tiger conservation act of 1994. African Wildlife Update [On-line periodical]. 1994. Available at: http://www.africanwildlife.org/ex_articl/rhintig.html.

Of course, there are many other categories of source material that might be listed in a CBE-formatted references page, far too numerous to mention here. If you want specific information on citing material derived from sources such as articles in an anthology, conference presentations, CD-Roms, and so forth, consult the *CBE Manual,* or one of the many research texts available in your school's library; these contain detailed information on every facet of correct documentation.

Conclusion

The best method of ensuring that you follow the proper style of citation is to ask your professor which format he or she favors. Professors will usually make this information to students at the time of assigning a given writing task, but professors are occasionally absent-minded (hence the movie of the same name) might forget to provide this important information. When in doubt, be sure to ask your professor or teaching assistant which documentation style they want you to use.

One further piece of advice: rather than worrying about every little detail such as comma placement in parenthetical citations, or whether you separate a volume number from a date using a semicolon or a colon when writing full citations, common sense will usually advice; it may help to keep these general principles in mind:

- When in doubt about a professor's preferences, follow general guidelines of the MLA style for writing in humanities classes, APA for social science writing, and CBE for science writing.
- Having picked one citation style, use it *consistently* throughout your essay.
- Remember that parentheses are used to provide in-text citations according to MLA and APA rules; endnotes for citations can be used in some other styles, including CBE.

- In-text citations are short, containing only essential information: author, date and page number. Only author and page number are given in MLA style.
- Full citations, regardless of the type of source, generally contain the information necessary for a reader to locate specific sources. Author's name, title, title of work in which specific title appears, place and name of publisher, date of publication, and page numbers of source. Generally these items of information are reported in the order given here.

INDEX